Adobe® Illustrator® CS

SSROOM
IN A BOOK®

www.adobepress.com

Adobe

Adobe® Illustrator® CS Classroom in a Book® for Windows® and Mac OS

Adobe Systems Incorporated, 345 Park Avenue, San Jose, California 95110, USA

Adobe Press books are published by Peachpit Press, Berkeley, CA. To report errors, please send a note to errata@peachpit.com.

Printed in the U. S. A.

ISBN# 0-321-19380-6

9 8 7 6 5 4 3

Contents

Getting Started

Adobe® Illustrator® is the industry-standard illustration program for print, multimedia, and online graphics. Whether you are a designer or a technical illustrator producing artwork for print publishing, an artist producing multimedia graphics, or a creator of Web pages or online content, the Adobe Illustrator program offers you the tools you need to get professional-quality results.

About Classroom in a Book

Adobe Illustrator CS Classroom in a Book® is part of the official training series for Adobe graphics and publishing software from Adobe Systems, Inc.

The lessons are designed so that you can learn at your own pace. If you're new to Adobe Illustrator, you'll learn the fundamentals you'll need to master to put the program to work. If you are an experienced user, you'll find that Classroom in a Book teaches many advanced features, including tips and techniques for using the latest version of Adobe Illustrator.

Although each lesson provides step-by-step instructions for creating a specific project, there's room for exploration and experimentation. You can follow the book from start to finish or do only the lessons that correspond to your interests and needs. Each lesson concludes with a review section summarizing what you've covered.

Prerequisites

Before beginning to use Adobe Illustrator CS Classroom in a Book, you should have a working knowledge of your computer and its operating system. Make sure you know how to use the mouse and standard menus and commands, and also how to open, save, and close files. If you need to review these techniques, see the printed or online documentation included with your Windows or Mac OS documentation.

Note: *When instructions differ by platform, Windows commands appear first, and then the Mac OS command, with the platform noted in parentheses. For example, "press Alt (Windows) or Option (Mac OS) and click away form the artwork." Common commands may be further abbreviated with the Windows command first, followed by a slash and the Mac OS commands, without any parenthetical reference. For example, "press Alt/Option;" or Ctrl/Command-click."*

Installing the program

Before you begin using Adobe Illustrator CS Classroom in a Book, make sure that your system is set up correctly and that you've installed the required software and hardware.

You must purchase the Adobe Illustrator CS software separately. For complete instructions on installing the software, see the "How to Install" Readme file on the application CD.

Installing the Classroom in a Book fonts

The Classroom in a Book lesson files use the fonts that installed with Adobe Illustrator CS. If it is necessary to reinstall these font files, you can perform a custom installation from your Adobe Illustrator software CD to reinstall only the fonts. See the "How to Install" Readme file on the application CD.

Copying the Classroom in a Book files

The Classroom in a Book CD includes folders containing all the electronic files for the lessons. Each lesson has its own folder. You must install these folders on your hard disk to use the files for the lessons. To save room on your hard disk, you can install the folders for each lesson as you need them.

To install the Classroom in a Book files:

1 Insert the Adobe Illustrator Classroom in a Book CD into your CD-ROM drive.

2 Create a folder on your hard disk and name it AICIB.

3 Do one of the following:

- Copy the Lessons folder into the AICIB folder.
- Copy only the single lesson folder you need.

Restoring default preferences

The preferences file controls how palettes and command settings appear on your screen when you open the Adobe Illustrator program. Each time you quit Adobe Illustrator, the position of the palettes and certain command settings are recorded in the preferences file. If you want to restore the tools and palettes to their original default settings, you can delete the current Adobe Illustrator CS preferences file. (Adobe Illustrator creates a preferences file if one doesn't already exist the next time you start the program and save a file.)

You must then restore the default preferences for Illustrator before you begin each lesson. This ensures that the tools and palettes function as described in this book. When you have finished the book, you can restore your saved settings.

To save your current Illustrator preferences:

1 Exit Adobe Illustrator.

2 Locate the AI Prefs (Windows) or Adobe Illustrator CS Preferences (Mac OS), as follows.

• *In Windows, the AI Prefs is located in the Document and Settings\username\Application Data\Adobe\Adobe Illustrator CS Settings folder.*

Note: You may have to choose Folder Options from the Control panel to show hidden files to locate this preferences, from the Folder Options window click on Views. Check the radio button to the left of Show Hidden Files or Folders.

• *In Mac OS X, it is located in the Mac OS X\Users\Home\Library\Preferences\Adobe Illustrator CS Settings folder. An easy way to locate the preference file is to click on Home in the title bar of any open window in the Finder.*

Note: *If you cannot locate the preferences file use your operating systems Find command.*

If you can't find the file, either you haven't started Adobe Illustrator yet or you have moved the preference file. The preferences file is created after you quit the program the first time, and is updated thereafter.

3 Delete or rename the AI Prefs file (Windows) or Adobe Illustrator CS Prefs file (Mac OS).

4 Start Adobe Illustrator.

To locate and delete the Adobe Illustrator preferences file quickly each time you begin a new lesson, create a shortcut (Windows) or an alias (Mac OS) for the Illustrator CS Settings folder.

To restore your saved settings after completing the lessons:

1 Exit Adobe Illustrator.

2 Drag the preference file from the desktop back into the Adobe Illustrator Settings folder.

3 In the warning dialog box that appears, confirm you'll replace the existing file.

Note: *You can rename the preferences file with your current settings, rather than moving it or throwing it away. To restore your current settings when you have finished the lessons, change the preferences filename back. Exit Illustrator, and return the renamed preferences file to the Illustrator CS Settings folder.*

Additional resources

Adobe Illustrator CS Classroom in a Book is not meant to replace documentation that comes with the program. Only the commands and options used in the lessons are explained in this book. For comprehensive information about program features, refer to these resources:

• Online Help, which you can view by choosing Help > Illustrator Help. (For more information, see Lesson 1, "Getting to Know the Work Area.")

• Training and support resources on the Adobe Web site (www.adobe.com), which you can view by choosing Help > Online Support if you have a connection to the World Wide Web.

Adobe Certification

The Adobe Training and Certification Programs are designed to help Adobe customers improve and promote their product-proficiency skills. The Adobe Certified Expert (ACE) program is designed to recognize the high-level skills of expert users. Adobe Certified Training Providers (ACTP) use only Adobe Certified Experts to teach Adobe software classes. Available in either ACTP classrooms or on site, the ACE program is the best way to master Adobe products. For Adobe Certified Training Programs information, visit the Partnering with Adobe Web site at http://partners.adobe.com.

A Quick Tour of Adobe Illustrator

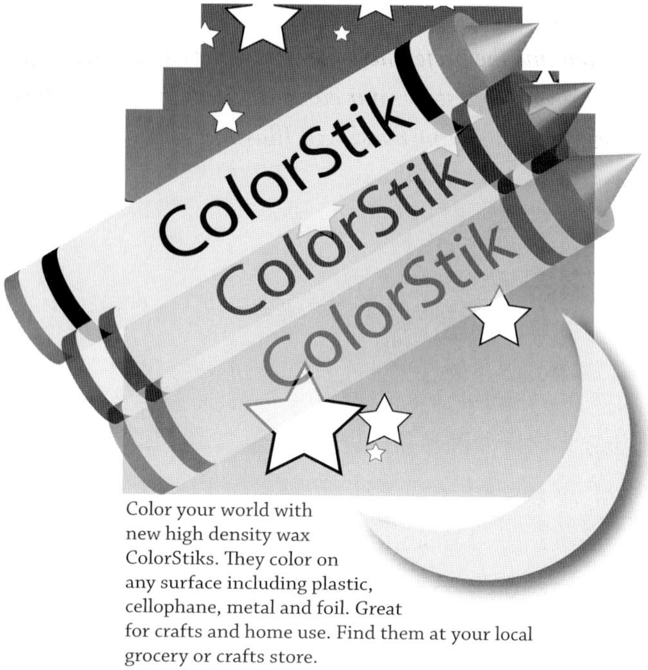
ColorStik
ColorStik
ColorStik
Color your world with new high density wax ColorStiks. They color on any surface including plastic, cellophane, metal and foil. Great for crafts and home use. Find them at your local grocery or crafts store.

This interactive demonstration of Adobe Illustrator is designed to give an overview of key features of the program in about one hour.

Getting started

You'll work in one art file during this tour. All art files are located on the Adobe Classroom in a Book CD that is located on the inside back cover of this book. Make sure that you copy the AICIB folder from the CD to your hard drive before starting this exercise. Before you begin, you need to restore the default preferences for Adobe Illustrator. Then you'll open the finished art file for this lesson to see what you'll create.

Note: *If you're new to Adobe Illustrator or to vector-drawing applications, you may want to begin with Lesson 1, "Getting to Know the Work Area."*

1 To ensure that the tools and palettes function exactly as described in this tour, delete or deactivate (by renaming) the Adobe Illustrator CS preferences file. See "Restoring default preferences" on page 4.

2 Start Adobe Illustrator. When the Welcome Screen appears choose Open Document, or File > Open.

3 Open the tour_done.ai file in the Lesson00 folder, located inside the Lessons folder within the AICIB folder on your hard drive.

Note: *The tour file uses an OpenType font named Chaparral Pro Regular. Illustrator CS comes with Chaparral Pro and a variety of other OpenType fonts so you can use these features in your work right away. See Lesson 11 for more information on fonts.*

Zoom Out to make the finished artwork smaller, and leave it on your screen as you work. Use the Hand tool (✋) to reposition the artwork in the upper left of the page then drag the lower right corner to make the window smaller. If you don't want to leave the image open, choose File > Close.

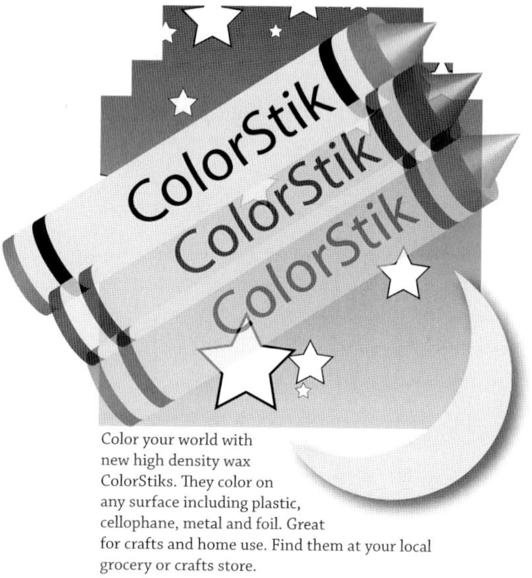
ColorStik
ColorStik
ColorStik
Color your world with new high density wax ColorStiks. They color on any surface including plastic, cellophane, metal and foil. Great for crafts and home use. Find them at your local grocery or crafts store.

The completed Tour illustration.

For a color illustration of the finished artwork in this lesson, see the color section.

Now open the start file to begin the tour.

5 To open the start file, choose File > Open, and open the tour_start.ai file in the Lesson00 folder, located inside the Lessons folder within the AICIB folder on your hard drive.

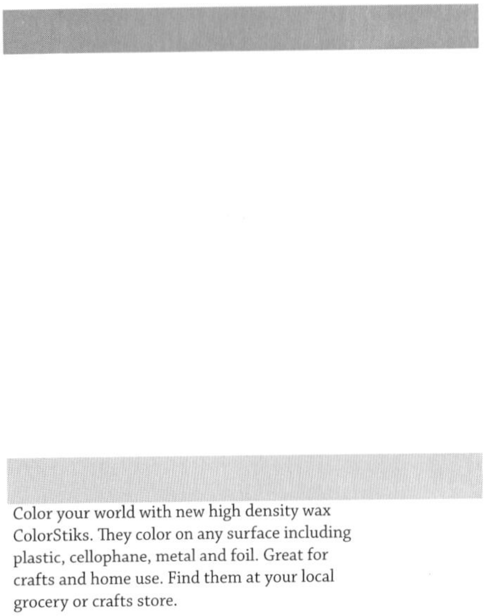

Color your world with new high density wax
ColorStiks. They color on any surface including
plastic, cellophane, metal and foil. Great for
crafts and home use. Find them at your local
grocery or crafts store.

The start file.

6 Choose File > Save As, name the file **colorstik.ai**, and leave the type of file format set to Adobe Illustrator®, and click Save. Leave the options at the defaults and click OK.

Creating a basic blend

Illustrator includes a variety of methods for creating blends from one object to another, giving you the opportunity to create interesting effects that transition colors and shapes. In this example we will create a smooth color blend by using the existing rectangles on the document.

1 First, use the Selection tool (↖) to select the topmost rectangle in the document window. Hold down the Shift key and click to add the bottom rectangle to the selection,

2 Use Object > Blend > Make. As a default this creates a smooth color blend. Other options are available from Object > Blend > Blend Options. For this exercise Smooth Color should be selected. Blends are discussed in more detail in Lesson 12.

3 Choose Select > Deselect.

4 Choose File > Save.

Setting default colors

As you start to create in Adobe Illustrator you'll discover that Illustrator objects have a stroke (outline) and a fill. Learn more about what you can do with strokes and fills in Lesson 5, Painting. For this part of the exercise you'll want the stroke and fill at the default of black and white.

1 To assure that you are set at default colors of white fill and black stroke locate the fill and stroke icons at the bottom of the toolbar.

2 Click on the small black and white swatch in the lower left to reset to the default colors.

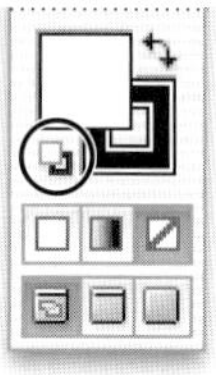

Click to reset the default colors.

Drawing a star

Adobe Illustrator includes tools to create shapes such as rectangles, circles, polygons stars and more. In this step we will create a star to fill the background.

1 Hold down the mouse button on the Rectangle tool () in the toolbox to display a group of tools. Select the Star tool (), and then click, and release anywhere on the artboard.

2 Clicking once with the Star tool rather than dragging it in the artwork lets you precisely specify the shape's dimensions.

3 In the Star dialog box, specify the shape of the star. (We specified 20 pt for Radius 1, 10 pt for Radius 2, and 5 for the number of points on the star.) Click OK.

Creating a symbol

Now that the star is created we will use it as an Illustrator symbol. Symbols are art objects you create and store in the Symbols palette. The symbol can then be applied using the Symbol Sprayer Tool.

1 From the Window menu choose Symbols. A Symbol window appears showing the default symbols already provided.

2 With the star selected Alt-click (Windows) or Option-click (Mac OS) on the New Symbol button at the bottom of the Symbols Palette. By holding down the Alt/Option key you are given the opportunity to name the symbol as it is added to the palette.

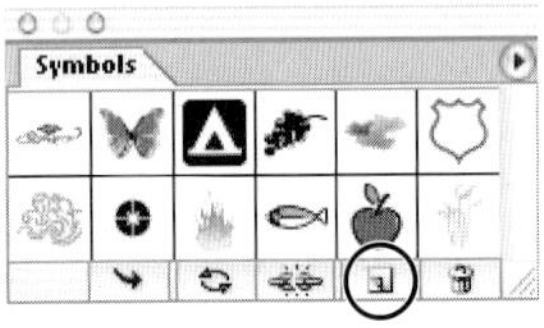

Alt or Option-click on the New Symbol button to add the star.

3 Name the symbol **star** and click OK. The star has now been added to the Symbols palette.

4 We won't need the original star that you created. Select it with the Selection tool and press the delete key to eliminate it, or choose Edit > Clear.

Applying the symbol using the Symbol Sprayer

Now that the symbol has been added, apply it using the Symbol Sprayer tool.

1 Select the Symbol Sprayer from the toolbar ( ).

2 From the Symbols palette select the Star symbol you just added.

3 Position the mouse over the color blend created earlier then click and drag to "spray" the stars over the blend.

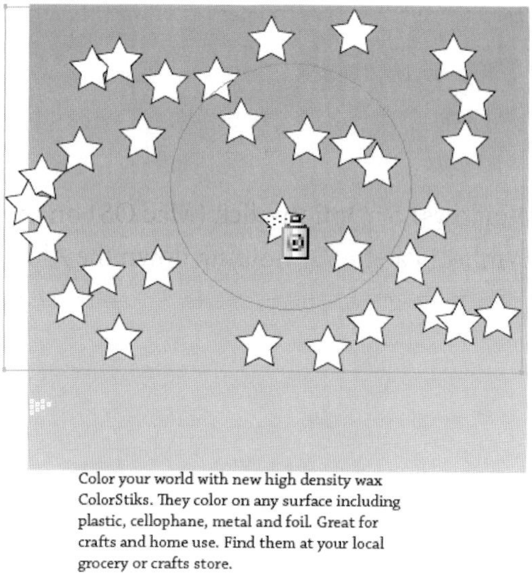

Color your world with new high density wax ColorStiks. They color on any surface including plastic, cellophane, metal and foil. Great for crafts and home use. Find them at your local grocery or crafts store.

Click and Drag to apply the star symbol.

Variations of the symbol

By using the Symbolism tools you can change the size and spacing of the stars you just created.

1 Hold down on the Symbol Sprayer tool ( )and drag to the right to display the additional hidden tools in the group and select the Symbol Sizer Tool ( ).

2 Position the cursor over any star and note that when you click and hold the mouse, the star becomes larger. To make the star smaller hold down the Alt key (Windows) or the Option key (Mac OS) while holding down the mouse.

The Symbol Sizer tool.

3 Experiment with enlarging and reducing the star symbols, stopping when you are satisfied with the results.

4 Choose File > Save.

Spacing out the stars

In this next step you will reorganize the placement of some of the star symbols by using the Symbol Shifter tool.

1 Click and hold on the recently used Symbol Sizer tool and drag to select the Symbol Shifter tool ( ).

2 Position the tool over various stars and click and drag to randomly reposition the stars.

The Symbol Shifter tool.

Creating a clipping mask

A clipping mask allows the user to define a shape to mask other objects. In Adobe Illustrator this allows the designer to create artwork that can then fill virtually any shape. In this next exercise we will create a custom shape and mask our blend and stars into it.

An example of two objects before and after using the clipping mask feature.

Creating three rectangles for the final shape.

1 Select the Rectangle tool (). Click on the default color swatches on the toolbar to make the fill white and the stroke black, or press D. This is the key command for returning to default fill and stroke.

Instead of clicking and dragging to create the first of three rectangles, click and release once on the artboard. Input the values **315 pt** for the Width, and **265 pt** for the Height in the Rectangle dialog box..

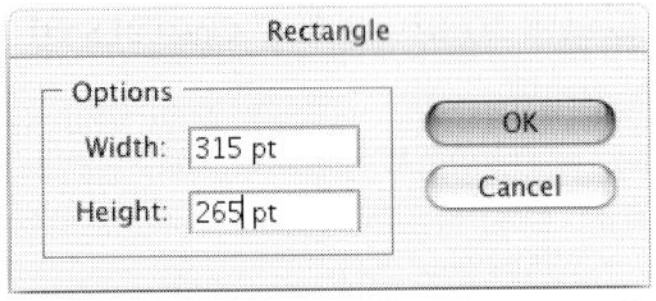

Enter specific values for the rectangle by clicking once on the artboard.

Note: *Even if your measurements are not in points you can enter "pt" after the numerical value. Adobe Illustrator will recognize the measurement as points.*

2 Click and release on the artboard again and enter the values **265 pt** for the Width, and **60 pt** for the Height to make the second rectangle.

3 Click and release one more time and enter the values **215 pt** for the Width, and **60 pt** for the Height for the third and final rectangle.

4 Select the large rectangle and position it over the gradient star artwork created earlier.

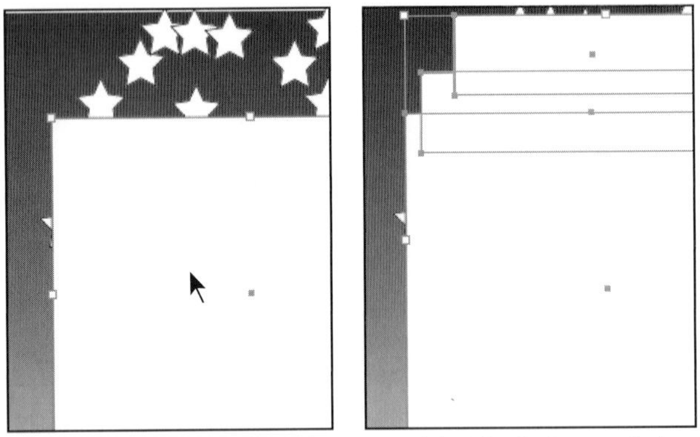

Drag the largest rectangle to the center of the blend, then stack the other two rectangles on top.

5 Position the other two rectangles so that they are stacked on top of the large one, with the smallest rectangle on the top. The tops and bottoms should overlap slightly, but don't worry about alignment.

6 Choose Select > Deselect and File > Save.

Using the align feature

Illustrator has many precision tools available to make the job of precise positioning more efficient. In this step we will utilize the Align palette to align the centers of your three rectangles before combining them into one larger shape.

1 Using the Selection tool (↖), click on one of the rectangles. Then press down the Shift key and click on the other two rectangles. Pressing the Shift key while clicking on objects adds to the current selection.

2 Let go of the Shift key and Lock the large rectangle's position by giving it one last click.

Note: *By clicking on an object before using the Alignment features you essentially lock the position down, forcing the other selected objects to move into alignment with the locked object.*

3 Choose Window > Align to show the Align palette.

4 Select Horizontal Align Center. The selected rectangles align horizontally.

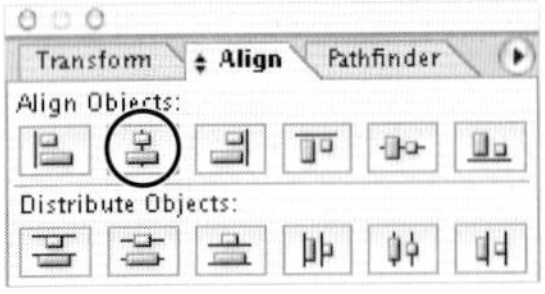

The Horizontal Align Center button.

5 Choose Select > Deselect and File > Save.

Using the pathfinder feature

For a designer, Illustrator offers the ability to create new interesting shapes from multiple existing shapes. The Pathfinder palette will be used to create an "Art Deco" shape from the three rectangles.

1 Using the Selection tool (), shift click to select all three rectangles.

2 Choose Window > Pathfinder to bring forward the Pathfinder palette.

3 Alt-click (Windows) Option-click (Mac OS) the Add to Shape Area button in the Pathfinder palette.

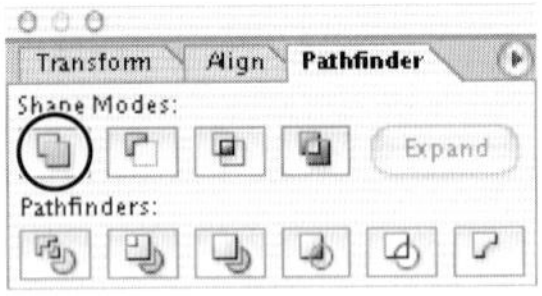

The Add to Shape Area button.

Note: *If you click the Add to Shape Area button without holding down the Alt/Option key, the shapes become a compound shape. They are still three separate paths but appear as though they are combined into one shape. You can release a compound shape and it reverts to the original shapes. By Alt/Option-clicking the Add to Shape Area button, you permanently combine the shapes (also called expanding) into one shape. You cannot retrieve the original shapes once a compound shape has been expanded, but it will keep the file less complex as we add more elements.*

Creating a clipping mask

Now you will create a clipping mask over the blend and stars artwork.

1 Choose Select > Select All, to activate the stars, blend and new shape that you created.

2 Deselect the text area by holding down the Shift key and clicking on it.

3 Select Object > Clipping Mask > Make. The blend and stars now appear, only in the area of the mask.

4 File > Save.

The blend and stars masked in the combined shape.

Using the new 3-D effect

Making objects appear three-dimensional is a new feature that is easy to implement, yet produces impressive results. The trick is creating the correct shape for the result that you want. In this image we will create the three-dimensional shape of a crayon. The shape has already been created and saved as another file. You will start by copying that shape and pasting it into the working documents.

1 Choose File > Open, and open crayon.ai file in the Lesson00 folder, located inside the Lessons folder within the AICIB folder on your hard drive.

2 From the menu items choose Select > All and then Edit > Copy.

3 At the very bottom of the Window menu you will find all open documents listed, select colorstik.ai to bring that document window to the front and then Edit > Paste.

4 Move the crayon shape off to the left so as to not interfere with the current artwork.

Creating the three-dimensional crayon.

We will now turn the basic shape into a three-dimensional shape using the Revolve effect. You can revolve an open or closed path around an axis in a counterclockwise direction to create a 3D object.

1 Select the crayon shape with the Selection tool.

2 Choose Effect > 3D > Revolve. Position the 3D Revolve Options window so the crayon is visible.

3 Click on the preview checkbox to see how the shape appears while using the Revolve effect.

4 As a default the angle that the three dimensional shape is created is Off-axis Front. To customize the angle click on the cube in the position preview pane, then click and drag. Position the cube so that the crayon is on an angle pointed toward the upper right.

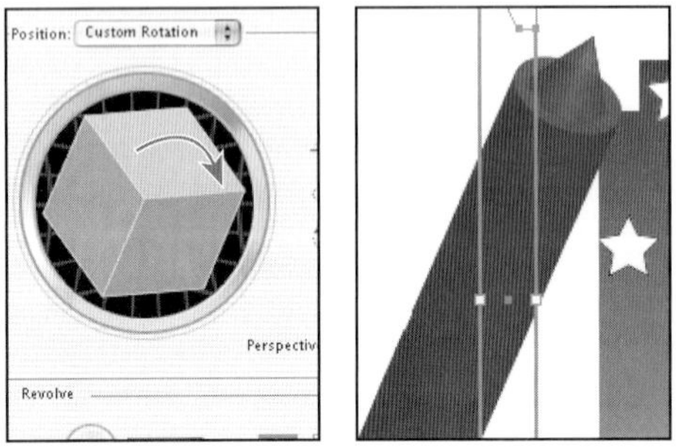

Click and drag the cube to change and revolve it in space.

5 Click OK.

6 File > Save.

Adding a label

As you may have noticed, while you revolved your crayon in space, your shape has many sides to it. In this next exercise you will locate the surface that is visible and apply a label to the crayon.

1 Select the crayon and choose Window > Appearance.

The Appearance palette lists the attributes of the crayon, including the 3D Revolve effect.

2 Double-click on 3D Revolve in the Appearance palette to open the 3D Revolve options window. Any revisions to the present Revolve effect must be made by opening the options from the Appearance palette.

3 Click on the Map Art button on the upper right of the Revolve Options window and turn on the preview for this window.

4 Select the surface of the object. In this instance we select 1 of 4, the surface of the crayon where a label would normally appear.

5 Use the Map Art feature to select a symbol to wrap around the object. Select from the pop-up menu the Symbol named "**label**."

6 In the window pane beneath, click and drag the label symbol so that it is visible. The light gray area is visible in this view.

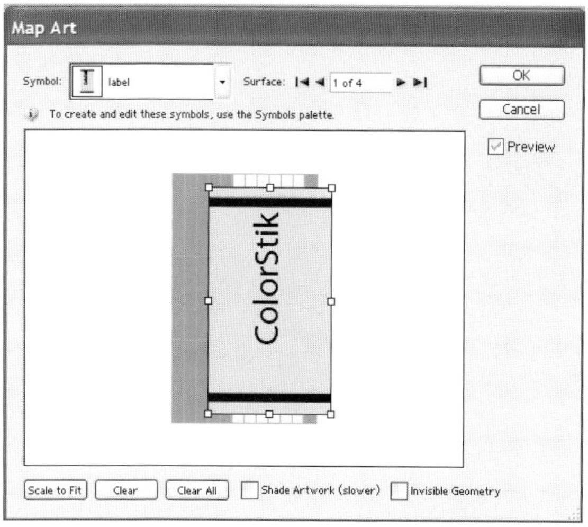

Select the symbol and the surface that you want to map.

7 Click OK to finalize the symbol placement, and OK again for the 3D filter.

8 File > Save.

Cloning the crayon

The finished artwork has three crayons in it. Instead of creating each one, you will duplicate the original.

1 Select the crayon with the Selection tool (↖) and drag it to position it over the masked image of the stars.

Note: *When the revolved object is selected the original anchor points are visible. This can be confusing at times, but is a benefit if you need to edit the shape.*

2 After the crayon is positioned, hold down the Alt (Windows) or Option (Mac OS) key and drag down to create a clone of the original crayon.

Note: *You must hold down the Alt/Option key the entire time that you are dragging the crayon. A clone of the crayon will appear when the mouse is released.*

3 Repeat the clone so there are three crayons.

Clone using the Selection tool and Alt/Option key modifier.

Changing the color of the crayon.

The 3D Effect is an intelligent effect that allows you to change the color of the crayon and still retain the shading and dimension.

1 Make sure the Swatches palette is forward. If not, choose Window > Swatches.

2 Select the bottom crayon, then click on a blue swatch.

Change the color of the crayon with the Swatches palette.

3 Click on the top crayon and choose green from the swatches palette, leave the middle crayon red.

Applying transparency

In Adobe Illustrator you have the ability to apply various levels of transparency to objects. Blending modes are also available. Transparency and blending modes are discussed in greater detail in Lesson 6.

In this next section we will apply Transparency to two of the crayons. If the Transparency palette is not visible choose Window > Transparency.

1 Leaving the top-most crayon untouched, select the middle crayon and in the Transparency window reduce to 75%. You can do this by dragging the pop-up slider, or by typing **75** into the text box.

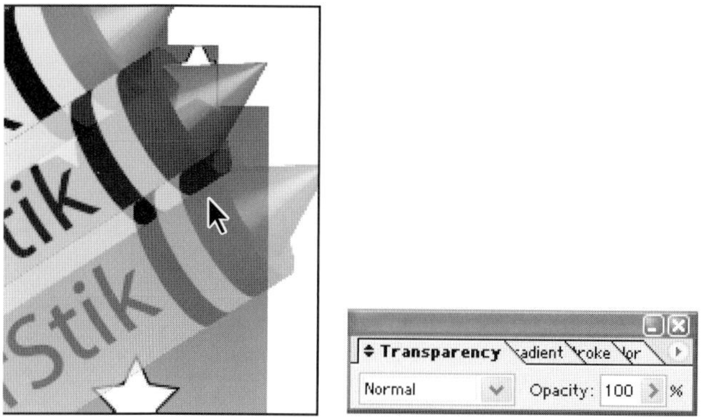

The Transparency palette.

2 Select the bottom Crayon and assign **50%** Transparency.

3 File > Save.

Creating the crescent shape

You will now create the shape of a crescent moon by using the Pathfinder palette. If your Swatches palette is not visible choose Window > Swatches.

1 Choose Select > Deselect to make sure no objects are selected.

2 Click once on the Fill swatch at the bottom of the toolbar and then click on the yellow swatch in the Swatches palette. Click once on the Stroke swatch and click on the None swatch (⧄)in the Swatches palette.

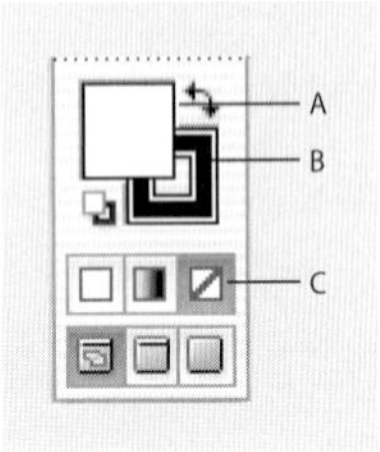

A. Fill. B. Stroke.
C. None.

3 Select the Ellipse tool (◯) from the toolbar. The Ellipse tool is in the same group of shapes as the Rectangle, Rounded Rectangle, Polygon, Star and Lens Flare tools. If it is not immediately visible, hold down on the Shape tool and drag to select the Ellipse tool.

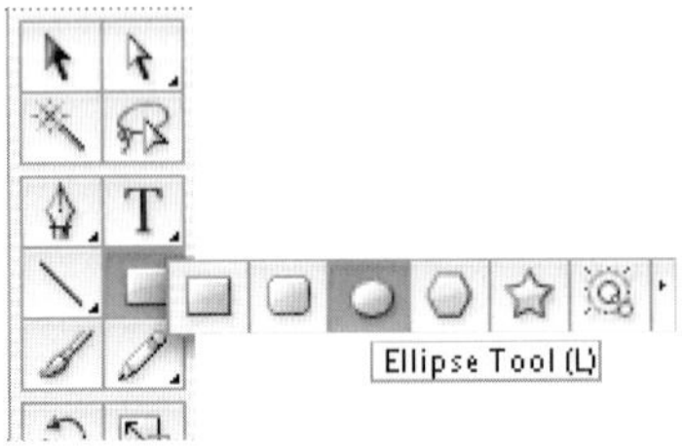

Click and drag to select the Ellipse tool if it is not visible.

4 Hold down Shift-Alt (Windows) or Shift-Option (Mac OS) then click and drag to draw a circle that's almost half the size of our masked frame. (Holding down Shift constrains the ellipse to a circle. Holding down Alt/Option draws from the center rather than from the left side.) If you can't get this to work the first time use Edit > Undo to try again.

***Note:** If you are having difficulty creating the circle, practice in the scratch area. When you have a circle that you are happy with, use the Selection tool to click and drag it into position.*

5 If you want to be certain that the circle is not too large or small choose Window > Transform. The Width and Height should be approximately 200 pt. You can type **200** in the text boxes for W and H if you wish.

Create a circle for the moon.

6 With the circle still selected use the Selection tool (↖) and hold down the Alt key (Windows) or Option key (Mac OS) while dragging up and slightly to the left. This clones a new circle that overlaps the original. When subtracted this will form the inner part of our crescent shape.

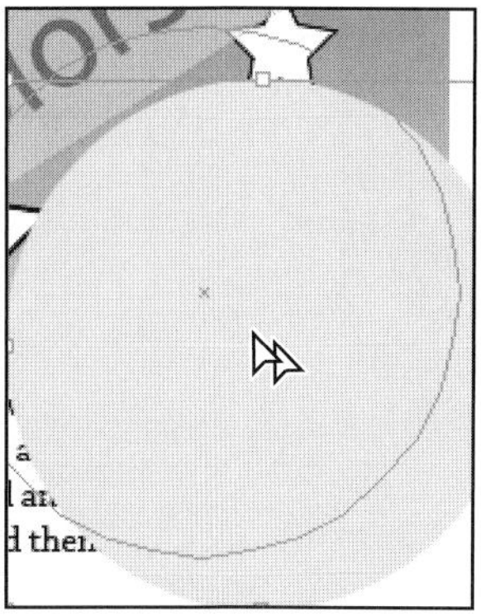

Clone and Overlap the circle.

7 With the cloned circle still selected, use the Selection tool and Shift-click on the original circle, to select both objects.

Locate the Pathfinder palette, and Alt-click (Windows) or Option-click (Mac OS) the Subtract from Shape Area button in the Pathfinder palette. This forms the crescent shape of the moon. Remember, Alt/Option+clicking expands the two shapes into one, subtracting the overlapping circle from the other.

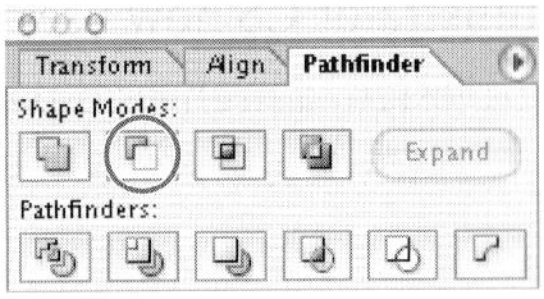

Subtract the topmost circle to form a crescent shape.

Adding live effects

To add more dimension to this image you will add a drop shadow to the crescent shape. In order to do this without permanently affecting the object, you will use the Effects feature. This feature is discussed in more detail in Lesson 10.

1 Select the newly created crescent shape.

2 Choose Effect > Stylize > Drop Shadow. Note that you have many options from which to choose. For this exercise we will leave it at the default settings and click OK.

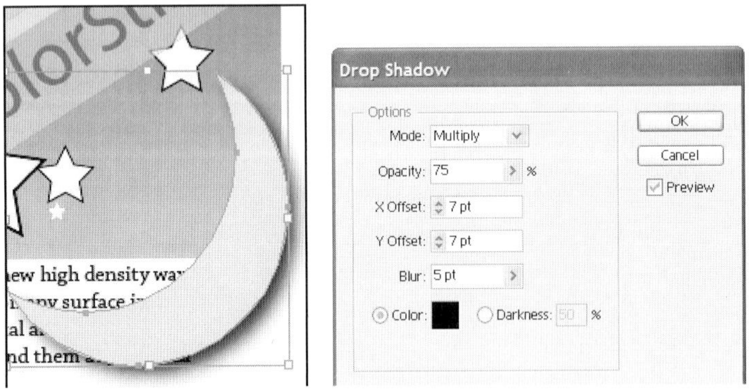

The Drop Shadow Effect.

Note: *The Filter and the Effect menu items might look repetitive, but they are very different in how they apply their attributes. When using the Drop shadow effect it can be selected, edited, and even deleted using the Appearance palette, whereas the Drop Shadow filter creates a separate object which is not easily changed, or ungrouped.*

Wrapping text around artwork

Our final step is to wrap text around the crescent shape. Illustrator CS now uses the same type engine and offers the same features as Adobe InDesign, a high-end page layout program. The intuitive text wrap option offers more flexibility than in previous versions.

1 Drag the crescent shape over the text if it is not overlapping already. The text wrap has not been applied yet, so the crescent shape is covering up some of the text.

2 Select Object > Text Wrap > Make Text Wrap. Leave the default text offset set to 6 pt, this is the distance that the text will be pushed away from the crescent shape. Click OK.

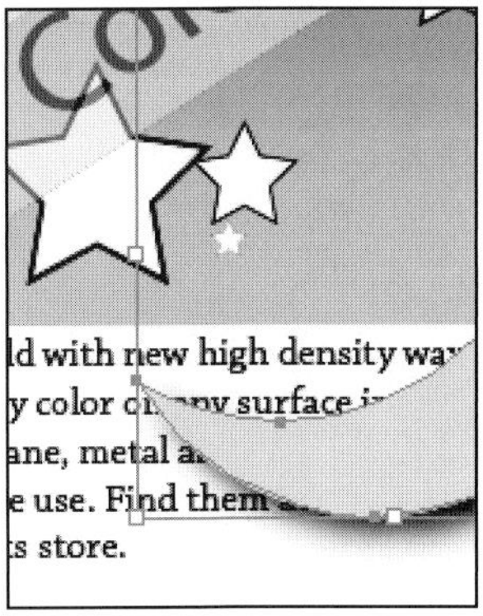

Overlap the moon into the text area.

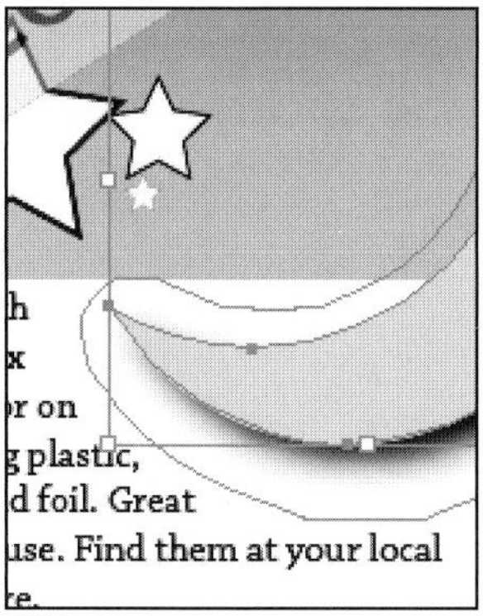

The Text Wrap feature applied.

If you are not happy with the wrap, reposition the crescent shape or change the amount of offset by choose Object > Text Wrap > Text Wrap Options. See Lesson 11 for more information about the text wrap feature.

3 Choose File > Save then Choose File > Close.

Congratulations! You have completed the initial tour of Adobe Illustrator CS. You are now ready to start creating on your own and progress through the rest of the lessons.

Lesson 1

1 Getting to Know the Work Area

To make the best use of the extensive drawing, painting, and editing capabilities in Adobe Illustrator, it's important to learn how to navigate the work area. The work area consists of the artboard, the scratch area, the toolbox, and the default set of floating palettes.

In this introduction to the work area, you'll learn how to do the following:

- Use the Welcome Screen.
- Open an Adobe Illustrator file.
- Select tools from the toolbox.
- Use viewing options to enlarge and reduce the display of a document.
- Work with palettes.
- Use online Help.

Getting started

You'll be working in one art file during this lesson, but before you begin, restore the default preferences for Adobe Illustrator. Then open the finished art file for this lesson to see an illustration.

1 To ensure that the tools and palettes function exactly as described in this lesson, delete or deactivate (by renaming) the Adobe Illustrator CS preferences file. See "Restoring default preferences" on page 2.

2 Double-click the Adobe Illustrator icon to start the Adobe Illustrator program.

When started Adobe Illustrator displays a Welcome Screen with bulleted options.

The Welcome Screen.

Use the Welcome Screen to find out what's new in Illustrator CS, gain access to tutorials and CD extras. CD extras include fonts, sample files. The Welcome Screen also offers the option to create a new document from scratch, or from a template, or to open an existing document.

Note: *If you prefer not to have the Welcome Screen appear at startup, uncheck the Show this dialog at startup checkbox. You can open the Welcome Screen at any time by selecting it from the Help menu.*

How Does an Illustrator template work?

New with Illustrator CS is the ability to save and create files as templates. Choose File > Save as Template to save a file as an .ait (Adobe Illustrator Template) file. When a new file is created based on the template, an untitled document is created, leaving the original untouched.

Any existing Illustrator document may also be Opened as a template file by selecting File > New From Template, again creating a new untitled document and leaving the original intact.

For this lesson we will open an existing file.

3 Click on the Open Document button in the lower right of the Welcome Screen or choose File > Open, and open the L1strt.ai file in the Lesson01 folder, located inside the Lessons folder within the AICIB folder on your hard drive.

For an illustration of the finished artwork in this lesson, see the color section.

When the file is opened and Illustrator CS is fully launched the menu bar, the toolbox, and five palette groups appear on the screen. (The Transparency/Stroke/Gradient palette group is docked with the Color/Attributes palette group.)

4 Choose File > Save As, name the file **Parrots.ai**, and select the Lesson01 folder in the Save In menu. Leave the type of file format set to Adobe Illustrator® Document, and click Save, leaving the Illustrator Options set at the defaults. Click OK.

About the work area

In Adobe Illustrator, the work area occupies the entire space within the Illustrator window and includes more than just the printable page containing your artwork. The printable and nonprintable areas are represented by a series of solid and dotted lines between the outermost edge of the window and the printable area of the page.

Imageable area *is bounded by the innermost dotted lines and represents the portion of the page on which the selected printer can print. Many printers cannot print to the edge of the paper. Don't get confused by what is considered non-imageable.*

Non-imageable area *is between the two sets of dotted lines representing any nonprintable margin of the page. This example shows the non-imageable area of an 8.5" x 11" page for a standard laser printer.*

The Imageable and Non-imageable area is determined by the printer selected in the Print options dialog box. (See Lesson 17 for more information about assigning a printer.) If you are saving an Illustrator document to be placed in a layout program, such as InDesign, the Imageable and Non-imageable areas are irrelevant, the artwork outside of the bounds will still appear.

Edge of the page *is indicated by the outermost set of dotted lines.*

Artboard *is bounded by solid lines and represents the entire region that can contain printable artwork. By default, the artboard is the same size as the page, but it can be enlarged or reduced. The U.S. default artboard is 8.5"x 11", but it can be set as large as 227"x 227".*

A. *Imageable area.* ***B.*** *Nonimageable area.* ***C.*** *Edge of page.* ***D.*** *Artboard.* ***E.*** *Scratch area.*

Scratch area *is the area outside the artboard that extends to the edge of the 227-inch square window. The scratch area represents a space on which you can create, edit, and store elements of artwork before moving them onto the artboard. Objects placed onto the scratch area are visible on-screen, but they do not print.*

–From Adobe Online Help.

Viewing artwork

When you open a file, it is displayed in Preview view, which displays artwork the way it will print. When you're working with large or complex illustrations, you may want to view only the outlines, or wireframes, of objects in your artwork, so that the screen doesn't have to redraw the artwork each time you make a change.

1 Choose View > Outline. Only the outlines of the objects are displayed. Use this view to find objects that might not be visible in Preview.

2 Choose View > Preview to see all the attributes of the artwork. If you prefer keyboard commands, Ctrl+Y (Windows) or Command+Y (Mac OS) toggles between these two modes.

3 Choose View > Overprint•Pixel Closeup (at the bottom of the menu) to zoom in to a preset area of the image. This custom view was added to the document.

Note: *To save time when working with large or complex documents, you can create your own custom views within a document to quickly jump to specific areas and zoom levels. You set up the view that you want to save and then choose View > New View. Name the view; it is saved with the document.*

4 Choose View > Overprint Preview to view any lines or shapes that are set to overprint. This view is helpful for those in the print industry who need to see how inks interact when set to overprint. See Lesson 17, "Printing Arwork and Producing Color Separations" for more information on overprinting.

5 Choose View > Pixel Preview to view how the artwork will look when it is rasterized and viewed on-screen in a Web browser.

Outline view.

Preview view.

Overprint preview.

Pixel preview.

Working with tiled artwork

Illustrator is generally not meant to create multi-page documents. That would be more of a function of a page layout program such as InDesign. Illustrator can tile multiple pages for the purposes of accommodating artwork that is too large for an output device.

What is Tiling?

By default, Illustrator prints your artwork on a single sheet of paper. However, if the artwork is larger than the page sizes available on your printer, you can print onto multiple sheets of paper.

Artboard divided into multiple page tiles .

Dividing the artboard to fit a printer's available page sizes is called tiling. You can choose a tiling option in the Setup section of the Print dialog box. To view the page tiling boundaries on the artboard, choose View > Show Page Tiling.

When you divide the artboard into multiple page tiles, the pages are numbered from left to right and from top to bottom, starting with page 1. These page numbers appear on-screen for your reference only; they do not print. The numbers enable you to print all of the pages in the file or specify particular pages to print.

–From Adobe Online Help, "Dividing the artboard into multiple page tiles".

Using the Illustrator tools

The Illustrator toolbox contains selection tools, drawing and painting tools, editing tools, viewing tools, and the Fill and Stroke color selection boxes. As you work through the lessons, you'll learn about each tool's specific function.

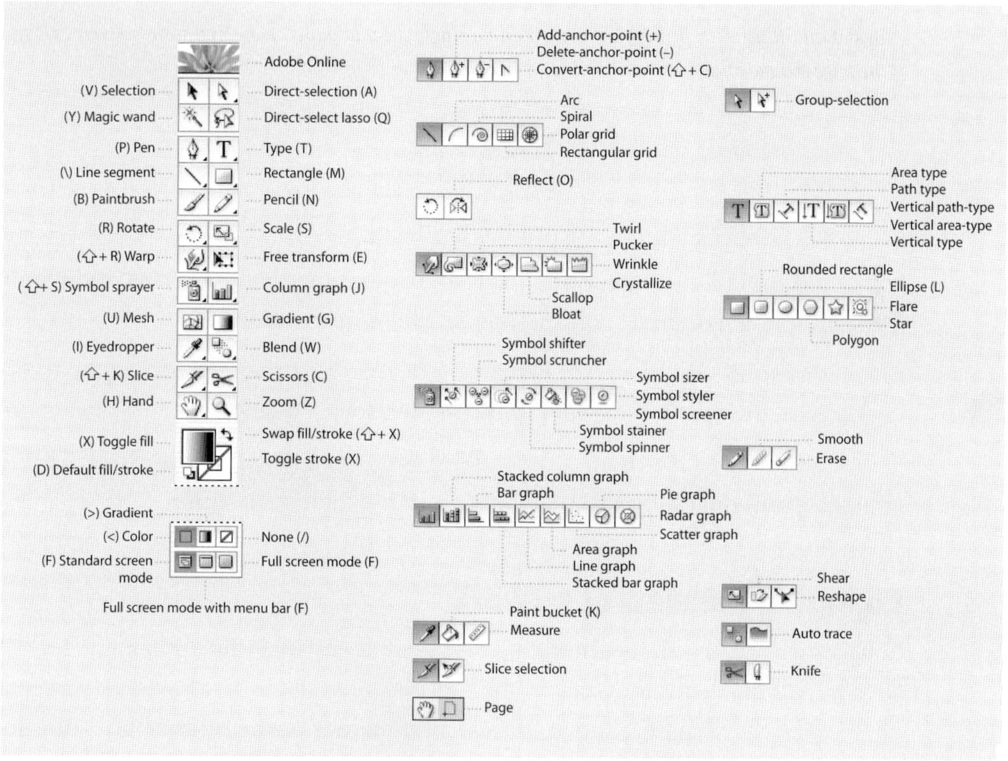

1 To select a tool, either click the tool in the toolbox or press the tool's keyboard shortcut. For example, you can press M to select the Rectangle tool from the keyboard. Selected tools remain active until you click a different tool.

2 If you don't know the keyboard shortcut for a tool, position the pointer over the tool to display the tool's name and shortcut. (All keyboard shortcuts are also listed in the Keyboard Shortcuts section in Online Help. You'll learn to use Online Help later in the lesson.)

Some of the tools in the toolbox display a small triangle at the bottom right corner, indicating the presence of additional hidden tools.

Name and shortcut .

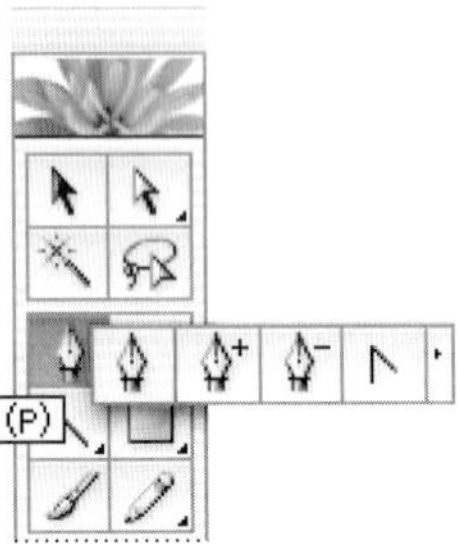

Hidden tools.

3 Select hidden tools in either of the following ways:

• Click and hold down the mouse button on a tool that has additional hidden tools. Then drag to the desired tool, and release the mouse button.

• Hold down Alt (Windows) or Option (Mac OS), and click the tool in the toolbox. Each click selects the next hidden tool in the hidden tool sequence.

• Click and drag to the right of the hidden tools and release on the arrow. This tears off the tools from the toolbar so that you can access them at all times.

Changing the view of artwork

You can reduce or enlarge the view of artwork at any magnification level from 3.13% to 6400%. Adobe Illustrator displays the percentage of the artwork's actual size in the title bar, next to the filename, and at the lower left corner of the Adobe Illustrator document window. Using any of the viewing tools and commands affects only the display of the artwork in Illustrator, not the actual size of the artwork.

Using the View commands

To enlarge or reduce the view of artwork using the View menu, do one of the following:

- Choose View > Zoom In to enlarge the display of the Parrots.ai artwork.
- Choose View > Zoom Out to reduce the view of the Parrots.ai artwork.

Each time you choose a zoom command, the view of the artwork is resized to the nearest predefined zoom amount. The preset zoom levels appear at the lower left corner of the window in a hidden menu, indicated by a triangle next to the percentage.

You can also use the View menu to fit the artwork to your screen, or to view it at actual size.

1 Choose View > Fit in Window. A reduced view of the entire document is displayed in the window. A helpful keyboard command for this view is Ctrl+0 (Windows) or Command+0 (Mac OS).

***Note:** With a Scratch area that extends to the 227" area you can easily lose sight of your illustration. By using View > Fit in Window or the keyboard shortcuts or Ctrl+0 (Windows) or Command+0 (Mac OS) our artwork is recentered in the viewing area.*

2 To display artwork at actual size, choose View > Actual Size. The artwork is displayed at 100%. (The actual size of your artwork determines how much of it can be viewed on-screen at 100%.)

3 Choose View > Fit in Window before continuing to the next section.

Using the Zoom tool

In addition to the View commands, you can use the Zoom tool to magnify and reduce the view of artwork. Use the View menu to select predefined magnification levels or to fit your artwork inside the document window.

1 Click the Zoom tool ( ) in the toolbox to select the tool, and move the cursor into the document window. Notice that a plus sign appears at the center of the Zoom tool.

2 Position the Zoom tool over the parrot in the upper left corner of the illustration and click once. The artwork is displayed at a higher magnification.

3 Click two more times over the upper left parrot. The view is increased again, and you'll notice that the area you clicked is magnified. Next you'll reduce the view of the artwork.

4 With the Zoom tool still selected, position the pointer over the upper left parrot and hold down Alt (Windows) or Option (Mac OS). A minus sign appears at the center of the Zoom tool ( ).

5 With the Alt/Option key still depressed, click in the artwork twice. The view of the artwork is reduced.

A much more controlled and effective zoom is achieved by dragging a marquee to magnify a specific area of your artwork.

6 With the Zoom tool still selected, hold down the mouse button and drag over the area of the illustration you want to magnify; watch as a marquee appears around the area you are dragging, then release the mouse button. The area that was included in the marqued area is now enlarged to fit the size of the document window.

7 Drag a marquee around the lower parrot.

The percentage at which the area is magnified is determined by the size of the marquee you draw with the Zoom tool (the smaller the marquee, the larger the level of magnification).

Area selected.

Resulting view.

***Note:** Although you can draw a marquee with the Zoom tool to enlarge the view of artwork, you cannot draw a marquee to reduce the view of artwork.*

You can also use the Zoom tool to return to a 100% view of your artwork, regardless of the current magnification level.

8 Double-click the Zoom tool in the toolbox to return to a 100% view.

Because the Zoom tool is used frequently during the editing process to enlarge and reduce the view of artwork, you can select it from the keyboard at any time without deselecting any other tool you may be using.

9 Before selecting the Zoom tool from the keyboard, click any other tool in the toolbox and move it into the document window.

10 Now hold down spacebar+Ctrl (Windows) or spacebar+Command (Mac OS) to select the Zoom tool from the keyboard. Click or drag to zoom in on any area of the artwork, and then release the keys. The tool you selected in the previous step is displayed.

11 To zoom out using the keyboard, hold down spacebar+Ctrl+Alt (Windows) or spacebar+Command+Option (Mac OS). Click the desired area to reduce the view of the artwork, and then release the keys.

12 Double-click the Zoom tool in the toolbox to return to a 100% view of your artwork.

Scrolling through a document

You use the Hand tool to scroll to different areas of a document. Using the Hand tool allows you to push the document around much like you would a piece of paper on your desk.

1 Click the Hand tool (✋) in the toolbox.

2 Drag downward in the document window. As you drag, the artwork moves with the hand.

As with the Zoom tool, you can select the Hand tool from the keyboard without deselecting the active tool.

3 Before selecting the Hand tool from the keyboard, click any other tool except the Type tool in the toolbox and move the pointer into the document window.

4 Hold down the spacebar to select the Hand tool from the keyboard, and then drag to bring the artwork back into view.

You can also use the Hand tool as a shortcut to fit all the artwork in the window.

5 Double-click the Hand tool to fit the document in the window.

***Note:** The spacebar shortcut will not work when you are on the Type tool, it will add spaces if you are in a text area, or create a new text area.*

Using the Navigator palette

The Navigator palette lets you scroll through a document. This is useful when you need to see the entire illustration in one window and edit it in a zoomed in view.

1 Make sure that the Navigator palette is at the front of its palette group. (If necessary, click the Navigator palette tab, or choose Window > Navigator.)

2 In the Navigator palette, drag the slider to the right to about 200% to magnify the view of the parrots. As you drag the slider to increase the level of magnification, the red outline in the Navigator window decreases in size.

3 Position the pointer inside the Navigator window. The pointer becomes a hand.

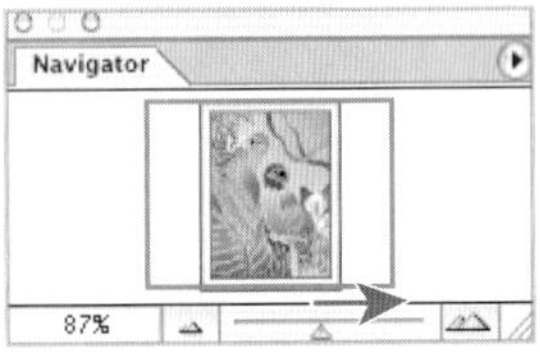

Dragging slider to 200%.

200% view of image.

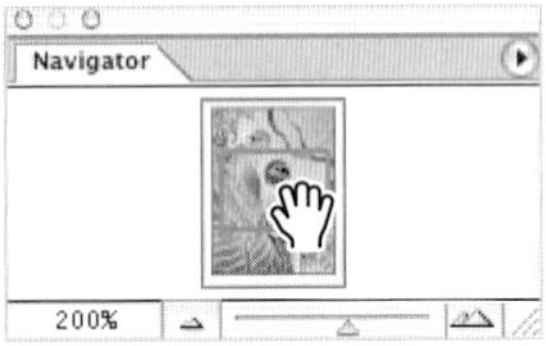

View in Navigator palette.

4 Drag the hand in the Proxy Preview area of the Navigator palette to scroll to different parts of the artwork.

You can also drag a marquee in the Navigator palette to identify the area of the artwork you want to view.

5 With the pointer still positioned in the Navigator palette, hold down on the Ctrl (Windows) or Command (Mac OS). When the hand changes to a magnifier, drag a marquee over an area of the artwork. The smaller the marquee you draw, the greater the magnification level in the document window.

Working with palettes

Palettes help to make modifying artwork easier by readily giving you access to many of Illustrator's functions. By default, they appear in stacked groups. To show or hide a palette as you work, choose the appropriate Window command. Selecting a Window command, as indicated by a check mark, displays the selected palette at the front of its group; deselecting a Window command conceals the entire palette group.

You can reorganize your work space in various ways. Try these techniques:

• To hide or display all open palettes and the toolbox, press Tab. To hide or display the palettes only, press Shift+Tab.

• To make a palette appear at the front of its group, click the palette's tab.

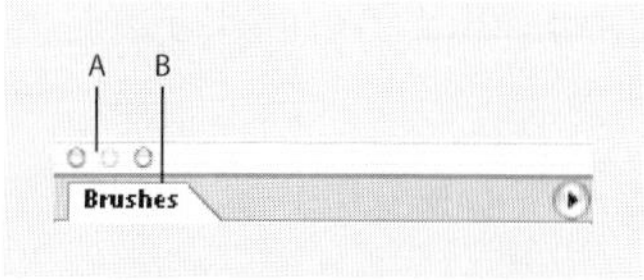

A. Title bar. B. Tab.

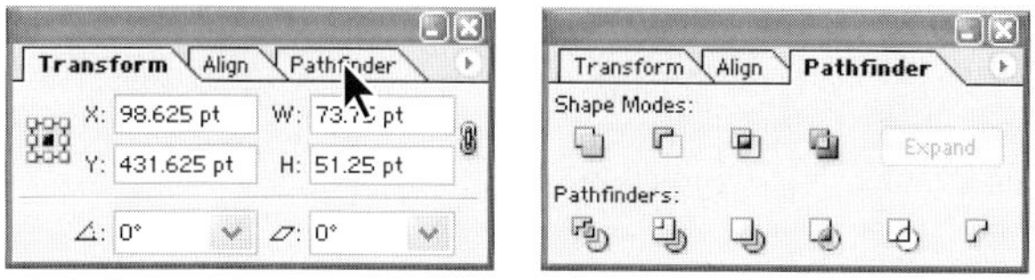

Click the Attributes tab to move the palette to the front.

To move an entire palette group, drag its title bar.

To rearrange or separate a palette group, drag a palette's tab. Dragging a palette outside of an existing group removes it from the group.

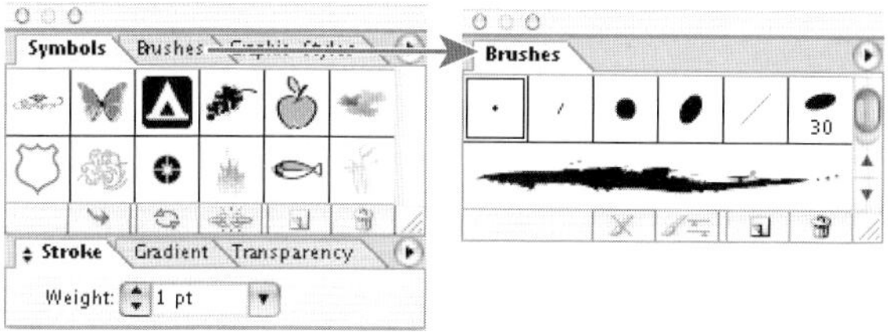

Palettes are grouped.

Drag a palette by its tab to separate the palette from its group.

• To move a palette to another group, drag the palette's tab to that group.

• To display a palette menu, position the pointer on the triangle in the upper right corner of the palette, and hold down the mouse button.

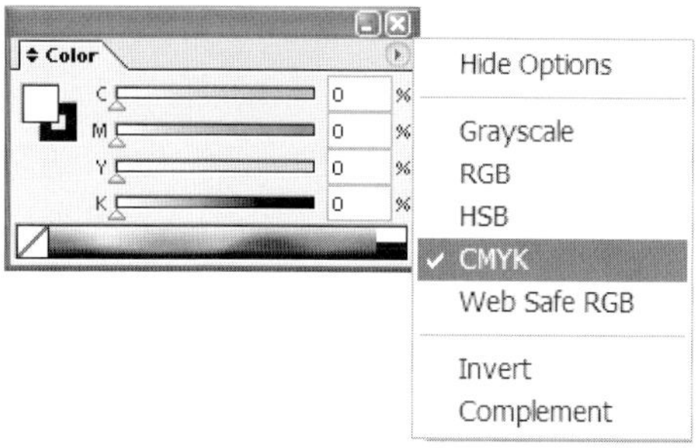

• If a palette has the option to change the height, you can drag its lower right corner. (You cannot change the height of the Align, Attributes, Color, Info, Magic Wand, Options, Pathfinder, Stroke, Transform Type or palette.)

• To collapse a group to palette title bars only, click the minimize/maximize box (Windows) or the resize box (Mac OS); click the box again to expand the palette group.

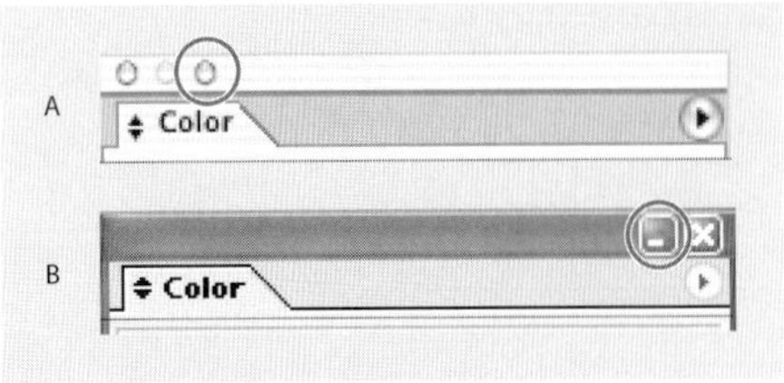

Click to collapse or expand palette.

***A.** Mac OS. **B.** Windows.*

• To cycle through the available sizes for a palette, double-click a palette's tab or single-click on the double triangles to the left of the palette name. (Not all palettes have the double triangles.) You can still access the menu of a collapsed palette.

Using context menus

In addition to the menus at the top of your screen, context-sensitive menus display commands relevant to the active tool, selection, or palette.

To display context-sensitive menus, position the pointer over the artwork, palette list, scrollbar or Document magnification level. Then click with the right mouse button (Windows) or press Ctrl and hold down the mouse button (Mac OS). (In Windows, you can also use context-sensitive Help or press F1 to get online Help. See "Using online Help" on the following page.)

Here you see the options for the Pen tool, displayed in its context-sensitive menu. (You access these same options by selecting the Edit or Object menu.)

Using online Help

For complete information about using palettes and tools, you can use online Help. Online Help includes keyboard shortcuts and additional information, including full-color galleries of examples. All the illustrations in online Help are in color.

Online Help is easy to use, because you can look for topics in these ways:

- Scanning a table of contents.
- Searching for keywords or phrases.
- Using an index.
- Jumping from topic to topic using related topic links.

Displaying the online Help contents

First you'll look for a topic using the Contents screen.

To properly view online Help topics, you need to have a recent browser, Internet Explorer, Safari, Netscape for instance, with JavaScript active.

1 To display the Help Contents menu, choose Help > Illustrator Help, or press F1 (Windows).

2 Drag the scroll bar or click the arrows to navigate through the contents. The contents are organized in a hierarchy of topics, much like the chapters of a book.

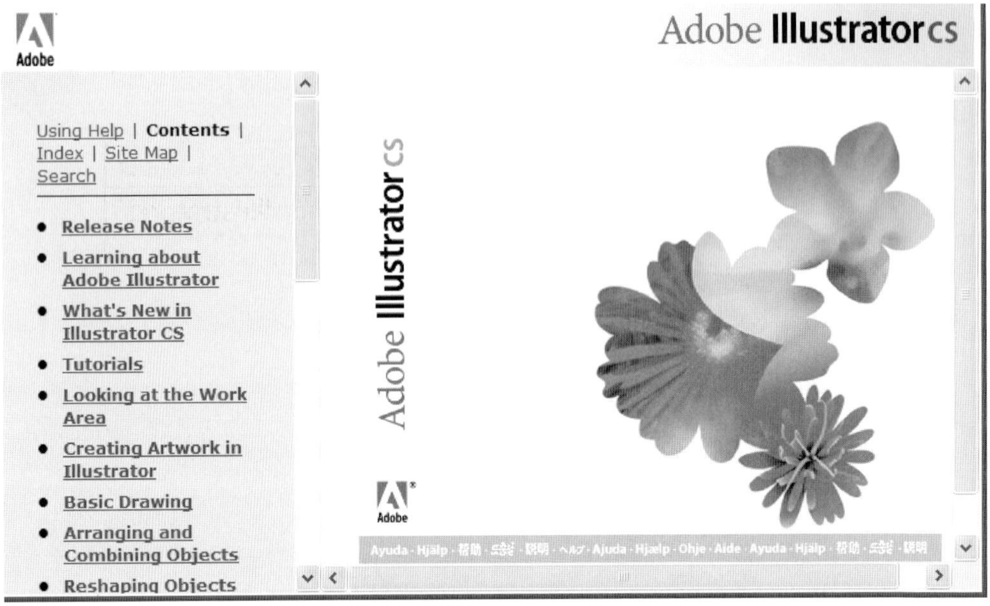

Illustrator Help Contents screen.

3 Position the pointer on the Looking at the Work Area chapter, and click it to display its contents.

4 Click on the topic of Using tools and commands.

5 Locate the Overview of tools (1 of 5) topic, and click to display it. An illustration of the Selection tools and shortcut information appears.

The online Help system is interactive. You can click any blue text, called a link, to jump to another topic. When the pointer changes into a hand it indicates a link, and appears when you move the mouse over a link or a hotspot.

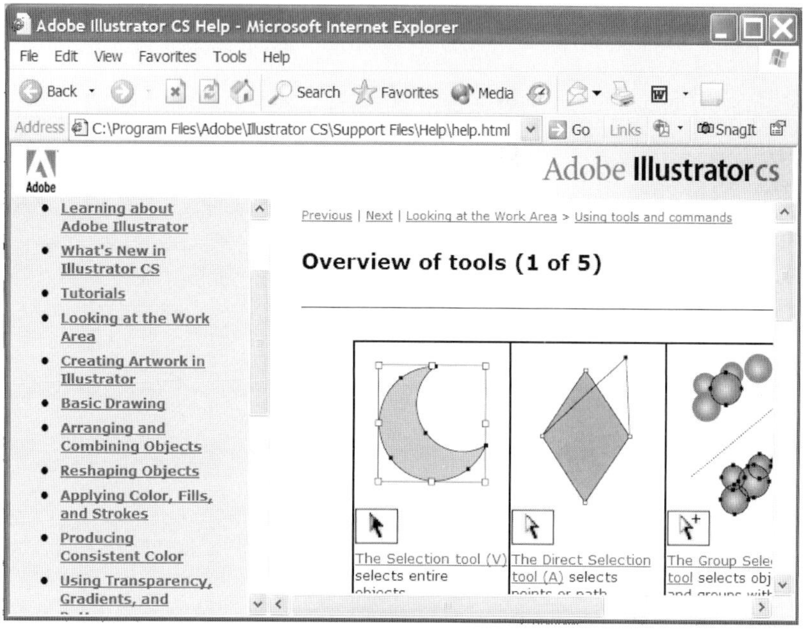

Using keywords, links, and the index

If you can't find the topic you are interested in by viewing the Contents page, then you can try searching using Search. You can search using keywords or phrases.

1 Click Search, and type **Brushes** in the text box. Click the Search button to go to that topic. A list appears of the items containing information about brushes.

2 Click Creating and editing brushes to learn about creating brushes. Notice that there are several subtopics available for further research.

3 Click Creating a calligraphic brush to read step-by-step instructions on how to create a calligraphic brush.

You can also locate a topic using the Index.

4 Click Index to go to an alphabetical listing of topics. You will see an alphabet.

5 Click the letter *H* to get a listing of all the topics starting with H.

6 Click the 1 or 2 next to the Hand tool entry to get information about the Hand tool and its functions.

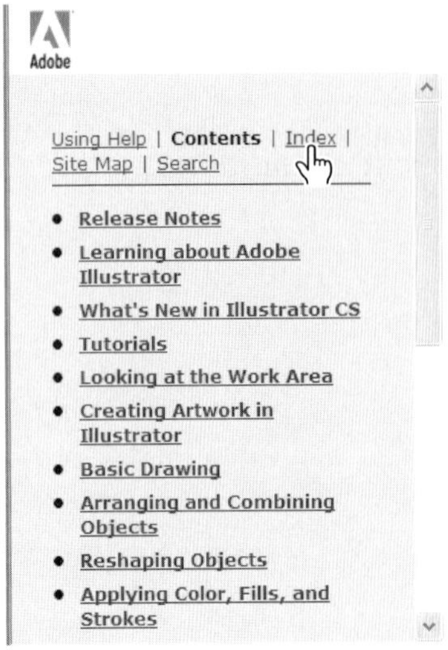

Click Index for alphabet.

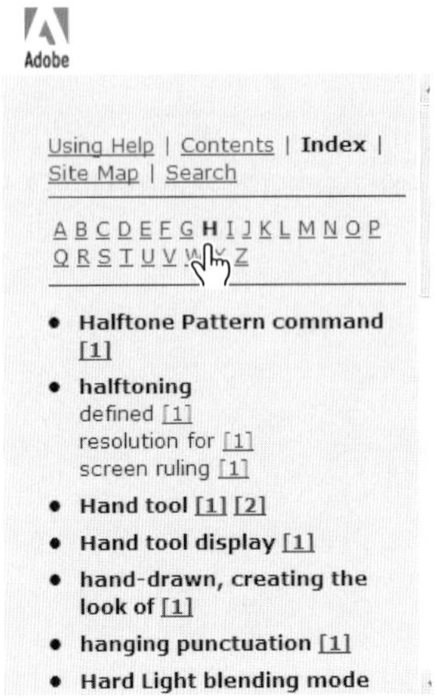

Click letter for topics; then click number.

Using Adobe online services

Another way to get information on Adobe Illustrator or on related Adobe products is to use the Adobe online services. Selecting the Illustrator Online menu item takes you directly to the product page on Adobe.com that lists the latest information on Illustrator.

Visiting the Adobe Web site

If you have an Internet connection and a Web browser installed on your system, you can access the U.S. Adobe Systems Web site (at http://www.adobe.com) for information on services, products, tutorials, tips, and community events on Illustrator.

1 If you have an Internet connection, from Adobe Illustrator, choose Help > Illustrator Online, or click the icon at the top of the toolbox.

2 When you have finished browsing the Adobe page, close and exit the browser.

Review questions

1 Describe two ways to change your view of a document.

2 How do you select tools in Illustrator?

3 Describe three ways to change the palette display.

4 Describe two ways to get more information about the Illustrator program.

Review answers

1 You can select commands from the View menu to zoom in or out of a document, or fit it to your screen; you can also use the Zoom tool in the toolbox, and click or drag over a document to enlarge or reduce the view. In addition, you can use keyboard shortcuts to magnify or reduce the display of artwork. You can also use the Navigator palette to scroll artwork or change its magnification without using the document window.

2 To select a tool, you can either click the tool in the toolbox or press the tool's keyboard shortcut. For example, you can press V to choose the Selection tool from the keyboard. Selected tools remain active until you click a different tool.

3 You can click a palette's tab or choose Window > Palette Name to make the palette appear. You can drag a palette's tab to separate the palette from its group and create a new group, or drag the palette into another group. You can drag a palette group's title bar to move the entire group. Double-click a palette's tab to cycle through a palette's various sizes. You can also press Shift+Tab to hide or display all palettes.

4 Adobe Illustrator contains online Help, plus keyboard shortcuts and some additional information and full-color illustrations. Illustrator also has context-sensitive help about tools and commands, and online services, including a link to the Adobe Systems Web site, for additional information on services, products, and Illustrator tips.

Lesson 2

2 Selection Basics

Choosing the correct selection method to make changes to objects is essential. In this lesson, you will learn how to correctly locate and select objects using the Selection tools, as well as protect objects by hiding and locking. Later, build on these methods by integrating layers.

In this lesson, you'll learn how to do the following:

- Differentiate when to use the Selection, Direct Selection, or Group Selection tools.

- How to group and ungroup items.

- How to clone items with the Selection tool.

- How to lock and hide items for organizational purposes.

- How to save selections for future use.

Getting started

You probably know the saying, "You have to select it, to affect it." When changing colors, size, adding effects or any number of attributes you must first select the object to which you are applying the changes. Consider this lesson a primer in the fundamentals of the Selection tools. More advanced selection techniques using layers are available and discussed in Lesson 7, "Working with Layers."

Before you begin, you'll need to restore the default preferences for Adobe Illustrator. Then open the art file that you will be working with.

1 To ensure that the tools and palettes function exactly as described in this lesson, delete or deactivate (by renaming) the Adobe Illustrator CS preferences file. See "Restoring default preferences" on page 2 in the Introduction.

2 Start Adobe Illustrator.

3 Choose File > Open, and open the L2strt_01.ai file in the Lesson02 folder, located inside the Lessons folder within the AICIB folder on your hard drive.

Using the Selection tool

4 Choose the Selection tool (➤). Position the mouse over the different star shapes without clicking. Note the icon that appears as you pass over objects (➤▪), indicating that there is an object that can be selected under the pointer. Click on the yellow star in the upper left corner. A bounding box with eight handles appears.

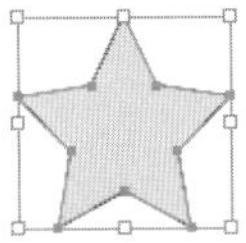

The Bounding Box.

The bounding box is used for transformations such as resizing and rotating; it also indicates that this item is selected and ready to be edited. This could mean changing the size, color, position, or any number of other things.

5 Using the Selection tool, click on the star to the right and notice that the first star is now deselected and only the second star is selected.

6 Add another star to the selection by holding down the Shift key and clicking on the first star. Both stars are now selected.

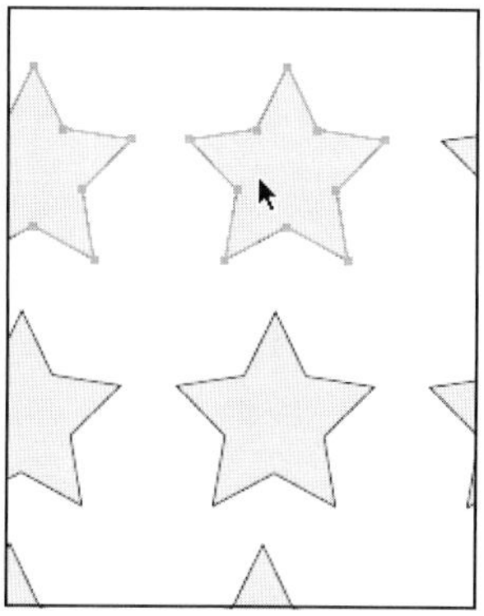

Add other items to a selection by holding down the Shift key.

7 Reposition the stars by clicking in the center of either selected star and dragging. Since both are selected, they travel together.

Note: *If selecting an item without a fill, you must click on the stroke (border).*

8 Deselect the stars by clicking on the artboard where there are no objects. If you prefer, choose Select > Deselect.

9 Revert to Saved by choosing the F12 key or File >Revert. In the Revert dialog box, click Revert.

The Direct Selection tool

1 With the same file, L2strt_01.ai, open, switch to the Direct Selection tool (). Again, don't click, but move the mouse over the different points on the stars with the Direct Selection tool. When the Direct Selection tool is over an anchor point of an unselected or selected path or object, it has a hollow square next to it. Click on the top point of the first star and drag the anchor point. Note that only the point you dragged is solid, representing that it is selected, while the other points in the star are hollow and not selected.

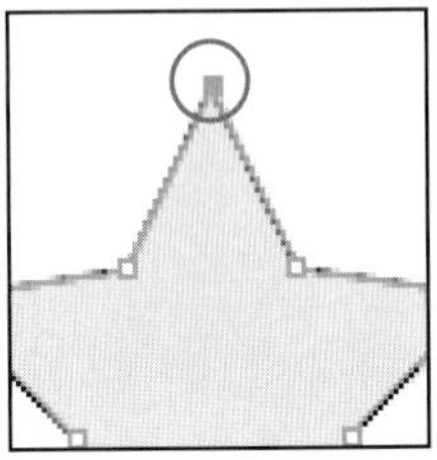

Only the point that is selected is solid.

2 With the Direct Selection tool still active, click and drag just the individual point. This allows you to edit the shape of an object. Try clicking on other points, and notice that the initial point is then deselected and you can edit other points individually.

3 File > Revert.

Note: *Using the Shift key, you can also select individual points to move them together.*

Marquee select

Some selections may be easier to make by creating a marquee around the objects that you want to select.

1 With the same file, L2start_01.ai, open switch to the Selection tool (). Instead of shift+clicking to select the first two stars, position the mouse above the upper left star and then click and drag downward and to the right to create a marquee that overlaps just the top points of the stars.

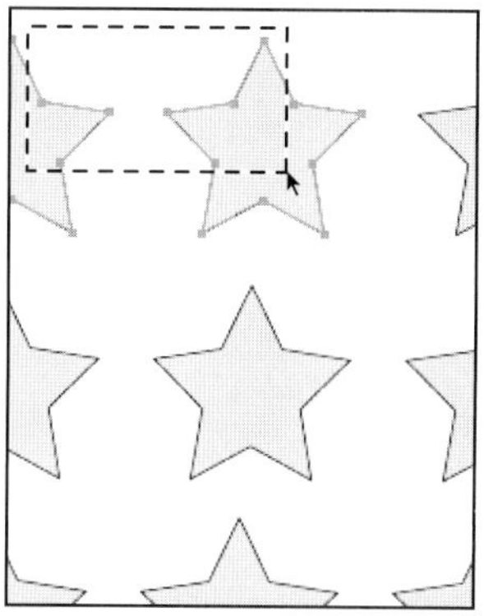

When dragging with the Selection tool, you only need to encompass a small part of an object to include it in the selection.

2 Try dragging a marquee starting outside the stars and crossing over all three anchor points in the top row. All stars become active.

3 Select > Deselect or click where there are no objects.

4 Using the same method, but with the Direct Selection tool, click outside the first star and drag to select the top points of each of the stars in the top row.

Click and drag across the top points.

Only the top points become selected. Click on one of the anchor points and drag to see how they reposition together. Use this method when selecting a single point as well; that way, you don't have to zoom in to hit exactly the anchor point that is to be edited.

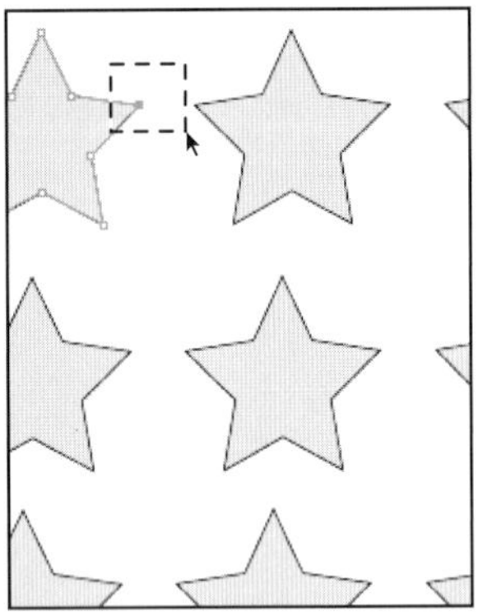

Select anchor points with a marquee.

5 File > Revert.

Grouping items

You can combine several objects into a group so that the objects are treated as a single unit. This way, you can move or transform a number of objects without affecting their attributes or relative positions.

1 With the same file, L2start_01.ai, open, switch to the Selection tool (). Click outside the top left of the first star and drag a marquee that touches each star on the first row to select all three.

2 Choose Object > Group, then choose Select > Deselect.

3 With the Selection tool click on the first star, notice that since it is grouped with the other two stars, all three become selected.

Adding to a group

Groups can also be nested; that is, they can be grouped within other objects or groups to form larger groups.

1 With the top group of three stars still selected, Shift+click on the first star in the second row. With this added to the selection, choose Object > Group.

2 Shift+click on the middle star in the second row and also choose Object > Group. Repeat this for the third star in the second row.

3 Select > Deselect when finished.

You have created groups within groups. This is a common technique used when designing artwork, but can be confusing when editing existing files where grouping has been used.

4 Choose the Selection tool (↖) and click on any one of the grouped stars. They all become selected.

5 Click off the stars to a blank area on the artboard to deselect them.

6 Hold down on the Direct Selection tool and drag to the right to access the Group Selection tool (↖+).

7 Click once on the first star. Only the star becomes active. Click again and the initial group of three stars becomes active. As you continue to click, each individual group created becomes selected.

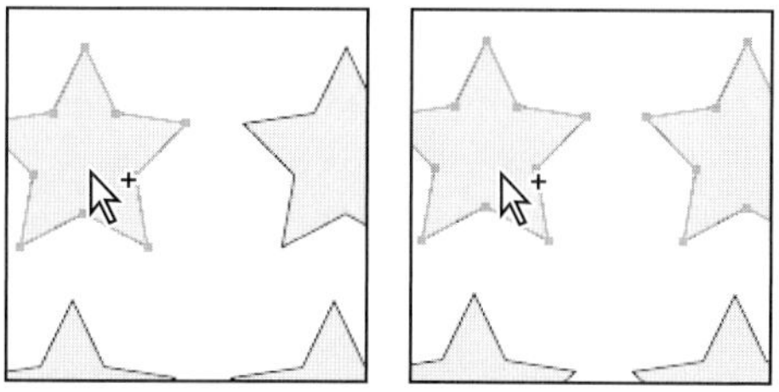

The Group Selection tool allows you add selections within groups.

8 Ungroup items by choosing Object > Ungroup. Note that you will have to repeat this action for each of the groups created. In other words, to get these back to individual stars we would have to choose Object > Ungroup four times.

Read Lesson 7, "Working with Layers." If you have a complex setup of nested groups and want to ungroup just one item, you can locate and select that item much easier using layers, and you don't have to ungroup.

9 File > Close without saving.

Applying the selection techniques

In this next lesson, you will use some of the techniques discussed as well as several others.

1 Choose File > Open, and open the L2strt_02.ai file in the Lesson02 folder, located inside the Lessons folder within the AICIB folder on your hard drive.

2 Make sure that the entire artboard is visible by choosing View > Fit in Window. On the right you see the completed project, on the left are the objects needed to create the finished dog.

3 Start this lesson by hiding the palettes; you won't need them for this lesson. Hold down Shift+Tab to hide the palettes, or hide palettes individually or by groups using the Window menu.

(Pressing Shift+Tab switches between hiding and showing the palettes. Pressing Tab alone hides or shows the toolbox and palettes.)

4 With the Selection tool (), select the brownish-red circle. To avoid grabbing a bounding box handle and resizing the circle, click and drag the center of the circle to slide it to its new location as the nose of the dog.

5 Using the Selection tool, drag both ears, the tuft of hair, and the mouth into position.

Note: Be careful with the mouth. It contains two objects, so using the Selection tool Shift+click to select the top and bottom objects and move them together.

Use the Selection tools to move parts into place.

6 Select the dog's head (light brown shape) and choose Object > Lock > Selection to keep it in position. You will not be able to select it until you choose Object > Unlock All. Leave it locked for now.

You are using is the solid arrow, or Selection tool (), to activate an entire object and move it. Each object that you select is made up of several anchor points. To activate these anchor points individually, switch to the Direct Selection tool ().

7 Click on the anchor point in the first peak, or tuft, of hair. When the individual point is selected it appears as a solid point (active), whereas the other anchor points are hollow (inactive). Click and drag the individual anchor point to change its position.

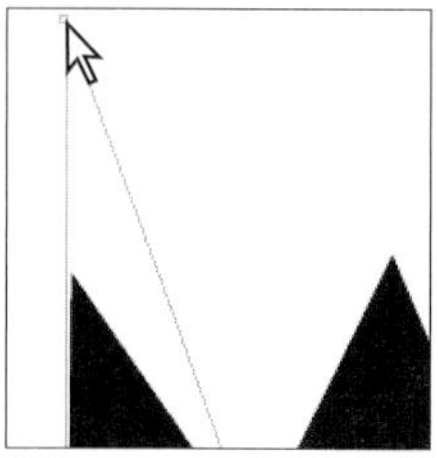

Using the Direct Selection tool, click and drag individual anchor points.

8 Individually select other anchor points in the hair shape and position them in different directions. You are giving a ruffled look to the dog's hair.

9 Choose the Selection tool. The eye is made of several parts. Using either the marquee selection technique or the Shift key to select all three parts of the eye. Choose Object > Group. Drag the eye into a position on the face to create a left eye.

10 While still on the Selection tool, hold down the Alt (Windows) or Option key (Mac OS) and drag the selected eye to the right to clone the left eye and position it as the right eye. Make sure that you release the mouse before releasing the Alt/Option key. The dog now has two eyes.

Note: *If you also hold down the Shift key when cloning, the newly cloned object is constrained and snaps to a straight, 45°, 90°, or 180° angle.*

11 File > Save and close the file.

Hiding selections

As you create more complicated artwork, existing objects may get in the way and make it difficult to make selections. A common technique when designing in Adobe Illustrator is to Hide selected artwork, which can be done by choosing Object > Hide > Selection. A hidden object can not be moved or selected; it is essentially as though that object no longer exists on the art board. Bring all hidden objects back at the same time by choosing Object > Show All.

Advanced selection techniques

When working on complex artwork, selections may become more difficult to control. In this lesson, we combine some of the lessons already covered with some additional features that will make selecting the correct items easier.

1 File > Open the file named L2strt_03.ai in the Lesson02 folder of AICIB lessons. Have both the Swatches and Stroke palettes open. If they are not visible, choose Window > Swatches and Stroke.

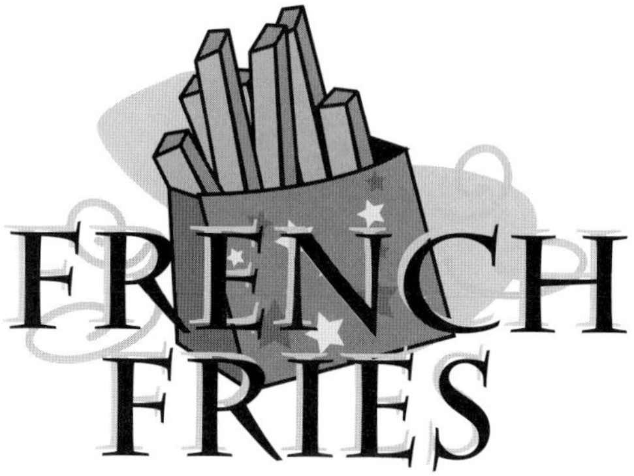

2 Note that the large words, ***French Fries***, cover and make it difficult to select items underneath. Using the Selection (↖) tool, select the words, French Fries, and choose Object > Hide > Selection or use Ctrl+3 (Windows) or Command+3 (Mac OS). The words will come back in the exact same location when we choose Object > Show All at the end of the lesson.

3 Changing the fill of all the yellow stars to white could be time-consuming, but using the Select Same feature reduces the trouble. Select any one yellow star and then choose Select > Same > Fill and Stroke. All the other stars become selected. Make sure that the fill box is forward in the toolbar and select white from the Swatches palette. The stars all change to white.

4 Select one of the shapes creating the french fries and then choose Select > Same > Stroke Weight. The french fry shape had a 3 pt stroke so all strokes that are **3** pt are now activated. Using Window > Stroke palette, type **5** into the textbox to increase the weight to 5 pt. Keep these items selected.

5 There are times when you will want to refer back to a selection more than once. With your previous selection still active, choose Select > Save Selection. Name the selection **5 pt stroke**.

6 Deselect the selection and choose Select > 5 pt stroke from the bottom of the Select menu to make the selection again.

7 Choose Object > Show All to bring back the words ***French Fries***.

8 Save and close the file.

Exploring on your own

Experiment with shapes by creating a shape object, circle, star, rectangle, or whatever. Clone it several times using the Alt/Option key. Apply different colors and strokes to the shapes and reselect them using the Select Same menu item. Try to clone while using the Shift key to constrain the angle of the newly created object. Try cloning multiple items at the same time.

Review questions

1 Why might an object that has no fill not become selected when you click on it?

2 How can you select one item in a group?

3 How do you edit the shape of an object?

4 What should be done after spending much time creating a selection that is going to be used repeatedly?

5 If something is blocking your view of a selection, what can you do?

Review answers

1 Items that have no fill must be selected by clicking on the stroke.

2 Using the Group Selection tool, you can click once for an individual item within a group. Continue to click to add the next grouped items to the selection. Read lesson 7, Layers to see how you can use layers to make complex selection easy.

3 Using the Direct Selection tool, you can select one or more individual anchor point and make changes to the shape of an object.

4 For any selection that you will need to use again, choose Select > Save Selection. Name the file and reselect it at any time from the Select menu.

5 If something is blocking your access to a selection, you can choose Object > Hide > Selection. The object is not deleted, just hidden in the same position until you choose Object > Show All.

Lesson 3

3 Creating Basic Shapes

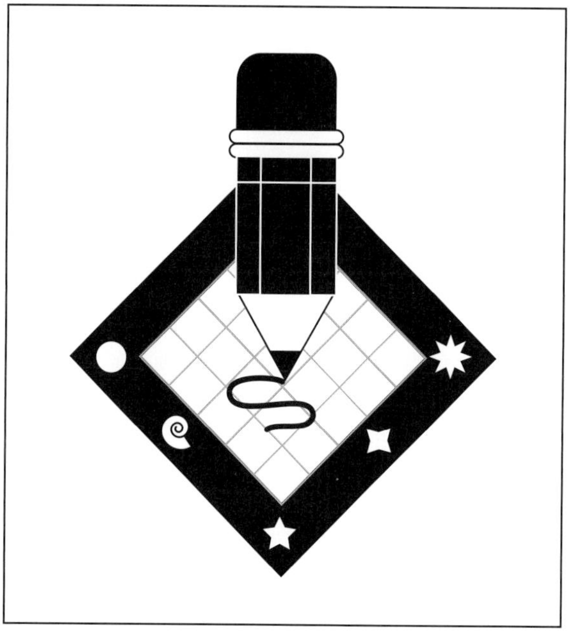

Many objects in the Adobe Illustrator program can be created by starting with basic shapes and then editing them to create new shapes. In this lesson, you will use some basic shapes to create a logo.

In this lesson, you'll learn how to do the following:

- Use tools and commands to create basic shapes.
- Copy and combine objects to create new shapes.
- Use rulers, guides, and grids as drawing aids.
- Use Selection tools to select and change parts of objects.
- Paint objects.
- Scale objects using the bounding box.

Getting started

Before you begin, you'll need to restore the default preferences for Adobe Illustrator. Then you'll open the finished art file for this lesson to see what you've created.

1 To ensure that the tools and palettes function exactly as described in this lesson, delete or deactivate (by renaming) the Adobe Illustrator CS preferences file. See "Restoring default preferences" on page 2 in the Introduction.

2 Start Adobe Illustrator.

3 Choose File > Open, and open the L3end.ai file in the Lesson03 folder, located inside the Lessons folder within the AICIB folder on your hard drive.

4 If you like, choose View > Zoom Out to make the finished artwork smaller, adjust the window size, and leave it on your screen as you work. (Use the Hand tool (✋) to move the artwork where you want it in the window.) If you don't want to leave the image open, choose File > Close.

Now create the start file to begin the lesson.

5 Choose File > New to open a new, untitled document. Leave the Color Mode and Artboard Size at the default settings, and click OK.

6 Choose File > Save As, name the file **Logo.ai**, and select the Lesson03 folder in the Save In menu. Leave the Type of File Format option set to Adobe Illustrator® Document, and click Save. In the Illustrator Native Format Options leave at the defaults and click OK.

Setting up the document

You'll begin the lesson by setting the ruler units to inches, displaying a grid to use as a guideline for drawing, and closing the palettes that you won't use.

1 Close all the palettes by clicking their close boxes or by holding down Shift and pressing Tab once. For now, you won't need to use them.

You can also hide or show the palettes by choosing their Window commands. If a palette is grouped with others, choosing the Window command hides or shows the group. (Pressing Shift+Tab switches between hiding and showing the palettes. Pressing Tab alone hides or shows the toolbox and palettes.)

2 Choose View > Show Grid to display a grid that's useful for measuring, drawing, and aligning shapes. This grid won't print with the artwork.

3 Choose View > Show Rulers to display rulers along the top and left side of the window. The ruler units are set by default to points.

You can change ruler units for all documents or for only the current document. The ruler unit of measure applies to measuring objects, moving and transforming objects, setting grid and guide spacing, and creating ellipses and rectangles. (It does not affect the units in the Character, Paragraph, and Stroke palettes. These are controlled by the options in the Units & Undo Preferences dialog box.)

4 Choose File > Document Setup to change the ruler units for only this document. In the Document Setup dialog box, for Units choose Inches, leave the other settings unchanged, and click OK.

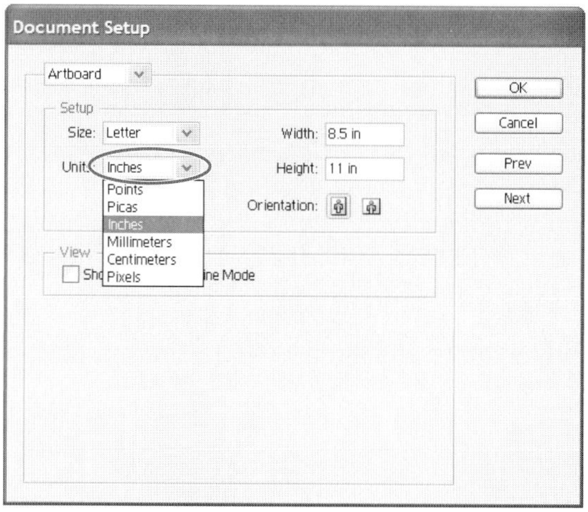

You can also set the default ruler units for all documents by choosing Edit > Preferences > Units & Undo (Windows) or Illustrator > Preferences > Units & Undo (Mac OS).

Using basic shape tools

In this lesson, you'll create a simple logo using the basic shape tools. The shape tools are organized in two groups in the toolbox, under the ellipse and Rectangle tools. You can tear these groups off the toolbox to display in their own palettes.

1 Hold down the mouse button on the Rectangle tool (▭) until a group of tools appears, and then drag to the tear-off triangle at the end and release the mouse button.

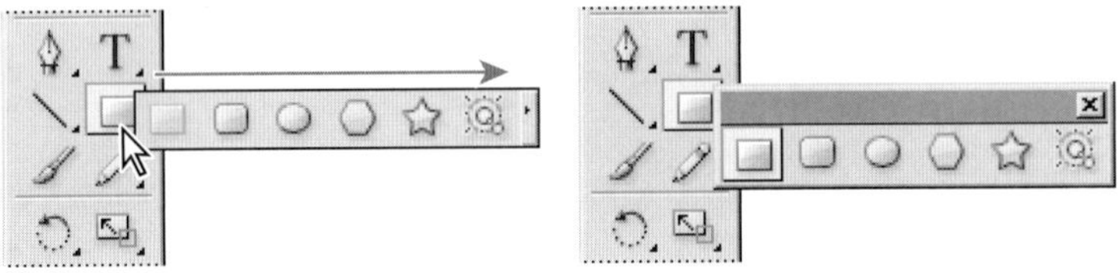

Tearing off tool group

2 Move the Rectangle tool group away from the toolbox.

Drawing the pencil shape

In Adobe Illustrator, you control the thickness and color of lines that you draw by setting stroke attributes. A stroke is the paint characteristics of a line or the outline of an object. A fill is the paint characteristics of the inside of an object. The default settings will let you see the objects you draw with a white fill and a black outline.

First you'll draw a series of rectangles and triangles that make up the pencil. You'll display Smart Guides to align your drawing.

1 Select the Zoom tool (🔍) in the toolbox, and click in the middle of the window once or twice until you are zoomed in to 150%. (Notice that 150% is displayed in the bottom left corner of the window.)

2 Choose View > Smart Guides to turn them on. Smart Guides automatically snap the edges of objects to nearby objects or their intersect points as you move them. Smart Guides also show Text Label Hints that display information on the position the pointer is currently snapped to (such as "center") as you manipulate the pointer.

You'll display the Info palette to check the dimensions of the rectangle you draw.

How Smart Guides work

When Smart Guides are turned on and you move the cursor over your artwork, the cursor looks for objects, page boundaries, and intersections of construction guides to snap to that are within the tolerance range set in Smart Guides Preferences.

You can use Smart Guides in the following ways when you create, move, and transform objects:

• When you create an object with the pen or shape tools, use the Smart Guides to position the new object's anchor points relative to the other object.

• When you move an object, use the Smart Guides to align to the point on the object that you have selected. You can align to the anchor point at the corner of a selected object near the bounding box. To do so, select the object just inside the bounding box handle. If the tolerance is 5 points or greater, you can snap to the corner point from 5 points away.

• When the Transform Tools option is selected in Smart Guides Preferences and you transform an object, Smart Guides appear to assist the transformation.

Note: *When Snap to Grid is turned on, you cannot use Smart Guides (even if the menu command is selected).*

-From Adobe Online Help "Using Smart Guides".

3 Choose Window > Info to display the Info palette.

4 Select the Rectangle tool ( ), and drag it to draw a rectangle that's 0.75 inch wide and 1 inch tall. (Use the rulers and the grid as guides.) This will be the body of the pencil.

When you release the mouse button, the rectangle is automatically selected and its center point appears. All objects created with the shape tools have a center point that you can drag to align the object with other elements in your artwork. You can make the center point visible or invisible (using the Attributes palette), but you cannot delete it.

5 In the Info palette, note the rectangle's width and height. If necessary, choose Edit > Undo, and redraw the rectangle.

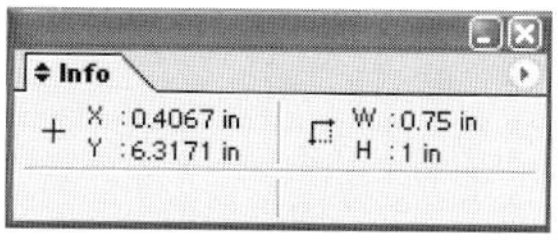

Info palette displays rectangle's width and height .

You'll draw another rectangle centered inside the first one to represent the two vertical lines on the pencil.

6 With the Rectangle tool still selected, position the pointer over the center point of the rectangle, hold down Alt (Windows) or Option (Mac OS), and drag out from the center point to draw a rectangle that's centered inside it. Release the mouse button when the rectangle is the same height as the first rectangle (1 inch).

Holding down Alt/Option as you drag the Rectangle tool draws the rectangle from its center point rather than from its top left corner. Smart Guides indicate when you've snapped to the first rectangle's edge, by displaying the text label hint "path."

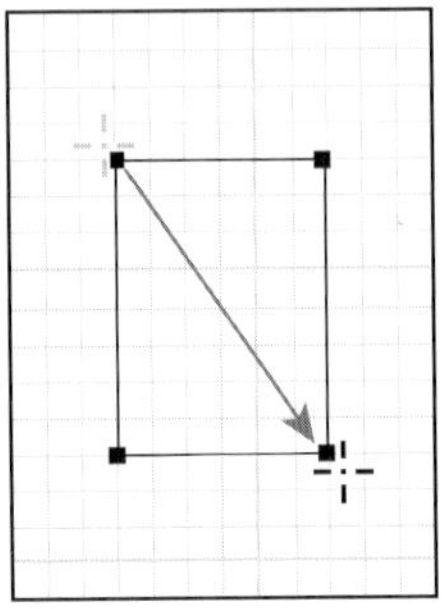

Drag to draw first rectangle.

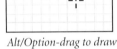

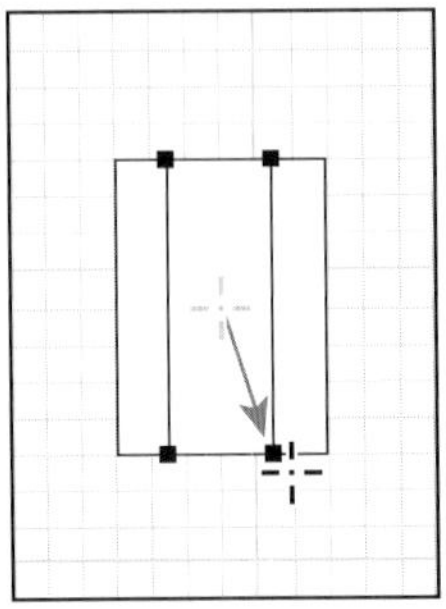

Alt/Option-drag to draw second rectangle.

Besides dragging a tool to draw a shape, you can click with the tool to open a dialog box of options. Now you'll create a rounded rectangle for the eraser by setting options in a dialog box.

7 Select the Rounded Rectangle tool (▢), and click once in the artwork to open the Rounded Rectangle dialog box. Type **0.75** in the Width text box, press Tab, and type **0.75** in the Height text box. Then press Tab again, and type **0.20** in the Corner Radius text box (the radius is the amount of the curve on the corners). Click OK.

To automatically enter identical Width and Height values in the Ellipse or either Rectangle dialog box, enter a Width or Height value, and then click the name of the other value to enter the same amount.

You'll use Smart Guides to help you align the eraser to the top of the pencil body.

8 Choose View > Hide Bounding Box to hide the bounding boxes of selected objects. This will prevent you from accidentally distorting the eraser shape when you move and align it.

The bounding box appears as a temporary boundary around selected objects. With the bounding box, you can move, rotate, duplicate, and scale objects easily by dragging the selection or a handle (one of the hollow squares surrounding the selected objects). When you release the mouse button, the object snaps to the current border created by the bounding box, and you see the object's outline move.

9 With the Rounded Rectangle tool still selected, hold down Ctrl (Windows) or Command (Mac OS) to select the Selection tool ( ) temporarily. Select the right edge of the eraser without releasing the mouse button, and then drag the eraser to the right side of the pencil body (Smart Guides indicate the path of the right side). Release the mouse button to drop the eraser on top of the pencil body.

10 Then hold down Ctrl (Windows) or Command (Mac OS), select the bottom edge of the eraser, and drag it up to the intersect point at the top of the pencil body. Release the mouse button.

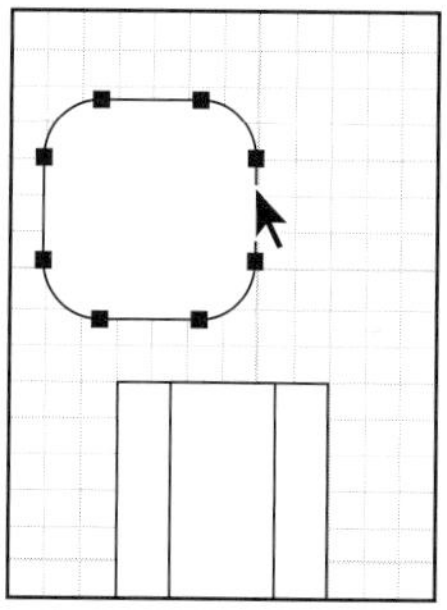

Select right edge of eraser shape.

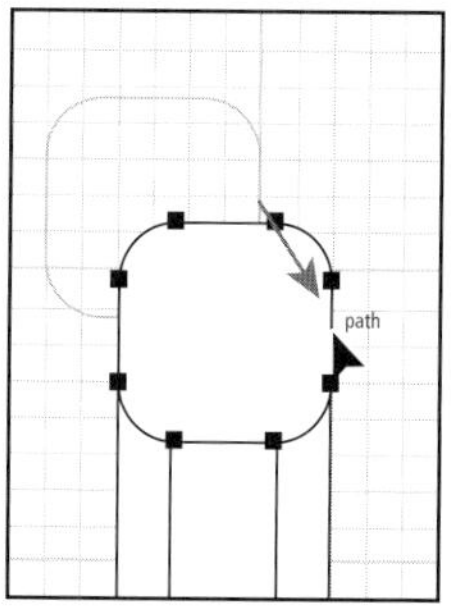

Drag eraser to path on pencil body.

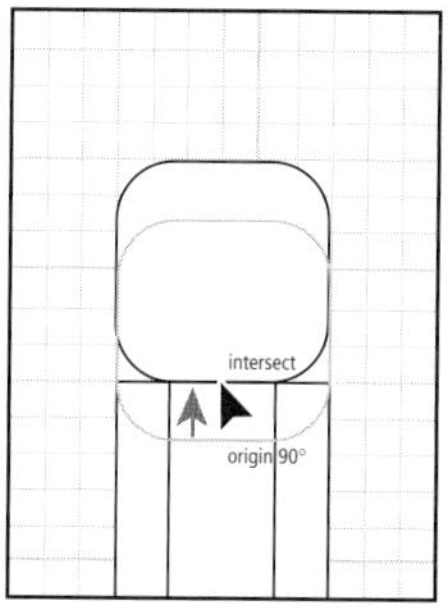

Drag bottom of eraser to top of pencil body.

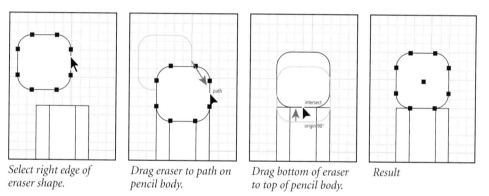

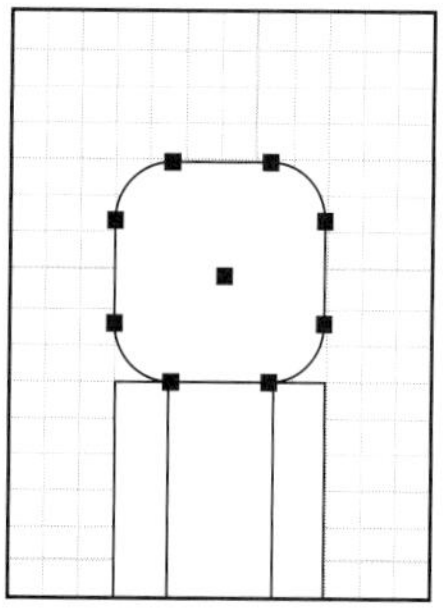

Result

Next you'll create two shapes to represent the metal bands connecting the eraser to the pencil.

11 To create the first band, click once anywhere in the artwork to open the Rounded Rectangle dialog box again. Type **0.85** in the Width text box, **0.10** in the Height text box, and **0.05** in the Corner Radius text box. Click OK.

12 Click the Selection tool ( ) to select the band, select the bottom left anchor point, and move the band to the top of the pencil body. Release the mouse button. (Smart Guides snap the anchor point to the top corner of the pencil body.)

13 With the band still selected, hold down Alt (Windows) or Option (Mac OS), select the anchor point again, drag straight up to make a copy, and move it above the original band. Release the mouse button. (Smart Guides snap the anchor point of the new copy to the top of the original band.)

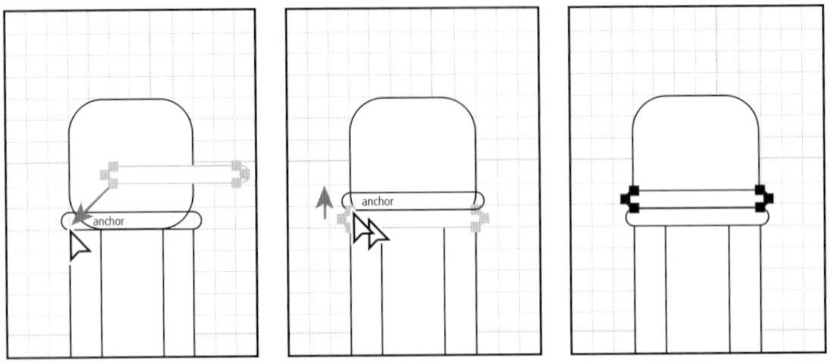

Move first metal band between eraser and pencil body. *Alt/Option-drag a copy above first metal band.* *Smart Guides snap objects into position.*

You've been working in Preview view. This default view of a document lets you see how objects are painted (in this case, with a white fill and black stroke). If paint attributes seem distracting, you can work with just the wireframe view of an object.

Now you'll draw two triangles to represent the pencil tip and its lead using Outline view.

14 Choose View > Outline to switch from Preview view to Outline view.

Illustrator lets you control the shape of polygons, stars, and ellipses by pressing certain keys as you draw. You'll draw a polygon and change it to a triangle.

15 Select the Polygon tool (), and position the pointer over the center point of the two rectangles.

16 Drag to begin drawing a polygon, but don't release the mouse button. Press the Down Arrow key three times to reduce the number of sides on the polygon to a triangle, and move the mouse in an arc to rotate one side of the triangle to the top. Before you release the mouse button, hold down the spacebar and drag the triangle down to position it below the pencil body. Release the mouse button when the triangle is positioned.

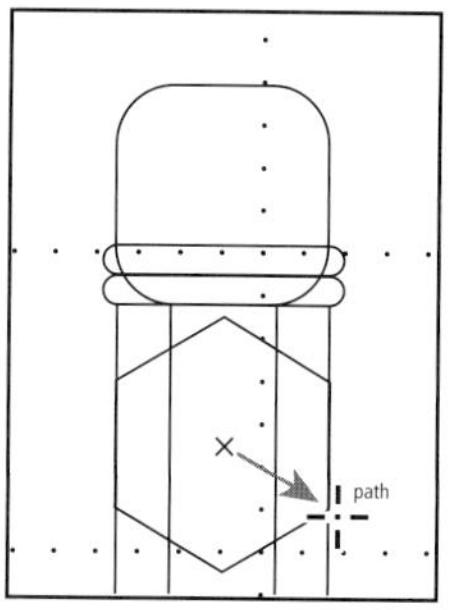

Drag to draw polygon; don't release mouse button.

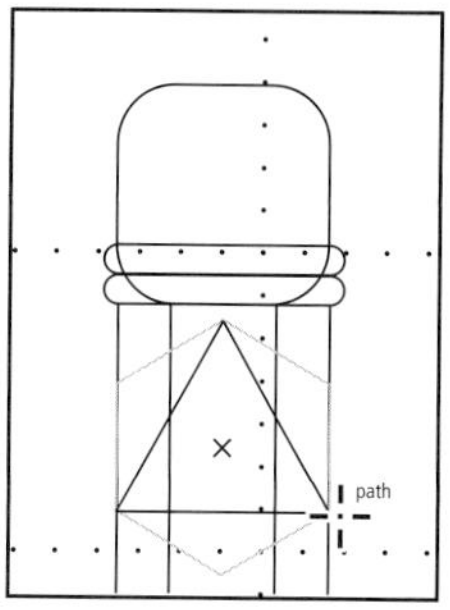

Press Down Arrow key three times.

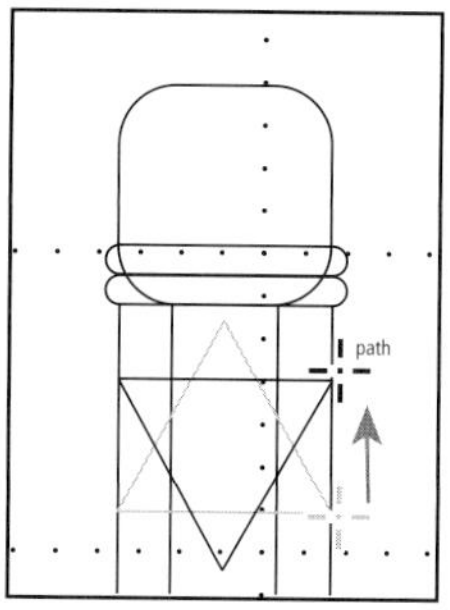

Drag to rotate triangle.

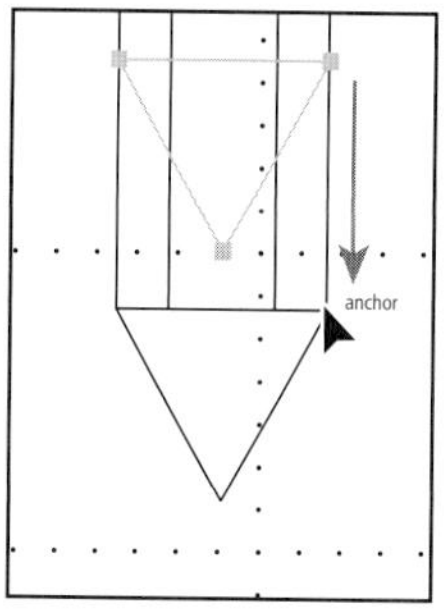

Hold down spacebar and move triangle.

Now you'll create the second triangle for the pencil's lead tip using the Scale tool.

17 With the triangle still selected, select the Scale tool ( ) in the toolbox and then Alt+click (Windows) or Option+click (Mac OS) the bottom corner point of the triangle.

Clicking the corner point of the triangle sets the reference point from which the new triangle will scale. Holding down Alt/Option as you click displays the Scale dialog box.

18 In the Scale dialog box, type **30%** in the Scale text box and click Copy. (Don't click OK.)

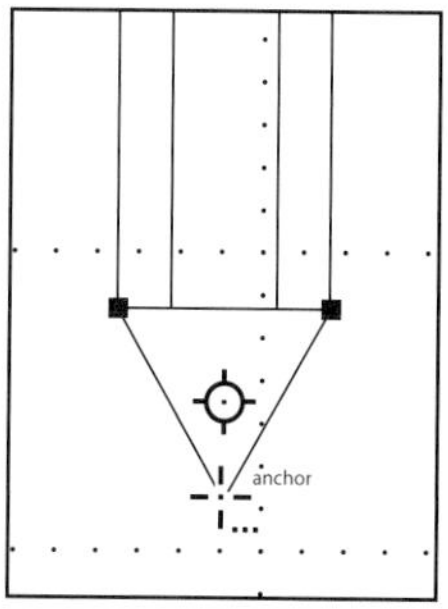

Alt/Option-click to set scaling reference point.

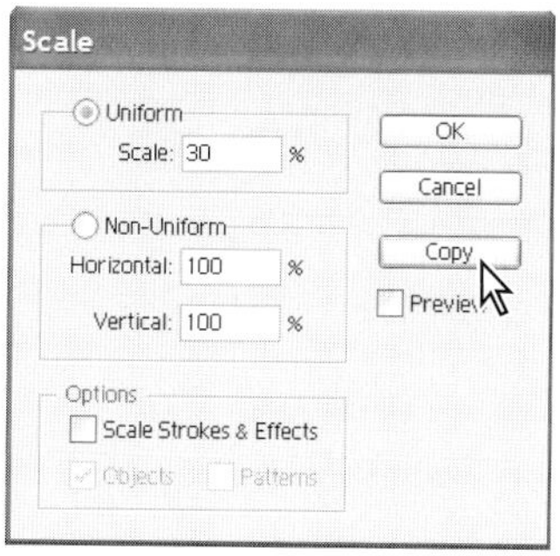

Set scale value.

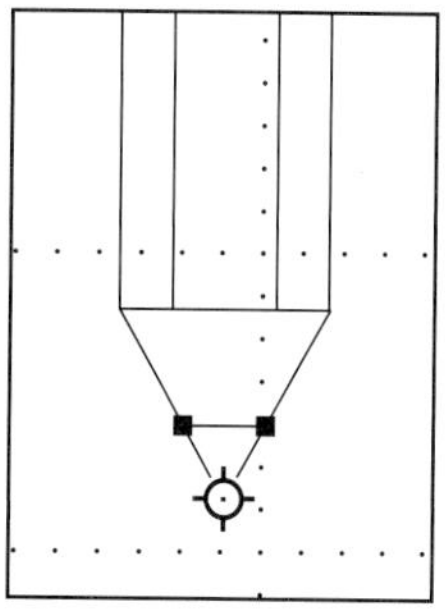

Result.

Next you will use the line Segment tool to quickly draw a horizontal line segment near the top of the pencil.

19 Select the line Segment tool (\), and position the pointer over the left side of the pencil near the top. Click where you want the line to begin, and drag to where you want the line to end. As you drag, hold down Shift to constrain the line horizontally.

Note: *The Line and Arc Segment tool Options dialog boxes display the values of the last segment created. You can reset to the default values in the dialog box by pressing Alt (Windows) or Option (Mac OS) and clicking Reset.*

20 Choose File > Save to save your work.

Drawing the piece of stationery

You can draw the diamond-shaped piece of stationery for the logo in a couple of ways. One way is to draw four-sided polygons (using the same methods you used to draw the triangles for the pencil tip). Another way is to draw using the Rectangle tool, the Rotate tool, and the Transform palette.

1 Select the Rectangle tool (□) in the toolbox, and position the pointer over the center point of the pencil body. Hold down Shift+Alt (Windows) or Shift+Option (Mac OS) and drag the tool to draw a square of any size from the center of the pencil.

Holding down Shift as you drag the Rectangle tool constrains the rectangle to a square. Holding down Alt/Option draws the rectangle from its center point rather than from the top left corner.

Now you'll use the Transform palette to enter precise dimensions for the square.

2 Choose Window > Transform to open the Transform palette.

3 Type **2.25** in the W (width) text box and **2.25** in the H (height) text box. Press Enter or Return to apply the changes.

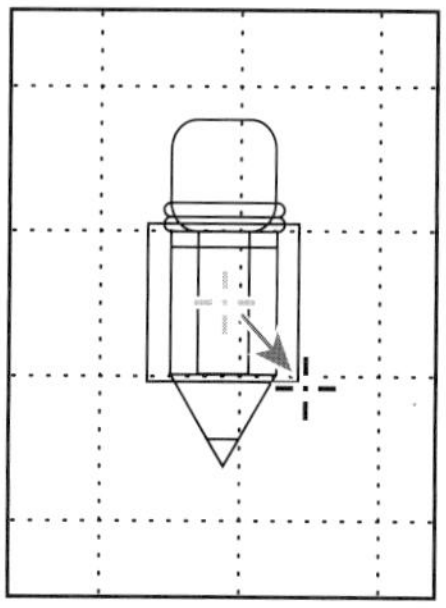

Draw a rectangle of any size from pencil's center.

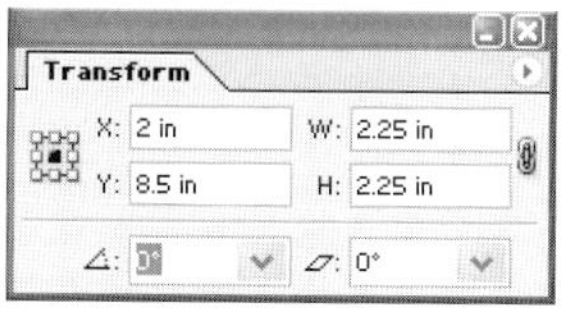

Set dimensions with Transform palette.

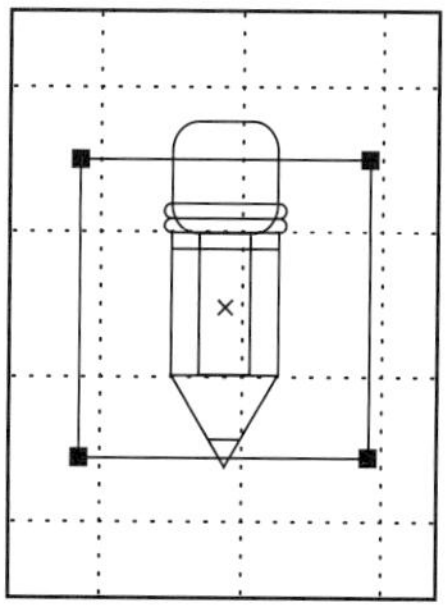

Result.

Next you'll create a smaller square that's centered inside the first one.

4 With the square still selected, choose Edit > Copy to copy the square to the Clipboard. Then choose Edit > Paste in Front to paste the copy of the square directly on top of the first one.

5 In the Transform palette, type **1.5** in the W (width) text box and **1.5** in the H (height) text box. Press Enter or Return to apply the changes.

6 Choose File > Save to save your work.

For information on using the transform tools and Transform palette in Illustrator, see Lesson 8, "Transforming Objects."

Drawing with the Rectangular Grid tool

With the grid tool, you can create complex grids in one click-and-drag motion. You can use either the Rectangular Grid tool or the polar grid tool to create rectangular grids or concentric circles, respectively, of a specified size with a specified number of dividers.

Now you'll add a grid to the stationery. Unlike the view grid, this grid can print.

1 To make this next part of the lesson easier to visualize, choose View > Hide Grid.

2 Select the Hand tool in the toolbox (✋), and move to a clear area of the artboard so that you have a clear area in which to work for the next step.

3 Hold down the mouse button on the line Segment tool (⟍) until a group of tools appears, and then drag to the tear-off triangle at the end and release the mouse button.

First you'll practice how to draw a grid manually with the grid tool.

4 Select the Rectangular Grid tool (▦), and position the pointer in a blank area of the artboard.

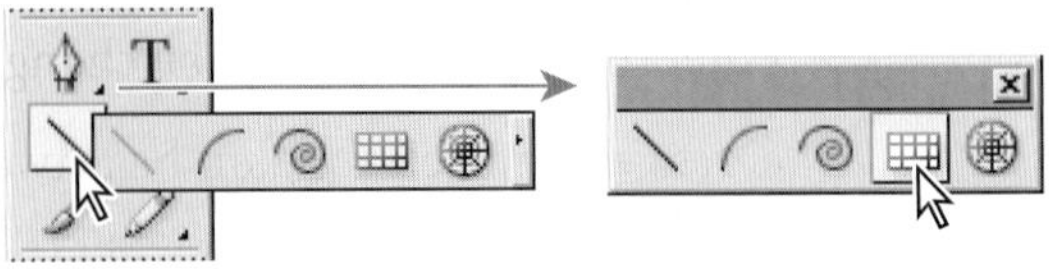

Tearing off tool group.

5 Begin dragging without releasing the mouse, and experiment changing the number of horizontal and vertical lines in the grid by pressing the arrow keys. Without releasing the mouse button, press the Up and Down Arrow keys as you drag to change the number of horizontal lines in the grid; press the Right and Left Arrow keys to change the vertical lines in the grid until you have a grid that is five by five. Do not release the mouse button as you try the next few steps.

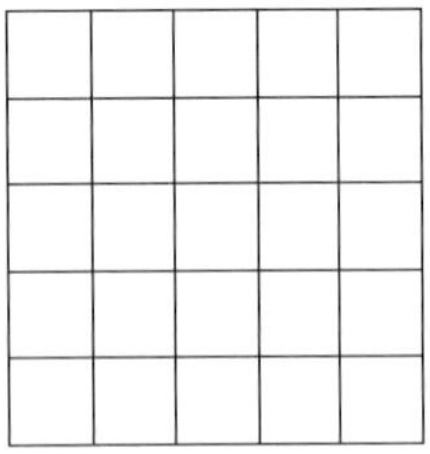

5 columns by 5 rows.

6 While still drawing the grid, press the C, X, F, and V keys to change the space between the cells. C adds spacing to the cells on the left, and X adds spacing to those on the right. F adds spacing to the top cells, and V adds spacing to the bottom ones.

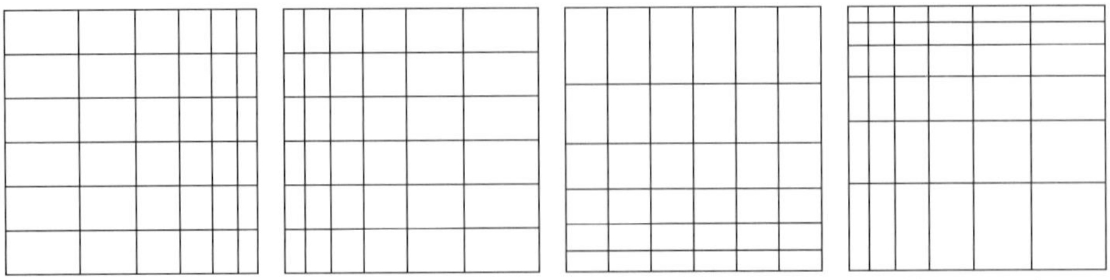

C adds space on left. *X adds space on right.* *F adds space on top.* *V adds space on bottom.*

7 Because there is no shortcut to revert the space between the cells to the original setting, press the C or X keys as needed to equalize the horizontal spacing; and press the F or V keys as needed to equalize the vertical spacing until the grid is evenly spaced. The grid should have **25** (5 by 5) evenly spaced cells.

Next you'll adjust the grid to fit into the stationery using the Transform palette.

8 With the grid still selected, in the Transform palette enter **1.5** in the W (width) text box and **1.5** in the H (height) text box. Press Enter or Return to apply the changes.

You can also draw a grid precisely by selecting the grid tool, clicking in the artwork to display the Rectangular Grid tool Options dialog box, and then setting values.

9 Select the Selection tool (➘) in the toolbox. Position the pointer over the top right anchor point and move the grid to reposition it within the smaller stationery square at the same corner point. Notice that the pointer turns white when the points intersect.

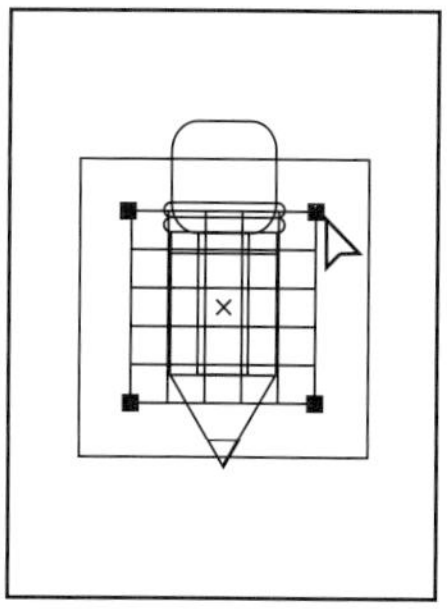

Reposition grid over smaller stationery square.

Now you'll rotate the grid and squares to create the diamond shape.

10 Using the Selection tool, drag to marquee-select the large and small squares and the grid. Be careful not to select any of the pencil.

11 Select the Rotate tool (◌) in the toolbox and position the pointer over the bottom right corner of the larger square. Shift-drag the corner to the left or right until a corner is at the top. (Smart Guides help to constrain the rotation to 45°.)

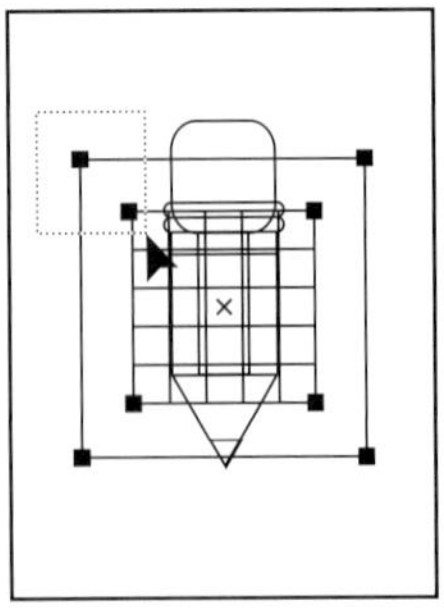

Use the Selection tool to marquee-select the grid and squares.

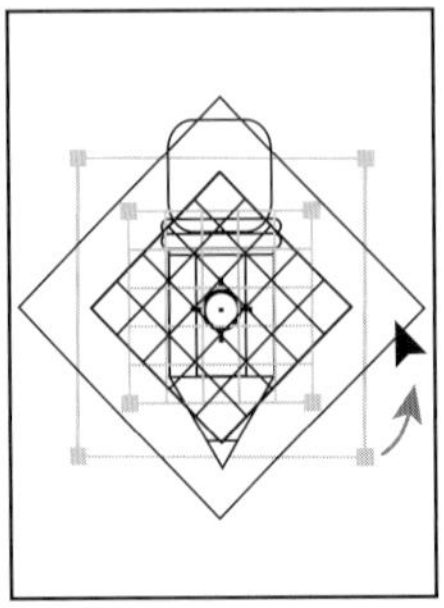

Use Rotate tool to turn selected objects 45°.

12 With the grid and two squares still selected, hold down Ctrl (Windows) or Command (Mac OS) to get the Selection tool, and drag the top corner point of the larger square to move the squares down to just below the metal bands securing the eraser to the pencil.

13 Choose View > Preview, and then choose Object > Arrange > Send to Back to move the squares and grid behind the pencil.

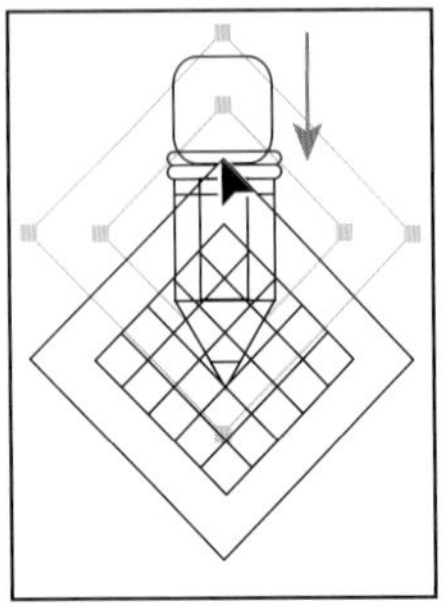

Drag squares down.

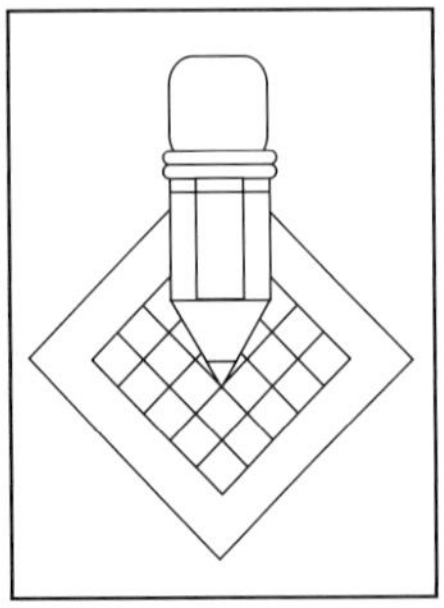

Arrange squares in back of pencil.

14 Choose Select > Deselect to deselect the artwork, and then choose File > Save to save your work.

Decorating the stationery border

You'll decorate the border of the piece of stationery with a circle, a spiral, and some star shapes, using different methods to create the shapes.

1 Double-click 150% in the status bar in the bottom left corner of the window, type 200, and press Enter or Return to zoom in to a 200% view of the artwork.

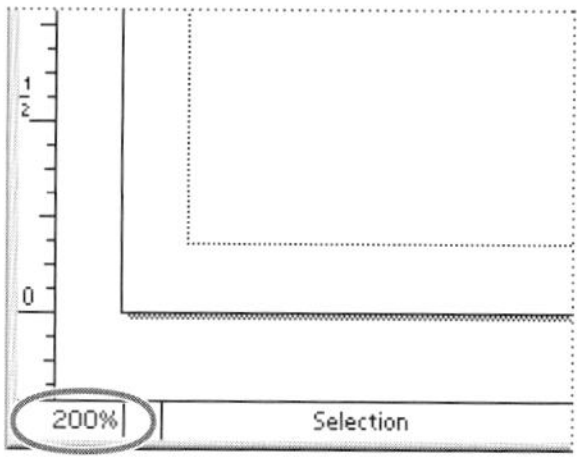

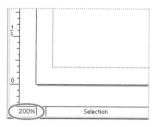

2 Select the Ellipse tool (), and position the pointer in the left corner of the stationery border. Hold down Shift + Alt (Windows) or Shift + Option (Mac OS) and drag the tool to draw a small circle.

Holding down Shift as you drag the Ellipse tool constrains the shape to a circle; holding down Alt/Option draws it from its center point.

3 Now select the Spiral tool () next to the Rectangular Grid tool (), and position it in the bottom left side of the stationery about midway between the two corners. Drag the tool to draw a small spiral, release the mouse, and then use the arrow keys to adjust the spiral's position.

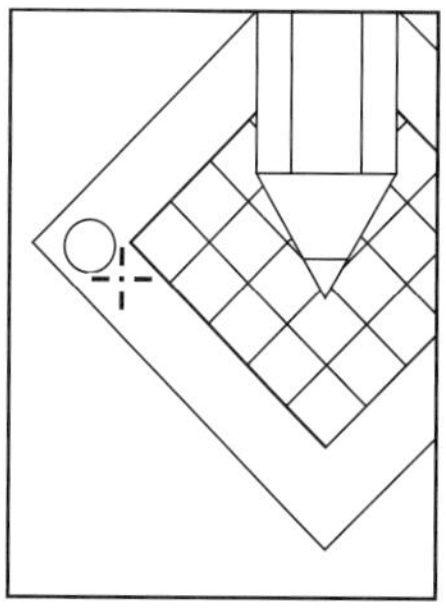
Press Shift + Alt/Option and drag to draw circle.

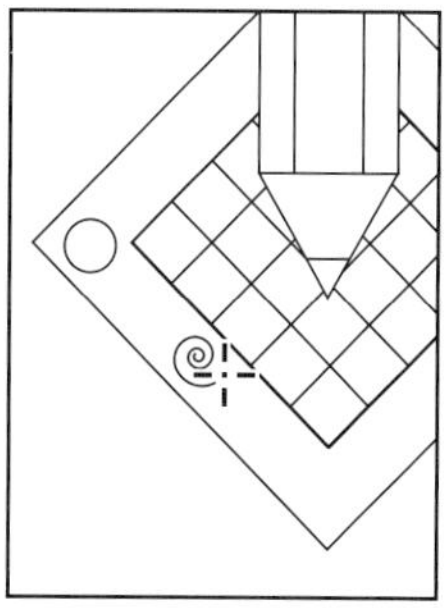
Draw spiral.

You can drag the Spiral tool to draw spirals, or click once to open the Spiral dialog box and specify the characteristics before drawing the spiral. Illustrator lets you specify the radius, number of segments, and percent of decay (amount that the spiral uncoils).

Drawing spirals

The Spiral tool creates a spiral-shaped object of a given radius and number of winds; that is, the number of turns that the spiral completes from start to finish.

To draw a spiral by specifying dimensions:

1. Select the Spiral tool, and click where you want to place the center of the spiral.

By default, the Spiral dialog box displays the dimensions of the last spiral you drew. The unit of measure is determined by the unit of measure established in the Document Setup or Units & Undo Preferences dialog box.

2. In the Radius text box, enter the distance from the center to the outermost point in the spiral.

3. In the Decay text box, enter the amount by which each wind of the spiral should decrease relative to the previous wind.

4. Click the arrows or enter the number of segments in the Segments text box. Each full wind of the spiral consists of four segments.

5. For Style, select the counterclockwise or clockwise option to specify the direction of the spiral, and click OK.

-From Adobe online Help, "Drawing Simple Lines and Shapes".

Now you'll draw some stars using different methods.

4 Select the Star tool (☆) and position the pointer in the bottom corner of the stationery. Drag the tool to draw the first star shape. By default, the star tool draws a five-pointed star.

5 With the star tool still selected, click in the bottom right side of the stationery (midway between the two corners) to create a second star. By default, the Star dialog box displays the dimensions of the last star you drew. In the Star dialog box, type **4** in the Points text box, and click OK.

6 To draw the last star, start dragging the star tool in the right corner of the stationery, but don't release the mouse button. As you drag, press the Up Arrow key to increase the number of points on the star (we created an eight-sided star), and then, before releasing the mouse button, hold down the spacebar and move the star into position in the corner of the border.

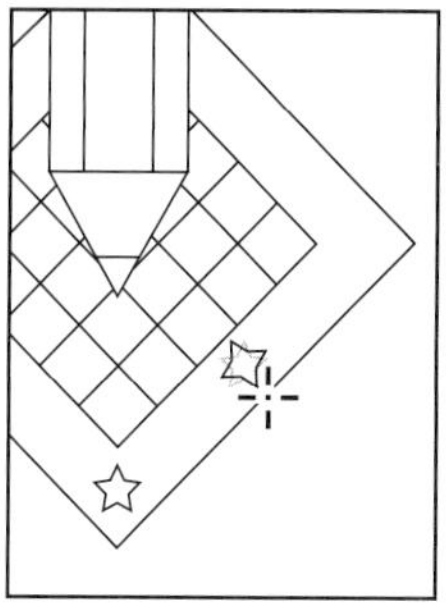

Draw star.

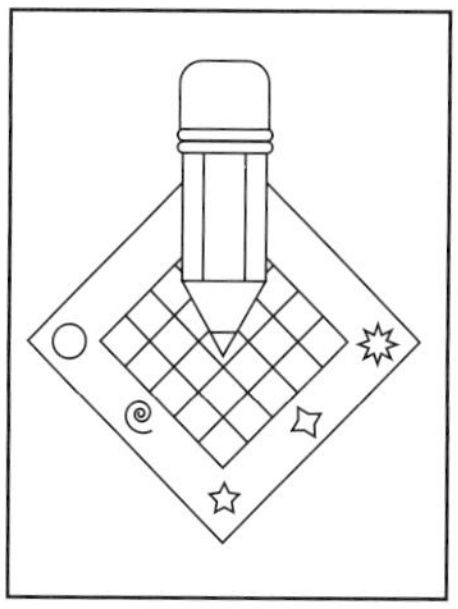

Press Up Arrow key to add star points.

7 Ctrl+click (Windows) or Command+click (Mac OS) away from the artwork to deselect the star, and choose File > Save.

Tips for drawing polygons, spirals, and stars

You can control the shapes of polygons, spirals, and stars by pressing certain keys as you draw the shapes. As you drag the polygon, spiral, or star tool, choose any of the following options to control the shape:

- To add or subtract sides on a polygon, points on a star, or number of segments on a spiral, press the Up Arrow key or the Down Arrow key while creating the shape. This will not work if you have already released the mouse. The tool remains set to the last value you specified until you reset the number.
- To rotate the shape, move the mouse in an arc.
- To keep a side or point at the top, hold down Shift.
- To keep the inner radius constant, start creating a shape and then hold down Ctrl (Windows) or Command (Mac OS). To undo this effect start creating the shape and then hold down Ctrl+Alt (Windows) or Command+Opt (Mac OS) while dragging.
- To move a shape as you draw it, hold down the spacebar. (This also works for rectangles and ellipses.)
- To create multiple copies of a shape, hold down the ~ (tilde) key as you draw.

Now you're ready to add a fresh coat of paint.

Painting the logo

In Adobe Illustrator, you can paint both the fill and the stroke of shapes with colors, patterns, or gradients. You can even apply various brushes to the path of the shapes. For this logo, you'll use a simple method to reverse the default fill and stroke of your shapes, painting the fill with black and the stroke with white.

1 Select the Selection tool (↖) in the toolbox, and then click the eraser shape to select it.

2 Click the Swap Fill and Stroke button in the toolbox.

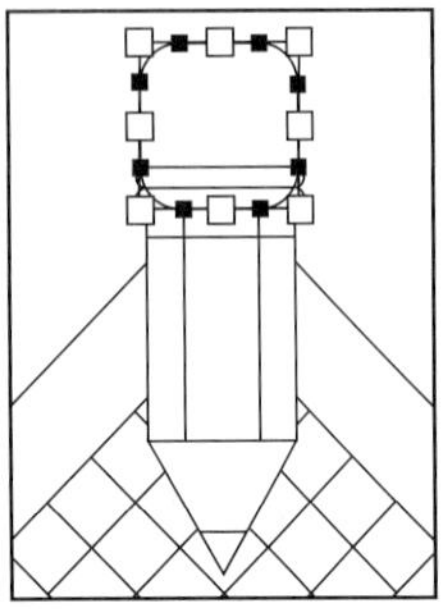

Select eraser shape.

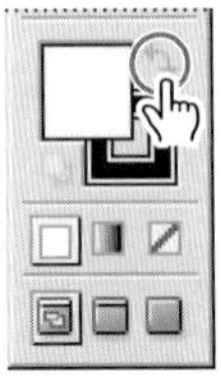

Swap Fill and Stroke.

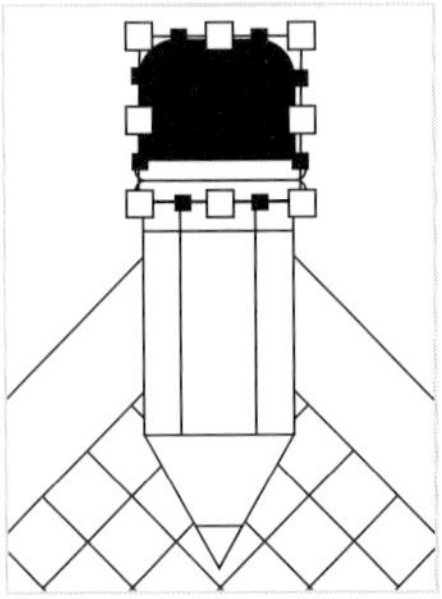

Result.

The black stroke of the rounded rectangle is transposed with the rectangle's white fill.

Next you'll paint the grid with a white fill and the stroke with a 50% screen of black.

3 Click anywhere on the grid, and choose Window > Color to open the Color palette.

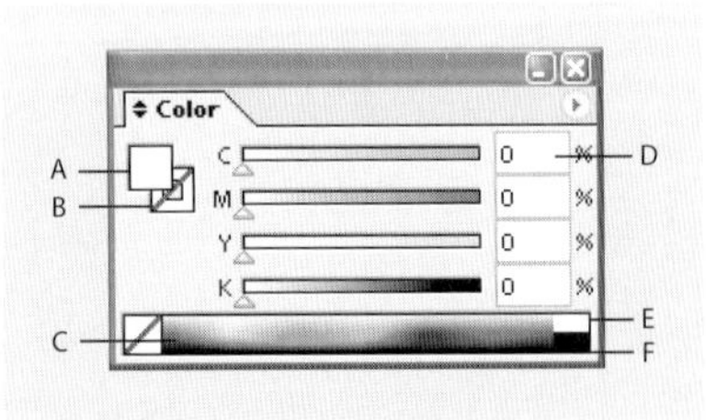

A. *Fill box.* ***B.*** *Stroke box* ***C.*** *Color bar.* ***D.*** *Color value.* ***E.*** *White color box.* ***F.*** *Black color box.*

4 In the Color palette, make sure that the Fill box is selected (in front of the Stroke box); then click the white color box to the right of the color bar to paint the fill color of the grid white.

5 In the Color palette, click the Stroke box to bring it in front of the Fill box. The color value of the stroke is 100% black.

6 Change the black value from 100% black to 39% black by either typing **39** in the color value field or dragging the slider under the color bar to the left until the value is 39%.

7 Click the line beneath the bands on the pencil to select the line. In the Color palette, click the White swatch at the right of the color bar to stroke the band white.

8 Click one of the two rectangles that make up the pencil body to select it, and then Shift-click to select the other rectangle. Click the Swap Fill and Stroke button in the toolbox to swap the white fills of the pencil body with the black strokes and paint the pencil black with a white stroke.

9 Select the designs around the border by Shift-clicking them. Then select the Default Fill and Stroke button.

10 Click the outer rectangle (not the inner rectangle) of the stationery border to select it, and click the Swap Fill and Stroke button.

Now you'll paint the pencil's lead tip with both a black fill and a black stroke.

11 Click the small triangle that represents the lead tip to select it.

12 In the toolbox, click the Default Fill and Stroke button, and then drag the black Stroke box onto the Fill box to paint the triangle black.

To complete the design, you'll draw a curvy line using the Pencil tool.

13 Click away from the artwork to deselect it.

14 With the Fill box selected, click the None button in the toolbox to indicate no fill setting. The Stroke is set to the default of black.

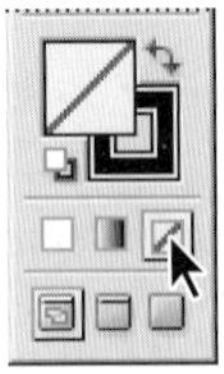

15 Select the Pencil tool () in the toolbox and draw a curvy line below the pencil's tip in the logo.

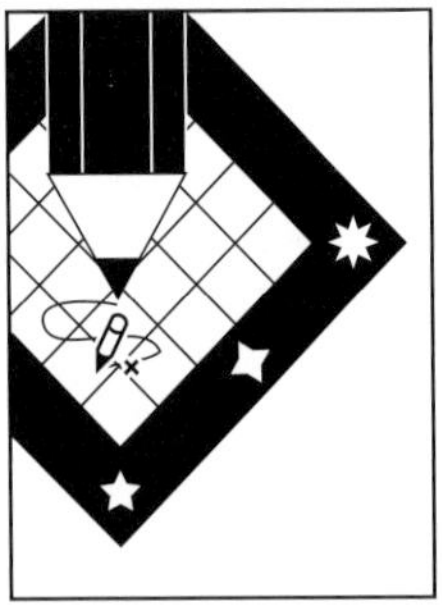

The curvy line remains selected after you draw it.

16 To adjust the path of the curvy line, drag the Pencil tool along part of the selected line and then continue dragging.

17 If the Stroke palette isn't visible, choose Window > Stroke to display it, and then increase the stroke weight of the selected line to **3 pt** in the Weight text box. Press Enter or Return.

 For information on drawing and editing shapes with the Pencil tool, see "Drawing freeform paths with the Pencil tool" in online Help.

Copying and scaling shapes

A final step in creating logos is to scale the artwork to a 1-inch square and make sure that the resized logo still presents a clear image. You'll use the bounding box feature in Illustrator to make a scaled copy of the logo.

1 Double-click the Zoom tool (🔍) in the toolbox to zoom out to 100%.

2 Choose View > Show Grid to redisplay the grid.

3 Choose View > Show Bounding Box to display the bounding boxes of selected objects.

4 Choose Edit > Preferences > General (Windows) or Illustrator > Preferences > General (Mac OS), and select the Scale Strokes & Effects option. Leave the other settings as they are, and click OK.

The Scale Strokes & Effects preference scales stroke weights and effects automatically, whether you scale objects by dragging or by using the Scale dialog box. You can also choose this command from the Transform palette menu.

5 Choose Select > All to select all the objects in the logo, and then click the Selection tool (▶) in the toolbox to select their bounding box.

6 Hold down Alt (Windows) or Option (Mac OS) and drag the pointer from the center of the objects to the outside of the bounding box to make a copy of the logo.

7 Position the copy of the logo below the original, and line up the left corner point on the logo with a grid line to make it easier to measure as you scale the copy.

8 Using the Selection tool, select the bottom right corner point of the bounding box, hold down Shift, and drag the corner up and to the left to scale down the logo. Release the mouse button when the logo is about an inch wide.

Holding down Shift as you drag the corner of the bounding box scales the objects proportionally.

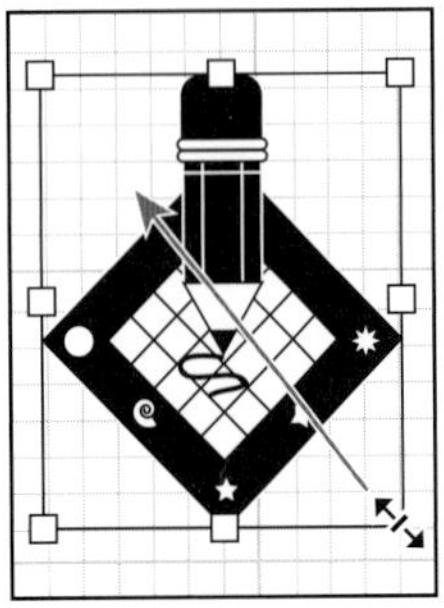

Shift-drag to scale proportionally.

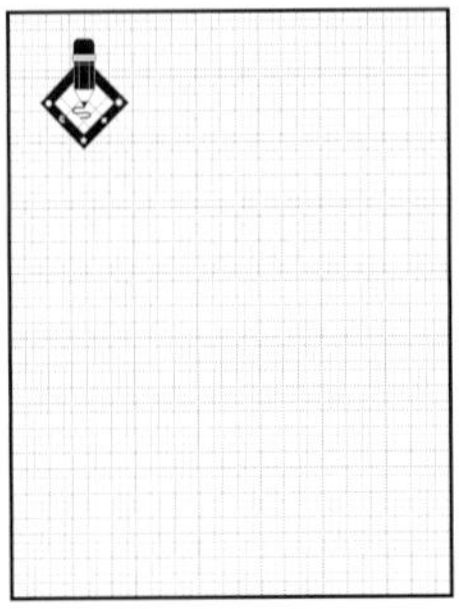

Result.

You can use various zoom options to zoom in on the smaller logo and check its clarity. Illustrator's Navigator palette is useful for moving around in the artwork at a higher magnification.

9 Choose Window > Navigator to open the Navigator palette, and then click the Zoom In button (△) at the bottom of the palette several times to zoom to 600%. As you click, the artwork in the window disappears and the red box in the Navigator palette becomes smaller.

The red square shows you where objects are located in relation to the artwork in the window. You can drag the red square to move the focus, or you can click where you want the red square to go.

10 In the Navigator palette, position the pointer so the hand is pointing to the smaller logo and click to move the red square over it.

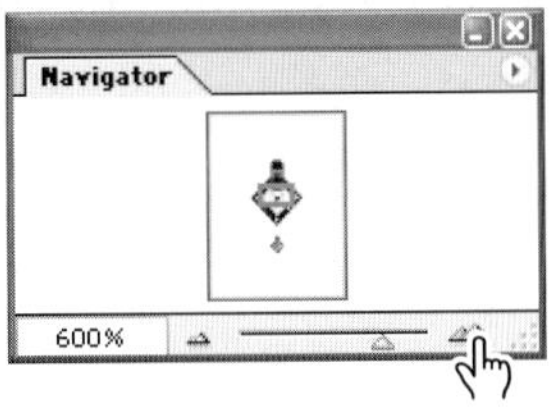

Click to zoom in.

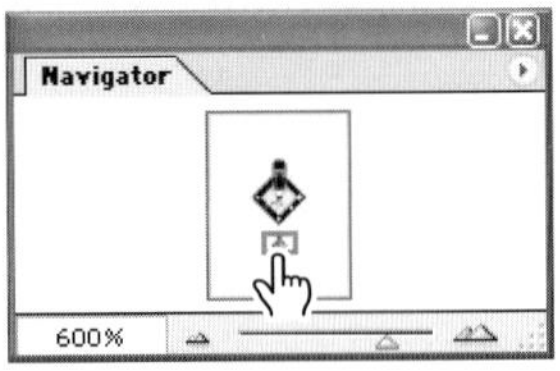

Click to move red view box.

For more information on using the Navigator palette, see Lesson 1, "Getting to Know the Work Area."

11 Choose View > Hide Grid to hide the grid and clear the background.

12 Double-click the Hand tool (✋) in the toolbox to fit the artwork in the window.

13 Choose File > Save to save your artwork. Choose File > Close to close the file.

You've now completed the basic shapes lesson and created the logo artwork.

For information on different ways you can add color to the logo, see Lesson 5, "Painting."

Review questions

1 What are the basic shape tools? Describe how to tear or separate a group of shape tools away from the toolbox.

2 How do you draw a square?

3 How do you draw a triangle?

4 Describe three ways to specify the size of a shape.

5 What is a quick way to transpose the color of an object's stroke with its fill color?

6 What is the difference between a view grid and a grid drawn with the Rectangular Grid tool?

7 How do you draw a rectangular grid? How can you control the size of the grid and its cells?

Review answers

1 There are six basic shape tools: Ellipse, Polygon, Star, Spiral, Rectangle, and Rounded Rectangle. To separate a group of tools from the toolbox, hold the pointer over the tool that appears in the toolbox and press the mouse button until the group of tools appears. Without releasing the mouse button, drag to the triangle at the end of the group, and then release the mouse button to tear off the group.

2 To draw a square, select the Rectangle tool (▭) in the toolbox. Hold down Shift and drag to draw the square, or click to enter equal dimensions for the width and height in the Rectangle dialog box.

3 To draw a triangle, select the Polygon tool ( ) in the toolbox, start dragging to draw the shape, and press the Down Arrow key to reduce the number of sides to three. Or click to enter the radius and number of sides in the Polygon dialog box.

4 To specify the size of a shape, you can do any of the following:

- Select the shape and specify new dimensions in the W (width) and H (height) text boxes in the Transform palette.

- Select the shape and then select the Scale tool ( ) in the toolbox. Alt/Option-click to set the point of origin and specify the dimensions in the Scale dialog box (click Copy to make a scaled copy of the selected object).

- Select the shape, and drag a side or corner handle of the shape's bounding box to resize its width, height, or both. (Shift-drag a corner handle to resize the selection proportionally.)

5 A quick way to transpose the color of an object's stroke with its fill color is to select the object and then click the Swap Fill and Stroke button in the toolbox.

6 The view grid is used as a guide for drawing and will not print with the artwork. A grid drawn with the grid tool can print.

7 To create a rectangular grid, you select the Rectangular Grid tool, and in the artboard either drag to draw a grid of the desired dimensions, or click to set the grid's origin and options. If you create a grid by dragging, you can use the Up and Down Arrow keys to add or remove horizontal or vertical lines, or the Right and Left Arrow keys to add or remove vertical lines. In addition, the F and V keys add space to the top and bottom cells, respectively, and the C and X keys add space to the left and right cells, respectively.

Lesson 4

4 Drawing with the Pen tool

The Pen tool is a powerful tool for drawing straight lines, Bézier curves, and complex shapes. While the Pencil tool is easier for drawing and editing free from lines, the Pen tool is easier for drawing more precisely. You'll practice using the Pen tool on a blank artboard and then use the Pen tool to create an illustration of a pear.

In this lesson, you'll learn how to do the following:

- Draw straight lines
- Use Template layers
- End path segments and split lines.
- Draw curved lines.
- Select and adjust curve segments.
- Draw two types of curves, smooth and pointed.
- Edit curves, changing from smooth to pointed, and vice versa.

Getting started

The first part of this lesson involves manipulating the Pen tool on a blank artboard.

1 To ensure that the tools and palettes function exactly as described in this lesson, delete or deactivate (by renaming) the Adobe Illustrator CS preferences file. See "Restoring default preferences" on page 2.

2 Open the file named L4strt_01.ai from the Lesson04 folder, located inside the Lessons folder within the AICIB folder on your hard drive. The top portion of the artboard shows the path that you will create. Use the bottom half of the page for this exercise.

3 Use Ctrl+0 or Command+0 (zero) to fit the entire page into the window and then close all the palettes, except for the tools, by clicking their close boxes or by holding down Shift and pressing Tab once. You won't need to use them for this lesson.

4 Select the Pen tool (✒). Notice that when the pen has not yet placed its first point, an "x" appears to the right of the pen icon. This means you are starting a new path. Click and release once near the top of the page. Then, move the mouse away from the original anchor point, and the "x" no longer appears.

Note: *If instead of the pen icon you see a crosshair, the caps lock key is active. Caps Lock On turns tool icons into crosshairs for greater precision use.*

5 Move the mouse to the right and click once to create the next anchor point in the path.

Note: *The first segment you draw will not be visible until you click a second anchor point. Also, if direction handles appear, you've accidentally dragged with the Pen tool; choose Edit*

> Undo, and click again. (Direction handles are used to reshapes curved paths, but do not print)

The first point connects to the new anchor point. Click back under the initial anchor point to create a zigzag pattern. Your zigzag is complete when it has a total of six anchor points.

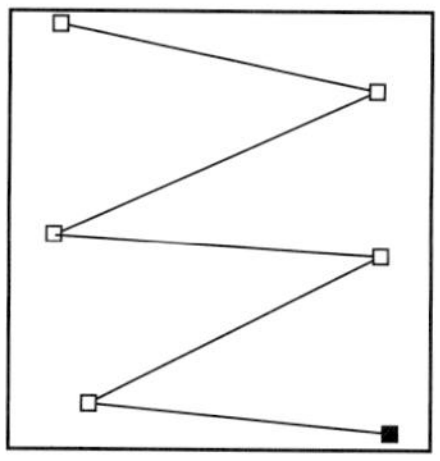

Click and release from point to point to create the zigzag.

Choose the Selection tool (). One of the many benefits of using the Pen tool is that you can create custom paths and continue to edit the anchor points that make up the path. You can learn more about the Selection tools by reviewing Lesson 2, "Basics of Selecting Objects"; here you will see how the Selection tools relate to the Pen tool.

6 Using the Selection tool, click on the zigzag path and note how all the anchor points become solid, signifying that all anchor points are selected. Click and drag the path to a new location anywhere on the artboard and notice that all the anchor points travel together, maintaining the zigzag path.

7 Deselect the zigzag path any one of these four ways:

a Use the Selection tool and click on an empty section of the artboard.

b Use Select > Deselect from the menu.

c While on the Pen tool, hold down the Ctrl (Windows) or Command (Mac OS) key and click to deselect; this temporarily gives you the Selection tool. When the Control or Command key is released, you return to the Pen tool.

d Click once on the Pen tool. Even though it looks like the path is still active, it will not connect to the next anchor point created.

8 Choose the Direct Selection tool () and click on any one point in the zigzag. Using the marquee selection technique with the Direct Selection tool can make selecting individual anchor points easier. The selected anchor point turns solid, while the rest are hollow.

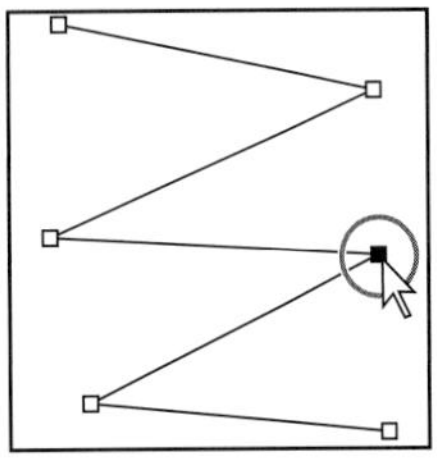

Only the active point appears solid.

9 With the anchor point selected, click and drag. The anchor point is moving but the others are stationary. This is how you edit a path.

10 At times you will need to recreate just one line segment in a path. Choose Select > Deselect, then with the Direct Selection tool (), click on any line segment that is between two anchor points and choose Edit > Cut.

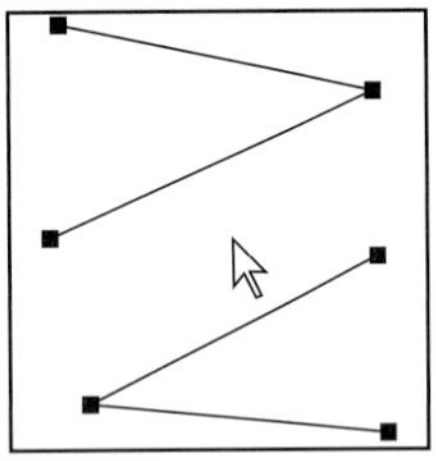

Select just a segment of a path.

11 Return to the Pen tool and position the pointer over one of the anchor points that was connected to the line segment. Note that the icon of the Pen has a forward slash () to the right of it, signifying a continuation of an existing path. Click and release the mouse.

12 Position the pointer over the other point that was connected to the original line segment. An icon of a circle (✎ₒ) with a line through it appears. This signifies that you are reconnecting to another path.

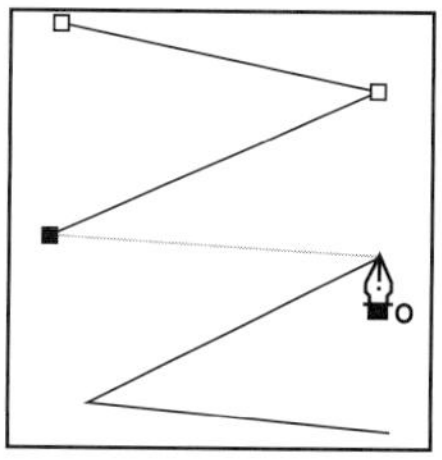

Reconnect the paths.

13 File > Save and close this file.

Creating straight lines

In Lesson 3 you discovered that using the Shift key in combination with shape tools constrains the shape of objects you create using Illustrator. This is also true with the Pen tool, except that the procedure constrains the paths you create in multiples of 45°.

In this part of the lesson, you will learn how to draw straight lines.

1 Open the file named L4strt_02.ai from the Lesson04 folder, located inside the Lessons folder within the AICIB folder on your hard drive. The top portion of the artboard shows the path that you will create. Use the bottom half of the page for this exercise.

2 Select the Pen tool (✎) and click once in the work area of the page.

3 Hold the Shift key down and click about an inch to the right of the original anchor point.

4 While holding down the Shift key, click with the mouse and try to replicate the path in the exercise file.

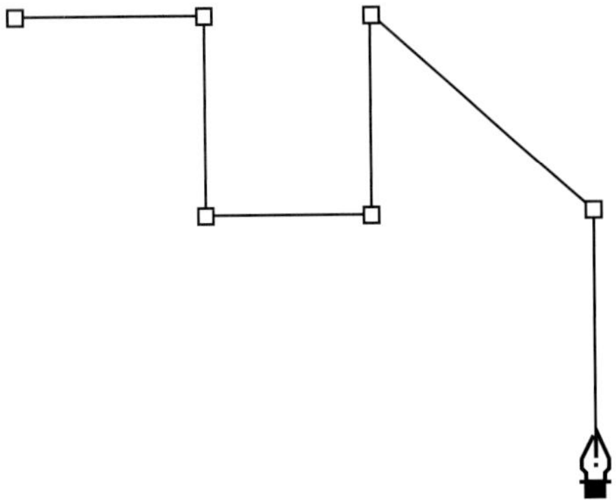

Hold down the Shift key while clicking to constrain the path.

5 File > Save and close the file.

Creating curved paths

In this part of the lesson, you'll learn how to draw smooth, curved lines with the Pen tool. In vector-drawing programs such as Adobe Illustrator, you draw a curve, called a Bézier curve, curves with control points. By setting anchor points and dragging direction handles (controls) you can define the shape of the curve. Although drawing curves this way takes some getting used to, it gives you the greatest control and flexibility in creating paths.

1 Before we get started with a lesson file, choose File > New to create a new letter-sized document in Adobe Illustrator, leaving settings at the page defaults. Consider this page a "scratch" page to practice the Bézier curve.

2 Click and release the mouse anywhere on the page to create the initial anchor point. Then click in another location on the page (don't release the mouse), and drag creating a curved path.

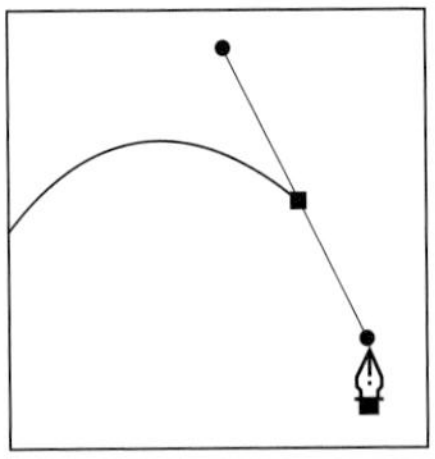

Click and drag to create a curved path.

Continue clicking and dragging at various locations on the page. The goal for this exercise is not to create anything specific, but to get you accustomed to the feel of the Bézier curve.

Notice that as you click and drag, direction handles appear that end in round direction points. The angle and length of the direction handles determine the shape and size of the curved segments. Direction lines do not print and are not visible when the anchor is inactive.

3 Choose Select > Deselect.

4 Choose the Direct Selection tool (↖) and select a curved segment to display the direction handles again. Moving the direction points reshapes the curves.

Note: *Anchor points are square, and, when selected, appear filled; unselected, they appear unfilled, like hollow squares. Direction points are round. These lines and points do not print with the artwork.*

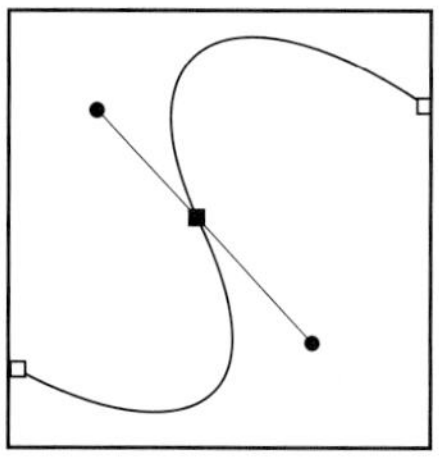

Select anchor points to access the direction handles.

4 Choose File > Close and do not save this file.

Components of a path

A smooth anchor point always has two direction handles that move together as a single, straight unit. When you drag the direction anchor point of either direction line on a smooth anchor point, both direction handles move simultaneously, maintaining a continuous curve at that anchor point.

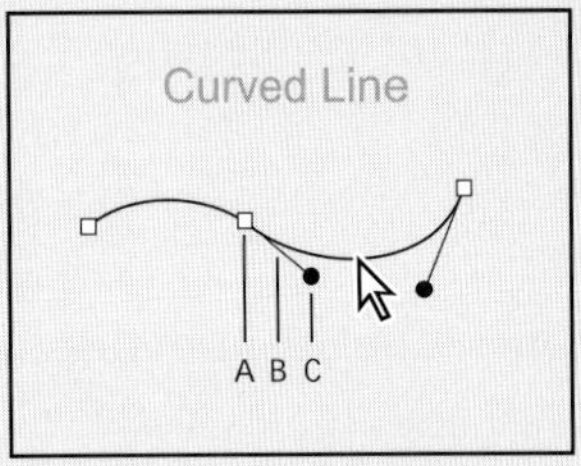

A. Anchor point . B. Direction line.
C. Direction point (or handle).

In comparison, a corner point can have two, one, or no direction handles, depending on whether it joins two, one, or no curved segments, respectively. Corner point direction handles maintain the corner by using different angles. When you drag a direction point on a corner point's direction line, the other direction line, if present, does not move.

Building a curve

In this part of the lesson, you will learn how to control the direction handles in order to control curves.

1 Open the file named L4strt_03.ai from the Lesson04 folder. On this page you can see the paths that you will create. A template layer has been created in this file so that you can practice using the Pen tool by tracing. (See Lesson 7, "Working with Layers," for information about creating layers.) The work area below the path is for additional practice on your own.

2 Press Z to switch to the Zoom tool and drag a marquee around the first curve.

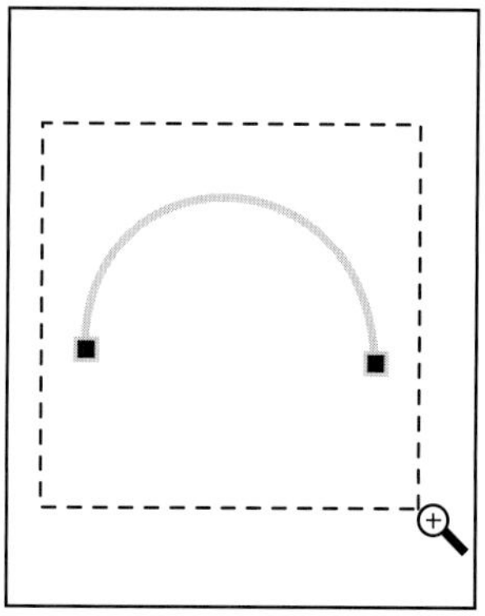

Zoom in to a specified area by dragging a marquee when on the Zoom tool.

3 Select the Pen tool (✎) and click and hold at the base of the left side of the arch and drag up to create a direction line going the same direction as the arch. It helps to remember to always follow the direction of the curve. Release the mouse when the direction line is slightly above the arch.

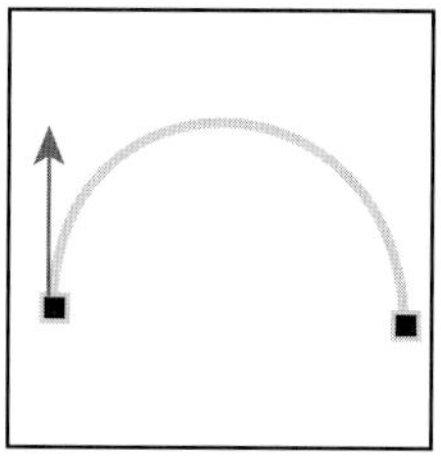

When a curve goes up, the direction line should also go up.

***Note:** The artboard may scroll as you drag the anchor point. If you lose visibility of the curve choose View > Zoom out until you see the curve and anchor point. Pressing the spacebar will temporarily give you the Hand tool and allow you to reposition the artwork.*

4 Click on the lower right base of the arch path and drag down. Release the mouse when the top direction line is slightly above the arch.

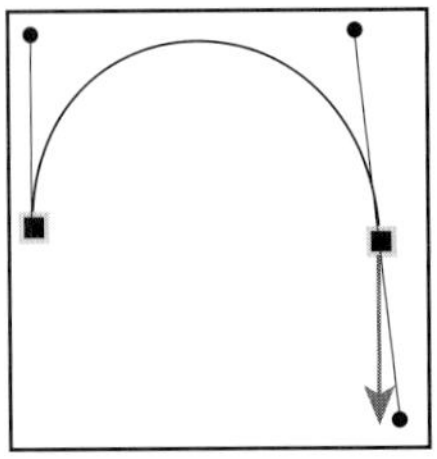

To Control the path pay attention to where the direction handles fall.

5 If the path you created is not aligned exactly with the template, return to the Direct Selection tool and select the anchor points one at a time. Then adjust the direction handles until your paht follows the template more accurately.

Note: *Pulling the direction handle longer makes a higher slope, while pulling it shorter makes the slope flatter.*

6 Save the file by choosing File > Save.

7 What you created is an open path; now you are going to create the second path on this page. If you click with the Pen tool while the original path is still active, the path will connect. To avoid doing this, use the Selection tool and click on the artboard anywhere there are no other objects, or choose Select > Deselect.

Note: *You can also hold down the Ctrl (Windows) or Command (Mac OS) key to temporarily switch you to the selection tool. Hold down command and click on the artboard where there are no objects to deselect.*

8 Click and drag at the left base of path "B," again in the direction of the arch. Click and drag down on the next square point, adjusting the arch with the direction handle before you release the mouse. Don't worry if it is not exact; you can correct this with the Direct Selection tool (↖) when the path is complete.

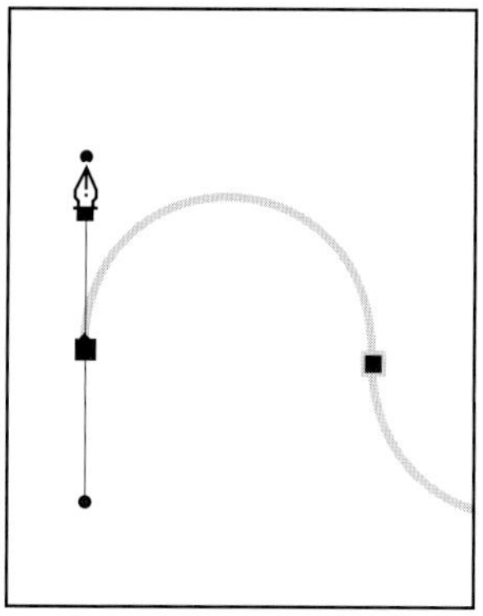

Click and drag up to create the upward arch.

Continue along the path, alternating between clicking and dragging up and down. Put anchor points only where you see the square boxes. If you make a mistake as you draw, you can undo your work by choosing Edit > Undo. Adobe Illustrator, by default, lets you undo a series of actions—limited only by your computer's memory—by repeatedly choosing Edit > Undo.

You have the ability to undo multiple times in Adobe Illustrator. To set the minimum number of undos, choose Edit > Preferences > Units & Undo (Windows) or Illustrator > Preferences > Units & Undo (Mac OS).

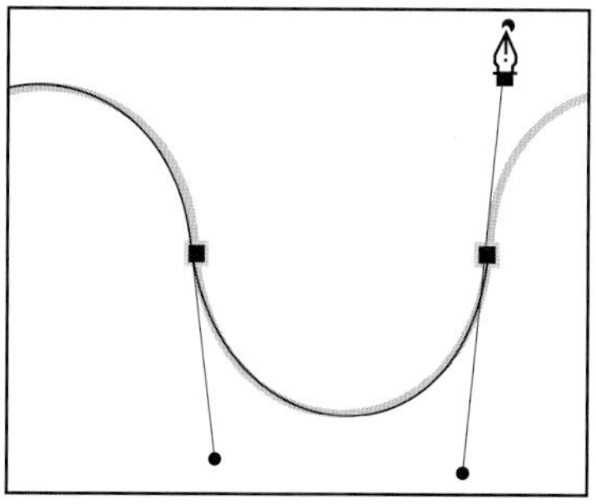

Alternate between dragging up and down with the Pen tool.

9 When the path is complete, choose the Direct Selection tool and select an anchor point. When the anchor is selected, the direction handles reappear and you can readjust the slope of the path.

10 Practice repeating these paths in the work area.

11 File > Save and close the file.

Curves and corner anchor points

When creating curves, the directional handles help to determine the slope of the path. Returning to a corner point requires a little extra effort. In this next portion of the lesson, we will practice converting curve points to corners.

1 Open the file named L4strt_04.ai from the Lesson04 folder. On this page you can see the path that you will create. Use the top section as a template for the exercise. Create your paths directly on top of those that you see on the page. The work area below is for additional practice on your own.

2 Use the Zoom tool and drag a marquee around the top path.

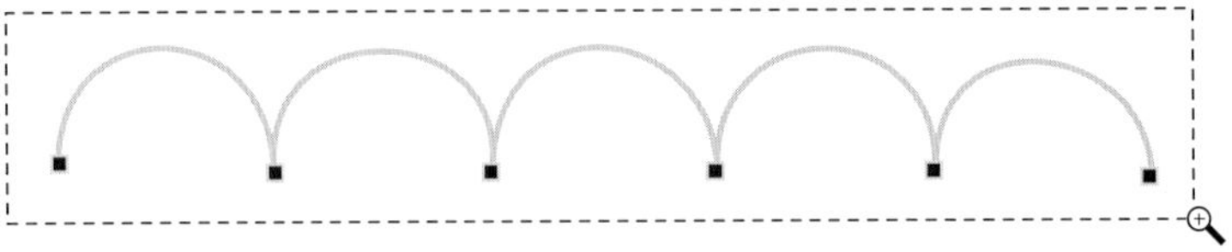

You will get a much more accurate path when you are zoomed in.

3 Choose the Pen tool (✒) and click on the first anchor point and drag up, then click on the second anchor point and drag down, just as you have been doing for previous exercises.

4 Hold down Alt (Windows) or Option (Mac OS) and position the mouse over either the last anchor point created or its direction handle. Look for the caret (^) symbol and click and drag up when it is visible.

An alert window will appear if you don't click exactly on the anchor point. If that apperas click OK and try again.

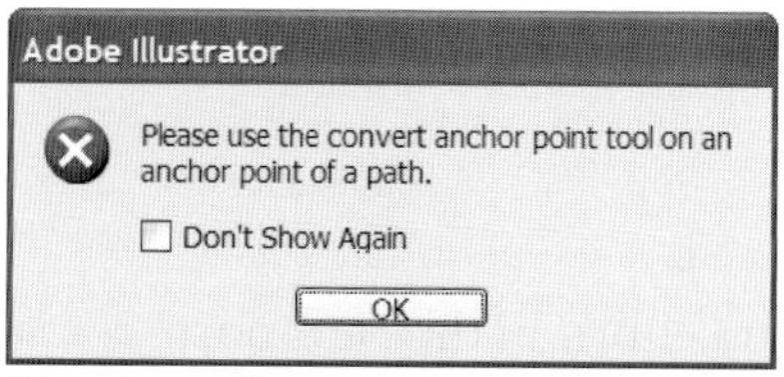

This alert will appear if you do not click on the anchor point.

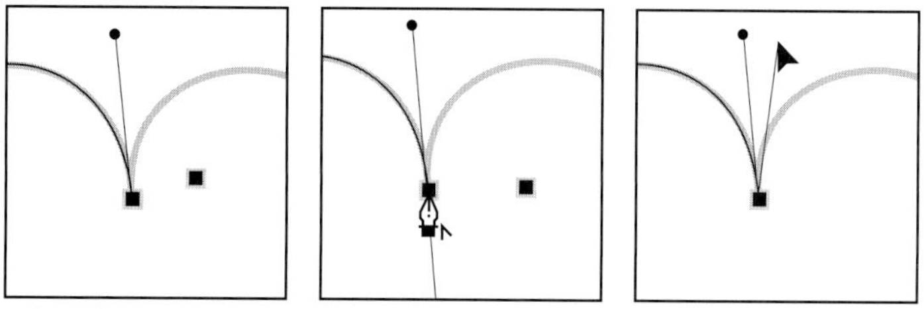

When the caret is visible, click and drag.

You can practice adjusting the direction handles with the Direct Selection tool (↖) when the path is completed.

5 Release the Alt/Option key and click on the next square point on the template path and drag down.

6 Hold down the Alt/Option key again and grab the last anchor point or direction line and pull it up for the next curve. Remember, you must see the caret (^) or you will create an additional loop.

7 Continue this pattern of clicking and dragging and using the Alt/Option key to create corner points until the path is completed. Use the Direct Selection tool to fine-tune the path, and then deselect the path.

8 File > Save.

9 Choose View > Fit in Window. You can also use Ctrl+0 (zero) (Windows) or Command+0 (Mac OS). Use the Zoom tool to drag a marquee around the second path and enlarge its view.

10 With the Pen tool, click on the first anchor point and drag up, then click and drag down on the second anchor point. This motion of creating an arch should be familiar to you by now. You will now go from the curve to a straight line. Simply pressing Shift and clicking will not produce a straight line, since this last point is a curved anchor point.

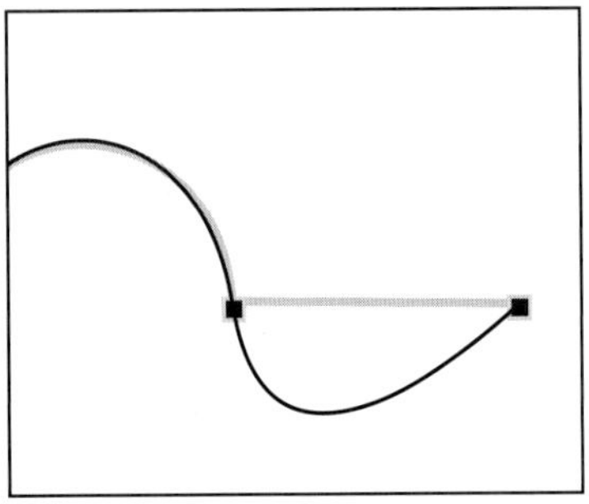

The path when a curved point is not turned into a corner point.

11 To create the next path as a straight line, click on the last point created. Then hold down the Shift key and click to the next point.

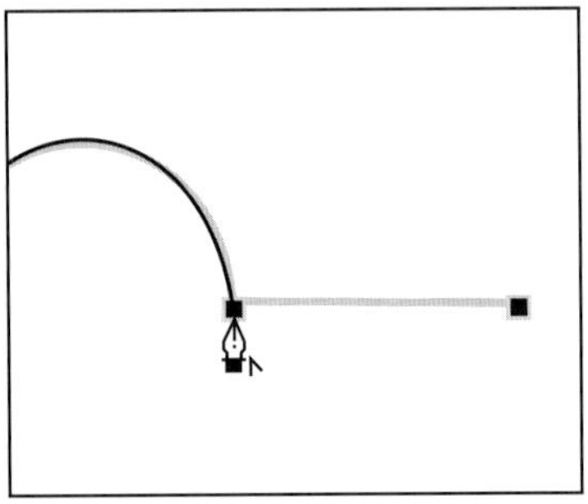

Click on the last anchor point created to force a straight path from it.

12 For the next arch, click and drag down (since the arch is going down).

13 Click on the next point and drag up to complete the downward arch.

14 Click and release on the last anchor point of the arch.

15 Shift+click to the last point.

16 Click and drag up and then click and drag down on the last point to create the final arch.

17 Practice repeating these paths in the lower portion.

18 File > Close the file.

Creating the pear illustration

In this next part of the lesson, you'll create an illustration of a pear pierced by an arrow. This procedure will incorporate what you have learned in the previous exercises as well as teach you some additional pen techniques.

1 Choose File > Open, and open the L4end.ai file in the Lesson04 folder, located inside the Lessons folder within the AICIB folder on your hard drive.

2 Choose View > Zoom Out to make the finished artwork smaller and leave it on your screen as you work. (Use the Hand tool (✋) to move the artwork where you want it in the window.) If you don't want to leave the image open, choose File > Close.

For an illustration of the finished artwork in this lesson, see the color section of this manual.

Now open the start file to begin the lesson.

3 Choose File > Open, and open the L4start.ai file in the Lesson04 folder.

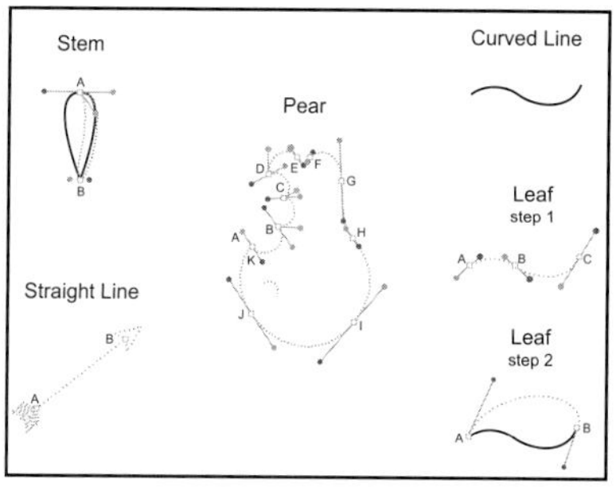

3 Choose File > Save As, name the file **Pear.ai**, and select the Lesson04 folder in the Save In menu. Leave the type of format set to Adobe Illustrator® Document, and click Save. In the Illustrator Options palette, leave the options set at the defaults and click OK.

Creating the arrow

You'll begin by drawing the straight line for the arrow. The template layer allows you to follow along directly over the artwork.

1 Choose View > Straight Line to zoom into the left corner of the template.

Separate views that show different areas of the template at a higher magnification were created for this document and added to the View menu.

To create a custom view, choose View > New View. For information, see "Viewing Artwork" in online Help.

2 Choose View > Hide Bounding Box to hide the bounding boxes of selected objects. Selecting the Pen tool ( ) in the toolbox, move the pointer to the dashed line of the arrow in the artwork. Notice that the Pen tool pointer has a small "x" next to it. If you recall, this indicates that clicking will begin a new path.

3 Click point A at the left end of the line to create the starting anchor point — a small solid square.

Click point B at the right end of the line to create the ending anchor point.

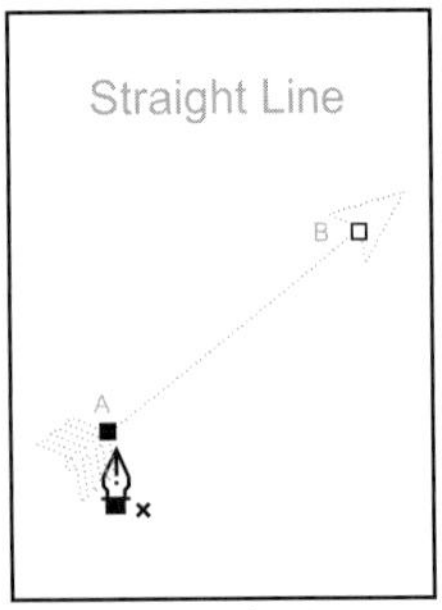

Click once to begin a straight line.

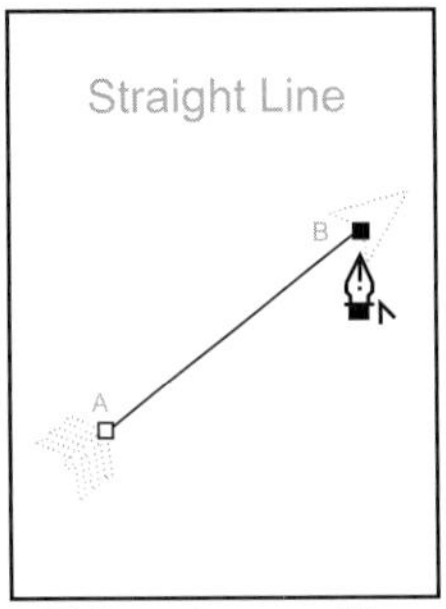

Click again to end it.

When you click a second time, a caret (^) appears next to the Pen tool. The caret indicates that you can split the anchor point to create a direction line for a curve by dragging the Pen tool from this anchor point. The caret disappears when you move the Pen tool away from the anchor point.

4 Remember that you must end the path before you can draw other lines that aren't connected to this path. Choose Select > Deselect, or use any of the other methods discussed in the previous exercises.

Now you'll make the straight line thicker by changing its stroke weight.

5 With the Selection tool (↖) from the toolbox, click the straight line to select it.

6 Choose Window > Stroke to display the Stroke palette.

7 In the Stroke palette, type **3 pt** in the Weight text box and press Enter or Return to apply the change.

Splitting a path

To continue creating the arrow for this illustration, you'll split the path of the straight line using the Scissors tool and adjust the segments.

1 With the straight line still selected, select the Scissors tool (✂) in the toolbox and click in the middle of the line to make a cut.

Cuts made with the Scissors tool must be on a line or a curve rather than on an endpoint.

Where you click with the Scissors tool, you will see a newly selected anchor point. The scissors tool actually creates two anchor points each time you click, but because they are on top of each other, you can see only one.

2 Select the Direct Selection tool (↖) in the toolbox and position it over the cut. The small hollow square on the pointer indicates that it's over the anchor point. Select the new anchor point, and drag it up to widen the gap between the two split segments.

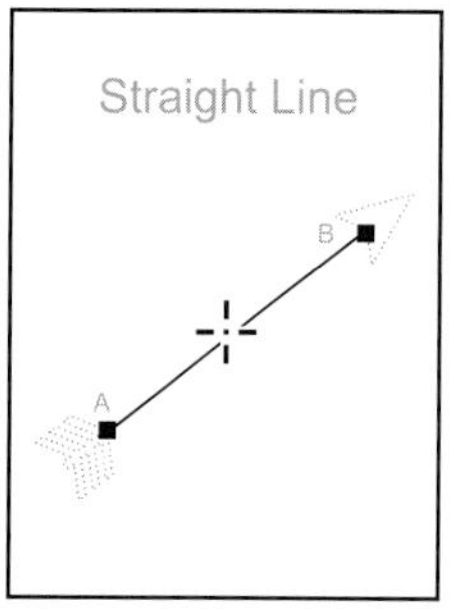

Click with the Scissors tool to cut the line.

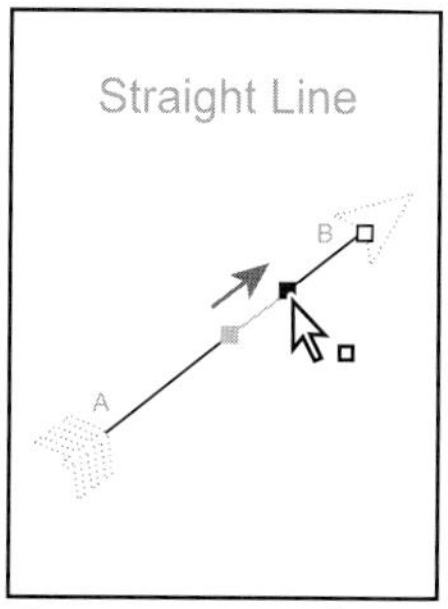

Drag to separate the new line segments.

Adding arrowheads

Adobe Illustrator lets you add pre-made arrowheads and tails to open paths by applying an Effect. The Add Arrowhead feature is available under the Filter menu as well as the Effect menu. The benefit to using an Effect is that the arrow dynamically changes with the stroke that it was created on. A filter, on the other hand, has no relationship to the stroke.

When a path with the Add Arrowhead Effect is changed the arrow head follows the path, whereas the Filter arrowhead remains in its created position. Read more about effects and how to use them in Lesson 10.

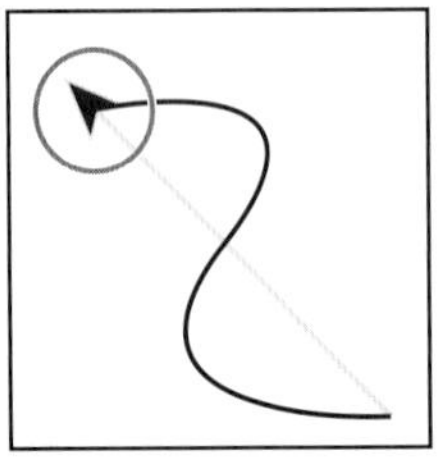

The Add Arrowhead Filter.

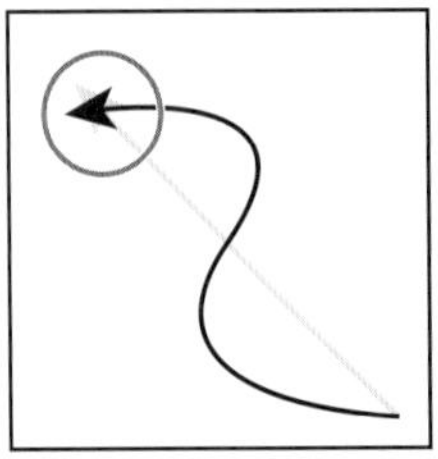

The Add Arrowhead Effect.

Now you'll add an arrowhead to the ending point of one line segment and a tail to the starting point of the other line segment.

1 With the top line segment selected, choose Filter > Effect > Stylize > Add Arrowheads.

Note: *Choose the top, or first, Effect > Stylize command. The second Effect > Stylize command applies painted or impressionistic effects to bitmap images.*

2 In the Add Arrowheads dialog box, leave the Start section set to **None**. For the End section, click an arrow button to select the number **2** style of arrowhead (a thumbnail preview appears in the dialog box), and click OK.

Illustrator adds the arrowhead to the end of the line (the last anchor point created on the uncut line).

3 Using the Direct Selection tool (), select the bottom line segment, and choose Effect > Stylize > Add Arrowheads to open the dialog box again. Select the number **18** style of arrowhead from the Start section, select **None** for the End section, and click OK to add a tail to the starting point of the line.

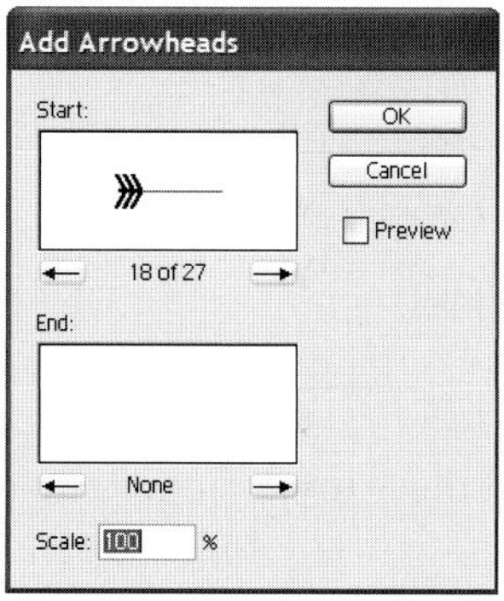

You can reapply the same arrowhead style to other selected objects by choosing Effect > Stylize > Add Arrowheads.

4 Choose Select > Deselect to deselect the artwork, and then choose File > Save.

Drawing curves

In this part of the lesson, you will review drawing curves by drawing the pear, its stem, and a leaf. You'll examine a single curve and then draw a series of curves together, using the template guidelines to help you.

Selecting a curve

1 Choose View > Curved Line to display a view of a curved line on the template.

2 Using the Direct Selection tool (), click one of the segments of the curved line to view its anchor points and its direction handles, which extend from the points. The Direct Selection tool lets you select and edit individual segments in the curved line.

By selecting a curve, you also select the paint attributes of the curve, so that the next line you draw will have those same attributes. For more on paint attributes, see Lesson 5, "Painting."

Drawing the leaf

Now you'll draw the first curve of the leaf.

1 Choose View > Leaf or scroll down to see the guides for Leaf step 1.

Instead of dragging the Pen tool to draw a curve, you will drag it to set the starting point and the direction of the line's curve. When you release the mouse button, the starting point is created and two direction handles are formed. Then you drag the Pen tool to the end of the first curve and to set the starting point and direction of the next curve on the line.

2 Select the Pen tool (✒) and position it over point A on the template. Press the mouse button and drag from point A to the red dot. Then release the mouse button.

Next you'll set the second anchor point and its direction handles.

3 Press the mouse button and drag from point B to the next red dot. Release the mouse button. Illustrator connects the two anchor points with a curve that follows the direction handles you have created. Notice that if you vary the angle of dragging, you change the amount of curve.

4 To complete the curved line, drag the Pen tool from point C on the template to the last red dot and release the mouse button.

5 Control-click (Windows) or Command-click (Mac OS) away from the line to indicate the end of the path. (You must do this to indicate when you have finished drawing a path. You can also do this by clicking the Pen tool in the toolbox, or by choosing Select > Deselect.)

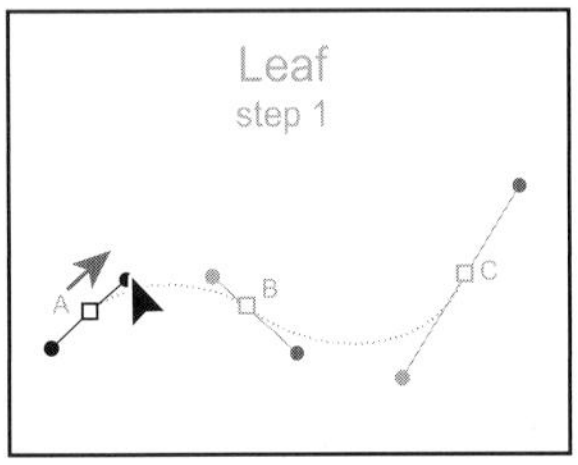

Drag to start the line and set direction of first curve.

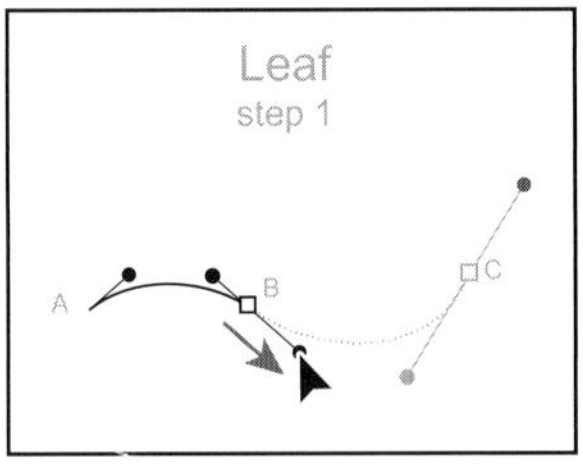

Drag to end first curve and set direction of second curve.

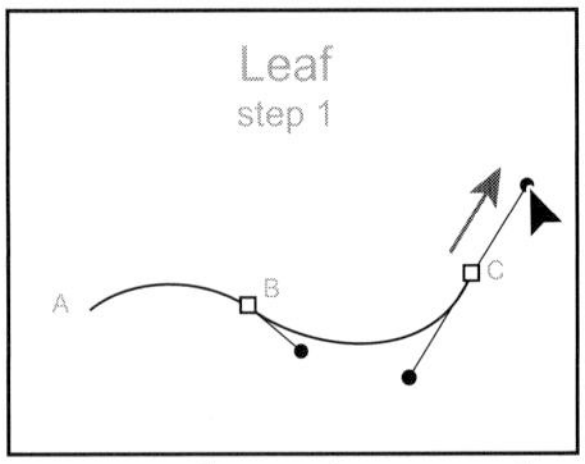

Drag to end second curve and adjust its direction.

Drawing different kinds of curves

Now you'll finish drawing the leaf by adding to an existing curved segment. Even after ending a path, you can return to the curve and add to it. The Alt (Windows) or Option (Mac OS) key lets you control the type of curve you draw.

1 Scroll down to the instructions on the template for Leaf step 2.

You'll add a corner point to the path. A corner point lets you change the direction of the curve. A smooth point lets you draw a continuous curve.

2 Position the Pen tool over the end of the line at point A. The slash next to the Pen tool indicates that you'll continue the path of the existing line, rather than start a new line.

3 Hold down Alt (Windows) or Option (Mac OS) and notice that the status bar in the lower left corner of the window displays "Pen: Make Corner." Now Alt/Option-drag the Pen tool from anchor point A to the red dot. Then release the mouse button.

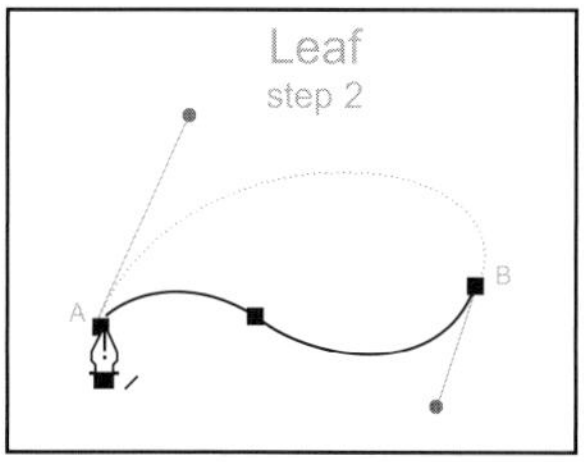

A slash indicates Pen tool is aligned with anchor.

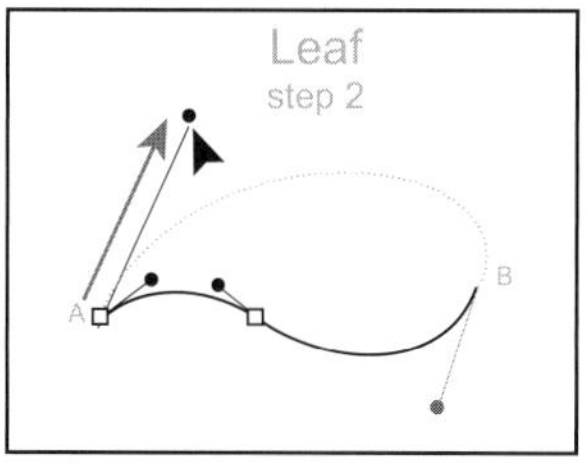

Alt/Option-dragging creates corner point.

So far, all the curves you have drawn have been open paths. Now you'll draw a closed path, in which the final anchor point is drawn on the first anchor point of the path. (Examples of closed paths include ovals and rectangles.) You'll close the path using a smooth point.

4 Position the pointer over anchor point B on the template. A small, open circle appears next to the Pen tool indicating that clicking will close the path. Press the mouse button and drag from this point to the second red dot.

Notice the direction handles where you close the path. The direction handles on both sides of a smooth point are aligned along the same angle.

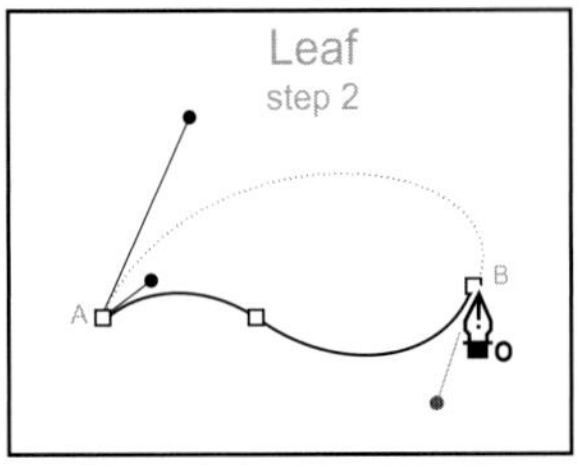

A small circle indicates clicking with Pen tool closes the path.

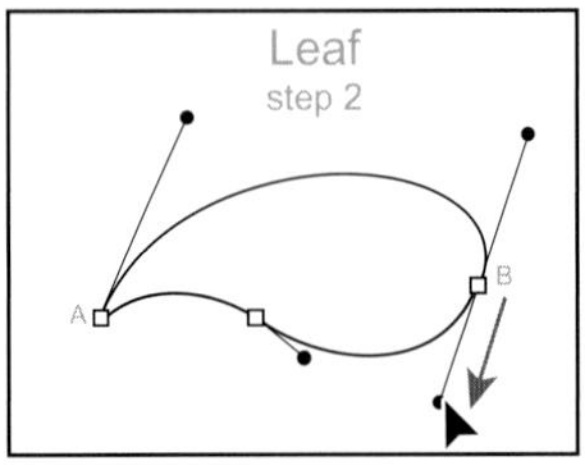

Drag to red dot to lengthen curved line.

5 Control-click (Windows) or Command-click (Mac OS) away from the line, and choose File > Save.

Changing a smooth curve to a corner and vice versa

Now you'll create the leaf stem by adjusting a curved path. You'll be converting a smooth point on the curve to a corner point and a corner point to a smooth point.

1 Choose View > Stem to display a magnified view of the stem.

2 Select the Direct Selection tool (↖) in the toolbox, position the pointer over point A at the top of the curve to display a hollow square on the pointer, and then click the anchor point to select it and display its red direction handles for the smooth point.

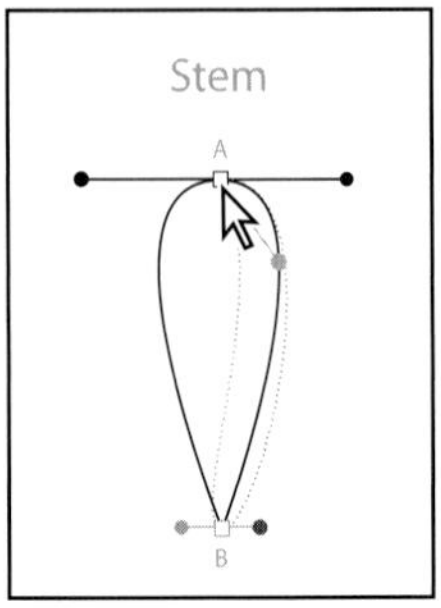

3 Select the Convert Anchor Point tool (↖) from the same group as the Pen tool in the toolbox, or use the shortcut for Convert Anchor Point tool by pressing Alt (Windows) or Option (Mac OS).

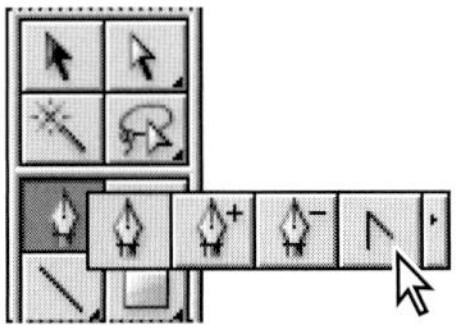

4 Using the Convert Anchor Point tool, select the left direction point (on top of the red dot) on the direction line, drag it to the gold dot on the template, and then release the mouse button.

Dragging with the Convert Anchor Point tool converts the smooth anchor point to a corner point and adjusts the angle of the left direction line.

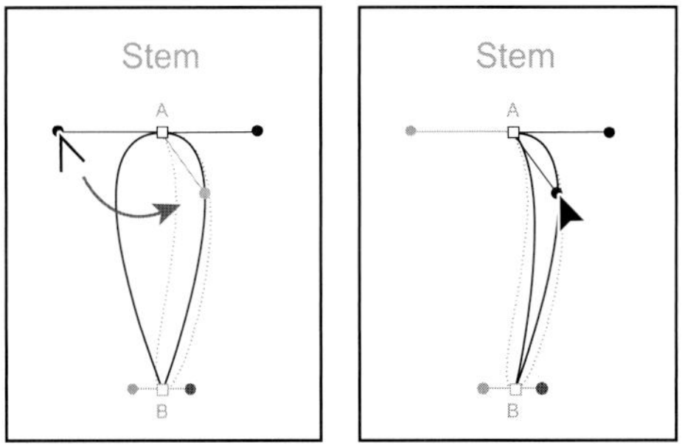

Use Convert Anchor Point tool to convert curves to corners.

5 Using the Convert Anchor Point tool, select the bottom anchor point and drag from point B to the red dot to convert the corner point to a smooth point, rounding out the curve, and then release the mouse button.

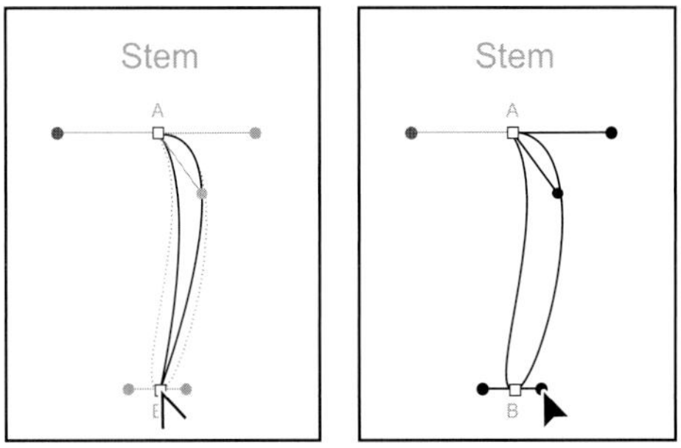

Use Convert Anchor Point tool to convert corners to curves.

Two direction handles emerge from the anchor point, indicating that it is now a smooth point.

When using the Convert Anchor Point tool, keep these guidelines in mind:

• Drag from the curve's anchor point for a smooth point and continuous curve.

• Click the curve's anchor point or drag a handle (direction point) of the curve for a corner point on a discontinuous curve.

6 Choose File > Save.

Drawing the pear shape

Now you'll draw a single, continuous object that consists of smooth points and corner points. Each time you want to change the direction of a curve at a specific point, you'll hold down Alt (Windows) or Option (Mac OS) to create a corner point.

1 Choose View > Pear to display a magnified view of the pear.

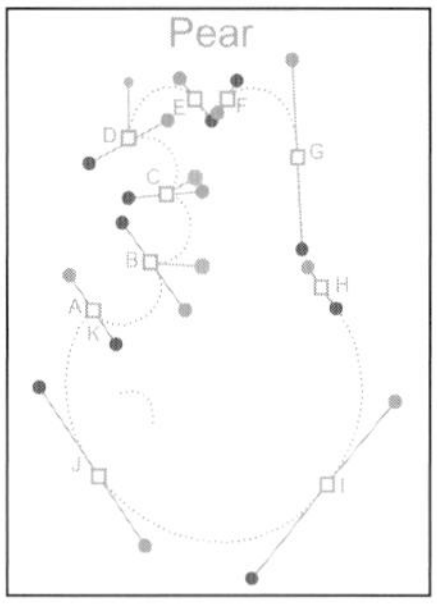

First you'll draw the bite marks on the pear by creating corner points and changing the direction of the curve segments.

2 Select the Pen tool (♠) from the same group as the Convert Anchor Point tool (↖). Drag the Pen tool from point A on the template to the red dot to set the starting anchor point and direction of the first curve. Release the mouse button.

3 Drag the Pen tool from point B to the red dot—but don't release the mouse button—and, while holding down Alt (Windows) or Option (Mac OS), drag the direction handle from the red dot to the gold dot. Release the mouse button.

4 Continue drawing to points C and D by first dragging from the anchor point to the red dot and then Alt/Option-dragging the direction handle from the red dot to the gold dot.

At the corner points B, C, and D, you first drag to continue the current segment, and then Alt/Option-drag to set the direction of the next curved segment.

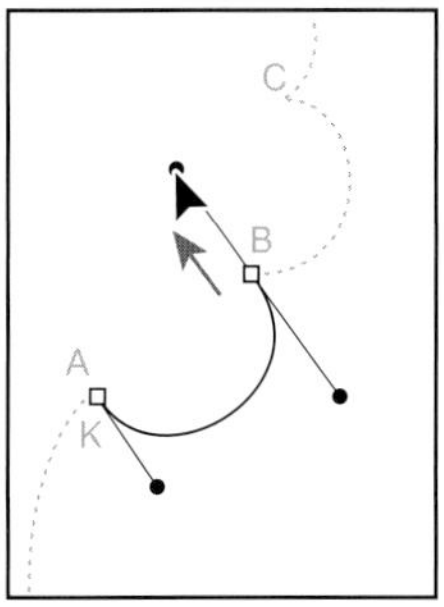

Drag to adjust curve.

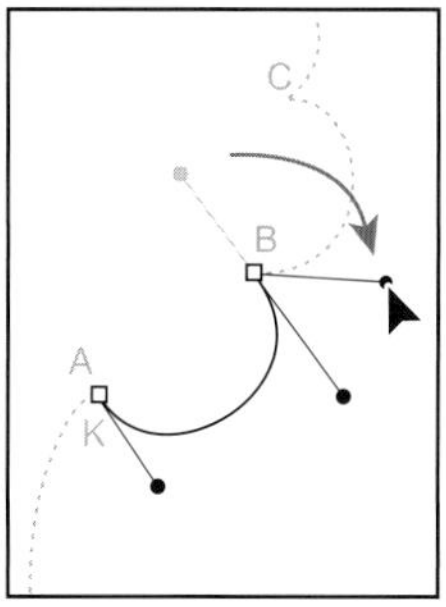

Alt/Option-drag direction point to set corner point.

Next, you'll complete your drawing of the pear by creating smooth points.

5 Drag each of the points from E through J to their red dots, and then click anchor point K to close the pear shape. Notice that when you hold the pointer over anchor point K, a small open circle appears next to the pen, indicating that the path will close when you click.

6 Hold down Control (Windows) or Command (Mac OS) and click away from the path to deselect it, and then choose File > Save.

Editing curves

To adjust the curves you've drawn, you can drag either the curve's anchor points or its direction handles. You can also edit a curve by moving the line.

1 Select the Direct Selection tool (↖) and click the outline of the pear.

Clicking with the Direct Selection tool displays the curve's direction handles and lets you adjust the shape of individual curved segments. Clicking with the Selection tool selects the entire path.

2 Click the anchor point G at the top right of the pear to select it, and adjust the segment by dragging the top direction handle as shown in the illustration.

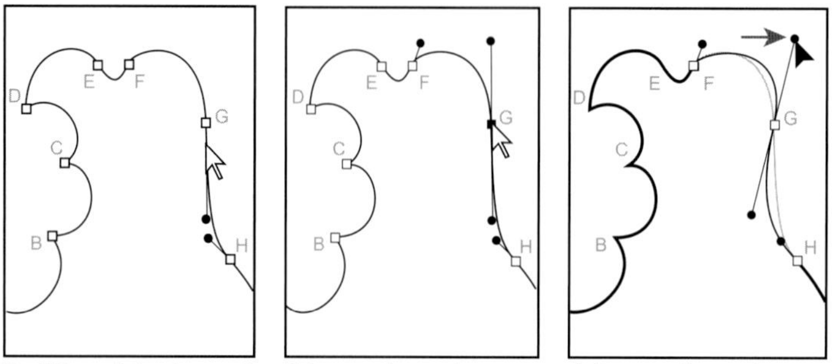

Use Direct Selection tool to select individual segments. *Select anchor point.* *Adjust anchor point.*

3 In the toolbox, click to select the Fill box. Then click the None box to change the Fill to None.

4 Now select the Pen tool ( ) and drag to draw the small curve on the pear where the arrow pierces it. (Use the dashed line on the template as a guide.)

Note: *If you can't see the dashed, curved line on the template, make sure that the Fill in the toolbox is set to None and that the Stroke is set to black.*

5 Choose File > Save.

Tips for drawing curves

Keep the following guidelines in mind to help you draw any kind of curve quickly and easily:

- *Always drag the first direction point in the direction of the bump of the curve, and drag the second direction point in the opposite direction to create a single curve. Dragging both direction points in the same direction creates an S curve.*

- *When drawing a series of continuous curves, draw one curve at a time, placing anchor points at the beginning and end of each curve, not at the tip of the curve.*

- *Use as few anchor points as possible, placing them as far apart as possible.*

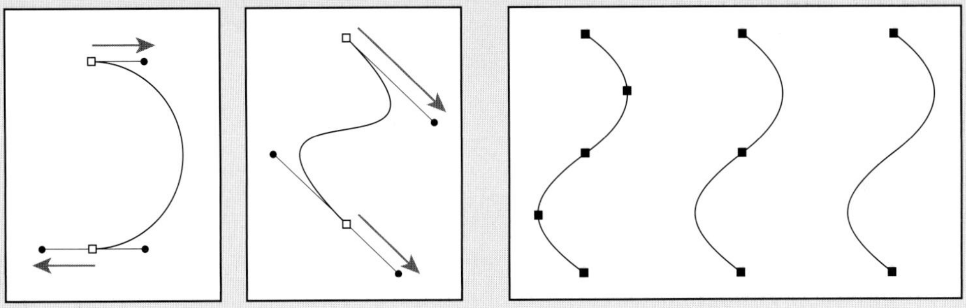

Drag in opposite direction to create a smooth curve. *Drag in same direction to create an S curve.* *Less to more-efficient curves.*

For information on adding, deleting, and moving anchor points on a path, see "About Drawing" in online Help.

Finishing the pear illustration

To complete the illustration, you'll make some minor modifications and assemble and paint all the objects. Then position parts of the arrow to create the illusion of the pear being pierced.

Assembling the parts

1 Double-click the zoom tool (🔍) to zoom to 100%.

2 Choose Window > Layers to display the palette.

3 In the Layers palette, click the template icon that's next to the Template layer name to hide the template.

4 Choose View > Show Bounding Box so that you can see the bounding boxes of selected objects as you transform them.

5 Select the Selection tool (↖) in the toolbox, and Shift-click to select the two single curved lines that you no longer need for the leaf. Press Backspace (Windows) or Delete (Mac OS) to delete them.

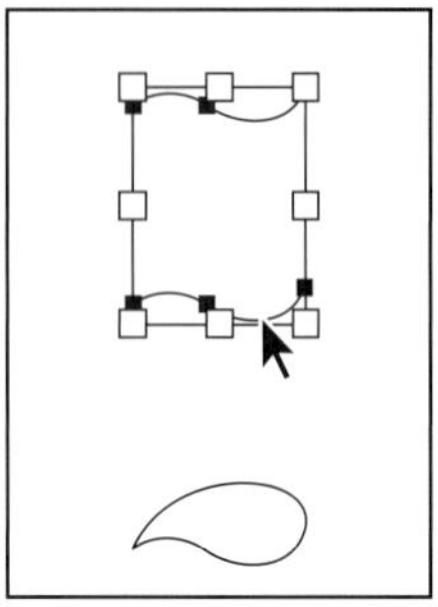

Select and delete extra lines.

Now you'll make the stem and leaf smaller and rotate them slightly using the Transform commands.

6 Select the stem and choose Object > Transform > Scale. Select Uniform and enter **50%** in the Scale text box. Select the Scale Strokes & Effects Option, and click OK.

The Scale Strokes & Effects Option scales stroke weights and effects automatically. You can also set this Option as a preference (choose Edit > General > Preferences).

7 Choose Object > Transform > Rotate. Enter **45** in the Angle text box, and click OK.

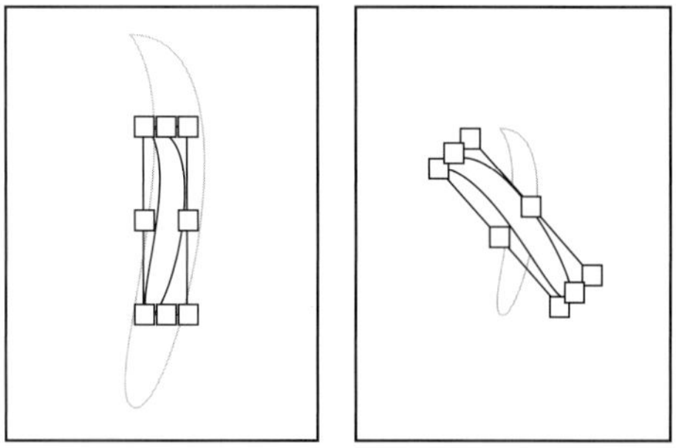

Scale stem 50%. *Rotate stem 45°.*

Now you'll repeat the scaling and rotation on the leaf.

8 Select the leaf and choose Object > Transform > Scale. Leave the settings as they are, and click OK to scale the leaf by 50%. Then choose Object > Transform > Rotate, enter **15** in the Angle text box, and click OK.

You can also scale and rotate objects by using the scale and rotate tools, respectively, or by using the free transform tool to do either. For information, see Lesson 6, "Transforming Objects."

9 Select the selection pointer, and move the stem and the leaf to the top of the pear.

10 Move the parts of the arrow over the pear to make it look as if the arrow is entering the front of the pear and exiting the back.

Objects are arranged in the order in which they are created, with the most recent in front.

11 Select the bottom part of the arrow, and Shift-click to select the curve where the arrow pierces the pear. Then choose Object > Arrange > Bring to Front to arrange them in front of the pear.

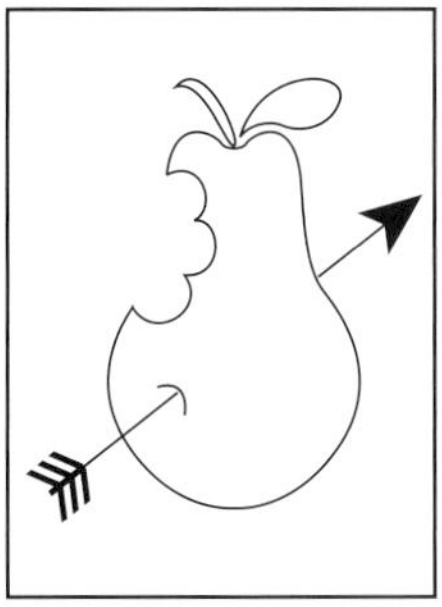

Painting the artwork

Now paint the objects as you like. In our color illustration, we have removed the stroke on the leaf, the stem, and the pear, and we've painted the fills with custom-made gradients called Pear leaf, Pear stem, and Pear body, which are provided in the Swatches palette. We painted the arrow with a dark blue color, and then we added some detail lines to the leaf, the stem, and the round part of the pear using the paintbrush tool and the Pen tool. We also stroked the curve where the arrow pierces the pear.

1 Choose Window > Swatches to display the Swatches palette.

2 Select an object, and then select a swatch in the Swatches palette to paint the object with a color, pattern, or gradient.

To learn how to create your own gradients, see Lesson 12, "Blending Shapes and Colors." To learn more about painting options in Illustrator, see Lesson 5, "Painting," and Lesson 15, "Creating Airbrush Effects."

3 In the Color palette, drag the None icon up and drop it on the Stroke box to remove the stroke of a selected object.

4 Choose File > Save to save your work, then File > Close to close the file.

You've completed the lesson on drawing straight lines and curves. For additional practice with the Pen tool, try tracing over images with it. As you practice more with the Pen tool, you'll become more adept at drawing the kinds of curves and shapes you want.

Exploring on your own

Now that you've used the Pen tool to draw a pear with precise Bézier curves, try drawing the pear using the Pencil tool to create a hand-drawn look. You can edit lines that you draw using the Pencil tool to change their shape, and you can use the Smooth tool and Erase tool to edit the drawing further.

1 Open the L4start.ai file again, and save it as **Pear2.ai**.

2 Select the Pencil tool (✐) in the toolbox, and draw the pear in one continuous line without releasing the mouse button. To close the path, hold down Alt (Windows) or Option (Mac OS)—a small circle will appear on the pointer—and continue dragging to draw the end of the line connected to the starting point.

Anchor points are set down as you draw with the Pencil tool, and you can adjust them once the path is complete. The number of anchor points is determined by the length and complexity of the path and by the tolerance values set in the Pencil tool Preferences dialog box. (Double-click the tool to display its preferences dialog box.)

Note: *You can draw and edit brushed paths with the paintbrush tool by using the same methods as those used for paths drawn with the Pencil tool. (See Lesson 5, "Working with Brushes.")*

3 Use the Pencil tool (✐) to edit the shape of the pear by redrawing segments on the path.

Changing a path with the Pencil tool

If the path you want to change is not selected, select it with the Selection tool. Or Control-click (Windows) or Command-click (Mac OS) the path to select it.

Position the Pencil tool on or near the path to redraw, and drag the tool until the path is the desired shape.

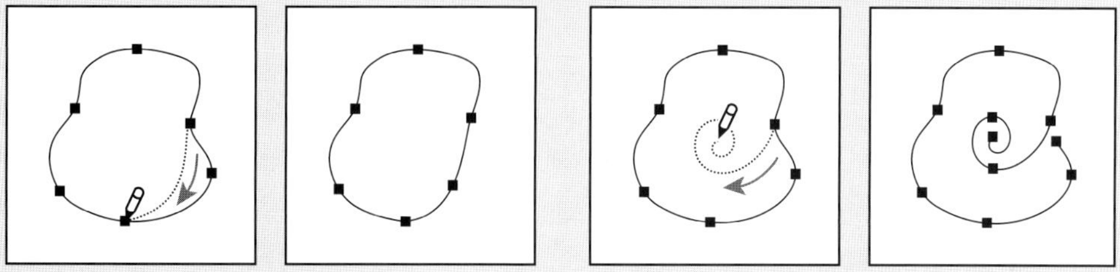

Using the Pencil tool to edit a closed shape. *Using the Pencil tool to create an open shape.*

Depending on where you begin to redraw the path and in which direction you drag, you may get unexpected results. For example, you may unintentionally change a closed path to an open path, change an open path to a closed path, or lose a portion of a shape.

–From "Adjusting Paths" in online Help.

4 Use the Smooth tool ( ), in the same group as the Pencil tool ( ) in the toolbox, to round out the shape of a curved segment (deleting anchor points if necessary).

The number of anchor points is determined by the length and complexity of the new path, as well as by the tolerance values set in the Smooth tool Preferences dialog box.

Smoothing the path with the Smooth tool

The Smooth tool lets you smooth out an existing stroke or section of a path. The Smooth tool retains the original shape of the path as much as possible.

To use the Smooth tool:

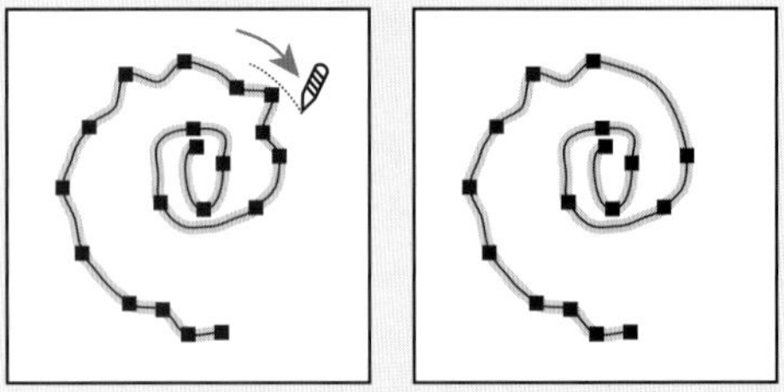

Stroke before and after using the Smooth tool.

1. If the path you wish to smooth is not selected, select it with the Selection tool. Or Ctrl-click (Windows) or Command-click (Mac OS) the path to select it.

2. Do one of the following:

- *Select the Smooth tool ( ), located in the same group as the Pencil tool ( ) in the toolbox.*
- *When the pencil or paintbrush tool is selected, hold down Alt (Windows) or Option (Mac OS) to change the pencil to the Smooth tool.*

3. Drag the tool along the length of the path segment you want to smooth out. The modified stroke or path may have fewer anchor points than the original.

4. Continue smoothing until the stroke or path is the desired smoothness.

–From "Adjusting Paths" on online Help.

5 Use the Erase tool ( ), in the same group as the Pencil tool ( ) in the toolbox, to erase segments on the path of the pear, then redraw them using the Pencil tool ( ).

Erasing the path with the Erase tool

The Erase tool lets you remove a portion of an existing path or stroke. You can use the Erase tool on paths (including brushed paths), but not on text or meshes.

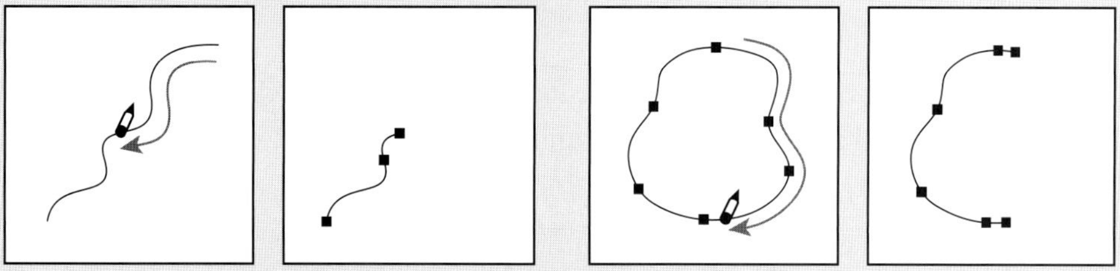

Strokes before and after using the Erase tool.

To use the Erase tool:

1. Select the Erase tool ( ), in the same group as the Pencil tool ( ) in the toolbox.

2. Drag the tool along the length of the path segment you want to erase (not across the path). For best results, use a single, smooth, dragging motion.

Anchor points are added to the ends of the new paths.

–From "Adjusting Paths" on online Help.

Review questions

1 Describe how to draw straight vertical, horizontal, or diagonal lines using the Pen tool.

2 How do you draw a curved line using the Pen tool?

3 How do you draw a corner point on a curved line?

4 How do you change a smooth point on a curve to a corner point?

5 Which tool would you use to edit a segment on a curved line?

Review answers

1 To draw a straight line, you click twice with the Pen tool—the first click sets the starting anchor point, and the second click sets the ending anchor point of the line. To constrain the straight line vertically, horizontally, or along a 45° diagonal, hold down Shift as you click with the Pen tool.

2 To draw a curved line using the Pen tool, you hold down the mouse button and drag to create the starting anchor point and set the direction of the curve, and then you click to end the curve.

3 To draw a corner point on a curved line, hold down Alt (Windows) or Option (Mac OS) and drag the direction handle on the endpoint of the curve to change the direction of the path, and then continue dragging to draw the next curved segment on the path.

4 Use the Direct Selection tool (↖) to select the anchor point, and then use the Convert Anchor Point tool (⊳) to drag a direction handle to change the direction.

5 To edit a segment on a curved line, select the Direct Selection tool (↖) and drag the segment to move it, or drag a direction handle on an anchor point to adjust the length and shape of the segment.

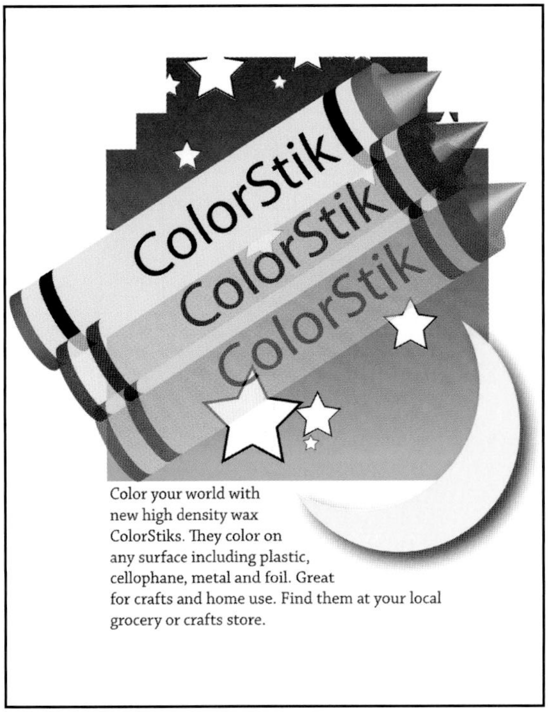
ColorStik
ColorStik
ColorStik
Color your world with new high density wax ColorStiks. They color on any surface including plastic, cellophane, metal and foil. Great for crafts and home use. Find them at your local grocery or crafts store.

Tour

Lesson 1

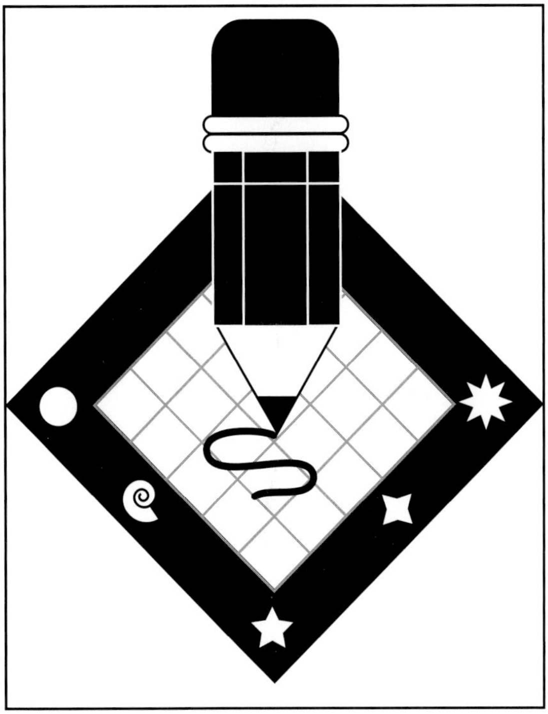

Lesson 3

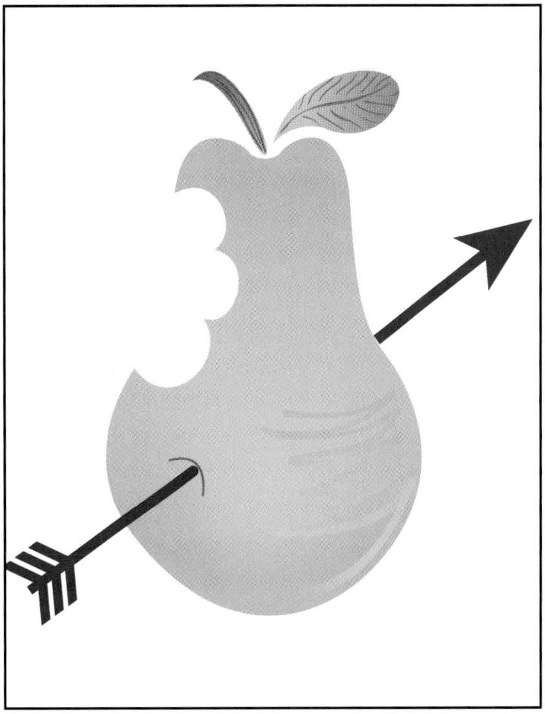

Lesson 4

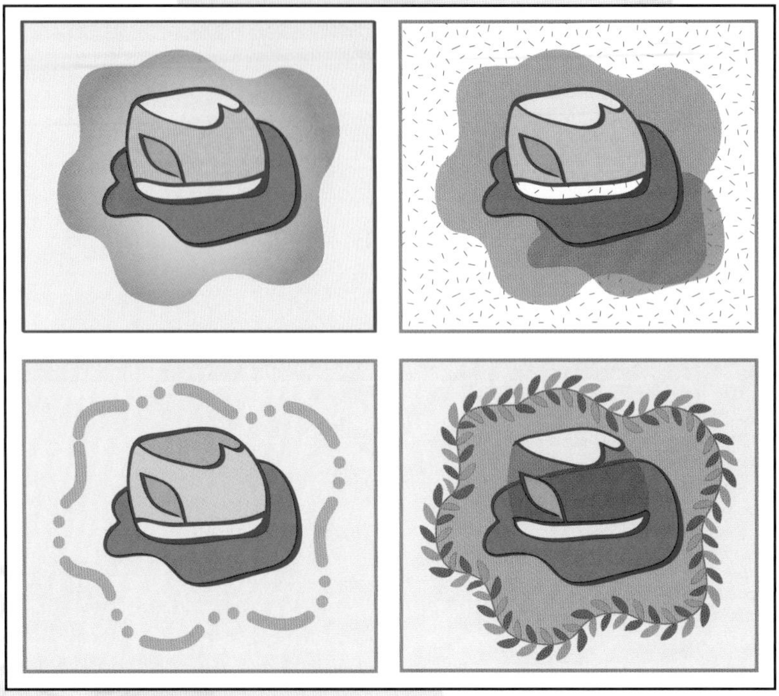

Lesson 5

Lesson 6

Lesson 7

Lesson 8

Lesson 9

Lesson 10

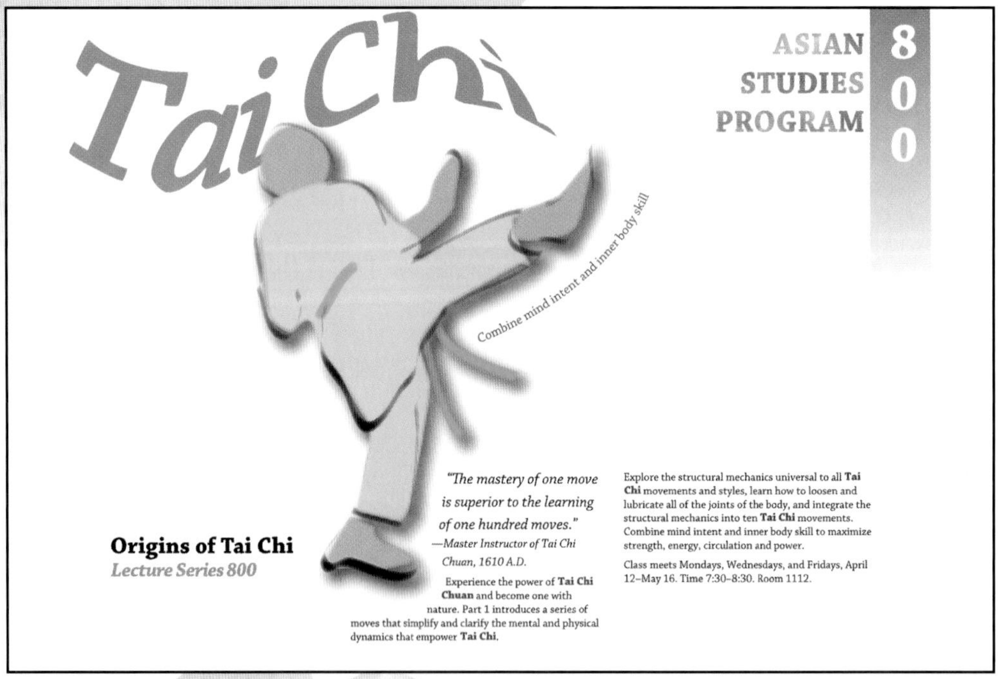

Tai Chi
ASIAN STUDIES PROGRAM
800
Combine mind intent and inner body skill
"The mastery of one move is superior to the learning of one hundred moves."
—Master Instructor of Tai Chi Chuan, 1610 A.D.
Experience the power of Tai Chi Chuan and become one with nature. Part 1 introduces a series of moves that simplify and clarify the mental and physical dynamics that empower Tai Chi.
Explore the structural mechanics universal to all Tai Chi movements and styles, learn how to loosen and lubricate all of the joints of the body, and integrate the structural mechanics into ten Tai Chi movements. Combine mind intent and inner body skill to maximize strength, energy, circulation and power.
Class meets Mondays, Wednesdays, and Fridays, April 12–May 16. Time 7:30–8:30. Room 1112.
Origins of Tai Chi
Lecture Series 800

Lesson 11

Lesson 12

Lesson 13

Lesson 14

Lesson 15

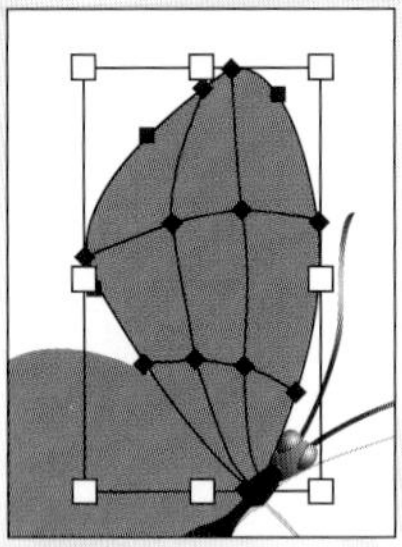

Flat appearance (no highlighting).

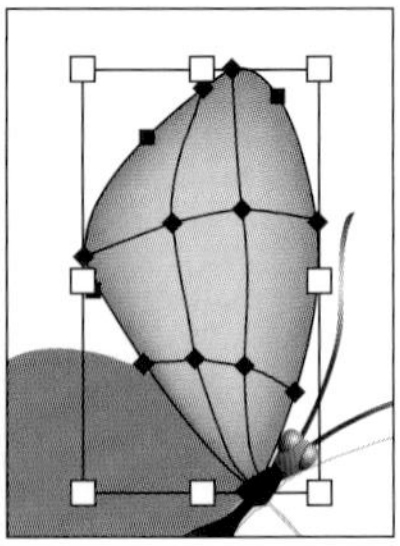

To Center highlighting.

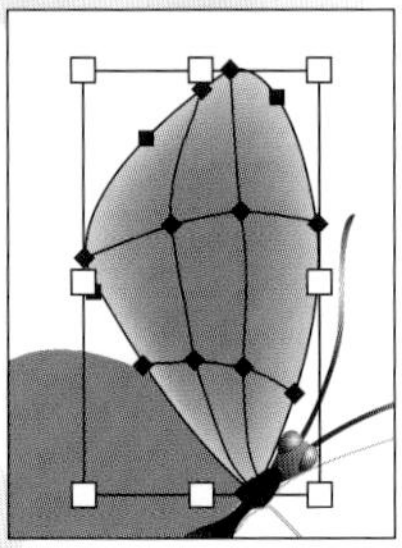

To Edge highlighting.

Modifying a gradient mesh

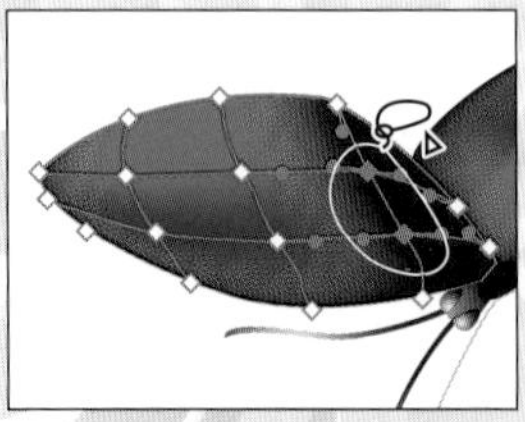

Mesh points selected before applying color.

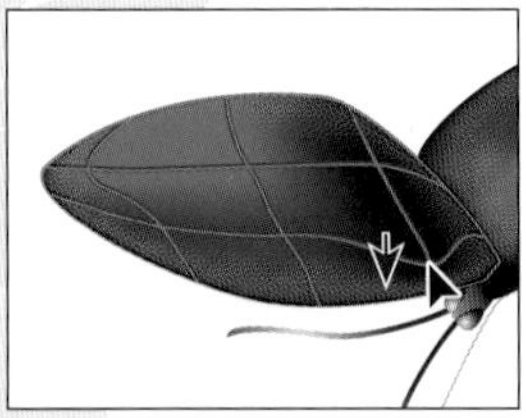

Moving a mesh point vertically.

Mesh point added with a new color applied.

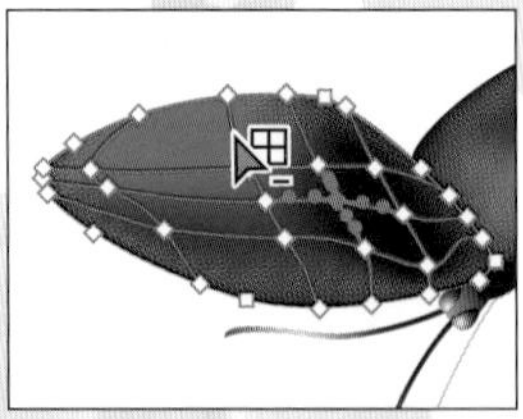

Deleting a mesh line.

Result of color blending.

Lesson 16

Lesson 17

CMYK and RGC color models

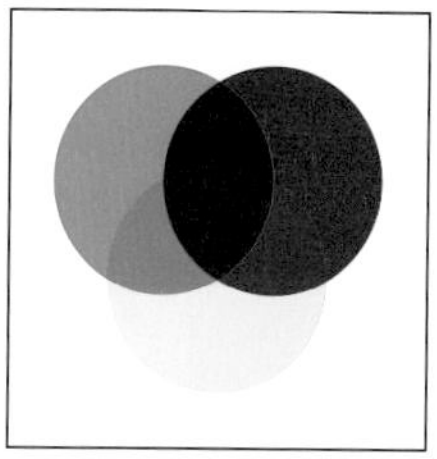

Subtractive Colors.

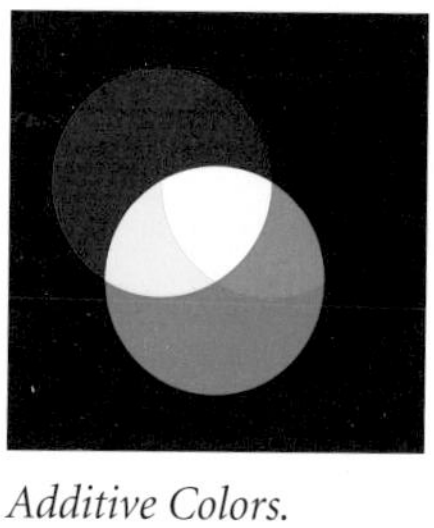

Additive Colors.

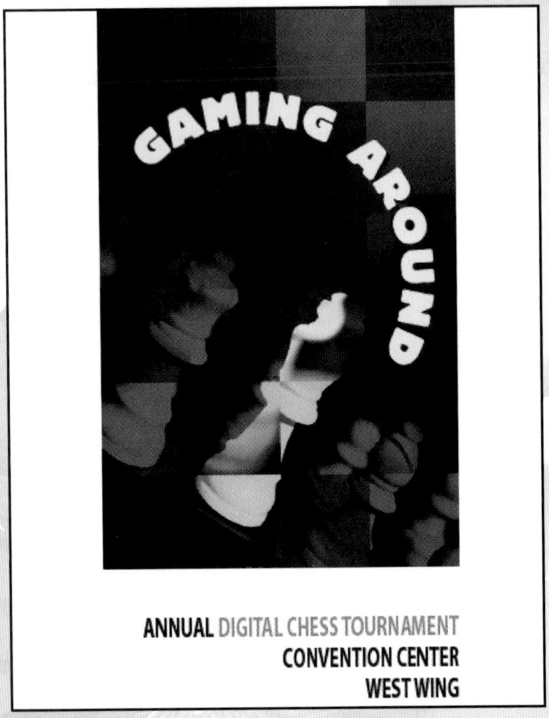
GAMING AROUND
ANNUAL DIGITAL CHESS TOURNAMENT
CONVENTION CENTER
WEST WING

Lesson 18

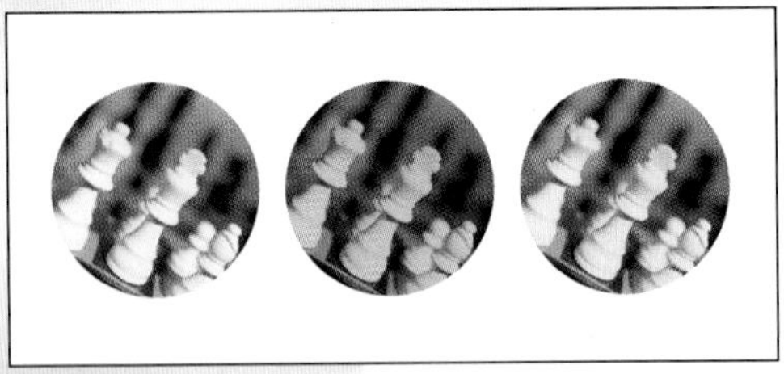

Adjust Color Filter on placed photo: Original, and after increasing Magenta and Yellow.

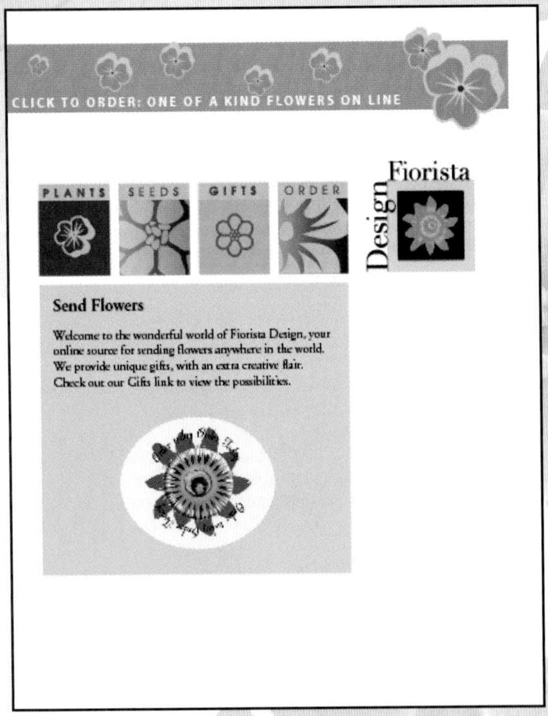
CLICK TO ORDER: ONE OF A KIND FLOWERS ON LINE
PLANTS
SEEDS
GIFTS
ORDER
Fiorista
Design
Send Flowers
Welcome to the wonderful world of Fiorista Design, your online source for sending flowers anywhere in the world. We provide unique gifts, with an extra creative flair. Check out our Gifts link to view the possibilities.

Lesson 19

Dithering Examples

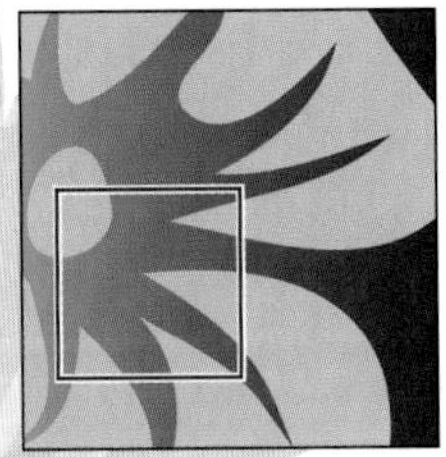

Artwork painted with the CMYK colors.

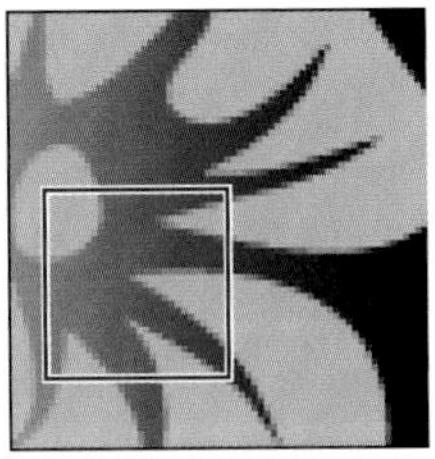

Colors dithered in GIF image.

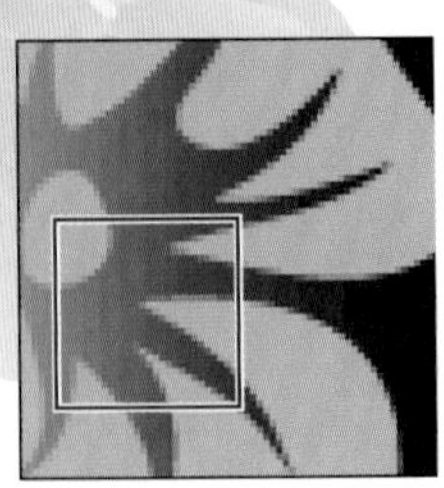

No color dithering in GIF image.

Lesson 5

5 Painting

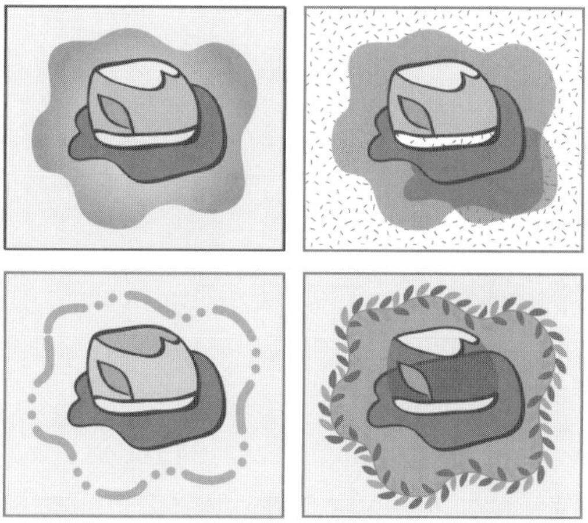

The Color and Swatches palettes let you apply, modify, and save colors in your artwork. You can paint with HSB, RGB, Web-safe RGB, or CMYK colors; grayscale, global process, and spot colors; patterns; and gradients of blended colors With the Brushes palette, you can apply art or patterns to the path of an object.

In this lesson, you'll learn how to do the following:

- Paint with, create, and edit colors.
- Name and save colors and build a color palette.
- Copy paint and appearance attributes from one object to another.
- Adjust the saturation of a color.
- Paint with gradients, patterns, and brushes.

Getting started

In this lesson, you'll learn about the variety of paint options in the Adobe Illustrator program as you paint an illustration of four hats. Before you begin, you'll restore the default preferences for Adobe Illustrator. Then you will open the finished art file for this lesson to see what you'll create.

1 To ensure that the tools and palettes function exactly as described in this lesson, delete or deactivate (by renaming) the Adobe Illustrator CS preferences file. See "Restoring default preferences" on page 2.

2 Start Adobe Illustrator.

3 Choose File > Open, and open the L5end.ai file in the Lesson05 folder, located inside the Lessons folder within the AICIB folder on your hard drive.

4 If you like, choose View > Zoom Out to make the finished artwork smaller and leave it on your screen as you work. (Use the Hand tool (✋) to move the artwork where you want it in the window.) If you don't want to leave the image open, choose File > Close.

For an illustration of the finished artwork in this lesson, see the color section of this manual.

Now open the start file to begin the lesson.

5 Choose File > Open, and open the L5start.ai file in the Lesson05 folder.

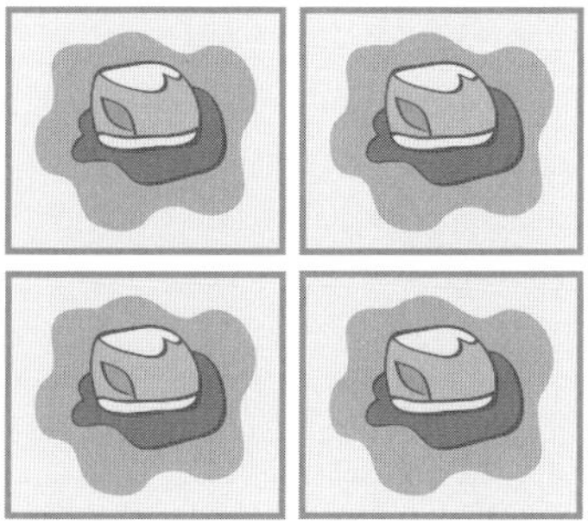

6 Choose File > Save As, name the file Hats.ai, and select the Lesson05 folder in the Save In menu. Leave the type of format set to Adobe Illustrator® Document, and click Save. In the Illustrator Options dialog box, accept the default settings by clicking OK.

Filling with color

Painting objects with colors, gradients, or patterns is done using a combination of palettes and tools–including the Color palette, the Swatches palette, the Gradient palette, the Stroke palette, and the paint buttons in the toolbox–that let you select and change an object's paint and line attributes.

You'll begin by filling an object with color. Filling an object paints the area enclosed by the path.

When you reset the defaults, the Color and Swatches palettes appear automatically on-screen when starting Adobe Illustrator.

(If the Color and Swatches palettes aren't visible, display them by choosing Window > Color and Window > Swatches; a check mark indicates that the palettes are open on-screen.)

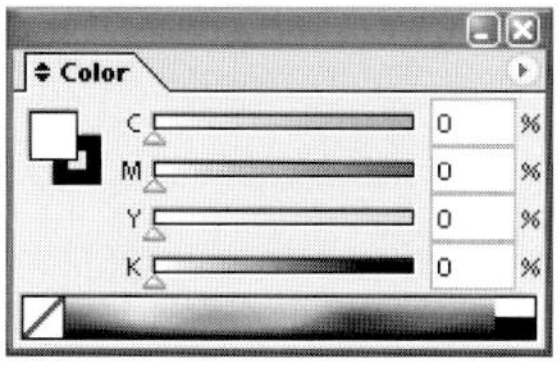

Default Color palette.

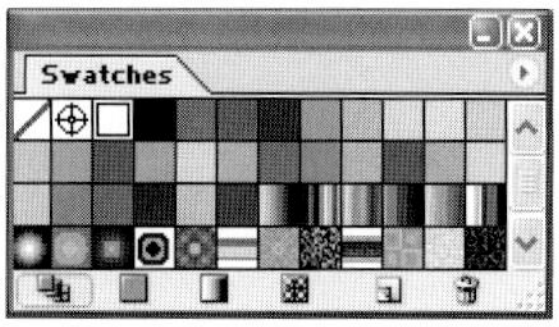

Default Swatches palette.

1 Choose View > Hide Bounding Box. The bounding box is useful for moving and resizing objects. You won't need this option for this lesson.

2 Choose the Selection tool () in the toolbox, and then click the rectangular border around the top left block in the artwork to select the object.

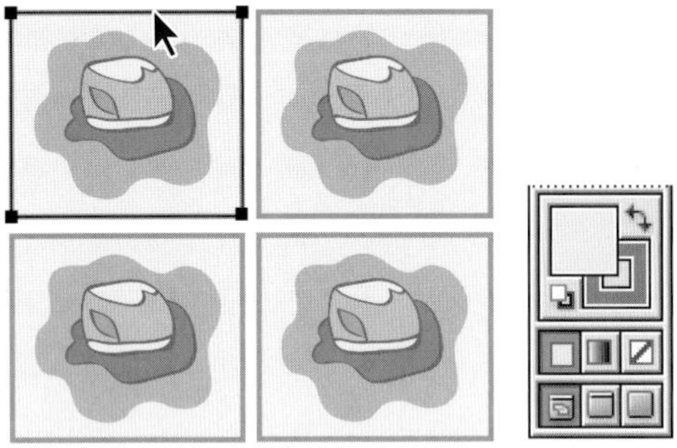

The selected object's paint attributes appear in the toolbox.

In the toolbox, notice that the Fill box appears in the foreground, indicating that it is selected. (This is the default.) The box has a fill of a warm grey color. In the background behind the Fill box, the Stroke box has a turquoise outline, indicating that the rectangle is outlined in turquoise. When the Stroke box or Fill box is in the background, its color is not the current selection.

The fill and stroke attributes of the selected object also appear in the Appearance palette. Appearance attributes can be edited, deleted, saved as Graphic Styles, and applied to other objects, layers, and groups. You'll use this palette later in this lesson.

The Transparency palette displays the selected object's opacity and blending mode, both of which can affect the color of your artwork. You'll change transparency and blending modes later in this lesson. For more information on the Transparency palette, see "Using the Transparency Palette" in online Help.

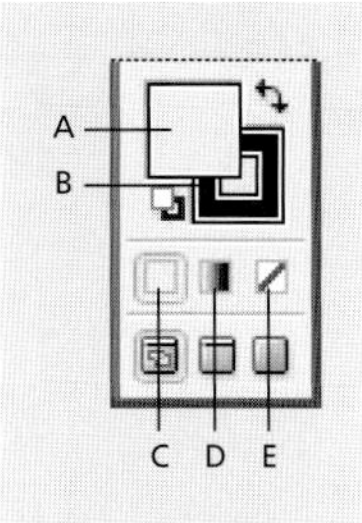

A. Fill. B. Stroke. C. Color. D. Gradient. E. None.

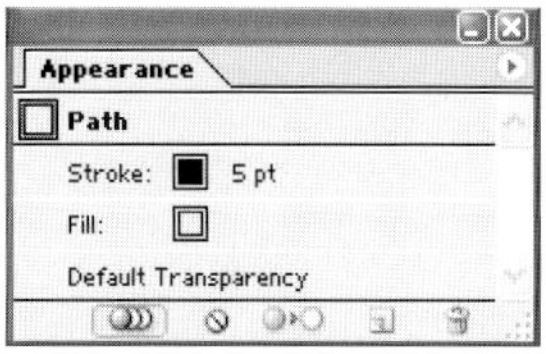

Appearance palette reflects selected object's paint attributes.

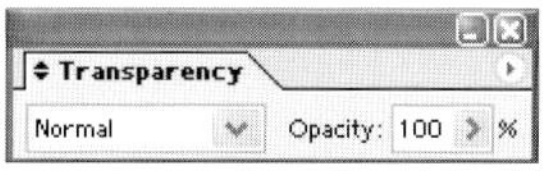

Transparency palette displays opacity and blending mode.

On the Color palette hold down the mouse button on the triangle in the upper right corner of the palette and choose Show Options from the palette menu. The Color palette displays the current color for the fill and stroke, and its CMYK sliders show the colors' percentages of cyan, magenta, yellow, and black. At the bottom of the Color palette is the color bar. Now you'll use it to select a fill color of yellow.

3 In the Color palette, position the Eyedropper pointer (✎) over the color bar. Hold down the mouse button and drag the eyedropper across the colors. As you drag, the color updates in the Fill boxes in the toolbox, in both the Color and Appearance palettes, and in the artwork.

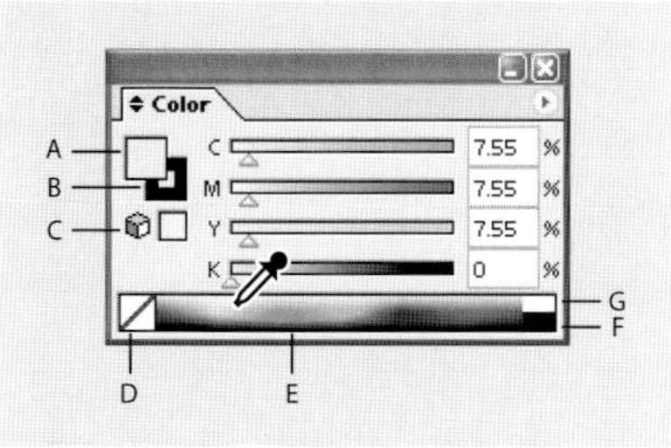

A. Fill box. B. Stroke box. C. Out of Web Color Warning. D. None button. E. Color bar. F. Black color box. G. White color box.

The color bar lets you quickly and visually select a fill or stroke color from a spectrum of colors. You can also choose white or black by clicking the appropriate color box at the right end of the color bar.

4 Now click a yellow color in the color bar to select the color. You can adjust the color by dragging the CMYK sliders in the Color palette. (We selected a yellow color with these values: C = 3.53%, M = 4.31%, Y = 48.63%, and K = 0%.) The color is updated in the Fill boxes in the toolbox and the Color palette, as well as in the artwork.

The paint attributes you choose are applied to all new objects you create until you change the attributes again. Depending on the last paint attribute applied, either the Fill box or the Stroke box appears selected and frontmost in the toolbox.

Stroking with color

Next, you'll outline the squiggly area around the bottom left hat. Painting just the outline of an object is called *stroking*.

1 Using the Selection tool (), click the squiggly shape around the hat in the bottom left rectangle to select it.

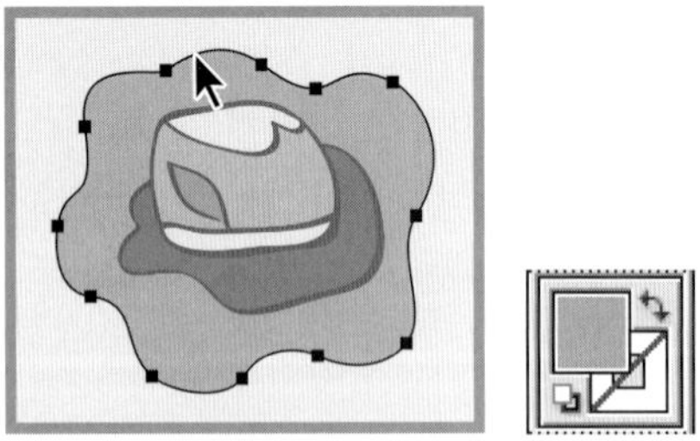

Select squiggly shape in bottom left rectangle.

The Fill box in the toolbox displays a pale green color. The Stroke box in the background has a red slash, indicating the squiggly shape's stroke is unpainted (a stroke value of "None").

You'll start by swapping the fill color with the stroke color.

2 Click the Swap Fill and Stroke button to reverse the colors of the selected object's fill and stroke.

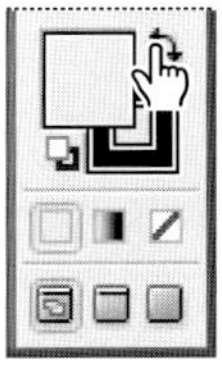

The Fill box now has no fill (a fill of "None"), and the Stroke box has a pale green color. (The color will become apparent in the next step.) With a fill of None, you can see through to the fill underneath—in this case, the gray color of the rectangle's fill.

Now you'll change the weight of the line that you just stroked using the Stroke palette. *Stroke weight* is the thickness of a line. The Stroke palette is grouped with the Transparency and Gradient palettes. The line has a weight of 1 point.

3 If the Stroke palette is not visible, choose Window > Stroke. Then type **7** in the Weight text box and press Enter or Return to change the stroke weight to **7** points. The squiggly line now stands out.

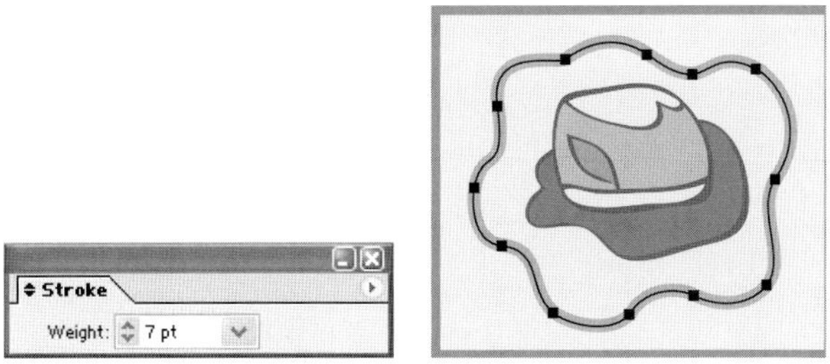

Change the Stroke weight to make the squiggly line stand out.

Next, you'll use the Stroke palette's options to change the line from solid to dashed.

4 In the Stroke palette, hold down the mouse button on the triangle in the upper right corner of the palette and choose Show Options from the palette menu. (You can use this same technique for choosing options from other palette menus.)

You use the Stroke palette options to specify how to cap the ends, join the corners, and make lines dashed or dotted.

5 In the Stroke palette, select the Dashed Line option. The Dash and Gap text boxes become active.

To create a dashed or dotted line, you specify first the length of the dash (or dot) and then the gap, or spacing, between the dashes. You can create a dashed or dotted line with as few as two values or as many as six values. The more values you enter, the more complex the pattern.

6 Type the following values in the Dash and Gap text boxes, pressing Tab after each entry to advance to the next text box: **12, 0, 12, 0, 12**. Leave the last Gap box empty. Press Enter or Return to apply the change.

Now you'll select a cap for the lines to create a dotted-line effect.

7 In the Cap options area of the Stroke palette, click the Round Cap button (the middle button). Click away from the artwork to deselect it and see the result.

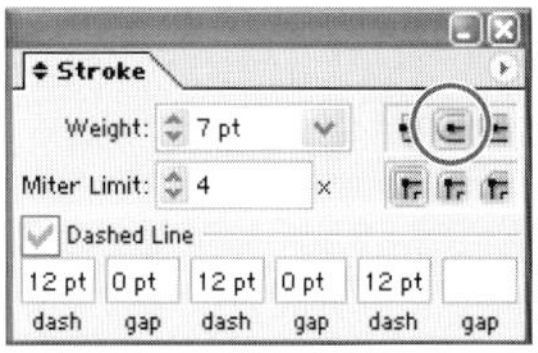

Select Round Cap for dashed line.

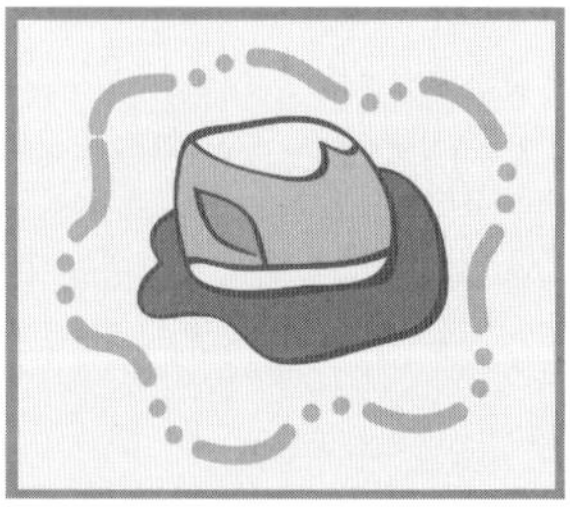
Result.

For examples of other effects you can create, and information on stroking lines, see "Changing stroke attributes" in online Help.

You can select objects by a common paint attribute (such as their stroke color or weight) and change them all at once.

8 Select the border of one of the rectangles, and click the Stroke box in the toolbox to select the rectangle's stroke.

9 Choose Select > Same > Stroke Weight to select the strokes all the objects that have the same stroke weight in the artwork (in this case, all of the rectangles).

10 In the Stroke palette, type **2** in the Weight text box and press Enter or Return to globally change the stroke weight to 2 points.

11 Click away from the artwork to deselect it, and choose File > Save.

Building custom swatches

Now you'll learn how to create your own custom colors by mixing, naming, and saving them in the Swatches palette.

Mixing your own color

You'll start to create a custom color using the CMYK sliders in the Color palette. First you'll mix a fill color.

1 In the toolbox, click the Fill box to make it active.

2 Using the Selection tool (↖), click the middle of the hat in the bottom left rectangle to select it.

Select Fill box.

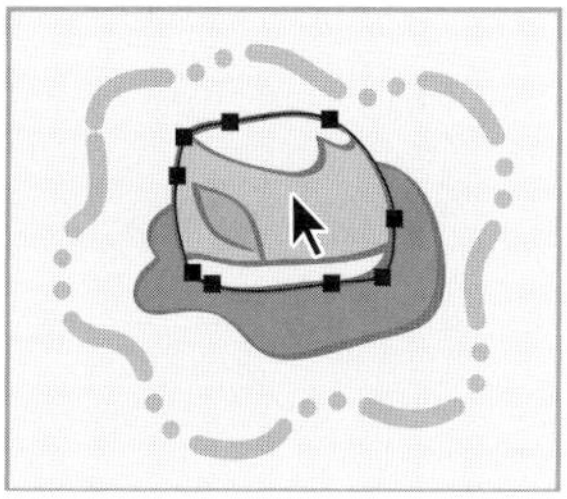

Select middle of hat in bottom left rectangle.

In the Color palette, notice that the hat color is grayscale–that is, a percentage of black–and only the K (black) slider shows a value. The color bar changes to display a scale ramp from white to black.

Now you'll change the color model to CMYK so that you can mix colors.

3 In the Color palette, choose CMYK from the palette menu.

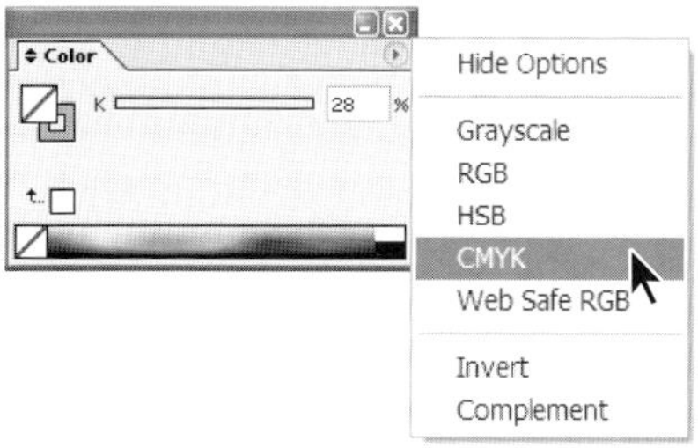

The Color palette lets you edit and mix colors–either colors that you create or colors that you have selected from the Swatches palette, from an object, or from a color library. In this case, you're selecting colors using the CMYK color model.

Now you'll select an orange color for the middle of the hat.

4 In the Color palette, drag the CMYK sliders to select a light orange color, or type values in the text boxes and press Enter or Return to apply the changes. (We specified C = 0%, M = 25%, Y = 54%, and B = 0%.)

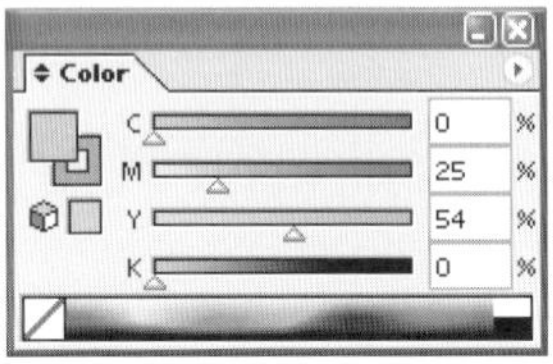

You can use the different color models in conjunction with the Color palette sliders to precisely select a color by its different color values. However, if you mix color models (such as CMYK and RGB) in the same file, Illustrator will convert the colors to the mode in which the file is saved.

For information on the color models that Illustrator uses, see "About color models and color modes" in online Help.

5 Click away from the artwork to deselect it, and choose File > Save.

Saving a color swatch

The Swatches palette stores the colors, gradients, and patterns that have been preloaded into Adobe Illustrator, as well as those you create and save for reuse. New colors added to the Swatches palette are saved with the current file. Opening a new artwork file displays the default set of swatches that comes with the Adobe Illustrator program.

Add the light orange color you just mixed to the Swatches palette so it will be stored with this artwork file. You can select a color to add from either the Fill or Stroke boxes in the toolbox, or from the Color palette. Even though you deselected the artwork, the light orange color is still the current color in the Fill box in both the toolbox and the Color palette.

1 Drag the orange color from the Fill box and drop it in the Swatches palette. It appears in the first empty spot in the palette.

As you drag a color into the Swatches palette, an outline appears around the palette, indicating that it is active and that you are about to drop the color.

Now you'll add another color to the Swatches palette.

2 Using the Selection tool (), select the top left rectangle that you painted with a yellow fill.

3 Make sure that the Fill box is selected in the toolbox, and then click the New Swatch button at the bottom of the Swatches palette to store the color.

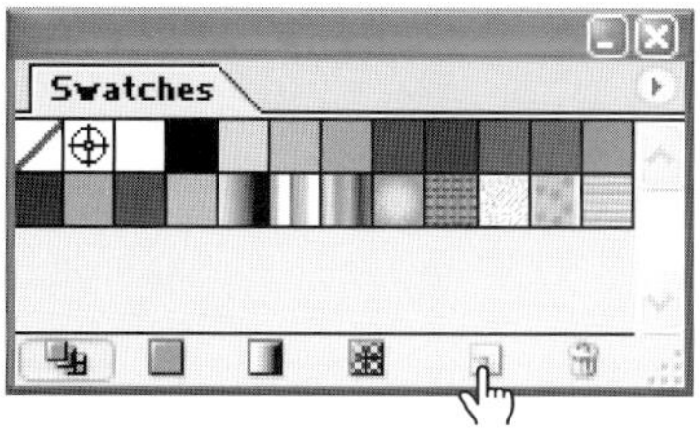

Click New Swatch button to store a color.

You can make your own custom set of swatches for the file by deleting swatches from the Swatches palette that you don't use.

4 Click away from the artwork to deselect it, and then click the black swatch (C = 0%, M = 0%, Y = 0%, K = 100%) in the Swatches palette to select it. Click the Delete Swatch button at the bottom of the Swatches palette, and then click Yes in the warning dialog box to delete the swatch.

If you want to add a color back into the Swatches palette, you can drag the color directly from the Color palette or from the Fill or Stroke boxes in the toolbox. You can also restore the default set of colors to your artwork.

5 Choose Window > Swatch Libraries > Default_CMYK to retrieve the default set of swatches for CMYK files. (These swatches may look different from the swatches in your Swatches palette.)

6 In the Default_CMYK palette, select the black color swatch you deleted in step 4, and then choose Add to Swatches from the palette menu to copy the selected swatch back to your customized Swatches palette. The color appears as the last color in the bottom row of the Swatches palette.

You can add swatches from any color library palette to the Swatches palette.

7 Click the close box of the Default_CMYK palette to close it, and choose File > Save.

Naming a swatch

You can give swatches unique names so you can quickly locate them in the Swatches palette. All colors—whether process or spot colors—can be named while still retaining all the characteristics of the particular color mode (for example, RGB, Web-Safe RGB, HSB, or grayscale modes).

1 Double-click the yellow swatch you saved in the Swatches palette, or select it and choose Swatch Options from the Swatches palette menu.

2 In the Swatch Options dialog box, name the color (for example, "background-yellow") and click OK.

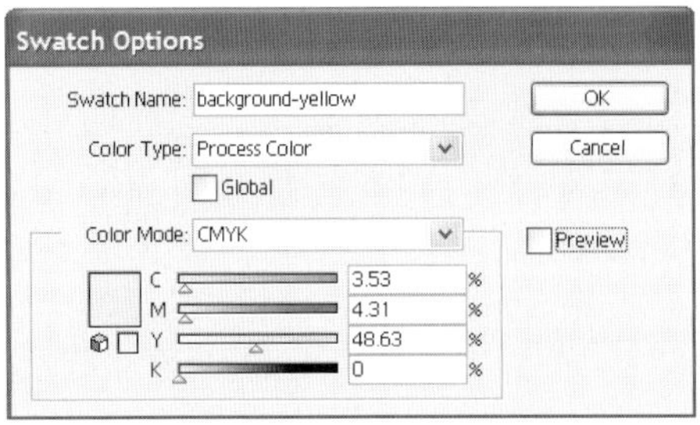

The Swatches palette lets you name, store, and select three types of colors: individual and global process colors (these include grayscale and CMYK, RGB, Web-Safe RGB, and HSB color models), and global spot colors. Spot colors are special, premixed colors used instead of, or in addition to, process color inks; they require their own separations and their own plates on press.

Working with process colors, spot colors, and registration colors

It is important to understand the different types of color used in Adobe Illustrator—global process color, non-global process color, spot color, and registration color—because the color type determines how colors are updated throughout the document, as well as how they are separated and printed.

Process colors *are the four inks used in traditional color separations: cyan, magenta, yellow, and black. In Illustrator, all five color models that are used in a CMYK file—that is, CMYK, RGB, Web-Safe RGB, HSB, and Grayscale—will result in process colors. Avoid using process colors in documents intended for online viewing only, because CMYK has a smaller color gamut than a typical monitor.*

Global process colors *are process colors that automatically update throughout the document when the swatch is edited; that is, every object containing such a color changes when the corresponding swatch is modified.*

Non-global process colors *also can be assigned to any of the five color models (CMYK, RGB, Web-Safe RGB, HSB, and Grayscale), and do not automatically update throughout the document when the color is edited. Process colors are non-global by default; a non-global process color can be changed to a global process color using the Swatch Options dialog box.*

Spot colors *are special, premixed colors that are used instead of, or in addition to, CMYK inks, and require their own separations and their own plates on a printing press. When a spot color swatch is edited, the color is updated globally throughout the document.*

You can assign any of the five color models to a spot color. Specific spot colors may or may not fall within the CMYK gamut; for example, a spot color may be a neon or metallic ink that is not within the CMYK gamut, or it may be a shade of green that falls within the gamut.

Registration colors *are applied to objects that you want to print on all plates in the printing process, including any spot color plates. Registration colors are typically used for crop marks and trim marks.*

Now you'll change the display of the Swatches palette so that you can locate the color by its name.

3 Choose List View from the Swatches palette menu to display the swatches by name and see the swatch you just named.

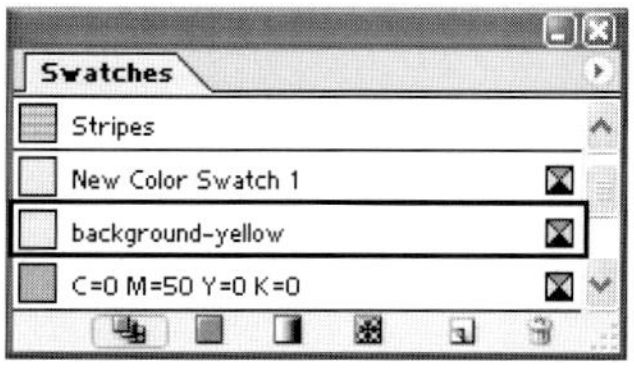

You can change how swatches are displayed in the palette—either as large or small swatches or by name. When you display swatches by name, the Swatches palette also displays icons indicating the color model and color type (individual process color, global process color, or global spot color).

Copying paint attributes

Adobe Illustrator lets you copy paint attributes of objects (such as their fill and stroke colors) in various ways and apply the attributes to other objects.

You'll use the Eyedropper tool to copy colors from your artwork into the Color palette. Also called *sampling*, copying colors lets you replicate paint attributes even when you don't know their exact values.

1 Select the Eyedropper tool ( ) in the toolbox.

2 In the bottom left rectangle, click the orange brim of the hat to sample its color. This action picks up the fill and stroke attributes of the hat brim and displays them in the Color palette.

By default, the Eyedropper tool samples all paint attributes of an object. However, you can restrict which attributes are sampled (by double-clicking the Eyedropper tool and selecting options in the dialog box).

3 To quickly apply the current paint attributes to the top of the hat, hold down Alt (Windows) or Option (Mac OS) to temporarily switch to the Paint Bucket tool ( ), and then click inside the top of the hat to apply the paint.

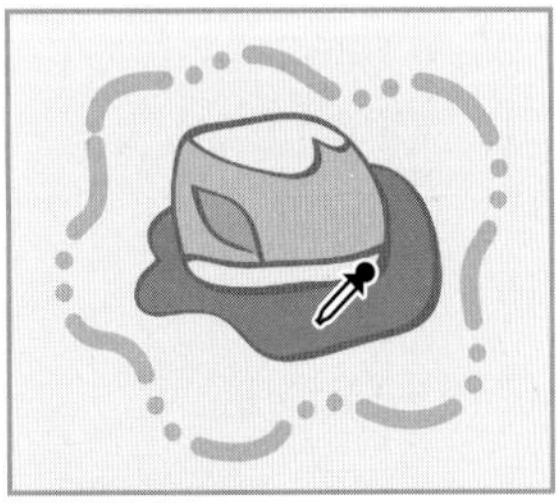

Select attributes with eyedropper.

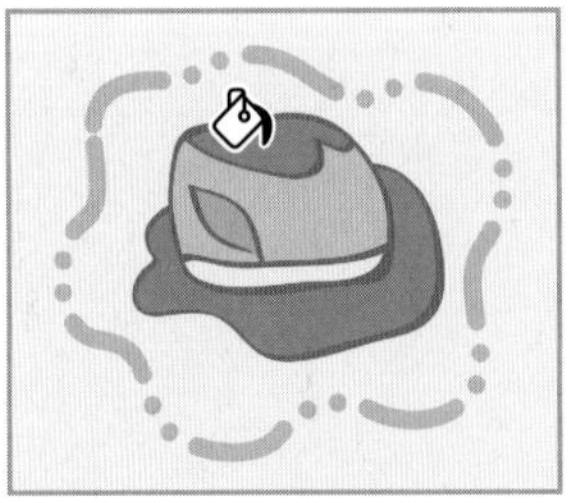

Apply with paint bucket.

Copying appearance attributes

Adobe Illustrator lets you copy appearance attributes that include both the fill and the stroke of an object as well as its transparency and effects.

You'll create a drop shadow shape and change its transparency. Then you'll apply the shadow's appearance to another shape using the Appearance palette. You can save and name appearance attributes using the Graphic Styles palette.

1 Select the Selection tool (↖) in the toolbox, and click the hat brim in the upper right rectangle.

2 Hold down Alt (Windows) or Option (Mac OS) and drag the brim slightly down and to the right. Release the mouse button to leave a copy of the hat brim. This copy will become a drop shadow.

3 Choose Object > Arrange > Send Backward to move the shadow shape underneath the hat brim. You should still be able to see both the shadow shape and the hat brim.

4 With the object (in this case, the hat's shadow) still selected, use the Color palette to change its stroke to None.

5 Change the fill to a medium brown. (We specified C = 49%, M = 65%, Y = 100%, and B = 0%.)

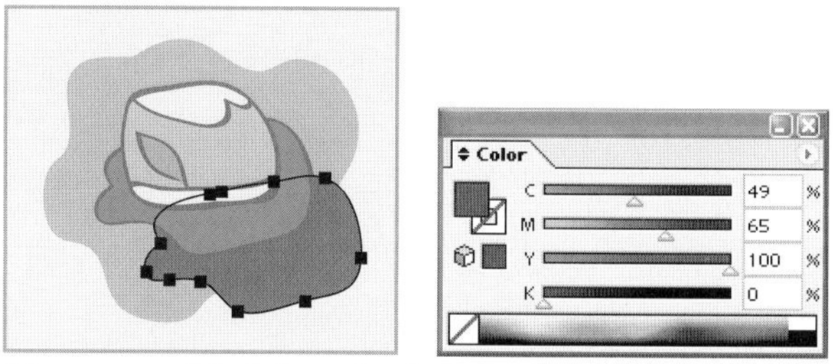

Move a copy of the brim and paint it brown.

6 Click the Transparency tab to bring the palette to the front of its group. Then choose Show Options from the palette menu to expand the Transparency palette.

7 With the shadow shape still selected, in the Transparency palette type **50** in the Opacity percentage box or use the slider, and press Return or Enter to change the opacity of the shadow shape to 50%.

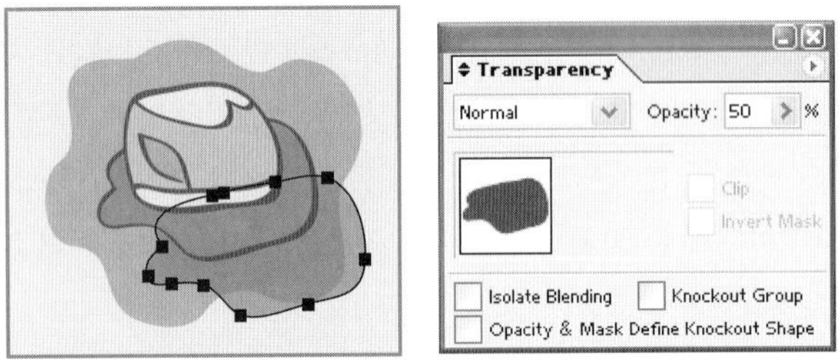

Change shadow's transparency to 50%.

8 In the Appearance palette, click the Path thumbnail to select it. Drag the Path thumbnail from the Appearance palette until the pointer is over the bottom right hat side. Release the mouse button to apply the appearance to the hat side and make it a transparent medium brown as well.

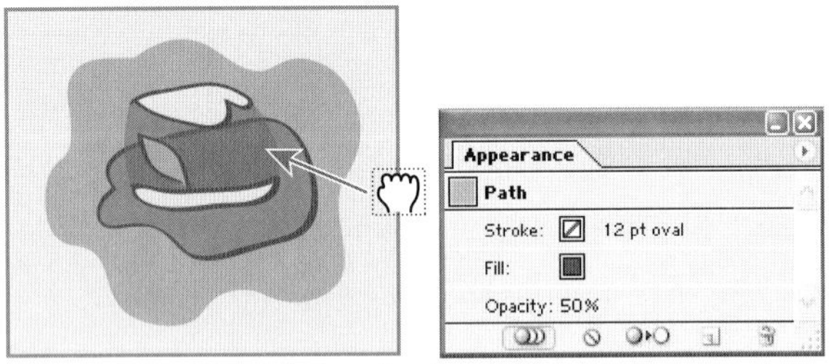

Drag and drop the Path thumbnail onto the shape.

9 Click away from the artwork to deselect it, and choose File > Save.

For more information on using the Appearance and Style palettes, see Lesson 10, "Applying Appearance Attributes, Styles, and Effects."

Saturating a color

Next, you'll adjust the saturation of the new color you added to the hat's top by changing the percentage of black in the color.

1 Using the Selection tool (), click the top of the hat in the bottom left rectangle to select it. Make sure that the Fill box in the toolbox is selected.

2 In the Color palette, hold down Shift and drag the M slider to the left to desaturate the color. As you Shift-drag, the sliders all move in tandem, changing the color intensity.

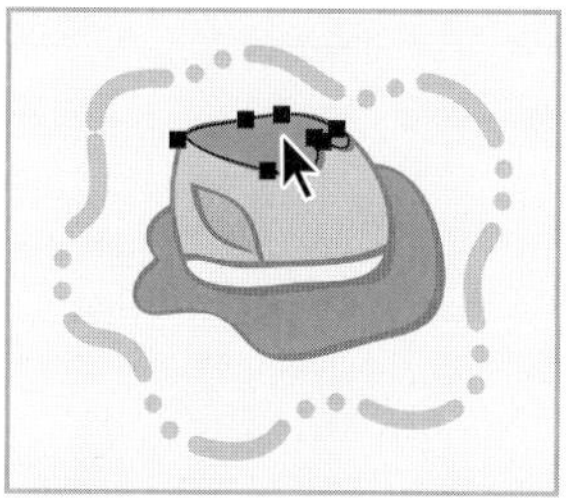

Select top of hat.

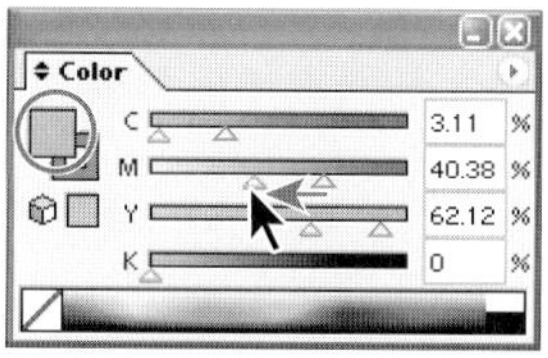

Shift-drag left to desaturate the magenta in the color mix.

Adjusting the saturation lets you change the strength of a color without affecting the hue. (However, if you drag a slider that is set to 0%, you will change the hue or color of the object, rather than the color's saturation.)

3 Click away from the artwork, and choose File > Save.

Painting with patterns and gradients

In addition to process and spot colors, the Swatches palette can also contain pattern and gradient swatches. Adobe Illustrator provides sample swatches of each type in the default palette and lets you create your own patterns and gradients.

To learn how to create your own gradients, see Lesson 12, "Blending Shapes and Colors."

For information on how to create patterns, see "Working with patterns" in online Help.

Now you'll fill some objects with a pattern, working with the hat in the top right rectangle.

1 Using the Selection tool (), click in the center of the hat ribbon shape in the top right rectangle. The Fill box in the toolbox shows that the shape's current fill is gray.

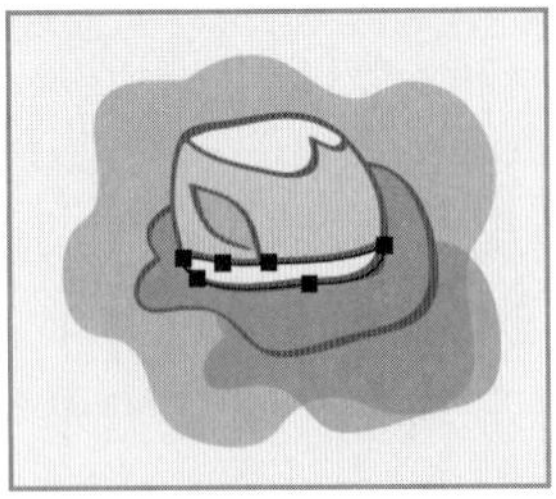

Select hat ribbon shape in top right rectangle.

The buttons at the bottom of the Swatches palette let you display swatches grouped as solid colors, gradients, or patterns.

2 In the Swatches palette, click the Show Pattern Swatches button (the fourth button from the left). All the pattern swatches appear.

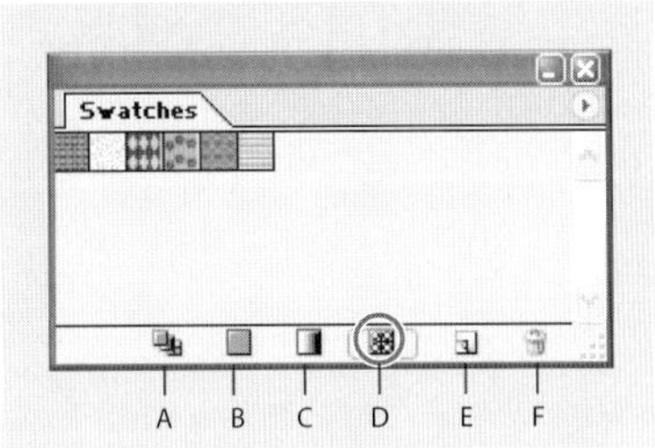

A. *Show All Swatches.* ***B.*** *Show Color. Swatches.* ***C.*** *Show Gradient. Swatches.* ***D.*** *Show Pattern Swatches.* ***E.*** *New Swatch.* ***F.*** *Delete Swatch.*

3 Click a pattern in the palette to select it, and fill the hat ribbon. (We selected the Confetti pattern.)

4 Now select the background of the top right rectangle. Make sure that the Fill box is selected, and click the same pattern swatch so the rectangle's fill with the same pattern.

Fill hat ribbon with a pattern.

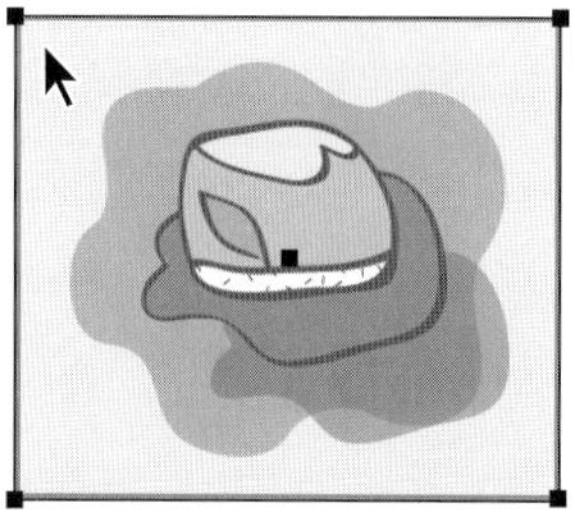

Select background of top right rectangle.

Fill background with same pattern.

Now you'll apply a gradient to the first block in the illustration.

5 In the top left rectangle, select the squiggly line around the hat, and make sure that the Fill box is selected in the toolbox.

6 In the Swatches palette, click the Show Gradient Swatches button (third button from the left) to show only gradient swatches in the palette.

7 Click a gradient to apply to the fill of the squiggly shape. (We selected the Yellow Orange Radial gradient.)

Painting with a Pattern brush

Brushes can be applied to existing paths or objects. There are four types of brushes in the Brushes palette: Calligraphic, Scatter, Art, and Pattern. For information on how to create your own custom brushes, see Lesson 14, "Working with Brushes and Scribbles."

Now you'll paint the stroke of a shape with a Pattern brush.

1 Use the Selection tool (↖) to select the squiggly shape around the hat in the bottom right rectangle.

2 Choose Window > Brushes to display the Brushes palette.

3 Choose List View from the Brushes palette menu, and scroll down to see the Pattern brushes. Click a name to select a brush, and apply it to the squiggly shape around the hat. (We selected the Laurel Pattern brush.)

The type of brush (Calligraphic, Scatter, Art, or Pattern) is indicated by an icon to the right of the brush name.

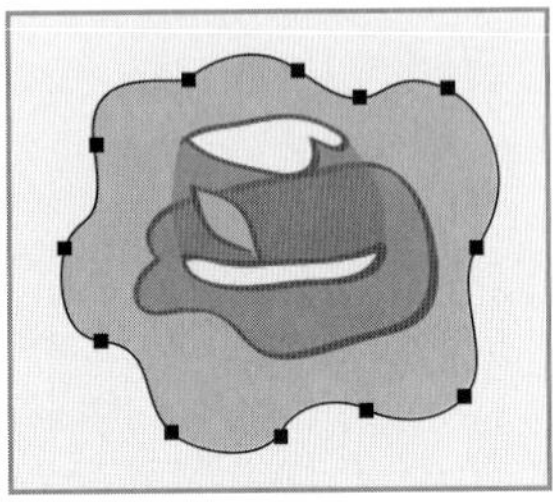

Select the squiggly shape in bottom right rectangle.

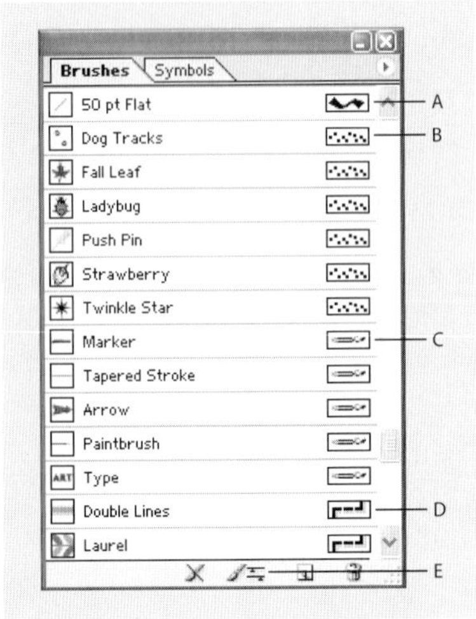

A. Calligraphic. ***B.*** *Scatter.* ***C.*** *Art.* ***D.*** *Pattern.* ***E.*** *Options of Selected Object.*

Apply a Pattern brush.

You can change the size and other characteristics of the pattern after it is applied to the selected object.

4 With the squiggly shape still selected, in the Brushes palette click the Options of Selected Object button (second button from the left) at the bottom of the palette.

5 In the Stroke Options (Pattern Brush) dialog box, select the Preview option to view different settings applied to the artwork without closing the dialog box.

6 Try out different settings to see how they affect the pattern on the squiggly shape, pressing Tab to move between the options. (We entered 75% in the Scale text box.) When you're satisfied with the settings, click OK to apply them to the artwork.

7 Choose File > Save.

8 Close the file.

You've completed painting the hat artwork using a variety of painting tools.

See these topics to learn more about the following painting techniques:

• For information on using brushes, creating your own custom brushes, and using the Brushes palette, see Lesson 14, "Working with Brushes and Scribbles."

• For how to create other blending effects, see Lesson 12, "Blending Shapes and Colors."

• For more on transparency, styles, appearance attributes, and effects, see Lesson 10, "Using Appearance, Attributes, Styles and Effects."

Review questions

1 Describe at least three ways to fill an object with color

2 How can you save a color?

3 How do you name a color?

4 How do you restore the original set of colors in the Swatches palette?

5 How do you paint a shape with a transparent color?

6 How can you desaturate a color?

7 What is a quick way to view all the pattern swatches in the Swatches palette?

8 What are the four types of brushes you can use to paint the fill or stroke of objects?

Review answers

1 To fill an object with color, select the object and the Fill box in the toolbox. Then do one of the following:

• Click a color in the color bar in the Color palette.

• Drag the color sliders or type in values in the text boxes in the Color palette.

• Click a color swatch in the Swatches palette.

• Select the Eyedropper tool ( ), and click a color in the artwork.

• Drag and drop an appearance thumbnail onto a shape in the artwork.

• Choose Window > Swatch Libraries to open another color library, and click a color swatch in the color library palette.

2 You can save a color for painting other objects in your artwork by adding it to the Swatches palette. Select the color, and do one of the following:

- Drag it from the Fill box and drop it over the Swatches palette.
- Click the New Swatch button at the bottom of the Swatches palette.
- Choose New Swatch from the Swatches palette menu.

You can also add colors from other color libraries by selecting them in the Color Library palette and choosing Add to Swatches from the palette menu.

3 To name a color, double-click the color swatch in the Swatches palette or select it and choose Swatch Options from the palette menu. Type the name for the color in the Swatch Options dialog box.

4 To restore the original set of colors in the Swatches palette, choose Window > Swatch Libraries > Default. This palette contains all the original swatches that appear by default before you customize the Swatches palette.

5 To paint a shape with a transparent color, select the shape and fill it with any color. Then adjust the opacity percentage in the Transparency palette to less than 100%.

6 To desaturate a color, select the color and Shift-drag a slider to the left in the Color palette. Shift-dragging the slider causes the other sliders to move in tandem so the hue won't change.

7 A quick way to view all the pattern swatches in the Swatches palette is to click the Show Pattern Swatches button at the bottom of the palette.

8 The four types of brushes are Calligraphic, Scatter, Art, and Pattern.

Lesson 6

6

Applying Transparency and Blending Modes

The Transparency features in Adobe Illustrator gives you the capability of creating artwork beyond expectations. Using commands in the Transparency palette, you can create special effects, such as knocking out underlying colors or creating graduated transparencies or blends.

In this lesson you will learn how to do the following:

- Use the Transparency palette.
- Change the opacity of objects.
- Use blending modes.
- Use group options for transparency.
- Apply Opacity Masks.

Getting started

In Adobe Illustrator CS, you can add transparency to artwork in a variety of ways. You can vary the degree of transparency of an object's fill or stroke (or both), a group of objects, or a layer from 100% opacity (completely solid) to 0% opacity (completely transparent). When you decrease an object's opacity, the underlying artwork becomes visible through the surface of the object.

Using features in the Transparency palette, you can also create special effects, such as knocking out underlying colors or creating graduated transparencies or blends. Transparency can be applied to multiple objects, groups and even to entire layers. In this lesson you will focus on the transparency palette and its capabilities. Learn how to apply transparency to layers in Lesson 7, "Working with Layers" and use with the Appearance palette in Lesson 10, "Using Appearance Attributes, Styles and Effects".

Changing the opacity of an object

Transparency is applied from 0%-100% exposing or covering the underlying objects. The transparency palette in its simplest form offers the ability to adjust the opacity of the selected object(s). Additional hidden options will change blending modes and mask the effects of the transparency palette.

1 To ensure that the tools and palettes function exactly as described in this lesson, delete or deactivate (by renaming) the Adobe Illustrator CS preferences file. See "Restoring default preferences" on page 2.

2 Start Adobe Illustrator.

3 Choose File > Open, and open the 06_end.ai file in the Lesson06 folder, located inside the Lessons folder on your hard drive.

4 If you like, choose View > Zoom Out to make the finished artwork smaller and leave it on your screen as you work. (Use the Hand tool (✋) to move the artwork where you want it in the window.) If you don't want to leave the image open, choose File > Close.

For an illustration of the finished artwork in this lesson, see the color section.

Now open the start file to begin the lesson.

5 Open the document named 06_start.ai from the CIB_lessons folder. If the Transparency palette is not visible, select Window > Transparency

6 Choose File > Save As, name the file **radio.ai**, and select the Lesson06 folder in the Save In menu. Leave the type of file format set to Adobe Illustrator® Document, and click Save. In the Illustrator Options dialog box, leave at the defaults and click Save.

7 Using the Selection tool (↖) select the first wave on the left and type in the Transparency palette text box **90%**.

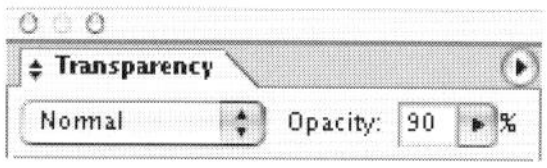

Use the Opacity textbox to change the Opacity of the waves.

8 Select the second wave (middle) and type in the value of **80%**.

9 Select the third (right) wave and type in the value of **70%**.

The waves at a 90%, 80% and 70% opacity.

Notice that when you decrease the opacity of an object the underlying text in this artwork becomes more visible.

10 File > Save. Keep this file open if you plan to continue on to the next exercise.

Changing the blending modes

The pop-up menu on the left of the transparency palette offers several choices for blending modes. You will apply three of the blending modes; Multiply, Difference, and Screen. For a full definition of each of the blending choices see Online Help..

1 Select the first wave. Using the Blending mode pop-up menu change the blending mode from Normal to **Multiply**.

The Multiply blending mode makes underlying objects darker.

Multiply multiplies the underlying color with the overlapping object's color. The resulting color is always a darker color. Multiplying any color with black produces black. Multiplying any color with white leaves the color unchanged. The effect is similar to drawing with multiple magic markers. This blending mode is used often for drop shadows.

2 Select the second wave and change the blending mode to **Difference**.

Difference creates the effect of seeing underlying objects as a color film negative. Using it subtracts either the overlaying color from the underlying color or the underlying color from the overlaying color, depending on which has the greater brightness value. Blending with white inverts the underlying color values. Blending with black produces no change.

3 Lastly, select the third wave and change the blending mode to **Screen**.

Screen multiplies the inverse of the overlying and underlying colors. The resulting color is always a lighter color. Screening with black leaves the color unchanged, and screening with white produces white. The effect is similar to projecting multiple slide images on top of each other.

4 File > Save.

Isolating the blending

This rather simple concept helps to maintain blending modes through groups and layers, but not affect the underlying objects. Isolate Blending is a option that is hidden in the palette. To show the Transparency options click and hold on the palette menu in the upper of the Transparency palette. Choose to Show Options.

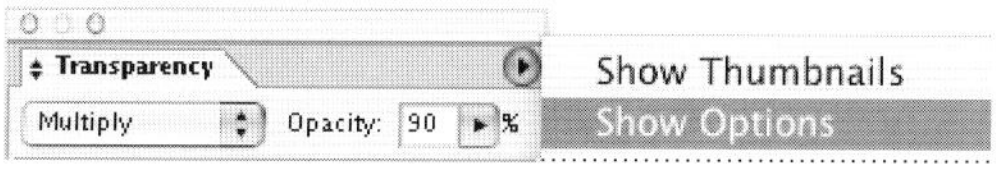

Access the Transparency palette options from the palette menu.

When you apply a blending mode to an object, the effect of the blending mode is normally seen on any objects that lie beneath the object's layer or group.

Using the Isolate Blending option changes the behavior of a blending mode so that only members of the targeted layer or group are affected, and objects beneath the group are unaffected, by the blending modes.

Note: *The Isolate Blending option is only useful when used on groups or layers that contain at least one object with a blending mode other than Normal applied to them. The option also works on individual objects that have had blending modes other than Normal applied to overlapping strokes or fills.*

1 Choose Select > waves. Waves is a saved selection that has been created to make the selection of the three waves easier. Read more about saving selections in Lesson 2.

2 Change the blending mode to **Multiply**. Note how the Multiply mode darkened the underlying intersecting parts of the waves.

3 Choose Object > Group to group the wave shapes together.

4 From the Transparency palette, check the Isolate Blending checkbox. Note that now the waves blending mode only affect each other and not the letters below. Uncheck the Isolate Blending checkbox to see the effect.

5 While the waves are still selected, change the blending mode for the group to Multiply.

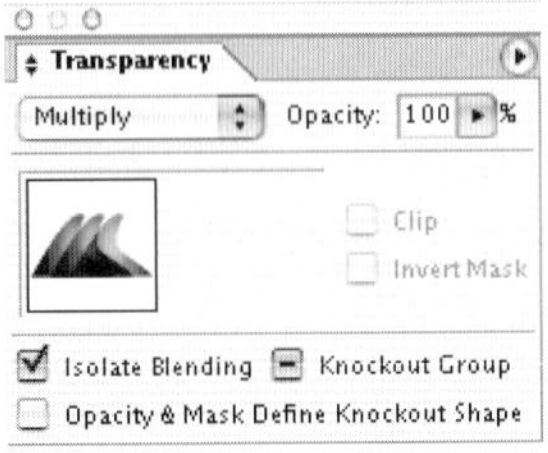

Use Isolate blending to show restrict modes within a selected group or layer.

6 File > Save and File.

What does Knockout Group do?

The Knockout Group option cycles through three states: on (check mark), off (no mark), and neutral (gray or dash).

Neutral–Use the neutral option when you want to group artwork without interfering with the knockout behavior determined by the enclosing layer or group.

On–Check On to prevent transparency from revealing underlying objects witin the group.

Off–Use the off option when you want to ensure that a layer or a group of transparent objects will never knock each other out.

Knockout Group Neutral.

Knockout Group On The waves do not show through to each other.

Knockout Group Off The waves do show through to each other.

Using an opacity mask

Add some transparency dazzle by using Opacity masks. An Opacity mask allows you to set varying levels of transparency on an object using other artwork as a mask. Anything that can be created or built in Illustrator can be used as a mask, even placed files, like images from Photoshop.

This feature may, at first glance, appear to be complicated, but once you understand the concept you can take your illustrations beyond the basics. An Opacity mask can be created by using selections or manually editing the mask after it has been created. In this lesson you will create an opacity mask by using a placed Photoshop image. Then make additional edits to the mask.

Placing a Photoshop file

In this part of the lesson you will place a Photoshop document to be used as the Opacity mask. Using Photoshop files or other placed images can open up entire new avenues for designing in Illustrator. Its the perfect way to integrate the two applications and get remarkable results.

1 With the radio.ai file still open choose File > Place. Place is used to place external objects into Adobe Illustrator such as Photoshop images and text.

2 From the Lesson06 folder choose the file named numbers.psd. Don't press Place yet.

3 In the lower left hand corner check the Link checkbox if it is not checked, then press Place.

The reason we picked to link the image rather than embedding it is to maintain editing capability for the placed image. If you were to update the numbers.psd file in Photoshop, the placed image in radio.ai would also be updated. Click Place.

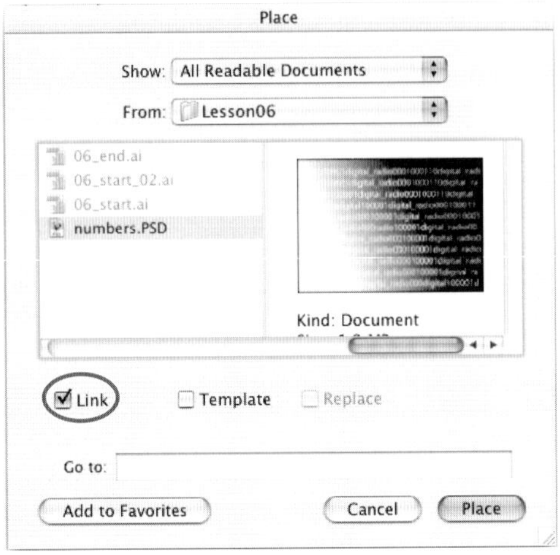

Placing a Linked Photoshop file.

Linking files vs. embedding

The Place command lets you import artwork into an Illustrator document in one of two ways: by creating a link to an external file or by embedding a copy of the file in the Illustrator document. The option you choose depends on how you plan to edit the artwork:

- *Linked artwork remains independent of the Illustrator document, resulting in a smaller Illustrator file. You can modify linked artwork using transformation tools and effects; however, you cannot select and edit individual components in the artwork. A preference you set for updating links determines whether the artwork in the Illustrator document changes when the linked file changes outside of Illustrator.*
- *Embedded artwork is copied into the Illustrator document, resulting in a larger Illustrator file. If the artwork contains multiple components, you can edit them discretely. For example, if the artwork contains vector data, Illustrator converts it to paths, which you can then modify using Illustrator tools and commands. Illustrator also preserves the object hierarchy (such as groups and layers) in artwork embedded from certain file formats.*

The Links palette lets you identify, select, monitor, and update objects in the Illustrator artwork that are linked to external files.

–From Online Help "Placing artwork".

4 If you do not have the Transparency palette options visible, choose Window > Transparency. Click and hold on the palette menu in the upper right corner of the Transparency palette and choose to Show Options.

5 From the Select menu choose waves to activate the previously saved selection of the three waves. A Thumbnail is visible with the selected objects on the left side.

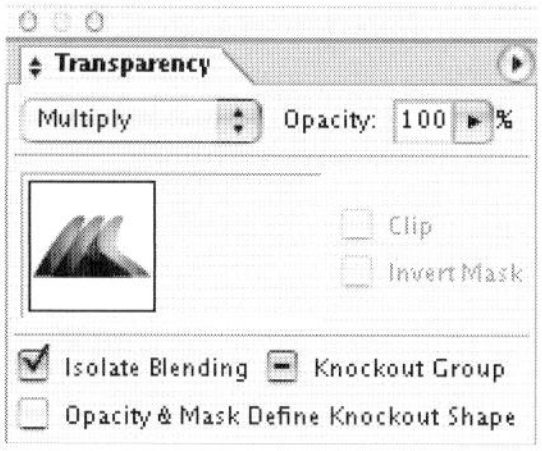

Thumbnails for the Opacity mask.

6 Hold down the Shift key and click on the placed image. You must select at least two objects or groups to make an Opacity Mask. The topmost selected object or group is used as the mask.

7 From the Transparency palette, choose the palette menu and select Make Opacity Mask. The placed image, is converted into an Opacity mask, shown as a thumbnail image in the lower section of the pallete.

The image, now used as a mask, allows the underlying waves to appear.

With both the waves and placed image selected choose Make Opacity mask.

Result.

8 File>Save.

Clipping & inverting an opacity mask

Located in the Appearance palette menu are these additional options.
When experimenting on your own understand that the New Opacity Masks are Clipping option sets the mask background to black. Therefore, black objects, such as black type, used to create an opacity mask with the Clip option selected will not be visible. To see the objects, use a different color or deselect the New Opacity Mask are Clipping option from the Transparency palette menu.

Defining the knockout shape

Use the Opacity & Mask Define Knockout Shape option to keep the knockout effect proportional to the object's opacity–in areas of the mask that are close to 100% opacity, the knockout effect will be strong; in areas with less opacity, the knockout effect will be weaker.

Editing an opacity mask

An opacity mask works much like a mask in Adobe Photoshop. The concept is rather simple. The mask overlays the selected artwork, covering entirely where the mask is solid or partially showing through the artwork based upon the shades of colors on the mask. White is 100% opaque, Black is 100% transparent, grays have varying levels of opacity based upon the lightness or darkenss of the shade. (All colors change to grayscale on a mask.)

To help make this concept become more clear you will edit the mask that you created.

1 Select the mask thumbnail (right). Notice that by clicking on the thumbnail of the mask a border appears, indicating that the mask is active. Any object created with the mask side of the thumbnail view selected will become part of the mask.

2 Choose Select > Deselect so that you do not change the objects attributes.

3 Use the Fill and Stroke swatches on the toolbar change the fill to Black and the Stroke to None.

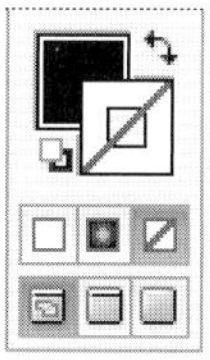

Change the Fill to Black and the Stroke to None.

4 Select the Rectangle tool (▭) and click and drag outside the upper left of the logo and down to the lower right, totally encompassing the artwork.

In the Opacity Mask thumbnail, you can see that by creating the black rectangle you have made the waves totally transparent.

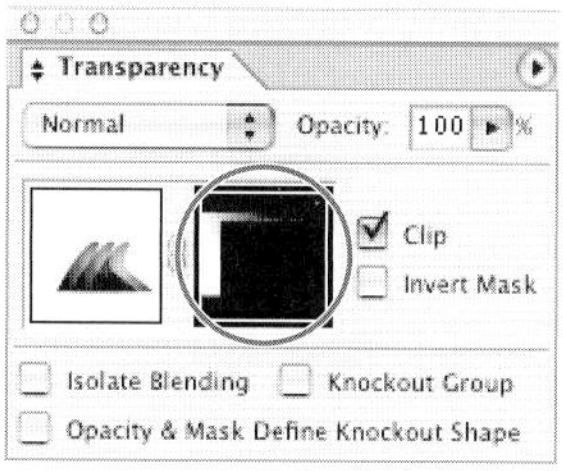

Creating the black rectangle on the Opacity Mask makes the waves transparent.

5 With the rectangle in the mask tumbnail still selected, make sure the Fill swatch is forward and click on various swatches on the Swatches palette to see how they affect the mask. Darker colors make the wave artwork more transparent, and lighter colors make the waves more opaque or visible. When you are finished experimenting, choose the Capri Stripes swatch from the Swatches palette for the final fill.

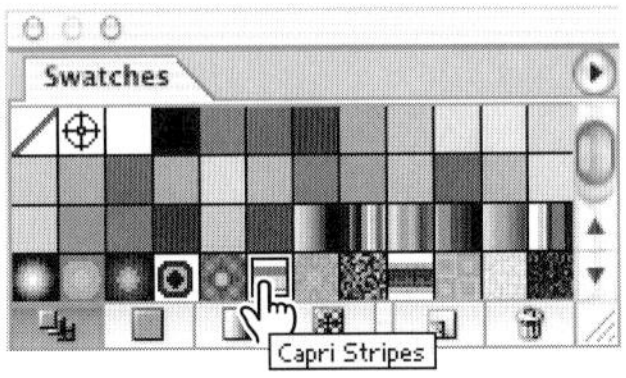

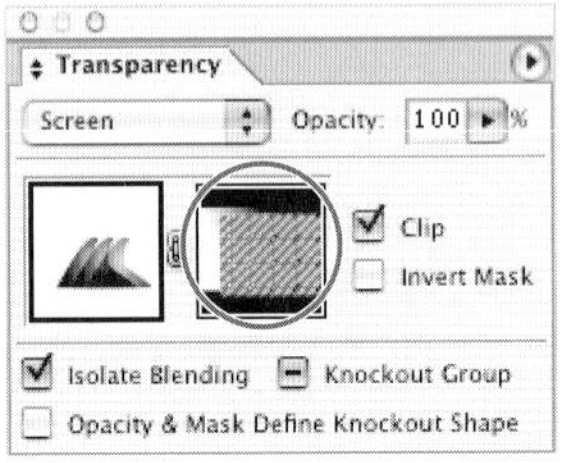

Choose the Capri Stripes swatch. *The Opacity mask and thumbnail reflect the change.*

6 With the rectangle in the mask thumbnail still selected, use the Transparency palette to change the opacity to **50%**. The pattern now creates a more subtle opacity mask over the existing number art, exposing 50% of the wave artwork.

Next you will change the angle of the pattern inside the rectangle.

7 With the rectangle in the mask thumbnail still selected, double-click on the Rotate tool (). You want to rotate the pattern, but not the entire rectangle. Check Preview and then enter **45°** into the angle textbox. At the bottom of the Rotate dialog window uncheck Objects and check Patterns. Click OK.

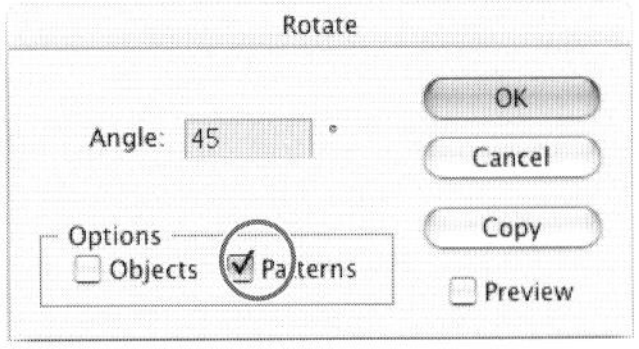

Change the angle of the pattern, but not the object.

8 Return to the original art by clicking on the left thumbnail in the Transparency palette.

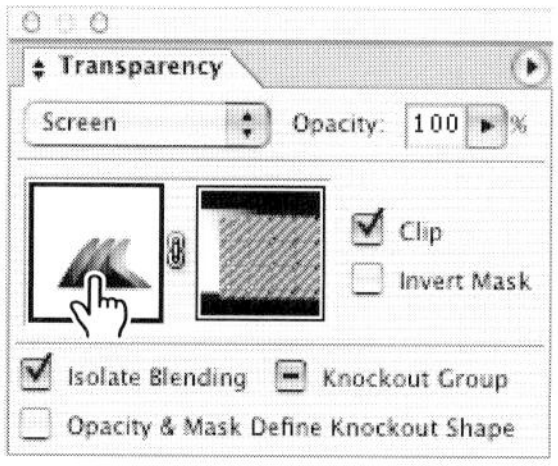

To continue working on the original art, click on the left thumbnail.

9 File > Save.

You have now completed the exercise. You can leave the file open to experiment on your own or close the file.

Note: *You can disable or remove an Opacity mask using the Transparency palette menu.*

Exploring on your own

Understanding the transparency feature opens up new ideas and avenues for creating innovative designs. On your own, create a colored object such as a rectangle and place an image on top of it. Select both and use the Create Opacity Mask from the Transparency palette options.

Also experiment with various blending modes to create the illusion of additional colors and shapes in your artwork.

Creating a spot color image in Illustrator

Create an image in a tint for watermark using PMS colors. This technique is fun to try and gives an extra boost to jobs that might only allow for one or two colors/

1 Create a shape that is large enough to accommodate a Photoshop image you have selected.

2 Fill the shape with any color, we especially like to take advantage of the Pantone colors for this technique. Choose Window > Swatch Libraries > Pantone Solid Coated to see the Pantone Swatches palette.

3 File > Place. Choose any image and position it on top of the shape.

4 From the Transparency palette menu choose Make Opacity Mask.

The image as a tinted image, using the spot color that you defined.

Review questions

1 What is a blending mode and how is it applied?

2 Can a placed object be modified with the Transparency palette?

3 Can an Opacity mask be removed?

4 How can I stop a group of objects from affecting the underlying artwork

Review answers

1 Blending modes allow you to vary the way that colors in objects interact or blend with the underlying objects. Modes can be selected from the pop-up menu in the upper left of the Transparency palette.

2 Yes, a placed object can be modified with the Transparency palette, just like any object that would be created in Adobe Illustrator.

3 Yes, an Opacity mask can be removed using the palette menu from the Transparency palette. Select Release Opacity Mask.

4 If the objects are grouped you can select Isolate Blending from the Transparency palette.

Lesson 7

7 Working with Layers

Layers let you organize your work into distinct levels that can be edited and viewed as individual units. Every Adobe Illustrator document contains at least one layer. Creating multiple layers in your artwork lets you easily control how artwork is printed, displayed, and edited.

In this lesson, you'll learn how to do the following:

- Work with the Layers palette.
- Create, rearrange, and lock layers, nested layers, and groups.
- Move objects between layers.
- Paste layers of objects from one file to another.
- Merge layers into a single layer.
- Apply a drop shadow to a layer.
- Make a layer clipping mask.
- Apply an appearance attribute to objects and layers.

Getting started

In this lesson, you'll finish the artwork of a wall clock as you explore the various ways to use the Layers palette. Before you begin, you must restore the default preferences for Adobe Illustrator and then you will open the finished art file for this lesson to see what you'll create.

1 To ensure that the tools and palettes function exactly as described in this lesson, delete or deactivate (by renaming) the Adobe Illustrator CS preferences file. See "Restoring default preferences" on page 4.

2 Start Adobe Illustrator.

3 Choose File > Open, and open the L07end.ai file in the Lesson07 folder, located inside the Lessons folder within the AICIB folder on your hard drive.

Separate layers are used for the objects that make up the clock's frame, striped clock face, hands, and numbers—as indicated by their layer names in the Layers palette.

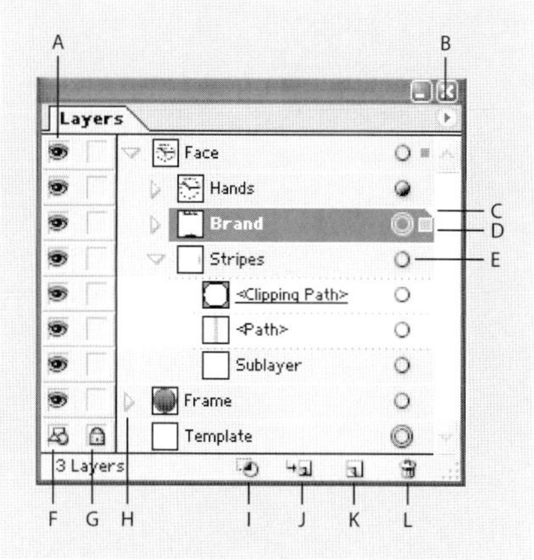

A. *Eye icon (Hide/Show).*
B. *Layers palette menu.*
C. *Current layer indicator.*
D. *Selection indicator.*
E. *Target and appearance indicator.*
F. *Template layer icon.*
G. *Edit column (Lock/Unlock).*
H. *Expand/Collapse triangle.*
I. *Make/Release Clipping Mask.*
J. *Create New Sublayer button.*
K. *Create New Layer button.*
L. *Delete button.*

4 If you like, you may leave the file open as a visual reference. Do this by reducing the size of your window then selected View > Fit in Window. If you don't want to leave the image open, choose File > Close.

For an illustration of the finished artwork in this lesson, see the color section.

To begin working, you'll open an existing art file.

5 Choose File > Open, and open the L07start.ai file in the Lesson07 folder, located inside the Lessons folder within the AICIB folder on your hard drive.

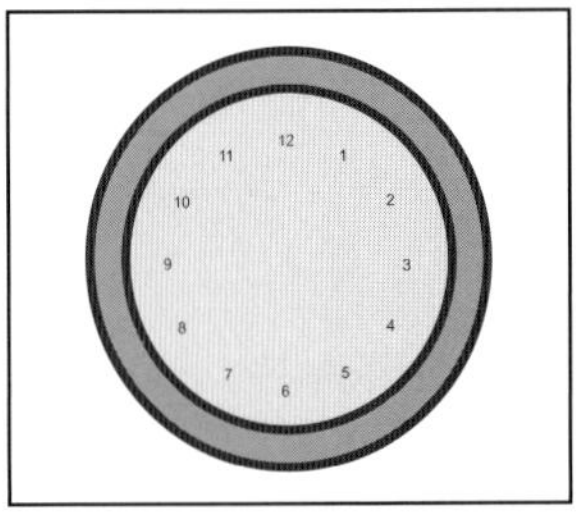

The artwork contains some of the basic objects for the clock illustration.

6 Choose File > Save As, name the file **Clock.ai**, and select the Lesson07 folder. Leave the type of file format set to Adobe Illustrator® Document, and click Save. In the Illustrator Options dialog box, leave at the defaults and click OK.

Using layers

Using the Layers palette, you can create multiple levels of artwork that reside on separate, overlapping layers, sublayers, and groups in the same file. Layers act like individual, clear sheets containing one or more objects. Where no filled (or nontransparent) objects overlap, you can see through any layer to the layer below.

You can create and edit objects on any layer without affecting the artwork on any other layer. You can also display, print, lock, and reorder layers as distinct units.

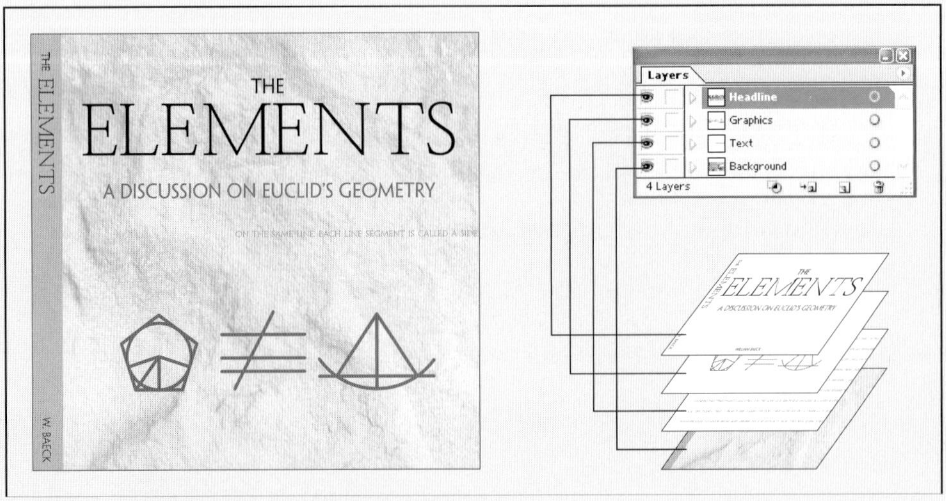

Example of composite art and how layers break out individually.

Creating layers

Every document in Illustrator contains one layer by default. You can rename the layer and add more layers at any time as you create the artwork. Placing objects on separate layers lets you easily select and edit them by their organization. For example, by placing type on a separate layer, you can change the type all at once without affecting the rest of the artwork.

You'll change the layer name to "Clock," and then you'll create another layer.

1 If the Layers palette isn't visible on-screen, choose Window > Layers to display it.

Layer 1 (the default name for the first layer) is highlighted, indicating that it is active. The layer also has a triangle (◥), indicating that objects on the layer can be edited when you use the tools.

2 In the Layers palette, double-click the layer name to open the Layer Options dialog box. Type **Clock** in the Name text box, and then click OK.

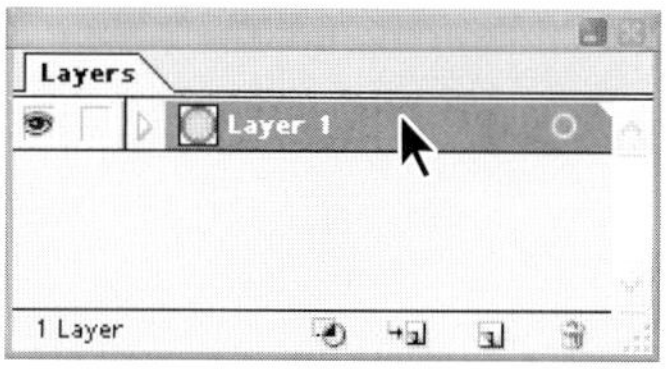

Double-click layer name.

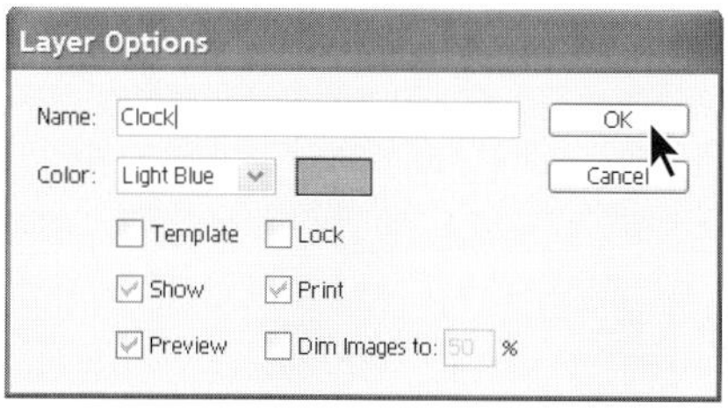

Change layer name to Clock.

Now you'll create a sublayer for the clock numbers.

3 Alt-click (Windows) or Option-click (Mac OS) the Create New Sublayer button (+▣) at the bottom of the Layers palette to create a new sublayer and display the Layer Options dialog box.

(If you simply want to create a new sublayer without setting any options or naming the layer, you can click the Create New Sublayer button. New sublayers created this way are numbered in sequence, for example, Layer 2.)

4 In the Layer Options dialog box, type **Numbers** in the Name text box, and click OK. The new sublayer appears directly beneath its main layer name (Clock) and is selected.

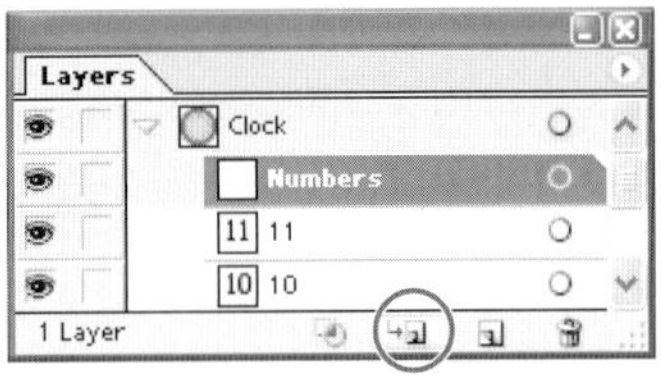

Create sublayer named Numbers.

Moving objects and layers

By rearranging the layers in the Layers palette, you can reorder layered objects in your artwork. You can also move selected objects from one layer or sublayer to another.

First you'll move the clock numbers onto their own sublayer.

1 In the Layers palette, grab the thumbnail for the 11 object and drag it onto the thumbnail for the Numbers layer. Release the mouse button when you see the large black triangles at either end of the Numbers layer in the palette. (The large triangles indicate that you are adding something to that layer.)

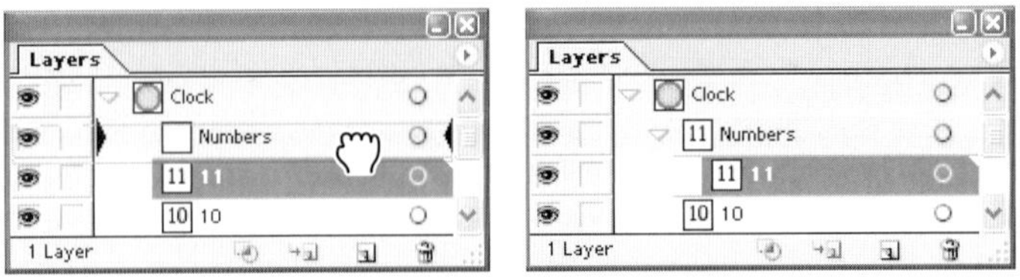

Grab thumbnail and move it onto sublayer thumbnail.

2 Repeat step 1 for each of the twelve numbers in the Layers palette.

To select multiple layers or sublayers quickly, select a layer and then Shift-click additional layers.

3 Choose Select > Deselect. Then choose File > Save.

4 To simplify your work, click the triangle to the left of the Numbers layer to collapse the layer view.

Now you'll move the face of the clock to a new layer to use later when you add the stripes, hands, and brand name of the clock, and you'll rename the Clock layer to reflect the new organization of the artwork.

5 In the artwork, click behind the numbers to select the clock face. In the Layers palette, the object named <Path> becomes active (as indicated by the small square selection indicator (■) in the far right column.

6 Alt-click (Windows) or Option-click (Mac OS) the Create New Layer button at the bottom of the Layers palette, or choose New Layer from the Layers palette menu.

7 In the Layer Options dialog box, enter **Face** in the Name text box, choose a different layer color from the pop-up menu (such as Orange), and click OK.

The new Face layer is added above the Clock layer and becomes active.

8 In the Layers palette, select the small square selection indicator on the <Path> layer, and drag it directly up to the right of the target indicator (◎) on the new Face layer.

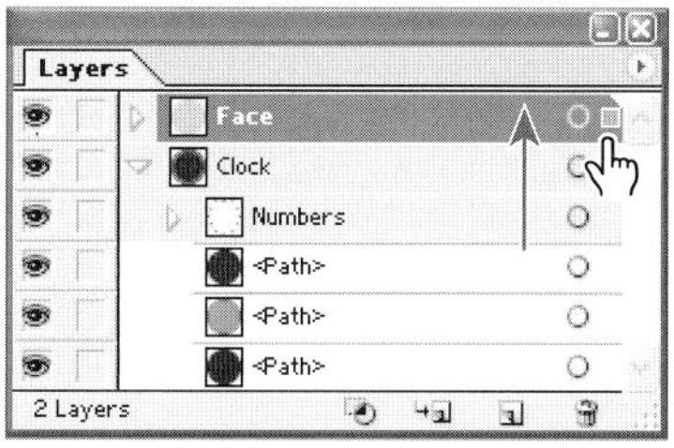

Drag selection indicator up to move object to another layer.

This action moves the selected object to the new layer. The color of the selection lines in the artwork changes to the color of the new Face layer (such as Orange).

Now that the Face layer is on top of the Clock layer and the Numbers layer, the clock numbers are covered up. You'll move the Numbers sublayer onto a different layer and rename the Clock layer to reflect the new organization of the artwork.

9 In the Layers palette, drag the Numbers sublayer thumbnail onto the Face layer thumbnail. Release the mouse button when you see the indicator bar with large black triangles at either end of the Face layer in the palette.

Now you can see the numbers again.

10 Double-click the Clock layer to display the Layer Options dialog box, and change the layer name to **Frame**. Then click OK.

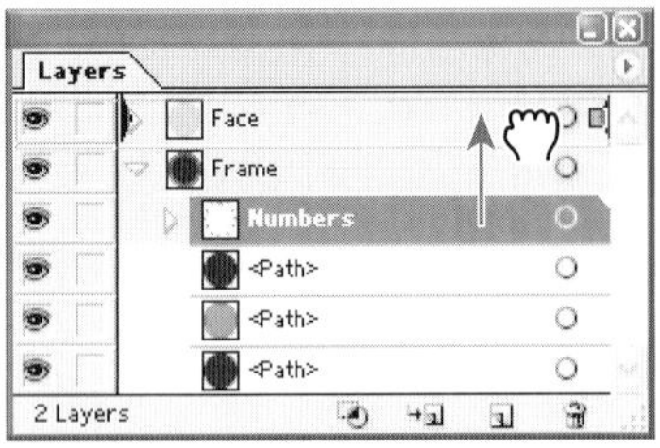

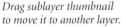

Drag sublayer thumbnail to move it to another layer.

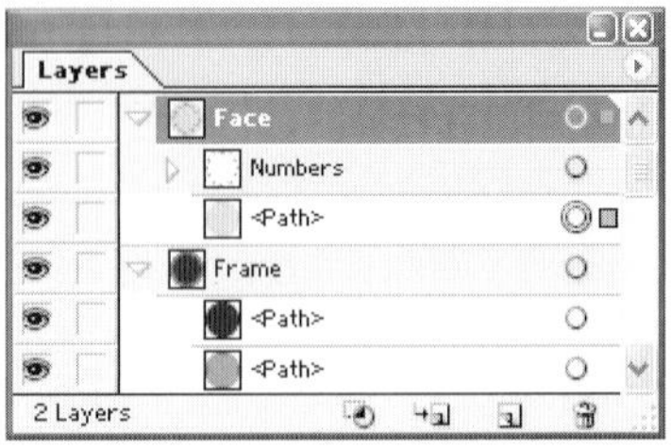

Change layer name.

11 Choose Select > Deselect to deselect all active objects, and then choose File > Save.

Locking layers

As you edit objects on a layer, use the Layers palette to lock other layers and prevent selecting or changing the rest of the artwork.

Now you'll lock all the layers except the Numbers sublayer so that you can easily edit the clock numbers without affecting objects on other layers. Locked layers cannot be selected or edited in any way.

1 To simplify your work, click the triangle to the left of the Frame layer to collapse the layer view.

2 Click the edit column to the right of the eye icon on the Frame layer to lock the layer.

The padlock icon (🔒) indicates that a layer and all its objects are locked.

3 Click the edit column to the right of the eye icon on the <Path> layer below the Numbers layer.

You can unlock individual layers by clicking the padlock icon to make it disappear from the edit column. Clicking again in the edit column relocks the layer. Holding down Alt (Windows) or Option (Mac OS) as you click in the edit column alternately locks and unlocks all other layers.

Now you'll change the type size and font of the numbers.

4 In the Layers palette to the right of the Numbers layer, click the selection column to select all objects on that layer.

A quick way to select all the type or objects on a layer is to click the selection column—the blank area to the right of the target indicators—in the Layers palette.

The Numbers layer now has a large red square, indicating that everything on the layer is selected.

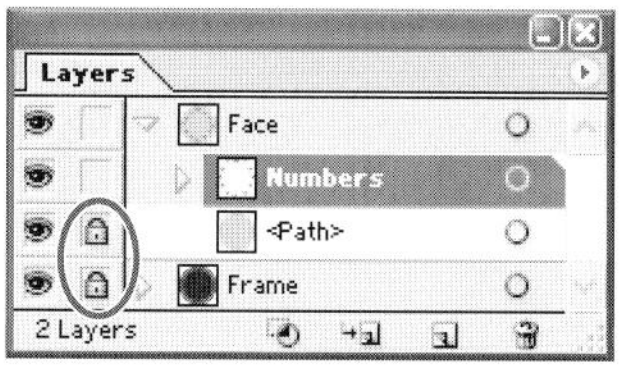

Click the edit column to lock layer.

5 Choose Window > Type > Character to display the Character palette.

6 In the Character palette, select another font or size for the group of numbers. (We used Myriad Pro Bold, size 28 points.)

Note: *Myriad Pro is an OpenType font included with Illustrator CS. Click on Cool Extras on the Welcome Screen for more information about fonts.*

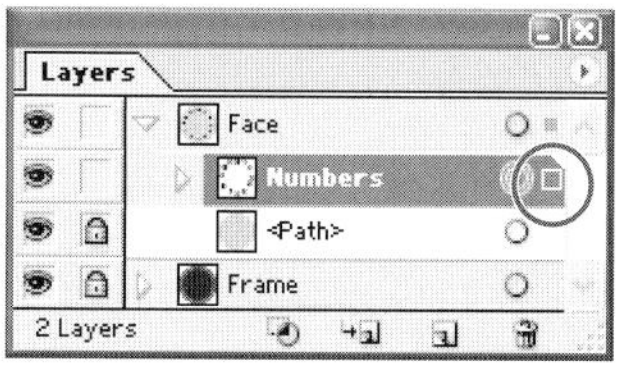

Click the selection column.

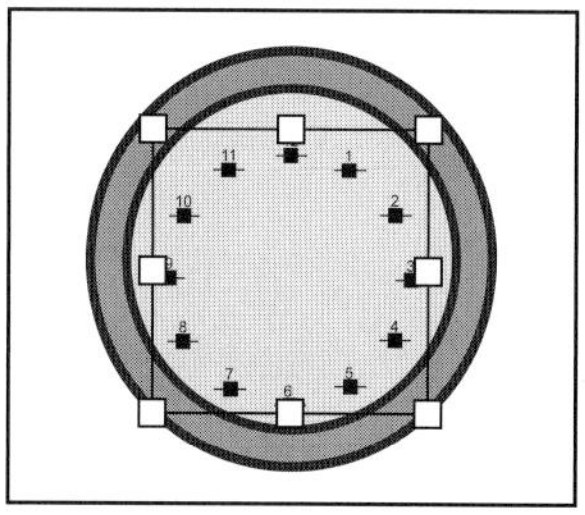

All type is selected.

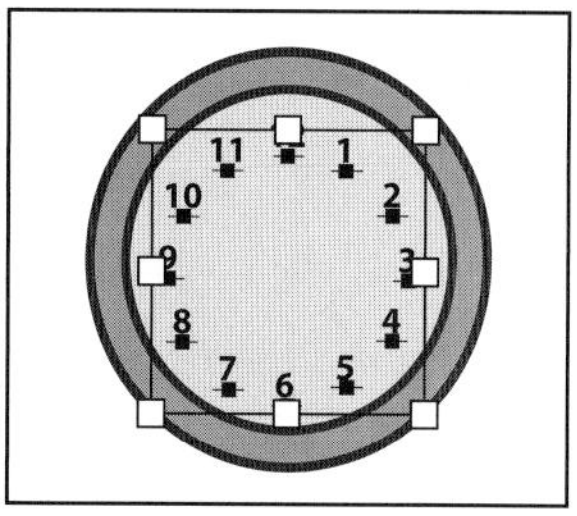

Change font and size globally.

7 If you wish, use the Color palette or Swatches palette to change the color of the selected numbers.

8 In the Layers palette, click the padlock icons next to the <Path> and the Frame layers to unlock them.

Viewing layers

The Layers palette lets you hide layers, sublayers, or individual objects from view. When a layer is hidden, objects on the layer are also locked and cannot be selected or printed. You can also use the Layers palette to display layers or objects in either Preview or Outline to view independently from other layers in the artwork.

Now you'll edit the frame on the clock, using a painting technique to create a three-dimensional effect on the frame.

1 In the Layers palette, click the Frame layer to select it, and then Alt-click (Windows) or Option-click (Mac OS) the eye icon (👁) next to the Frame layer name to hide the other layers.

Alt/Option-clicking the layer eye icon alternately hides and shows a layer. Hiding layers also locks them and prevents them from being changed.

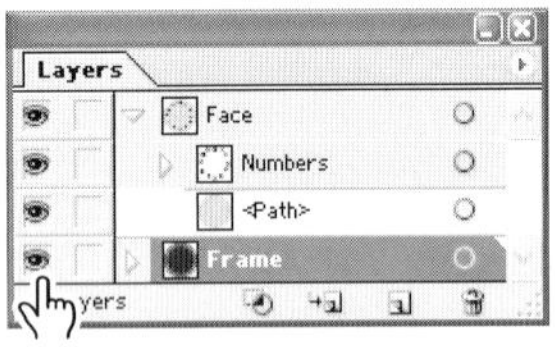

Alt/Option-click eye icon.

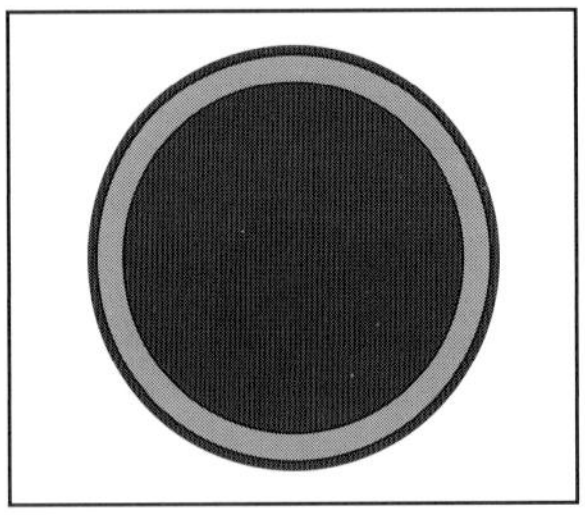

Only objects on Frame layer appear.

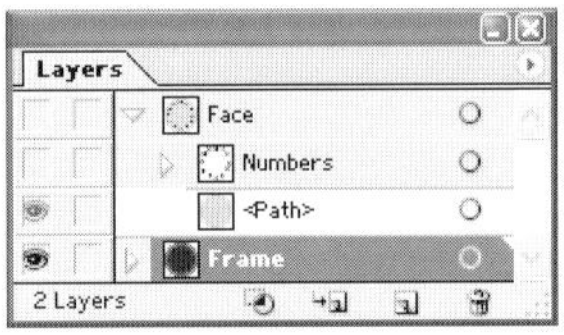

Only Frame layer is showing and unlocked.

2 Using the Selection tool (↖), click the inside circle of the frame to select it. Then holding down the Shift key, click the next largest circle to add it to the selection.

3 With the two inner circles selected, make sure that the Fill box is selected in the toolbox, and then click the Clock.frame swatch in the Swatches palette to paint the circles with a custom gradient.

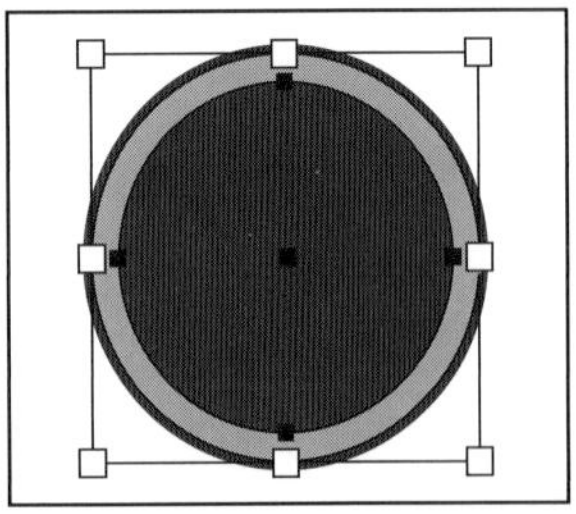

Select two inner circles.

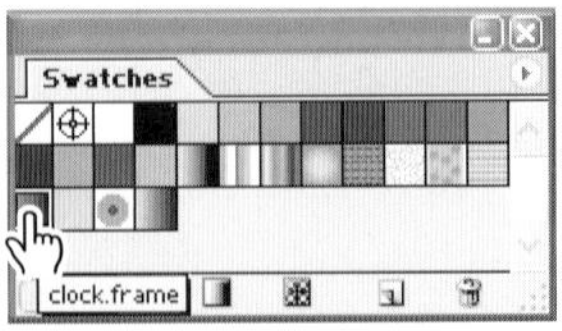

Paint with gradient fill.

4 Shift-click the second largest circle to deselect it and keep the inside circle selected.

5 Select the Gradient tool (■) in the toolbox. Drag the tool in a vertical line from the top of the circle straight down to the bottom to change the direction of the gradient.

The Gradient tool works only on selected objects that are filled with gradients. To learn more about using the Gradient tool, see Lesson 12, "Blending Shapes and Colors."

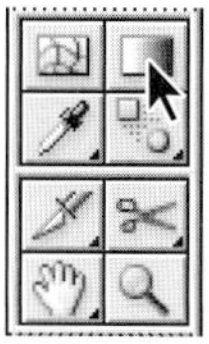
Select Gradient tool.

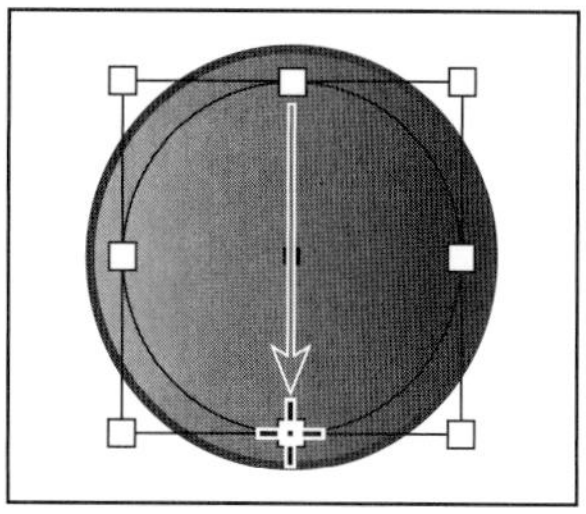
Drag over selected object.

6 Choose Select > Deselect to deselect the artwork, and then choose File > Save.

7 In the Layers palette, choose Show All Layers from the palette menu.

As you edit objects in layered artwork, you can display individual layers in Outline view, keeping the other layers in Preview view.

8 Ctrl-click (Windows) or Command-click (Mac OS) the eye icon next to the Face layer to switch to Outline view for that layer.

This action lets you see the gradient-filled circle behind the clock face. Displaying a layer in Outline view also is useful for viewing the anchor points or center points on objects without selecting them.

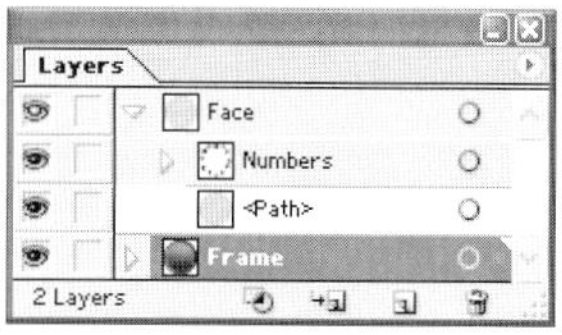

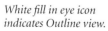

White fill in eye icon indicates Outline view.

Preview view of other layers shows through Face layer in Outline view.

9 Ctrl/Command-click the eye icon next to the Face layer to return to Preview view for that layer.

Pasting layers

To complete the clock, you'll copy and paste the finishing parts of artwork from another file. You can paste layered files into another file and keep all the layers intact.

1 Choose File > Open, and open the Details.ai file, located in the Lesson07 folder, inside the Lessons folder within the AICIB folder on your hard drive.

Clock.ai file.

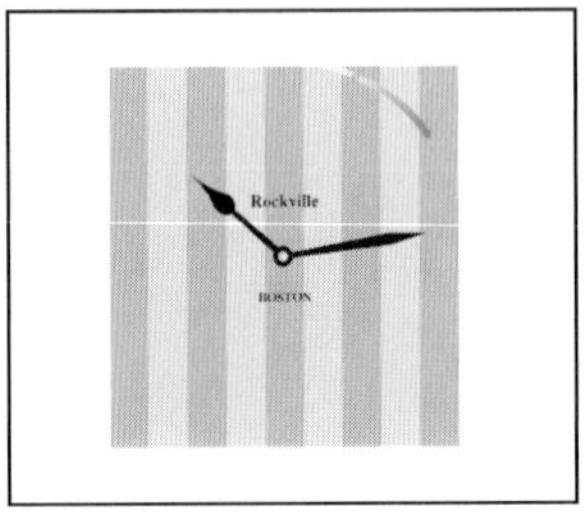

Details.ai file.

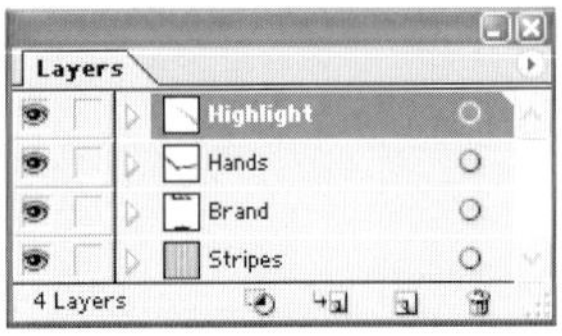

Layers palette for Details.ai file.

2 If you want to see how the objects are organized on the layers, Alt/Option-click the eye icons in the Layers palette to alternately display each layer and hide the others. You can also click the triangles (▸) to the left of the layer names to expand and collapse the layers for further inspection. When you've finished, make sure that all the layers are showing and that they are fully collapsed.

If a layer is hidden, its objects are locked and cannot be selected or copied.

3 Choose Select > All and then Edit > Copy to select and copy the clock details to the Clipboard.

4 Choose File > Close and click No (Windows) or Don't Save (Mac OS) to close the Details.ai file without saving any changes.

5 In the Clock.ai file, choose Paste Remembers Layers from the Layers palette menu to select the option. (A check mark next to the option indicates that it's selected.)

Selecting the Paste Remembers Layers option indicates that when multiple layers from another file are pasted into the artwork, they're added as individual layers in the Layers palette. If the option is not selected, all objects are pasted into the active layer.

6 Choose Edit > Paste In Front to paste the details into the clock.

The Paste In Front command pastes the objects from the Clipboard to a position relative to the original position in the Details.ai file. The Paste Remembers Layers option causes the Details.ai layers to be pasted as four separate layers (Highlight, Hands, Brand, Stripes) from the original file at the bottom of the Layers palette.

7 Drag the Layers palette by its lower right corner to resize it and display all the layers in the palette. As you can see, some of the layers need to be repositioned.

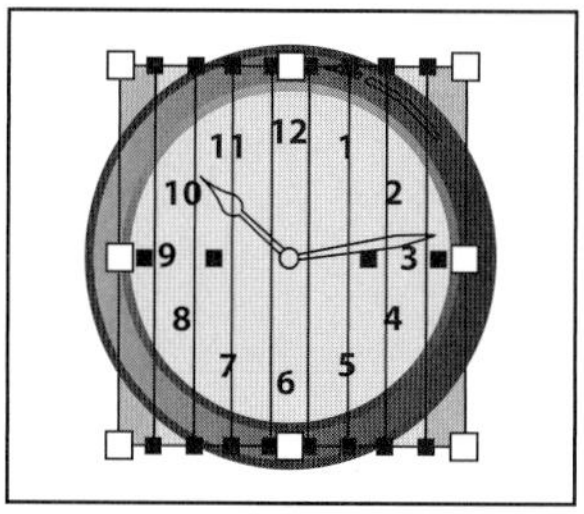

Paste artwork from Details.ai file.

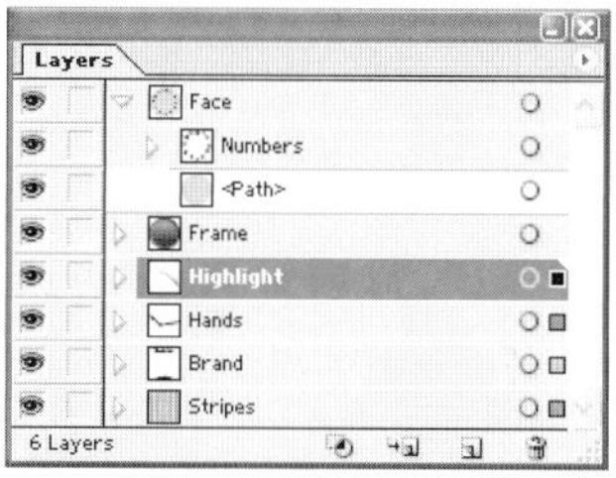

Layers are added from Details.ai file.

Now you'll move the brand and hands into the Face layer and the highlight in front of the Frame layer.

8 Select the Selection tool (), and click away from the artwork to deselect it.

9 In the Layers palette, select the Highlight layer, and drag it up between the <Path> sublayer and Frame layer. Release the mouse button when the indicator bar with large black triangles extends the full column width above the Frame layer. (You want to create a separate layer, not a sublayer.)

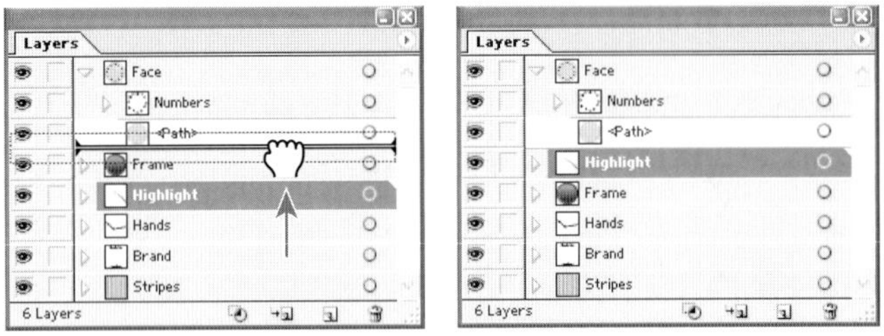

Move Highlight layer up above Frame layer.

10 Shift-click the Hands and Brand layers in the Layers palette.

11 Drag the selected layers up between the Numbers and <Path> sublayers; when the insertion bar appears between those sublayers, release the mouse button to make the Hands and Brand layers sublayers of the Face layer.

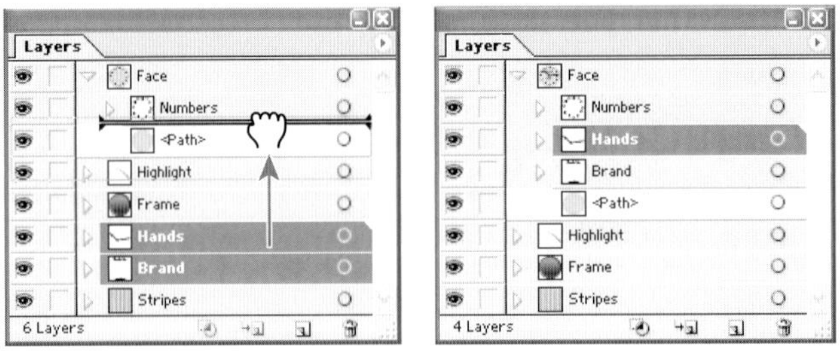

Drag Hands and Brand layers up into Face layer.

12 Choose File > Save to save the changes.

Creating clipping masks

The Layers palette lets you create clipping masks to control how artwork on a layer (or in a group) is hidden or revealed. A *clipping mask* is an object or group of objects whose shape masks artwork below it so that only artwork within the shape is visible.

Now you'll create a clipping mask with the circle shape in the Face layer. You'll group it with the Stripes sublayer so that only the stripes show through the circle shape.

1 In the Layers palette, drag the Stripes layer up until the insertion bar's double lines are highlighted above the <Path> layer within the Face layer. Release the mouse button when the indicator bar appears.

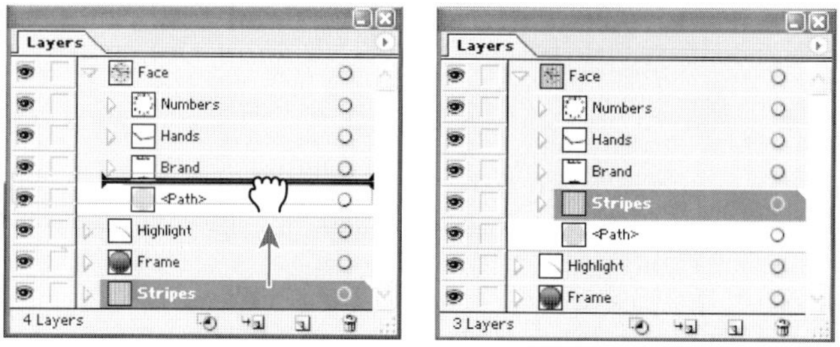

Drag Stripes layer up above <Path> sublayer within Face layer.

A masking object must reside above the objects it will mask in the Layers palette. Since you want to mask only the stripes, you'll move the circular <Path> object to the top of the Stripes sublayer before you create the clipping mask.

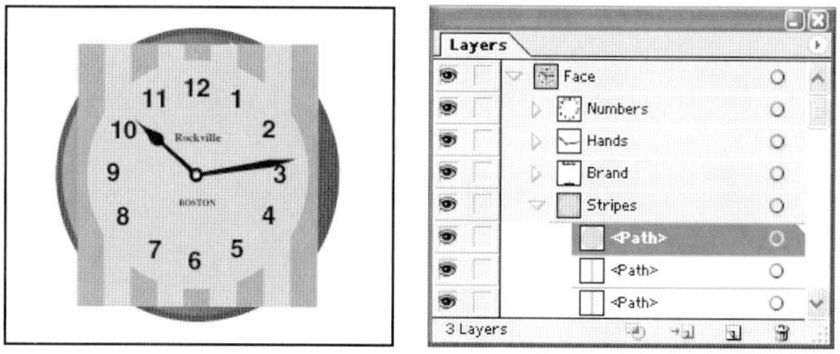

Drag circle named <Path> into Stripes layer.

2 Drag the <Path> layer with the circle color fill onto the Stripes thumbnail to add it to that layer as the top sublayer.

3 In the Layers palette, click the triangle (▸) to the left of the Stripes layer to expand the layer view.

4 Make sure that the <Path> with the circle color fill is the topmost sublayer in the Stripes layer, moving it if necessary. (Clipping masks are always the first object in a layer or group.)

5 Select the Stripes layer to highlight it. Then click the selection area to the right of the Stripes layer to select all the stripes and the colored circle path.

6 Click the Make/Release Clipping Mask button at the bottom of the Layers palette. Notice that all the layer's dividing lines are now dotted and the first path's name has changed to <Clipping Path>. The clipping path name is also underlined to indicate that it is the masking shape.

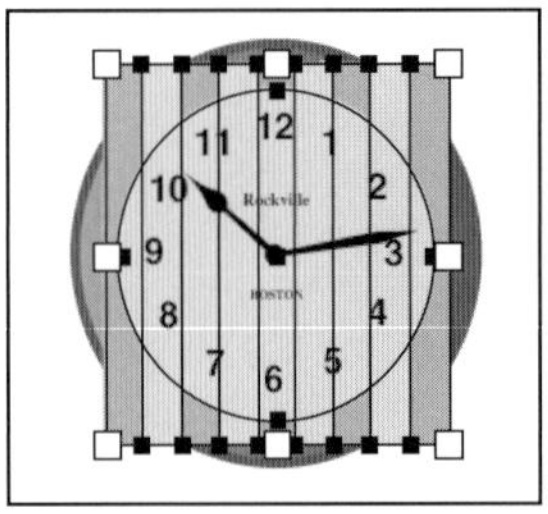

Select Stripes layer.

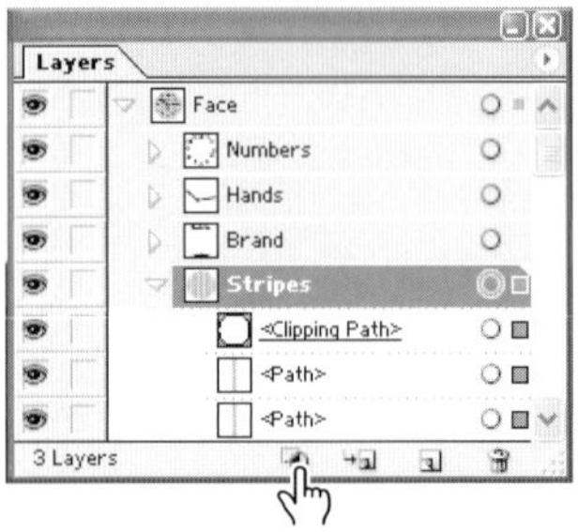

Click Make/Release Clipping Mask button.

Result.

7 Click the triangle next to the Stripes layer name to collapse the layers in the Layers palette.

8 Choose Select > Deselect. Then choose File > Save.

Merging layers

To streamline your artwork, you can merge layers. Merging layers combines the contents of all selected layers onto one layer.

1 In the Layers palette, click the Numbers layer to highlight it, and then Shift-click to highlight the Hands layer.

Notice the current layer indicator (◥) shows the last highlighted layer as the active layer. The last layer you select will determine the name and color for the merged layer.

2 Choose Merge Selected from the Layers palette menu to merge the objects from the Numbers layer into the Hands layer.

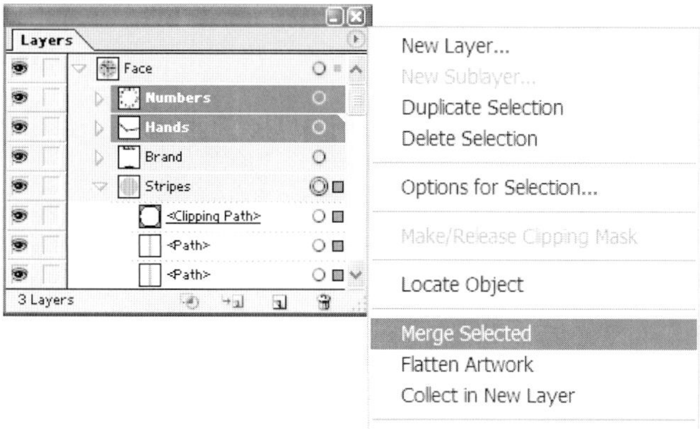

The objects on the merged layers retain their original stacking order, and are added above the objects in the destination layer.

3 Now click the Highlight layer to highlight it, and then Shift-click to highlight the Frame layer.

4 Choose Merge Selected from the Layers palette menu to merge the objects from the Highlight layer into the Frame layer.

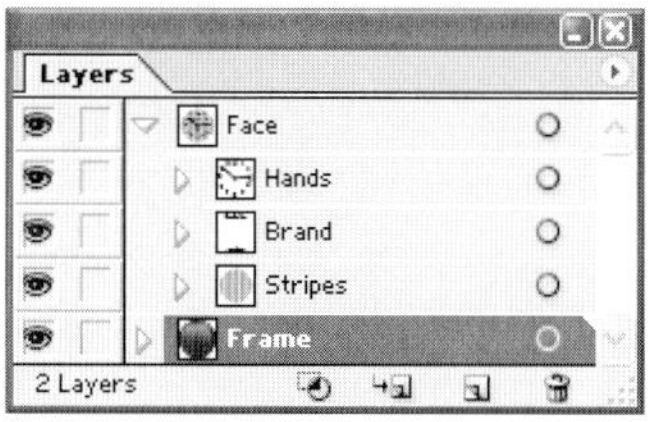

5 Choose File > Save.

Applying appearance attributes to layers

You can apply appearance attributes such as styles, effects, and transparency to layers, groups, and objects with the Layers palette. When an appearance attribute is applied to a layer, any object on that layer will take on that attribute. If an appearance attribute is applied only to a specific object on a layer, it affects only that object, not the entire layer.

You will apply an effect to an object on one layer. Then you'll copy that effect to a layer to change all objects on that layer.

1 In the Layers palette, collapse the Face layer and expand the Frame layer to reveal all its objects.

2 Select the bottom path in the Frame layer.

3 To the right of the bottom path's layer name, click the target indicator (◎) to target the bottommost object. Clicking the target indicator indicates that you want to apply an effect, style, or transparency change.

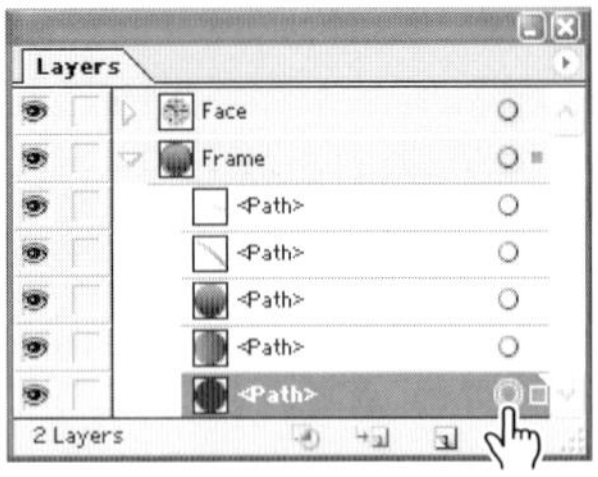

Click the target indicator to target the bottom path.

4 Choose Effect > Stylize > Drop Shadow. Leave the settings at their default values and click OK. A drop shadow appears on the outer edge of the clock.

Note: *Select the first Stylize option from the Effect submenu. Effect > Stylize > Drop Shadow command.*

5 Notice that the target indicator is now shaded, indicating that the object has appearance attributes applied to it.

6 Click the Appearance tab to bring the palette to the front of its group. (If the Appearance palette isn't visible on-screen, choose Window > Appearance.) Notice that Drop Shadow has been added to the list of appearance attributes for the selected shape.

Apply drop shadow effect to clock edge.

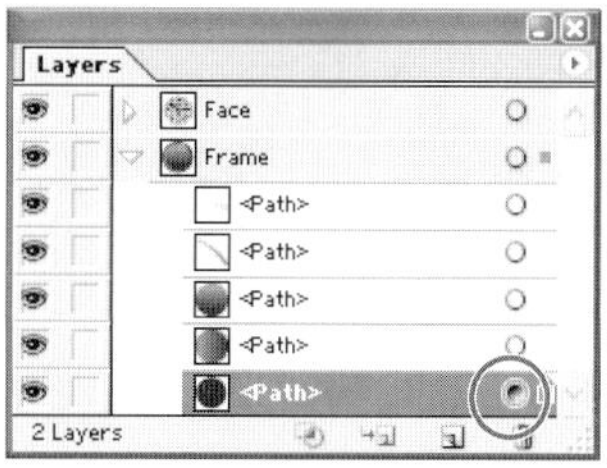

Shaded target indicator indicates appearance attributes.

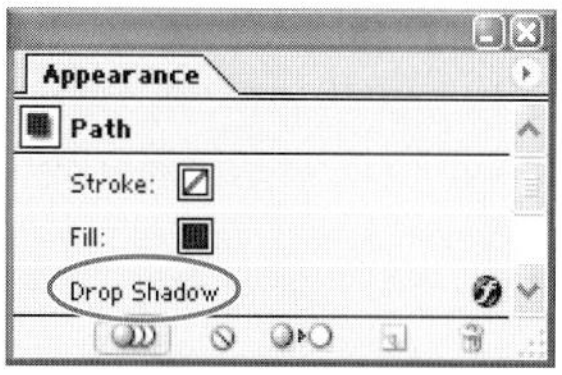

Appearance palette lists selection's attributes.

You will now use the Layers palette to copy an appearance attribute onto a layer and then edit it.

7 Expand the Face layer to reveal its contents. Drag the bottom right corner of the Layers palette to display the entire list.

8 Hold down Alt (Windows) or Option (Mac OS) and drag the shaded target indicator of the <Path> sublayer to the target indicator of the Hands layer, without releasing the mouse button. The hand pointer with a plus sign indicates that the appearance is being copied.

9 When the target indicator of the Hands layer turns light gray, release the mouse button. The drop shadow is now applied to the entire Hands layer, as indicated by the shaded target indicator.

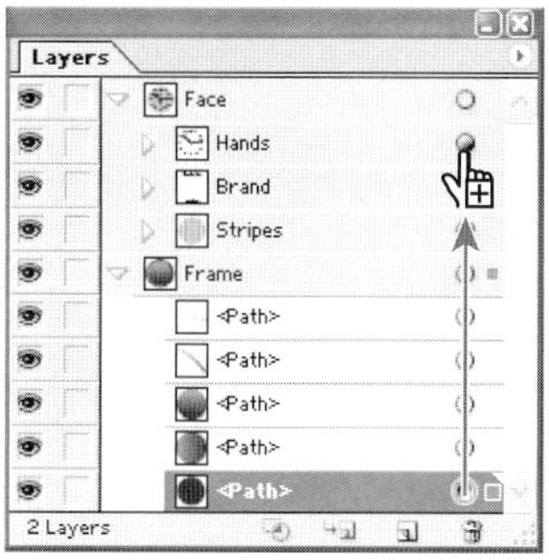

Drag target indicator to copy effect.

Result.

Now you'll edit the drop shadow attribute for the type and clock hands, to tone down the effect.

10 In the Layers palette, click the target indicator for the Hands layer. This automatically selects the objects on the Hands layer and deselects the object on the Frame layer.

11 In the Appearance palette, double-click the Drop Shadow attribute. In the Drop Shadow dialog box, enter **3 pt** for the X and Y offsets and the Blur amount. Click OK.

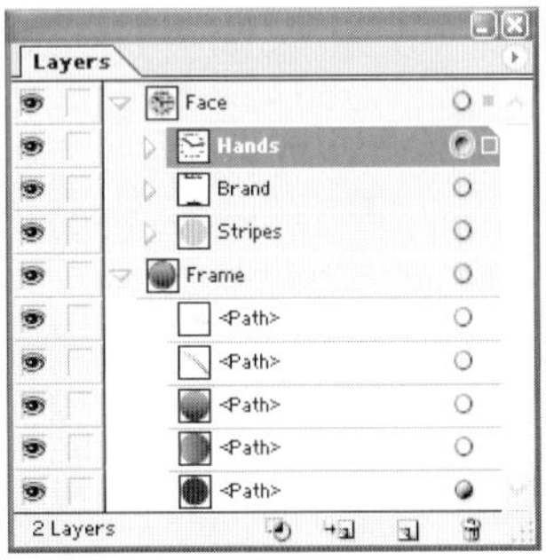

Target Hands layer.

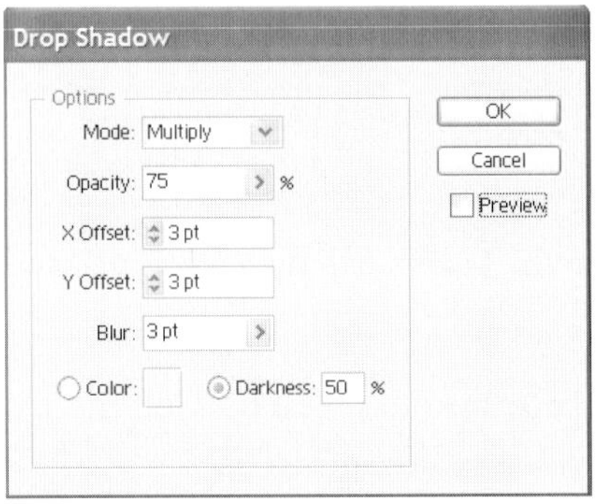

Edit Drop Shadow effect.

Result.

For more information on appearance attributes, see Lesson 10, "Using Appearance Attributes, Styles, and Effects."

12 Choose Select > Deselect.

13 Choose File > Save. Choose File > Close to close the file.

You have completed building a layered file.

In some cases after the artwork is complete, you may want to place all the layers of art onto a single layer and delete the empty layers. This is called flattening artwork. Delivering finished artwork in a single layer file can prevent accidents such as hiding layers, and not printing parts of the artwork, from happening.

To flatten specific layers without deleting hidden layers, select the layers you want to flatten, and then choose Merge Layers from the Layers palette menu.

Merging and flattening artwork

Merging and flattening are similar in that they let you consolidate paths, groups, and sublayers. With merging, you can select which items you want to consolidate; with flattening, all visible items in the artwork are consolidated in a single, parent layer. With either option, the stacking order of the artwork remains the same.

To merge artwork into a single layer or group:

1. *Select the items that you want to merge in the Layers palette.*

2. *Choose Merge Selected from the Layers palette menu. Items will be merged into the layer or group that you selected last. In flattened artwork, all visible layers are merged into the selected layer, and hidden layers are deleted. If you flatten a hidden layer that contains artwork, you can choose to delete the artwork along with the hidden layer, or make all artwork visible and flatten it into one layer. In most cases, you won't want to flatten a file until you finish editing individual layers.*

To flatten artwork:

1. *Make sure that all the layers you want to flatten are visible.*

2. *Select the layer into which you will flatten the artwork. You cannot flatten artwork into hidden, locked, or template layers. Doing this results in the topmost layer that is not hidden, locked, or a template being chosen instead. Regardless of the layer you select, the options for the layer and the stacking order of the artwork don't change.*

3. *Choose Flatten Artwork from the Layers palette menu.*

If artwork is present on a hidden layer, a dialog box prompts you to choose whether to make all artwork visible and flatten it into one layer, or delete the artwork along with the layer.

–From online Help, "Merging Layers".

For information on opening layered Photoshop files in Illustrator and working with layered Illustrator files in Photoshop, see Lesson 18, "Combining Illustrator Graphics and Photoshop Images".

For a complete list of shortcuts that you can use with the Layers palette, see "Keyboard Shortcuts" in online Help or the printed *Quick Reference Card.*

Exploring on your own

When you print a layered file, only the visible layers print in the same order in which they appear in the Layers palette—with the exception of template layers, which do not print even if they're visible. Template layers are locked, dimmed, and previewed. Objects on template layers neither print nor export.

Now that you've learned how to work with layers, try creating layered artwork by tracing an image on a template layer. We've provided a bitmap photo image of a goldfish that you can use to practice with, or use your own artwork or photo images.

1. Choose File > New to create a new file for your artwork.

2. Choose File > Place. In the dialog box, select the Goldfish.eps file, located in the Lesson07 folder, inside the Lessons folder within the AICIB folder on your hard drive; or locate your file containing the artwork or image you want to use as a template and click Place to add the placed file to Layer 1.

For information on importing files, see "About imported artwork" and "Opening and placing artwork" in online Help.

3. Create the template layer by choosing Template from the Layers palette menu or choosing Options for Layer 1 and selecting Template in the Layer Options dialog box.

4. Click the New Layer button to create a new layer on which to draw.

5. With Layer 2 active, use any drawing tool to trace over the template, creating new artwork.

6. Create additional layers to separate and edit various components of the new artwork.

7. If you wish, delete the template when you've finished to reduce the size of the file.

You can create custom views of your artwork with some layers hidden and other layers showing, and display each view in a separate window. To create a custom view, choose View > New View. To display each view in a separate window, choose Window > New Window.

For information on custom views, see "Viewing artwork" in online Help.

Review questions

1 Name two benefits of using layers when creating artwork.

2 How do you hide layers? Display individual layers?

3 Describe how to reorder layers in a file.

4 How can you lock layers?

5 What is the purpose of changing the selection color on a layer?

6 What happens if you paste a layered file into another file? Why is the Paste Remembers Layers option useful?

7 How do you move objects from one layer to another?

8 How do you create a layer clipping mask?

9 How do you apply an effect to a layer? How can you edit that effect?

Review answers

1 Benefits of using layers when creating artwork include: You can protect artwork that you don't want to change, you can hide artwork that you aren't working with so that it's not distracting, and you can control what prints.

2 To hide a layer, you click the eye icon (👁) to the left of the layer name; you click in the blank, leftmost column to redisplay a layer.

3 You reorder layers by selecting a layer name in the Layers palette and dragging the layer to its new location. The order of layers in the Layers palette controls the document's layer order—topmost in the palette is frontmost in the artwork.

4 You can lock layers several different ways:

• You can click in the column to the left of the layer name; a padlock icon appears, indicating that the layer is locked.

• You can choose Lock Others from the Layers palette menu to lock all layers but the active layer.

• You can hide a layer to protect it.

5 The selection color controls how selected anchor points and direction lines are displayed on a layer, and helps you identify the different layers in your document.

6 The Paste commands paste layered files or objects copied from different layers onto the active layer by default. The Paste Remembers Layers option keeps the original layers intact when the objects are pasted.

7 Select the objects you want to move and drag the square selection indicator icon (■) (to the right of the target indicator) to another layer in the Layers palette.

8 Create a clipping mask on a layer by selecting the layer and clicking the Make/ Release Clipping Mask button. The topmost object in the layer will become the clipping mask.

9 Click the target indicator (◎) for the layer to which you want to apply an effect. Then choose an effect from the Effect menu. To edit the effect, make sure that the layer is selected; then double-click the name of the effect in the Appearance palette. The effect's dialog box will open, and then you can change the values.

Lesson 8

8 Transforming Objects

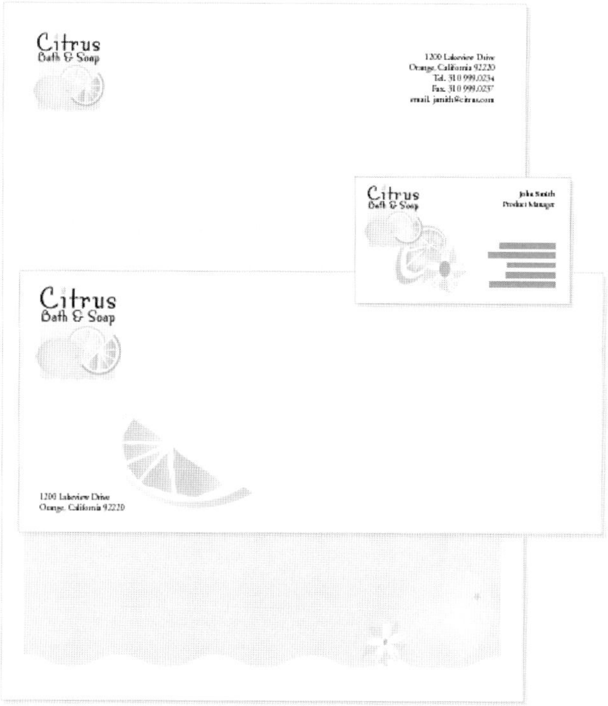

You can modify objects in many ways as you create your artwork—including quickly and precisely controlling their size, shape, and orientation. In this lesson, you'll explore the various transform tools, commands, and palettes as you create three pieces of artwork.

In this lesson, you'll learn how to do the following:

- Select individual objects, objects in a group, and parts of an object.
- Move, scale, and rotate objects using a variety of methods.
- Reflect, shear, and distort objects.
- Adjust the perspective of an object.
- Create symbols for artwork that you'll reuse.
- Repeat transformations quickly and easily.
- Experiment using variables to create different versions of a design.

Getting started

In this lesson, you'll transform parts of a logo to use in three pieces of artwork to create a letterhead design, an envelope, and a business card template. Before you begin, you'll restore the default preferences for Adobe Illustrator; then you'll open a file containing a composite of the finished artwork to see what you'll create.

1 To ensure that the tools and palettes function exactly as described in this lesson, delete or deactivate (by renaming) the Adobe Illustrator CS preferences file. See "Restoring default preferences" on page 2.

2 Start Adobe Illustrator.

3 Choose File > Open, and open the L8comp.ai file in the Lesson08 folder, located inside the Lessons folder within the AICIB folder on your hard drive.

This file contains a composite of the three pieces of finished artwork. The Citrus Bath & Soap logo in the top left corner of the letterhead is the basis for all the modified objects. The logo has been resized for the letterhead, envelope, and business card.

Note: *You can also view the individual pieces of finished artwork by opening the files L8end1.ai, L8end2.ai, and L8end3.ai in the Lesson08 folder.*

4 If you like, choose View > Zoom Out to reduce the view of the finished artwork, adjust the window size, and leave it on your screen as you work. (Use the Hand tool (✋) to move the artwork where you want it in the window.) If you don't want to leave the image open, choose File > Close.

For an illustration of the finished artwork in this lesson, see the color section.

To begin working, you'll open an existing art file set up for the letterhead artwork.

5 Choose File > Open to open the L8start1.ai file in the Lesson08 folder, located inside the Lessons folder within the AICIB folder on your hard drive.

This start file has been saved with the rulers showing, custom swatches added to the Swatches palette, and blue guidelines for scaling the logo and objects on the letterhead.

6 Choose File > Save As, name the file **Letterhd.ai**, and select the Lesson08 folder in the Save in Menu. Leave the type of file format set to Adobe Illustrator® Document, and click Save. In the Illustrator Options dialog box, accept the default settings by clicking OK.

Scaling objects

You scale objects by enlarging or reducing them horizontally (along the x axis) and vertically (along the y axis) relative to a fixed point of origin that you designate. If you don't designate an origin, the objects are scaled from their center points. You'll use three methods to scale the logo and two objects copied from the logo.

First you'll use the Transform palette to scale down the logo by entering new dimensions and designating the point of origin from which the logo will scale.

1 Using the Selection tool (↖) in the toolbox, click the logo to select the group of objects (type, background, lemon, orange slice, lime slice) that make up the logo.

2 Choose Window > Transform to display the Transform palette. (A check mark indicates that the palette is displayed on-screen.)

The Transform palette contains a small grid of squares, or reference points, that represent points on the selection's bounding box. All values in the palette refer to the bounding boxes of the objects.

3 Click the reference point in the top left corner of the grid (as shown in the illustration) to set the point of origin from which the objects will scale. Type **83.75** in the W text box, and then press Tab and type **88.5** in the H text box. Now press Enter or Return to scale down the logo to fit inside the blue guideline.

By default, the ruler units of measure are set to points.

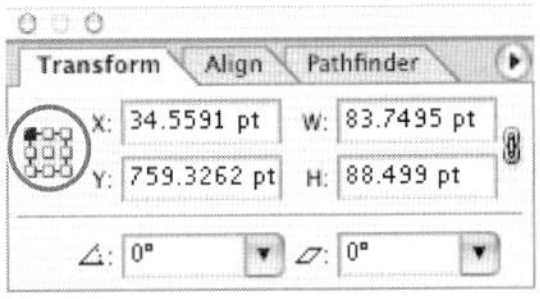

Set reference point, width, and height.

Result.

Next you'll copy the background object in the logo and scale the new object by dragging its bounding box to fit the background of the letterhead.

4 With the logo still selected, choose Object > Ungroup to ungroup the larger group in the logo. (Smaller subgroups remain grouped.)

Ungrouping the background object from the other objects lets you make copies that are separate from the group.

5 If desired, use the Zoom tool (🔍) to zoom in on the logo.

6 Using the Selection tool (➤), click away from the logo to deselect it, and then click below the word Bath to select the light-blue background object in the logo. Hold down Alt (Windows) or Option (Mac OS) and drag from the center of the object down to copy the object and move it to the bottom left corner of the page, aligning it with the guides. You can press the arrow keys to nudge the object into place.

Note: *Holding down Alt/Option as you drag an object duplicates it.*

Next, you'll make this background object the background for the page.

7 Drag the top right corner of the new object's bounding box up to the top right side of the blue letterhead guide, to just below the return address.

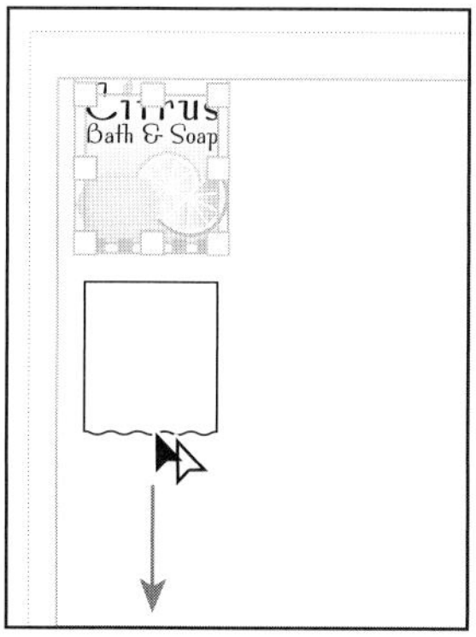

Move copy of object from logo.

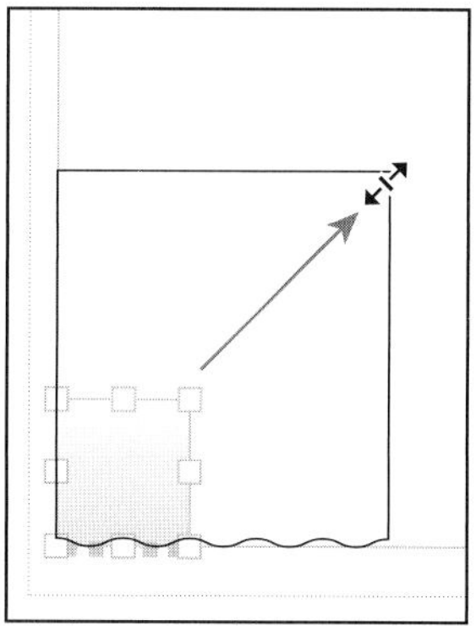

Scale new background to fit letterhead.

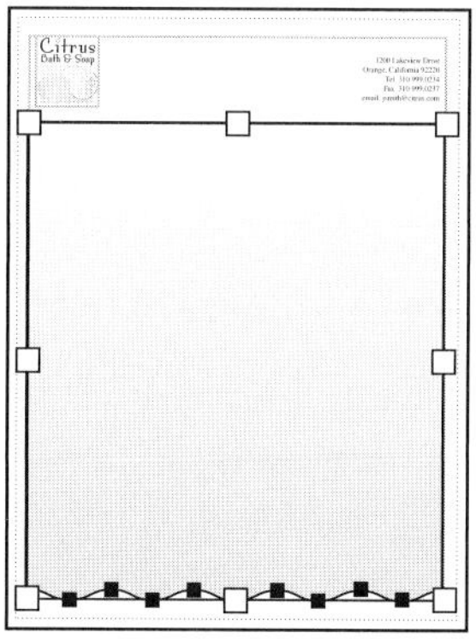

Result.

You'll use the Swatches palette to paint the background with a lighter gradient. To learn how to create your own custom gradients, see Lesson 12, "Blending Shapes and Colors."

8 Click the Swatches tab to bring the palette to the front of its group. With the background selected, hold the pointer over the swatches in the Swatches palette until you see their names. Then click the New Background swatch to paint the object with a lighter gradient.

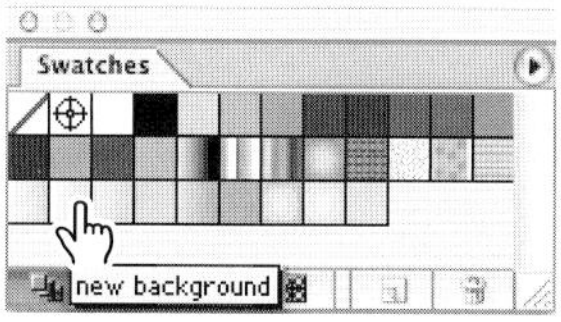

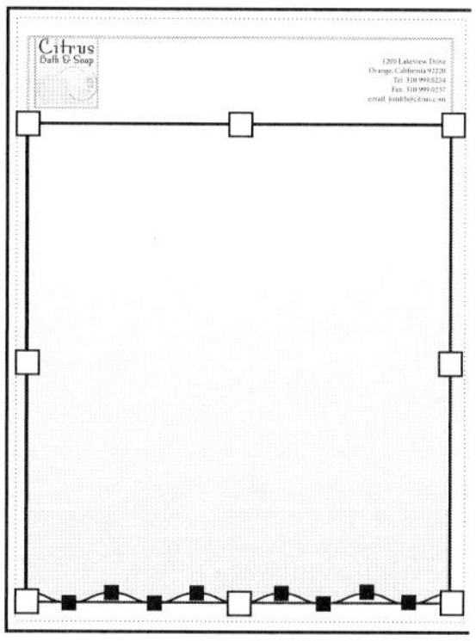

9 With the background object still selected, choose Object > Lock > Selection to lock the object and deselect it. Locking the background object makes it easier to select other objects you'll add to the artwork.

You can also lock all artwork above the selected object—for example, if you want to edit an object in the background that has objects on top of it—or all objects on other layers. In addition, you can use the Layers palette to lock objects. Once objects are locked, they cannot be selected or edited. You can quickly lock multiple objects, groups of objects, and sublayers by locking the parent layer.

The lemon in the logo is comprised of two objects grouped together. Now you'll copy the lemon and place it at the bottom of the letterhead.

10 Select the lemon in the logo, and Alt-drag (Windows) or Option-drag (Mac OS) to copy and move the new lemon to the bottom right corner of the letterhead guide.

You'll use the Scale tool to resize the new lemon and set a fixed point for the scaling.

11 Select the Scale tool in the toolbox, hold down Alt (Windows) or Option (Mac OS), and click the bottom right corner point of the letterhead guide.

Clicking the corner point of the guide sets the point of origin from which the lemon will scale. Holding down Alt/Option as you click displays the Scale dialog box.

12 In the Scale dialog box, type **300%** in the Scale text box and click OK to make the lemon three times larger.

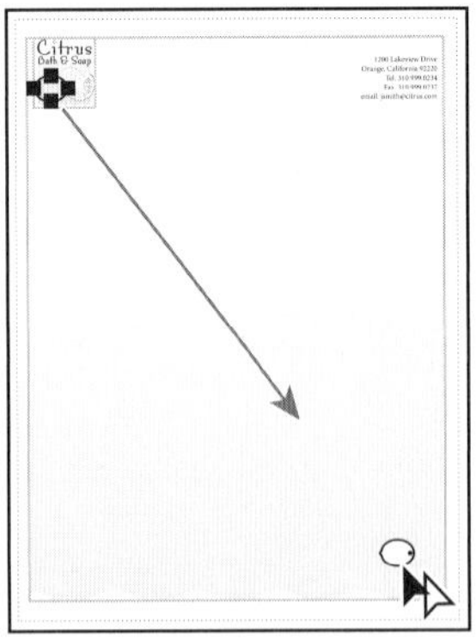

Move copy of lemon.

Set point of origin.

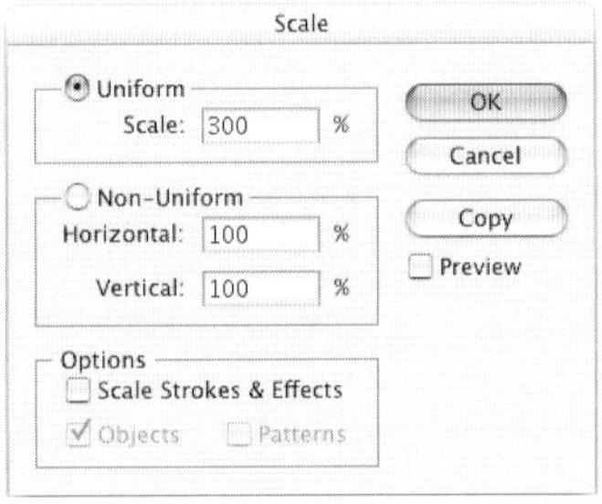

Scale dialog box.

Rotating objects

Objects are rotated by turning them around a designated point of origin. You can rotate objects by displaying their bounding boxes and moving the pointer to an outside corner. Once the rotate pointer appears, just click to rotate the object around its center point. You can rotate objects using the Transform palette to set a point of origin and a rotation angle. You can also rotate objects using the Rotate tool to drag the object or set its rotation angle.

You'll rotate the lemon 30° around its center point using the Rotate tool.

1 With the lemon selected, select the Rotate tool () in the toolbox.

Notice that the lemon's point of origin is still at the bottom right corner of the letterhead.

2 Begin dragging the selected lemon. Notice how the movement is constrained to a circle rotating around the point of origin. Continue dragging until the lemon is in its original position on the letterhead, and then release the mouse button. You can also choose Edit > Undo Rotate.

3 Now, with the lemon still selected, double-click the Rotate tool in the toolbox.

When an object is selected and you double-click the Rotate tool in the toolbox, the object is rotated exactly from the center of the object. (This also applies to the Scale tool.)

4 In the Rotate dialog box, type **30** in the Angle text box, then click OK to rotate the lemon 30° around its center point.

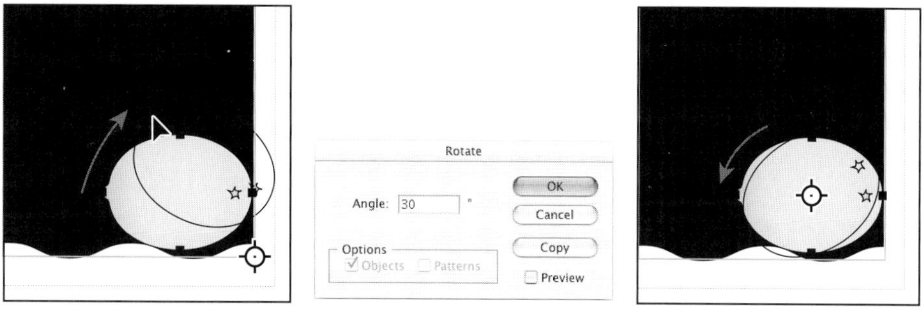

Rotating around different points of origin.

Next you'll select one of the two objects making up the lemon – without ungrouping the lemon – so that you can paint that part of it a lighter color.

5 Select the Group Selection tool () in the same group as the Direct Selection tool () in the toolbox. Hold down Shift and click the stem's core (not the lemon body) to deselect it. The Group Selection tool lets you select or deselect individual objects or subgroups within a group.

6 With the lemon body thus selected, click a color in the Color palette or a swatch in the Swatches palette to paint the lemon a lighter gradient. (We used the Pale Yellow gradient.)

7 Choose File > Save.

Distorting objects

Various tools and filters let you distort the original shapes of objects in different ways. For example, the wavy line on the bottom of the background object in the logo and on the letterhead was created by applying the Zig Zag distort filter to the straight edge.

Converting straight lines to zigzags

The Zig Zag filter adds anchor points to an existing line and then moves some of the points to the left of (or upward from) the line and some to the right of (or downward from) the line. You can specify the number of anchor points to create and the distance to move them. You can also choose whether to create smooth anchor points for a wavy-line effect or corner anchor points for a jagged-line effect.

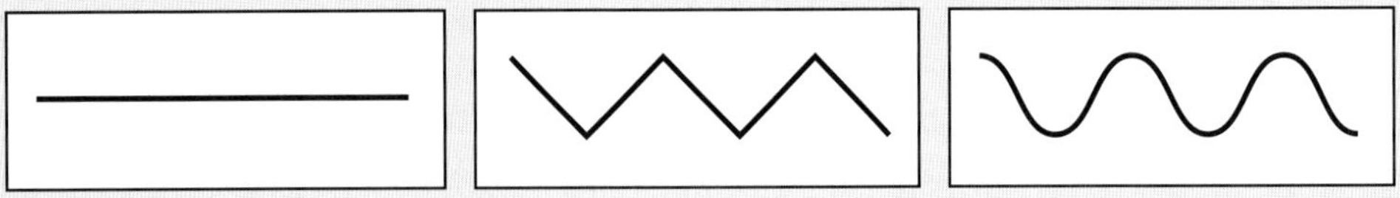

Original line. *Line with four corner ridges applied.* *Line with four smooth ridges applied.*

To convert straight lines to zigzags:

1. *Do one of the following:*

• *To apply the distortion permanently, use any selection tool to select the line you want to convert. Then choose Filter > Distort > Zig Zag.*

• *To apply the distortion as an effect that can be removed, select an object or group, or target a group or layer in the Layers palette. (For more on targeting, see Lesson 7, "Working with Layers.") Then choose Effect > Distort & Transform > Zig Zag.*

2. *Select how you wish to move points: Either Relative by a percentage of the object's size or Absolute by a specific amount.*

3. *For Size, enter the distance you want to move points on the line, or drag the slider.*

4. *For Ridges per Segment, enter the number of ridges per line segment you want, or drag the slider.*

5. *Select the type of line to create:*
Smooth to create smooth points for a wavy line, or Corner to create corner points for a jagged line.

6. *Click Preview to preview the line.*

7. *Click OK.*

Now you'll create a flower, first using the Twist distort filter to twirl the shape of a star, and then the Pucker & Bloat distort filter to transform another star in front of it.

To begin, you'll draw a star for part of the flower and use the Twist filter and Info palette to distort it.

1 Select the Star tool (☆) from the same group as the Rectangle tool (□) in the toolbox, and position the pointer in the artwork next to the lemon. Drag the tool to draw a five-pointed star that's about the same size as the lemon.

The star is painted with the paint attributes of the last selected object (in this case, the lemon).

2 With the star still selected, click a color swatch in the Swatches palette to paint the star with that color. (We selected the Lime Green swatch in the Swatches palette.) Leave the stroke set to None.

Now you'll distort the star using the Twist distort filter. This filter twists objects around their centers.

Twist distortion can be applied to objects two ways. Applying it as a filter permanently distorts the object. Applying it as an effect maintains the original shape and lets you remove or edit the effect at any time using the Appearance palette. You will be use both methods in the following exercise. Read more about using effects in Lesson 10, "*Applying Apperance Attributes, Styles and Effects.*"

3 Choose Filter > Distort > Twist. Type in the value of **35°** in the Twist dialog box and click OK.

Now you'll draw another star that's centered on top of the first star.

4 With the star selected, choose Window > Attributes to display the Attributes palette. Then click the Show Center button (▣) to display the star's center point.

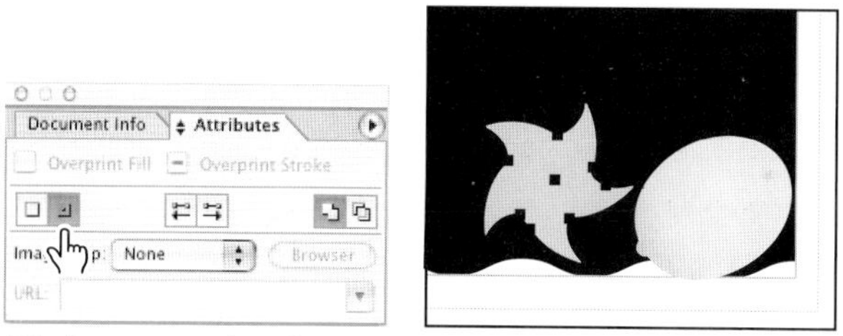

Display center point of star.

5 Select the Star tool again, hold down Alt (Windows) or Option (Mac OS), and drag from the center point to draw another star over the center of the first one. Before you release the mouse button, drag the star in an arc to rotate it so the points appear between the points of the star behind it. Keep the star selected.

6 In the Attributes palette, click the Show Center button (▫) to display the second star's center point.

7 Click the Color tab behind the Attributes palette to bring the Color palette to the front, or choose Window > Color. Click the White color box at the right end of the color bar to paint the star's fill white. Then click the Stroke box to select the star's stroke, and click a color either in the color bar or in the Swatches palette to paint the star's stroke. (We selected the Yellow color swatch.)

Now you'll distort the frontmost star using the Pucker & Bloat effect. This effect distorts objects inward and outward from their anchor points.

8 With the white star selected, choose Effect > Distort & Transform > Pucker & Bloat.

Applying it as an effect maintains the original shape and lets you remove or edit the effect at any time.

9 In the Pucker & Bloat dialog box, select the Preview option, and drag the slider to distort the star (we selected 50%). Click OK.

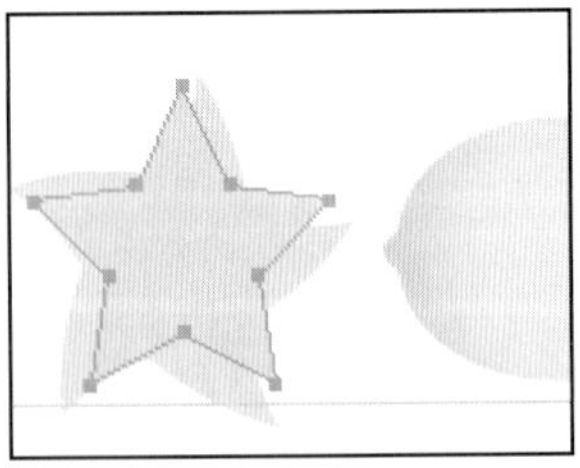
Draw star shape.

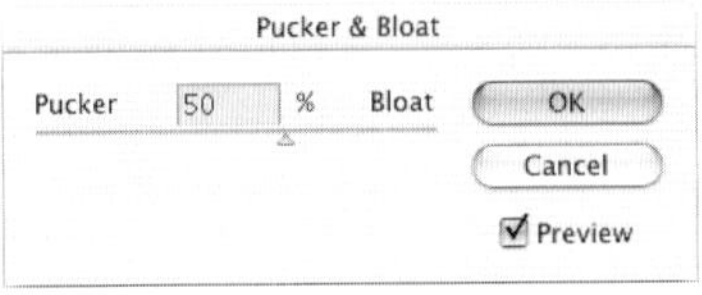

Apply Pucker & Bloat effect.

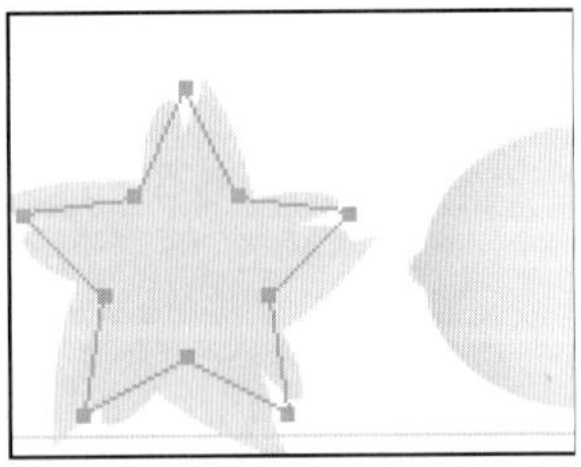
Result.

10 Keep the artwork selected, and choose File > Save.

Shearing objects

Now you'll complete the flower with an orange center, scale it, and shear it. Shearing an object slants, or skews, the sides of the object along the axis you specify, keeping opposite sides parallel and making the object nonsymmetrical.

1 Click the Appearance tab behind the Info palette to bring the Appearance palette to the front of its group. (If the Appearance palette isn't visible on-screen, choose Window > Appearance to display it.)

The Appearance palette displays the fill, stroke, effects, and transparency of the last object created. By default the next shape you create will retain all these attributes. Because the next shape will have different attributes, you will change this default setting.

2 Click the New Art Maintains Appearance button at the bottom of the Appearance palette.

The next shape will maintain only the stroke and fill attributes of the last shape.

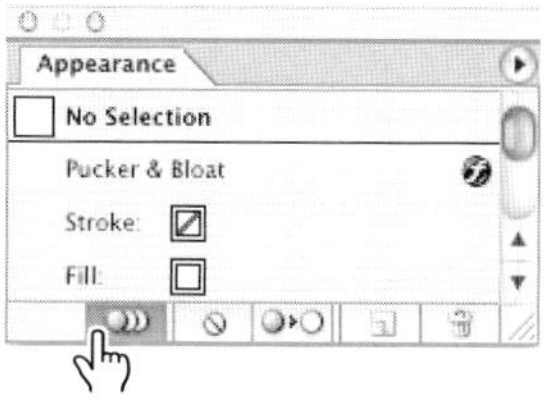

Clicking New Art Maintains Appearance button.

3 Select the Ellipse tool (◯) from the same group as the Star tool (☆) in the toolbox.

4 With the stars still selected and their center points visible, press Alt (Windows) or Option (Mac OS), position the Ellipse tool's crosshairs over the stars' center points, and drag to draw an oval from the center.

5 Click the Fill box in the toolbox to select the object's fill. In the Swatches palette, click the Orange swatch to paint the oval a light orange color.

6 In the Color palette, drag the None icon and drop it on the Stroke box to remove the stroke.

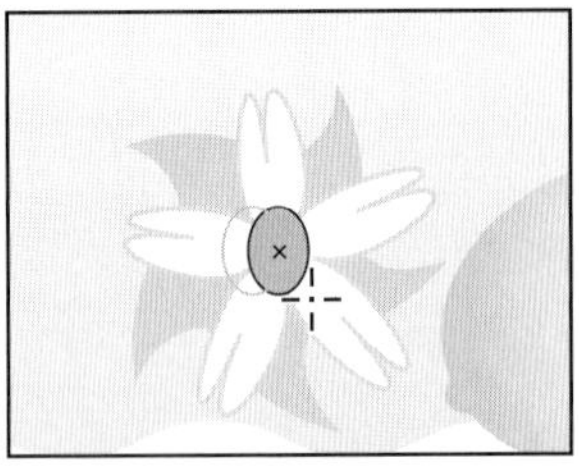

Draw oval shape and paint fill.

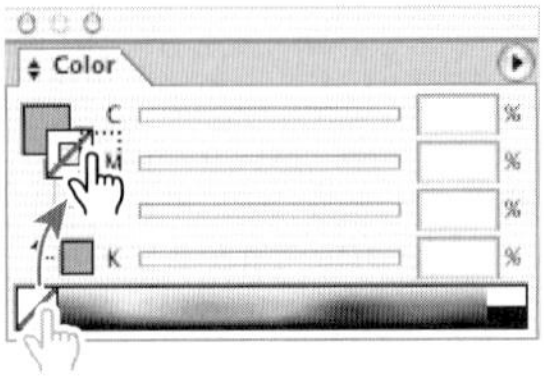

Drag and drop None button over Stroke box.

Now, you'll group and then shear the flower.

7 Select the Selection tool (), Shift-click to select the three parts of the flower, and choose Object > Group to group them together.

8 In the Transform palette, type **10°** (10 degrees) in the Shear text box, and press Enter or Return to apply the shearing effect on the flower.

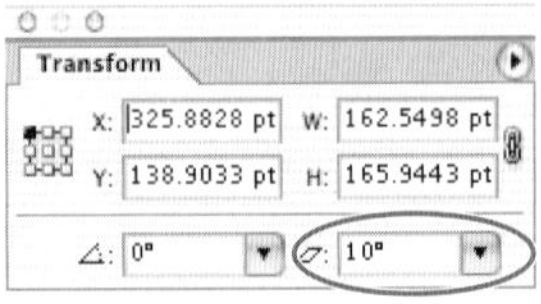

Enter 10° shear angle.

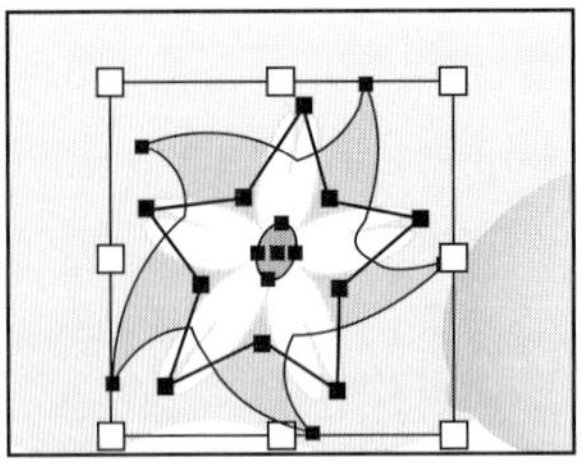

Result

9 Type **0.75 in** (inches) in the W text box and **0.75 in** (inches) in the H text box to scale the flower down to three-quarters of an inch.

Although the default unit of measure is set to points, when you type inches (or in) in the text boxes, Illustrator calculates the equivalent measurement in points.

You can have Illustrator convert unit values and perform mathematical operations in any text box that accepts numeric values. To automatically multiply or divide the size of an object by a number you specify, enter an asterisk (*) or a slash (/) and a number after the value in either the W or the H text box, or in both text boxes, and press Enter or Return to scale the object. For example, enter /2 after the values in the W and H text boxes to scale the object by 50%.

10 Using the Selection tool, drag the flower next to the lemon in the bottom right corner of the page.

11 Choose Select > Deselect to deselect the artwork, and then choose File > Save.

You've completed the letterhead artwork. Keep the file open so that you can use its artwork later in the lesson.

Positioning objects precisely

You can use the Transform palette to move objects to exact coordinates on the x and y axes of the page and to control the position of objects in relation to the trim edge.

To learn how to produce crop marks for the trim edge, see "Setting Marks and Bleeds Options" in online Help.

You'll create the envelope by first pasting a copy of the logo into the envelope artwork, and then specifying the exact coordinates on the envelope where the pasted logo will go.

1 Double-click the Hand tool ( ) in the toolbox to fit the artwork in the window.

2 Using the Selection tool ( ), draw a marquee around the logo so that all the objects in it are selected.

3 Choose Edit > Copy to copy the logo to the Clipboard.

Now you'll open the start file for the envelope artwork.

4 Choose File > Open to open the L8start2.ai file in the Lesson08 folder, located inside the Lessons folder within the AICIB folder on your hard drive.

5 Choose File > Save As, name the file **Envelope.ai**, and select the Lesson08 folder. Leave the type of file format set to Adobe Illustrator® Document, and click Save. In the Illustrator Options dialog box, accept the default settings by clicking OK.

6 Choose Edit > Paste.

You'll move the pasted logo to within 1/4-inch of the top left corner of the envelope by specifying the x and y coordinates in relation to the ruler origin. The ruler origin is the point where 0 appears on each ruler. We changed the ruler origin in this file to begin at the top left corner of the envelope, and the ruler units to inches.

For more information, see "Using Rulers" in online Help.

7 In the Transform palette, click the top left reference point and then type **0.25 in** (18 pt) in the X text box and **–0.25 in** (a negative coordinate) in the Y text box. Press Enter or Return to apply the last setting you typed.

Copy the logo from the letterhead.

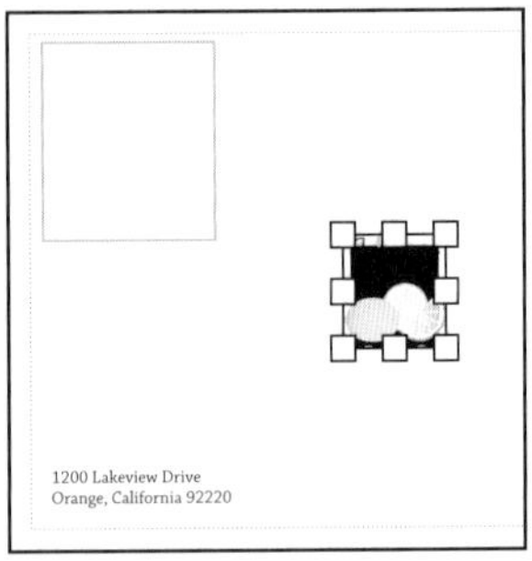

Paste into the envelope.

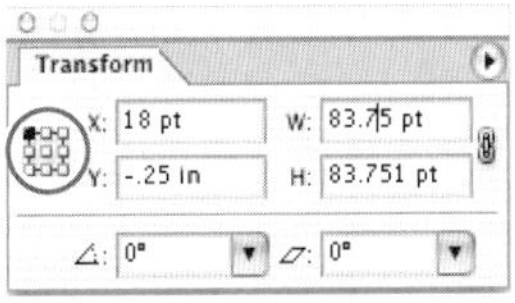

Select top left reference point and enter x and y coordinates.

***Note:** You can also move selected objects to exact x and y coordinates by choosing Object > Transform > Move and entering coordinates in the Move dialog box.*

8 With the logo still selected, drag the bottom right corner of the bounding box to scale the logo and make it fit within the blue square guideline.

9 Click away from the artwork to deselect it, and then choose File > Save.

Reflecting objects

Objects are reflected by flipping them across an invisible vertical or horizontal axis. Copying objects while reflecting creates a mirror image of the objects. Similar to scaling and rotating, in reflecting you either designate the point of origin from which an object will reflect or use the object's center point by default.

Now you'll use the Reflect tool to make a mirror image of the orange slice in the logo.

1 Use the Selection tool (↖) to select the orange slice in the logo.

2 Zoom in, if necessary.

3 Select the Reflect tool nested with the Rotate tool in the toolbox, hold down Alt (Windows) or Option (Mac OS), and click the right edge of the orange slice.

Clicking the edge of the object designates the point of origin. Holding down Alt/Option as you click displays the Reflect dialog box.

4 In the Reflect dialog box, make sure that the Vertical option is selected and **90°** is entered in the Angle text box. Then click Copy (don't click OK).

Note: *You can also use the Transform palette to reflect selected objects by choosing Flip Horizontal or Flip Vertical from the palette menu.*

5 Click the Selection tool to select the bounding box of the new orange slice and move the object down below the logo, Shift-dragging the selection to constrain the move. Then Shift-drag the bounding box to enlarge the orange slice (as shown in the illustration).

Move reflected copy down and rescale it.

Changing the perspective

Now you'll use the Free Transform tool to change the perspective of the orange slice.

1 With the orange slice selected, select the Free Transform tool () in the toolbox.

2 Position the double-headed arrow pointer over the bottom left corner of the object's bounding box, and select the bottom left corner handle (don't release the mouse button). Holding down Shift+Alt+Ctrl (Windows) or Shift+Option+Command (Mac OS), slowly drag upward to change the perspective of the object.

Holding down Shift as you drag scales an object proportionally, holding down Alt/Option scales an object from its center point, and holding down Ctrl/Command as you drag distorts an object from the anchor point or bounding box handle that you're dragging.

3 Select the Group Selection tool () in the toolbox, and click away from the orange slice to deselect it. Then Shift-click to select the segments of the orange slice and its rind. (Don't select the inner white pith of the rind.)

4 In the Swatches palette, select the Pale Orange gradient swatch to paint the selected objects with a lighter gradient.

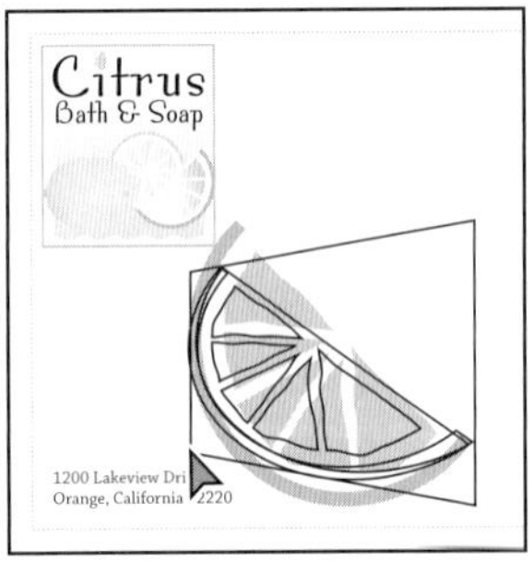

Change perspective.

Select colored parts.

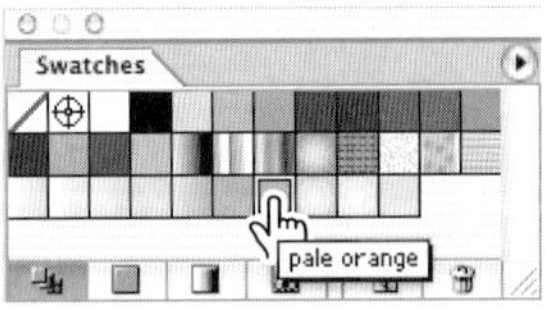

Paint with lighter gradient.

5 Choose Select > Deselect.

6 Choose File > Save. You can either minimize the file and leave it open on your desktop, or close the file. You'll use it later in this lesson.

Using the Free Transform tool

The Free Transform tool is a multipurpose tool that, besides letting you change the perspective of an object, combines the functions of scaling, shearing, reflecting, and rotating.

Now you'll use the Free Transform tool to transform objects that you copy from the logo into a business card.

1 Choose File > Open, and open the L8start3.ai file in the Lesson08 folder, located inside the Lessons folder within the AICIB folder on your hard drive.

2 Choose File > Save As, name the file **Buscards.ai**, and select the Lesson08 folder. Leave the type of file format set to Adobe Illustrator® Document, and click Save. In the Illustrator Options dialog box, accept the default settings by clicking OK.

3 Click the Navigator tab behind the Info palette to bring the Navigator palette to the front of its group. (If the Navigator palette isn't visible on-screen, choose Window > Navigator to display it.) In the Navigator palette, click the Zoom In button (⛰) a few times to zoom to 200%, and then move the red view box over the top left corner of the artwork.

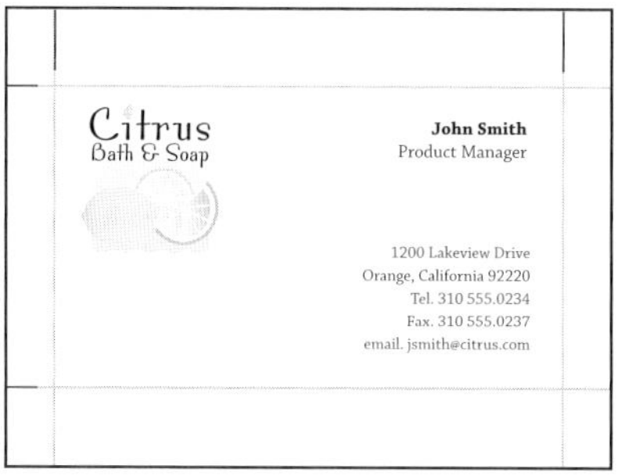

4 Choose the Selection tool (↖), and click to select the lime slice in the logo. Then, Alt-drag (Windows) or Option-drag (Mac OS) to make a copy of the object. Position the new lime slice below and slightly to the right of the logo.

Now you'll use the Free Transform tool to scale, distort, and rotate the new lime slice.

5 With the lime slice still selected, select the Free Transform tool( ) in the toolbox. Holding down Shift+Alt (Windows) or Shift+Option (Mac OS), drag the bottom right corner down to scale the object from its center and make the lime slice bigger.

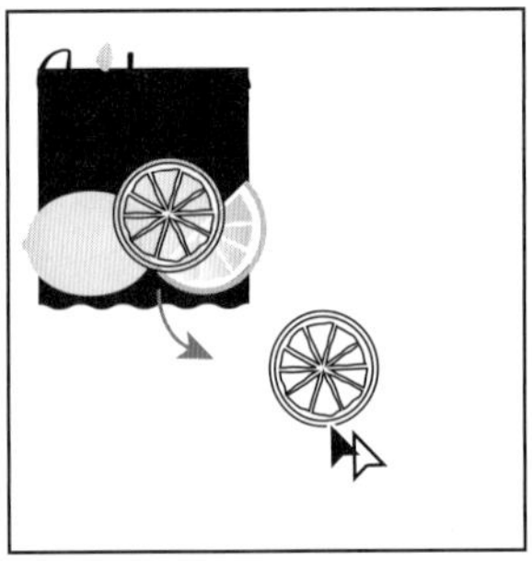

Make copy of lime slice.

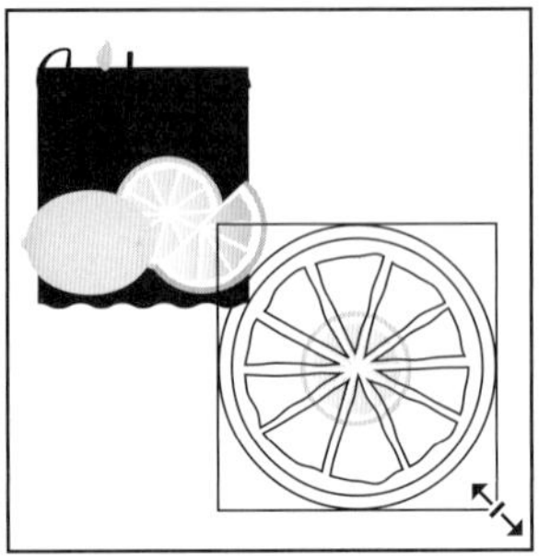

Use Free Transform tool to scale object.

Although you can scale objects using the Selection tool, scaling with the Free Transform tool lets you perform other transformations without switching tools.

6 To distort the lime slice using the Free Transform tool, select the bottom right corner of the object's bounding box, but don't release the mouse button. Begin dragging, and then hold down Ctrl (Windows) or Command (Mac OS) and slowly drag toward the opposite corner of the object.

(You can use the Free Transform tool to shear an object by dragging a side handle rather than a corner handle of the bounding box.)

7 To slightly rotate the lime slice, position the Free Transform tool just outside the bottom right corner of the object's bounding box until you see the rotate pointer, and then drag to rotate the object.

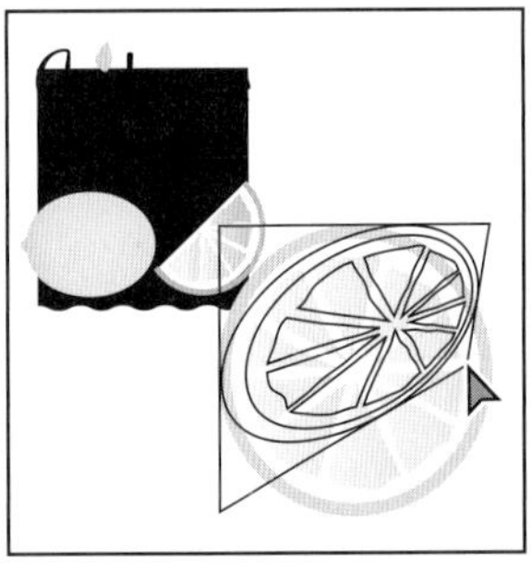

Distort object using Free Transform tool.

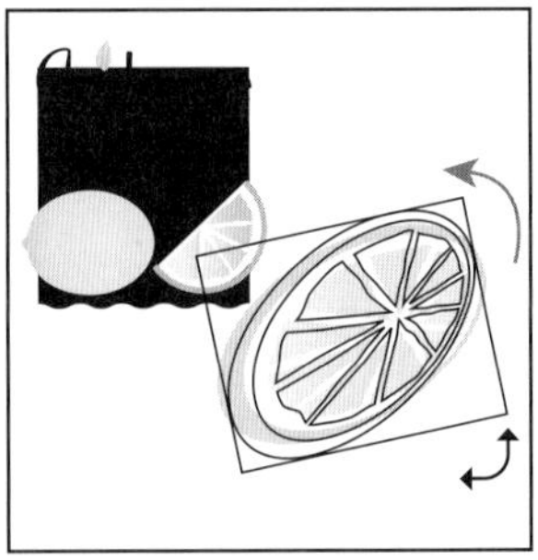

Rotate object using Free Transform tool.

8 With the lime slice selected, select the Group Selection tool (⁺) in the toolbox and Shift-click the inner white pith of the rind to deselect it. In the Swatches palette, select the Pale Green gradient swatch to paint the lime slice with a lighter gradient.

9 Select the Selection tool ( ), and drag a marquee to select the entire slice (including the inner white pith of the rind). Then choose Object > Arrange > Send to Back, and move the slice to tuck it underneath the logo.

Now you'll explore a slightly different way of distorting objects. Free Distort lets you distort a selection by moving any of its four corner points. It can be used either as a filter to apply a permanent change or as an effect to apply a change that can be removed.

10 With the lime slice still selected, choose Filter > Distort > Free Distort.

***Note:** Choose the top Filter > Distort command. The bottom Filter > Distort commands work only on bitmap images).*

11 Drag one or more of the handles to distort the selection. Click OK.

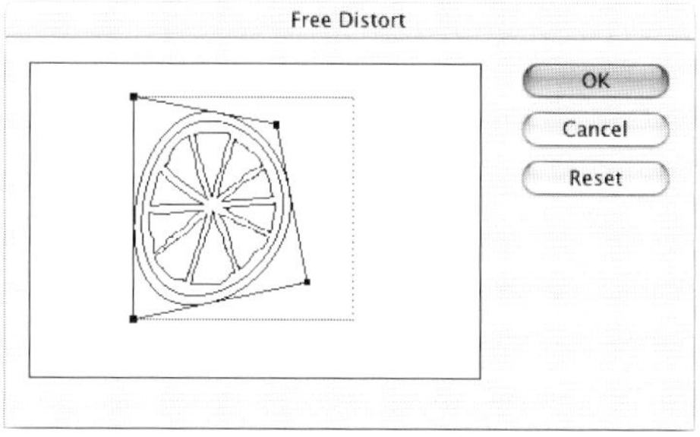

Previewing a free distortion.

12 Click outside of the artwork to deselect it, and choose File > Save.

Making multiple transformations

Now you'll create multiple copies of the business card and replicate the symbol instances in a few easy steps.

1 Double-click the Hand tool ( ) in the toolbox to zoom out and fit the artwork in the window.

2 Choose Select > All to select all the objects on the business card.

3 Choose Object > Transform > Transform Each.

The Move options in the Transform Each dialog box let you move objects in a specified or random direction. Now you'll move a copy of the selected objects down 2 inches from the original objects.

4 In the Transform Each dialog box, enter **–2 in** in the Move Vertical text box, leave the other settings as they are, and click Copy (don't click OK).

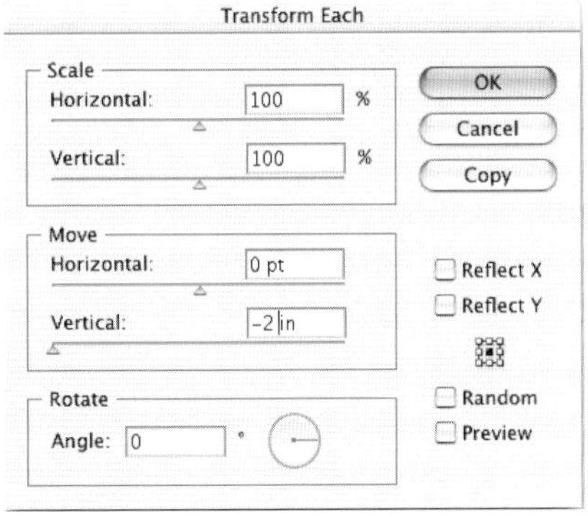

Move object down 2 inches and copy it.

5 Choose Object > Transform > Transform Again to create a third copy.

Now you'll use the keyboard shortcut to repeat the transformations.

6 Press Ctrl+D (Windows) or Command+D (Mac OS) twice to transform two additional times, creating a total of five cards in the column.

Note: *You can also apply multiple transformations as an effect, including scaling, moving, rotating, and reflecting an object. After selecting the objects, choose Effect > Distort & Transform > Transform. The dialog box looks the same as the Transform Each dialog box. Transforming as an effect has the advantage of letting you change or remove the transformation at any time.*

Next you'll use some shortcuts to make a copy of the column.

7 Press Ctrl+A (Windows) or Command+A (Mac OS) to select everything on the five business cards, and right-click (Windows) or Ctrl-click (Mac OS) in the window to display a shortcut menu. Choose Transform > Transform Each from the shortcut menu.

8 This time in the Transform Each dialog box, enter **3.5 in** in the Move Horizontal text box and **0 in** in the Move Vertical text box. Leave the other settings as they are, and click Copy (don't click OK).

9 To clear the window so that you can view the finished artwork, press Ctrl (Windows) or Command (Mac OS) and click outside the artwork to deselect it. Then choose View > Guides > Hide Guides to hide the blue guidelines, and press Tab to close the toolbox and palettes.

Pressing Tab toggles between hiding and showing the toolbox and all of the palettes. Pressing Shift+Tab alternately hides or shows only the palettes.

10 Choose File > Save and File > Close.

Exploring on your own

You can update text, graph data, linked files, or graphics dynamically and change them in your artwork using certain variables. For example, you can create a series of business cards in which individual names and titles change, but all other information remains constant.

The Variables feature lets designers create highly formatted graphics as templates (called data-driven graphics), and then collaborate with developers to control the links between a template and its content. For more complex applications, you could, for example, produce 500 different Web banners based on the same template. In the past, you had to manually fill in the template with data (images, text, and so on). With data-driven graphics, however, you can use a script referencing a database to speedily generate the Web banners for you.

In Illustrator, you can turn any piece of artwork into a template for data-driven graphics. All you need to do is define which objects on the artboard are dynamic (changeable) using variables. In addition, you can create different sets of variable data to easily view what your template will look like when it is rendered.

Making text dynamic

To get an idea of the power and usefulness of the Variables feature, you can try out this procedure using the business card artwork in the lesson.

1 Choose File > Open, and open the L8start3.ai file in the Lesson08 folder, located inside the Lessons folder within the AICIB folder on your hard drive.

2 Choose File > Save As, name the file **Buscard2.ai**, and select the Lesson08 folder. Leave the type of file format set to Adobe Illustrator® Document, and click Save. In the Illustrator Options dialog box, accept the default settings by clicking OK.

3 Using the Zoom tool, zoom in on the business card artwork in the upper left corner.

4 Choose Window > Variables to display the Variables palette.

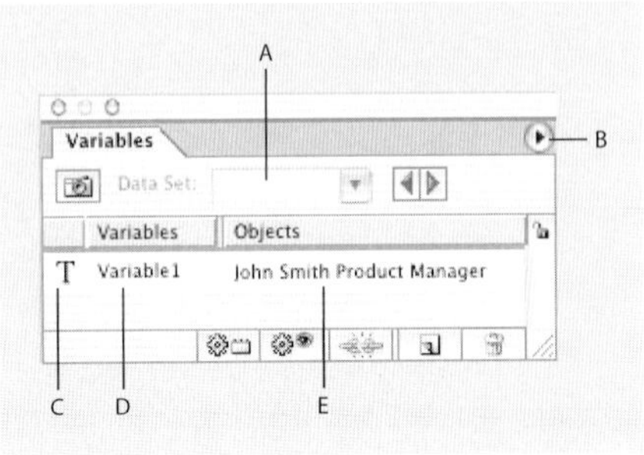

A. Data set. B. Palette menu. C. Variable type. D. Variable name. E. Name of bound object.

You'll create some text variables so that you can change the name and title on the business cards. This technique lets you create a series of business cards with a name and title that you can easily modify for other employees. You could also create variables for the address, for example, so that you can change the address for different branch offices.

5 Using the Selection tool, in the artwork select the name and title "John Smith, Product Manager."

6 At the bottom of the Variables palette, click the Make Text Dynamic button. A new variable, named Variable1, appears in the palette.

The (T) icon appears to the left of the variable, indicating that it's a text string. The Objects column lists the object to which the variable is bounded—in this case, the text you selected in step 5.

7 Double-click the variable, and in the Variable Options dialog box name it name_title. The type already is set to Text String. Click OK.

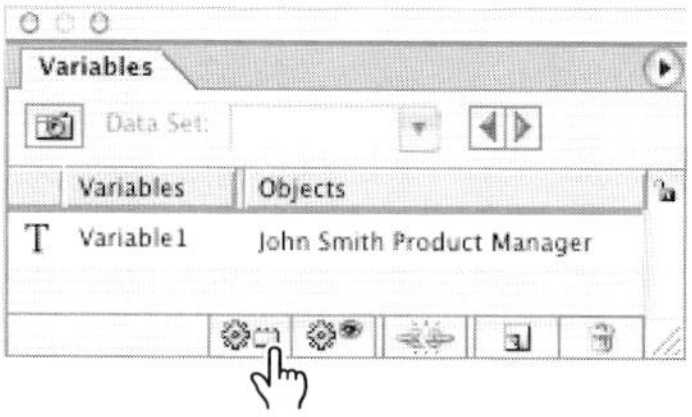

Make Text Dynamic button.

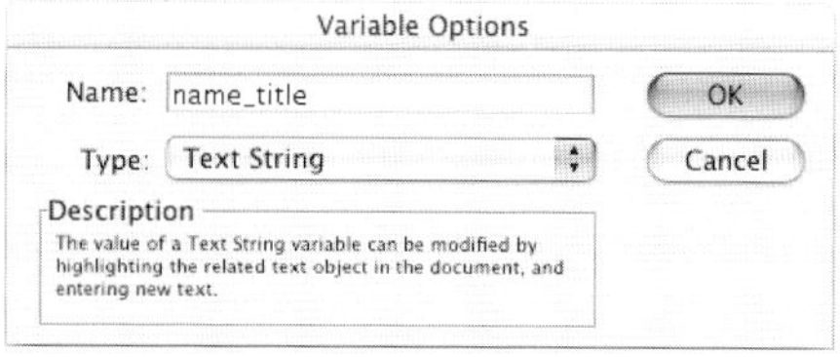

Variable Options dialog box.

You can create four types of variables in Illustrator: Graph Data, Linked File, Text String, and Visibility. A variable's type indicates which object attributes are changeable. For example, you can use a Visibility variable to show or hide any object in your template. The Graph Data, Linked File, and Text String variables make those respective objects dynamic, while the Visibility variable makes any object's visibility dynamic.

8 In your artwork, make sure that the text "John Smith, Product Manager" is still selected.

9 In the Variables palette, click the Capture Data Set button in the upper left of the palette to capture the information. Data Set 1 appears in the Data Set pop-up menu as your first variable.

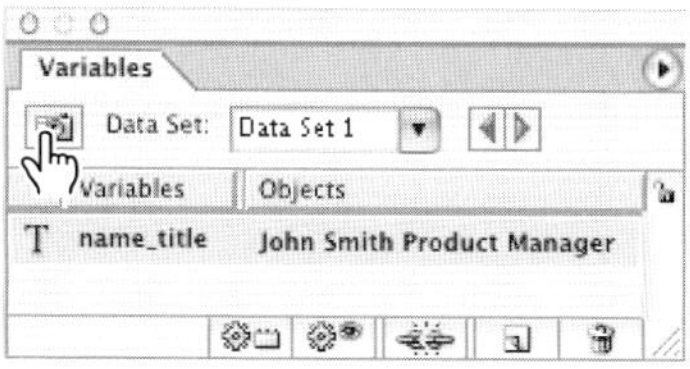

Capture Data Set button and Data Set 1 in Variables palette.

A data set is a collection of variables and associated data. When you create a data set, you capture a snapshot of the dynamic data that is currently displayed on the artboard. You can switch between data sets to upload different data into your template.

Now you'll revise the text and create another data set.

10 Select the Type tool in the toolbox. In the artwork, drag to select the text "John Smith, Product Manager." Then type **Maggie Riley, Marketing Manager** to replace the text.

11 Notice that the Data Set 1 variable now appears in italics in the Variables palette. The italics indicate that the variable has been edited. You can modify a data set after you create it, as you'll do now.

12 In the Variables palette, click the Capture Data Set button in the upper left of the palette to capture the information. Data Set 2 appears in the pop-up menu as the current variable.

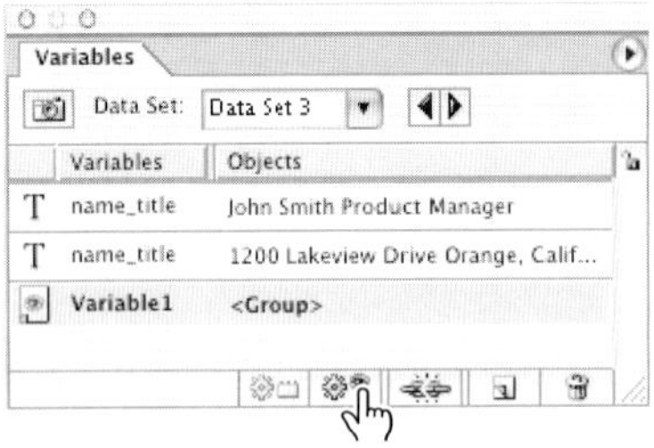

Capturing new data set.

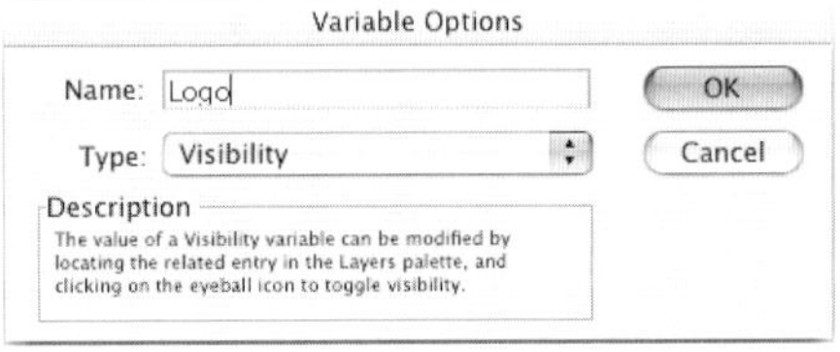

Data Set 2.

Creating variables is a two-step process. First you define the variable, and then you bind it to an object attribute to make the object variable. The type of object and type of variable determine what attributes of the object can change. You can bind a Visibility variable to any object to make the object's state of visibility dynamic. If the object is text, a linked image, or a graph, you can also make the object's content dynamic.

13 To create another variable for the address, click in a blank area of the Variables palette to deselect the variable you just created. If you want to create a new variable that matches the type of the selected object, make sure that no variable is selected in the Variables palette.

14 Use the Selection tool (↖) to select the address text.

15 Click the Make Text Dynamic button at the bottom of the Variables palette. A text string variable with the first line of the address as the object appears in the palette. You can double-click the variable and rename it. (We renamed it address.)

16 Using the Type tool (T), revise the telephone number and e-mail address.

(We used 310 555.5678 and mriley@citrus.com.)

17 Click the Capture Data Set button at the top left of the Variables palette to capture this information. You've created Data Set 3.

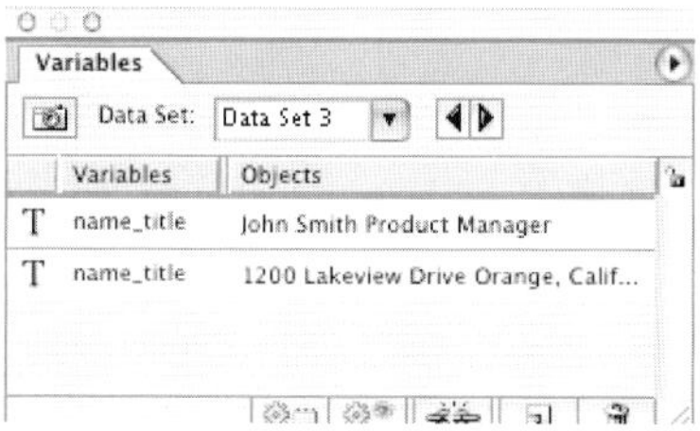

Data Set 3.

18 To view the variables you just created, click the Next Data Set button (▸) to the right of the Data Set menu to scroll through the variables.

Notice that Data Set 2 lists the wrong telephone number and e-mail address for Maggie Riley. You can easily delete data sets.

19 With Data Set 2 selected in the Variables palette, choose Delete Data Set from the Variables palette menu, and click Yes at the alert message.

You could create a series of data sets for business card information, and then use a batch process to update all or part of the information—such as the names and titles, branch office addresses, and telephone numbers.

20 Choose File > Save.

Making artwork dynamic

You can also use variables to create artwork for clients that contains different iterations of a design. Now you'll change the visibility of some elements in the artwork.

1 Click in a blank area of the Variables palette to deselect the variable you just created.

2 Choose Window > Layers to display the Layers palette. You use the Layers palette to hide or show artwork.

3 Using the Selection tool, drag a marquee to select just the logo in the artwork. If you accidentally select the business card border or text, Shift-click to deselect those objects.

You can also use the Layers palette to select all the objects in a layer or group.

4 Choose Object > Group to group the selected artwork so that it's easier to work with.

5 Expand the Layers palette and Layer1 so that you can see its contents. Notice that the <Group> sublayer is selected, as indicated by the selection indicator to the right of the layer name.

You'll create a variable to show or hide the selection. You can use the Visibility variable to selectively hide or show any object, group, or layer in your artwork. You can also create graph data, linked file, and text string variables to make your graphs, linked images, or text dynamic.

6 In the Variables palette, click the Make Visibility Dynamic button. A new variable, titled Variable1 and with its object listed as <Group>, appears in the palette.

7 Double-click Variable1 to display the Variable Options dialog box. Rename the variable by typing **Logo**. Its type already is set to Visibility because you clicked the Make Visibility Dynamic button. Click OK to rename Variable1 as Logo in the Variables palette.

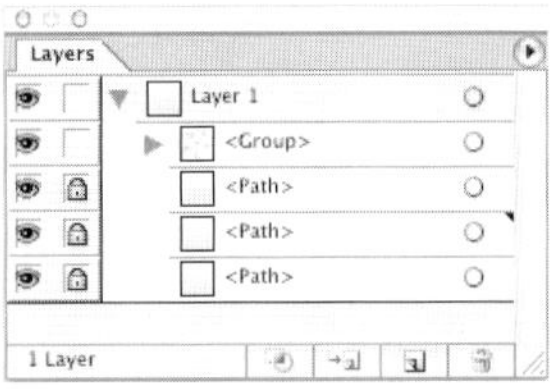

Select object.

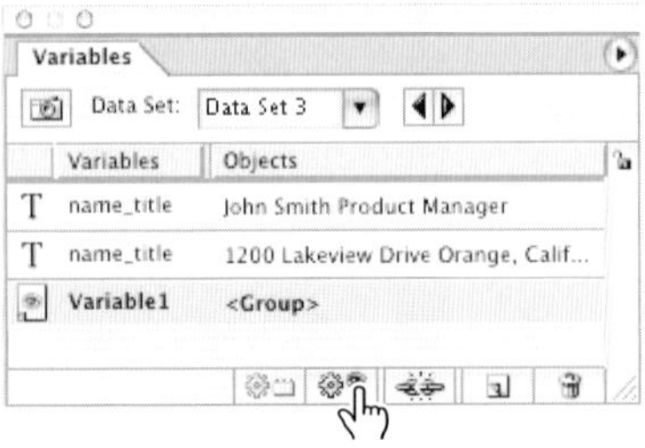

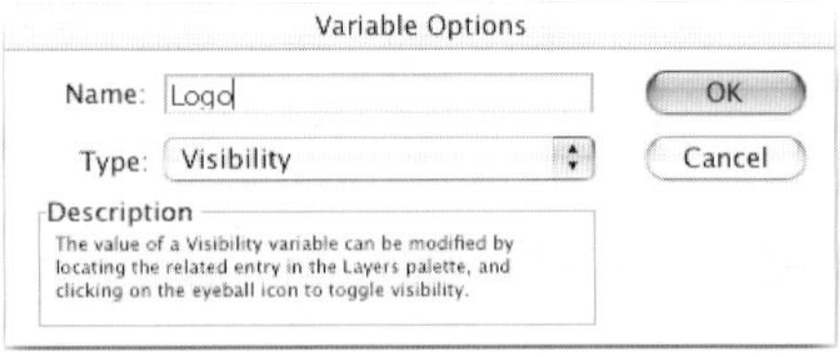

Click Make Visibility Dynamic button. *Name variable.*

Now you'll hide the logo artwork.

8 In the Layers palette, click the eye icon to the left of the selected <Group> sublayer to hide the logo and its artwork.

9 In the Variables palette, notice that Data Set 3 now appears in italics, indicating that you have edited the data set.

10 Click the Capture Data Set button in the upper left of the palette to capture the information. Data Set 4 appears in the Data Set pop-up menu.

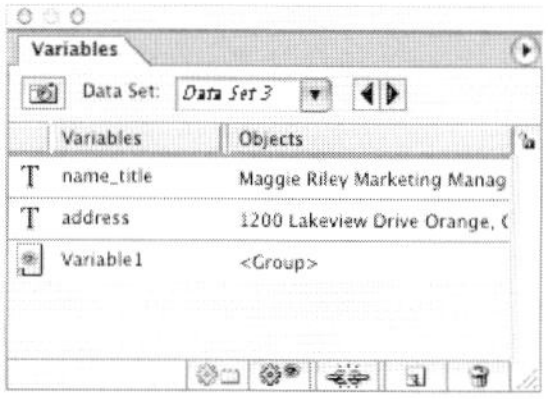

Lime sublayer selected in Layers palette.

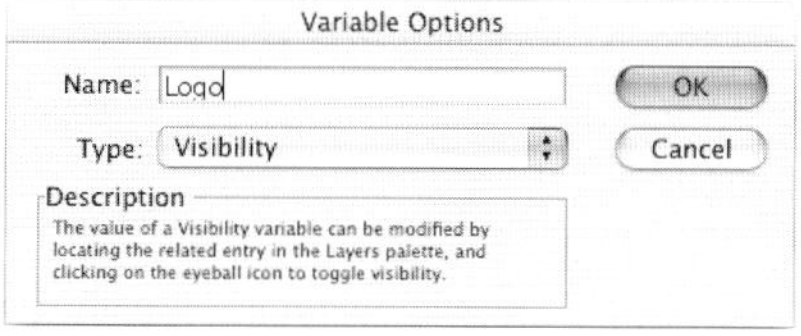

Editing data set.

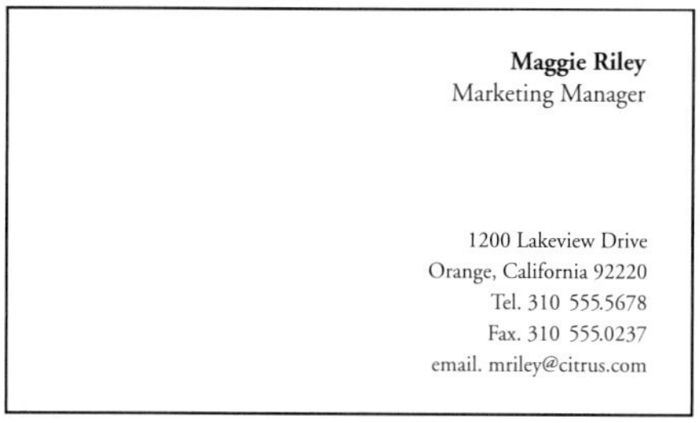

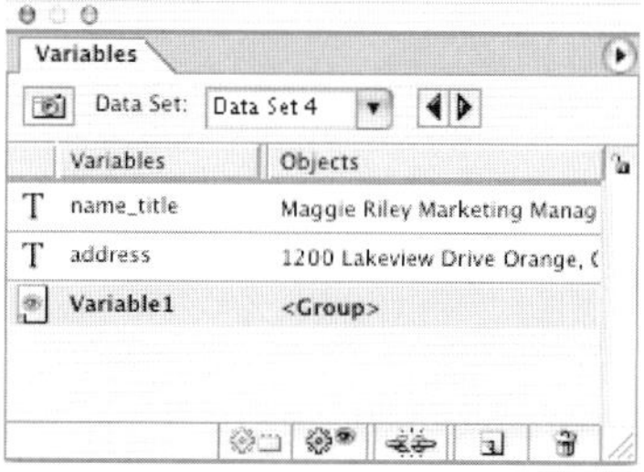

Data Set 3 and logo hidden in artwork.

11 To view the variables you just created, click the Next or Previous Data Set button to the right of the Data Set menu to scroll through the variables.

12 Choose File > Save. Then choose File > Close to close the file.

For more information on data-driven graphics and variables, see "Automating Tasks" in online Help.

Review questions

1 How can you select and manipulate individual objects in a group?

2 How do you resize an object? Explain how you determine the point from which the object resizes. How do you resize a group of objects proportionally?

3 What transformations can you make using the Transform palette?

4 What does the square diagram indicate in the Transform palette, and how will it affect your transformations?

5 What's an easy way to change perspective? List three other types of transformations you can perform with the Free Transform tool.

6 How do you create a variable? What are some uses for variables in your artwork?

Review answers

1 You can use the Group Selection tool () to select individual objects or subgroups of objects within a group and change them without affecting the rest of the group.

2 You can resize an object several ways: by selecting it and dragging handles on its bounding box, or by using the Scale tool, the Transform palette, or Object > Transform > Scale to specify exact dimensions. You can also scale by choosing Effect > Distort & Transform > Transform.

To determine the point of origin from which an object scales, select a reference point in the Transform palette or in the Transform Effect or Transform Each dialog box, or click in the artwork with the Scale tool. Holding down Alt (Windows) or Option (Mac OS) and dragging the bounding box or double-clicking the Scale tool will resize a selected object from its center point.

Shift-dragging a corner handle on the bounding box scales an object proportionally, as does specifying either a uniform scale value in the Scale dialog box or multiples of the dimensions in the Width and Height text boxes in the Transform palette.

3 You use the Transform palette for making the following transformations:

• Moving or strategically placing objects in your artwork (by specifying the x and y coordinates and the point of origin).

• Scaling (by specifying the width and height of selected objects).

• Rotating (by specifying the angle of rotation).

• Shearing (by specifying the angle of distortion).

• Reflecting (by flipping selected objects vertically or horizontally).

4 The square diagram in the Transform palette indicates the bounding box of the selected objects. Select a reference point in the square to indicate the point of origin from which the objects as a group will move, scale, rotate, shear, or reflect.

5 An easy way to change the perspective of selected objects is to select the Free Transform tool (), hold down Shift+Alt+Ctrl (Windows) or Shift+Option+Command (Mac OS), and drag a corner handle on the bounding box.

Other types of transformations you can do with the Free Transform tool are distorting, scaling, shearing, rotating, and reflecting.

6 To create a variable, you make a selection in your artwork, and then bind a variable to the object. The type of object and type of variable determine what attributes of the object can change. You can bind a Visibility variable to any object to make the object's visibility dynamic, or changeable. If the object is text, a linked image, or a graph, you can also make the object's content dynamic.

Using variables is a quick way to make artwork versions for a client that shows different iterations of the same design. You can also use variables to automate tedious design tasks, such as designing and updating business cards for hundreds of employees. You can use variables to update text, graph data, linked files, or graphics, and change them dynamically in your artwork.

Lesson 9

9 Working with Placement and Order of Objects

Using custom and ruler guides can help you produce quality artwork, such as logos, from scanned art. Combine object arrangement or painting order with transparency and masking options to create dramatic results that vary based on which shapes are in front or behind.

In this lesson you will learn how to do the following:

- Turn scanned artwork into a template.
- Use and create guides.
- Re-create a scanned logo and convert into vector art.
- Constrain objects.
- Clone objects.
- Rearrange object order.
- Integrate transparency with placement of objects.
- Create a clipping mask.

Getting started

In this lesson you'll digitally re-create a logo that is supplied to you as a low-resolution scan. This is a simple technique that can be applied to a multitude of projects including creating artwork form Photographs, or update your company's logo into a scalable vector form that can be used over and over again without degradation.

Before you begin, you'll restore the default preferences for Adobe Illustrator, and then open a file containing the final version of the finished logo to see what you are going to create.

1 To ensure that the tools and palettes function exactly as described in this lesson, delete or deactivate (by renaming) the Adobe Illustrator CS preferences file. See "Restoring default preferences" on page 2 in the Getting Started section.

2 Start Adobe Illustrator.

3 Choose File > Open to open the file named 09_logo_end.ai in the Lesson09 folder within the AICIB folder on your hard drive.

Recreate this logo digitally with the Pen tool.

If you like, choose View > Zoom Out to reduce the view of the finished artwork, adjust the window size, and leave it on your screen as you work. (Use the Hand tool ( ) to move the artwork where you want it in the window.) If you don't want to leave the image open, choose File > Close.

To begin working, you'll open an existing art file set up for the logo artwork.

4 Choose File > Open to open the 09_logo_start.ai file in the Lesson09 folder, located inside the Lessons folder within the AICIB folder on your hard drive.

This start file contains locked vector text for a fish supply chain, but not the artwork needed to complete the logo. Many times a client provides the only working logo that he or she has, and it's already printed–perhaps even on a napkin! With no digital information, you can recreate the client's logo with the Pen tool.

5 Choose File > Save As, name the file **vwlogo.ai**, and choose the Lesson09 folder in the Save In menu. Leave the type of file format set to Adobe Illustrator® Document, and click Save. In the Illustrator Options dialog box leave at the defaults and click OK.

Placing a scan as a template

Bitmapped files and files from other programs, such as Photoshop, can be placed into Illustrator to be used as a template that you can trace over.

6 Choose File > Place and locate the file named vw_logo.psd. In the Place dialog box, uncheck link, because you will delete the image later. Check Template, then click Place.

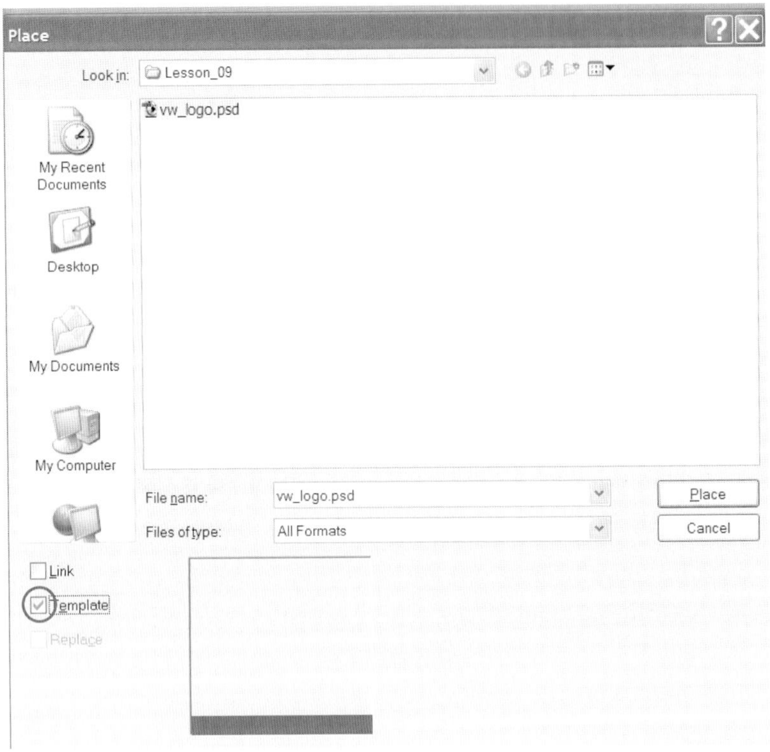

A scanned image placed as a template.

To see the result of Step 6, choose Window > Layers. The scanned artwork appears dimmed and is locked in placed on a layer underneath your working layer. A template icon appears to the left of the named layer.

7 Double-click on the template layer to view and change options. By checking Template when the logo was placed Illustrator created two layers, one locked template layer and an unlocked work layer for you to create artwork.

As a default Template layers are:

- Named with the name of the placed image.
- Visible at a dimmed view of 50%.
- Locked.
- Non-Printing.

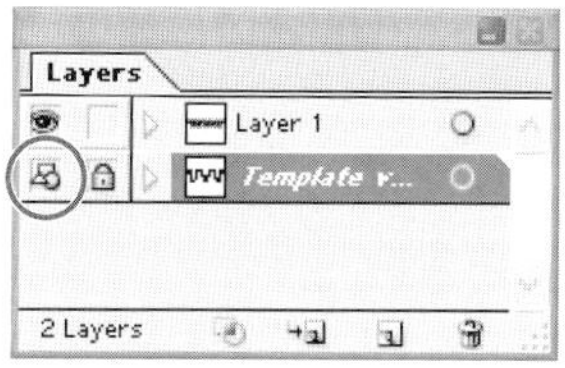

The logo placed as a template.

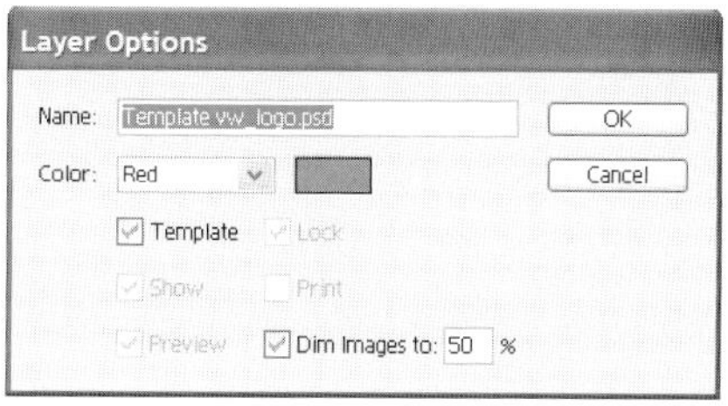

Uncheck Template for additional options.

8 Uncheck Template to change options. In this case you want to be able to reposition the placed logo. Lock automatically becomes unchecked when Template is unchecked. Click OK.

9 Using the Selection tool (↖) reposition the placed logo so that it is centered on top of the existing text.

10 Double-click on the Template layer again and re-check Template.

11 In the Layers palette click on Layer 1 to target it for the next part of the lesson.

Creating custom guides

You should be getting an idea of the direction that you are headed. Using Template layers is very much like the workflow you would use with artwork placed underneath a piece of tracing paper.

Before you start any project that requires some level of accuracy you should set up guides. In this lesson you will use standard ruler guides, as well as custom guides that you create yourself from pen paths.

1 First, make rulers visible choose View > Show Rulers or Ctrl+R (Windows) or Command+R (Mac OS).

Using and creating guides

There are two kinds of guides that can be used in Illustrator:

- *Standard ruler guides are non-printing straight lines that run vertically or horizontally on the page.*
- *Guide objects are created by converting an object into a guide. This can be helpful when aligning objects on a diagonal line, or if you need a shape to be a guide.*

New guides are locked in place. However, you can use View > Guides to unlock a guide to select, move, delete, or modify it, or revert from a custom guide back to a path.

2 Click and hold on the horizontal ruler. Drag a ruler guide from the ruler to the bottom (or baseline) of the placed artwork.

Note: *As a default, all guides are locked. To reposition a guide, uncheck View > Guides > Lock Guides.*

3 Drag another ruler guide to the top of the placed artwork.

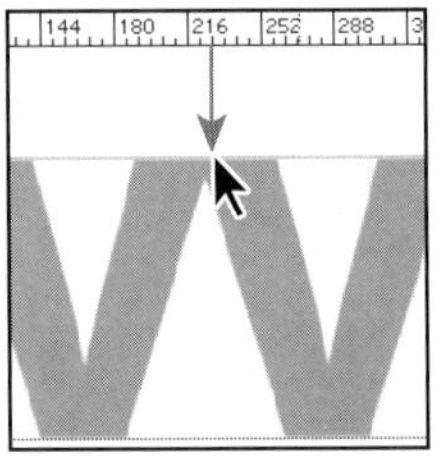

Horizontal guides are located at the top and bottom of the artwork.

4 Click on the vertical ruler and drag out, creating ruler guides to surround both sides of the logo.

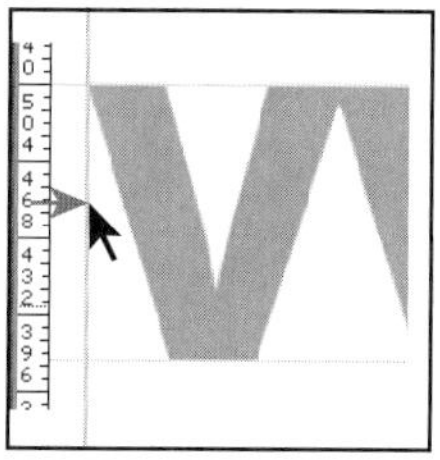

Create vertical guides using the vertical ruler.

***Note:** Holding down Alt (Windows) or Option (Mac OS) while clicking on the rulers and dragging will change the orientation of the guide. The horizontal ruler produces a vertical guide and the vertical ruler produces a horizontal guide.*

You'll now create pen paths that will be converted into custom guides. This makes it easier to keep angles consistent throughout the artwork. The paths that you are creating should overshoot the top and bottom so that you can make adjustments to them with less difficulty.

5 Select the Pen tool (✒) and click below the baseline of the first "v." Then click over the top of the "v" following the angle. If you did not get it exactly along the angle, switch to the Direct Selection tool (↖) and activate the end points individually to adjust them.

Follow the angle of the first "v" in the artwork.

6 Choose Select > Deselect to deactivate the path and create another path that follows the inside of the first "v."

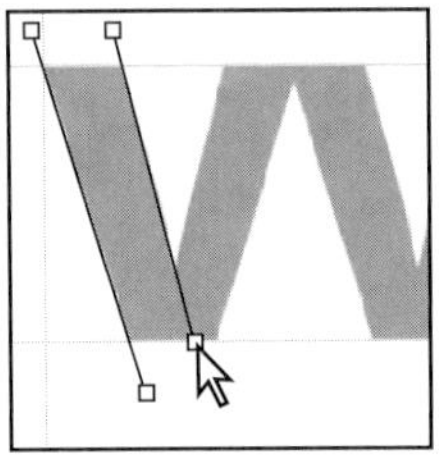

Use the Direct Selection tool to adjust the path.

7 Choose the Selection tool (), click on the first path created. Shift+click on the second path that you created to add it to the selection.

Instead of creating the other side of the "v" with the Pen tool and risking inaccuracies, you will use the Reflect tool.

8 To mirror these same angled paths, double-click on the Reflect tool (), which is hidden in the Rotate tool (). In the Reflect tool options, select Angle, type **90°**, and click Copy (not OK).

9 Using the Selection tool (), begin moving the reflected paths into position over the other side of the first "v." Hold down the Shift key to constrain the paths to a horizontal movement as you drag them.

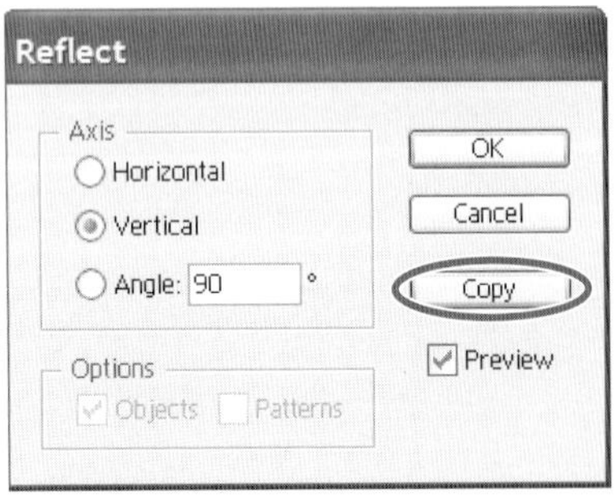

Set the Reflect options and Click Copy instead of OK.

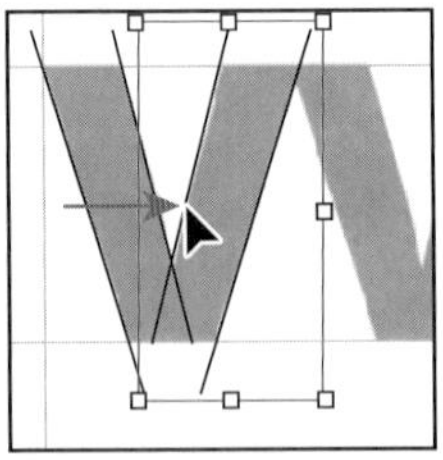

Reposition the reflected paths to align with the other side of the "v."

10 Instead of recreating paths for each "v" shape, you will clone them two times. Using the Selection tool, select all four paths, then hold down Alt (Windows) or Option (Mac OS) and drag the cloned copy over top of the next "v" shape in the artwork. If you hold down the Shift key after you start dragging the paths will be constrained to moving in a straight path. You must release the mouse before releasing the Alt/Option to have the clone to occur.

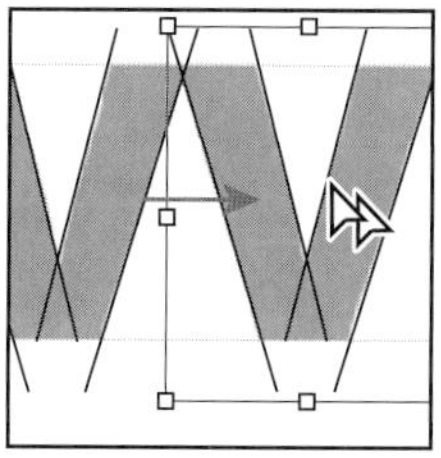

Look for a double arrow icon before you drag when cloning.

If the clone is not exactly on top of the second "v" shape, choose Edit > Undo and try again. It is important that you do this in one movement so that distance can be duplicated precisely in creating the final "v" shape.

11 Choose Object > Transform > Transform Again or Control+D (Windows) or Command+D (Mac OS) to duplicate the cloned paths the exact same distance that you moved the first cloned paths.

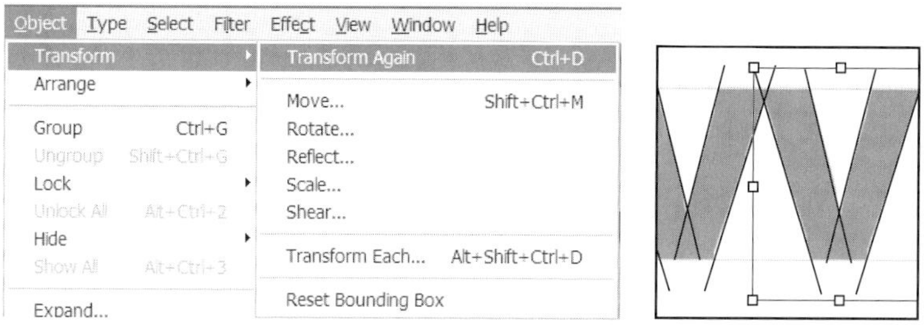

Transform Again repeats the clone and move distance.

12 If necessary, fine-tune any paths with the Direct Selection tool ( ). Then choose Select > Select All, Control+A (Windows) or Command+A (Mac OS). Since you only want to change the paths that you created in guides Shift+click on the text underneath the place logo (Victor Welling Fashions) to deselect it.

13 With the paths selected, choose View > Guides > Make Guides. You have created custom guides, which can be changed back into paths at any time using Choose View > Guides > Release Guides after unchecking View > Guides > Lock. Leave them as guides for the rest of this lesson.

Tips for editing guides

Choose View > Guides > Lock Guides to lock or unlock the guide. When a guide is locked, a check mark appears next to the Lock Guides command.

Select the guide you want to move, delete, or release, and do one of the following:

- *Move the guide by dragging or copying.*
- *Delete the guide by pressing Backspace or Del (Windows) or Delete (Mac OS), or by choosing Edit > Cut or Edit > Clear.*
- *Delete all guides at once by choosing View > Guides > Clear Guides.*
- *Release guide objects, turning them back into regular graphic objects, by choosing View > Guides > Release Guides.*
- *Hide Guides by choosing View > Guides > Hide Guides.*

Creating the vector logo

1 Before you start using your guides to create the pen path, click on the Fill swatch on the toolbar and change it to None. Click on the Stroke swatch on the toolbar and change it to black. Choose Window > Stroke and set it to **1 pt**. This will make it easier to see the path as you create it.

2 If your guides are unlocked Choose View > Guides > Lock Guides to keep all the guides in place.

3 Select the Pen tool ( ). and starting at the lower left base of the first "v" click and release, then continue from point to point using your guides for accuracy.

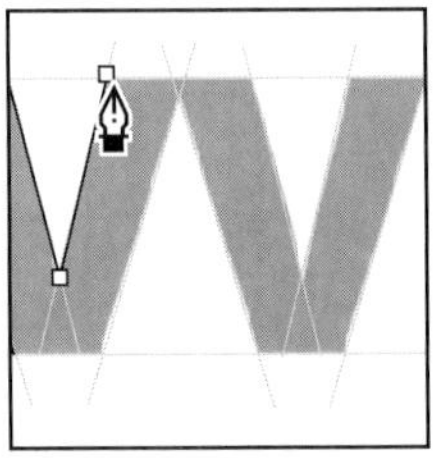

Use your guides to create the pen path.

5 When you come back to the starting point of your path, look for the close path (✎) symbol to appear, then click. Leave the path selected and press Shift+X to swap the fill and stroke colors, leaving you with a black fill and no stroke.

6 Next, turn off the visibility of the template layer by clicking on the visibility icon to the left of the named Template layer.

7 Choose View > Guides > Hide Guides.

You have now successfully change a scanned logo into digital artwork. Your last step is to delete the Template layer.

8 In the Layers palette click and drag the Template layer to the Trash icon in the lower right of the palette.

9 File > Save.

Applying the warp and pathfinder features

Now that you have recreated the main part of the logo you can take advantage of some of the other features in Adobe Illustrator like Warp and Pathfinder.

1 First, select the Rectangle tool (▭) and create a long thin rectangle that will serve as the first stripe across the logo.

2 Change the Fill to Black and the Stroke to None.

Create the first strip using the Rectangle tool.

3 Next, choose the Selection tool and Alt+drag (Windows) or Option+drag (Mac OS) the rectangle to create a clone of the original and the next stripe. Remember, you can hold down the Shift key AFTER you start dragging to constrain the movement to a straight path. Position the stripe correctly in one movement, if you can't get it in one movement the first time choose Edit > Undo or Ctrl+Z (Windows) or Command+Z (Mac OS) and try it again.

Use Alt/Option to clone the stripe in one movement.

4 Choose Object > Transform >Transform Again or Control+D (Windows) or Command+D (Mac OS)

This repeats the original clone and movement. Repeat the Transform again until you have covered the "vw" pen path with stripes.

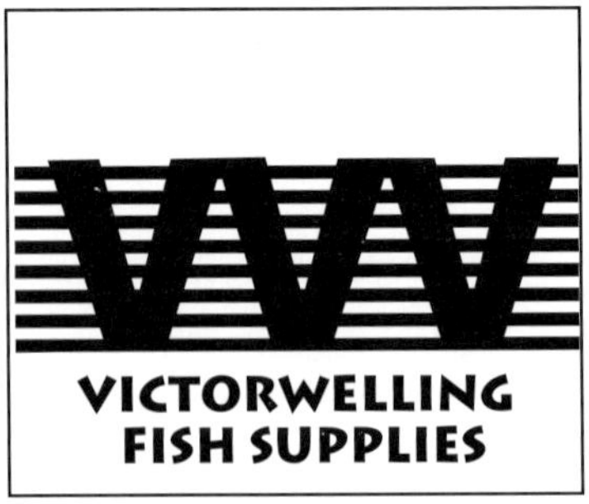

The logo with the completed stripes.

Applying the warp effect

1 Shift+click to select all of the strips and choose Effect > Warp > Flag. Check on the Preview checkbox and change the settings until you are satisfied. (We used the settings **of 100% for the Bend and 49% for the Horizontal Distortion.) Click OK.**

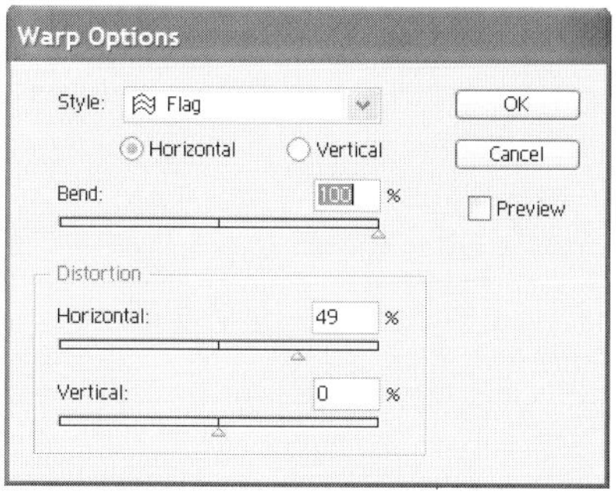

Since this is an Effect, you can open Window > Appearance and double-click on the Flag effect at any time to make changes or even drag it to the trash in the Appearance palette to delete it, restoring the rectangles back to their original shape.

Using the Pathfinder palette

2 With the stripes still selected Shift+click on the "vw" path, adding it to the selection.

3 Choose Window > Pathfinder to show the Pathfinder palette.

4 Click on the last button on the top row, Exclude.

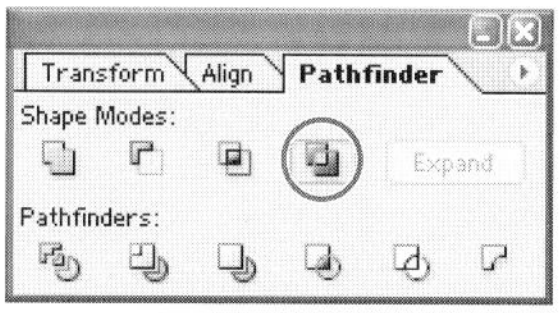

Exclude eliminates overlapping shape areas.

5 File > Save and File > Close.

Arrangement and object order

The Adobe Illustrator application stacks successively drawn objects, with the first object drawn on the bottom, much like a stack of papers on your desk. As you add items to the stack, they will cover the previously created objects underneath.

This arrangement, or stacking order is important not only because it affects the way items look when they overlap, but also because the stacking order plays a large part in the creation of masks and the way objects appear when transparency is applied.

In this part of the lesson you will change object order to create an illustration for a fish store.

1 Choose File > Open and open the file named 09_fish_end.ai in the Lesson09 folder within the AICIB folder on your hard drive.

If you like, choose View > Zoom Out to reduce the view of the finished artwork, adjust the window size, and leave it on your screen as you work. (Use the Hand tool (✋) to move the artwork where you want it in the window.) If you don't want to leave the image open, choose File > Close.

2 To begin working, you'll open an existing art file set up for the illustration. Choose File > Open to open the 09_fish_start.ai file located in the Lesson09 folder.

This start file contains the artwork needed to complete the illustration; however, you will need to rearrange it and add some objects.

3 Choose File > Save As, name the file **fishart.ai**, and select the Lesson09 folder.

4 Leave the Format option set to Adobe Illustrator Document, and click Save. In the Illustrator Options dialog box, leave all the settings at the defaults and click OK.

5 Using the Selection tool (↖), activate the plant in the lower left corner. Clone (duplicate) the plant by holding down Alt (Windows) or Option (Mac OS) and dragging the plant next to itself so that it is overlapping slightly. Press Control+D (Windows) or Command+D (Mac OS) or use Object > Transform > Repeat Transform to repeat the clone until you have six copies of the original plant.

6 Locate the Transparency palette under View > Transparency. Click on the second plant from the left and use the Blending mode pop-up menu in the Transparency palette to change the mode to Multiply. The second plant shows through to the original plant since it was created after the first, and is thereby on top of the original plant. Read more about blending modes in lesson 6, "Applying Transparency and Blending Modes."

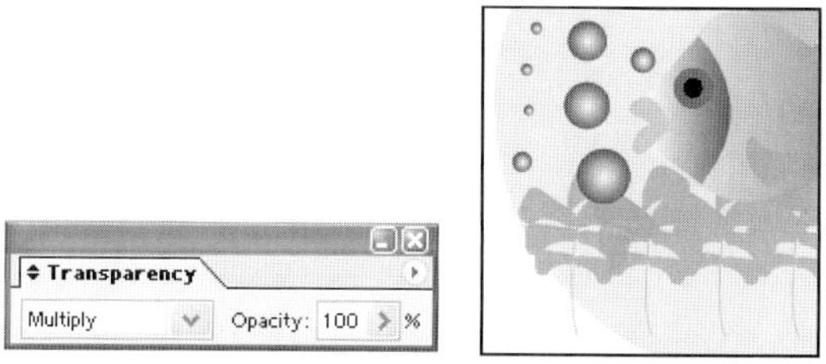

Change the blending mode to multiply to show through the plant.

7 Choose every other plant and change each to the Multiply mode.

8 Choose Select > Bubbles to activate a saved selection of the bubbles. Change the Blending mode for the bubbles to Screen and the Transparency to **50%**.

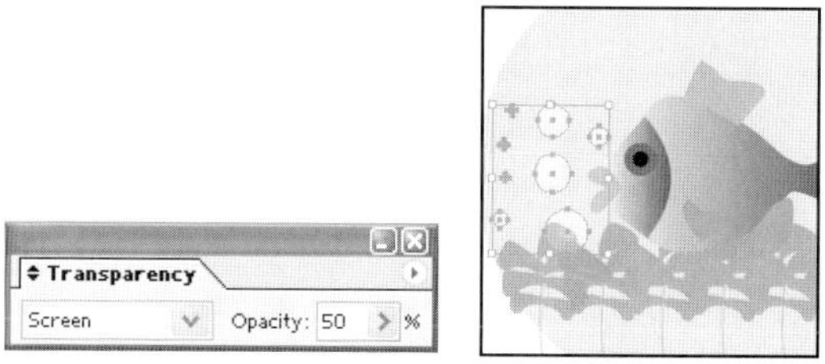

9 Create a rectangle that encompasses the fish and plant artwork. Exact size is not important. This will serve as the water in the illustration. Choose to fill the rectangle with the gradient named Midday Sky from the Swatches palette. With the rectangle still selected, change the blending mode to Multiply in the Transparency palette, leave the transparency slider set to 50%.

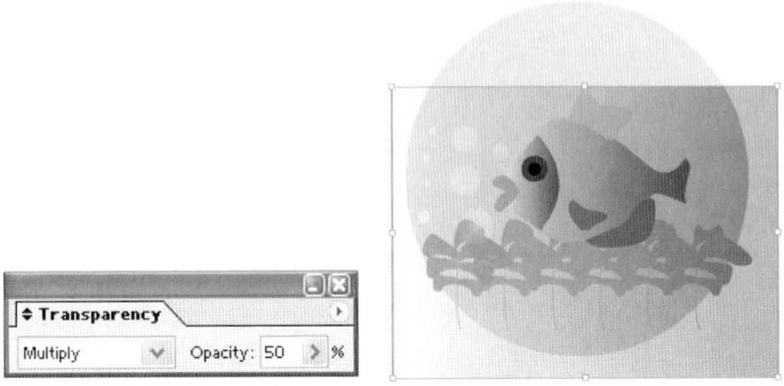

Surround the fish and plants with a rectangle to create the water.

10 File > Save.

Applying an effect

11 Using the Zig Zag effect, you will give this water ripples. Choose Effect > Distort and Transform > Zig Zag. Set the options as follows:

- size: **10**
- ridges per segment: **20**
- points: **smooth**.

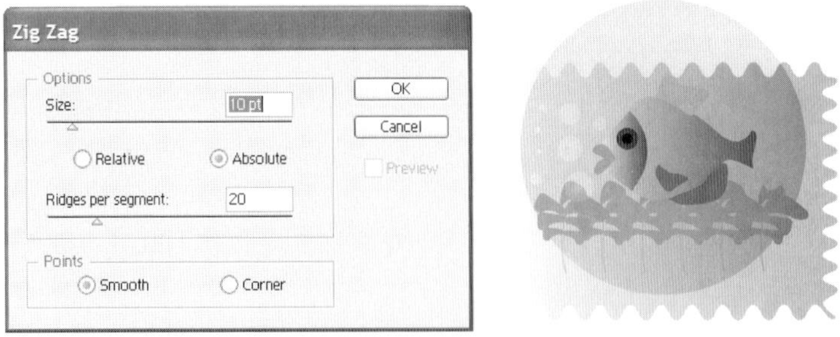

Set the options to create a wavy effect using Zig Zag.

11 Click OK.

Creating a clipping mask

In this next step you will turn the yellow circle into a clipping mask. When complete, the modified circle will act as a window showing through only the artwork located within the boundaries of that shape.

12 Select the yellow circle with the Selection tool (↖).

13 Choose Object > Arrange > Bring to Front. A Clipping Mask object must be at the top of the painting order.

Changing the stacking order

You can change the stacking order (also called the painting order) of objects in your artwork at any time using Object > Arrange commands.

Layers also affect the order in which items appear. Arrangements involving layers are discussed in the next lesson.

*The **Bring to Front** and **Send to Back** commands let you move an object to the top or the bottom of the stack of objects on its layer, while the **Bring Forward** and **Send Backward** commands let you move an object just one object forward or backward in the stack of objects.*

If the object is part of a group, the object is moved to the front or back of the group.

14 Choose Select > Select All or Control+A (Windows) or Command+A (Mac OS).

15 Choose Object > Clipping Mask > Make to mask all the artwork into the topmost object, the circle.

Create a mask from the topmost object.

16 File > Save.

Putting the logo together

1 Choose File > Open and locate the logo you created and saved in the Lesson09 folder named vwlogo.ai.

2 Choose Select > Select All, then Edit > Copy to copy the logo. Then choose Window to locate the fishart.ai document.

Illustrator lists all open documents at the bottom of the Window menu.

3 Edit > Paste the logo onto the fishart.ai document.

4 With the logo still selected choose Window > Layers to show the Layers palette.

5 From the Layers palettechoose the palette menu in the upper right choose New Layer. Name the layer **Logo** and click OK.

6 In the Layers palette notice the selection square to the right of Layer 1. This indicates that there is a selection on that layer. Drag the selection square up to the layer you just created named Logo. The selection handles change indicating that the logo has now been moved to a different layer.

7 Lock Layer 1 by clicking on the empty square to the left of the layer name.

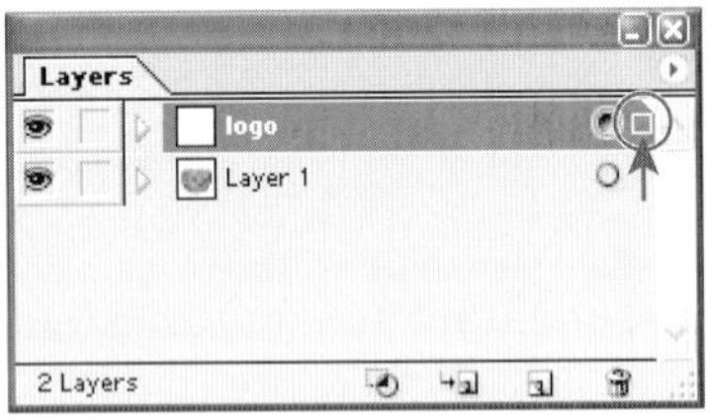

Drag the selection square to the new layer.

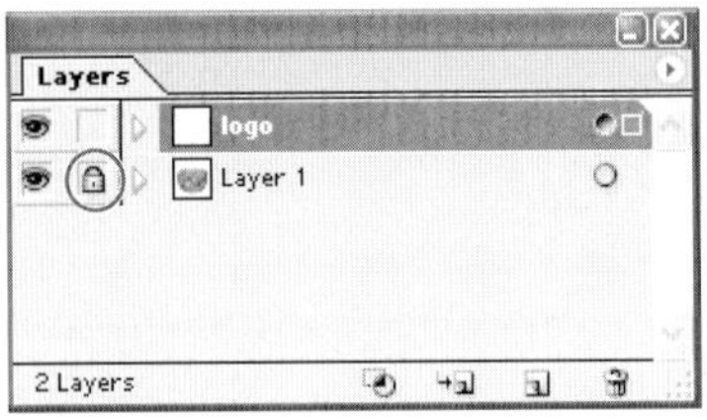

Lock Layer 1.

8 Now that the fish art is locked you can choose Select > Select All to activate just the logo. Reposition the logo on top of the fish art.

9 Using the Fill and Stroke swatches in the toolbar, select the entire logo and change the fill to White and the Stroke to None.

10 Click off the art to deselect it.

10 Select only the top portion of the logo (VW).

11 If the Transparency palette is not visible choose Window > Transparency and change the Blending mode to Lighten and the opacity to **50%**.

You are now finished with the logo. Choose File > Save and File > Close.

Exploring on your own

Experiment with different shapes and various transparency settings. Overlap the shapes and rearrange the painting order using the Object > Arrange menu items to create new colors and effects.

Review questions

1 What makes a custom guide different from a ruler guide?

2 What steps do you take to make a scan into a template?

3 How can you use Transform Again?

4 What is the difference between Bring Forward and Bring to Front?

5 Where must an object be in the painting in order to be used as a clipping mask?

Review answers

1 A custom guide is different from a ruler guide in that it can be created from any path or shape. A ruler guide is only horizontal or vertical and is created by dragging the guide from the rulers.

2 To make a scan into a template, it is best to scan it into Photoshop at a larger size than you'll need. This makes creating the path easier. Then choose File > Place from

Adobe Illustrator and check Template in the Place dialog box. Using guides and the Pen tool, re-create the placed scan and then drag the template layer to the trash icon in the Layers palette.

3 Use Transform Again to duplicate cloned items the exact same distance from the original artwork as the first. Use this to repeat the last move you made or transformation such as Rotate, or Scale.

4 Bring Forward will only bring the selected object ahead of the item created right before it. This is not the same as Bring to Front, which will immediately place the selected object at the top of the stacking order.

5 When you are creating a clipping mask, the object acting as the mask must be at the top of the painting order. Always make sure by selecting the object and choosing Object > Arrangement > Bring to Front.

Lesson 10

10 Applying Appearance Attributes, Styles, and Effects

You can alter the look of an object without changing its structure using appearance attributes—fills, strokes, effects, transparency, blending modes, or any combination of these object properties. You can edit or remove appearance attributes at any time. You can also save them as styles and apply them to other objects. At any time, you can edit an object that has a style applied to it, plus edit the style—an enormous time-saver!

In this lesson, you'll learn how to do the following:

- Create an appearance attribute.
- Reorder appearance attributes and apply them to layers.
- Copy and remove appearance attributes.
- Add an effect to an appearance and edit an effect.
- Save an appearance as a style.
- Apply a style to a layer.
- Select appropriate resolution settings for printing or exporting files with transparency.

Getting started

In this lesson, you'll enhance the basic design for a Web page by applying appearance attributes and styles to the page's type, background, and three buttons. Before you begin, you'll restore the default preferences for Adobe Illustrator. Then you will open the finished art file for this lesson to see what you'll create.

1 To ensure that the tools and palettes function exactly as described in this lesson, delete or deactivate (by renaming) the Adobe Illustrator CS preferences file. See "Restoring default preferences" on page 2 in the Introduction.

2 Start Adobe Illustrator.

3 Choose File > Open, and open the L10end.ai file located in the Lesson10 folder inside the Lessons folder within the AICIB folder on your hard drive.

The artwork in this file is a design mock-up of a Web home page. The design for the completed page includes several styles and effects, including overlapping gradients, transparent type, drop shadows, and texturized and shaded graphics.

4 If you like, choose View > Zoom Out to make the design mock-up smaller, adjust the window size, and leave it on-screen as you work. (Use the Hand tool (✋) to move the artwork where you want it in the window.) If you don't want to leave the artwork open, choose File > Close.

For an illustration of the finished artwork in this lesson, see the color section..

Using appearance attributes

You can apply appearance attributes to any object, group, or layer by using effects and the Appearance and Styles palettes. An appearance attribute is an aesthetic property–such as a fill, stroke, transparency, or effect–that affects the look of an object, but does not affect its basic structure. An appearance attribute can be changed or removed at any time without changing the underlying object or any other attributes applied to the object.

The advantage to using the Appearance palette to add effects or other attributes is that these effects or other attributes can be selected and edited at any time.

For example, if you apply a drop shadow effect to an object, at any time you can change the drop shadow distance, blur, or color. You can also copy that effect and apply it to other shapes, groups, or layers. You can even save it as a style and use it for other objects or other files. In contrast, if you create a drop shadow by applying the Drop Shadow filter to an object, you cannot edit the filter results, copy the filter effect, or apply it to other objects globally.

The Appearance palette contains the following types of editable attributes:

• Fill–lists all fill attributes (fill type, color, transparency, and effects).

• Stroke–lists some stroke attributes (stroke type, brush, color transparency, and effects). All other stroke attributes are displayed in the Stroke palette.

• Transparency–lists opacity and blending mode.

• Effect–lists commands in the Effect menu.

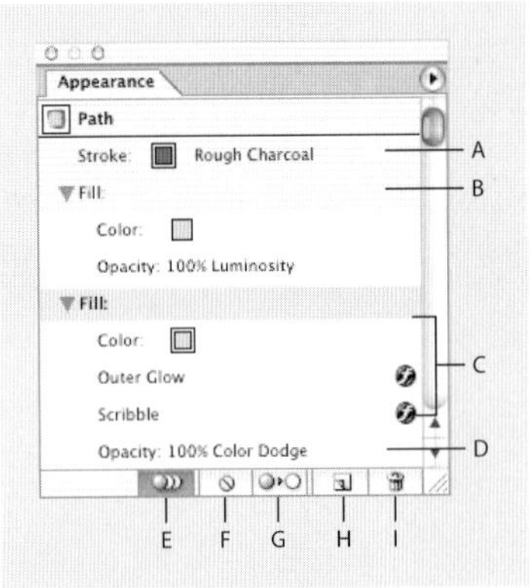

A. *Stroke color and paintbrush name.*
B. *Fill color and opacity.*
C. *Second fill color and effects.*
D. *Fill opacity and blending mode.*
E. *New Art Has Basic Appearance.*
F. *Clear Appearance.*
G. *Reduce to Basic Appearance.*
H. *Duplicate Selected Item.*
I. *Delete Selected Item.*

Note: *Later in this lesson you will learn about flattening artwork using effects that take advantage of transparency. Flattening is an easy and necessary step for files that will be printed. If your artwork is to be printed, make sure that you create files in the CMYK color mode. Flattening is not necessary if your final output is for the Web.*

Adding appearance attributes

You'll start by selecting the star shape and adding to its basic appearance using the Appearance palette.

1 Choose File > Open, and open the L10start.ai file, located in the Lesson10 folder inside the Lessons folder within the AICIB folder on your hard drive.

2 Choose File > Save As, name the file **StarArt.ai**, and select the Lesson10 folder in the Save In window. Leave the type of file format option set to Adobe Illustrator® Document, and click Save. In the Illustrator Options dialog box accept the defaults and click OK.

3 Using the Selection tool (), select the star shape.

4 In the Layers palette, expand the Star Button layer so that you can see its contents. Notice that the star shape is selected, as indicated by the square to the right of the layer name, and its path is targeted, as indicated by the double-circle (target) icon to the right of the path name.

5 Notice the stroke and fill attributes of the star shape listed in the Appearance palette. (If the palette isn't visible on-screen, choose Window > Appearance to display it; a check mark indicates that the palette is open on-screen.)

Star selected.

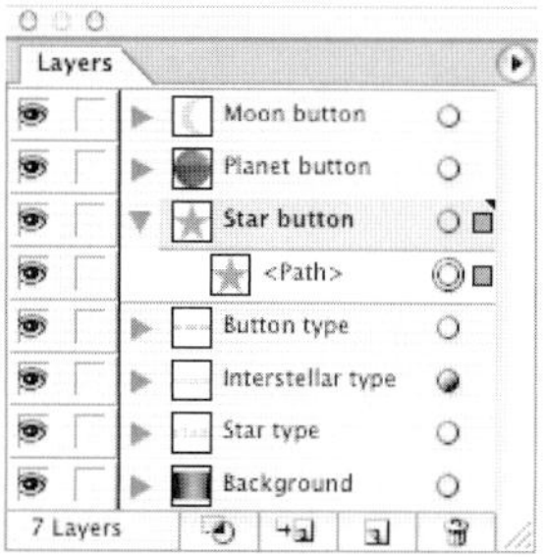

Expanded Star Button layer.

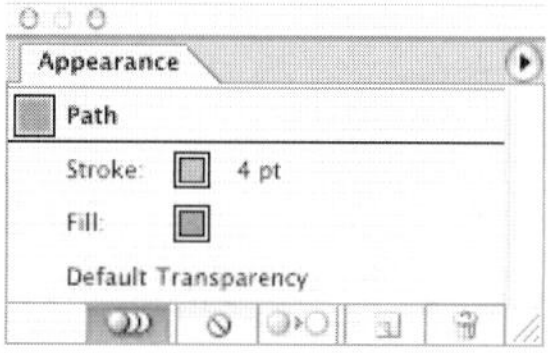

Stroke and fill attributes.

6 In the Appearance palette, click the Stroke attribute to select it.

Selecting the Stroke attribute lets you change just the stroke in the artwork.

7 In the Transparency palette, choose Multiply from the blending modes pop-up menu.

You can expand and collapse attributes in the Appearance palette by clicking the triangle (▸) to the left of the attribute in the palette list.

8 While remaining on the Selection tool, press Ctrl+spacebar (Windows) or Command+spacebar (Mac OS) and click the star shape to zoom in on it to about 200%. Inspect the stroke around the star to see how it has changed. The effect of the Multiply blending mode is similar to drawing on a page with transparent marker pens.

Strokes are centered on a path outline-half of the stroke color overlaps the filled star shape and half of the stroke color overlaps the background gradient.

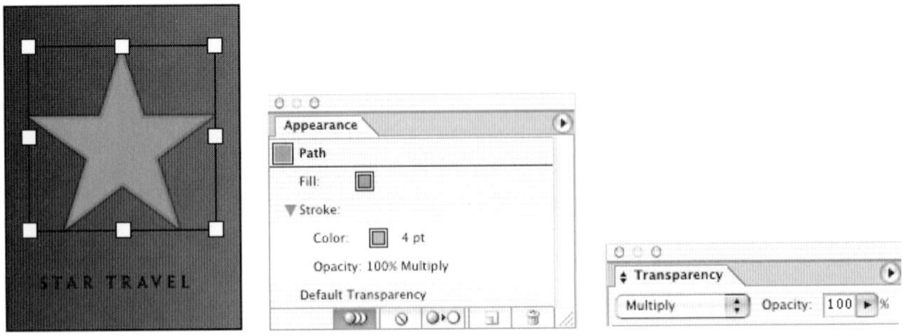

Star shape with Multiply blending mode applied.

Reordering appearance attributes

Now you'll change the appearance of the Multiply blending mode by rearranging the attributes in the Appearance palette.

1 Resize the Appearance palette so that you can view all its contents. Click the Fill attribute and drag it above the Stroke attribute. (This technique is similar to dragging layers in the Layers palette to adjust their stacking order.)

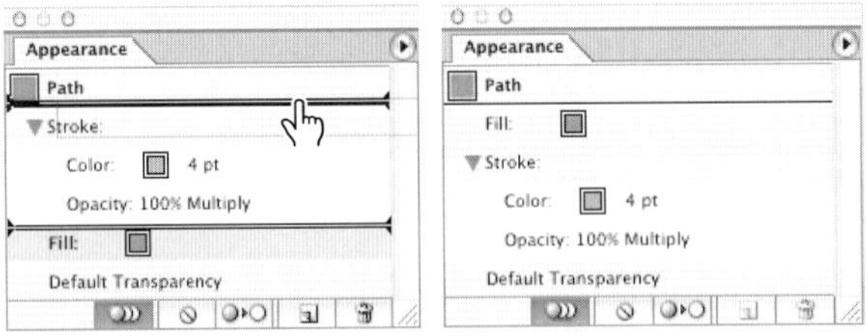

Drag Fill attribute above Stroke attribute.

Result.

Moving the Fill attribute above the Stroke attribute changes the look of the Multiply blending modes on the stroke. Half the stroke has been covered up. Blending modes work only on objects that are beneath them in the stacking order.

You'll now add another stroke to the object using the Appearance palette.

2 With the star shape still selected, choose Add New Stroke from the Appearance palette menu. A stroke is added to the top of the appearance list. It has the same color and stroke weight as the first stroke.

3 In the Color palette, choose RGB from the palette menu, and then use the sliders or text boxes to change the color to a dark orange. (We used a color mix of R=255, G= 73, and B=0.)

4 Click the Stroke palette tab to bring it to the front of its group. Then change the Stroke weight to **2 pt**. Press Enter or Return.

You'll rearrange the order of the appearance attributes to prepare for adding live effects in the next part of the lesson.

5 In the Appearance palette, click the triangle to the left of the 4-point Stroke attribute to collapse the attribute, then drag it to the very top of the Appearance attributes list. (It should be directly above the 2-point stroke.)

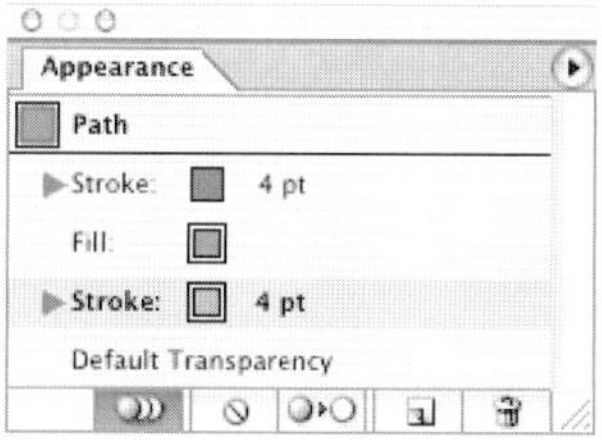

Add new stroke.

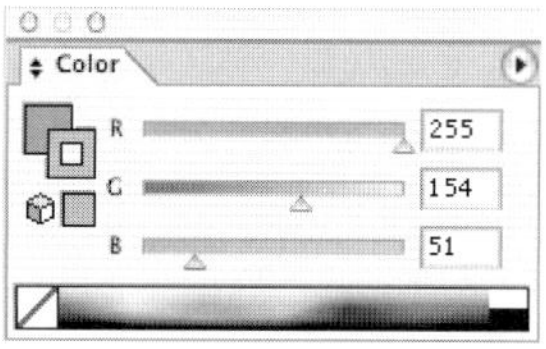

Change stroke color.

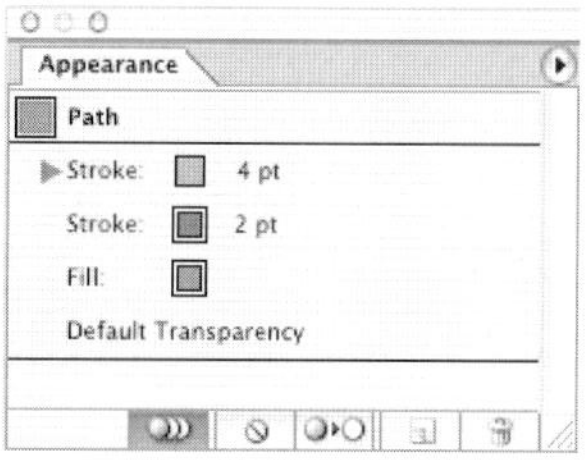

Rearrange stroke order.

6 Choose Select > Deselect and then File > Save to save the artwork.

Using live effects

The Effect menu commands alter the appearance of an object without changing the underlying object. Many Effect commands also appear in the Filter menu, but only the Effect commands are fully editable. Applying an effect to an object automatically adds the effect to the object's appearance attribute. You can select and edit the effect at any time by double-clicking on the effect in the Appearance palette.

You can apply more than one effect to an object. In this part of the lesson, you'll apply two effects to the star shape – an outer glow to make the star appear radiant and a texture using a Photoshop effect called Grain.

1 With the Selection tool (↖) select the star, choose Effect > Stylize > Outer Glow.

Note: Choose the top Stylize command in the Effect menu.

2 Click the Preview option and try different Opacity and Blur amounts until you are satisfied with the result. Leave the blend mode set to Screen. (We used 86% opacity and a 19 pt blur.) Don't click OK yet.

3 Click the color square next to the Mode menu to change the glow color. (We used a color mix of R=255, G=255, and B=51 to get a richer, brighter yellow.) Click OK to exit the Color Picker, and click OK again to apply the effect.

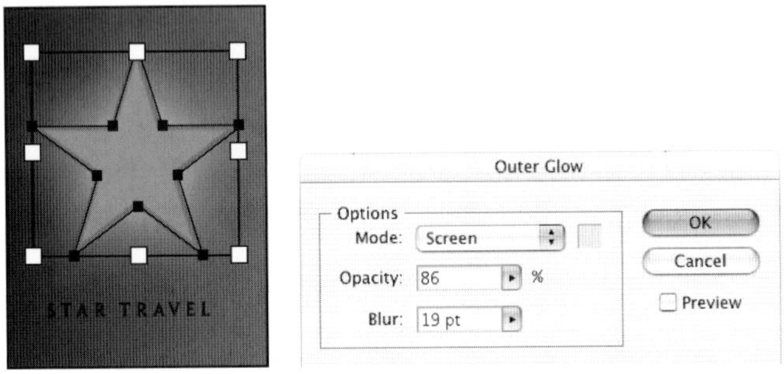

Adding Outer Glow effect.

Now you'll add a second effect to the star shape.

4 Choose Effect > Texture > Grain.

5 Adjust the settings until you are satisfied with the preview in the Grain dialog box. (We used an Intensity of 30, Contrast of 100, and Regular type.)

6 Click OK to see the result. Notice that Grain has been added to the list of attributes in the Appearance palette.

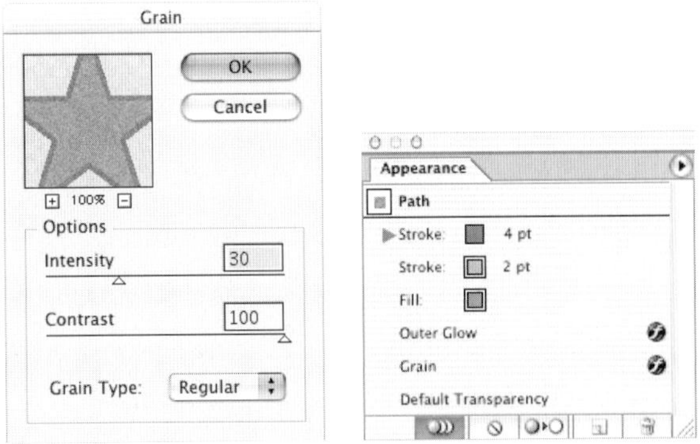

Adding Grain effect.

7 Choose File > Save to save your changes.

Editing an effect

Effects can be edited at any time. To edit an effect, you simply double-click its name in the Appearance palette to display that effect's dialog box. Changes you make will update the artwork.

Next you'll change the texture you applied to the star in the last section.

1 Make sure that the star is still selected.

2 If necessary, resize the Appearance palette to view all its contents. Then double-click the Grain attribute.

3 In the Grain dialog box, change the Type to Soft and click OK.

Now you'll adjust the blending mode of the star's fill to make it glow more.

4 With the star shape still selected, click the Fill attribute in the Appearance palette.

5 In the Transparency palette, choose Luminosity from the blending mode menu.

6 Choose File > Save to save the artwork.

Luminous fill added to effect.

Now you're ready to save the star's appearance as a style.

Using Graphic styles

A Graphic style is a named set of appearance attributes. By applying different Graphic styles, you can quickly and globally change the appearance of an object.

For example, you may have a symbol on a map that represents a city, with a Graphic style applied that paints the symbol green with a drop shadow. You can use that Graphic style to paint all the cities' symbols on the map. If you change your mind, you can change the fill color of the style to blue. All the symbols painted with that Graphic style will then be updated automatically.

The Graphic Styles palette lets you create, name, save, and apply various effects and attributes to objects, layers, or groups. Just like attributes and effects, styles are completely reversible. For example, you could apply a style to a circle that contains the Zig Zag effect, turning the circle into a starburst. You can revert the object to its original appearance with the Appearance palette, or you can break the link with that graphic style and edit one of its attributes without affecting other objects that are painted with the same graphic style.

Creating and saving a Graphic style

Now you'll save and name a new Graphic style using the appearance attributes you just created for the star button.

1 Click the Graphic Styles tab to bring the palette to the front of its group. (If the Graphic Styles palette isn't visible on-screen, choose Window > Graphic Styles; a check mark indicates that the palette is open on-screen.)

2 Position the Graphic Styles palette and the Appearance palette so that you can see both of them at the same time. Resize the Graphic Styles palette so that all the default styles are visible and there is empty space at the bottom.

3 Make sure that the star shape is still selected so that its appearance attributes are displayed in the Appearance palette.

The appearance attributes are stored in the appearance thumbnail, named Path in the Appearance palette.

4 In the Appearance palette, drag the appearance thumbnail onto the Graphic Styles palette.

5 Release the mouse button when a thick black border appears on the inside of the palette. The border indicates that you are adding a new style to the palette.

The path thumbnail in the Appearance palette will change to "Path: Graphic Style."

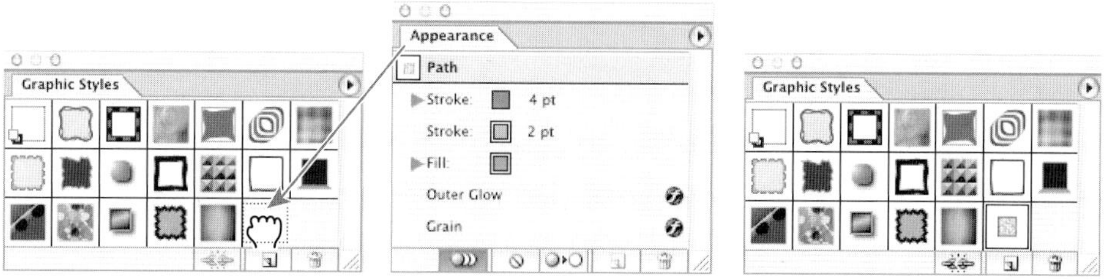

Drag object's appearance thumbnail onto Styles palette to save appearance attributes as new style.

6 In the Styles palette, choose Graphic Style Options from the palette menu. Name the new style **Grainy Glow**. Click OK.

7 Choose Select > Deselect to deselect the star shape, and then choose File > Save.

Applying a Graphic style to a layer

Once a style is applied to a layer, everything added to that layer will have that same style applied to it. Now you'll create a new style and apply it to a layer. Then you'll create a few new shapes on that layer to see the effect of the style.

1 In the Appearance palette, click the Clear Appearance button at the bottom of the palette. Then select the appearance name or thumbnail.

2 The Clear Appearance option removes all appearance attributes applied to an object, including any stroke or fill.

3 Choose Effect > Stylize > Drop Shadow.

Use the default settings. If desired, click the radio button to the left of the color swatch in the Drop Shadow dialog box, then click on the color swatch to change the shadow color. (We picked a red color of R=215, G=65, and B=4.) Click OK to exit the Color Picker, and click OK again to apply the effect.

Note: Because the Drop Shadow appearance has no stroke or fill, its thumbnail will be blank. But once attributes are applied to a shape, the drop shadow will appear.

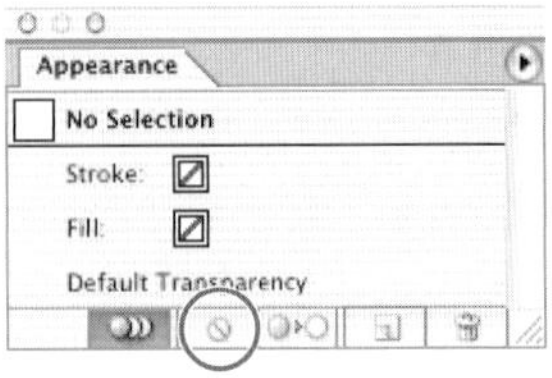

Clear appearances.

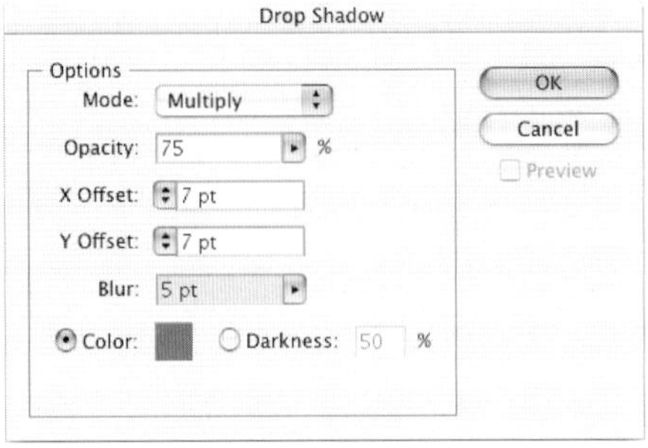

Choose Drop Shadow effect.

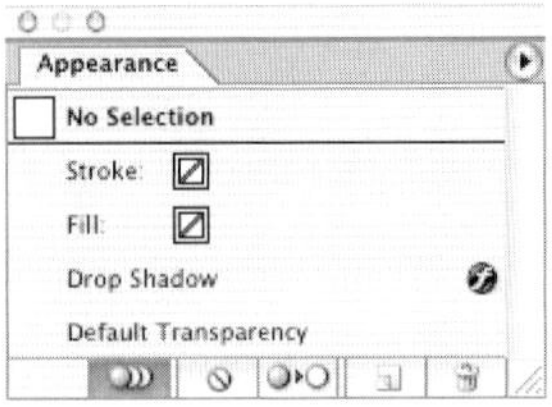

Result.

When creating a new style, the Style palette automatically uses the current appearance attributes displayed in the Appearance palette.

4 In the Graphic Styles palette, Alt-click (Windows) or Option-click (Mac OS) the New Style button at the bottom of the palette, and type **Drop Shadow** as the name of the new style. Click OK.

Now you'll target the Planet Button layer, to apply a drop shadow to all the shapes on that layer.

5 In the Layers palette, click the triangle to the left of the Planet Button layer to expand the layer. Then click the target indicator (◎) to the right of the Planet Button layer. (Be careful not to target the mesh-filled path (the Planet Button sublayer). If you target the path, only the planet shape will have a drop shadow.)

6 In the Styles palette, click the Drop Shadow style to apply the style to the layer.

7 Choose Select > Deselect to deselect the planet shape.

Now you'll test the layer effect by adding some shapes to the Planet Button layer.

8 Select the Star tool (☆) in the same group as the Rectangle tool (▭) in the toolbox.

9 Click the Color tab to bring the palette to the front of its group, or choose Window > Color to display it. In the Color palette, choose a fill color (we used R=129, G=23, B=136 for a purple color) and a stroke of None.

10 With the Planet Button layer still selected, in the artwork draw several small stars around the planet shape.

Because the Drop Shadow style contains only an effect and no stroke or fill, the objects retain their original stroke and fill attributes.

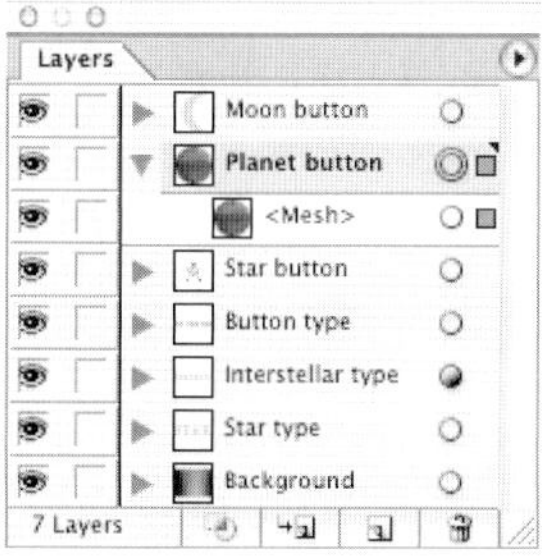

Layer targeted. *Style applied to layer.* *Stylized artwork added to layer.*

11 Notice the following icons on the right side of a layer in the Layers palette, indicating whether any appearance attributes are applied to the layer or whether it is targeted:

(◎) indicates that the layer, group, or object is targeted but has no appearance attributes applied to it.

(○) indicates that the layer, group, or object is not targeted and has no appearance attributes applied to it.

(●) indicates that the layer, group, or object is not targeted but has appearance attributes applied to it.

(◉) indicates that the group is targeted and has appearance attributes applied to it. This icon also designates any targeted object that has appearance attributes more complex than a single fill and stroke applied to it.

12 Choose File > Save to save the artwork.

Applying existing styles

Adobe Illustrator comes with a palette of pre-made styles that you can apply to your artwork. Now you'll finish the button designs by adding an existing style to the Moon Button layer.

A good habit to get into is using the Layers palette to select objects or layers to which you'll apply styles. An effect or style varies, depending on whether you're targeting either

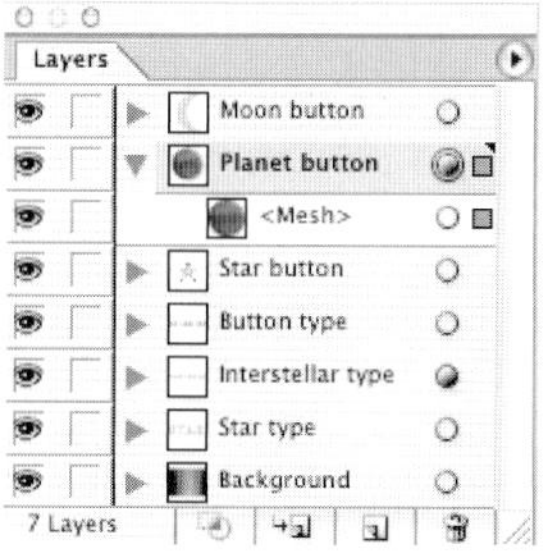

a layer or an object or group within a layer. Now you'll select the Moon button shape, not the layer.

1 In the Layers palette, click the triangle (▶) to expand the Moon Button layer.

2 Select the <Path> sublayer to select it. Then click the target indicator (◎) to the right of the <Path> sublayer to target it. Targeting the sublayer selects the path in the artwork.

Note: *If you target a layer or sublayer by mistake, Control/Command-click the target indicator to remove it.*

3 Click the Swatches tab to bring the palette to the front its group. In the Swatches palette, select the Moon gradient to fill the selected path.

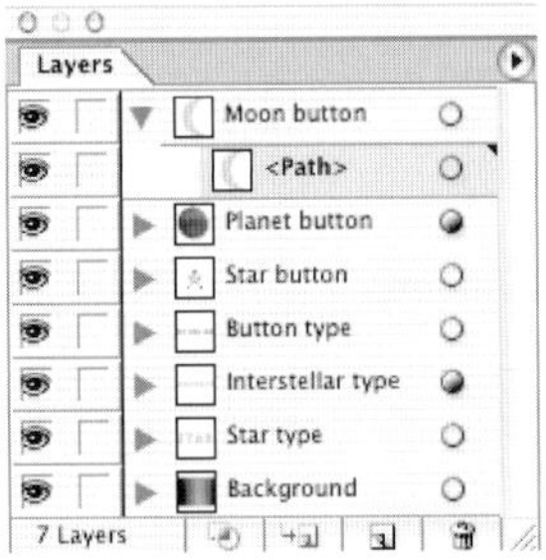

Select path in Layers palette.

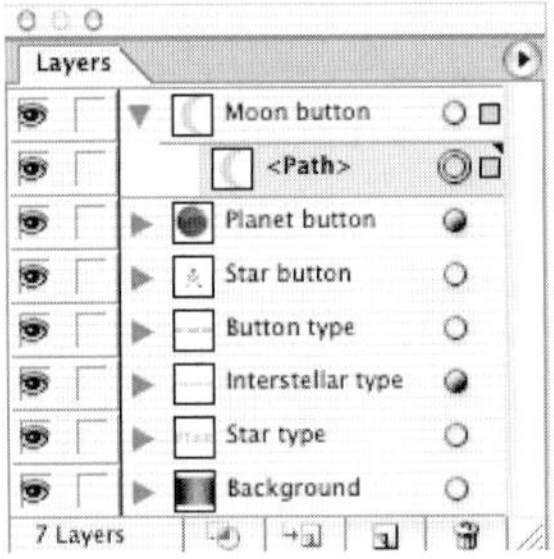

Target path in Layers palette.

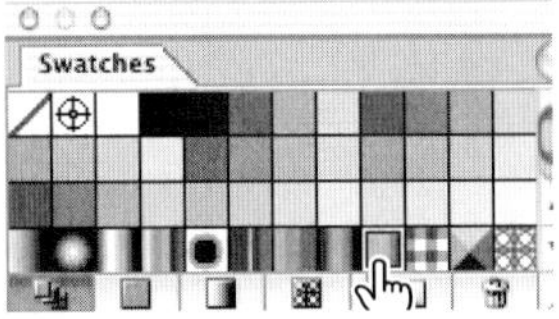

Change fill color to Moon gradient.

Now you'll apply a style to the Moon Button layer. The style contains a color, which you'll apply to the layer in place of the moon's existing color.

4 In the Layers palette, click the target indicator (◎) for the Moon Button layer.

5 Click the Styles tab to bring the palette to the front of its group. In the Styles palette, click the Green relief style (fourth row, left-most swatch) to apply it to the layer.

6 Choose File > Save to save the artwork.

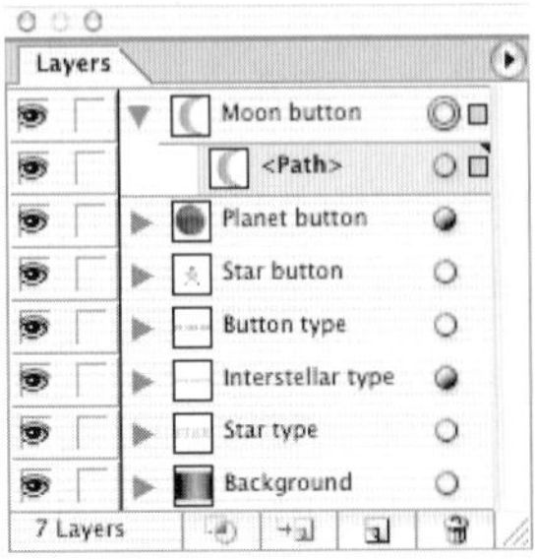

Layer selected.

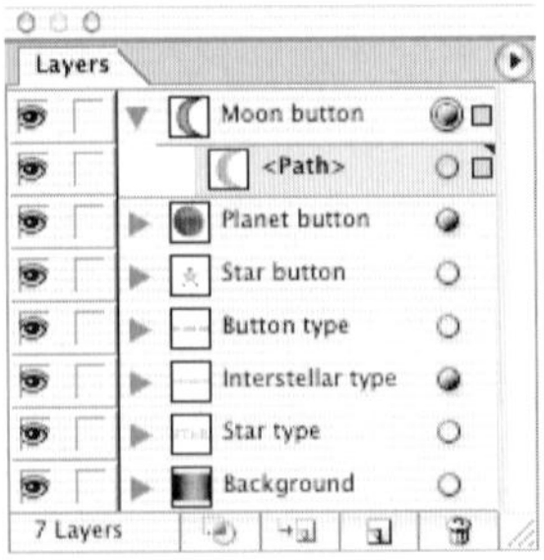

Style applied to layer.

Result.

Applying an appearance to a layer

You can also apply simple appearance attributes to layers. For example, to make everything on a layer 50% opaque, simply target that layer and change the opacity in the Transparency palette.

Next you'll target a layer and change its blending mode to soften the effect of the type.

1 In the Layers palette, click the downward triangle next to the Moon Button layer to collapse the layer.

2 If necessary, scroll to the Star Type layer. Then click the target indicator (○) for the Star Type layer. This action selects everything on the layer and targets all its objects.

3 In the Transparency palette, choose Soft Light from the blending mode menu.

4 Choose File > Save to save the artwork.

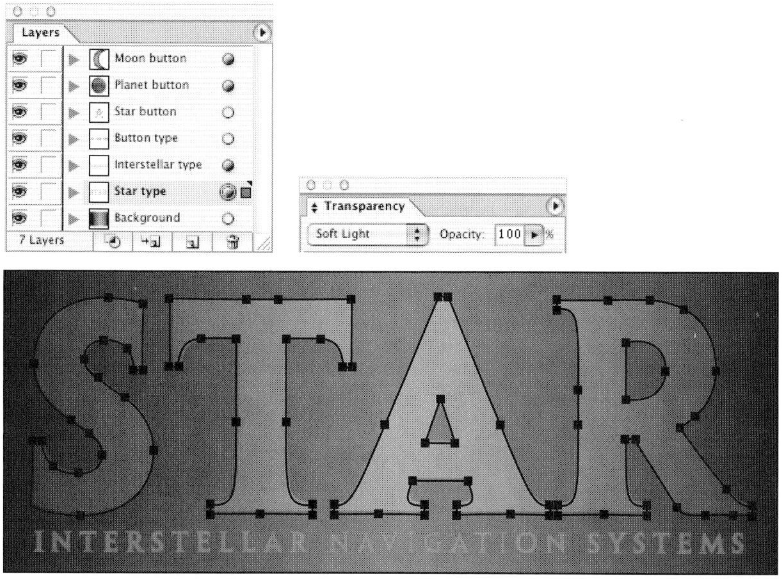

Star Type layer targeted; Soft Light mode applied; result.

Copying, applying, and removing styles and appearances

Once you've created several styles and appearances, you may want to use them on other objects in your artwork. You can use the Styles palette, the Appearance palette, the Eyedropper tool (), or the Paint Bucket tool () to apply and copy appearance attributes.

Next you'll apply a style to one of the objects using the Appearance palette.

1 Choose Select > Deselect.

2 Select the Selection tool (↖) in the toolbox, and click the star shape to select it.

3 In the Appearance palette, drag the appearance thumbnail (labeled "Path: Grainy Glow") onto the moon shape to apply those attributes to it.

You can apply styles or attributes by dragging them from the Styles palette or the Appearance palette onto any object. The object doesn't have to be selected.

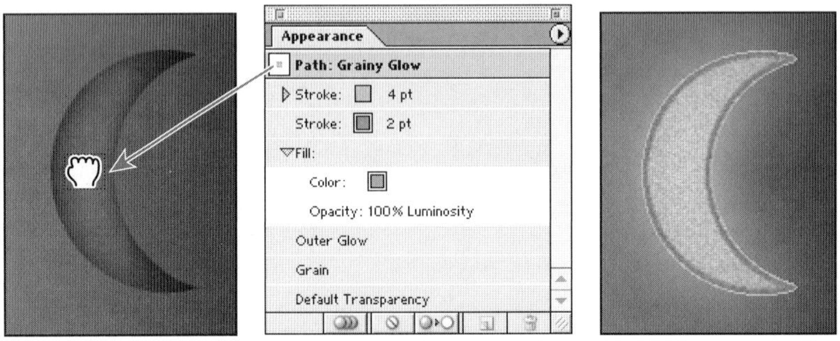

Star shape attributes. *Drag thumbnail onto new object to apply the same attributes.*

4 Control-click (Windows) or Command-click (Mac OS) away from the artwork to deselect it.

Next, you'll apply a style by dragging it directly from the Styles palette onto an object.

5 In the Styles palette, drag the Green relief style thumbnail onto the moon shape in the artwork.

6 Release the mouse button to apply the style to the shape.

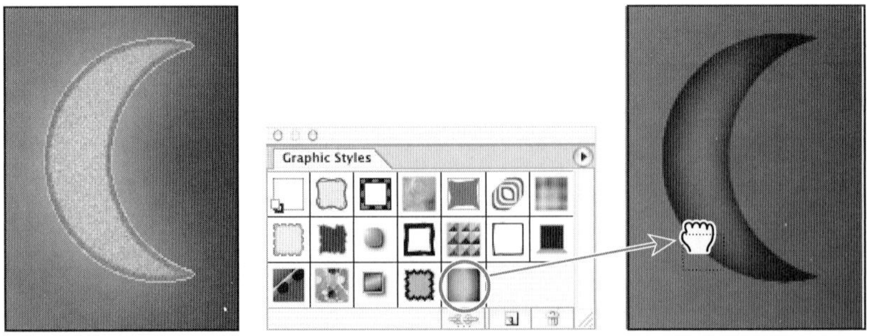

Drag style thumbnail onto object (selected or not) to apply the style.

Now you'll use the Layers palette to copy an attribute from one layer to another.

7 Expand the Layers palette to see all the layers. Then in the Layers palette, Alt-drag (Windows) or Option-drag (Mac OS) the appearance indicator from the Planet Button layer onto the appearance indicator of the Button Type layer.

Using Alt or Option copies one layer effect onto another, as indicated by the hand pointer with the plus sign. To move an appearance or style just from one layer or object to another, simply drag the appearance indicator.

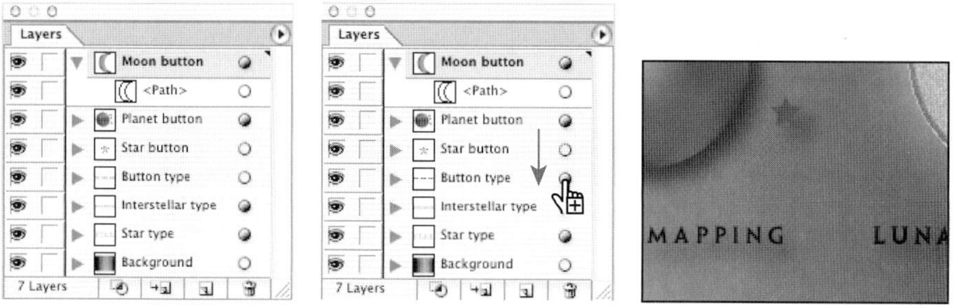

Alt/Option drag appearance attribute to copy it from one layer to another.

Now you'll remove an appearance from a layer using the Layers palette.

8 In the Layers palette, click the target indicator to the right of the Button Type layer.

9 Drag the appearance indicator to the Trash button at the bottom of the Layers palette to remove the appearance.

Another way to remove attributes of a selected object or layer is to use the Appearance palette. Select the object and then click the Reduce to Basic Appearance button at the bottom of the palette to return the object to its original state (including any stroke or fill) before the appearance attribute or style was applied.

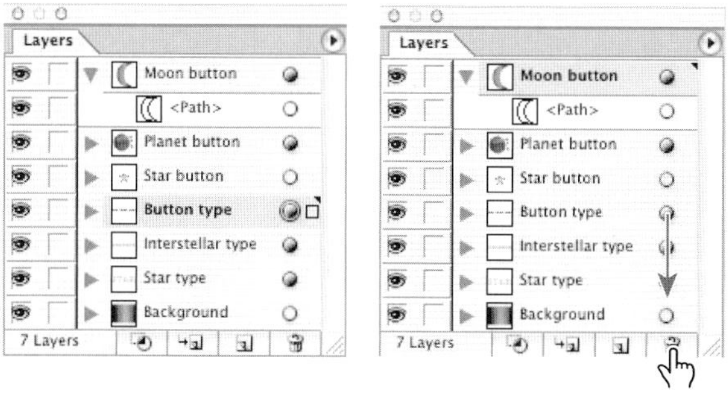

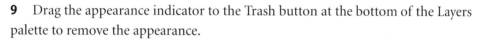

Drag appearance indicator to Trash button to remove attributes.

10 Choose File > Save, and then File > Close.

Saving and printing files with transparency effects

Now that you have learned to take advantage of Effects and the Appearance palette, you need to learn how to get them to print correctly. Many of the Effects used in this lesson take advantage of Illustrator's ability to create transparency. Transparency is applied to any object that has been modified to affect an underlying object. Illustrator, InDesign and Photoshop work seamlessly together and will maintain transparency from one application to the other if the proper workflow is followed. This simple workflow includes a step necessary for printing at the end, called Flattening.

Flattening is a term used to define the process of converting all transparent objects into a collection of opaque objects that retain the appearance of the original transparent objects when printed.

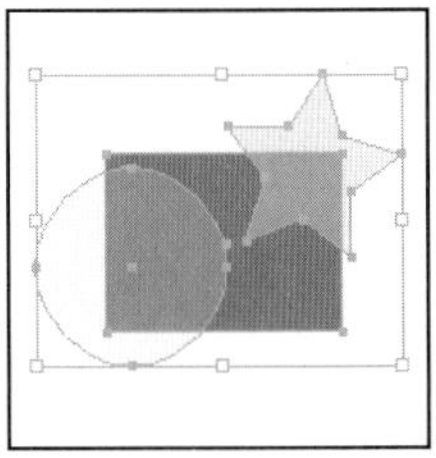

Objects before Flattening.

After Flattening.

Illustrator flattens artwork containing transparency before printing or saving the artwork. During flattening, Illustrator looks for areas where transparent objects overlap other objects and isolates these areas by dividing the artwork into components. Illustrator then analyzes each component to determine if the artwork can be represented using vector data or if the artwork must be rasterized.

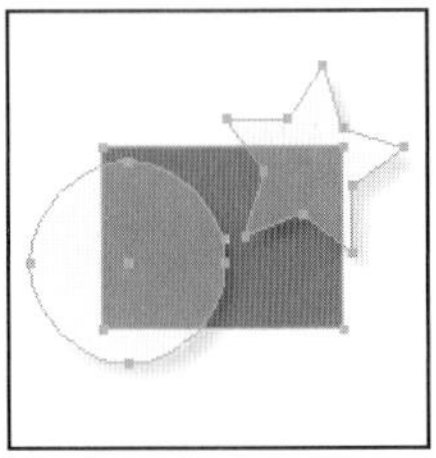

The drop shadow before flattening.

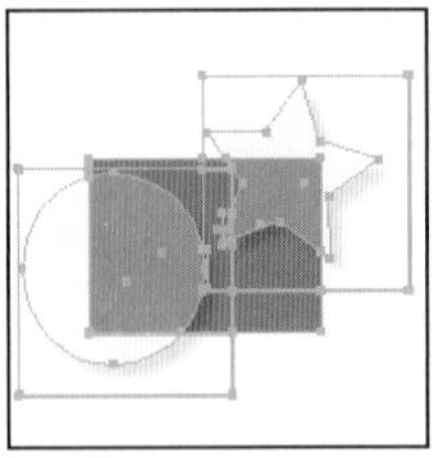

The rasterized drop shadow as a separate object after flattening.

In most cases, the flattening process produces excellent results. However, if your artwork contains complex, overlapping areas and you require high-resolution output, you can control the degree to which artwork is rasterized. To preserve as much of the vector art in your document as possible, use the Raster/Vector Balance slider in the Document Setup dialog box. Illustrator uses these settings to determine the quality, printing speed, or both, for your artwork.

What is Rasterization?

Rasterization is the process of changing vector graphics, vector fonts, gradients and gradient meshes into bitmap images for display and printing, essentially turning vector artwork into pixels. The higher the ppi (pixels per inch), the better the quality. The amount of ppi or dpi (dots per inch) is referred to as the resolution of the artwork.

Vector Object. *Rasterized at 72 ppi.* *Rasterized at 300 ppi.*

Specifying the resolution of filters and live effects

For this next exercise you will create several overlapping shapes with various levels of transparency.

1 Choose File > New and create a new CMYK document.

If you plan to print your transparent artwork, the document should be in CMYK mode.

2 Using the shape tools, create any three shapes and overlap them.

3 Assign a different color fill to each and assign None to the stroke.

4 Using the Transparency palette, apply varying levels of transparency to all three shapes. Exact amounts are not important, as long as you can see the underlying shapes.

5 With the three shapes selected choose Effect > Stylize > Drop Shadow. Accept the defaults and click OK.

6 With the three shapes still selected choose Effects > Pixelate > Pointilize. Leave at the default settings and click OK.

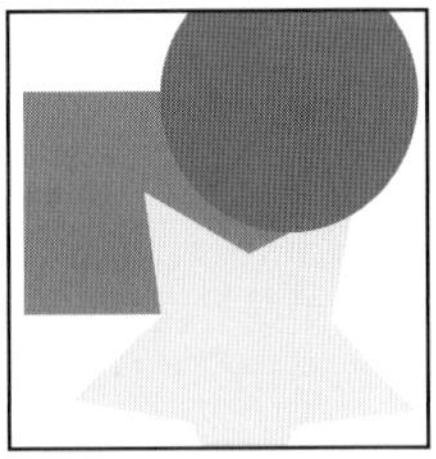

Create overlapping shapes with colored fills.

Apply Transparency.

Apply Effect.

7 Choose File > Save, name the file **shapes.ai**, and select the Lesson10 folder in the Save In menu. Leave the type of file format set to Adobe Illustrator® Document, and click Save. In the Illustrator Options dialog box, leave at the defaults and click Save.

Using Document Raster Effects Settings

1 Select the Zoom tool (🔍) in the toolbox. Position the zoom tool over any shape's drop shadow and click. Continue clicking on the center of the shapes until you have zoomed in to 300%. You should be able to see the pixelated texture of the drop shadow, and the pointilization effect.

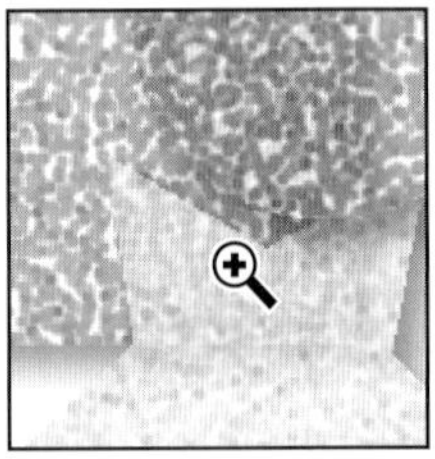

Zoom in to see the details.

Notice the edges of the star shape, with stair-stepping on the angled edges. This is due to the resolution setting for the raster effects. The default setting is 72 ppi.

You will change that setting to improve the quality of the shape's shadow.

2 Choose Effect > Document Raster Effects Settings.

3 Change the Resolution setting to Medium (150 ppi).

4 Leave the other settings as they are, and click OK.

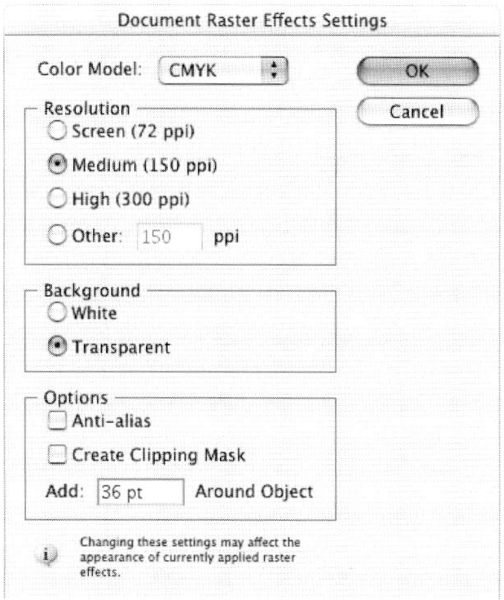

5 Notice that the shadow has become smoother and the pixels have become more precise.

If you were to increase the resolution to 300 ppi, the artwork would be even more well-defined. For this lesson you will leave the setting at 150 ppi.

Now that you have determined the quality of rasteration you want to occur, you will choose your flattening settings using the Flattener Preview palette.

Using the Flattener Preview palette.

If you are not sure what objects require flattening choose Window > Flattener Preview. Use the preview options in the Flattener Preview palette to highlight the areas affected by flattening artwork. Use this information to adjust the flattening options, and save custom flattener presets.

1 On the same shapes.ai file add another shape. Do not apply transparency or effects to this object

2 Fill it with a red color from the Swatches palette.

3 Use the Selection tool (↖) to drag the new opaque object on top of any other shape.

4 Choose Window > Attributes and click on the checkbox to Overprint Fill.

5 Choose View > Overprint Preview to show how your overprint will appear when printed.

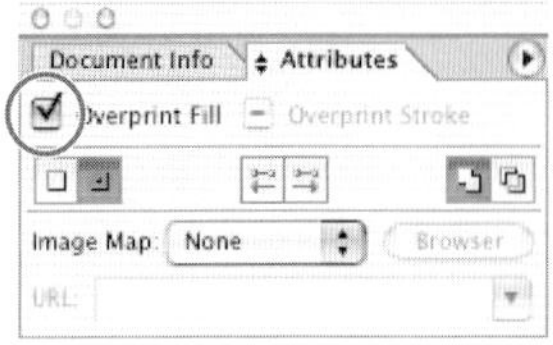

Check the Overprint fill box.

6 Choose Window > Flattener Preview. The Flattener Preview palette can remain open while you work on your artwork.

7 Click Refresh, and choose Transparent Objects from the Highlight pop-up menu . If necessary, click Refresh again.

All transparent objects are highlighted. Any other objects are gray.

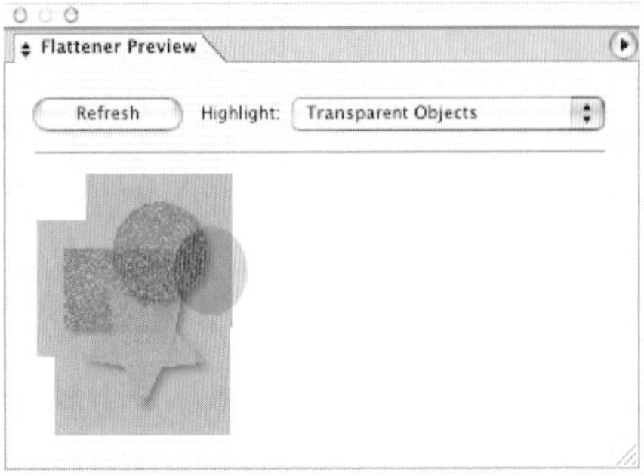

The Flattener Preview palette can show Transparent objects.

8 From the Highlight pop-up menu, choose All Affected Objects. More objects would appear highlighted if you had transparent objects on top of non-transparent objects.

9 Choose Show Options from the Flattener Preview palette menu.

In Options you can select different settings and preview the result. Note that the Flattening Preview palette does not actually perform the flattening.

Note: *As you change flattening options, click Refresh to update the display in the preview.*

10 From the Overprints pop-up menu, choose Simulate for the type of overprinting to use for the preview. Click Refresh.

• ***Preserve*** to retain overprinting for devices that support it. In most cases, only separations devices support overprinting.

• ***Simulate*** to maintain the appearance of overprinting in composite output.

• ***Discard*** to ignore any overprint settings that are present in your document.

11 From the Preset pop-up window, choose High Resolution from the available presets.

• ***Low Resolution*** is for quick proofs that will be printed on black-and-white desktop printers, as well as for documents that will be published on the Web or exported to SVG.

• ***Medium Resolution*** is for desktop proofs and print-on-demand documents that will be printed on PostScript color printers.

• ***High Resolution*** is for final press output and for high-quality proofs, such as separations-based color proofs.

You will now alter the High Resolution setting for your own custom settings.

12 Specify rasterization settings. Drag the Raster/Vector Balance slider to determine the percentage of rasterization. The settings vary from 0 on the left for the greatest rasterization to 100 on the right for the least rasterization on artwork. Select the highest setting to represent as much artwork as possible using vector data or select the lowest setting to rasterize all the artwork. For this exercise drag the slider to **90%**.

Note: *You will not see the rasterization in the Flattener Preview palette.*

Understand that rasterizing everything in a file degrades some of vector graphics' crisp edges, but maintaining too much of the vector artwork may make a file difficult to print due to your printer's memory limitations.

13 Specify an output resolution for art and text. In this case, leave the Line Art and Text Resolution at 1200.

If your final output will be separated and printed on a four-color press, you will want to specify a resolution of 1200. If your final output is to be a laser printer or color copier, you can select something lower, such as 600 or 800 dpi. In normal viewing conditions, no difference is visible, but the lower dpi takes less processing time and memory.

14 Set a separate resolution for the Gradients Mesh objects. Generally, these objects require less resolution than solid fill objects. Leave the setting at 300.

15 Leave the Convert All Text to Outlines unchecked. This ensures that the width of text, respectively, remains consistent during flattening.

16 Leave Convert All Strokes to Outlines unchecked. We do not have strokes in this artwork, but if we did, this option would convert all strokes to simple filled paths. This option ensures that the width of strokes stays consistent during flattening but will cause thin strokes to appear slightly thicker.

17 Leave the Clip Complex Regions option selected. When selected, this option ensures that the boundaries between vector artwork and rasterized artwork fall along object paths, but may result in paths that are too complex for the printer to handle.

18 Once you have determined which settings work best for your workflow, choose Save Transparency Flattener Preset from the palette menu in the upper right of the Flattener Preview.

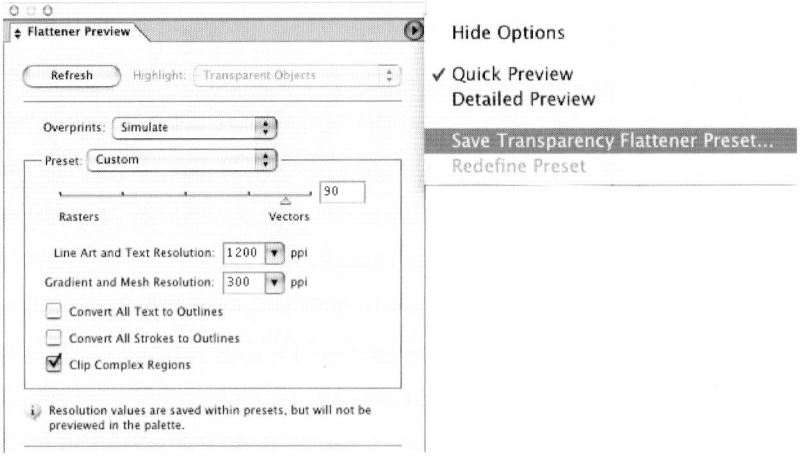

Save your settings as a preset.

19 Name the preset **shapes1** and click OK. You can close the Flattener Preview palette as well.

Note: *If you are unsure of which settings to use, contact your printer. A good print provider should be able to discuss the options with you and may even provide a preset that works in their workflow. Learn how to import presets later in this lesson.*

Assigning the Flattening preset

Using File > Document Setup, you can either create new flattening settings or assign presets to a document.

1 Choose File > Document Setup.

2 Choose Transparency from the pop-up menu in the Document Setup dialog box.

3 Choose the preset that you created (shapes1) in the Flattener Preview palette.

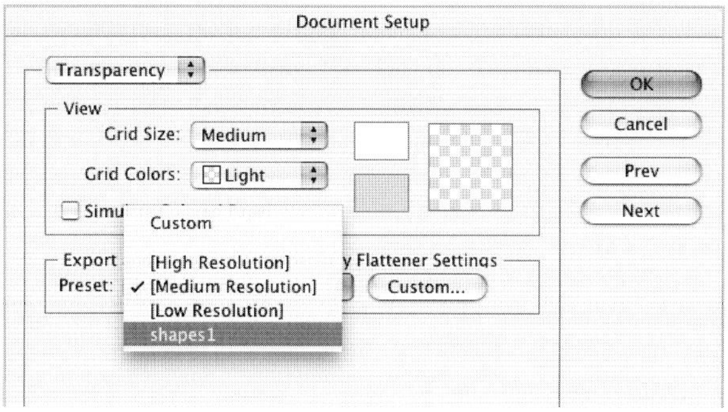

The transparency options in Document Setup.

4 Click OK.

5 Choose File > Save.

Note: *You can also create custom flattening settings in the Document Setup window by choosing Custom on the Preset pop-up window and selecting options.*

Saving a file with transparency

If saving a file that is to be used in other Adobe applications, such as InDesign or Photoshop, keep the transparency live by saving the artwork in the native Adobe Illustrator format. The transparency is supported in the other applications.

In this next exercise you will save your shape file in two different formats to place into an InDesign or Photoshop document.

1 Choose File > Save As, name the file **shapes1.ai**, and select the Lesson10 folder in the Save In menu. Leave the type of file format set to Adobe Illustrator® Document, and click Save. In the Illustrator Options dialog box, leave at the defaults and click OK.

2 Open Photoshop or InDesign and choose File > New. Create a letter-sized document.

3 Choose File > Place. Locate the file you saved in the Lesson10 folder named shapes1.ai and click Place.

Using Place to import your file allows the artwork to maintain its transparency.

Note: *Though you have the ability to drag and drop artwork from one Adobe application to another, transparency will not be supported.*

Saving in the EPS format

Save a file as an Encapsulated Postscript file to use in non-Adobe applications, or if you do not need to need the transparency to remain live.

1 Return to Adobe Illustrator.

2 Choose File > Save As, name the file **shapes2.eps**, and select the Lesson10 folder in the Save In menu. Set the type of file format to Illustrator EPS, and click Save.

3 In the EPS options window, select the preset you created earlier named shapes1. Click OK.

4 Return to the InDesign or Photoshop document.

5 Choose File > Place and select the file you just saved named shapes2.eps and click Place.

Notice that transparency is not supported. The transparent areas of the artwork do not interact with the rest of the document.

Native Adobe Illustrator File format.

EPS format.

6 Return to Illustrator and choose File > Close, or leave the file open to experiment with other flattening options.

Printing transparent artwork

If you have a printer connected, you can experiment with different flattening settings in the Print dialog box.

1 Choose File > Print.

2 Click on Advanced in the options window.

3 From the Preset pop-up menu, choose a transparency preset or click on Custom to create your own.

Exporting and importing flattening settings

Settings that you create can be accessed by using the Document Setup dialog box, but you can import settings that were created in other documents by choosing Edit > Transparency Flattener Presets.

Export from the document in which you created the preset. Use the Import button to make the settings available to any other document. This can be especially useful if you are working with a printer that can supply presets.

You are now finished with the discussion on flattening. More information can be found using online help or at Adobe.com.

Close any files that you have open.

Exploring on your own

Now that you've learned the basic steps to creating and using effects and styles, experiment with different combinations of appearance attributes to fashion interesting special effects. Try combining different styles to produce new ones.

For example, here's how to merge two existing styles to create a brand new style:

1 Choose File > New to open a new file.

2 If the Graphic Styles palette isn't visible on-screen, choose Window > Graphic Styles to display it.

3 In the Graphic Styles palette, select Transmogrifier style.

4 Add another graphic style to the selection by Control-clicking (Windows) or Command-clicking (Mac OS) the style named Double Scribble.

5 Choose Merge Graphic Styles from the Styles palette menu.

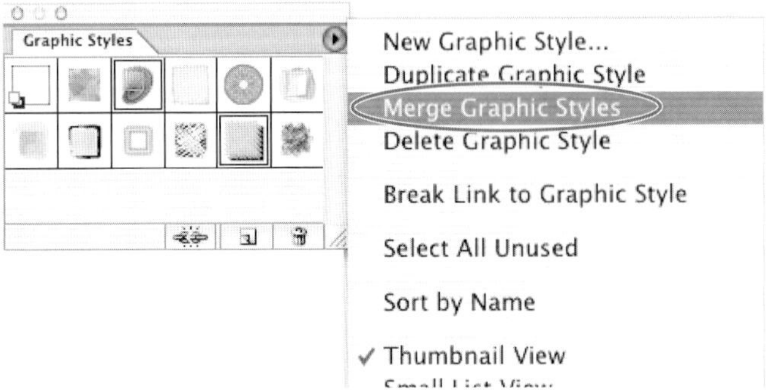

6 Name the new style **merged style** in the Style options dialog box, and click OK.

7 In the artwork, draw a shape and apply the new style.

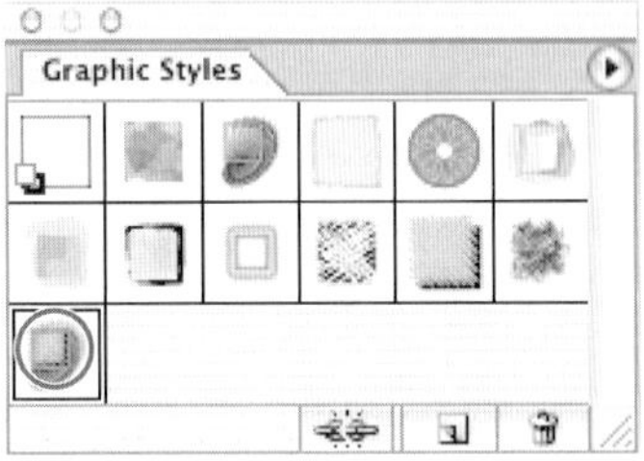

Merged styles.

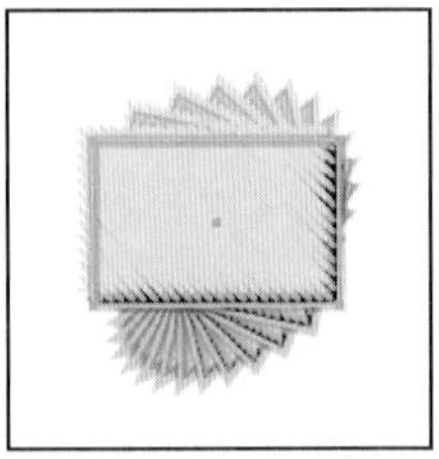

Result.

If you want to edit the style and save it again, do the following:

8 Deselect the artwork.

9 In the Appearance palette, drag the 7-point stroke to the top, above the three fills and the 3-point stroke.

10 Create a new shape or drag the appearance thumbnail onto the existing shape to view the results.

If you like the new effect, you can replace the first merged style with it.

11 To replace a style, Alt-drag (Windows) or Option-drag (Mac OS) the appearance thumbnail onto the style you are replacing in the Graphic Styles palette. The style being replaced displays a thick black border when you position the pointer over it.

12 Release the mouse button, and save the file.

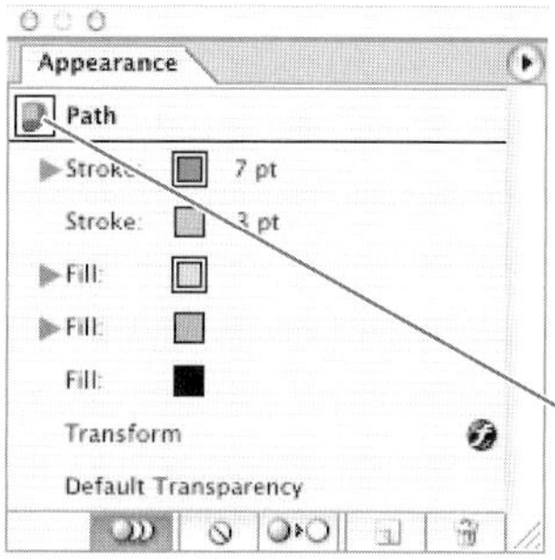

Select appearance thumbnail.

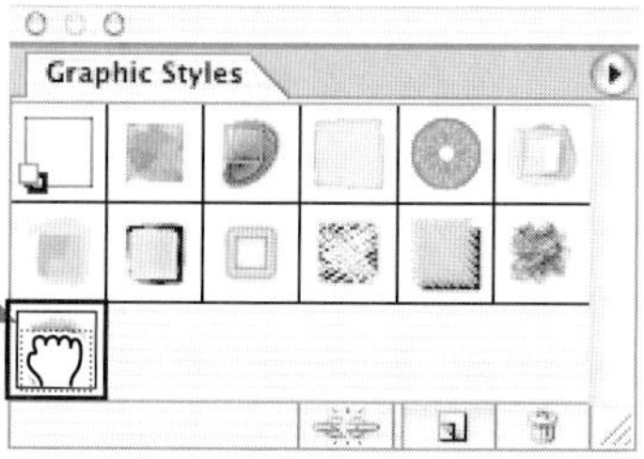

Alt/Option-drag onto style in Graphic Styles palette.

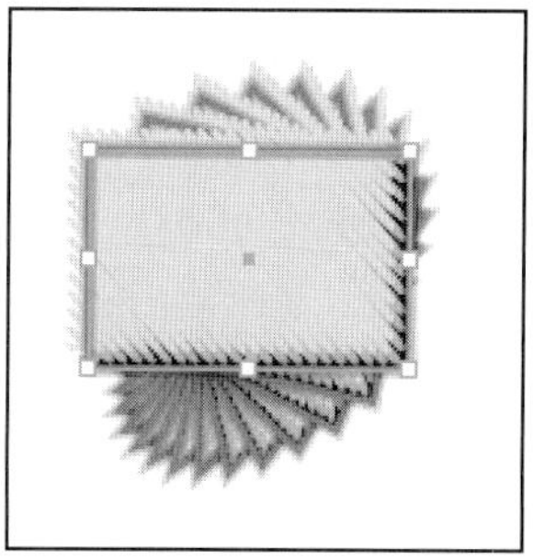

Result.

Review questions

1 Name two types of Appearance attributes.

2 How do you add a second stroke to an object?

3 What's the difference between a filter and an effect?

4 How do you edit an effect that is part of an object's appearance attributes?

5 What's the difference between applying a graphic style to a layer versus applying it to an object?

6 How do you remove an appearance using the Layers palette?

7 How do you set the resolution for a file that contains filter effects?

Review answers

1 The Appearance palette contains the following types of editable attributes:

- Fill attributes (fill type, color, transparency, and effects).
- Stroke attributes (stroke type, brush, color transparency, and effects).
- Transparency attributes (opacity and blending mode).
- Effects commands from the Effect menu.

2 From the Appearance palette, menu choose Add New Stroke. A stroke is added to the top of the appearance list. It has the same color and stroke weight as the first stroke.

3 Many commands in the Effect menu also appear in the Filter menu, but only the Effect menu commands are fully editable.

4 To edit an effect you simply double-click its name in the Appearance palette to display that effect's dialog box. You can then make changes and click OK to update them in the artwork.

5 Once a graphic style is applied to a layer, everything you add to that layer will have that style applied to it. For example, if you create a circle on Layer 1 and then move it to Layer 2, which has a Drop Shadow effect applied, the circle would adopt that effect. When a style is applied to a single object, nothing else on that object's layer is affected by the object's style. For example, if a triangle has a Roughen effect applied to its path, and you move it to another layer, it will still retain the Roughen effect.

6 In the Layers palette, click the target indicator of a layer. Drag the appearance indicator down to the Trash icon in the Layers palette to remove the appearance. You can also remove the appearance of a selected object or layer by using the Appearance palette. Select the object and click the Reduce to Basic Appearance button to return the object to its original state before the appearance attribute or style was applied.

7 You change the resolution in the Rasterize Effects Settings dialog box. Choose Effect > Document Raster Effects Settings. Change the Resolution setting to Low (72 ppi), Medium (150 ppi), High (300 ppi), or Other. Click OK.

Lesson 11

11 Working with type

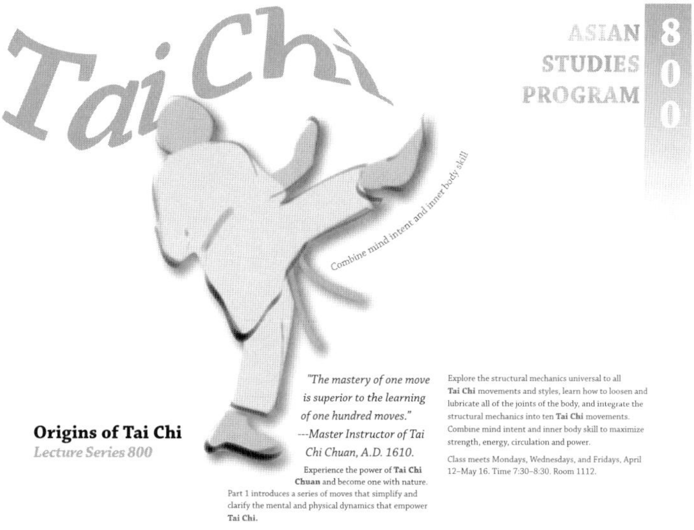

Tai Chi
ASIAN
STUDIES
PROGRAM
800
Combine mind intent and inner body skill
Origins of Tai Chi
Lecture Series 800
"The mastery of one move is superior to the learning of one hundred moves." ---Master Instructor of Tai Chi Chuan, A.D. 1610.
Experience the power of Tai Chi Chuan and become one with nature. Part 1 introduces a series of moves that simplify and clarify the mental and physical dynamics that empower Tai Chi.
Explore the structural mechanics universal to all Tai Chi movements and styles, learn how to loosen and lubricate all of the joints of the body, and integrate the structural mechanics into ten Tai Chi movements. Combine mind intent and inner body skill to maximize strength, energy, circulation and power.
Class meets Mondays, Wednesdays, and Fridays, April 12–May 16. Time 7:30–8:30. Room 1112.

One of the most powerful features of Adobe Illustrator is the ability to use type as a graphic element. Like other objects, type can be painted, scaled, rotated, and so on. You can also wrap type around objects, make it follow along the shape of a path, create type masks, import text files into containers, and modify the shapes of individual letters in a block of type.

In this lesson, you'll learn how to do the following:

- Create type in containers and along paths.
- Import text files into type containers.
- Apply an envelope effect to type, and edit the effect and the envelope contents.
- Adjust type attributes and formatting, including the font, leading, and paragraph alignment.
- Format text and adjust the text flow.
- Use OpenType.
- Create and use Styles.
- Wrap type around a graphic.
- Create stylized letterforms with outlined type.
- Create type masks.
- Create text on a path.
- Save a file in PDF format for online distribution and viewing.

Getting started

In this lesson, you'll create a Tai Chi lecture series poster. Before you begin, you'll need to restore the default preferences for Adobe Illustrator. Then you'll open the finished art file for this lesson to see what you'll create.

Also have Chaparral Pro installed in your system. Chaparral Pro is an OpenType® font that can be used on both Windows and Macintosh operating systems. You will find Chaparral Pro on the with the original Adobe Illustrator CS installation files. To find out more information about fonts that come with the installation, click on Cool Extras on the Welcome Screen.

1 To ensure that the tools and palettes function exactly as described in this lesson, delete or deactivate (by renaming) the Adobe Illustrator CS preferences file. See "Restoring default preferences" on page 4.

2 Start Adobe Illustrator.

Type in Illustrator CS

Illustrator CS uses a new Adobe Text Engine to provide the highest-quality text composition, support for Unicode and OpenType features, and time-saving Character and Paragraph styles.

In this lesson, all exercises have been updated to work with this new type engine. If you open legacy (previous versions) files you may get a message prompting you to update the type. Text created in previous versions of Illustrator must be updated before you can edit it.

You may notice the following types of layout changes in updated text:

- *Changes to character position attributes such as leading, tracking, and kerning.*
- *Words shifting to the next line in an area type object, which may update hyphenation.*
- *Words overflowing from an area type object or shifting to the next linked text block.*

To avoid these types of changes, you can choose not to update text. Text that has not been updated is called legacy text. You can view, move, and print legacy text, but you can't edit it. Legacy text has an x through its bounding box when selected.

To update all text in a document:

1. *Choose Type > Update All Legacy Text*

To update legacy text in a specific object:

2. *Select a Type tool, and click in the type you want to update.*

3. *A dialog box appears and explains the layout changes that may occur when you update the text.*

Choose one of the following options:

- *Update to update the legacy text without creating a copy.*
- *Copy Text Layer to preserve the legacy text on a layer below the updated text. This allows you to compare the layout of the legacy text to the updated text.*
- *Cancel to not update the legacy text.*

—From online Help, "Type enhancements".

3 Choose File > Open, and open the L11end.ai file in the Lesson11 folder, located inside the Lessons folder within the AICIB folder on your hard drive.

4 If you like, choose View > Zoom Out to make the finished artwork smaller and leave it on your screen as you work. (Use the Hand tool (✋) to move artwork where you want it in the window.) If you don't want to leave the image open, choose File > Close.

For an illustration of the finished artwork in this lesson, see the color section.

Now open the start file to begin the lesson.

5 Choose File > Open, and open the L11start.ai file in the Lesson11 folder, located inside the Lessons folder within the AICIB folder on your hard drive.

6 Choose File > Save As, name the file **TaiChi.ai**, and select the Lesson11 folder in the Save In menu. Leave the type of file format set to Adobe Illustrator® Document, and click Save. In the Illustrator Options dialog leave at the defaults and click OK.

7 Choose Window > Links palette. Notice that the Links palette displays a link, the image of the sky to the right of the artboard, which is an embedded image (it was pasted into the document).

8 Click the close box or choose Window > Links to close the Links palette.

For information on using the Links palette, see "Managing linked and embedded images" in online Help.

Adding type to a document

Adobe Illustrator lets you add type to a document several different ways. You can type directly in the artwork, copy and paste type from other documents, and import entire text files.

To begin adding type to your artwork, you'll type the Tai Chi title on the poster.

1 Select the Type tool (T) in the toolbox. Position the pointer so that the I-beam cross hair is in the top left corner of the artwork. Click and drag down and to the right using the guides that already exist in the document, then release.

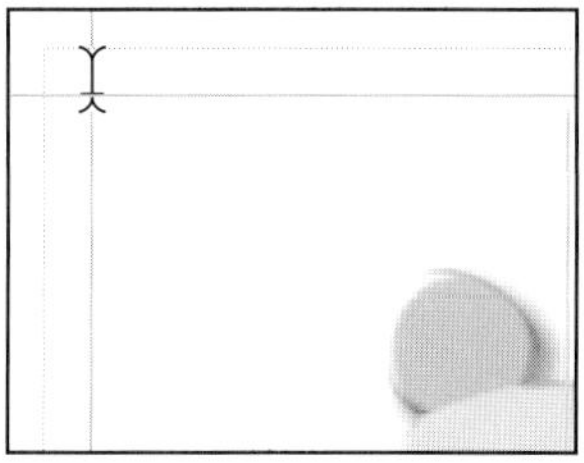

Position Type tool at intersection of guides.

The small horizontal line near the bottom of the I-beam–its cross hair–marks the position of the type baseline. The baseline is the line on which the type rests.

2 Click to set the type baseline where the guides intersect, and type **Tai Chi**.

By default, the type you create is 12-point Myriad Roman, filled with black, and stroked with None. The Fill and Stroke boxes in the toolbox display the type's current paint attributes.

Sampling type

Now you'll use the Eyedropper tool (✎) to pick up, or sample, the attributes of other type in the artwork and apply it to the Tai Chi title.

1 Click the Selection tool (↖) in the toolbox to select the words Tai Chi.

Clicking the Selection tool immediately after typing with the Type tool automatically selects the words you typed.

2 Click the Eyedropper tool () in the toolbox, and click anywhere in the line "Lecture Series 800" to sample the type's attributes (18-pt Chaparral Pro Bold Italix).

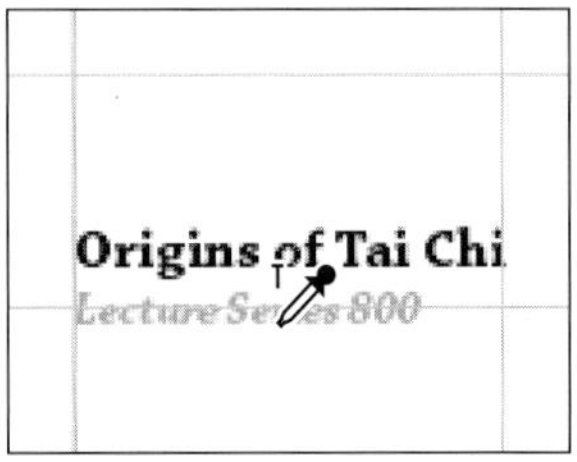

Sampling type attributes.

Sampled attributes are applied to any selected text, and the type colors appear in the Fill and Stroke boxes in the toolbox. In this case, 18-pt Chaparral Pro Bold Italic is applied to the Tai Chi text.

You can double-click on the Eyedropper tool in the toolbox to choose the attributes you want to copy.

Changing the character size

Now you'll use the Character palette to make the title bigger.

1 With the Tai Chi type still selected, choose Window > Type > Character to display the Character palette.

By default, the Character palette displays the selected font and its style, size, kerning, leading, and tracking values. If the type selection contains two or more attributes, the corresponding text boxes are blank. (*Leading* is the amount of space between lines or paragraphs. *Kerning* is the space between two characters. *Tracking* is the spacing between a string of characters.)

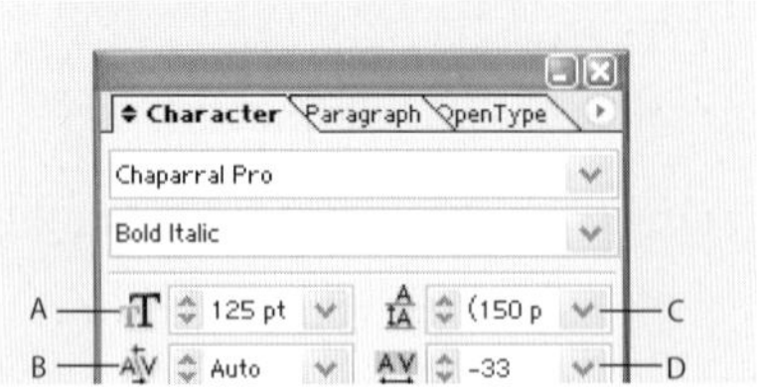

***A.** Font size. **B.** Kerning .**C.** Leading.*
***D.** Tracking.*

2 Type **120** in the Font Size text box, and press Enter or Return to increase the font size to 120 points.

You can use the Character palette to select or view a font and its attributes.

3 In the Character palette you have two pop-up menus, one used to select the font family and one to set the font style for the selected font. Notice that the selected font is the one that you sampled in the "Lecture Series 800" (Chaparral Pro Bold Italic.) Release the mouse button.

Choosing font from Character palette menu.

You can also select a font and size using the Font and Size submenus in the Type menu.

Reshaping text with an envelope

You'll add a simple envelope effect to the Tai Chi title to distort the text in the shape of the envelope and make the text follow the curve of the body. Envelopes are objects that distort or reshape selected objects.

1 Click the Selection tool (↖) in the toolbox.

2 With the Tai Chi title still selected, choose Object > Envelope Distort > Make With Warp.

3 In the Warp Options dialog box, select Preview to see how the effect will appear.

You'll select a preset warp shape for your envelope. You can also make an envelope using the topmost selected object in your artwork, or a mesh object or objects on your artboard—including text objects, paths, compound paths, meshes, blends, and raster images. You can use envelopes on all artwork except linked objects (with the exception of TIFF, GIF, and JPEG) or artwork to which a third-party plug-in is applied.

4 For Style, choose Flag. Select Horizontal for Bend, and enter an amount using the sliders or entering values in the text box. Then set the Horizontal and Vertical distortions. (We used a Horizontal Bend value of 62%, a Horizontal Distortion of –42%, and a Vertical Distortion of 10%.)

If you like, you can preview other styles and distortion values.

5 Click OK. Illustrator groups the envelope and the original artwork.

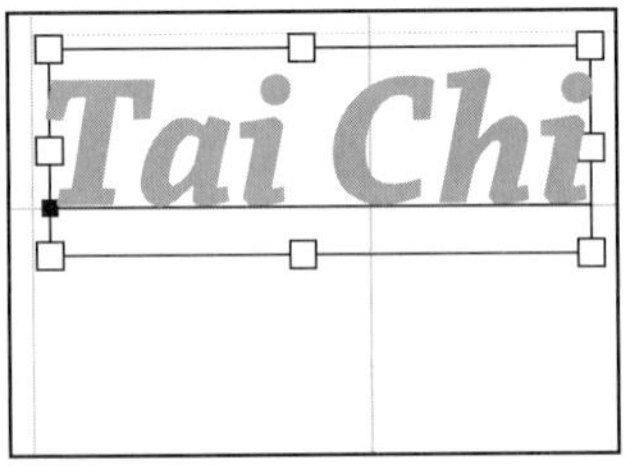

Select object to warp.

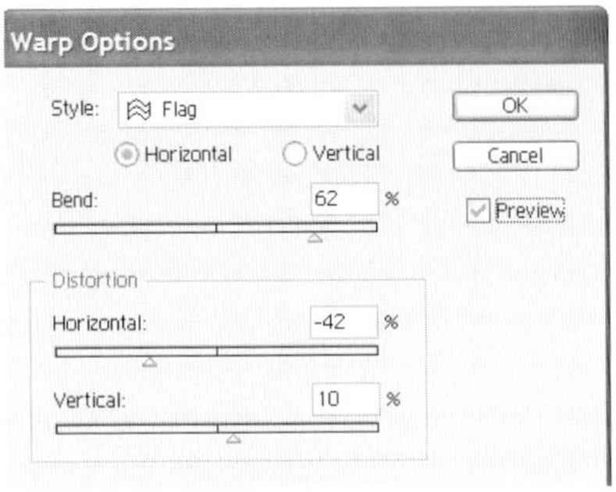

Set envelope's warp options.

Result.

Now you'll adjust the envelope slightly.

After you apply an envelope, you can continue to edit the original objects. You can edit either the envelope or the artwork, but not both at the same time. At any time you can also edit, delete, or expand an envelope.

6 Select the Mesh tool () in the toolbox.

7 Click the title text one-quarter of the way from the top baseline, and again one-quarter from the bottom baseline to create a series of two horizontal mesh lines with intersecting vertical mesh.

You'll use the Direct Selection tool () to adjust the mesh.

8 Select the Direct Selection tool (![]) in the toolbox. Drag the nodes (points on the grid) slightly to distort the text. You can also drag the direction lines to adjust the curve of the warp. Experiment by dragging the mesh points to various locations.

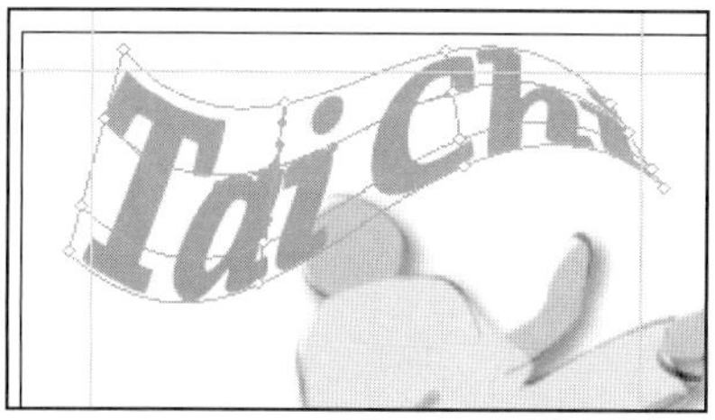

Click with Mesh tool to add mesh lines.

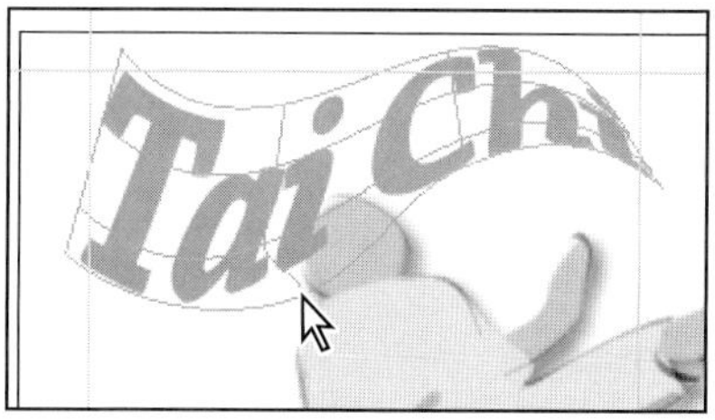

Adjust the mesh nodes and lines with the Direct Selection tool.

You can also select the envelope in the artwork, and choose Object > Envelope Distort > Reset With Mesh or Reset With Warp. Then select the desired options.

You can also edit the contents of an envelope. Now you'll change the font size.

9 Click the Selection tool in the toolbox to select the title text.

10 If you want to edit the text of an envelope, select the Type tool (T) in the toolbox. Then triple-click the text to select it, and type a new word. (We typed **Karate**.)

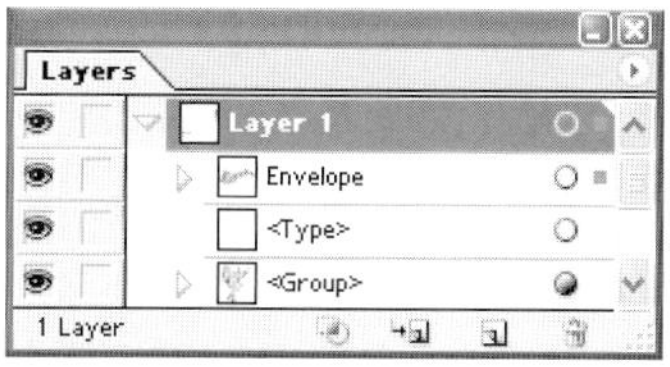

Selection indicator shows <Envelope> contents being edited.

Edit envelope contents.

11 Choose Edit > Undo. For this lesson, you'll use the original text.

12 In your artwork, use the Selection tool to reposition the title text so that the base of the T touches the left guide, and the top of the text touches the dotted line of the printing guide. Press the arrow keys to nudge the text into place.

Tai Chi

Repositioning text in an envelope.

13 Choose Select > Deselect to deselect your work. Choose File > Save.

Creating columns of type

Another way to add type to your document is to import a text file.

You'll create a container that overlaps the bottom leg of the figure so that later you can wrap the text around the leg. Then you'll divide the type container to hold three columns of type for this layout.

1 If necessary, double-click the Hand tool (✋) to fit all the artwork in the window.

2 Select the Type tool (T) in the toolbox. Using the vertical guides at the bottom right of the page for alignment, drag to draw a text container that spans from the intersecting guides beneath the figure's left knee to the lower page boundary and to the right guide.

3 Choose File > Place. Select the text file, Text.rtf, located in the Lesson11 folder, and click Place. Click OK to accept the defaults in the Microsoft Word Options dialog box. The placed text appears within the text container. You may see a plus sign in the lower right corner, indicating that not all the text is displayed. Resize the text area by dragging the handles to allow the text to fit.

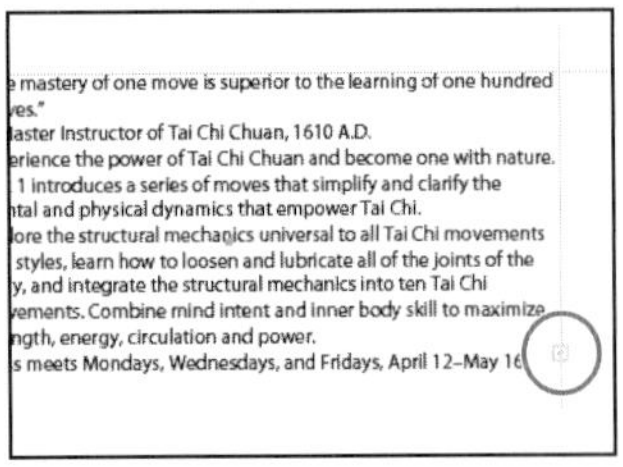
mastery of one move is superior to the learning of one hundred
es."
aster Instructor of Tai Chi Chuan, 1610 A.D.
rience the power of Tai Chi Chuan and become one with nature.
1 introduces a series of moves that simplify and clarify the
tal and physical dynamics that empower Tai Chi.
ore the structural mechanics universal to all Tai Chi movements
styles, learn how to loosen and lubricate all of the joints of the
y, and integrate the structural mechanics into ten Tai Chi
ements. Combine mind intent and inner body skill to maximize
ngth, energy, circulation and power.
s meets Mondays, Wednesdays, and Fridays, April 12–May 16

Placed text fills container drawn within guides.

Each area type object contains an in port and an out port, which enable linking to other objects and creating a linked copy of the type object. When a port is empty, it means that all the text is visible and the object isn't linked. An arrow in a port indicates that the object is linked to another object. A red plus sign in an out port indicates that the object contains additional text. This remaining unseen text is called overflow text.

Read more about in and out ports and how to use them in online Help, "Threading text between objects."

Illustrator supports more than a dozen text formats for Windows and Mac OS, including Microsoft Word®, Rich Text Format, and WordPerfect®. You can also bring text into Illustrator by copying and pasting text from the Clipboard. However, the copied text may lose its type attributes (such as its font and styles) when pasted into the document.

4 Choose View > Guides > Hide Guides.

You'll divide the type into two columns using the Area Type Options feature.

5 Click the Selection tool ( ) to select the text block automatically.

6 Choose Type > Area Type Options.

The Area Type Options dialog box is useful for changing the height, width, and gutter size between rows and columns.

- ***Width*** and ***Height*** represent the total size of the text area.
- ***Spans*** indicates the individual sizes of each row and column.
- ***Fixed*** can be checked to lock the row or width to fixed values. The width and height will not change when the text area is adjusted. The default is that the row or width will adjust to be larger or smaller as the text area is resized.
- ***Gutter*** is the space between the rows and columns.
- ***Offset*** determines how much of a margin of space is between the edge of the text area and where the text starts. The baseline can also be adjusted to determine where the first line of text starts.
- ***Text Flow*** lets you control the direction in which text flows (from left to right or up and down).

You'll divide the text container into columns and gutters.

7 In the Columns area, use the up and down arrows or type **2** in the Number text box to create two columns, and click OK.

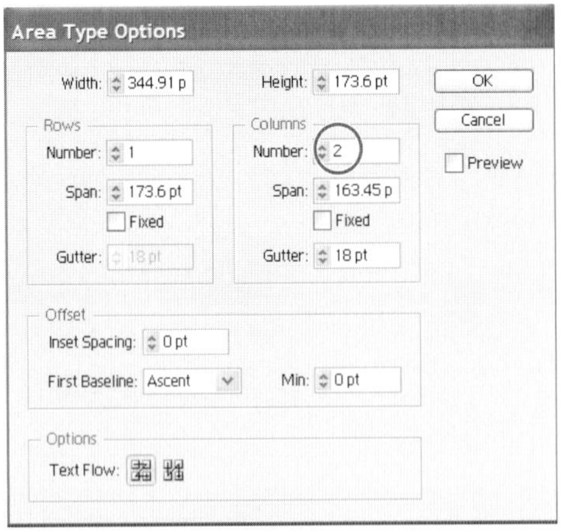
Area Type Options
Width: 344.91 p
Height: 173.6 pt
OK
Cancel
Preview
Rows
Number: 1
Span: 173.6 pt
Fixed
Gutter: 18 pt
Columns
Number: 2
Span: 163.45 p
Fixed
Gutter: 18 pt
Offset
Inset Spacing: 0 pt
First Baseline: Ascent
Min: 0 pt
Options
Text Flow:

A single text container is created with two columns in it. Text will flow from the first column into the second.

8 Before continuing, choose View > Zoom In to magnify your view of the type containers.

9 Click outside of the artwork to deselect the type columns, and choose File > Save.

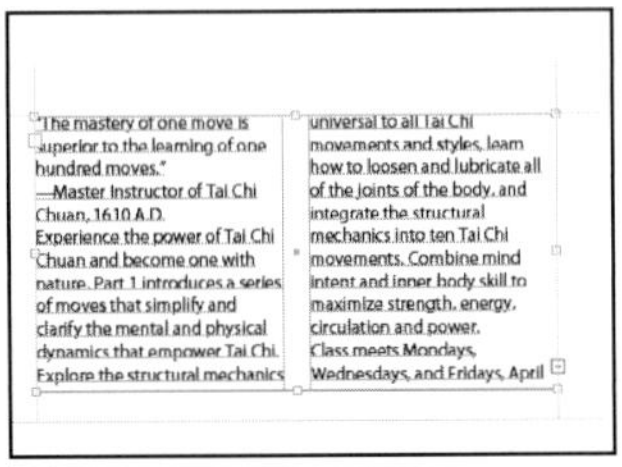
"The mastery of one move is superior to the learning of one hundred moves."
—Master Instructor of Tai Chi Chuan, 1610 A.D.
Experience the power of Tai Chi Chuan and become one with nature. Part 1 introduces a series of moves that simplify and clarify the mental and physical dynamics that empower Tai Chi. Explore the structural mechanics
universal to all Tai Chi movements and styles, learn how to loosen and lubricate all of the joints of the body, and integrate the structural mechanics into ten Tai Chi movements. Combine mind intent and inner body skill to maximize strength, energy, circulation and power.
Class meets Mondays, Wednesdays, and Fridays, April

Text container divided into two columns.

Changing character attributes of placed text

Next you'll format the type that you just imported. You'll change the character font of the placed text to match the rest of the poster, and reformat the first two paragraphs, which are a quote and a byline.

1 Select the Type tool (T), and click anywhere in one of the two text columns, then choose Select > All to select all the imported text.

2 In the Character palette, use the Font Menu (at the top of the palette) to choose a font (we choose Chaparral Pro).

Note: *Chaparral Pro is an OpenType face that is included with the original installer files of Adobe Illustrator CS. If you do not have it available, use another typeface and read on about OpenType features.*

What is OpenType?

If you frequently send files back and forth between platforms you should be designing your text files using the OpenType format.

OpenType is a new cross-platform font file format developed jointly by Adobe and Microsoft. Adobe has converted the entire Adobe Type Library into this format and now offers thousands of OpenType fonts.

The two main benefits of the OpenType format are its cross-platform compatibility (the same font file works on Macintosh and Windows computers), and its ability to support widely expanded character sets and layout features, which provide richer linguistic support and advanced typographic control.

OpenType fonts can include an expanded character set and layout features, providing broader linguistic support and more precise typographic control. Feature-rich Adobe OpenType fonts can be distinguished by the word "Pro," which is part of the font name and appears in application font menus. OpenType fonts can be installed and used alongside PostScript Type 1 and TrueType fonts.

–From www.adobe.com/type/opentype

3 In the Character palette enter sizes for the type and the leading in the Font Size and Leading text boxes. (We specified 10 in the Font Size text box and 12 in the Leading text box.) Press Enter or Return to apply the attributes.

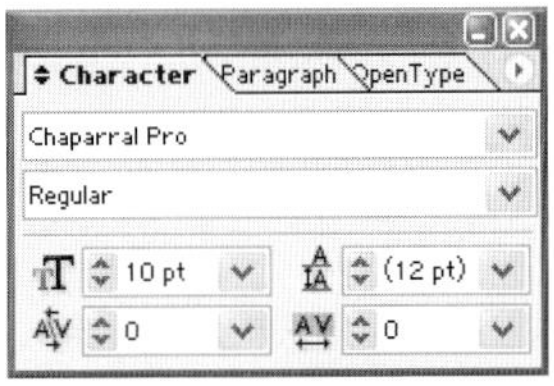

Choose font and size from the Character palette menu.

Next you'll select the first two paragraphs and format them as a quote and a byline.

4 First, choose Type > Show Hidden Characters to display all the hidden characters in the text, such as spaces and paragraph breaks.

5 Using the Type tool (T), triple-click inside the first paragraph to select only that paragraph. (You can also select it by dragging.)

6 In the Character palette, choose a font from the pop-up menu (we selected Chaparral Pro Italic), and enter sizes for the font and leading (we specified 14 points in the Font Size text box and 20 points in the Leading text box). Press Enter or Return to apply the changes.

7 Using the Type tool again, triple-click inside the second paragraph to select it, and experiment with different fonts and sizes for the byline. (We used Chaparral Pro Italic, 11 points for font size, and 16 points for leading.)

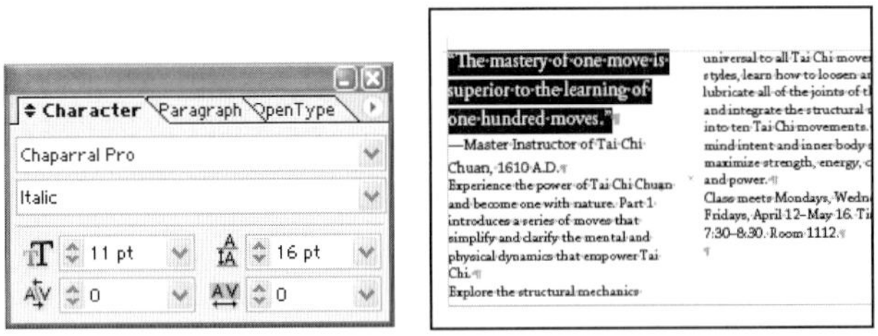

Select and reformat first two paragraphs.

8 Choose Type > Show Hidden Characters to turn off the display of hidden text characters.

9 Choose File > Save.

Changing paragraph attributes

You can set paragraph attributes (such as alignment or indenting) before you enter new type, or reset them to change the appearance of existing, selected type. If you select several type paths and type containers, you can set attributes for all of them at the same time.

Now you'll add more space leading before all the paragraphs in the column text.

1 Hold down Ctrl (Windows) or Command (Mac OS) to temporarily convert the Type tool (T) to the Selection tool (↖), and click the edge of the colums of text.

2 Click the Paragraph tab behind the Character palette to display the Paragraph palette, or choose Window > Type > Paragraph.

3 In the Paragraph palette click on the palette menu arrow in the upper right, then click on Show Options. Type **6** in the Space Before Paragraph text box (in the bottom left corner). Spacing before paragraphs, rather than pressing the Return key, is recommended when creating large text areas.

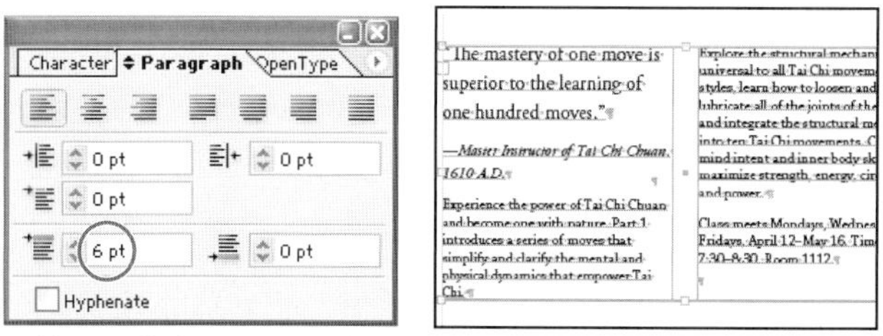
Character
Paragraph
OpenType
0 pt
0 pt
0 pt
6 pt
0 pt
Hyphenate
"The mastery of one move is superior to the learning of one hundred moves."
—Master Instructor of Tai Chi Chuan, 1610 A.D.

Add space before paragraphs.

4 Choose File > Save.

For information on other features you can use when working with type, such as kerning, tracking, tabs, and searching, see "Creating Type" in online Help.

Saving and Using Styles

New in Illustrator CS, you can save and use styles. This keeps text consistent and is helpful when text attributes need to be updated. Once a style is created, a change only needs to be completed to the created style, and all text with the style applied is updated.

There are two types of styles in Adobe Illustrator CS.

- ***Character***-This retains the text attributes and applies them to selected text only.
- ***Paragraph***-This retains text and paragraph attributes and applies them to the entire paragraph. In other words, if the Insertion point is between two letters and a paragraph style is applied, the entire paragraph is changed.

In this next lesson you will create a Character Style and apply it to selected text.

1 Using the Type tool (T) select Tai Chi Chuan in the first column of the paragraph text.

2 In the Character palette change the font style from regular to bold.

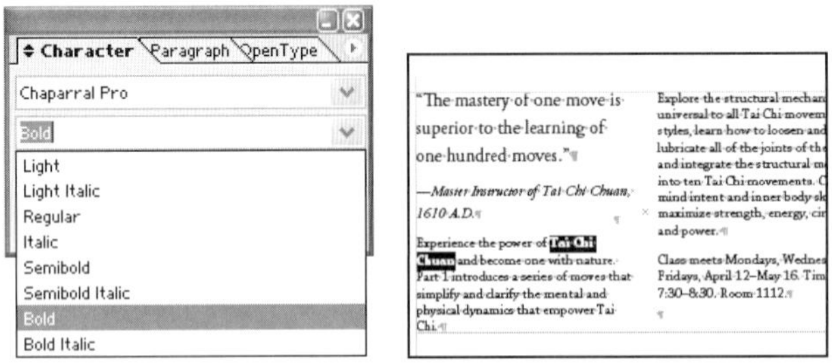

Leave the font the same but change the style using the style pop-up menu.

3 Click the Fill and select a red swatch from the Swatches palette.

The selected text is now bold and red.

Now you will save these attributes as a Character Style and apply it to other instances in the text.

4 Choose Window > Type > Character Styles.

5 Alt-click (Windows) or Option-click (Mac OS) on the Create New Style button at bottom of the Character Styles palette. Alt/Option + clicking on the New Style button allows you to name the style as it is added to the palette. You can also double-click at any time on the style to name and edit it.

6 Name the style **Bold** and click OK. The style records the attributes applied to your selected text.

Now you will apply that Character Style to other instances.

7 With the text still selected, click on the named style Bold in the Character Styles palette to assign the style to that text.

8 Select the words Tai Chi that follow in the paragraph and Alt-click (Windows) or Option-click (Mac OS) on the named style Bold in the Character Styles palette. The Alt/Option click is used to clear any attributes from the text that are not part of the Character Style.

9 Select other instances of the text Tai Chi and assign them the **Bold** style as well.

10 Choose Select > Deselect.

Perhaps you decide that the color just isn't working and you want to change it. Using styles, you only have to change the color once, and all instances are updated.

11 From the Character Styles palette choose the palette menu, then Character Style Options. Select a type attribute option from the window on the left, then assign specific attributes by selecting characteristics on the right.

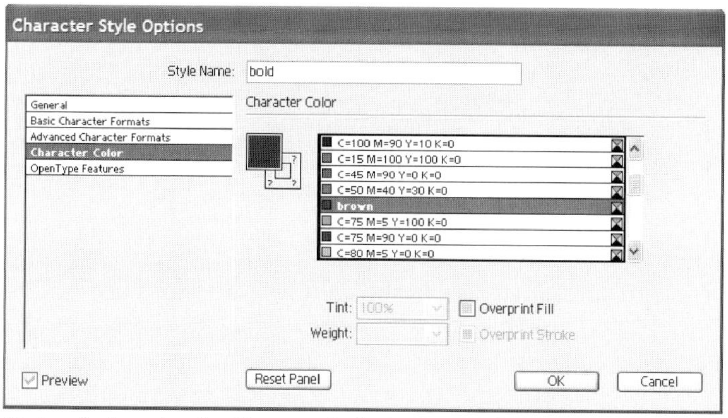

Update Styles using the Character Style Options Dialog box.

12 Click on Character Color. In the window that appears on the right choose the swatch named **brown**.

13 Click OK.

The assigned Character Styles now change from Red to Brown.

Paragraph Styles are created the same way but apply the selected attributes to the entire paragraph.

Wrapping type around a graphic

You can make type wrap around any graphic object in Illustrator. To complete the column layout, you'll wrap the left column of type around the bottom leg of the figure.

1 Using the Selection tool (↖), click and drag the two column text area on top of the standing leg.

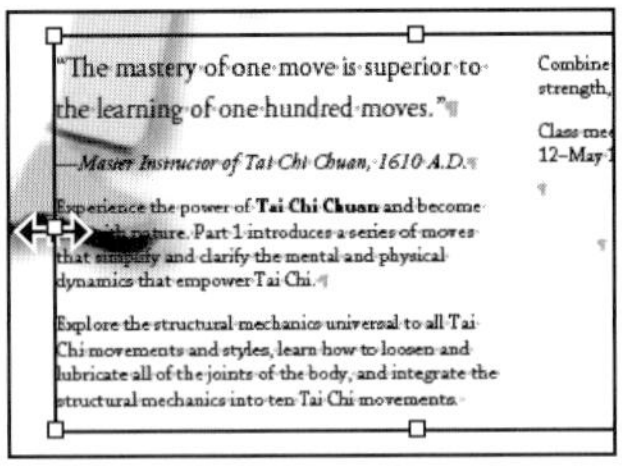

Objects around which you will wrap type must be in front of the type container.

2 Select the figure with the Selection tool. Choose Object > Arrange > Bring to Front.

3 Choose Object > Text Wrap > Make Text Wrap.

4 Check on the Preview and type in **6** for the text offset.

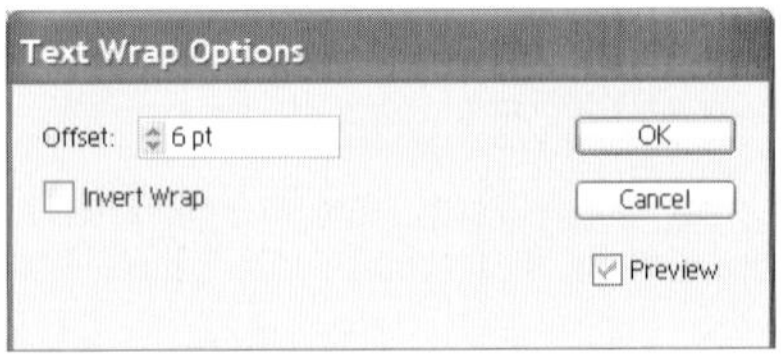

Type an offset.

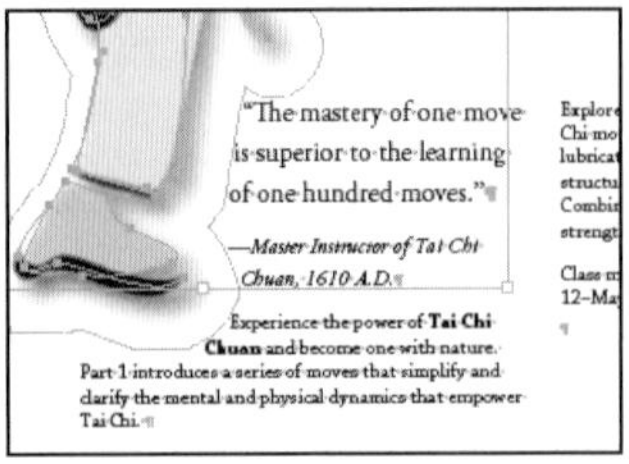

Result.

You can use the Type tool to click anywhere in the columns of placed text and make changes as you wish, such as typing some new words or correcting the spelling.

5 Change the wrap to a smaller amount by choosing Object > Text Wrap > Text > Wrap Options. Change the offset value to **5** and click OK.

6 Choose Select > Deselect to deselect the artwork.

7 Choose File > Save.

Typing along a path

Another way to create type in Illustrator is to enter type along a path. Now you'll add a freeform line of text to the poster.

1 With no objects selected, change the fill to **None** and the stroke to **Black**.

2 Select the Pencil tool ( ) in the toolbox, and drag it to draw a line along the back of the figure's raised leg. The line remains selected after you draw it.

3 Click the Character tab behind the Paragraph palette to display the Character palette, choose a font from the pop-up menu (we selected Adobe Garamond Regular), type 6 points in the Font Size text box, and press Enter or Return to set the new attributes.

4 Select the path Type tool ( ) from the same group as the Type tool in the toolbox, and click at the beginning of the line.

Clicking a line with the Path Type tool converts the line to an invisible path (without any fill or stroke color), and a blinking insertion point appears.

5 Type in the line of text **Combine mind intent and inner body skill.**

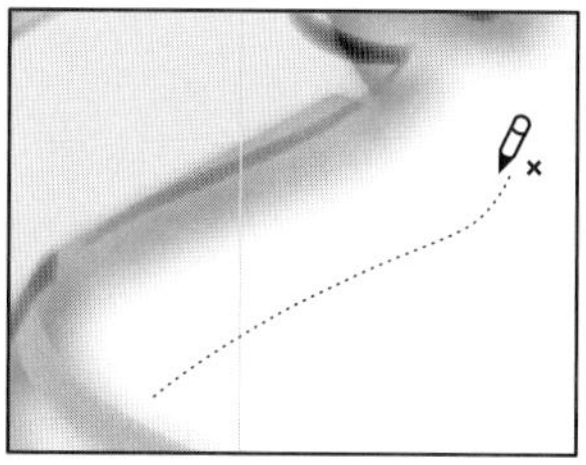
Draw a line.

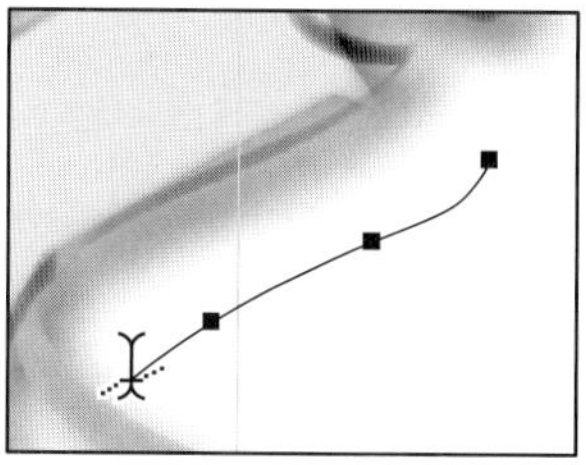
Convert line to type path.

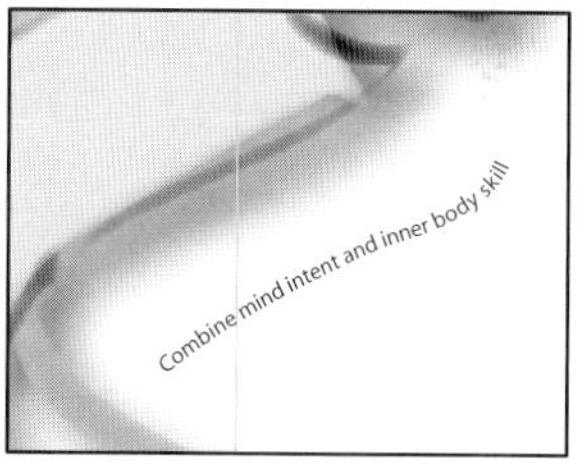

Type words along path.

Turning a path or object into a type path removes any stroke or fill from the path, even if it was originally stroked or filled. When you select a type path, changing the paint settings affects only the type, not the path.

6 To move the type path, use the Selection tool ( ).

7 Choose View > Hide Bounding Box so that it doesn't distract you.

8 To adjust the position of the type along the path, position the Selection tool over the type's start, center, or end bracket until a small icon appears next to the pointer. (If the pointer doesn't change, make sure the Selection tool is still selected.) Drag to the right or left to reposition the type on the path. (Dragging across the path flips the type.)

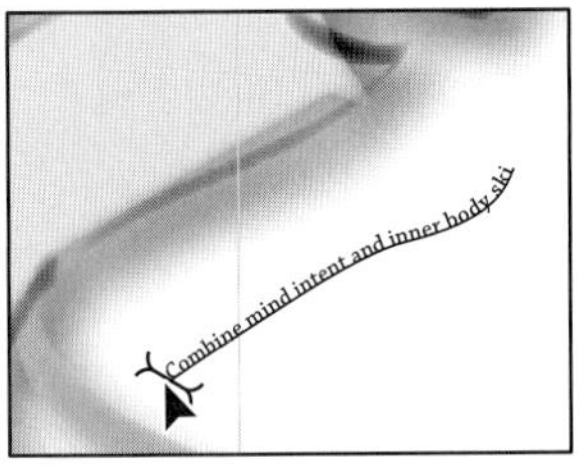
Combine mind intent and inner body ski

Adjusting type along path.

9 If you zoomed in on the artwork, double-click the Hand tool (✋) in the toolbox to fit the artwork in the window.

10 Choose Select > Deselect, and then choose File > Save.

Creating type outlines

You can modify the shapes of individual letters in a block of type by converting the block to type outlines or letterforms. When you create type outlines, each character becomes a separate object with compound paths outlining the character. This is helpful when creating logos or other artwork that is distributed to many people and might not have the same fonts that you used.

Now you'll create the number 800 and convert it into outlines.

1 Select the Line Segment tool (\) and position the cursor to the right of the filled rectangle in the upper right section of the page. Hold down the Shift key then click and drag downwards to create a path about as long as the rectangle. This creates a straight line constrained to 90°.

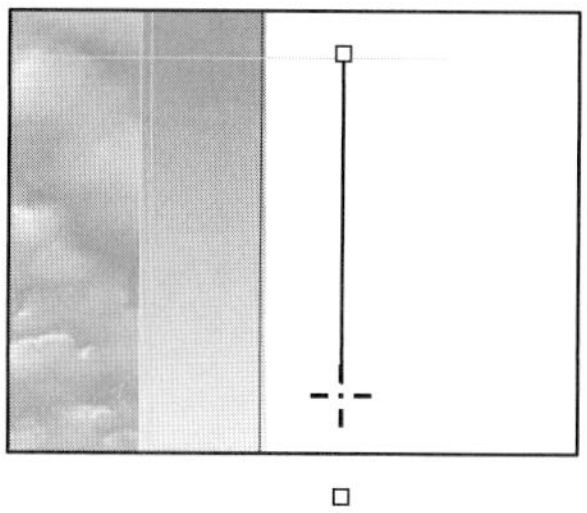

2 You will now deselect the Bold character style by choosing Window > Type > Character Styles and selecting No character style. Leaving the Bold character style selected affects any new type created in your document.

3 Select the Vertical Type tool (|T) and click on the top of the path.

This converts the path into a text path.

4 In the Character palette change the font size to **45 pts**. Choose a font face that you want to use. (We used Chaparral Pro Bold).

5 Type **800**. The text flows down from the top.

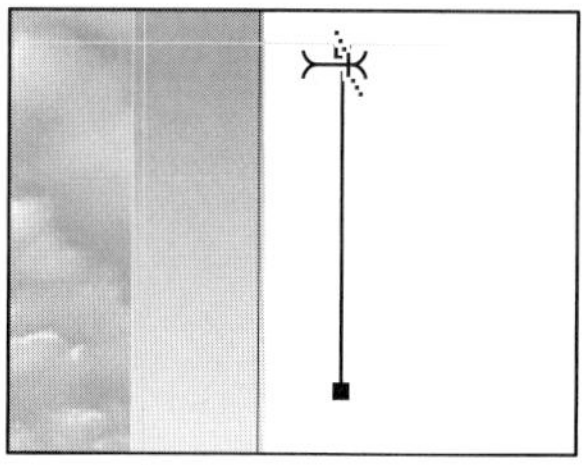

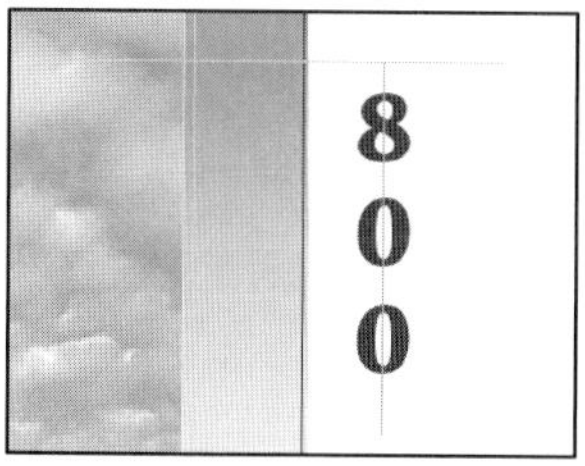

Using the vertical Type tool click on the path and type 800.

6 Use the Selection tool (↖) to select the type 800 and then choose Type > Create Outlines.

The type is converted to a set of compound paths around each number that can be edited and manipulated like any other object.

7 Click away from the artwork to deselect the numbers, and then select the Group Selection tool (↖+) from the same group as the Direct Selection tool in the toolbox.

The Group Selection tool lets you select individual outlines in a compound path.

8 Shift+click to select the outer paths of all three numbers, and press the Up Arrow key a few times to move the paths up, leaving the inner paths of all three in their original position.

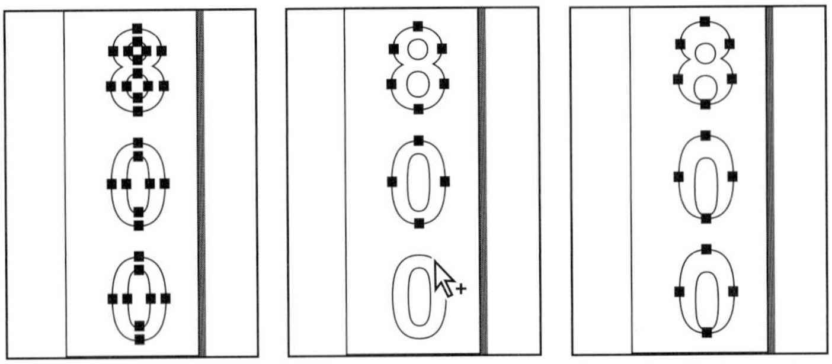

Create outlines. *Select the outer lines.* *Press the Up Arrow key.*

You can also change the shape of letterforms by using the Direct Selection tool to select path segments or anchor points in the outlines and dragging the direction lines in new directions.

9 Using the Selection tool, click and drag the number over the filled rectangle.

10 Make sure that Fill is forward in the toolbar and assign white as the fill, press the **X** key bring the stroke forward and change the stroke to None.

11 Click away from the artwork to deselect it.

12 File > Save.

Creating type masks

Masks crop part of an image so that only a portion of it is revealed through the shape or shapes that you create. You can use type as a mask without having to convert the type to outlines first. After creating a mask using type, you can still edit it—for example, by adjusting the font or size and even by typing in new text.

In this example, you'll create a mask using type and an embedded bitmap image. An image of a cloudy sky was pasted into the document to use as the background of the mask.

Now you'll add the heading "ASIAN STUDIES PROGRAM" in the top right corner of the poster and convert it to a type mask over the cloudy sky image.

1 Select the Type tool (T) from the same group as the Vertical Path Type tool (↓T) in the toolbox, and click in the sky next to the number **8**.

2 In the Character palette, choose a font from the pop-up menu (we chose Chaparral Bold), enter sizes for the font and the leading (we specified 28 points in the Font Size text box and 28 points in the Leading text box), and press Enter or Return to apply the settings.

3 Click the Paragraph tab to display the Paragraph palette. Click the Align Right button.

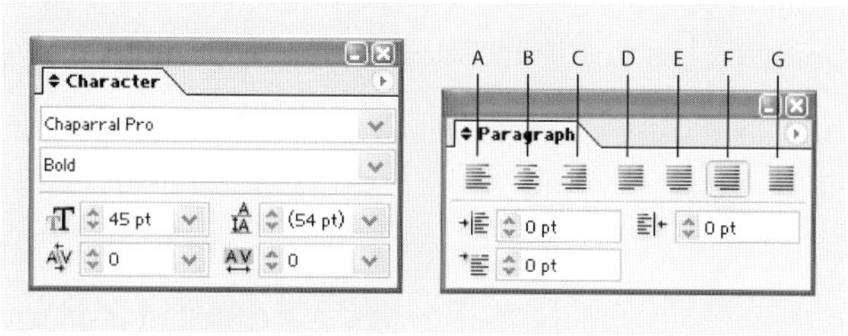

A. Align left. B. Align center. C. Align right. D. Justify with last line aligned left. E. Justify with last line aligned center. F. Justify with last line aligned right. G. Justify all lines.

4 Press the Caps Lock key to type in all uppercase letters. Type **ASIAN**, and then press Enter or Return to move the insertion point to the next line. Type **STUDIES**, press Enter or Return, and then type **PROGRAM**.

5 If necessary, click the Selection tool to reposition the text block so that it is on top of the sky image.

6 Shift-click to select the image behind it.

The object that will be the mask can be a single shape, multiple shapes, or type. The masking object (in this case, the type) must be on top of the artwork you want to mask.

7 Choose Object > Clipping Mask > Make to convert the front object into a mask and see through to the image.

Select type and sky image.

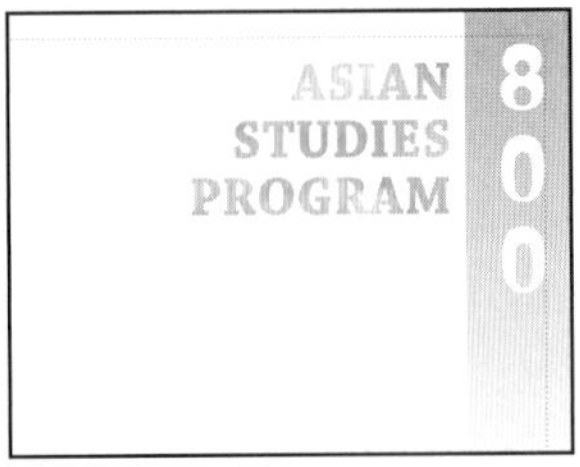

Apply clipping mask.

The type mask loses its paint attributes and is assigned a fill and stroke of None. Thus, if you moved the type away from the background image, you would no longer see the type mask in Preview view unless you select it or assign it new paint attributes.

Once you have created a mask, you can still adjust the artwork and the type (the mask) independently. For example, you can resize either the artwork (here an embedded photo) or the type, as well as rotate, skew, and reflect them.

8 Double-click the Hand tool (✋) in the toolbox to fit the artwork in the window.

9 Choose File > Save.

You've completed the artwork for the Tai Chi poster using various ways to work with type.

Saving your file for electronic distribution

Now you'll save a copy of the poster in Portable Document Format (PDF) so you can distribute it electronically, or link it to your Web site. When you save your artwork in PDF format, Illustrator creates an exact snapshot of the page that lets you view it online without the fonts, linked images, or software used to create it.

1 Choose File > Save As. In the dialog box, choose Illustrator PDF from the Save as Type (Windows) or Format (Mac OS) pop-up menu, name the file **TaiChi.pdf**. In the Save In menu, navigate to the Lesson11 folder, nd click Save.

2 In the Adobe PDF dialog box, leave the Preset at Illustrator Defaults.

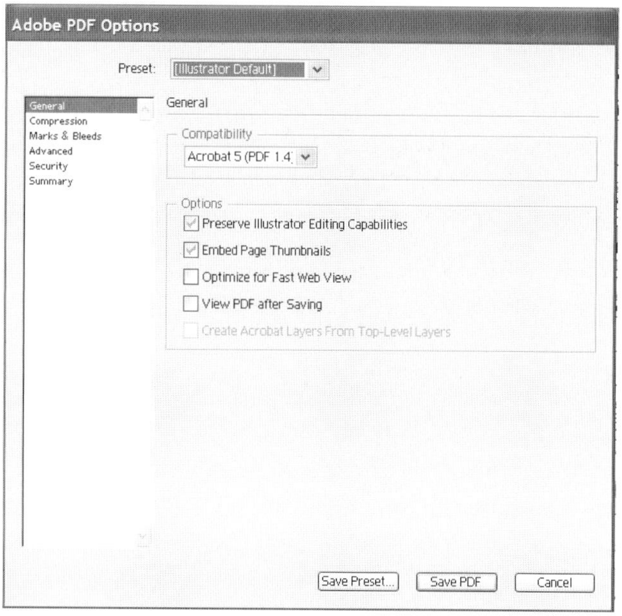

3 Leave the other settings as they are, and click Save PDF.

Presets Defined

Illustrator Default–*to create a PDF file in which all Illustrator data is preserved. PDF files created with this preset can be reopened in Illustrator without any loss of data.*

Press–*to create a PDF file that will be printed to imagesetters or platesetters as high quality final output. In this case, file size is not a consideration. The objective is to maintain all the information in an Adobe PDF file that a commercial printer or service provider will need to print the document correctly. This set of options converts color to CMYK; embeds all fonts used in the file; prints at a higher resolution; and uses other settings to preserve the maximum amount of information contained in the original document.*

Note: *Before creating an Adobe PDF file to send to a commercial printer or service provider, check with the provider to find out what the output resolution and other settings should be. You may need to customize the settings for a particular provider, and then provide them with a custom preset.*

Acrobat 6 Layered–*to create a PDF file in which top-level Illustrator layers are saved as Acrobat layers. This allows Adobe Acrobat 6 users to generate multiple versions of a document from a single file. For example, if a document will be published in multiple languages, you can place the text for each language in a different layer. Your printer or prepress service provider can then show and hide the layers in Acrobat 6 to generate different versions of the document.*

–From online Help. "Saving artwork in Adobe PDF".

Illustrator saves the copy of the poster as a PDF file that can be viewed electronically in Adobe Acrobat Reader® and linked to your Web pages to be viewed in a browser. Acrobat Reader – electronic publishing software for Windows, DOS, UNIX®, and Macintosh® – is provided on the Adobe Illustrator CD and is available on the Adobe Web site (http: //www.adobe.com) for free distribution.

4 To view the PDF file if you have Acrobat 5.0 or 6.0 installed, launch Acrobat. Then choose File > Open, and open the TaiChi.pdf file you just saved in the Lesson11 folder.

For information on saving Illustrator files in different formats, see "Saving and Exporting Artwork" in online Help.

For information on converting artwork to GIF and JPEG images for your Web pages, see Lesson 18, "Creating a Web Publication."

Review questions

1 Describe three ways to enter text into the artwork.

2 How do you change the leading between lines in a paragraph? How do you change the leading between paragraphs?

3 Describe two ways to change the font and size of type.

4 How can you divide a type container into smaller containers?

5 How do you create type that follows the shape of a path or an object?

6 What is a reason for converting type to outlines?

7 How do you create a type mask?

8 How do you create an envelope effect? How do you edit the effect?

9 How do you create a PDF version of an Illustrator document?

Review answers

1 To enter text in the artwork, do any of the following:

- Select the Type tool (T) and start typing.
- Import text from another file by choosing File > Place.
- Select the path Type tool, click on any path, and start typing.
- Click inside any shape, or click and drag a marquee with the Type tool. Then start typing or place a text file.

2 To change the leading between lines in a paragraph, select the paragraph and then enter a new leading value in the Character palette. (Choose Window > Type > Character to display the Character palette.) To change the leading (or space) between paragraphs, select the block of type and then enter a new leading value in the Space Before Paragraph text box in the Paragraph palette. (Choose Window > Type > Paragraph to display the Paragraph palette.)

3 To change the font and size of type, you can use the controls in the Character palette, or choose commands from the Font and Size submenus in the Type menu.

4 To divide a type container into smaller containers, select the container and choose Type > Area Type Options. In the Area Type Options dialog box, enter the number of horizontal or vertical containers, or both, into which you'll divide the container, their size, and the space between each container.

5 You can use the Path Type tool (↝) to type words along an existing path. You can also wrap a block of type around an object by selecting the object and choosing Object > Text Wrap > Make Text Wrap. (The object must be in front of the type.)

6 To create a PDF version of an Illustrator file, you choose File > Save a Copy; then for format or type, you select Adobe PDF.

7 Convert type to outlines when you want to transform (scale, reshape, and so on) letters individually in the word or block of type. Outlines are also useful for filling type with a gradient fill. Outlines also eliminate the need to send the font along with the file when sharing with others.

8 One way to create a type mask is to select the type that you want to be the mask, and select the object, bitmap image, or type that you want to show through the mask. (The masking type must be in front of any other objects.) Then choose Object > Clipping Mask > Make to create the type mask.

9 You create an envelope by selecting an object and then applying a preset warp shape or mesh using the Object > Envelope Distort > Make With Warp or Make With Mesh command. You can also select a top object that will act as the envelope, select another object to which you apply the envelope, and then choose Object > Envelope Distort > Make With Top Object.

You can edit either an envelope or its contents, but not both at the same time. To edit an envelope, you select the envelope and then choose Object > Envelope Distort > Reset With Warp or Reset With Mesh. You can also use the Selection tool or Mesh tool to edit the envelope. To edit an envelope's contents, you select the envelope and then choose Object > Envelope Distort > Edit Contents.

Lesson 12

12 Blending Shapes and Colors

Gradient fills are graduated blends of two or more colors. You use the Gradient palette to create or modify a gradient fill. The Blend tool blends the shapes and colors of objects together into a new blended object or a series of intermediate shapes.

In this lesson, you'll learn how to do the following:

- Create and save gradients.
- Add colors to a gradient.
- Adjust the direction of a gradient blend.
- Create smooth-color blends between objects.
- Blend the shapes of objects in intermediate steps.
- Modify a blend, including adjusting its path and changing the shape or color of the original objects.

Getting started

You'll explore various ways to create your own color gradients and blend colors and shapes together using the Gradient palette and the Blend tool.

Before you begin, you'll restore the default preferences for Adobe Illustrator. Then you'll open the finished art file for this lesson to see what you'll create.

1 To ensure that the tools and palettes function exactly as described in this lesson, delete or deactivate (by renaming) the Adobe Illustrator CS preferences file. See "Restoring default preferences" on page 2.

2 Start Adobe Illustrator.

3 Choose File > Open, and open the L12end.ai file in the Lesson12 folder, located inside the Lessons folder within the AICIB folder on your hard drive.

3 The chile peppers, CHILES type, and wavy lines are all filled with gradients. The objects that make up the inside of the bowl, the objects on the outside of the bowl, and the top and bottom wavy lines on the blanket have all been blended to create new objects.

4 If you like, choose View > Zoom Out to make the finished artwork smaller, adjust the window size, and leave it on your screen as you work. (Use the Hand tool (✋) to move the artwork where you want it in the window.) If you don't want to leave the image open, choose File > Close.

For an illustration of the finished artwork in this lesson, see the color section.

To begin working, you'll open an existing art file.

5 Choose File > Open, and open the L12start.ai file in the Lesson12 folder, located inside the Lessons folder within the AICIB folder on your hard drive.

6 Choose File > Save As, name the file **Chiles.ai**, and select the Lesson12 folder in the Save In menu. Leave the type of file format set to Adobe Illustrator® Document, and click Save. In the Illustrator Options dialog box, leave at the defaults and click OK.

7 Click the close box in the Layers palette or choose Window > Layers to close the Layers palette group. You won't need these palettes for this lesson.

Creating a gradient fill

Gradients can be used very much like colors to fill objects that you create. A gradient fill is a graduated blend between two or more colors. You can easily create your own gradients, or you can use the gradients provided with Adobe Illustrator and edit them for the desired effect.

To begin the lesson, you'll create a gradient fill for one of the chile peppers.

1 Using the Selection tool (↖), click to select the chile pepper in the back.

The pepper is painted with a solid color fill and no stroke, as indicated in the Fill and Stroke boxes in the toolbox. The Gradient button below the Fill and Stroke boxes indicates the current gradient fill (which is by default a black-and-white gradient until you select a gradient-filled object or a gradient swatch in the Swatches palette).

2 Click the Gradient button in the toolbox.

The default, black-and-white gradient appears in the Fill box in the toolbox and is applied to the selected chile pepper.

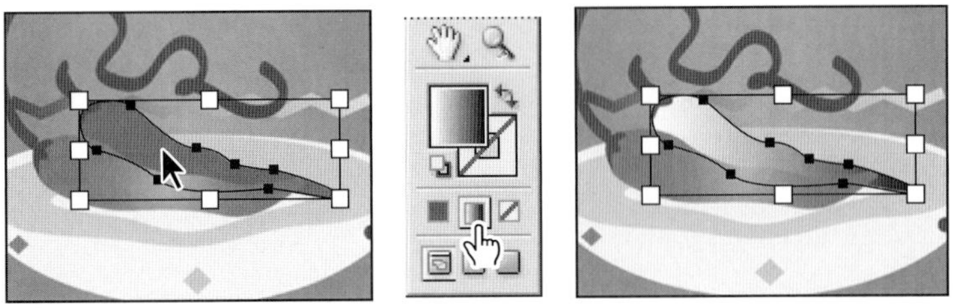

Click Gradient button to paint selected object with default or current gradient fill.

Choose Window > Gradient if your Gradient palette is not visible. You use the Gradient palette to create your own gradients and to modify the colors of existing gradients.

3 In the Gradient palette, position the pointer on the triangle in the upper right corner of the palette, press the mouse button, and choose Show Options from the palette's menu. (Use the same technique for choosing options from other palette menus.)

4 Now click the Gradient tab on the palette and drag it to move the palette to another area on your screen. This action separates, or undocks, the Gradient palette from any other palettes.

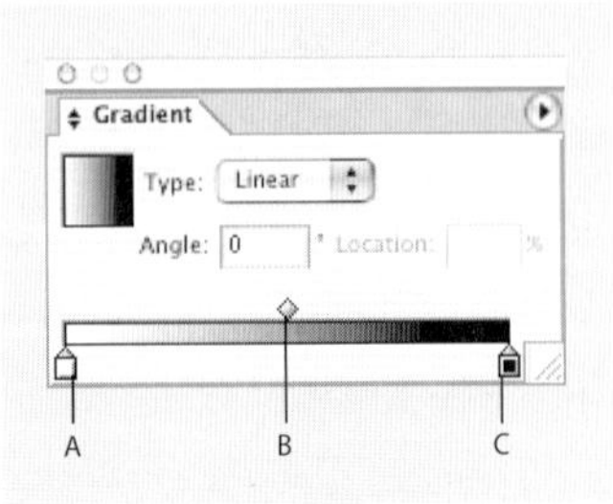

A. *Starting gradient stop.*
B. *Midpoint between blended colors.*
C. *Ending gradient stop.*

In the Gradient palette, the left gradient square, or stop, under the gradient bar marks the gradient's starting color; the right gradient stop marks the ending color. A gradient stop is the point at which a gradient changes from one color to the next. A diamond above the bar marks the midpoint where two colors blend equally.

5 Click the left gradient stop to select the starting color of the gradient. The tip of the gradient stop appears darker to indicate that it's selected.

In the Color palette, a gradient stop appears beneath the Fill box, indicating which color in the gradient is currently selected. Now you'll paint the selected color in the gradient with a new color.

6 In the Color palette, position the pointer on the triangle in the upper right corner of the palette, press the mouse button, and choose CMYK to switch from the Grayscale palette to the CMYK palette.

7 With the gradient stop selected, position the eyedropper pointer in the color bar at the bottom of the Color palette, and drag or click to select a new color. Notice the change to the gradient fill in the selected chile pepper.

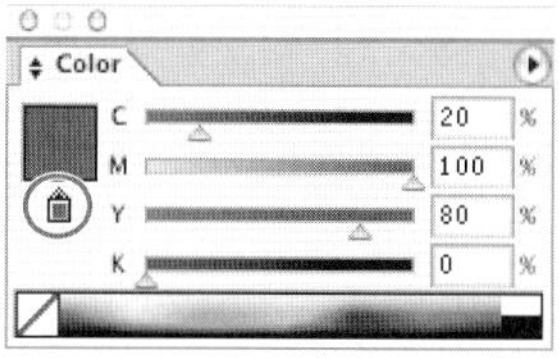

Gradient stop color selected.

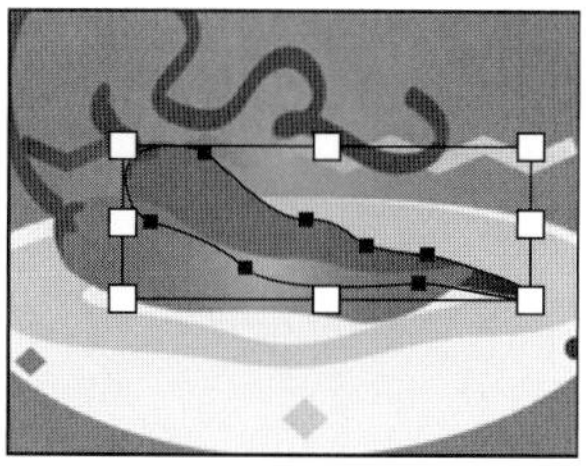

Result.

You can also drag the Color palette sliders or enter values in the percent text boxes to select a color. The selected gradient stop changes to reflect your choice.

8 With the left gradient stop still selected, enter these CMYK values in the Color palette: C=**20**, M=**100**, Y=**80**, and K=**0**. (To move between text boxes, press Tab.) Press Enter (Windows) or Return (Mac OS) to apply the last value typed.

9 In the Gradient palette, select the ending gradient stop on the right.

10 In the Color palette, choose CMYK from the palette menu to switch to the CMYK palette from the Grayscale palette.

11 Change the ending color by entering these values in the Color palette: C=**100**, M=**30**, Y=**100**, and K=**0**. (Press Tab to select each text box.) Press Enter or Return to apply the last value typed.

Now you'll save the new gradient in the Swatches palette.

12 Click the Swatches tab to bring the palette to the front of its group. (If the Swatches palette isn't visible on-screen, choose Window > Swatches to display it.)

13 To save the gradient, drag it from the Fill box in the toolbox or the Gradient palette and drop it on the Swatches palette; or select it in the Fill box in the toolbox or in the Gradient palette, and click the New Swatch button at the bottom of the Swatches palette.

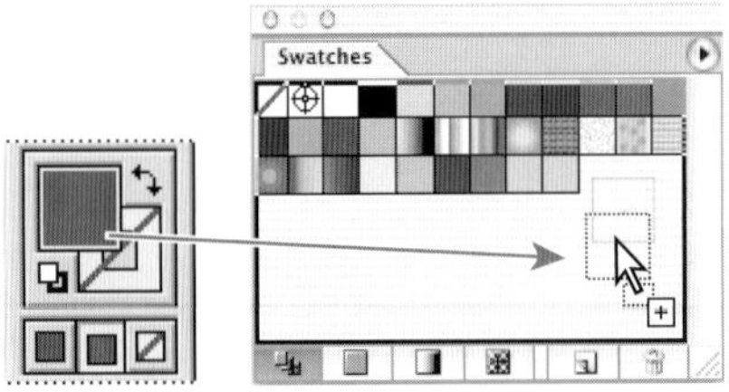

Drag gradient swatch from Fill box to Swatches palette.

14 In the Swatches palette, double-click the new gradient swatch to open the Swatch Options dialog box. Type **Pepper2** in the Swatch Name text box, and click OK.

15 To display only gradient swatches in the Swatches palette, click the Show Gradient Swatches button at the bottom of the Swatches palette.

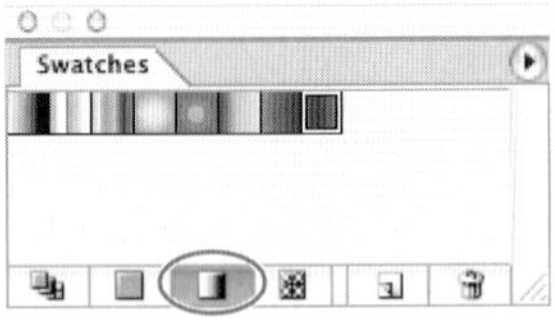

Display only gradient swatches.

16 Try out some of the different gradients in the selected chile pepper.

Notice that some of the gradients have several colors. You'll learn how to make a gradient with multiple colors later in this lesson.

17 Deselect the artwork by choosing Select > Deselect, and then choose File > Save.

Adjusting the direction of the gradient blend

Once you have painted an object with a gradient fill, you can adjust the direction that the gradient colors blend in the object. Now you'll adjust the gradient fill in the other chile pepper.

1 Use the Selection tool (↖) to select the chile pepper in front. Notice that it's painted with a radial-type gradient (as indicated in the Gradient palette).

You can create linear or radial gradients. Both types of gradient have a starting and an ending color of the fill. With a radial gradient, the starting color of the gradient defines the center point of the fill, which radiates outward to the ending color.

2 Select the Gradient tool (◨) in the toolbox.

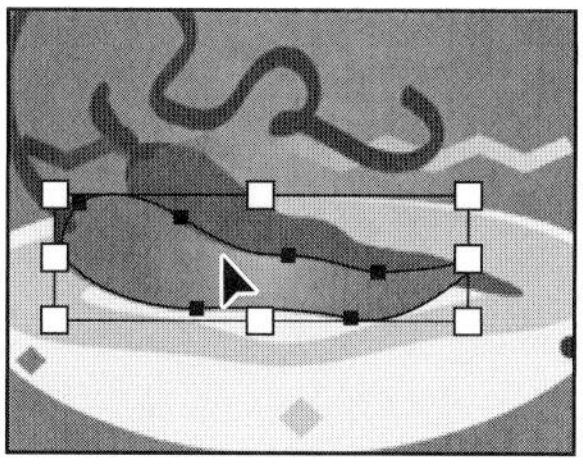

Select gradient-filled object.

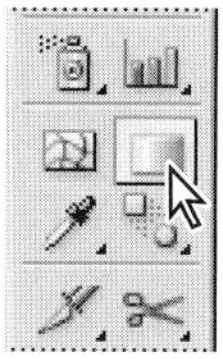

Select Gradient tool to adjust gradient.

The Gradient tool works only on selected objects that are filled with a gradient.

3 Click or drag the Gradient tool across the selected chile pepper to change the position and direction of the gradient's starting and ending colors.

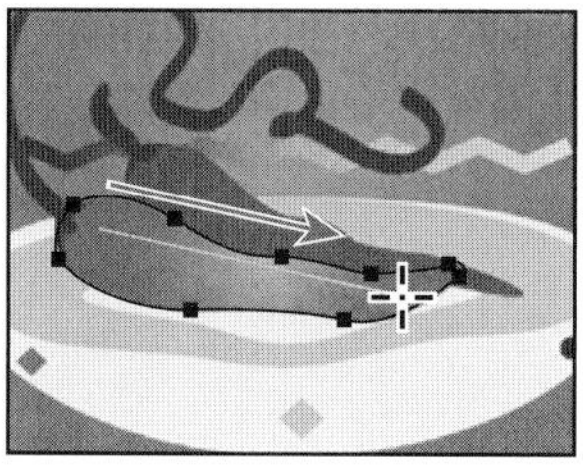

Drag Gradient tool at an angle.

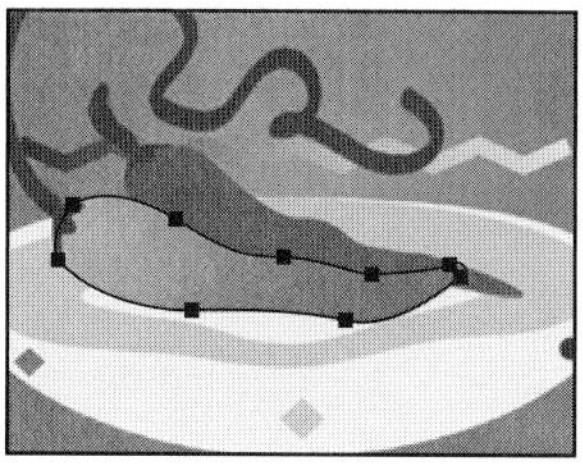

Result.

For example, drag within the pepper to create a short gradient with distinct color blends; drag a longer distance outside the pepper to create a longer gradient with more subtle color blends. You can also drag from the ending color to the starting color and vice versa to transpose the colors and reverse the direction of the blend.

4 Deselect the artwork by choosing Select > Deselect, and then choose File > Save.

Adding colors to a gradient

Every gradient in Adobe Illustrator has at least two gradient stops. By editing the color mix of each stop and by adding gradient stops in the Gradient palette, you can create your own custom gradients.

Now you'll paint some type that has been converted to path outlines with a linear gradient fill, and edit the colors in it.

1 Select the Magic Wand tool ( ), and click to select the letters in the type CHILES.

The *CHILES* type has already been converted to path outlines so you can fill it with a gradient. (To convert type to path outlines, select it and choose Type > Create Outlines. See Lesson 11, "Working with Type," for more information.)

2 Choose Object > Group to group the letters.

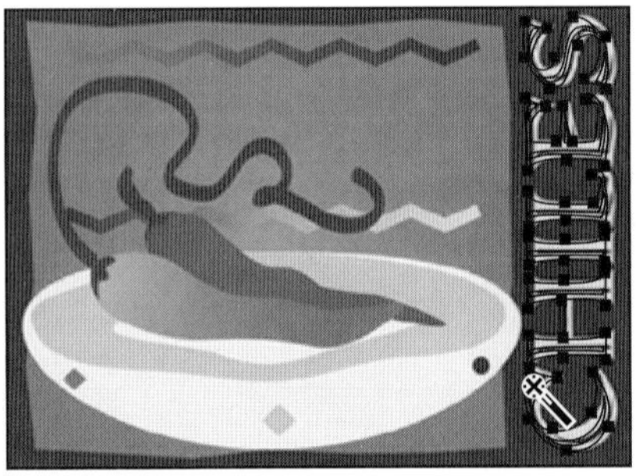

Select letter outlines and group type.

By grouping the letters, you'll fill each individual letter with the same gradient at once. Grouping them also makes it easier to edit the gradient fill globally.

3 In the toolbox, click the Gradient button (below the Fill and Stroke boxes) to paint the type outlines with the current gradient fill—in this case, with the radial gradient that was last selected in the chile pepper.

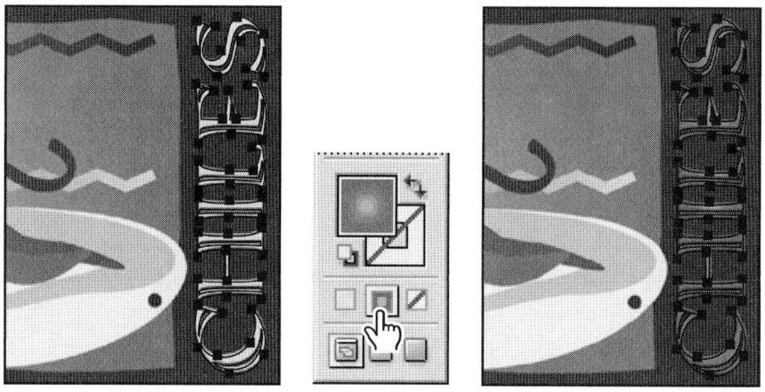

Paint selected type with last-selected gradient fill.

To edit the colors in a gradient, you click their gradient stops below the gradient bar.

4 In the Gradient palette, for Type choose Linear to change the fill to a linear gradient, and then click the left gradient stop to select it so that you can adjust the starting color of the gradient.

The Color palette displays the color of the currently selected gradient stop in the Fill box.

Now you'll change the display of the Swatches palette so that you can choose any color from it.

5 At the bottom of the Swatches palette, click the Show All Swatches button to display all the color, gradient, and pattern swatches in the Swatches palette.

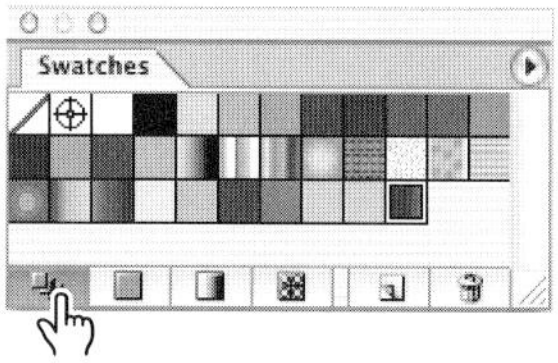

Display all swatches.

6 With the left gradient stop selected in the Gradient palette, hold down Alt (Windows) or Option (Mac OS) and click a color swatch in the Swatches palette to assign the color to the gradient. (We selected the Lime color swatch.)

Holding down Alt/Option as you click a color swatch applies the color to the selected gradient stop in the gradient rather than to the selected objects in the artwork.

Colors in gradients can be assigned as CMYK process colors, RGB process colors, Web Safe RGB colors, or spot colors. When a gradient is printed or separated, mixed-mode gradient colors are all converted to CMYK process color.

Now you'll add intermediate colors to the gradient to create a fill with multiple blends between colors.

7 In the Gradient palette, click anywhere below the gradient bar to add a stop between the other gradient stops.

You add a color to a gradient by adding a gradient stop. When you add a new gradient stop, a diamond appears above the gradient bar to mark the colors' new midpoint.

8 With the new gradient stop selected, hold down Alt (Windows) or Option (Mac OS) and click a color swatch in the Swatches palette to assign it to the gradient. (We selected the Yellow color swatch.)

Observe how the new color looks in the *CHILES* type.

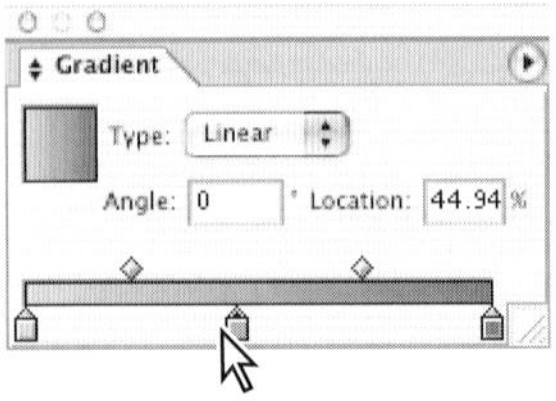

Select gradient stop and change middle color of gradient.

Result.

9 To adjust the midpoint between two colors, drag the diamond above the gradient bar to the right or left.

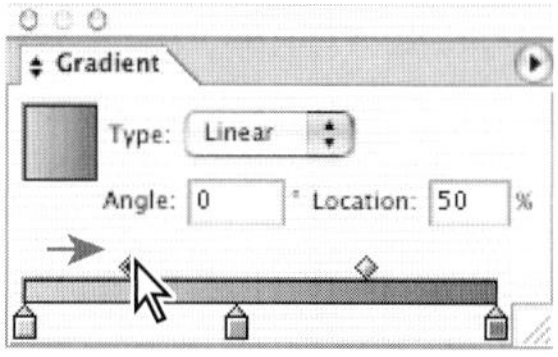

Drag diamond to adjust color midpoint.

Note: *You can delete a color in a gradient by dragging its gradient stop downward and out of the Gradient palette.*

Another way to apply a color to the gradient is to sample the color from the artwork using the Eyedropper tool.

10 Select the right gradient stop in the Gradient palette. Select the Eyedropper tool (✎) in the toolbox. Then hold down Shift and click a color in the artwork. (We sampled the light red color in the front chile pepper.)

Holding down Shift as you click with the Eyedropper tool applies the color sample to the selected gradient stop in the gradient rather than replacing the entire gradient with the color in the selected *CHILES* type.

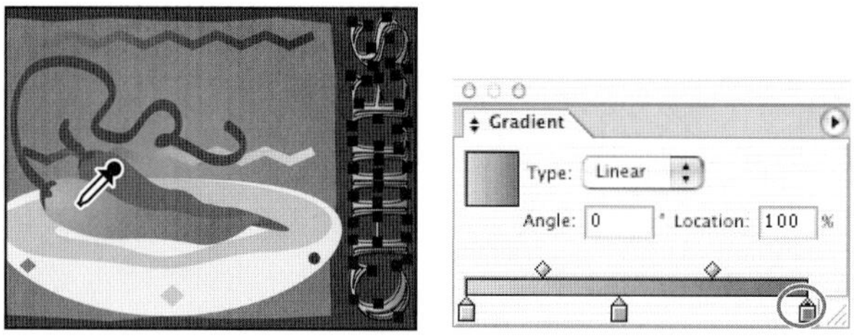

Shift-click to apply sample to selected stop in gradient.

Now you'll save the new gradient.

11 In the Swatches palette, choose New Swatch from the palette menu, type a name for the gradient in the Swatch Name text box (we named it "Chiles type"), and click OK to save the new gradient.

12 Deselect the artwork by choosing Select > Deselect, and then choose File > Save.

Creating smooth-color blends

You can choose several options for blending the shapes and colors of objects to create a new object. When you choose the smooth-color blend option, Illustrator combines the shapes and colors of the objects into many intermediate steps, creating a smooth graduated blend between the original objects.

For an example of smooth-color blends, see the color section.

Now you'll combine the two inner shapes of the bowl into a smooth-color blend.

1 Select the Selection tool (), click the smallest shape inside the bowl to select it, and then Shift-click to select the second shape inside the bowl.

Both objects are filled with a solid color and have no stroke. Objects that have strokes blend differently than those that have no stroke.

2 Choose Object > Blend > Blend Options.

3 In the Blend Options dialog box, for Spacing choose Smooth Color (selected by default), and click OK.

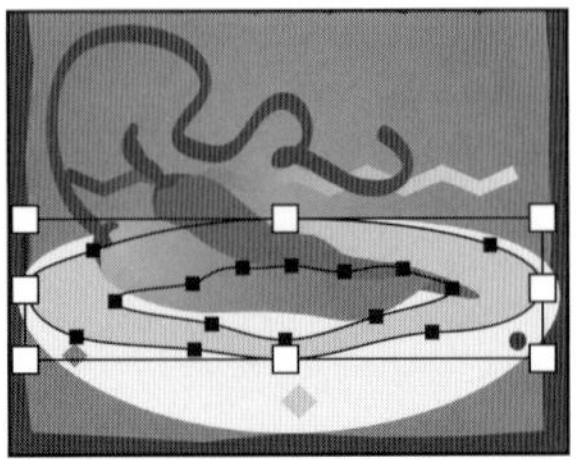

Select two inner shapes.

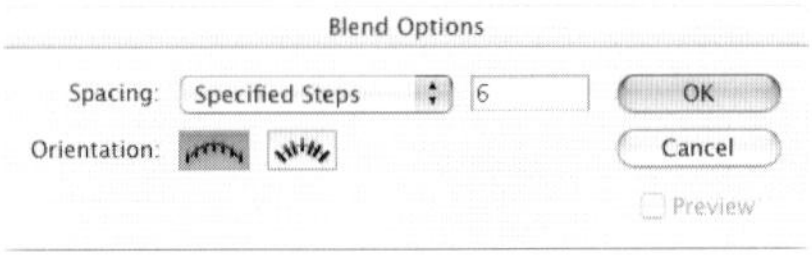

Set blend options.

This action sets up the blend options, which remain set until you change them. Now you'll apply the blend.

4 Choose Object > Blend > Make.

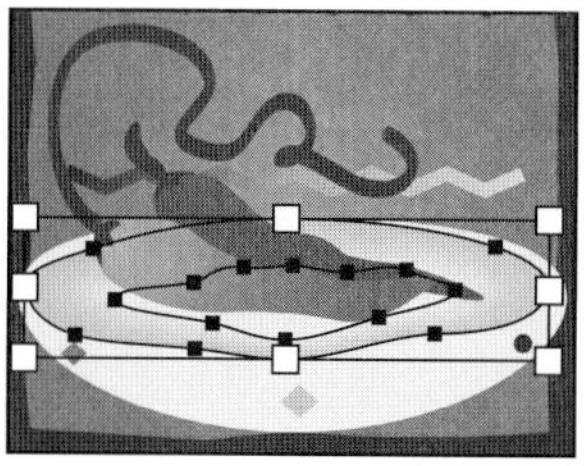

Result.

When you make a smooth-color blend between objects, Illustrator automatically calculates the number of intermediate steps necessary to create a smooth transition between the objects.

Note: *To release a blend and revert to the original objects, select the blend and choose Object > Blend > Release.*

Blending intermediate steps

Now you'll create a series of blended shapes between three different-colored shapes on the outside of the bowl by specifying the number of steps in the blend and using the Blend tool to create the blend.

1 Click away from the artwork to deselect it, and then double-click the Blend tool ( ) to open the Blend Options dialog box.

2 For Spacing, choose Specified Steps, type **6** for the number of steps, and click OK.

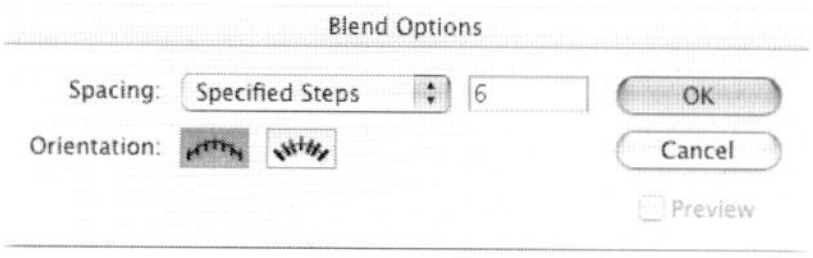

3 Using the Blend tool, click the red diamond with the tool's upper hollow square, and then click the green diamond to make a blend between them.

A new object is created that blends the shapes of the diamonds and their colors together in six steps.

4 Now click the blue circle to complete the blended path.

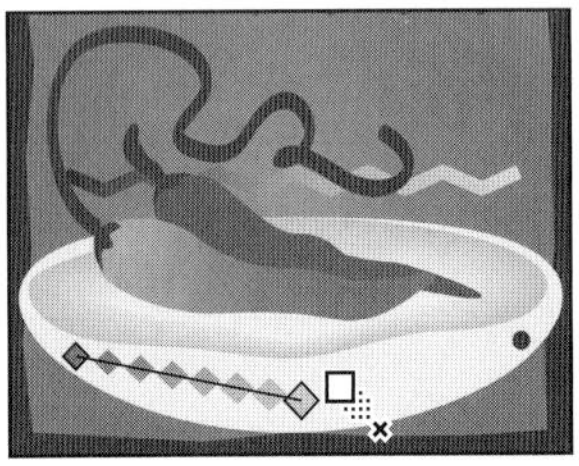

Click objects with Blend tool to create a blend.

Result.

Note: *To end the current path and continue blending other objects on a separate path, click the Blend tool in the toolbox first and then click the other objects.*

Modifying the blend

Now you'll modify the shape of the path or spine of the blend using the Convert Anchor Point tool (⌃).

1 Select the Convert Anchor Point tool from the same group as the Pen tool (✒) in the toolbox.

2 Select the endpoint of the spine at the center of the blue circle (don't release the mouse button). Drag slowly down until you see two direction lines, and continue dragging down and a little to the left until the path runs parallel to the bottom edge of the bowl.

3 Repeat step 2 with the endpoint of the spine at the center of the red diamond, but drag up instead of down.

Now you'll adjust the spacing between the center shapes on the blend.

4 Using the Convert Anchor Point tool, select the middle anchor point of the spine (at the center of the green diamond)—don't release the mouse button—and drag to the left to lengthen the direction line and stretch out the spacing between the blend steps.

Select end and middle anchor points and drag direction handles to reshape blend path.

A quick way to reshape the blend's path is to wrap it around another path or object. Select the blend, select the other object or path, and then choose Object > Blend > Replace Spine.

You can modify the blend instantly by changing the shape or color of the original objects. Now you'll delete an anchor point on an object and reshape the object to modify the blend.

5 Zoom in closer on the red diamond by using the Zoom tool ( ) or the Navigator palette.

6 Hold down Ctrl (Windows) or Command (Mac OS), and click the red diamond to select it.

7 Select the Delete Anchor Point tool ( ) from the same group as the Convert Direction Point tool in the toolbox and click a corner point on the red diamond to delete it.

Notice how changing the shape of the diamond affects the shape of the intermediate steps in the blend.

8 Select the Direct-Selection tool ( ) in the toolbox and drag another anchor point on the diamond out to extend the shape of the corner.

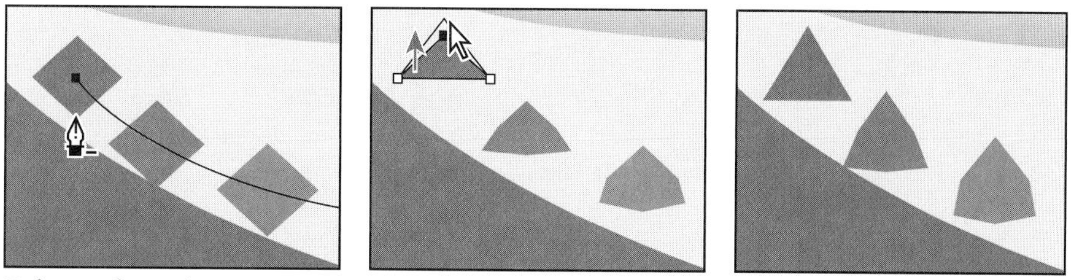

Delete anchor point on original object. *Drag anchor point to reshape object.* *Result.*

You can switch the starting and ending objects in the blend without affecting the shape of the spine by selecting the blend and choosing Object > Blend > Reverse Spine.

9 Choose File > Save.

For an example of modified blends, see figure 8-2 in the color section.

Combining blends with gradients

You can blend objects that are filled with gradients to create different effects of color blending. The two zigzag lines in the artwork are filled with gradients. (See "Exploring on your own" at the end of this lesson to learn how to create them.)

Now you'll blend the gradient-filled lines to create a multicolored blend in the artwork.

1 Double-click the Hand tool ( ) in the toolbox to fit the artwork in the window.

2 Select the Blend tool ( ) in the toolbox and click the top zigzag line to select the first object for the blend. Then click the corresponding point on the bottom zigzag line to create the blend. (If you don't click the corresponding point, you'll get a distorted result.)

The current blend settings for six specified steps are applied to the blend. You can change these settings for an existing blend.

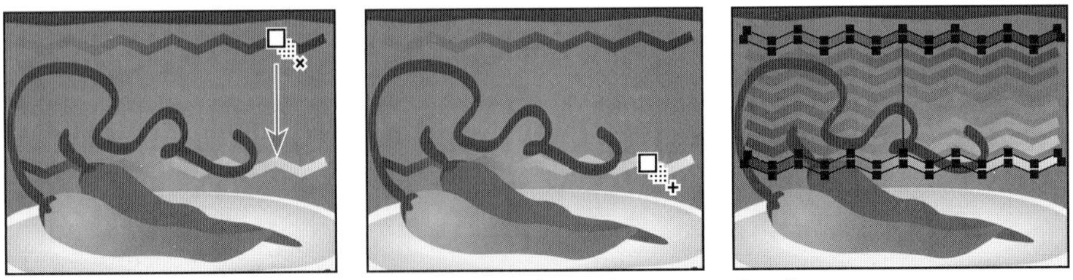

Click top line to select first object for blend. *Click corresponding point on bottom line.* *Result.*

3 Click the Selection tool ( ) to select the bounding box of the new blend, and choose Object > Blend > Blend Options.

4 In the Blend Options dialog box, select Preview, type a number in the text box (we specified 4 steps), and press Tab to see the effect in the artwork. Click OK.

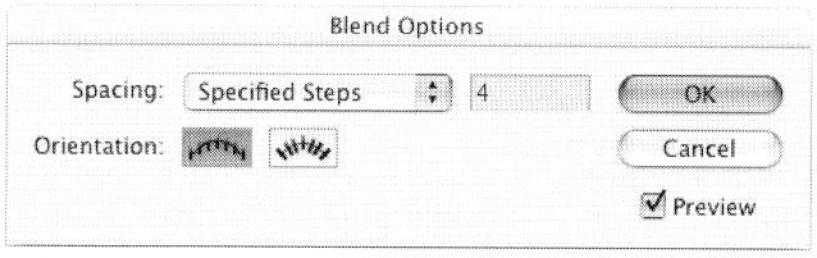

Change number of steps in the blend.

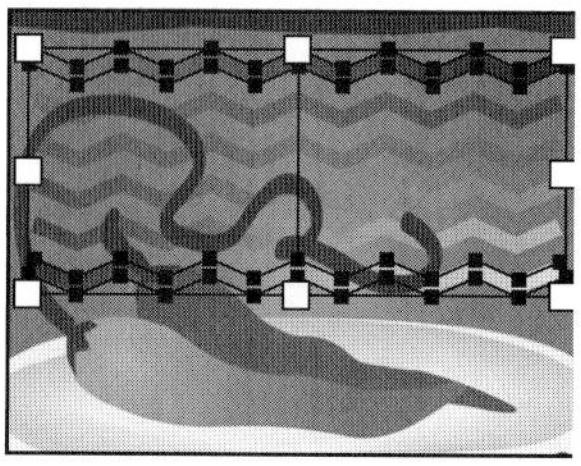
Result.

5 Click away from the artwork to deselect it.

Now you'll adjust the blend by changing a gradient color in one of the original objects.

6 Select the Direct-Selection tool (↖), and select one of the original zigzag lines. (We selected the bottom zigzag line.)

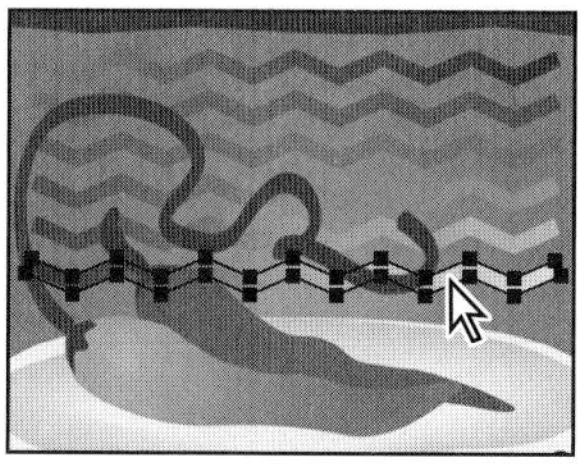
Select original object.

7 In the Gradient palette, click a gradient stop to select a color in the gradient fill. (We selected the right gradient stop to select the ending color of the gradient.)

8 Hold down Alt (Windows) or Option (Mac OS), and click a color in the Swatches palette to apply it to the selected gradient stop. (We selected the Teal color swatch.)

Holding down Alt/Option as you click applies the color swatch to the selected gradient stop rather than to the selected zigzag line.

You can paint the individual steps in the blend with separate gradients or colors by expanding the blend. Select the blend and choose Object > Blend > Expand.

9 To view your final artwork, press Tab to hide the toolbox and all the open palettes.

Pressing Tab toggles between hiding and showing the toolbox and palettes. Pressing Shift+Tab toggles between hiding and showing just the palettes (and not the toolbox).

10 Deselect the artwork.

11 Choose File > Save. Choose File > Close to close the file.

This completes the lesson. To learn how to use the Gradient Mesh tool to make colors in an object blend in multiple directions, see Lesson 15, "Creating Airbrush Effects." To learn how to use the color modes or transparency to blend colors together, see Lesson 10, "Applying Appearance Attributes, Styles, and Effects."

Exploring on your own

The two wavy lines in the artwork were created by applying the Zig Zag distort filter to two straight lines, and then they were converted to path outlines so that they could be filled with gradients.

To create a gradient-filled zigzag line like those in the artwork, do the following:

1 Choose File > New to create a new document and draw a straight line using the Pen tool.

2 Select the line, remove the fill, paint the stroke with a color, and increase the stroke weight to **10 pt**.

3 With the line selected, choose Filter > Distort > Zig Zag. (Choose the top filter command in the menu.)

4 In the Zig Zag dialog box, enter **0.15** in in the Size text box and **11** in the Ridges per segment text box. Click OK.

5 Choose Object > Path > Outline Stroke.

Notice that the stroke color has switched with the fill of None, so now you can fill the object with a gradient.

Review questions

1 What is a gradient fill?

2 Name two ways to fill a selected object with a gradient.

3 What is the difference between a gradient fill and a blend?

4 How do you adjust the blend between colors in a gradient?

5 How do you add colors to a gradient?

6 How do you adjust the direction of a gradient?

7 Describe two ways to blend the shapes and colors of objects together.

8 What is the difference between selecting a smooth-color blend and specifying the number of steps in a blend?

9 How do you adjust the shapes or colors in the blend? How do you adjust the path of the blend?

Review answers

1 A gradient fill is a graduated blend between two or more colors or tints of the same color.

2 Select an object and do one of the following:

• Click the Gradient button in the toolbox to fill an object with the default white-to-black gradient or with the last selected gradient.

• Click a gradient swatch in the Swatches palette.

• Make a new gradient by clicking a gradient swatch in the Swatches palette and mixing your own in the Gradient palette.

• Use the Eyedropper tool (✎) to sample a gradient from an object in your artwork, and then apply it to the selected object.

3 The difference between a gradient fill and a blend is the way that colors combine together–colors blend together within a gradient fill and between objects in a blend.

4 You drag one of the gradient's stops in the Gradient palette.

5 In the Gradient palette, click beneath the gradient bar to add a gradient stop to the gradient. Then use the Color palette to mix a new color, or in the Swatches palette, Alt-click (Windows) or Option-click (Mac OS) a color swatch.

6 You click or drag with the Gradient tool (■) to adjust the direction of a gradient. Dragging a long distance changes colors gradually; dragging a short distance makes the color change more abrupt.

7 You can blend the shapes and colors of objects together by doing one of the following:

• Clicking each object with the Blend tool ( ) to create a blend of intermediate steps between the objects according to preset blend options.

• Selecting the objects and choosing Object > Blend > Blend Options to set up the number of intermediate steps, and then choosing Object > Blend > Make to create the blend.

Objects that have painted strokes blend differently than those with no strokes.

8 When you select the Smooth Color blend option, Illustrator automatically calculates the number of intermediate steps necessary to create a seamlessly smooth blend between the selected objects. Specifying the number of steps lets you determine how many intermediate steps are visible in the blend. You can also specify the distance between intermediate steps in the blend.

9 You use the Direct Selection tool ( ) to select and adjust the shape of an original object, thus changing the shape of the blend. You can change the colors of the original objects to adjust the intermediate colors in the blend. You use the Convert-anchor-point tool ( ) to change the shape of the path, or spine, of the blend by dragging anchor points or direction handles on the spine.

Lesson 13

13 Working with Symbols

The Symbols palette lets you apply multiple objects by painting them onto the page. Symbols used in combination with the Symbolism tools offer options that make creating repetitive shapes, such as grass, or stars in the sky, easy and fun. You can also use the Symbol palette as a database to store artwork and map symbols to 3D objects.

In this lesson, you'll learn how to do the following:

- Create a Symbol.
- Apply Symbol Instances.
- Use the Symbolism Tools.
- Modify and redefine a symbol.
- Store and retrieve artwork in the Symbols palette.
- Use a symbol for 3d mapping.

Getting started

In this lesson you'll finish artwork for a poster. Before you begin, restore the default preferences for Adobe Illustrator; then open a file containing the final version of the finished artwork to see what you are going to create.

1 To ensure that the tools and palettes function exactly as described in this lesson, delete or deactivate (by renaming) the Adobe Illustrator CS preferences file. See "Restoring default preferences" on page 2.

2 Start Adobe Illustrator.

3 Choose File > Open and open the file named 13_symbol_end.ai in the Lesson13 folder within the AICIB folder on your hard drive.

If you like, choose View > Zoom Out to reduce the view of the finished artwork, adjust the window size, and leave it on your screen as you work. (Use the Hand tool (✋) to move the artwork where you want it in the window.) If you don't want to leave the image open, choose File > Close.

For an illustration of the finished artwork in this lesson, see the color section.

4 To begin working, you'll open an existing art file set up for the artwork. Choose File > Open to open the 13_symbol_start.ai file in the Lesson13 folder, located inside the Lessons folder within the AICIB folder on your hard drive.

5 Choose File > Save As, name the file **ballgame.ai** and select the Lesson13 folder in the Save In menu. Leave the type of file format set to Adobe Illustrator® Document, and click Save. In the Illustrator Options dialog box, leave at the defaults and click OK.

Creating a symbol

A Symbol is an art object that you store in the Symbols palette and can reuse over and over again. For example, if you create a symbol from an object in the shape of a blade of grass, you can then add instances of that grass multiple times to your artwork by spraying it on using the Symbol Sprayer tool. The grass instance is linked to the symbol in the palette and can be altered using Symbolism tools or edited and replaced, all instances of the symbol linked to that original symbol are also updated. You can turn that grass from brown to green instantly! Symbols can save time and greatly reduce file size.

Illustrator objects that can be used are; paths, compound paths, text, raster images, mesh objects, and groups of objects. Symbols can even include active objects, such as brush strokes, blends, effects, or other symbol instances in a symbol.

Note: *You cannot use non–embedded placed art as a symbol, nor can you use some groups, such as groups of graphs.*

You will first start by adding a crowd to this image.

6 Change the stroke to none and choose Custard from the Swatches palette for the fill.

7 Select the Ellipse tool and click and drag to create the shape of a head.

Create the shape of a head with the Ellipse tool.

8 If the Symbols palette is not visible choose Window > Symbols. Select the ellipse that you created and Alt-click (Windows) or Option-click (Mac OS) on the New Symbol button at the bottom of the Symbols palette. Name the symbol **face**.

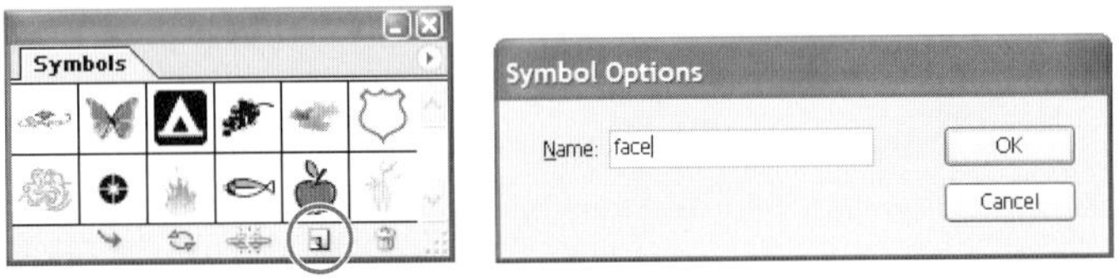

Add the ellipse to the Symbols palette.

Note: *Alt/Option-clicking on the new Symbol icon gives you the opportunity to name the symbol as it is being added to the palette.*

9 Using the Selection tool (↖) select and delete the original ellipse used to create the symbol.

Applying a symbol instance

Now you will use the Symbol Sprayer tool to apply the face to your illustration.

10 Select the Symbol Sprayer tool ( ) from the toolbar.

11 Click on the symbol that you created in the Symbols palette.

12 Click and drag using the Symbol sprayer much like an airbrush, or can of paint, to create a crowd with your symbol.

Use the Symbol Sprayer like an airbrush.

Symbol instances

Keep the following in mind when creating a symbol instance with the Symbol Sprayer:

- *All the symbols that appear from each spray become one instance set that you manipulate and edit as a whole.*
- *You can enlarge or reduce the spraying radius by using the bracket keys ,"[" for a smaller spraying radius, "]" for a larger spraying radius.*
- *Holding down the Alt (Windows) or Option (Mac OS) key while using the Symbol Sprayer deletes instances.*

13 While the symbol instance is still selected, choose Object > Arrange > Send to back. The crowd falls behind the baseball player.

Using the Symbolism tools

There are seven Symbolism tools hidden inside the Symbol Sprayer tool. Symbolism tools are used for changing the density, color, location, size, rotation, transparency, or style of symbol sets.

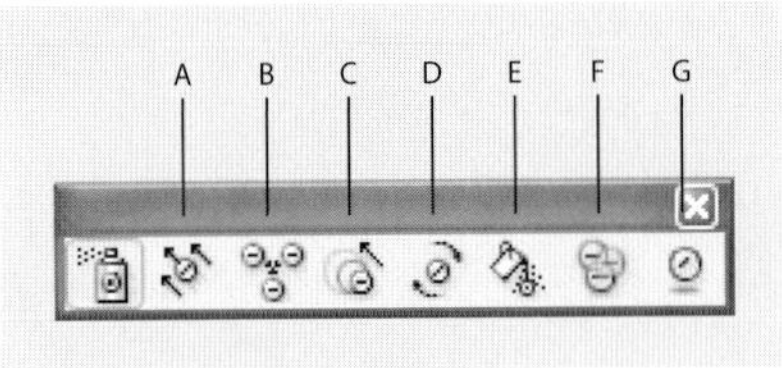

A. Symbol Shifter tool. B. Symbol Scruncher tool.
C. Symbol Sizer tool. D. Symbol Spinner tool.
E. Symbol Stainer tool. F. Symbol Screener tool.
G. Symbol Styler tool.

What do the Symbolism tools do?

Symbol Shifter tool - *The Symbol Shifter tool moves symbol instances around. It can also change the relative paint order of symbol instances in a set.*

Symbol Scruncher tool - *The Symbol Scruncher tool pulls symbol instances together or apart.*

Symbol Sizer tool - *Use the Symbol Sizer tool to increase or decrease the size of symbol instances in an existing symbol set.*

Symbol Spinner tool - *Use the Symbol Spinner tool to orient the symbol instances in a set. Symbol instances located near the cursor orient in the direction you move the cursor. As you drag the mouse, an arrow appears above the cursor to show the current orientation of symbol instances.*

Symbol Stainer tool - *Use the Symbol Stainer tool to colorize symbol instances. Colorizing a symbol instance changes the hue toward the tint color, while preserving the original luminosity so black or white objects don't change at all.*

Symbol Screener tool- *Use the Symbol Screener tool to increase or decrease the transparency of the symbol instances in a set.*

Symbol Styler tool - *The Symbol Styler tool applies the selected style to the symbol instance.*

You can switch to the Symbol Styler tool when using any other symbolism tool, by clicking a style in the Styles palette.

–For more information of Symbolism tools and their options see Online Help.

Using the Symbolism tools

In this next lesson you will use the Symbol Sizer and Stainer tools to alter the look of individual symbol instances.

1 Select the Sizer tool ( ) and click and drag over your symbol instances to scale up some of the faces. Hold down the Alt (Windows) or Option (Mac OS) while you are using the Symbol Sizer tool to reduce the size of the selected instances.

Note: *The Symbol Sizer works better when you click and release over symbol instances, rather than holding down. If the symbols resize too quickly for you, choose Edit > Undo and try again.*

Now you will apply colorization to the Symbols.

2 Select the color Malt from the Swatches palette. Select the Symbol Stainer tool ( ) and click and drag over the faces to add tints of the malt color.

The longer you hold down on the mouse, the more colorization occurs. Hold down the Alt (Windows) or Option (Mac OS) key to decrease the colorization amount.

Change the size and color using the Symbolism tools.

3 File > Save.

Editing symbols

In the next steps you will add an additional symbol, then edit and update it.

1 While on the Selection tool Control-click (Windows) or Command-click (Mac OS) anywhere on the document to make sure that no objects are selected.

2 Select None for the fill and Green from the Swatches palette for the stroke.

3 Using Window > Stroke set the stroke to **1 pt.**

4 Using the Line Segment tool (\) create several blades of grass. Use at least 10 line segments to make a tuft of grass.

Create blades of grass to be used as a symbol.

5 Switch to the Selection tool (↖) and marquee select the blades of grass. (You could also select one blade and Shift-click to add the others.)

6 With the blades of grass selected Alt (Windows) or Option (Mac OS) on the New Symbol button on the Symbols palette. Name the new symbol "grass."

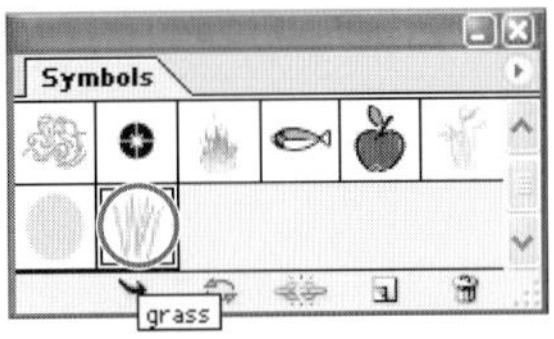

Create a new symbol from the grass.

7 Use the selection tool to delete the original blades of grass used to create the symbol.

8 Choose the Symbol Sprayer ( ) tool and click on the grass symbol you just added to the Symbols palette. Return to the artboard and click and drag to apply the grass symbol over the dirt.

9 Select the Symbol Scruncher tool ( ) and click and drag over the grass instances, scrunching them together. Use Alt (Windows) or Option (Mac OS) to unscrunch some of the instances of grass.

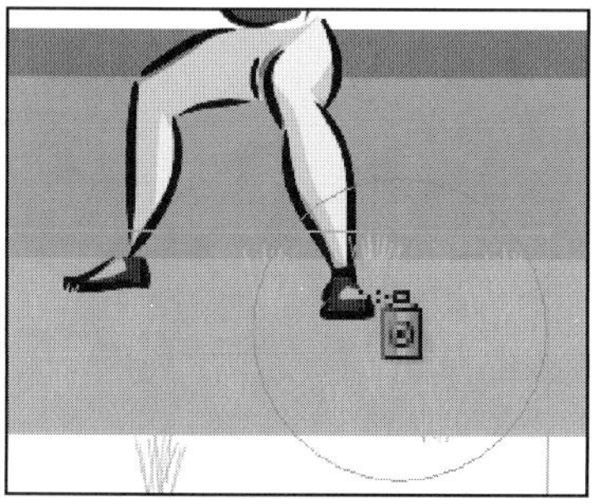

Spray on the grass using the Symbol Sprayer.

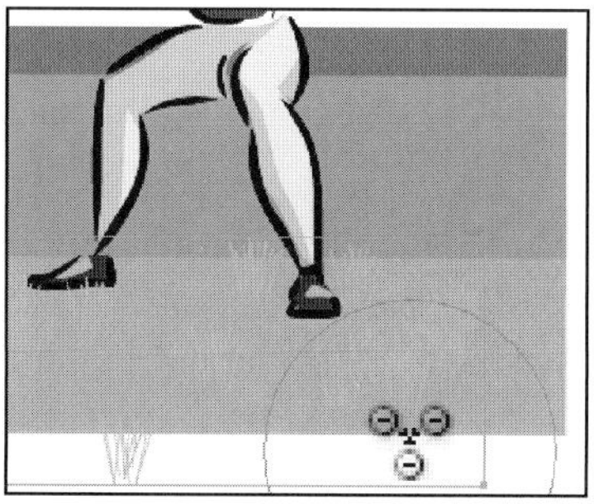

Scrunch the grass using the Symbol Scruncher.

10 File > Save.

Updating a symbol

Perhaps 1 pt blades of grass are too small. In this next section you will edit the blades of grass once and all instances will be updated.

1 To reactivate a symbol as an art object click on the Place Symbol Instance button at the bottom of the Symbols palette. This will place the symbol one time in the middle of your page.

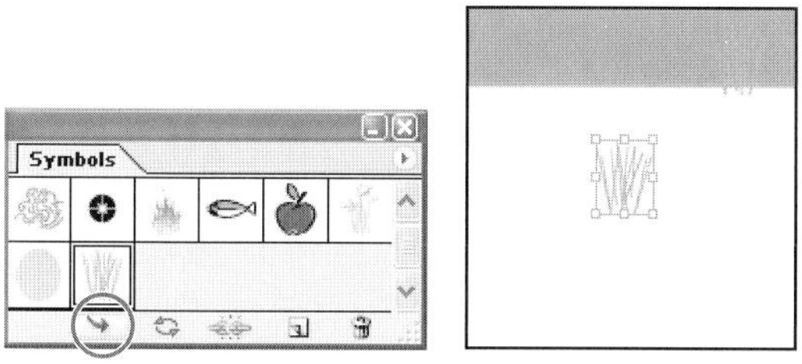

Click the Place Symbol Instance button to edit the symbol.

2 Using the Selection tool, move the blades of grass to a location that will let you view it alone.

3 Choose Object > Expand to put the artwork back into an editable mode. Leave the options of the Expand window at the defaults.

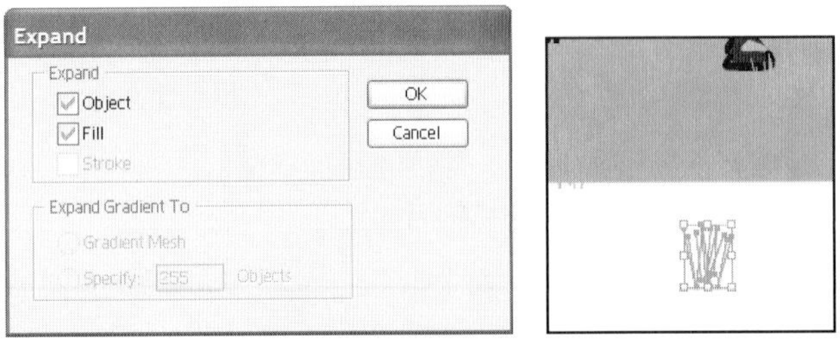

Expand puts the grass symbol back into an editable mode.

4 While the grass is selected, change the strokes to **2 pt** in the Stroke palette.

5 File > Save.

Now you will update all instances of the grass symbol with the new art.

6 Hold down the Alt (Windows) or Option (Mac OS) and drag the edited blades of grass on top of the original grass symbol in the Symbols palette. Release when you see a black border appear around the grass symbol.

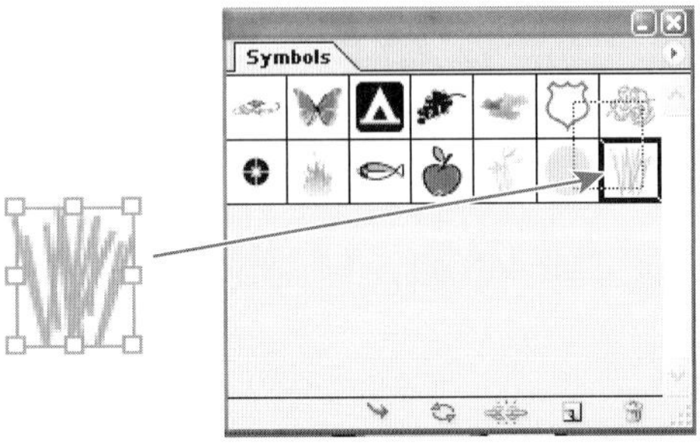

Replace the original symbol with the new one by Alt/Option dragging it on top or the original symbol.

The symbol instances are now using the thicker blades of grass.

7 File > Save this artwork.

Using the Symbols palette as a database

Save frequently used logos or other artwork as a symbol to readily access them when needed.

In this next lesson you will take the illustration you created and save it as a Symbol. You will then close the file and import it into a new document and make changes to it.

1 Choose Select > Select All to activate all the components of your illustration.

2 Alt+click (Windows) or Option+click (Mac OS) on the New Symbol button at the bottom of the Symbols palette. Name the symbol **baseball**.

3 Click and drag the baseball symbol back on to the page. This symbol can be placed back on to the page as many times as you need and can be a big help when using artwork repeatedly.

4 Choose File > Save and close the file.

5 Create a new document using File > New. Leave the settings at the defaults and click OK.

6 Choose File > Save and name the file **ballgame.ai** and select the Lesson13 folder in the Save In menu. Leave the type of file format set to Adobe Illustrator® Document, and click Save. In the Illustrator Options dialog box, leave at the defaults and click Save.

7 From the Symbols palette menu in the upper right choose Open Symbol Library > Other Library, locate the file we just saved named ballgame.ai in the lesson13 folder of the AICIB folder. A palette will appear named with the name of our original file. In it are any symbols created when the file was last saved.

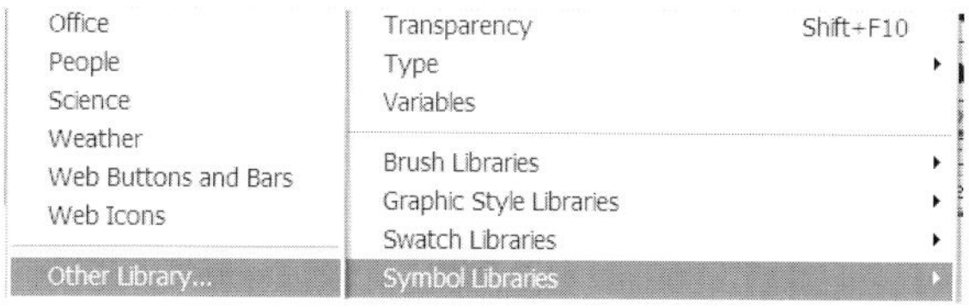

Take advantage of precreated symbols like borders and 3D effects in the palette menu of the Symbols palette.

8 Locate the symbol you named baseball and use the Place Symbol Instance button at the bottom of the Symbols palette or drag it out from the Symbols palette on to your page.

The artwork comes in the same size as the original but is considered an object, or symbol instance, until you expand it.

9 Choose Object > Expand. Leave the expand options at the default and click OK,

10 The artwork is now editable but is also grouped. Use the Direct Selection tool () to select the shirt and then click on various colors in the Swatches palette until you find one you like.

Need an extra source of clip art? Any of the symbols from the palette menu can be dragged out of the Symbols palette onto the page and expanded to have colors and sizes changed.

11 File > Save.

Mapping a symbol to 3D artwork

Symbols can be mapped to 3D artwork to create labels and textures. In this next lesson you will create a cereal box with your baseball player on the front panel and a text symbol on the top and side.

1 Choose Select > All with the Selection tool.

2 Double-click on the Scale tool () and enter the value of 50% in the Uniform textbox.

3 Choose Window > Type > Character, Ctrl+T (Windows) or Command+T (Mac OS) to open the Character palette. Choose any font, we selected Chaparral Pro Bold, and change the size to **45 pt**. Select the Type tool and click above the artwork to create a text insertion point. Type the word **Superstar**.

Add text to the graphic.

4 Choose Select > All and Alt+click (Windows) or Option+click (Mac OS) the New Symbol button on the Symbol palette. Name the Symbol **Superstar**.

5 Choose Select > Deselect.

Reduce the image to 50%.

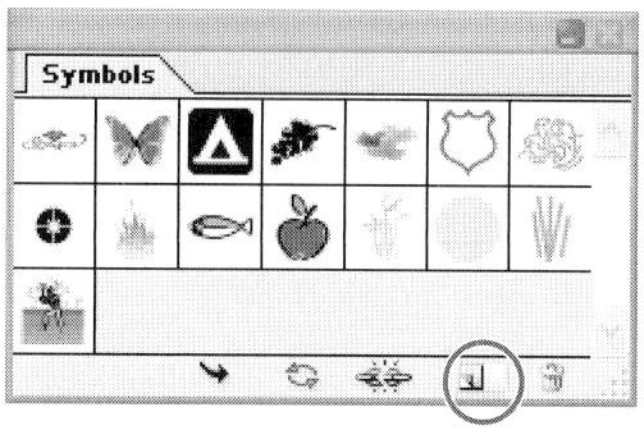

Alt/Option+click on the New Symbol button.

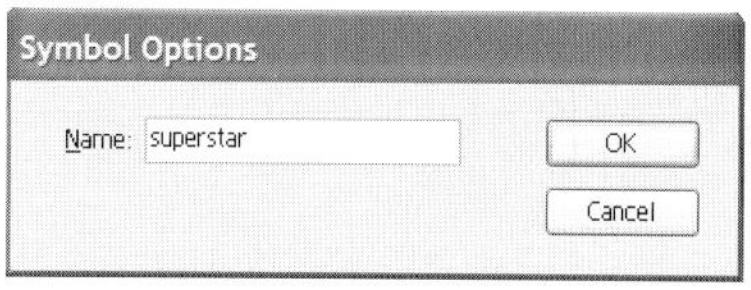

Name the Symbol.

Creating a symbol for the side panel

Now you will create the word *Cereal* that will be mapped to the boxes side panel.

1 Choose the Type tool (T) and select any font, (we choose Chaparral Pro Semibold). Leave the font size at 45 pt. Find a blank area on the artboard and click to create a text insertion point. Type the word **Cereal**.

2 Double-click on the Rotate (◌) tool to open the rotate options. Type **90** in the angle textbox and click OK.

3 With the text still selected Alt+Click (Windows) or Option+Click (Mac OS) on the New Symbol button on the Symbols palette to add this text as a Symbol. Name the Symbol **Cereal**.

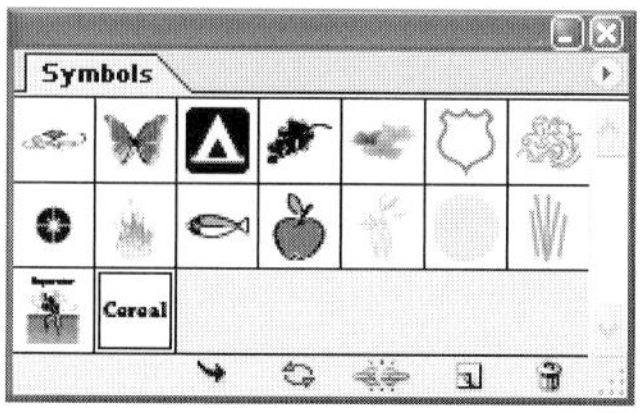

Add the text, Cereal, to the Symbols palette.

4 Select > All and use the Delete key to eliminate any artwork on the artboard.

5 Click on the Default color swatches at the bottom of the toolbar.

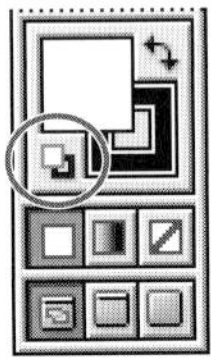

6 Choose the Rectangle tool (▢) and click once on the artboard. Enter the values **225 pt** for the width and **300 pt** for the height.

7 With the Rectangle still selected, choose Effect > 3D > Extrude and Bevel. Check on the preview.

Using the Extrude Effect you will make the rectangle appear to be three-dimensional. Read more details about the 3D Effect in Lesson 16, *Using the 3D Effect*, or in online Help.

8 Choose Off-Axis Front for the position and type **75** Extrude Depth. Leave this window open.

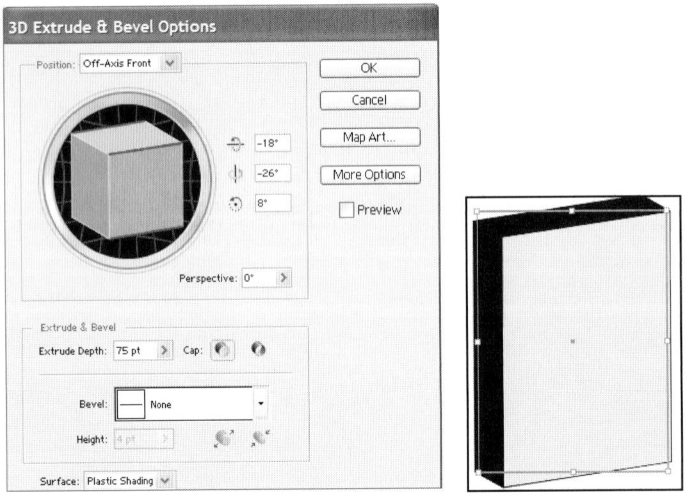

The Extrude and Bevel Effect adds dimension to our rectangle.

9 Click on More Options to change the light source. Change the surface to Diffuse Shading and the Shading Color to None.

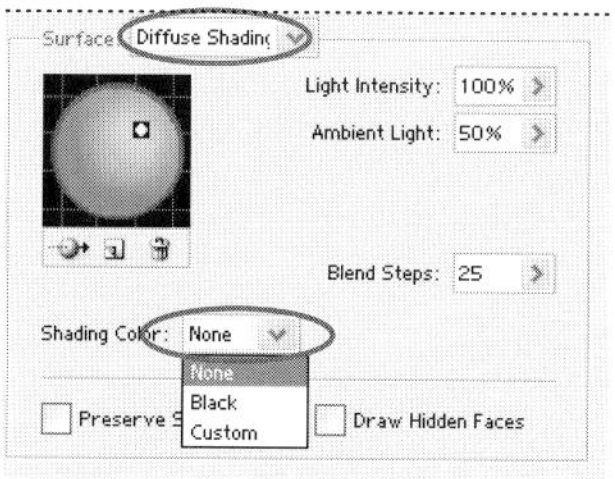

Additional light options are available by pressing More Options.

10 Change the direction of the light source by clicking on the light indicator on the image of the sphere and dragging it to the lower left.

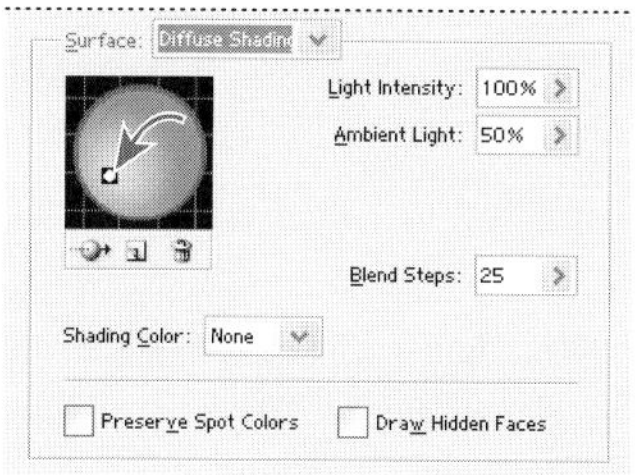

Click and drag the light to change its location.

For more information about lighting read Lesson 16, "Creating 3D Objects, or see Lighting an Object" in online Help.

Now you will map the symbols to our newly created cereal box.

11 Click on the Map Art button in the upper right. Check on the Preview.

12 Using the single arrows to the right of Surface click to navigate through the different faces of the box. Choose the surface 1 of 16 and click on the Symbol pop-up menu. Select your saved Symbol named Superstar.

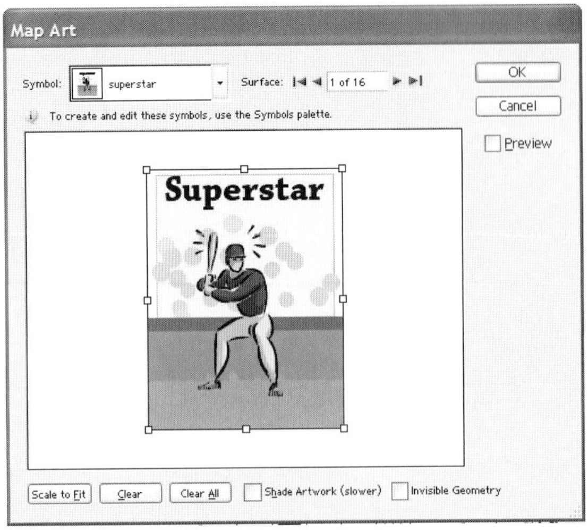

13 Click Scale to Fit to resize the artwork automatically.

14 Click on the right single arrow (▸) in the Surface textbox or type in **11** to get to the 11th surface. Choose the symbol named Cereal.

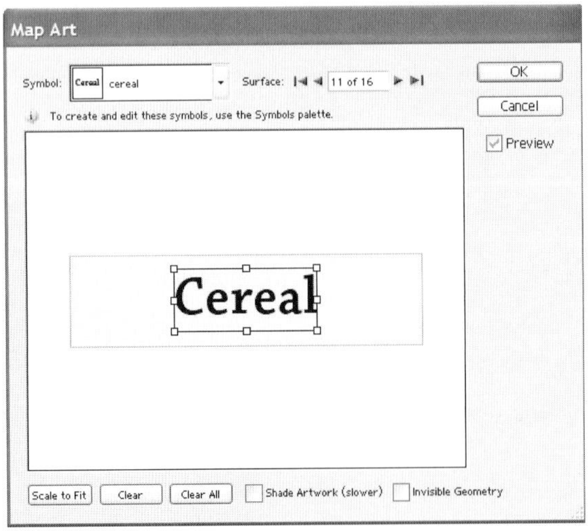

15 Click OK, and OK again.

16 You have completed the lesson. File > Save and File > Close.

Exploring on your own

Symbols do not have to be applied with the Symbol Sprayer. Try to integrate symbols into illustrations with repeated artwork such as maps that contain repeated icons and road signs to creative and customized bullets for text. Symbols make it easy to update logos in business cards or name tags, or any artwork created with multiple placements of the same art.

To place multiple symbol instances do the following:

1 Select the artwork that is to become a symbol.

2 Drag the art using the Selection tool (↖) into the Symbol palette. Delete the original art once it is in the Symbols palette.

3 To use the first instance, drag the symbol from the Symbol palette to a location on your artboard.

4 Drag as many instances of the symbol as you like, or Alt/Option drag the original instance to clone it to other locations.

5 The symbols are now linked to the original symbol in the Symbols palette. If it is updated all placed instances will be updated.

Note: *You can break the link between the placed symbol by right-clicking (Windows) or Control-clicking (Mac OS) and selecting Break Link to Symbol from the contextual menu.*

Review questions

1 What are three benefits of using a symbol?

2 Name the Symbolizer tool that is used for changing tints and shades of a symbol.

3 If you are using a Symbolizer on an area that has two different symbols applied, which one becomes affected?

4 How do you update an existing symbol?

5 What is something that cannot be used as a symbol?

6 Can you use symbols from other documents?

Review answers

1 Three benefits of using symbols are:

- Easy application of multiple shapes
- You can edit one symbol and all instances will be updated.
- You can map artwork to 3D objects.

2 The Symbol Stainer tool changes the tints and shades of a symbol

3 If you are using a Symbolizer tool over an area that has two different symbol instances, the symbol active in the Symbols palette will be the only instance affected.

4 To update existing symbol instances do the following:

a Use the Place Symbol button

b Expand the artwork.

c Make any changes.

d Alt/Option drag the new artwork on top of the original symbol in the Symbols palette.

5 Non-embedded images and groups of graphs cannot be used as symbols.

6 Yes, you can use symbols from saved documents by choosing Swatch Libraries > Other Libraries from the Symbols palette menu.

Lesson 14

14 Working with Brushes and Scribbles

The variety of brush types in Adobe Illustrator lets you create a myriad of effects simply by painting or drawing on paths. You can choose from the provided Art, Calligraphic, Pattern, and Scatter brushes, or create new ones from your Illustrator artwork. You can use the paintbrush tool or the drawing tools to apply brushes to artwork and use the new Scribble effect to add some freeform scribbles to the image.

In this lesson, you'll learn how to do the following:

• Draw with each of the four brush types—Art, Calligraphic, Pattern, and Scatter—using the paintbrush tool.

• Change brush color and adjust brush settings before and after applying brushes to artwork.

• Create new brushes from Adobe Illustrator artwork.

• Apply brushes to paths created with drawing tools.

• Use the new Scribble Effect for artwork and text.

Applying brushes to paths

Adobe Illustrator brushes let you apply artwork to paths to decorate paths with patterns, figures, textures, or angled strokes. You can modify the brushes provided with Illustrator, and you can create your own brushes. Brushes appear in the Brushes palette.

You apply brushes to paths using the paintbrush tool or the drawing tools. To apply brushes using the paintbrush tool, you choose a brush from the Brushes palette and draw in the artwork. The brush is applied directly to the paths as you draw. To apply brushes using a drawing tool, you draw in the artwork, select a path in the artwork, and then choose a brush in the Brushes palette. The brush is applied to the selected path.

You can change the color, size, and other features of a brush. You can also edit paths after brushes are applied.

Getting started

In this lesson, you'll learn to use the four brush types in the Brushes palette, including how to change brush options and how to create your own brushes. Before you begin, you'll need to restore the default preferences for Adobe Illustrator. Then you'll open the finished art file for this lesson to see what you'll create.

1 To ensure that the tools and palettes function exactly as described in this lesson, delete or deactivate (by renaming) the Adobe Illustrator CS preferences file. See "Restoring default preferences" on page 2.

2 Start Adobe Illustrator.

3 Choose File > Open, and open the L14end.ai file in the Lesson14 folder, located inside the Lessons folder in the AICIB folder on your hard drive.

4 If you like, choose View > Zoom Out to make the finished artwork smaller, adjust the window size, and leave it on your screen as you work. (Use the Hand tool (✋) to move the artwork where you want it in the window.) If you don't want to leave the image open, choose File > Close.

For an illustration of the finished artwork in this lesson, see the color section.

To begin working, you'll open an existing art file set up with guides to draw the artwork.

5 Choose File > Open to open the L14start.ai file in the Lesson14 folder inside the AICIB folder on your hard drive.

6 Choose File > Save As, name the file Brushes.ai, and select the Lesson14 folder. Leave the type of format set to Adobe Illustrator® Document, and click Save. In the Illustrator Options dialog box accept the defaults and click OK.

Using Art brushes

Art brushes stretch artwork evenly along a path. Art brushes include strokes resembling various graphic media, such as the Charcoal and Marker brushes. Art brushes also include images, such as the Arrow brush, and text, such as the Type brush, which paints the characters *A-R-T* along a path. In this section, you'll use the Charcoal brush to draw the trunk and limbs of a tree.

The start file has been created with guides that you can use to create and align your artwork for the lesson. Guides are paths that have been converted using the View > Make Guides command. The guides are locked and cannot be selected, moved, modified, or printed (unless they are unlocked).

For more information on guides, read lesson 9, Working with Placement and Order of Objects, see "Using guides" in online Help.

Drawing with the Paintbrush tool

Now you'll use the paintbrush tool to apply a brush to the artwork.

1 In the toolbox, click the Paintbrush tool ( ) to select it.

You select a brush in the Brushes palette to be applied to the artwork.

2 Click the Brushes tab to bring the Brushes palette to the front. (If the palette isn't visible on-screen, choose Window > Brushes.)

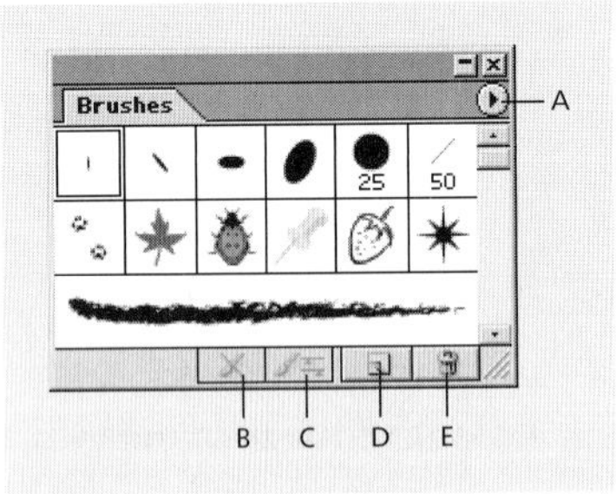

A. *Displays Brushes palette menu.*
B. *Remove Brush Stroke.*
C. *Options of Selected Object.*
D. *New Brush.* **E.** *Delete Brush.*

Brushes are arranged according to brush type, in the following order: Calligraphic, Scatter, Art, and Pattern.

By default, brushes appear as icons. You can also view brushes by name. When viewed by name, a small icon to the right of the brush name indicates the brush type.

3 In the Brushes palette, position the mouse button over the triangle in the top right corner of the Brushes palette, press the mouse button to display the palette menu, and choose List View.

You can choose which types of brushes are displayed in the Brushes palette to reduce the palette size and make it easier to find the brushes you want to use.

4 Choose Show Calligraphic Brushes from the palette menu. Then repeat the step to choose Show Scatter Brushes and Show Pattern Brushes and deselect those options, leaving only Art brushes visible in the palette. A check mark next to the brush type in the Brushes palette menu indicates that the brush type is visible in the palette.

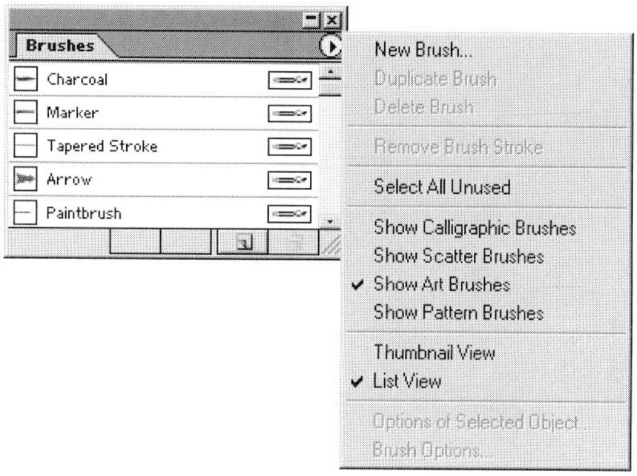

Showing and hiding brush types.

5 Select the Charcoal art brush in the Brushes palette.

Brushes are applied to paths as a stroke color. If you have a fill color selected when you apply a brush to a path, the path will be stroked with the brush and filled with the fill color. Use a fill of None when applying brushes to prevent the brushed paths from being filled. Later in this lesson you'll use a fill color with a brush. For more information on stroke and fill color, see Lesson 5, "Painting."

6 In the toolbox, click the Fill box and click the None box.

7 Use the Paintbrush tool to draw a long, upward stroke to create the left side of the tree trunk, tracing over the guides as you draw. Don't worry if your stroke doesn't follow the guide exactly. You'll remove the guides at the end of the lesson, so that they won't show through the finished artwork.

8 Draw a second upward stroke to create the right side of the tree trunk, using the guide to place your drawing.

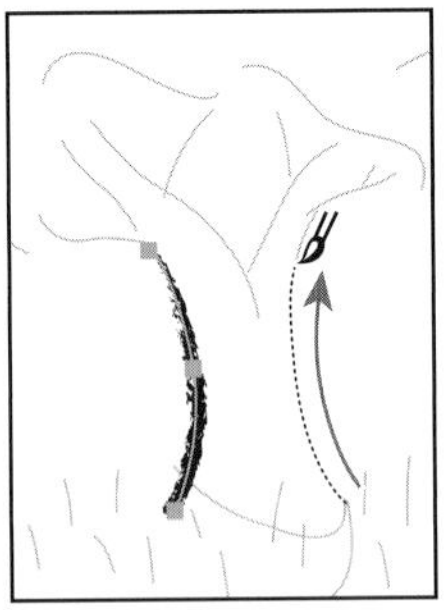

Draw with the paintbrush tool.

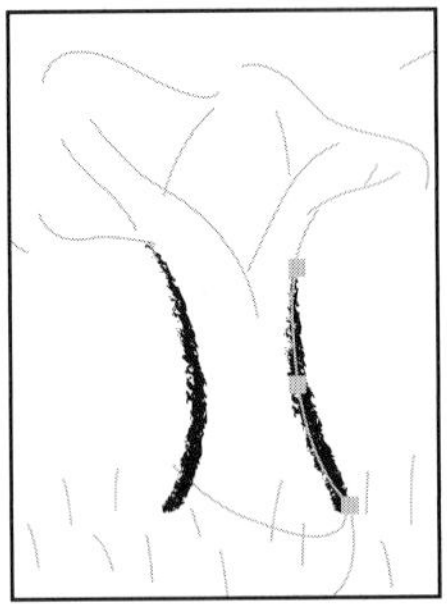

Last path drawn remains selected.

Each path remains selected after you draw it, until you draw another path.

9 Choose File > Save to save your work.

Editing paths with the paintbrush tool

When you draw with the Paintbrush tool, the last path you draw remains selected by default. This feature makes it easy to edit paths as you draw. If you draw over the selected path with the Paintbrush tool, the part of the selected path that you drew over is edited. You can disable or set a tolerance for path editing in the Paintbrush Tool Preferences dialog box.

Now you'll use the Paintbrush tool to edit the selected path.

1 Place the Paintbrush tool (![]) near the top of the selected path (the right side of the tree trunk) and draw upward.

The selected path is edited from the point where you began drawing over it. The new path is added to the selected path (instead of becoming a separate path).

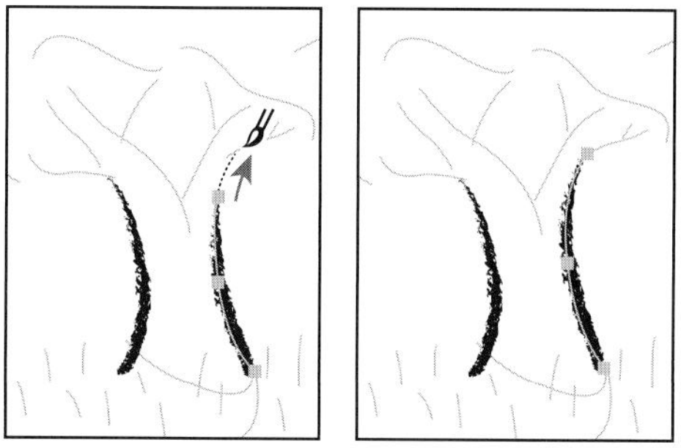

Draw over selected path to edit it. *Selected path is edited.*

When drawing with the paintbrush tool, you may want paths to remain unselected so that you can draw over paths without altering them and create layered or overlapping strokes. You can change the paintbrush tool preferences to keep paths unselected as you draw.

2 Choose Select > Deselect.

3 In the toolbox, double-click the paintbrush tool to display the Paintbrush Tool Preferences dialog box. You use this dialog box to change the way the paintbrush tool functions.

4 Click the Keep Selected option to deselect it, and click OK. Now paths will remain unselected as you draw, and you can draw overlapping paths without altering the earlier paths.

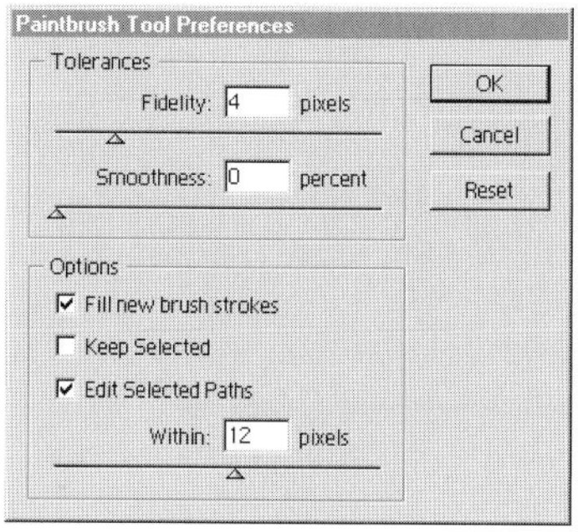

Now you'll draw the limbs of the tree.

5 Draw shorter strokes to create the limbs of the tree.

When the Keep Selected option is turned off, you can edit a path with the paintbrush tool by selecting the path with the Selection tool (or selecting a segment or point on the path with the direct-selection tool) and then redrawing the path with the paintbrush tool.

6 Press Ctrl (Windows) or Command (Mac OS) to toggle to the Selection tool (), and select a limb in the artwork that you want to redraw.

Pressing Ctrl/Command temporarily selects the Selection tool (or the Direct Selection or Group Selection tool, whichever was used last) when another tool is selected.

Draw with the paintbrush tool. *Path remains unselected.* *Select path to edit it.*

7 Use the Paintbrush tool to draw over the selected path.

You can also edit paths using the smooth tool and the erase tool (located under the Pencil tool in the toolbox) to redraw or remove parts of a path drawn with the Paintbrush tool. For information on using the smooth and erase tools, see "Exploring on your own" in Lesson 4, "Drawing with the Pen Tool."

After you apply a brush to an object, it's easy to apply another brush to the paths to change the appearance of the object.

8 Select the Selection tool () and drag a marquee to select the tree trunk and branches.

9 In the Brushes palette, click the Marker brush. The new brush is applied to the selected paths in the artwork.

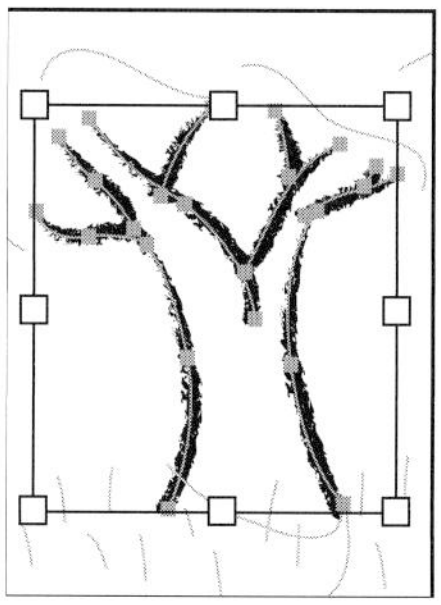

Charcoal strokes selected.

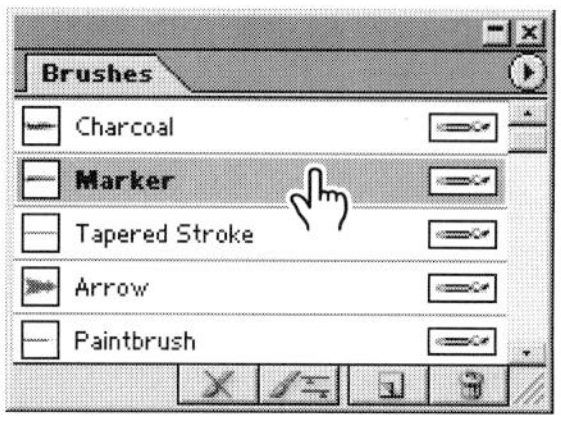

Selecting Marker brush.

Marker brush applied.

10 Click outside the artwork to deselect it and view the tree without selection highlights.

11 Drag a selection marquee to select the tree again.

12 Click several other brushes in the Brushes palette to see the effects of those brushes in the artwork. When you have finished, click the Charcoal brush again to reapply that brush.

13 Click outside the artwork to deselect it.

14 Choose File > Save to save your work.

As you complete the rest of this lesson, use the methods you learned in this section to edit paths as you draw with the paintbrush tool. You can use the brushes, editing paths with the Keep Selected option, if you want strokes to remain selected as you draw, or use the selection tool to select strokes to be edited.

Using Scatter brushes

Scatter brushes randomly spread an object, such as a leaf, a ladybug, or a strawberry, along a path. In this section, you'll use the Fall Leaf Scatter brush to create leaves on the tree. You'll start by adjusting options for the brush to change its appearance in the artwork.

Changing brush options

You change the appearance of a brush by adjusting its settings in the Brush Options dialog box, either before or after brushes have been applied to artwork. The changes you make appear when you apply the brush to artwork, but do not appear in the brush icon in the Brushes palette.

1 In the Brushes palette, choose Show Scatter Brushes from the palette menu to select that option. Then choose Show Art Brushes to deselect that option.

2 Double-click the Fall Leaf brush to open the Scatter Brush Options dialog box.

Brush options vary according to the type of brush. For Scatter brushes, you can set either fixed values or a (random) range of values for the brush size, spacing, scatter, and rotation. If you have a pressure-sensitive drawing tablet attached to your computer, you can also set the pressure of the stylus using the Pressure option.

3 Set the following values, either dragging the slider or entering values, and pressing Tab to move between the text boxes:

• For Size, set the size of the brush object relative to the default (100%) by choosing Random and entering **40%** and **60%.**

• For Spacing, set the distance between brush objects on a path relative to 100% (objects touching but not overlapping) by choosing Random and entering **10**% and **30**%.

• For Scatter, indicate how far objects will deviate from either side of the path, where 0% is aligned on the path, by choosing Random and entering **–40%** and **40%**.

• For Rotation relative to the page or path, enter **–180°** and **180°**; then choose Rotation Relative to Page.

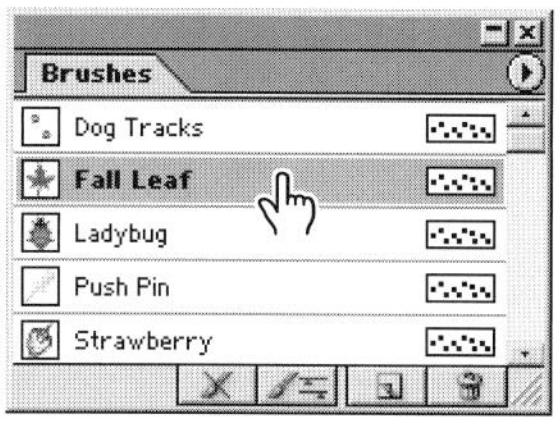

Select Fall Leaf brush.

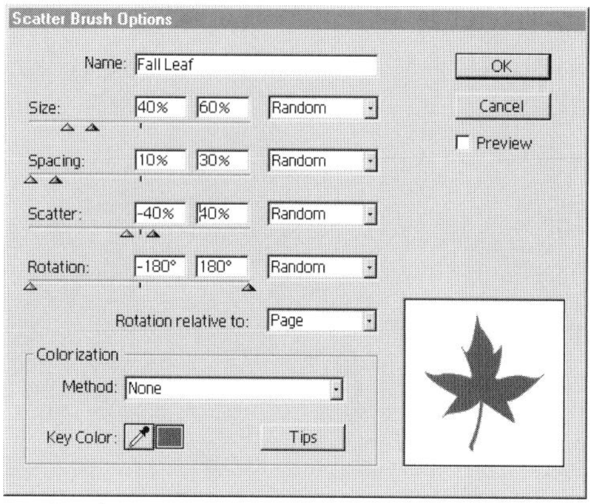

Set brush options.

4 Click OK.

In addition to the features you adjusted in this section, you can change the color of a brush. You'll change the color of the Fall Leaf brush and another brush later in this lesson.

Applying a scatter brush to paths

Now you'll use the Fall Leaf brush with its adjusted settings to draw leaves on the tree in the artwork. First you'll select and lock the tree. Locking an object prevents it from being altered while you work on other objects in the artwork.

1 Use the Selection tool (↖) to drag a marquee around all parts of the tree to select them.

2 Choose Object > Lock > Selection.

The bounding box around the tree disappears, and the tree is locked.

3 Select the Fall Leaf scatter brush.

4 Use the Paintbrush tool (🖌) to draw strokes with the Fall Leaf brush above the tree branches, using the guides to help place your paths. Remember that if you want to edit paths as you draw, you can use the Keep Selected option for the Paintbrush tool or select paths with the Selection tool.

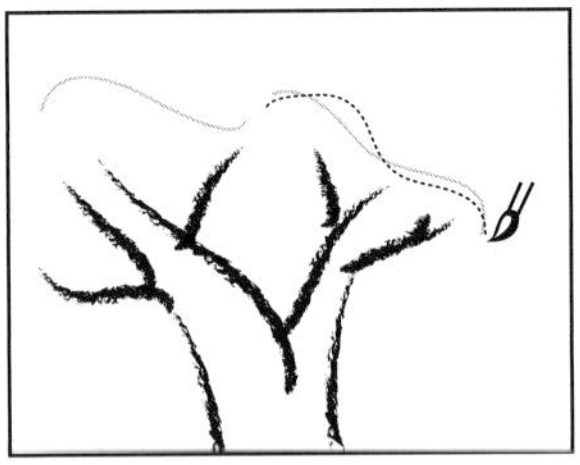

Drawing with paintbrush tool

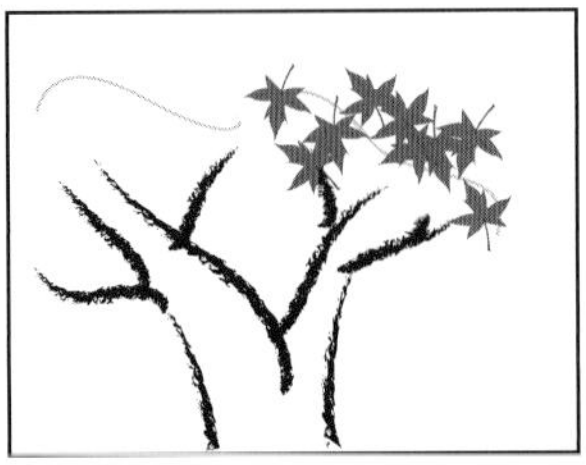

Fall Leaf brush applied to artwork

5 Choose File > Save.

Changing the color attributes of brushes

You'll change the color of the Fall Leaf brush in the artwork.

Before you change the brush color, it's helpful to understand how Illustrator applies color to brushes.

To change the color of Art, Pattern, and Scatter brushes, you use one of three *colorization methods*—models for applying color to the artwork in a brush. To change the color of Calligraphic brushes, you simply select the brush and choose a stroke color. (See Lesson 5, "Painting," for information on choosing a stroke color.) You can change the color attributes of a brush before and after you apply the brush to artwork.

When you apply a brush to artwork, Illustrator uses the current stroke color for the brush only if a colorization method is chosen. Selecting brush strokes and choosing a new stroke color applies that new color to the brush. If no colorization method is set, Illustrator uses the brush's default color. For example, the Fall Leaf brush was applied with its default color of red (not the current stroke of black) because its colorization method was set to None.

To colorize Art, Pattern, and Scatter brushes, you choose from three colorization methods—Tints, Tints and Shades, and Hue Shift:

• Tints displays the brush stroke in tints of the stroke color. Portions of the art that are black become the stroke color, portions that aren't black become tints of the stroke color, and white remains white. If you use a spot color as the stroke, Tints generates tints of the spot color. Choose Tints for brushes that are in black and white, or when you want to paint a brush stroke with a spot color.

• Tints and Shades displays the brush stroke in tints and shades of the stroke color. Tints and Shades maintains black and white, and everything between becomes a blend from black to white through the stroke color. Because black is added, you may not be able to print to a single plate when using Tints and Shades with a spot color. Choose Tints and Shades for brushes that are in grayscale.

• Hue Shift uses the key color in the brush artwork, by default the most prominent color in the art. Everything in the brush artwork that is the key color becomes the stroke color. Other colors in the brush artwork become colors related to the stroke color (the complement on the color wheel). Hue Shift maintains black, white, and gray. Choose Hue Shift for brushes that use multiple colors. You can change the key color. (If the original brush has only one color, the Hue Shift colorized brush also will contain only one color.)

***Note:** Brushes colorized with a stroke color of white may appear entirely white. Brushes colorized with a stroke color of black may appear entirely black. Results depend on the original brush colors.*

Changing the brush color using Hue Shift colorization

Now you'll change the color of the Fall Leaf brush using the Hue Shift colorization method.

1 Select the Selection tool (↖), and drag a selection marquee to select the Fall Leaf strokes in the artwork.

2 Click the Color palette tab to bring the palette to the front. (If the Color palette isn't visible on-screen, choose Window > Color.)

3 Select the Stroke box in the Color palette to bring it to the front. Then click in the color bar to select a color for the Fall Leaf brush. (We chose a lavender color.)

4 In the Brushes palette, double-click the Fall Leaf brush to view the Scatter Brush Options dialog box for the brush. Move the dialog box off to the side so that you can see your artwork as you work.

You'll select a colorization method for the brush. For brushes set to a default colorization method of None, you must choose a colorization method before you can change the brush color. Brushes set to the Tints, Tints and Shades, or Hue Shift colorization method, by default, automatically apply the current stroke color to the brush when you use it in the artwork.

Note: *To find a brush's default colorization setting, double-click the brush in the Brushes palette to view the Brush Options dialog box, and then select the setting in the Method pop-up menu in the Colorization section.*

5 In the Colorization section in the dialog box, choose Hue Shift from the Method pop-up menu.

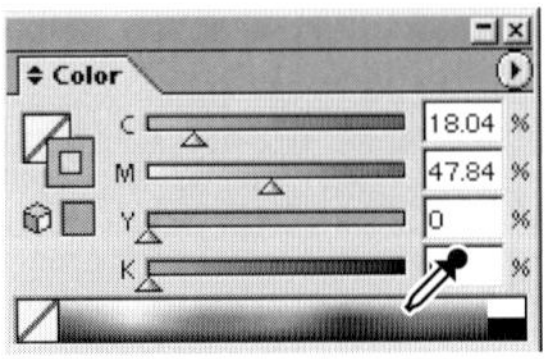

Select brush color.

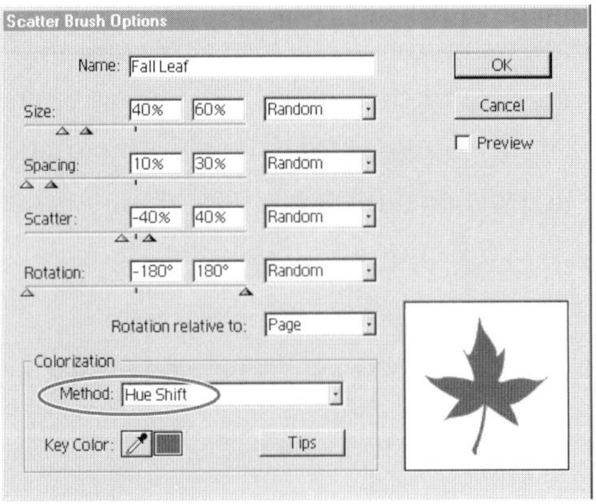

Set colorization method.

The Key Color swatch in the Colorization section indicates the brush color that will shift to the new stroke color. The Key Color box displays the default key color (in this case, the leaf's red color) or the key color you select. For this lesson, you'll use the default key color.

It can be useful to select a new key color if a brush contains several colors and you want to shift different colors in the brush. To select a different key color, you click the Key Color eyedropper in the dialog box and position the eyedropper on the desired color in the preview (such as one of the black veins in the leaf), and click. The new key color shifts to the stroke color when you use the brush in the artwork (and other colors in the brush will shift correspondingly).

6 Click Preview to preview the color to be applied by the colorization method.

The selected Fall Leaf strokes are colorized with the current stroke color (the color you selected in step 3). This color will appear when you apply the Hue Shift colorization method.

7 If desired, choose the Tints or Tints and Shades colorization method from the pop-up menu to preview the change. Then return to the Hue Shift method.

8 Click OK. At the alert message, click Apply To Strokes to apply the colorization change to the strokes in the artwork. You can also choose to change only subsequent brush strokes and leave existing strokes unchanged.

Once you select a colorization method for a brush, the new stroke color applies to selected brush strokes and to new paths painted with the brush.

9 In the Color palette, click the color bar in several different places to try other stroke colors for the selected brush strokes.

10 When you are satisfied with the color of the Fall Leaf brush strokes, click away from the artwork to deselect it.

11 Choose File > Save.

Changing the brush color using Tints colorization

Now you'll apply a new color to the Marker brush in the Art Brushes section of the Brushes palette, and use the brush to draw blades of grass in the artwork.

You'll begin by selecting the brush in the Brushes palette.

1 In the Brushes palette menu, choose Show Art Brushes. Then choose Show Scatter brushes to hide those brushes.

You'll display the Brush Options dialog box for the Marker brush to see the default colorization settings for the brush and change the brush size.

2 In the Brushes palette, double-click the Marker brush. The brush's original color is black.

3 In the Art Brush Options dialog box, note that the Marker brush is set by default to the Tints colorization method.

The Tints colorization method replaces black with the stroke color. Neither the Tints and Shades, nor the Hue Shift colorization method, works with black brushes. Both methods replace the original black color with black, leaving the brush unchanged.

4 In the Size section of the dialog box, enter **50%** for Width to change the size to a more appropriate scale for drawing in the artwork.

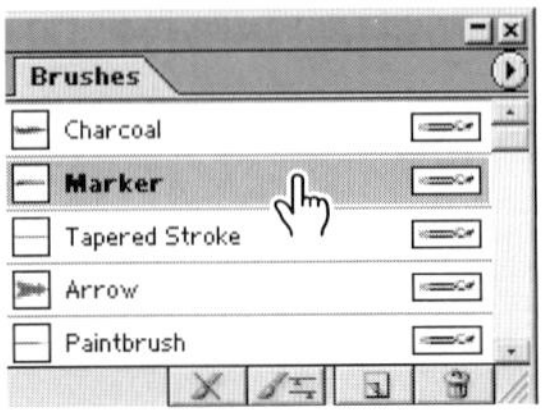

Marker brush selected.

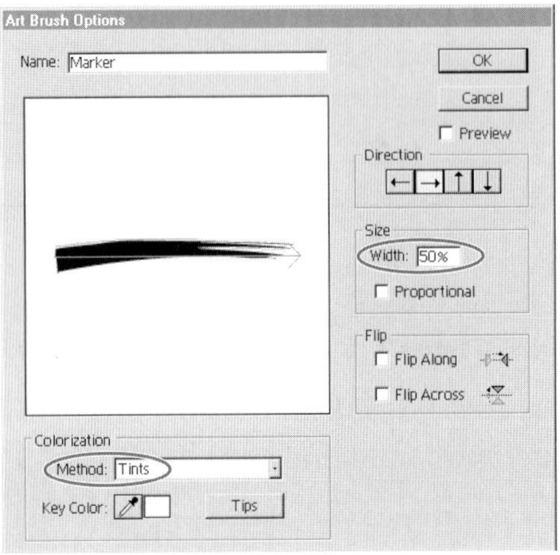

Marker brush with default Tints colorization method.

5 Click OK to accept the settings and close the dialog box.

Now you'll select a color for the grass, and draw the grass with the Marker brush.

6 In the Color palette, click in the color bar to select a color for the grass. (We chose a bright green.)

7 Use the Paintbrush tool ( ) to draw short, upward strokes around the base of the tree, applying the stroke color you selected in step 6. Use the guides to place your drawing. Don't paint the grass around the canoe; you'll paint this later in the lesson. Click off the page to deselect all items.

Note: *If you find strokes disappearing as you create new ones, uncheck Keep Selected from the paintbrush options.*

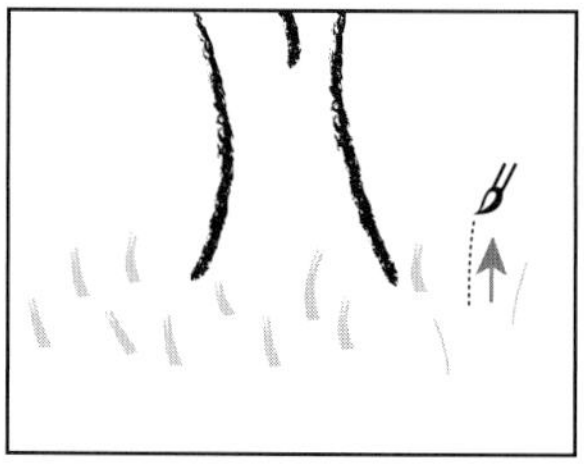

Because the Marker brush is all one color, the Tints colorization method applies the new stroke color as one color (rather than varied tints of the color). When the original brush contains several colors, the Tints colorization method applies a different tint for each color in the brush.

Using a fill color with brushes

When you apply a brush to an object's stroke, you can also apply a fill color to paint the interior of the object with a color. When you use a fill color with a brush, the brush objects appear on top of the fill color in places where the fill and the brush objects overlap.

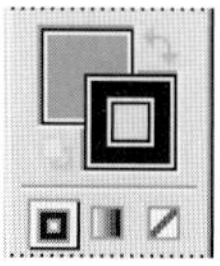

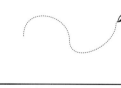

Choose fill color.

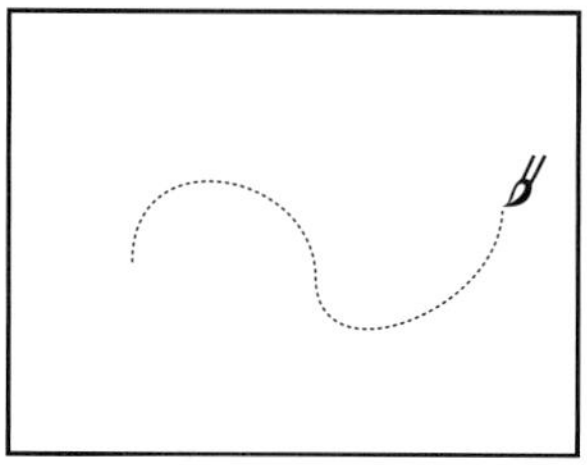

Draw with paintbrush.

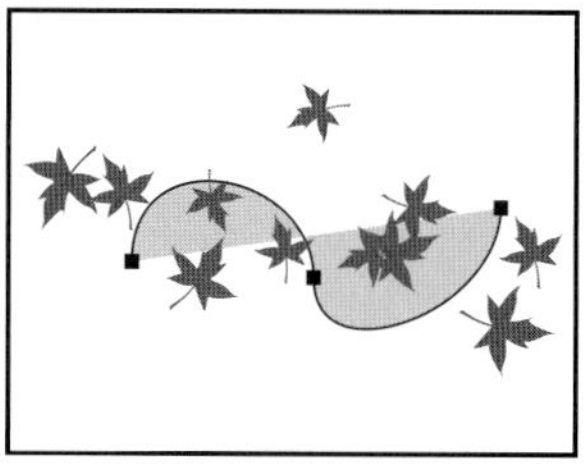

Brush objects appear on top of fill.

Now you'll use the paintbrush tool to draw a canoe at the edge of the grass with an Art brush. You'll begin by selecting the brush in the Brushes palette.

1 In the Brushes palette, select the Tapered Stroke brush.

The Tapered Stroke brush uses the Tints colorization method by default. To change the color of the Tapered Stroke brush, you'll simply select a stroke color.

2 In the Color palette, make sure that the Stroke box is selected. Then click in the color bar to select a color for the edges of the canoe. (We chose a dark orange.)

Now you'll use the paintbrush tool to draw the edges of the canoe. Use the guides to align your drawing.

3 Use the Paintbrush tool (🖌) to draw a crescent shape to make the side and bottom of the canoe:

- Draw a long stroke from left to right to make the side edge of the canoe. Do not release the mouse button.

- While still holding down the mouse button, draw a second long stroke beneath the first, from right to left, connecting the two strokes at the right endpoint of the object, to make a crescent shape. When you have drawn the second stroke, release the mouse button.

You may have to draw the crescent shape more than once to create a shape with a single path. Remember that you can edit paths as you draw. Use the direct-selection tool to select a segment of the path that you want to redraw.

Don't worry if your drawing doesn't match the guides exactly. What's important is drawing the shape as one path, without releasing the mouse button, so that you can fill the object correctly. (If a shape is made of separate paths, the fill color is applied to each path separately, yielding unpredictable results.)

4 Draw a third long stroke for the top side of the canoe. Then draw two shorter strokes for the crossbars. (Draw the top side and crossbars as separate paths, releasing the mouse button after each one.)

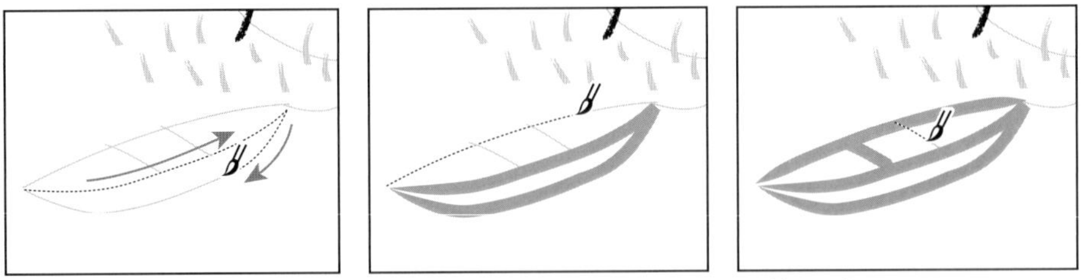

Draw crescent as one path. *Add top.* *Add crossbars.*

Now you'll fill the side of the canoe with a color.

5 Select the Selection tool (), and select the crescent shape you drew for the lower side and bottom of the canoe.

6 In the Color palette, select the Fill box. Then click in the color bar to select a fill color for the canoe. (We chose a yellowish orange.)

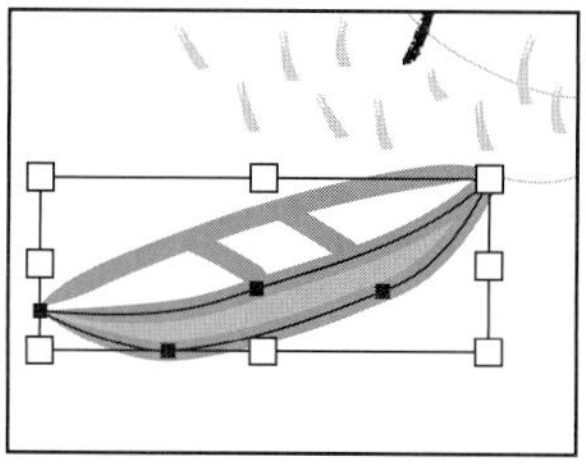

Selected shape is filled.

7 Click outside the artwork to deselect it.

8 Choose File > Save.

Using Calligraphic brushes

Calligraphic brushes resemble strokes drawn with the angled point of a calligraphic pen. Calligraphic brushes are defined by an elliptical shape whose center follows the path. Use these brushes to create the appearance of hand-drawn strokes made with a flat, angled pen tip.

You'll use a Calligraphic pen to draw water in front of the canoe. You'll begin by selecting the brush, and then choose a color for the brush.

1 In the Brushes palette, choose Show Calligraphic Brushes from the palette menu to select that option. Then choose Show Art Brushes from the menu to deselect that option.

2 In the Brushes palette, select the 12 pt Oval brush.

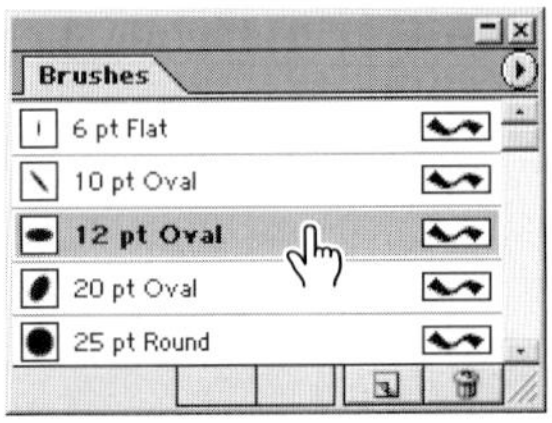

3 In the Color palette, click the Stroke box. Then click in the color bar to select a new color for the water. (We chose a light blue.)

Calligraphic brushes use the current stroke color when you apply the brushes to artwork. You do not use colorization methods with Calligraphic brushes.

4 In the Color palette, click the Fill box and then click the None box. A fill of None with brushes prevents paths from being filled when you apply the brush.

5 Select the Paintbrush tool (), and draw wavy lines for the water surface. The paths you draw use the stroke color you selected in step 3.

Now you'll change the shape of the 12 pt Oval brush in the Brush Options dialog box to change the appearance of the strokes made with the brush.

6 In the Brushes palette, double-click the 12 pt Oval brush to display the Calligraphic Brush Options dialog box.

You can change the angle of the brush (relative to a horizontal line), the roundness (from a flat line to a full circle), and the diameter (from 0 to 1296 points) to change the shape that defines the brush's tip, and change the appearance of the stroke that the brush makes. Now you'll change the diameter of the brush.

7 Enter **8 pt** for Diameter. In the Name text box, enter **8 pt Oval**. Notice that the weight of the Calligraphic brush strokes in the artwork decreases.

The Preview window in the dialog box shows changes you make to the brush.

8 Click OK. At the alert message, click Apply To Strokes to apply the change to the strokes in the artwork.

12 pt Oval brush.

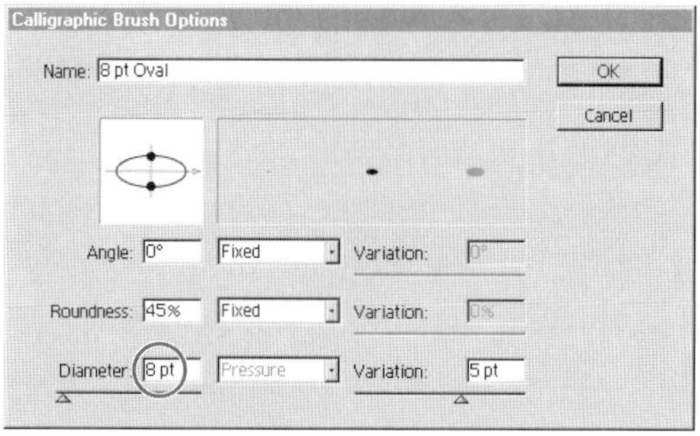

Selecting 8 pt Oval brush.

Result.

9 Ctrl/Command-click outside the artwork or choose Select > Deselect to deselect it.

10 Choose File > Save.

Using Pattern brushes

Pattern brushes paint a pattern made up of separate sections, or tiles, for the sides (middle sections), ends, and corners of the path. When you apply a Pattern brush to artwork, the brush applies different tiles from the pattern to different sections of the path, depending on where the section falls on the path (at an end, in the middle, or at a corner). You'll use the Rope Pattern brush to draw a rope from the canoe to the tree, with different tiles used for the rope's middle and end sections.

1 In the Brushes palette, choose Show Pattern Brushes from the palette menu to select that option. Then choose Show Calligraphic Brushes from the menu to deselect that option.

2 Double-click the Rope brush to display the Pattern Brush Options dialog box for the brush.

The Brush Options dialog box displays the tiles in the Rope brush. The first tile on the left is the Side tile, used to paint the middle sections of a path. The second tile from the right is the Start tile, used to paint the beginning section of a path. The last tile on the right is the End tile, used to paint the end of a path.

Pattern brushes can have up to five tiles – the Side, Start, and End tiles, plus an Outer Corner tile and an Inner Corner tile to paint sharp corners on a path. The Rope brush has no corner tiles because the brush is designed for curved paths, not sharp corners (just as a real rope creates loops or coils, not sharp angles). In the next part of this lesson, you'll create a Pattern brush that uses corner tiles.

Now you'll change the scale of the Pattern brush so that the brush is in scale with the rest of the artwork when you apply it.

3 In the Pattern Brush Options dialog box, enter 20% in the Scale text box, and click OK.

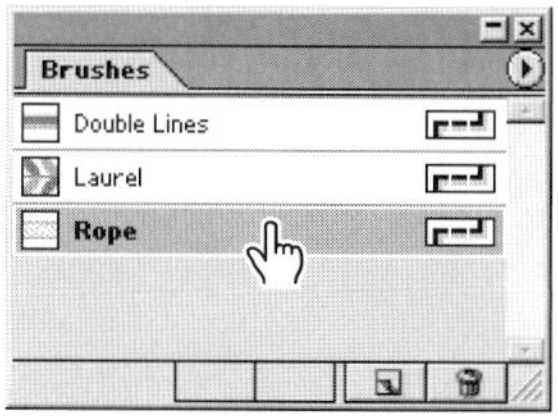

Rope brush.

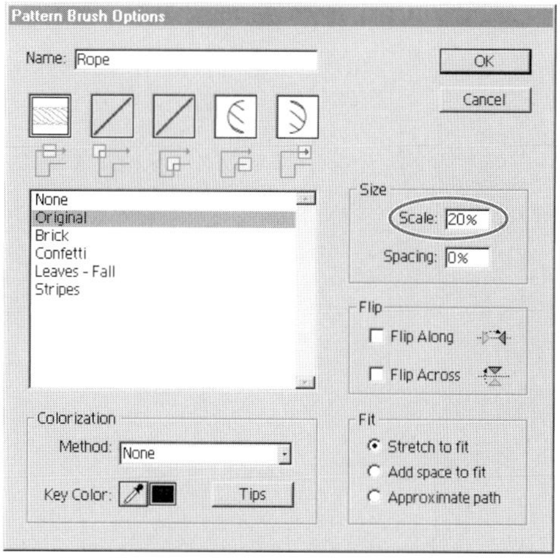

Rope brush with Side, Start, and End tiles scaled 20%.

4 Select the Paintbrush tool (), and draw a path that loops around the base of the tree. Then draw a second path that leads from the loop around the tree to the canoe.

Draw the rope as two separate paths, rather than one path, to avoid creating a path with a sharp angle. (Because the Rope brush does not include corner tiles, the brush uses Side tiles to paint sharp angles. The Side tiles appear severed at sharp corners, and the rope appears to be cut.)

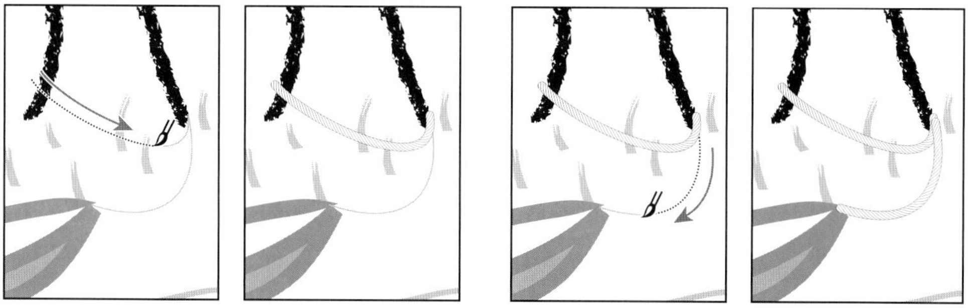

Apply Rope brush as two separate paths.

Now you'll select a blade of grass you created earlier in the lesson and move it in front of the rope to make the rope appear to lie behind the grass.

5 Select the Selection tool (), and then select a grass blade lying along the path of the rope. (Be careful not to select the rope along with the grass.)

If you like, you can Shift-click to select additional grass blades along the path of the rope.

6 Choose Object > Arrange > Bring to Front.

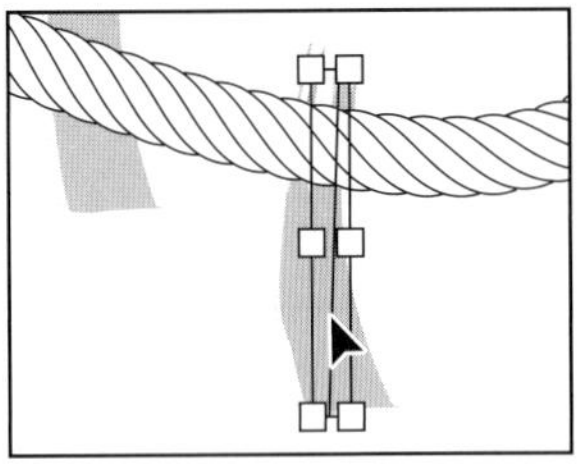

Select grass blade.

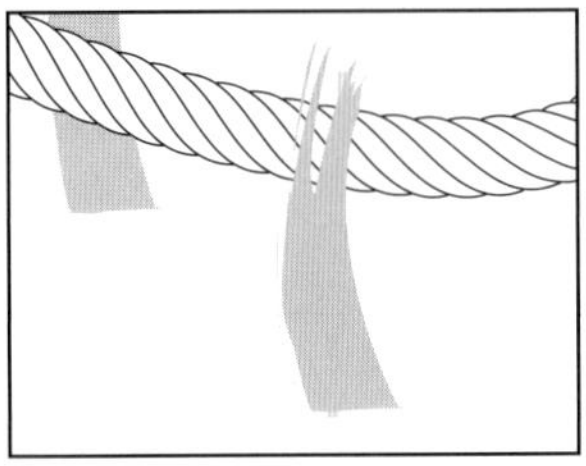

Bring grass to front.

7 Choose File > Save.

Tips for using brushes

When you work with brushes, keep the following points in mind:

- *You can often use Scatter brushes and Pattern brushes to achieve the same effect. However, one way in which they differ is that Pattern brushes follow the path exactly, whereas Scatter brushes do not.*

- *If you apply a brush to a closed path and want to control the placement of the end of the path, select the scissors tool and split the path. To change again, select the endpoints, choose Object > Path > Join, and use the scissors again.*

- *To select all brushstroke paths in the current artwork, choose Select > Object > Brush Strokes.*

- *For better performance when creating a brush from art that contains multiple overlapping paths filled with the same color and with no stroke, select the paths and click the Unite button in the Pathfinder palette before you create the brush.*

–From online Help "Using the Brushes palette".

Creating brushes

You can create new brushes of all four brush types, using artwork in an Illustrator file as the basis for the brush. In this section, you'll use artwork provided with the lesson to create a new Pattern brush with three tiles–a cloud for the Side tile, and a sun for the Outer Corner tile and Inner Corner tile.

Creating swatches for a Pattern brush

You create Pattern brushes by first creating swatches in the Swatches palette with the artwork that will be used for the Pattern brush tiles. In this section, you'll use the cloud and sun drawings included with the artwork file to create swatches.

1 Use the scroll bars, the hand tool, or the Navigator palette to display the scratch area to the right of the artboard to view the cloud and sun drawings located there.

For information on moving to different areas of the document window, see Lesson 1, "Getting to Know the Work Area."

The cloud and sun were created using the Marker brush. (You can use any drawing tool to create artwork for new brushes.) Each piece was then expanded using the Object > Expand Appearance command. If you used a brush to create art for the swatch, you must first expand the art before you can create a swatch in the Swatches palette.

You'll unlock the sun and cloud artwork, and then use the artwork to create swatches. The objects were locked to prevent them from being altered while you completed the earlier sections of the lesson.

2 Choose Object > Unlock All.

Bounding boxes and selection highlights appear around the sun and cloud, indicating that the objects are unlocked and selected. The tree, which you locked earlier in the lesson, is also unlocked and selected. (The tree can be unlocked, because you've finished drawing in the area of the tree.)

3 Click outside the artwork to deselect the objects.

4 Click the Swatches palette tab to view the Swatches palette. (If the palette isn't visible on-screen, choose Window > Swatches.)

Now you'll create a pattern swatch.

5 Select the Selection tool (), and drag the cloud onto the Swatches palette. The new swatch appears in the pattern swatches group.

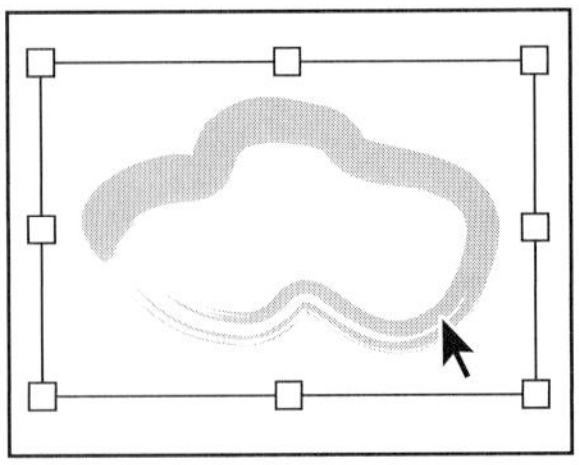

Select cloud.

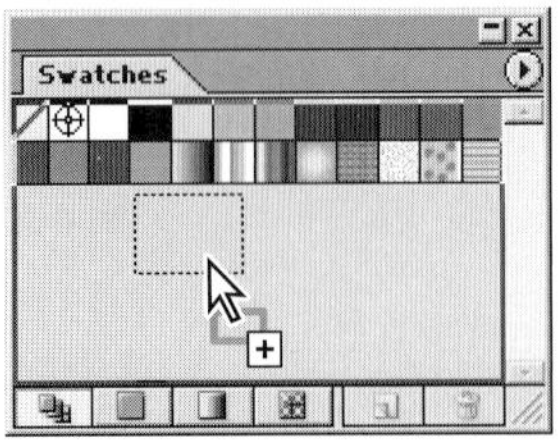

Drag it onto Swatches palette.

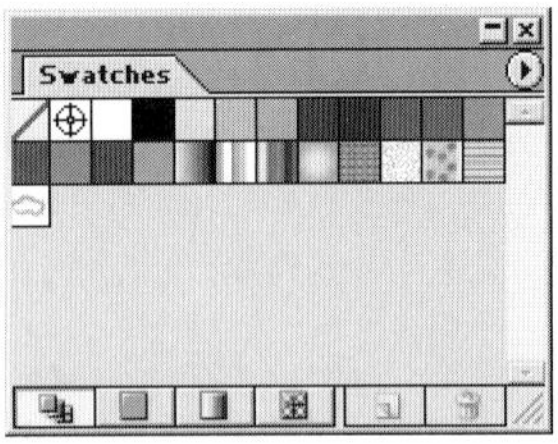

Cloud swatch is added to palette.

6 Click away from the artwork to deselect the cloud.

7 In the Swatches palette, double-click the cloud swatch. Double-clicking the cloud swatch changes the current fill or stroke box to that swatch and opens the Swatch Options dialog box.

8 Name the swatch **Cloud**, and then click OK.

9 Now repeat steps 5 through 8 to create a pattern swatch of the sun art:

- Use the Selection tool to drag the sun onto the Swatches palette. The new swatch appears in the pattern swatches group.
- Click away from the artwork to deselect the sun.
- In the Swatches palette, double-click the sun swatch.
- Name the swatch **Sun**, and then click OK.

For more information on creating pattern swatches, see "Working with Patterns" in online Help.

Creating a Pattern brush from swatches

To create a new Pattern brush, you apply swatches from the Swatches palette to tiles in the Brush Options dialog box. Now you'll apply the Cloud and Sun swatches to tiles for a new Pattern brush.

First you'll open a Brush Options dialog box for a new Pattern brush.

1 Click the Brushes palette tab to view the palette.

2 In the Brushes palette, click the New Brush button.

3 Select New Pattern Brush and click OK.

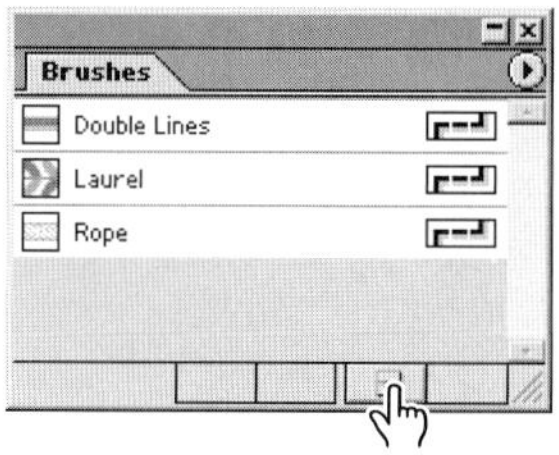

Create new brush.

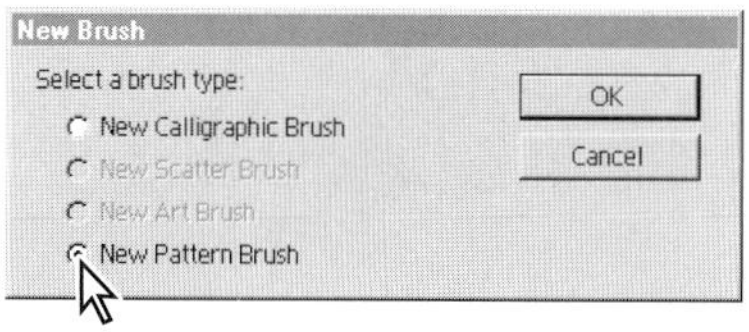

Select brush type.

You'll apply the Cloud swatch to the Side tile for the new Pattern brush.

4 In the Pattern Brush Options dialog box, select the Side tile box (the far left tile box).

5 In the pattern swatches scroll list, select the Cloud swatch. The Cloud swatch appears in the Side tile box.

Next you'll apply the Sun swatch to the Outer Corner tile and Inner Corner tile for the new Pattern brush.

6 In the Pattern Brush Options dialog box, select the Outer Corner tile box (the second tile box from the left). In the pattern swatches scroll list, select the Sun swatch. The Sun swatch appears in the Outer Corner tile box.

In the Pattern Brush Options dialog box, select the Inner Corner tile box (the middle tile box). In the pattern swatches scroll list, select the Sun swatch. The Sun swatch appears in the Inner Corner tile box.

You won't create a Start tile or End tile for the new brush. (You'll apply the new brush to a closed path in the artwork later in the lesson, so you won't need Start or End tiles at this time. When you want to create a Pattern brush that includes Start and End tiles, you add those tiles the same way as you did the Side and Corner tiles.)

7 In the Name text box, name the brush **Clouds and Sun**. Then click OK.

The Clouds and Sun brush appears in the Pattern brush section in the Brushes palette.

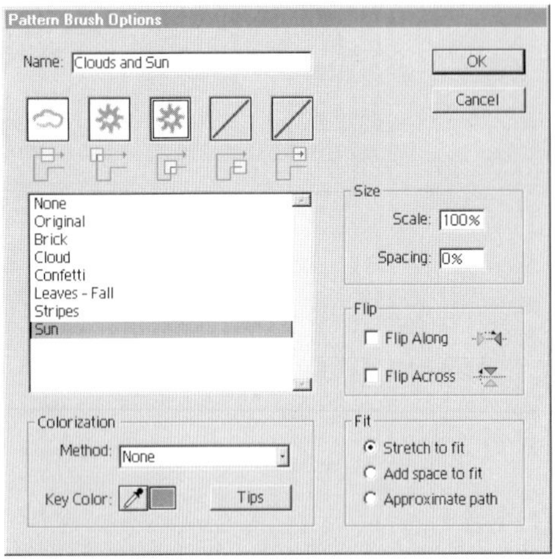

Note: *When you create a new brush, the brush appears in the Brushes palette of the current artwork only. If you open another file in Illustrator, the Clouds and Sun brush won't appear in that file's Brushes palette.*

To save a brush and reuse it in another file, you can create a brush library with the brushes you want to use. For more information, see "Using brush libraries" in online Help.

Painting with the Pattern brush

So far in this lesson you've used the paintbrush tool to apply brushes to paths. You can also apply brushes to paths created with any drawing tool—including the pen, pencil, ellipse, and rectangle tools—and the other basic shapes tools. In this section, you'll use the rectangle tool to apply the Clouds and Sun brush to a rectangular border around the artwork.

When you use drawing tools to apply brushes to artwork, you first draw the path with the tool and then select the brush in the Brushes palette to apply the brush to the path.

First you'll set the fill color to None.

1 In the toolbox, click the Fill box and click the None box.

2 Use the Navigator palette or the Zoom tool (🔍) to reduce the view of the artwork.

Now you'll draw a border with the rectangle tool, and apply the brush to the path.

3 Select the Rectangle tool (▭). Drag to draw a rectangle on the artboard, about 1/2-inch inside the imageable area on each side, as indicated by the guide.

4 In the Brushes palette, click the Clouds and Sun brush.

The rectangle path is painted with the Clouds and Sun brush, with the Cloud tile on the sides and the Sun tile on the corners.

Draw rectangle.

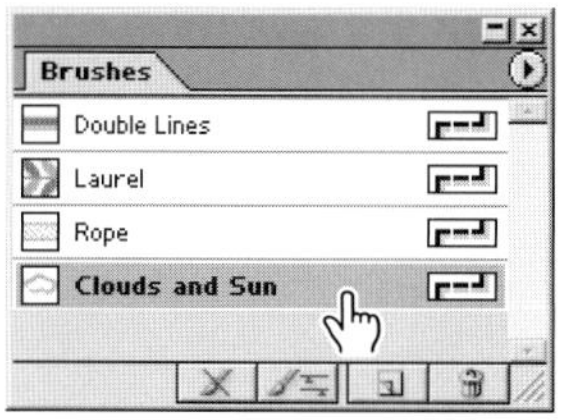

Select Pattern brush.

Brush is applied to rectangle path.

5 Ctrl-click (Windows) or Command-click (Mac OS) outside the art to deselect it.

Now you'll draw a curved path using the Clouds and Sun brush.

6 In the Brushes palette, double-click the Clouds and Sun Pattern brush to view the Brush Options dialog box for the brush.

You'll change the scale and spacing of the brush for a different look.

7 Under Size, enter **250%** for Scale, and **30%** for Spacing. Click OK.

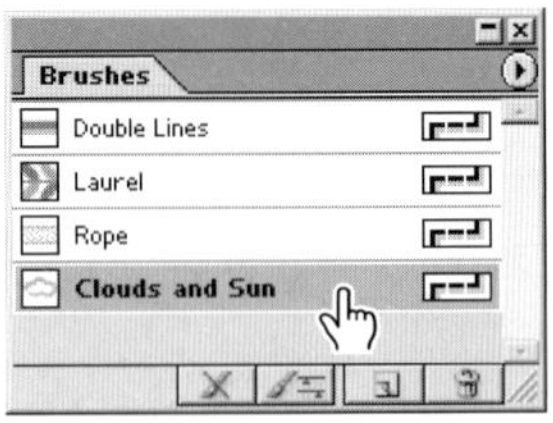

Select Clouds and Sun Pattern brush.

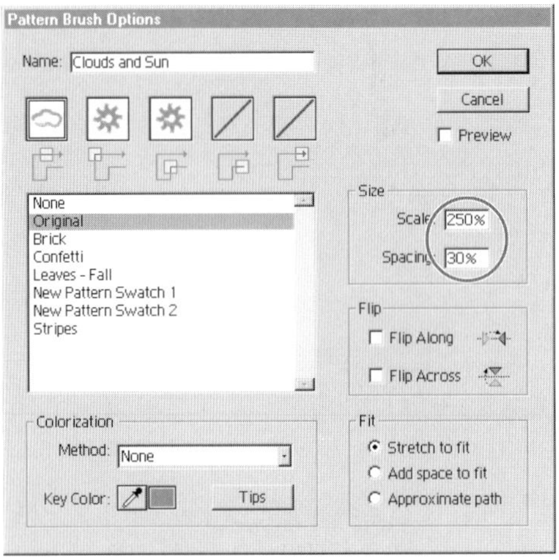

Change scale and spacing.

8 At the Brush Change alert message, click Leave Strokes to keep the border brush strokes as they are.

The Leave Strokes option preserves paths in the artwork that are already painted with the brush. The changes you made to the brush will apply to subsequent uses of the brush. Now you'll use the brush to paint a curved path in the artwork.

9 Select the Paintbrush tool (✐) and draw a smooth curve over the tree. Use the guides for placement.

Apply Pattern brush to path with paintbrush.

Result.

The path is painted with the clouds from the Clouds and Sun brush (the Side tile in the brush). Because the path does not include sharp corners, the Outer Corner tile and Inner Corner tile (the Sun tiles) are not applied to the path.

Applying the Scribble effect

The Scribble effect is a new feature in Illustrator CS that lets you apply loose or mechanical-like scribbling to fills and strokes. This includes fills of gradients and patterns.

You will create the lake water, grass and text using the Scribble Effect and its options.

1 Create a rectangle behind the tree to create the grass. Fill the rectangle with the Green swatch from the Swatches palette and give it a Stroke of None.

2 Create the rectangle for the lake water by following the guide that is behind the boat. Fill this rectangle with the gradient named *water* in the Swatches palette.

Create two rectangles using guides for the grass and lake.

3 Choose the Gradient tool (■). Change the direction and length of the gradient in the water by clicking in the lower section of the rectangle and dragging upwards. The distance that you drag and the direction determines the length and direction of the gradient. Do this as many times as you like until you are satisfied with the gradient.

You don't have to click and drag with the Gradient tool at the bottom of the rectangle or even in the rectangle. Get different effects by clicking in the middle of the rectangle and dragging up, or even clicking outside the rectangle and dragging up and over the top.

4 With the water still selected, choose Effect > Stylize > Scribble.

The Scribble effect options appear, giving you choices that range from changing the width of the scribbled stroke, to loopiness and tightness.

5 Choose options in the Scribble Options dialog box to make the blue look more like water. (We used the following settings; Angle 30°, Path Overlap -2.5 pt, Variation 5 pt, Stroke Width 10 pt. The curviness was set to be more angular with a setting of 0 (zero), but variations were made to make the strokes look less mechanical with a Curviness Variation setting of 18 %. Spacing between the strokes was set to 14 pt with a variation of .5 pt.) Click OK.

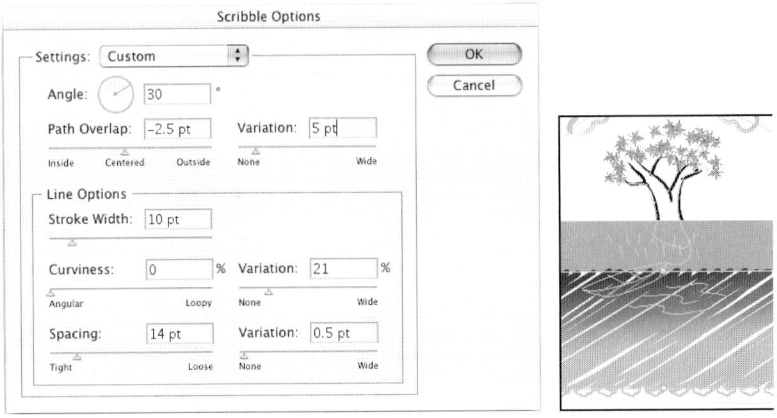

Using the Stroke Options to create water.

Now you create the grass using slightly different settings.

6 Using the Selection tool (↖) select the rectangle forming the grass and choose Effect > Stylize > Scribble. Don't choose the Scribble directly under the Effect menu. That will apply the last used settings of the Scribble effect without opening the options dialog box.

7 Using the options to create a tighter more mechanical scribble for the grass. (We used; Angle 90°, Path Overlap 0 (zero), Variation 5 pt, Stroke width 3 pt, Curviness 5 pt, Variation for Curviness 1 %, Spacing 5 pt, Variation for Spacing .5 pt.) Click OK.

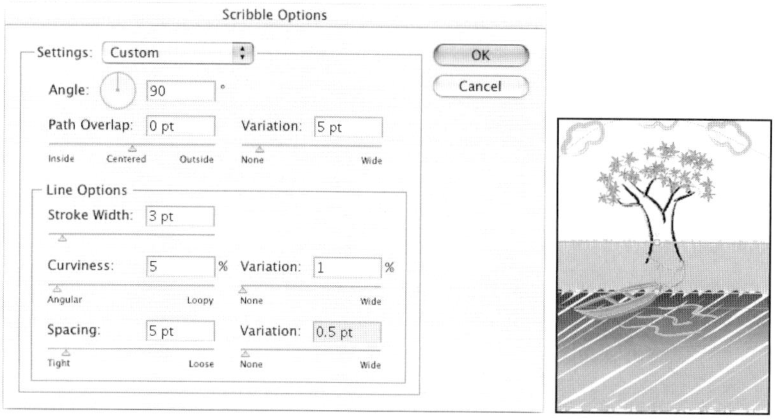

Changing the Scribble Options for the grass.

8 Using the Selection tool Shift-click on the water to select both the grass and water rectangles simultaneously.

9 Choose Object > Arrange > Send to Back to reveal the boat and ripples in the water again.

Now you will use the Scribble Effect on live text.

10 Select the Type tool (T) and click in the middle of the water rectangle. Before typing, set up your character attributes. If your Character palette is not visible choose Window > Type > Character. (We chose Myriad Pro Black, which comes with Adobe Illustrator CS. For more information about the fonts that come with your software choose Help > Welcome Menu and click on Cool Extras.) Change the font size and leading to **72 pt**. Use Window > Type > Paragraph to Align Center the text.

11 Type **LAKESIDE DESIGNS** in all caps, return after the word LAKESIDE.

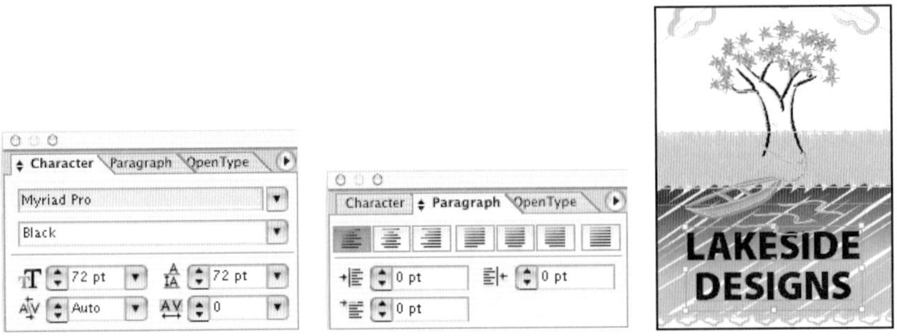

Choose the font style and alignment.

12 Use the Selection tool to select the text, choose Effect > Stylize > Scribble. Using the Scribble Options make the text look scribbled, but yet readable. We chose to tighten up the scribble with the following settings: Angle 0° (zero), Path Overlap 0 (zero), Variation .5 pt, Stroke Width 2 pt, Curviness 0 (zero), Curviness Variation 0 (zero), Spacing 3 pt, Variation for Spacing 0 (zero). Click OK.

The text is still live text. If you were to change the font or size, it would still maintain the scribbled look.

You've completed the artwork for the lesson. Now you'll remove the guides so you can view the artwork in its finished form.

When working with guides, you can temporarily hide guides by choosing View > Guides > Hide Guides. The guides disappear but are preserved in the artwork. You can display hidden guides by choosing View > Guides > Show Guides. You won't need the guides again in this lesson, so you'll delete them using the Clear Guides command.

13 Choose View > Guides > Clear Guides. The guides are deleted from the artwork.

14 Choose File > Save to save your work. Choose File > Close to close the file.

Exploring on your own

Here are some ideas you can try on your own.

Applying brushes to paths

Practice applying brushes to paths you create with drawing tools (just as you applied the Clouds and Sun Pattern brush to a path drawn with the rectangle tool in the final section of the lesson).

1 Choose File > New, to create a document for practice.

2 In the Brushes palette menu, make sure that Show Scatter Brushes is selected (indicated by a check mark next to the option). You can uncheck the other brush choices to see only the Scatter brushes.

3 Use the drawing tools (the pen or pencil tool, and any of the basic shapes tools) to draw objects. Use the default fill and stroke colors when you draw.

4 With one of the objects selected, click a brush in the Brushes palette to apply the brush to the object's path.

5 Repeat step 3 for each object you drew.

6 Display the Brush Options dialog box for one of the brushes you used in step 3, and change the color, size, or other features of the brush. After you close the dialog box, click Apply To Strokes to apply your changes to the brush in the artwork.

Creating brushes

Use one of the basic shapes tools to create artwork to use as a new Scatter brush.

1 Select a basic shape tool in the toolbox, and draw an object, keeping it selected.

2 Click the New Brush button at the bottom of the Brushes palette.

Note: *You can use more than one object to create the new brush. All selected objects in the artwork will be included in the brush. If you use a brush to create artwork for a new brush, remember to expand the brush strokes before creating the new brush.*

3 In the New Brush dialog box, select New Scatter Brush and click OK.

The Brush Options dialog box for the new brush appears, with the selected objects displayed in the brush example. The new brush is named Scatter Brush 1 by default.

4 Enter a name for the brush. Then click OK to accept the settings for the brush.

5 Select the paintbrush tool and draw a path. The new brush is applied to the path.

6 Double-click the new brush to display the Brush Options dialog box. Change the brush settings to try out different versions of the brush. When you have finished, click OK.

Using a brush library

Try out some of the brushes included in the brush libraries in Illustrator.

1 To open a brush library, choose Window > Brush Libraries.

2 Choose a library from the submenu. Illustrator includes nine brush libraries in addition to the default brush library that appears when you start the program.

You can also create your own brush libraries. See "Using brush libraries" in online Help.

Review questions

1 Describe each of the four brush types—Art, Calligraphic, Pattern, and Scatter.

2 What is the difference between applying a brush to artwork using the paintbrush tool and applying a brush to artwork using one of the drawing tools?

3 Describe how to edit paths with the paintbrush tool as you draw. How does the Keep Selected option affect the paintbrush tool?

4 How do you change the colorization method for an Art, Pattern, or Scatter brush? (Remember, you don't use colorization methods with Calligraphic brushes.)

5 How can you make the scribble effect more mechanical rather than loose and flowing?

Review answers

1 The following are the four brush types:

• Art brushes stretch artwork evenly along a path. Art brushes include strokes that resemble graphic media (such as the Charcoal brush used to create the tree, or the Marker brush used to create the grass). Art brushes also include objects, such as the Arrow brush.

• Calligraphic brushes are defined by an elliptical shape whose center follows the path. They create strokes that resemble hand-drawn lines made with a flat, angled calligraphic pen tip.

• Pattern brushes paint a pattern made up of separate sections, or tiles, for the sides (middle sections), ends, and corners of the path. When you apply a Pattern brush to artwork, the brush applies different tiles from the pattern to different sections of the path, depending on where the section falls on the path (at an end, in the middle, or at a corner).

• Scatter brushes scatter an object, such as a leaf, along a path. You can adjust the Size, Spacing, Scatter, and Rotation options for a Scatter brush to change the brush's appearance.

2 To apply brushes using the Paintbrush tool (), you select the tool, choose a brush from the Brushes palette, and draw in the artwork. The brush is applied directly to the paths as you draw. To apply brushes using a drawing tool, you select the tool and draw in the artwork; then you select the path in the artwork and choose a brush in the Brushes palette. The brush is applied to the selected path.

3 To edit a path with the paintbrush tool, simply drag over a selected path to redraw it. The Keep Selected option keeps the last path selected as you draw with the paintbrush tool. Leave the Keep Selected option turned on (the default setting) when you want to easily edit the previous path as you draw. Turn off the Keep Selected option when you want to draw layered paths with the paintbrush without altering previous paths. When the Keep Selected option is turned off, you can use the selection tool to select a path and then edit the path.

4 To change the colorization method of a brush, double-click the brush in the Brushes palette to view the Brush Options dialog box. Use the Method pop-up menu in the Colorization section to select another method. If you choose Hue Shift, you can use the default color displayed in the dialog box preview; or you can change the key color (the new color that will appear) by clicking the Key Color eyedropper, and clicking a color in the preview. Click OK to accept the settings and close the Brush Options dialog box. Click Apply to Strokes at the alert message if you want to apply the changes to existing strokes in the artwork.

Existing brush strokes are colorized with the stroke color that was selected when the strokes were applied to the artwork. New brush strokes are colorized with the current stroke color. To change the color of existing strokes after applying a different colorization method, select the strokes and select a new stroke color.

5 Using the Scribble Option, you can keep the choices for Curviness Variation and Spacing Variation to a minimum to make the scribble more mechanical.

Lesson 15

15 Creating Airbrush Effects

Converting shapes into mesh objects lets you blend colors in multiple directions within the shapes, for a watercolor or airbrush effect. It's easy to modify mesh objects. You can add or remove colors from points on the mesh, to adjust the direction and amount of color blending.

In this lesson, you'll learn how to do the following:

- Create a mesh object using two methods.
- Apply colors to a mesh.
- Edit a mesh for a variety of effects.
- Apply warp effects.
- Select objects in different groups and layers.
- Use Smart Guides to display information about mesh objects.

Getting started

In this lesson, you'll convert the shapes of two butterflies into meshes, paint them, and manipulate the color blending. Before you begin, you must restore the default preferences for Adobe Illustrator and then you will open the finished art file for the lesson to see what you'll create.

1 To ensure that the tools and palettes function exactly as described in this lesson, delete or deactivate (by renaming) the Adobe Illustrator CS preferences file. See "Restoring default preferences" on page 2.

2 Start Adobe Illustrator.

3 Choose File > Open, and open the L15end.ai file in the Lesson15 folder, located inside the Lessons folder within the AICIB folder on your hard drive.

4 If you like, choose View > Zoom Out to make the finished artwork smaller, adjust the window size, and leave it on your screen as you work. (Use the Hand tool (✋) to move the artwork where you want it in the window.) If you don't want to leave the image open, choose File > Close.

For an illustration of the finished artwork in this lesson, see the color section.

To begin working, you'll open an existing art file.

5 Choose File > Open, and open the L15start.ai file in the Lesson15 folder, located inside the Lessons folder within the AICIB folder on your hard drive.

6 Choose File > Save As, name the file **Butterfly.ai**, and select the Lesson15 folder in the Save In menu. Leave the type of format set to Adobe Illustrator® Document. Click Save. In the Illustrator Options dialog box, leave at defaults and click OK.

Setting Smart Guides preferences

Smart Guides are useful for working with mesh objects because they display information about the mesh without the need to select the object first. You'll set preferences for hiding the construction guides (which are useful for drawing and aligning objects) and text labels (which you won't need for this lesson), and you'll change the snapping tolerance (the distance that the pointer must be from an object before Smart Guides take effect).

1 Choose Edit > Preferences > Smart Guides & Slices (Windows) or Illustrator > Preferences > Smart Guides & Slices (Mac OS).

2 In the Preferences dialog box, deselect the display options for Text Label Hints and Construction Guides, and make sure that Transform Tools and Object Highlighting are selected. Enter 1 pt in the Snapping Tolerance text box. Click OK to set the preferences.

The Transform Tools option is useful for scaling, rotating, reflecting, and shearing objects. The Object Highlighting option displays mesh lines and anchor points when the mouse is positioned over the object.

3 Choose View > Smart Guides to activate them. (A check mark in the menu indicates that they're turned on.)

Painting with the Mesh tool

You can convert any object into a mesh object by using the Mesh tool and creating one mesh point at a time. Each time you click an object using the Mesh tool, a new color is added to the object.

First you'll paint a color on one of the tail wings on a butterfly, and then you'll paint the other tail wing with the same color.

1 Select the Zoom tool (🔍) in the toolbox and click the butterfly at the top of the artwork a few times to zoom in to 300% (as indicated in the lower left corner of the window). Then select the Hand tool (✋), and use it to move the butterfly to the center of the window.

2 Click a color in the Color palette or Swatches palette to specify the current fill. (We selected the Color 2 swatch.) To display the Swatches palette, click its tab to bring it to the front of its palette group.

3 Select the Mesh tool (▦) in the toolbox, and click in the center of the upper left tail wing to apply a mesh point with the currently selected color.

The tail wing is automatically converted to a mesh object. The first time you click an object with the Mesh tool, the object is converted to a mesh object with one mesh point and two intersecting mesh lines.

4 Now click in the center of the right tail wing to apply a mesh point with the same color and convert it to a mesh object.

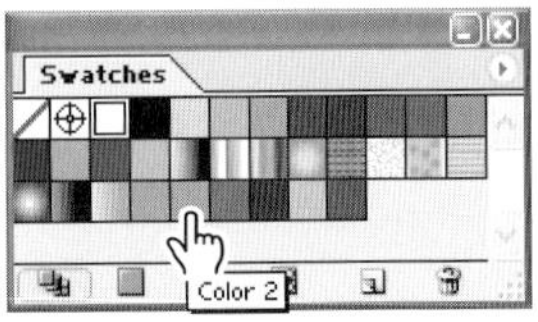

Select color.

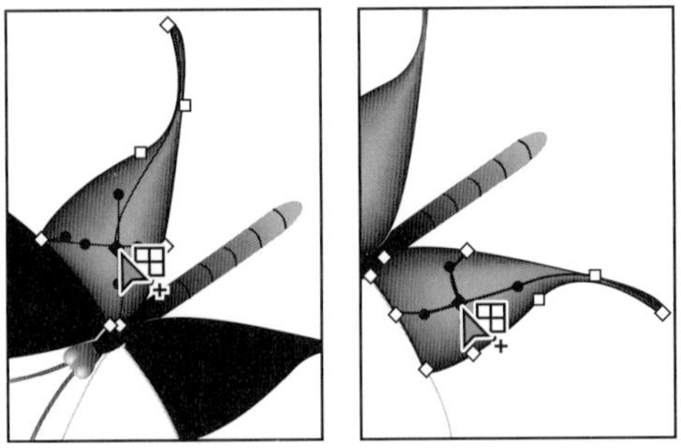

Click with Mesh tool to apply selected color.

5 Hold down Ctrl (Windows) or Command (Mac OS), and click away from the tail wing to deselect it, and then select another color from the Color or Swatches palette. (We selected the Color 3 swatch.)

6 Click in the left tail wing to add a mesh point with the new color, and then click in the right tail wing to add one with the same color.

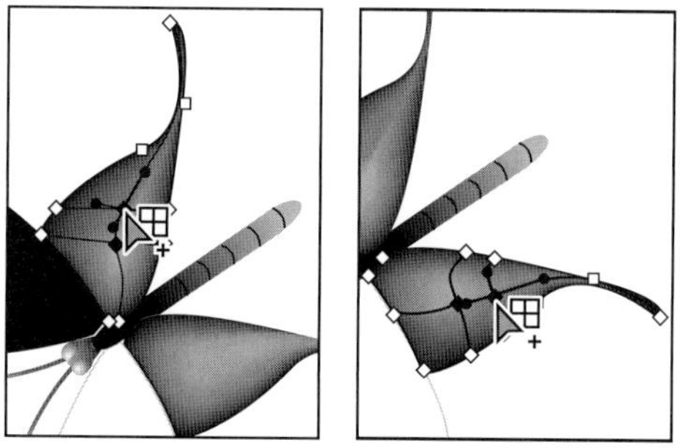

Add mesh points to mesh object with another color.

7 Control-click (Windows) or Command-click (Mac OS) away from the object to deselect it, and then continue adding a few more colors and mesh points.

8 When you have finished, choose File > Save.

Specifying the number of mesh lines

When you use the Mesh tool to create a mesh object, two intersecting mesh lines are created for every mesh point you create. Before converting an object to a mesh object, you'll specify its number of mesh lines using the Create Gradient Mesh command.

1 Select the Selection tool (↖) in the toolbox, and click the black forewing on the butterfly to select it.

2 Choose Object > Create Gradient Mesh.

3 In the Create Gradient Mesh dialog box, select the Preview option to see the changes to the selected object without closing the dialog box. Type **3** in the Rows text box; Leave the Columns set to 4 (the default) and leave the Appearance as Flat (the default). Click OK.

The black forewing is converted to a mesh object with three rows separated by two horizontal mesh lines and four columns separated by three vertical mesh lines.

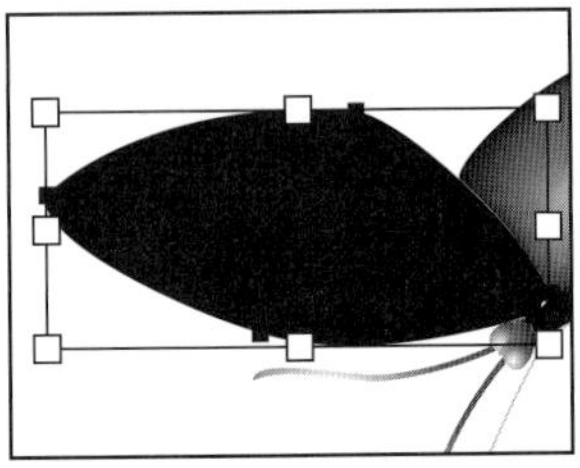

Select black forewing.

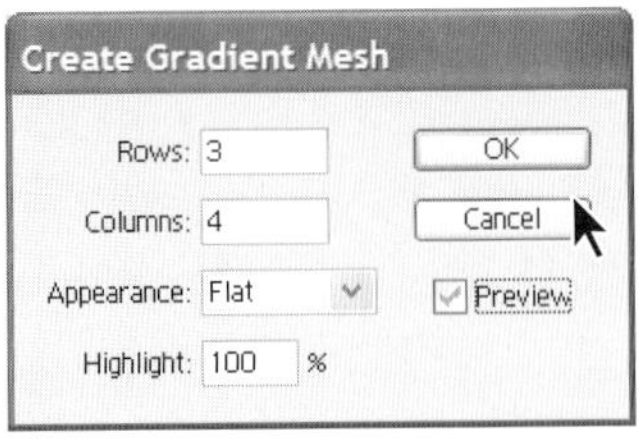

Apply mesh.

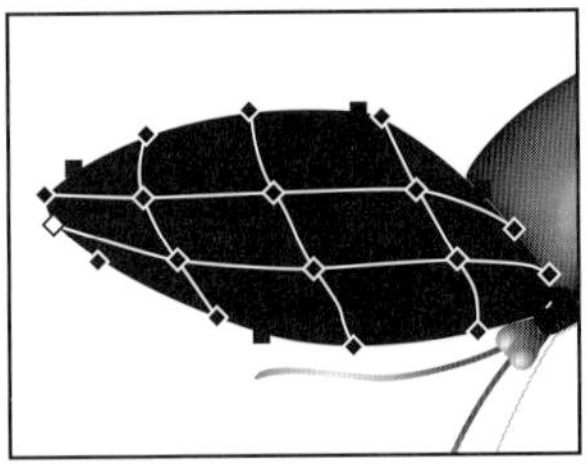

Result.

The mesh object is automatically selected when you create it.

4 Notice that the points in the selected object are all a solid color, indicating that they're selected. Also, the object has a mesh point at the intersection of every mesh line, anchor points at the ends of the mesh lines, and some anchor points on the segments of the outlining edge that are from the original object.

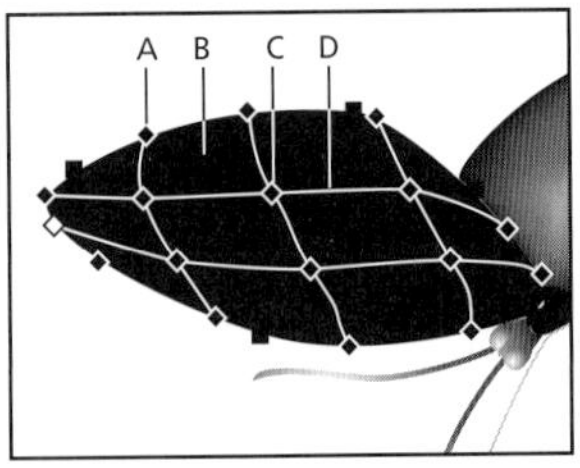

A. *Anchor point.* **B.** *Mesh patch.*
C. *Mesh point.* **D.** *Mesh line.*

For a color illustration of selected mesh objects, see the color section.

Applying colors to the mesh

You can select points on a mesh object using either the Direct Selection tool or the Mesh tool and paint them with different colors. Now you'll practice selecting mesh points using the Direct Selection tool and apply three colors to the butterfly's forewing.

1 Select the Direct Selection tool (), and click away from the object to deselect it. Then move the pointer over the top left side of the forewing. (Smart Guides display the mesh as you move the pointer over it.)

2 Click in the center of a mesh patch to select the four mesh points where the lines intersect. (We clicked in the patch above the top horizontal line and to the right of the left vertical line.)

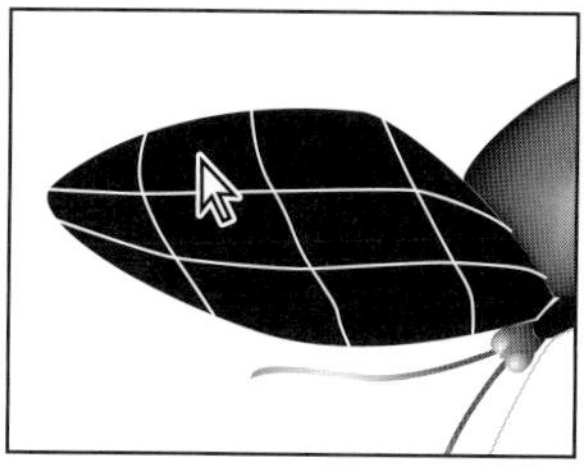

Position pointer over mesh patch.

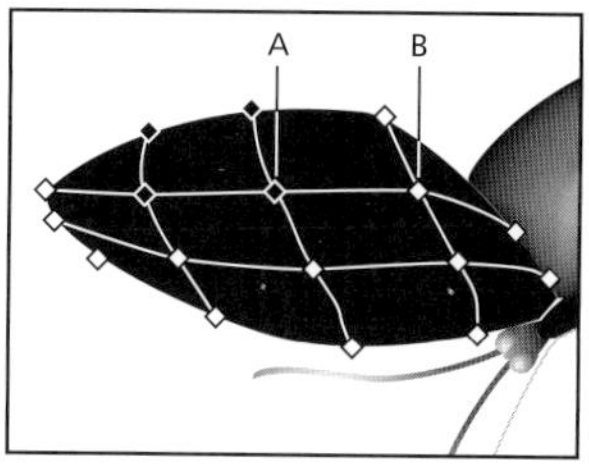

A. Selected mesh point.
B. Deselected mesh point.

Clicking with the Direct Selection tool in a mesh patch is an easy way to select all of the mesh points and direction handles on the lines surrounding the patch. All the other points become white diamonds, indicating that they're not selected.

3 Click a color in the Color palette or Swatches palette (we selected the Color 2 swatch) to apply it to the four selected points.

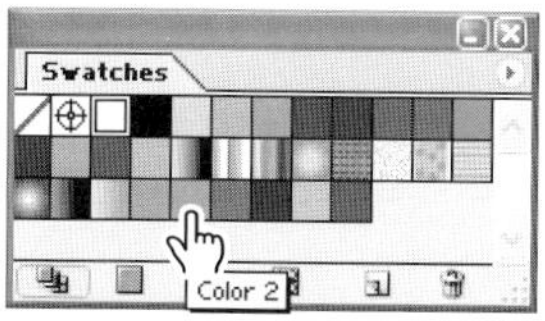

Select color.

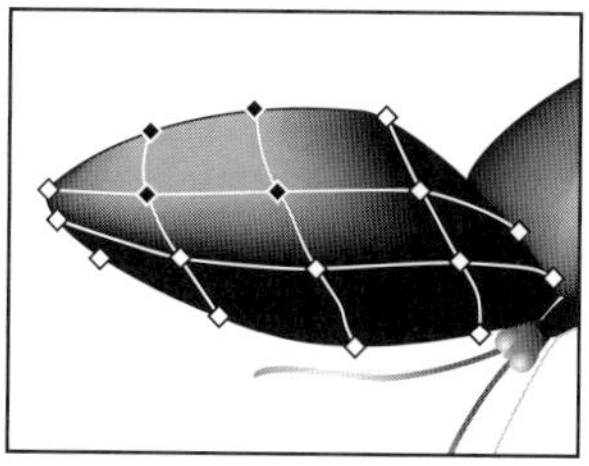

Result.

4 Select the Direct Select Lasso tool () in the toolbox.

5 With the forewing still selected, draw a selection marquee around the two left mesh points on the bottom horizontal line.

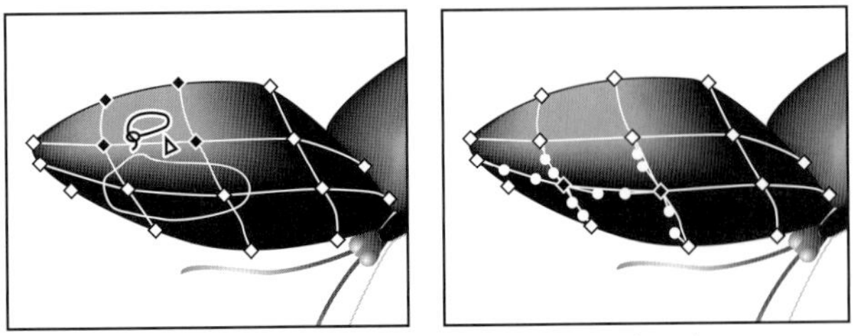

Draw selection marquee around mesh points to select them.

If you inadvertently select the wrong mesh points, draw the selection marquee again. You can also Control-click (Windows) or Command-click (Mac OS) away from the artwork to deselect it, Control/Command-click the artwork to reselect it, and then redraw the selection marquee.

6 Paint the two selected mesh points with a color from the Color palette or Swatches palette (we selected the Color 3 swatch).

7 Use the Direct Select Lasso tool to select the two middle mesh points on the right vertical mesh line. Select a third color in the Color palette or Swatches palette (we selected the Color 4 swatch) to paint the selected mesh points.

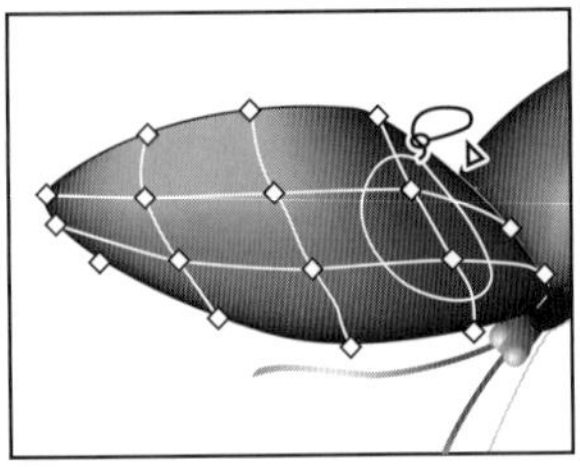

Select two right mesh points.

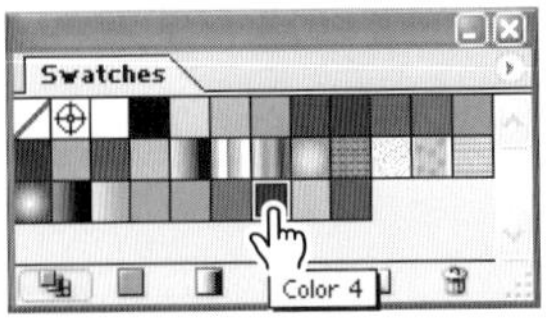

Select color.

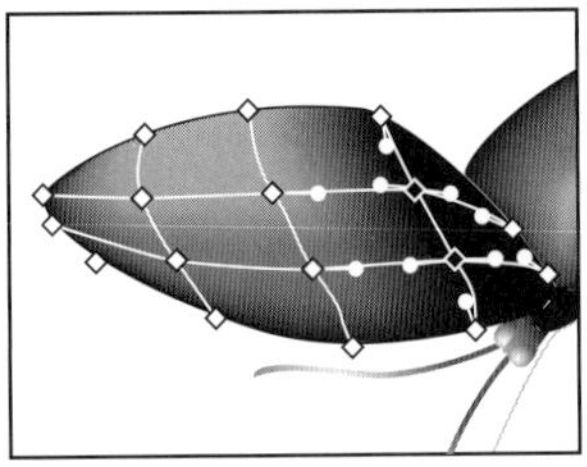

Result.

8 Choose File > Save.

Highlighting a mesh object

To give an object a three-dimensional appearance, you can create a mesh that highlights the center or the edge of an object. Now you'll create a mesh with highlighting.

1 Use the Hand tool (✋) to move the second butterfly at the bottom of the artwork to the center of the window.

2 Select the Selection tool (↖), and click the top forewing on the pink butterfly to select it.

3 Choose Object > Create Gradient Mesh.

4 In the Create Gradient Mesh dialog box, leave **3** entered in the Rows text box. Type **3** in the Columns text box, and make sure that the Preview option is selected.

5 For Appearance, choose To Edge in the dialog box; notice the change to the highlighting in the selected object. Then choose To Center from the pop-up menu.

To Edge creates a highlight on the edges of the object. To Center creates a highlight in the center of the object.

For a color illustration of highlighted mesh objects, see the color section.

Type a value between 0% and 100% in the Highlight text box (we entered 60%), and press Tab to see the change to the artwork without closing the dialog box.

6 A value of 100% applies a maximum white highlight to the object. A value of 0% applies no white highlight to the object.

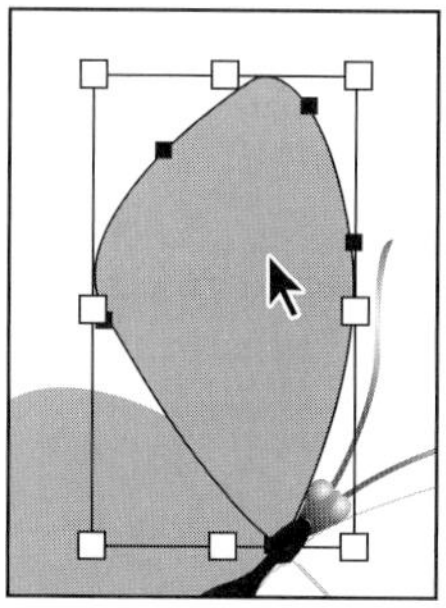

Select top forewing.

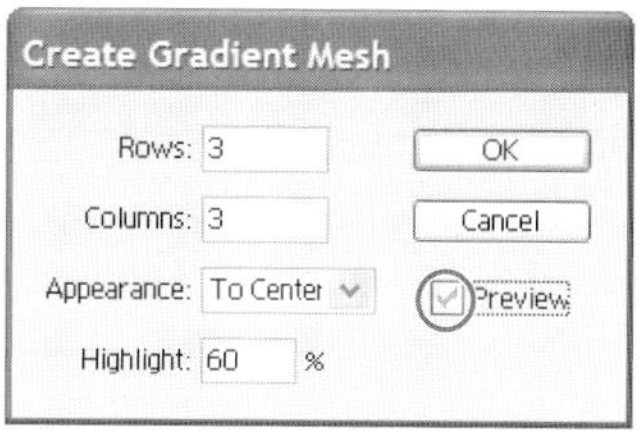

Apply highlight and preview.

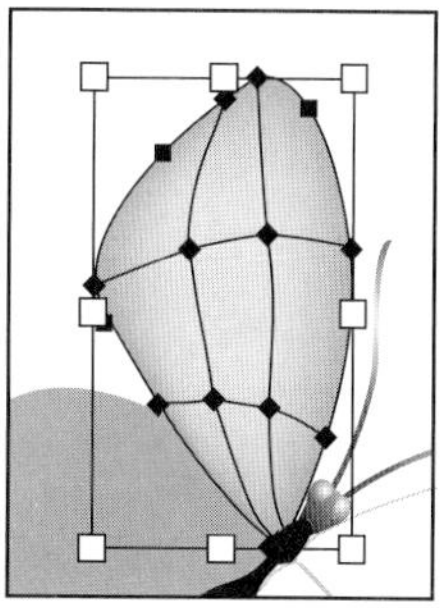

Result.

7 Click OK to close the dialog box and create the highlighted mesh object.

8 Select the Direct Select Lasso tool (), and drag to draw a marquee over the tip of the forewing to select the four upper left anchor points on the mesh.

9 With the anchor points selected, click a color in the Color palette or Swatches palette to apply it to the points. (We selected the Color 4 swatch.)

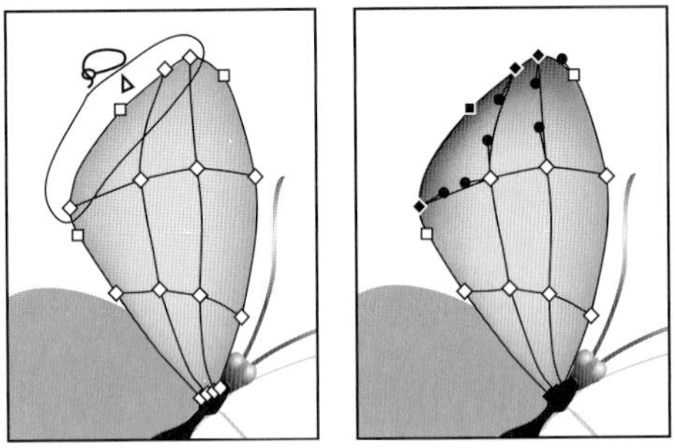

Drag Direct Select Lasso to select mesh points.

Editing mesh points

You can use the Mesh tool to select, add, and delete mesh points to change the way colors blend in a mesh object. Every mesh point has a set of direction handles that let you adjust the distance and direction that a color blends with neighboring colors in the mesh object.

First, you'll use the Mesh tool to select a mesh point and add a color to the butterfly's forewing.

1 Select the Mesh tool () in the toolbox and position the pointer over a mesh point. The plus sign on the pointer disappears when it's over a mesh point. Click to select the mesh point. (We selected the lower right mesh point where the right vertical line intersects with the bottom horizontal line.) Choose Edit > Undo if you add a mesh point by mistake.

2 Click a color in the Color palette or Swatches palette to apply it to the selected mesh point. (We selected the Color 5 swatch.)

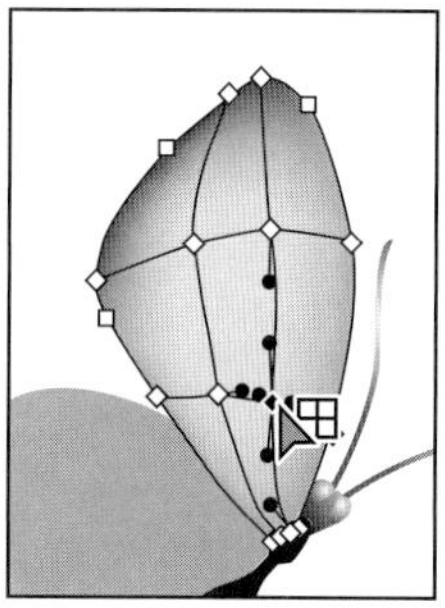
Select mesh point with Mesh tool.

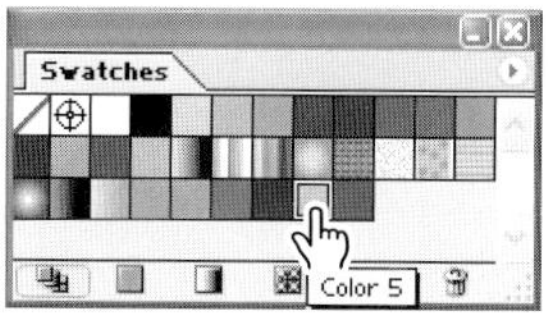

Select color.

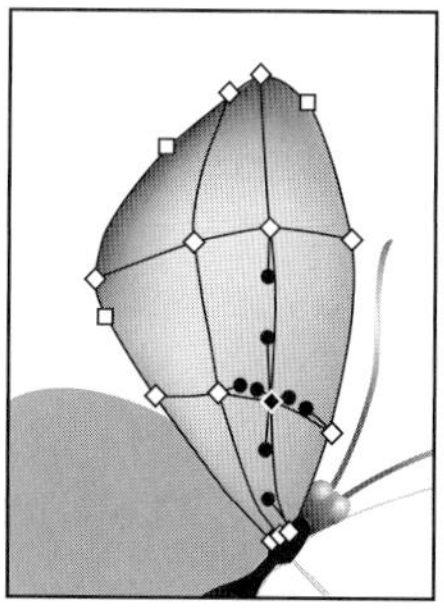
Result.

Now you'll use the Mesh tool to delete a mesh point on the forewing and see how the colors and highlighting readjust.

3 Using the Mesh tool, hold the pointer over the top left mesh point where the top horizontal line and left vertical line intersect. Hold down Alt (Windows) or Option (Mac OS) to display a minus sign on the pointer, and click the mesh point to delete it.

Deleting a mesh point also deletes the two intersecting mesh lines.

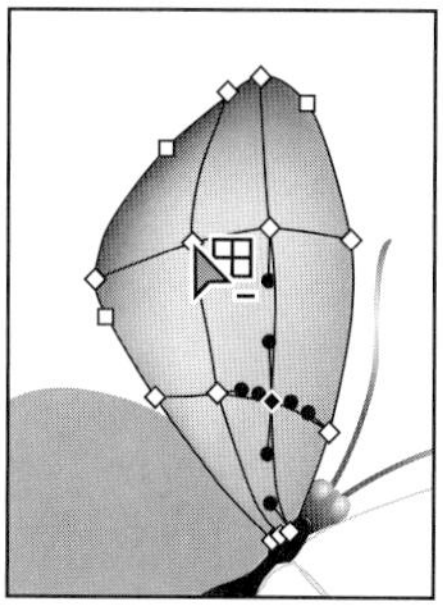
Delete mesh point.

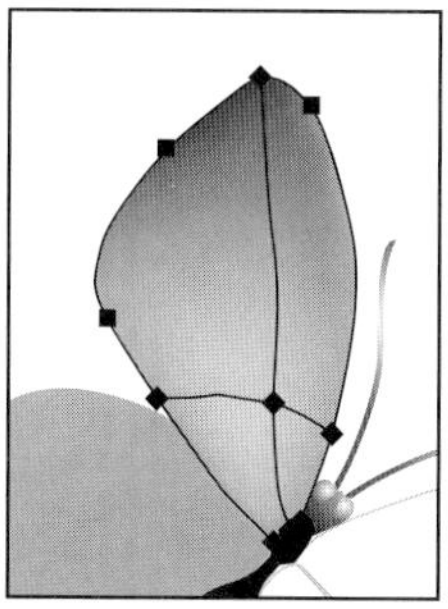
Result.

Notice that the highlighting from the center of the object is diminished as the remaining colors on the anchor points now blend with the original base color.

4 If you want to take a look at that change again, press Ctrl+Z (Windows) or Command+Z (Mac OS) to undo the deletion, and then press Shift+Ctrl+Z (Windows) or Shift+Command+Z (Mac OS) to redo it.

Now you'll use the Mesh tool to add a mesh point to the tail wing on the butterfly and then change the direction in which the color of the mesh point blends from the center.

5 With the Mesh tool selected, hold the pointer over the bottom tail wing, and click anywhere inside it to add a mesh point.

6 Click a color in the Color palette or Swatches palette to apply it to the new mesh point. (We selected the Color 5 swatch.)

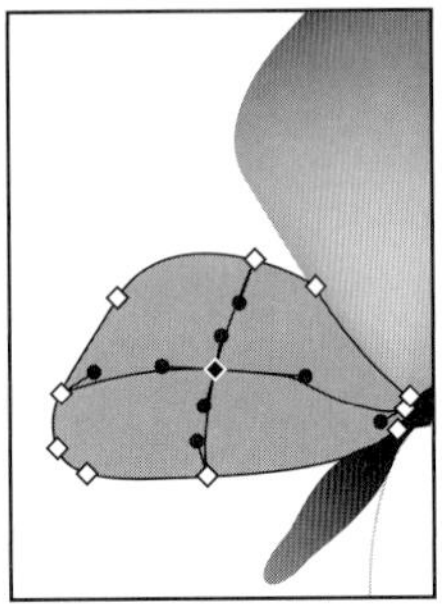

Click with Mesh tool to add mesh point.

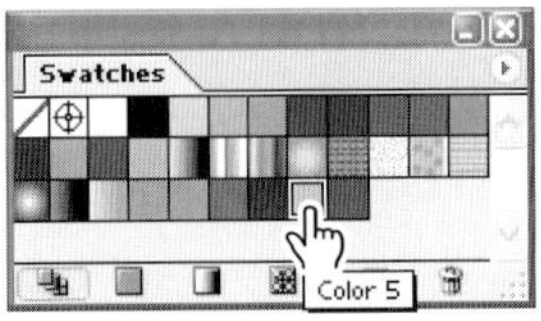

Select color.

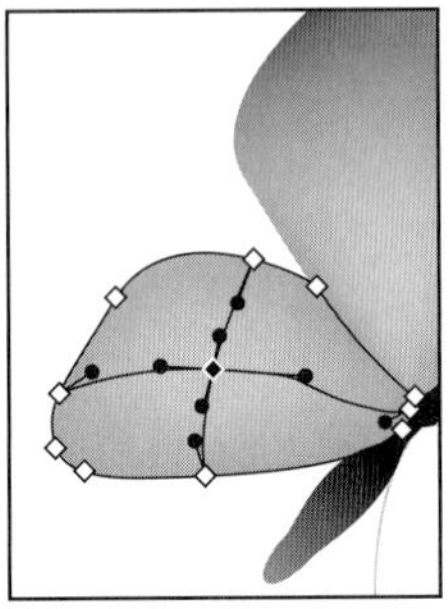

Result.

7 Select the Direct Selection tool ( ) in the toolbox. Drag a marquee over the bottom tip of the tail wing to select the anchor points along the edge, and click a color in the Color palette or Swatches palette to apply it to the selected points. (We selected the Color 4 swatch.)

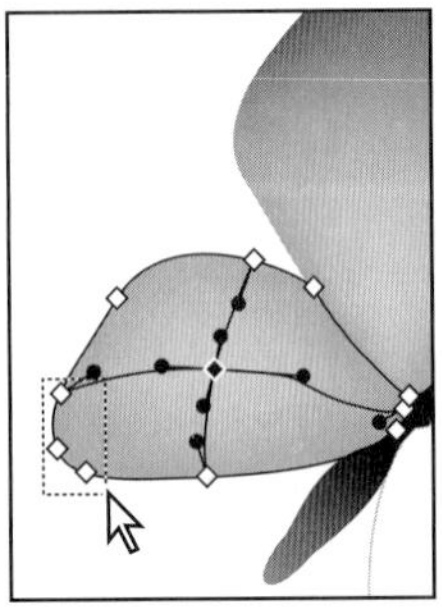

Select edge points.

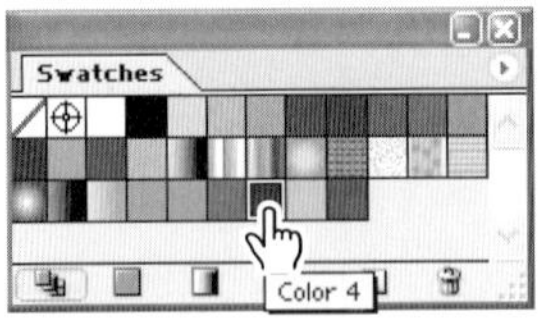

Select color.

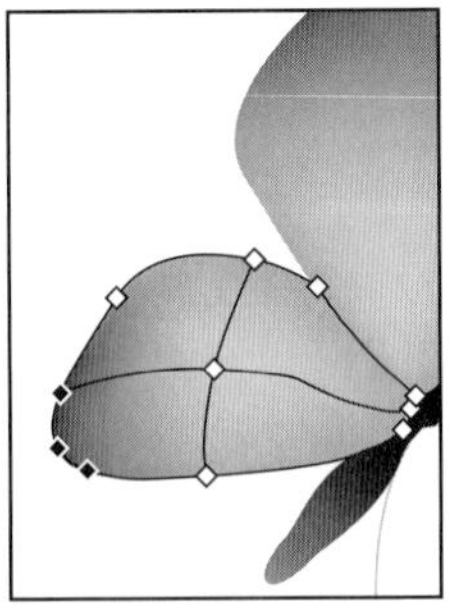

Result.

8 Select the Mesh tool ( ) in the toolbox, and click the mesh point you created in the center of the tail wing to select it. (The plus sign on the pointer disappears when it's over a mesh point.)

The selected mesh point displays four direction points (or handles) that lie along the mesh lines until you move them. Now you'll use the handles to adjust the direction and distance of the mesh point's color.

9 Using the Mesh tool, select the left direction handle (don't release the mouse button) and drag it to the left about midway to the edge of the object; then release the mouse button. Notice how the mesh point's color extends further out before it starts to blend with the other colors.

10 Select another direction handle and drag it in an arc to swirl the direction of the blending colors.

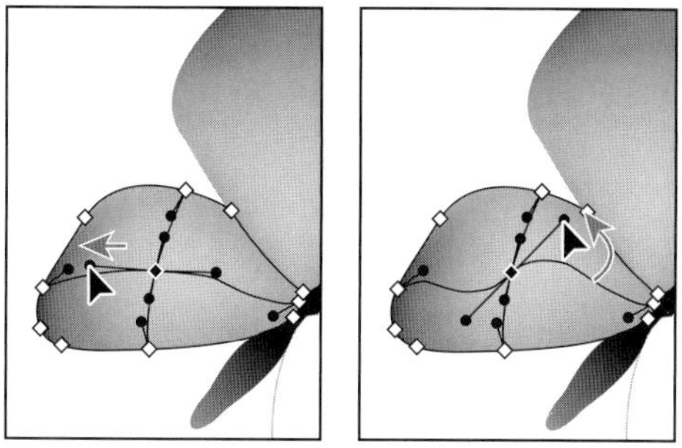

Drag direction handles to lengthen or swirl color blending.

11 Control-click (Windows) or Command-click (Mac OS) away from the object to deselect it.

12 Choose File > Save.

Reflecting mesh objects

You can use the Reflect tool and other tools in the toolbox on a mesh object just like any other type of object. Now you'll reflect a copy of the two wing parts to complete the butterfly.

1 Select the Selection tool (↖) in the toolbox, and Shift-click to select both the tail wing and the forewing on the bottom butterfly.

2 Select the Reflect tool (⧓) from the same group as the Rotate tool (↺) in the toolbox, hold down Alt (Windows) or Option (Mac OS), and click in the center of the butterfly's body, midway between the selected wing parts and the wing guides on the right.

Clicking the body of the butterfly designates the point of origin from which the object will reflect. Holding down Alt/Option as you click displays the Reflect dialog box.

3 In the Reflect dialog box, select the Angle option and type 46 in the degree text box. Click Copy. (Don't click OK.)

Depending on where you clicked to set the reflecting reference point in step 2, you may need to slightly adjust the position of the reflected copy using the arrow keys—or choose Edit > Undo and repeat steps 2 and 3.

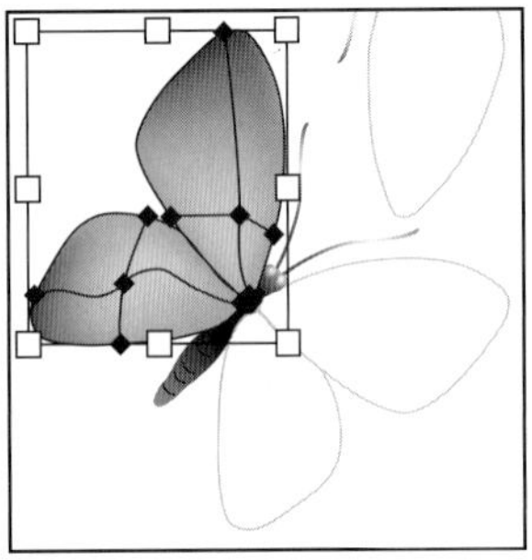

Select wing parts.

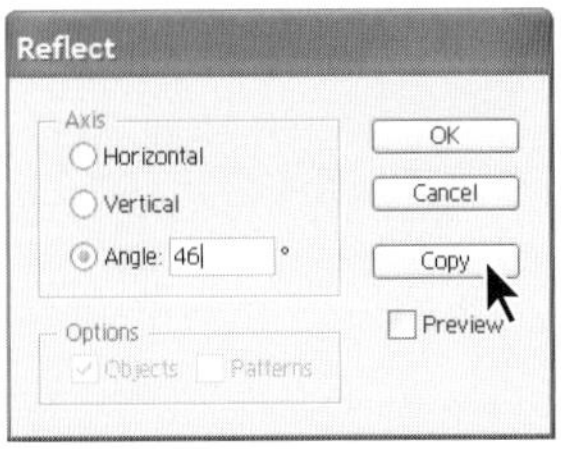

Reflect and copy.

Result.

4 Control-click (Windows) or Command-click (Mac OS) away from the object to deselect it.

5 Choose File > Save to save the artwork.

Modifying mesh lines

You'll use the Mesh tool to reshape mesh lines by moving mesh points on them, add mesh lines with an unpainted mesh point to the mesh, and delete a single mesh line in the forewing of the first butterfly.

1 Select the Hand tool (), and move the butterfly at the top of the artwork down to the center of your window.

2 Select the Mesh tool (), and position it over the left forewing. Select the left mesh point on the top horizontal line (don't release the mouse button); then hold down Shift, and drag the mesh point to the left.

As you drag to the left, the intersecting vertical mesh line is reshaped. Holding down Shift as you drag constrains the movement horizontally, leaving the horizontal mesh line unaffected.

3 Select the bottom mesh point on the right vertical line (don't release the mouse button), and Shift-drag to move it down without affecting the vertical mesh line.

Notice how the color blending readjusts to the new position of the mesh point.

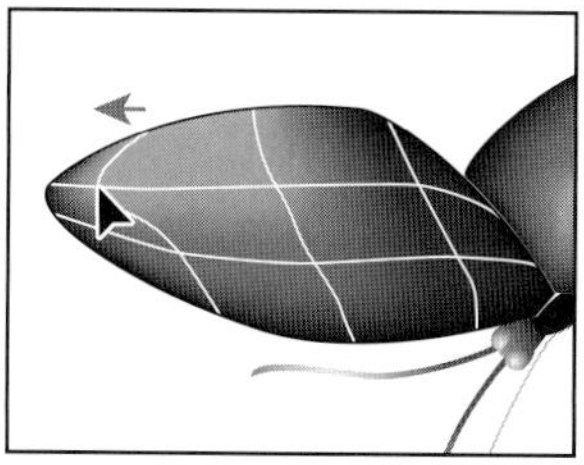

Shift-drag left to move mesh point along horizontal line.

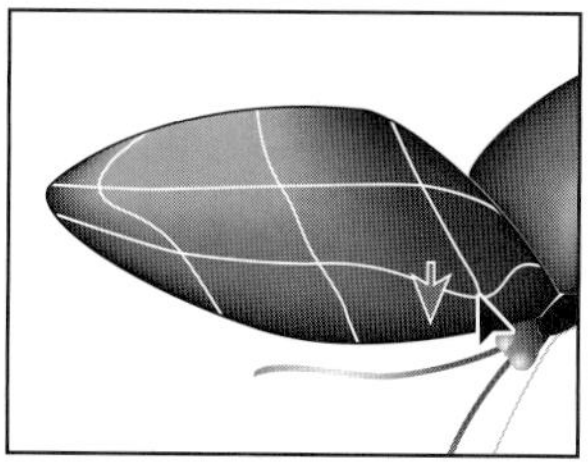

Shift-drag down to move mesh point along vertical line.

For a color illustration of the edited mesh point, see the color section.

You can add a mesh point to a mesh object without applying the current fill color to it or changing the existing colors in the object.

4 Control-click (Windows) or Command-click (Mac OS) away from the object to deselect it.

5 Select a new color fill by clicking a color in the Color palette or the Swatches palette. (We selected the Color 6 swatch.)

6 Using the Mesh tool, position the pointer in the center of a patch. (We chose the middle right patch; see the following illustration.) Shift-click to add a new mesh point with two intersecting mesh lines—without changing the color in the object. Notice that the Fill box in the toolbox changes to the existing color of the object where you clicked.

7 If you want to change the color of the new mesh point, click a new color in the Color palette or Swatches palette. (We selected the Color 6 swatch again.)

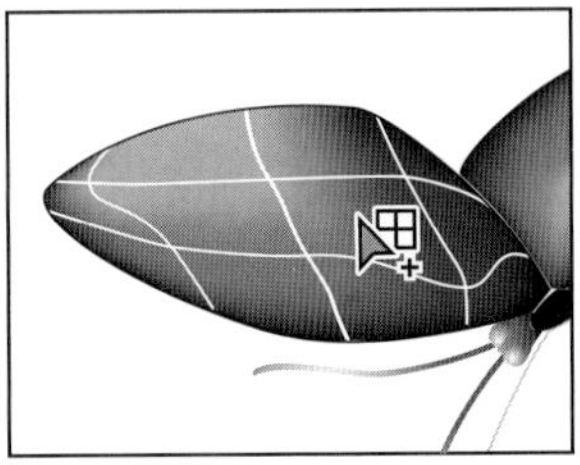

Shift-click to add unpainted mesh point.

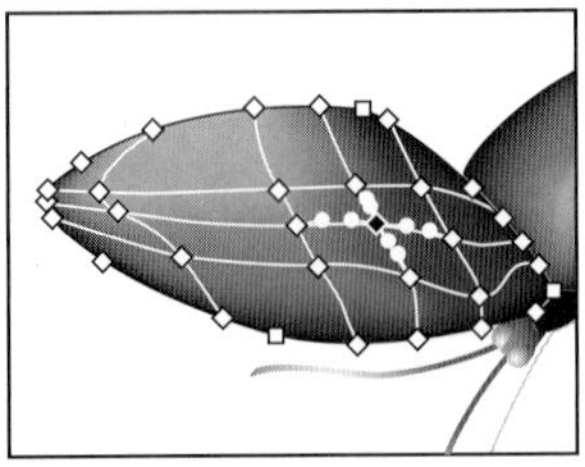

New mesh point picks up underlying mesh colors.

Note: *You can add anchor points to an existing mesh line by selecting the object and using the Add-Anchor-Point tool ( ).*

Now you'll delete a mesh line.

8 Using the Mesh tool, position the pointer over a mesh line and hold down Alt (Windows) or Option (Mac OS) to display a minus sign on the pointer. Alt/Option-click a segment (between two mesh points) on the mesh line to delete the line.

Notice how the color on the new mesh point spreads into the area where the line was.

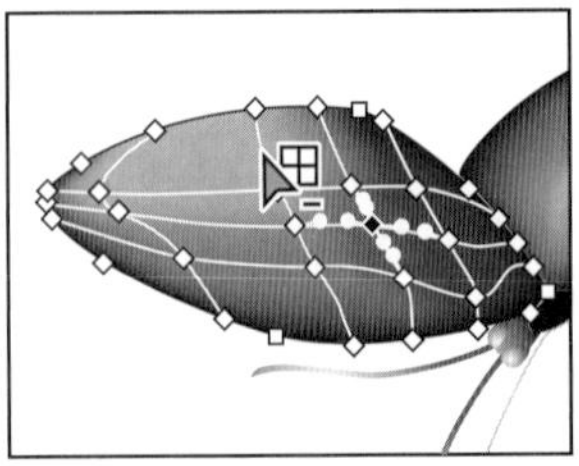

Position pointer over line to left of new mesh point.

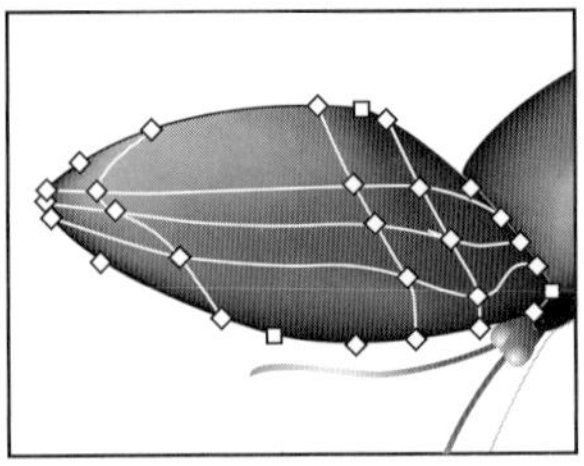

Alt/Option-click segment to delete mesh line.

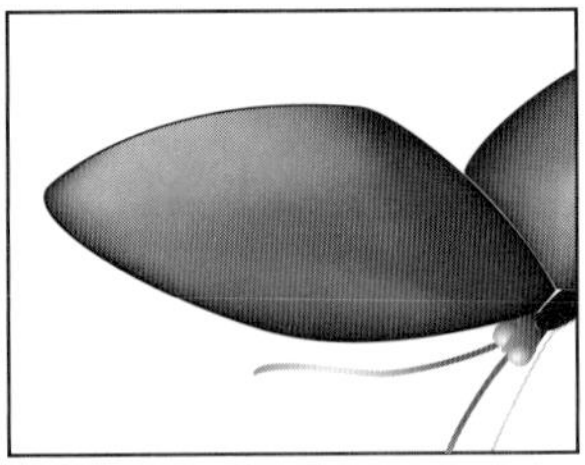

Result.

You'll complete the butterfly body by reflecting a copy of the forewing.

9 Select the Selection tool () in the toolbox to select the bounding box of the mesh object.

10 Select the Reflect tool () in the toolbox, and Alt-click (Windows) or Option-click (Mac OS) in the body of the butterfly, about midway between the existing wing and the wing guide.

11 In the Reflect dialog box, make sure that the Angle option is selected, type **36** in the degree text box, and click Copy. (Don't click OK.)

Depending on where you clicked in the body, you may have to adjust the position of the reflected copy by using the arrow keys.

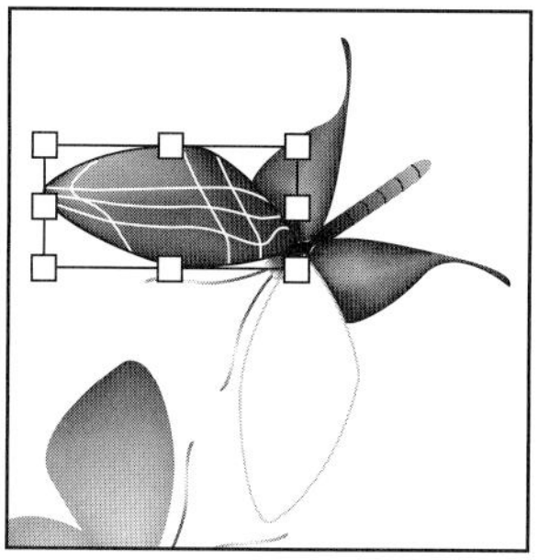
Select wing.

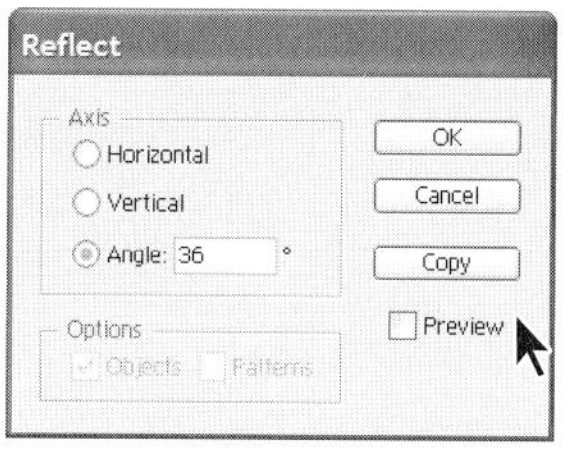

Reflect copy.

Result.

12 Choose Select > Deselect.

13 Choose File > Save to save your work.

Warping a mesh

Now you'll experiment with changing the shape of the butterfly wing and its meshes using the Warp tool. The Warp tool, along with the other Liquify tools, changes an object's shape.

1 Double-click the Warp tool () in the toolbox to select the tool and display its Options dialog box.

The Warp tool molds objects in the same way as if they were modeling–clay. Dragging or pulling parts of an object with the Warp tool causes the pulled areas to thin out. First you'll set the tool's options.

2 In the Warp Tool Options dialog box, enter **10 pt** for both the Global Brush Dimensions Width and Height to set the size of the tool cursor.

3 Set the Intensity to **25%**. The lower the intensity, the slower the rate of change when dragging the Warp tool.

4 Leave the remaining Warp options as is.

Detail specifies the spacing between points introduced into the object's outline; the higher the value, the more closely spaced are the points. Simplify is related to Detail and reduces superfluous points that do not noticeably affect the shape's overall appearance.

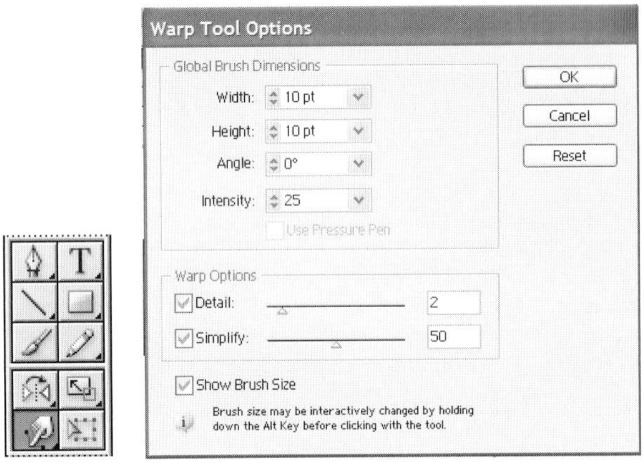

5 Click OK.

6 In the artwork, position the Warp tool over the right butterfly wing, and drag to warp the meshes. Continue to drag the tool and try out its effect.

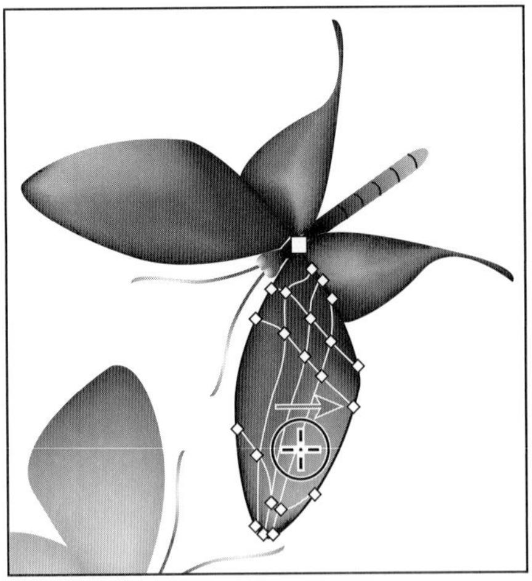

Drag Warp tool to warp mesh.

You can apply preset warp effects to paths, text, blends, and raster images. In addition, you can apply a warp effect as a live effect that can be removed at any time using the Effect menu. Once you apply the Warp effect, the warp appears in the Appearance palette, where you can save it as part of a style, select it for editing, expand it, or delete it. The effect also appears in the Layers palette, which displays the object as having an appearance applied.

If you don't like the effect, you can remove it before continuing with the lesson by choosing the File > Revert command.

7 Choose Select > Deselect. Choose File > Save to save your work.

Modifying shapes with liquify tools

Illustrator provides a variety of liquify tools for changing an object's shape. Using these tools alters the original object's shape. To distort objects with Liquify tools, simply draw over the object with the tool–the tool adds anchor points and adjust paths as you draw.

Note: *You cannot use Liquify tools on objects that contain text, graphs, or symbols.*

Use any of the following tools to distort an object:

Warp *tool ()–Molds objects in the same way as if they were modeling clay. When you drag or pull portions of an object using this tool, the pulled areas attenuate.*

Twirl *tool ()–Creates swirling distortions of an object.*

Pucker *tool ()–Deflates an object by moving control points toward the cursor.*

Bloat *tool ()–Inflates an object by moving control points away from the cursor.*

Scallop *tool ()–Adds scallop-like details to the outline of an object.*

Crystallize *tool ()–Adds crystal-like details to the outline of an object.*

Wrinkle *tool ()–Adds wrinkle-like details to the outline of an object.*

–From online Help.

Applying transparency to a mesh

Mesh objects can be transparent or opaque, just like non-mesh objects. Now you'll scroll down to the dragonfly in your lesson art. You'll create an iridescent mesh in the dragonfly's wing and then you'll adjust its transparency to make it appear translucent.

1 In the Layers palette, click to the left of both the Dragonfly and Leaves layers to display the artwork on those layers. If necessary, resize the Layers palette to view all the contents.

2 Press the spacebar to get the Hand tool (✋), and drag the image up until the dragonfly is visible in the center of the window.

3 Select the Direct Selection tool (▷) in the toolbox, and click in the center of the lower left wing of the dragonfly.

4 Apply a mesh to the dragonfly wing:

• Choose Object > Create Gradient Mesh.

• In the Create Gradient Mesh dialog box, enter **3** in the Rows text box, press Tab and enter **2** in the Columns text box, and make sure that the Preview option is selected.

• For Appearance, choose To Center to highlight the center of the object. Enter a highlight of **80%**. Click OK.

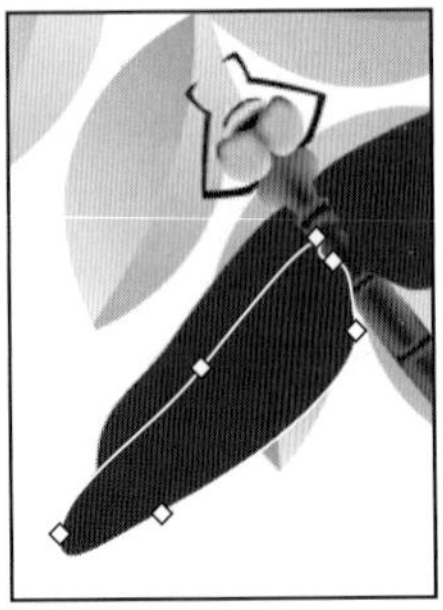

Select lower wing. *Create gradient mesh with highlight.* *Result.*

5 In the Layers palette, click the triangle (▷) to the left of the Dragonfly layer to view its contents.

6 Now click the triangle to the left of the Lower Wings sublayer to expand its view. This sublayer has two paths, named <Path> and <Mesh>. The solid square selection indicator (■) and the shaded target indicator (◯) show that the <Mesh> path is selected.

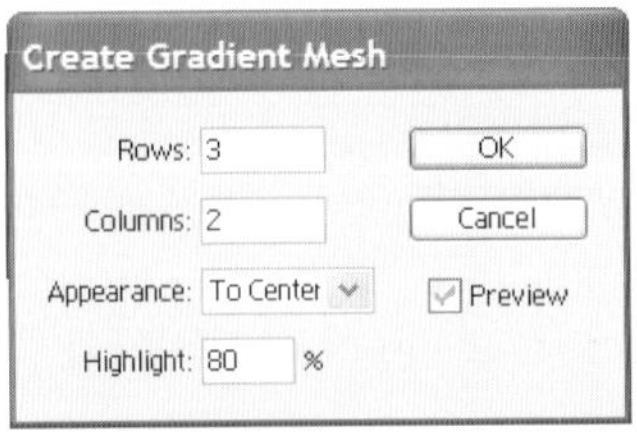

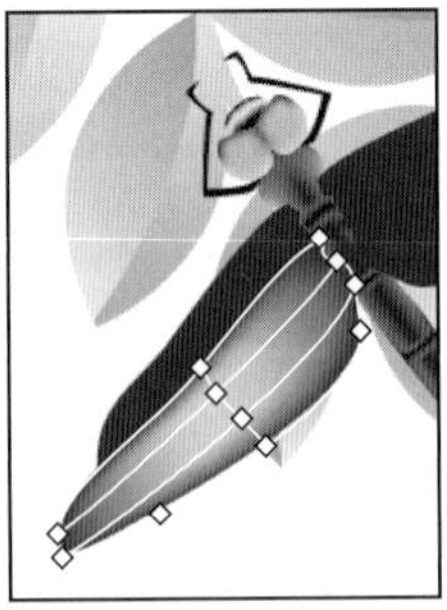

7 Click the selection indicator area for the <Path> sublayer to select the lower right wing.

Using the selection indicators in the Layers palette is a quick and easy way to select objects that are in different groups or on different layers.

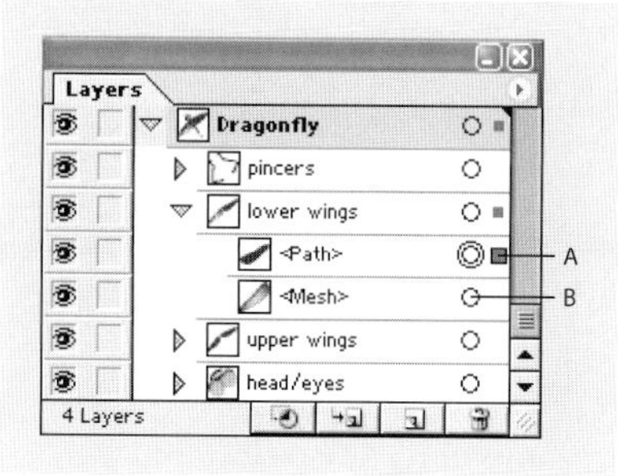

A. Selection indicator. B. Target indicator.

8 Repeat step 4 for the lower right wing. Notice that the sublayer's name changes to <Mesh> from <Path>.

9 In the Layers palette, click the triangle to the left of the Lower Wings sublayer to collapse it.

Now you'll repeat these steps to apply a mesh to the upper wings.

10 Click the triangle to the left of the Upper Wings sublayer to expand its view. This sublayer also has two paths.

11 Now apply a mesh to each of the upper right wings:

• To select the upper right wing, click the selection indicator area for the first <Path> sublayer. Repeat step 4.

• To select the upper left wing, click the target indicator for the second <Path> sublayer. Repeat step 4.

Now you'll select the wings using the Layers palette and adjust their transparency.

12 In the Layers palette, click the selection indicator area to the far right of the Upper Wings sublayer. Shift-click the selection indicator for the Lower Wings sublayer to add the wings to the selection. All four dragonfly wings are now selected.

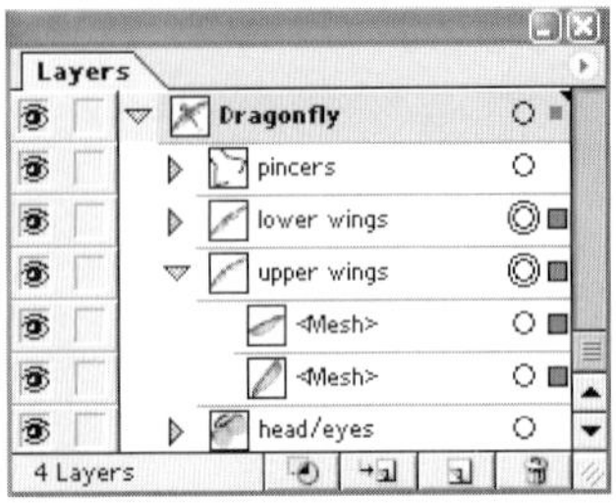

Shift-click target indicators to select multiple sublayers.

13 Choose Window > Transparency or click the Transparency palette tab to display the Transparency palette.

14 Use the Opacity slider to decrease the opacity of the dragonfly wings. (We used 29%.)

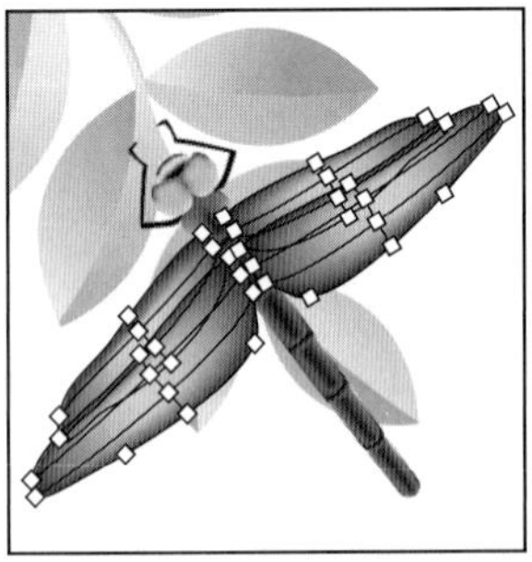

Select four wings.

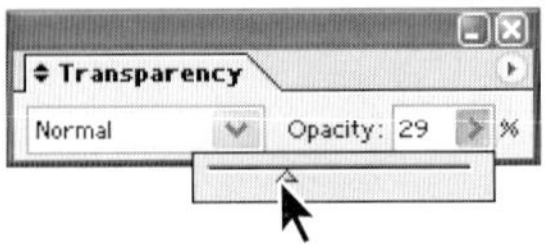

Change opacity.

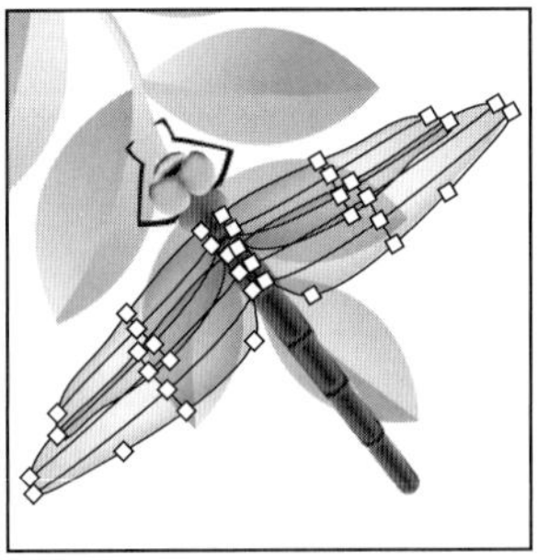

Result.

For a color illustration of the opacity change, see the color section.

Now you're ready to view the finished artwork. You'll clear the guides and selection lines.

15 Double-click the Zoom tool ( ) to zoom out to 100%.

16 Choose View > Smart Guides, and then choose Select > Deselect.

17 Choose File > Save to save the artwork. Choose File > Close to close your file.

This completes the lesson. You're ready to create your own watercolor or airbrush effects. To learn other ways to blend colors in objects, see Lesson 12, "Blending Shapes and Colors."

Tips for creating mesh objects

You can create a mesh object from any path object or any bitmap image (such as a photographic image imported from Adobe Photoshop). Keep these important guidelines in mind when creating mesh objects:

- *You cannot create gradient mesh objects from compound paths, text objects, or placed EPS files.*
- *Once a mesh object has been created, it cannot be converted back to a path object.*
- *When converting complex objects, use the Create Gradient Mesh command for the best results.*
- *When converting simple objects, use either the Mesh tool or the Create Gradient Mesh command. However, if you want to add a highlight to a particular spot, use the Mesh tool and click at the point you want the highlight to appear.*
- *To create a mesh object with a regular pattern of mesh points and mesh lines, use the Create Gradient Mesh command.*
- *When converting complex objects, Illustrator can add hidden anchor points to maintain the shape of a line. If you want to edit, add, or remove one or more of these anchor points, use the Add Anchor Point tool or the Delete Anchor Point tool.*
- *To improve performance and speed of redrawing, keep the size of mesh objects to a minimum. Complex mesh objects can greatly reduce performance. Thus, it is better to create a few small, simple mesh objects than to create a single, complex mesh object.*

–From online Help.

Review questions

1 Describe two methods for creating a mesh.

2 How do you change a color on the mesh?

3 How do you add a mesh point to a mesh object? How do you add the mesh point without adding a color?

4 How do you delete a mesh line?

5 Describe how to move a mesh point without affecting the intersecting line.

6 How do you make a mesh transparent?

7 How do you add a warp effect?

Review answers

1 To create a mesh, you select the Mesh tool and click an object; or you can select the object first, choose Object > Create Gradient Mesh, and specify the number of mesh lines and highlighting in the Create Gradient Mesh dialog box. Another way to create a mesh is to select a gradient-filled object, choose Object > Expand, and select the Mesh option in the Expand dialog box to expand the gradient.

2 To change a color on the mesh, use the Direct Selection tool or the Mesh tool to select the mesh point for the color, and then select a different color.

3 To add a mesh point to a mesh object, click in a mesh patch or on a mesh line segment with the Mesh tool. (You can also add anchor points to mesh lines using the Add Anchor Point tool.) To add the mesh point without adding a color, hold down Shift as you click.

4 To delete a mesh line, select the Mesh tool, and Alt/Option-click a segment on the line.

5 To move a mesh point without affecting the intersecting line, use the Mesh tool to select the point, and without releasing the mouse button, Shift-drag the mesh point.

6 To make a mesh transparent, select the mesh object and change its opacity in the Transparency palette.

7 To add a warp effect, select the Warp tool in the Liquify tool set in the toolbox. Then simply drag over the artwork you want to warp. To set tool options, double-click the Warp tool in the toolbox. You can also apply warp effects as live effects that can be removed at any time, using the Effect > Warp menu.

Lesson 16

16 Using the 3D Effect

It's easy to turn two-dimensional artwork into three-dimensional shapes using the new 3D effect. The new 3D effect also includes features that makes it easy to map artwork to all the surfaces, control lighting, and apply bevels.

In this lesson, you'll learn how to do the following:

- Use Warp Effects to create a banner logotype.
- Use Brush Libraries included with Illustrator CS.
- Create 3D objects from 2D artwork.
- Map artwork to the faces of the 3D objects.

Getting started

In this lesson, you'll create several three-dimensional objects using the new 3D Effects feature in Illustrator. Before you begin, you'll need to restore the default preferences for Adobe Illustrator. Then you'll open a file containing the finished artwork to see what you'll create.

1 To ensure that the tools and palettes function exactly as described in this lesson, delete or deactivate (by renaming) the Adobe Illustrator CS preferences file. See "Restoring default preferences" on page 2.

2 Start Adobe Illustrator.

3 Choose File > Open, and open the L16end.ai file in the Lesson16 folder, located inside the Lessons folder within the AICIB folder on your hard drive.

This file displays a completed illustration of a soap can, soap balls and a vase.

4 Choose View > Zoom Out to make the finished artwork smaller, adjust the window size, and leave it on your screen as you work. (Use the Hand tool (✋) to move the artwork where you want it in the window.) If you don't want to leave the image open, choose File > Close.

For an illustration of the finished artwork in this lesson, see the color section.

To begin working, you'll open an existing art file to which you will add 3D objects.

5 Choose File > Open, and open the L16strt1.ai file in the Lesson16 folder, located inside the Lessons folder within the AICIB folder on your hard drive.

6 Choose File > Save As, name the file Lemon.ai, and select the Lesson16 folder in the Save In menu. Leave the type of file format option set to Adobe Illustrator® Document, and click Save. In the Illustrator Options dialog box, leave the Illustrator options at their defaults and click OK.

Creating a banner logo with the Warp effect

You will use a Warp effect to create the banner logo. Warp effects distort objects, including paths, text, meshes, blends, and raster images. Because Warp effects are live, you can apply a warp to your artwork and then continue to modify or remove the effect at any time using the Appearance palette.

Creating the logotype

You can make a warp from objects in your artwork, or you can use a preset warp shape or a mesh object as an envelope.

1 Select the Selection tool (↖) in the toolbox. Then click to select the Lots O' Lemon type.

2 Choose Effects > Warp > Rise.

3 In the Warp Options dialog box, select Preview to preview the effect of changes.

4 Drag the Warp Options dialog box by its title bar so that you can see the dialog box and the selected type in the artwork.

5 Set the Bend amount to **93%** to create a ribbon effect. Click OK.

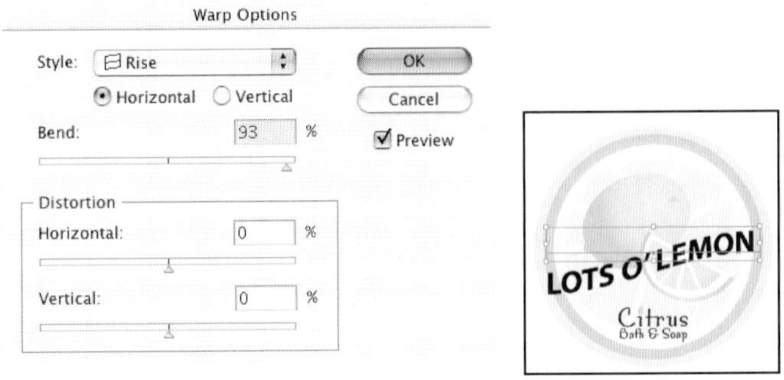

Use the Warp effect to distort the text.

6 Choose File > Save to save your work.

Stylizing the banner and logotype

To complete the banner and logotype, you'll add some sophistication by offsetting a stroke around the text and adding a colored drop shadow.

1 With the Selection tool, click on the logotype if it is not still selected.

2 If the Appearance palette is not visible, choose Window > Appearance.

Notice that the Appearance palette lists the Warp effect that has been applied to the text.

3 From the Appearance palette menu, choose Add New Stroke. Leave it set at 1 pt.

You can add multiple strokes to one object and apply different effects to each one, giving you the opportunity to create unique and interesting artwork.

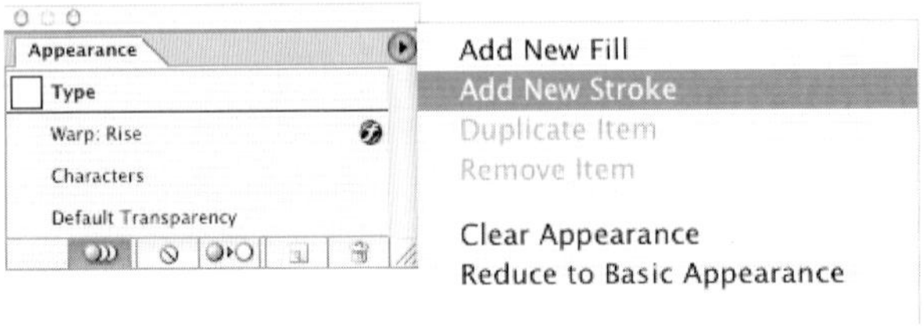

Add a new stroke.

4 With the Stroke selected in the Appearance palette, choose Effect > Path > Offset Path. Change the Offset to **2 pt** and click OK. This creates an outline around the text.

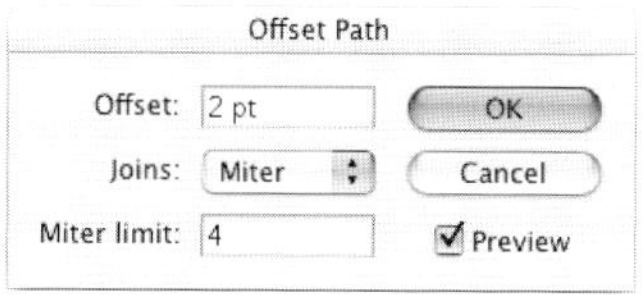

Apply the Offset Path effect.

Now you will add a colored drop shadow to the text.

5 In the Appearance palette, click on the word Type. This assures that the drop shadow applies to the text and not to just the offset stroke.

6 Choose Effect > Stylize > Drop Shadow, and check the Preview checkbox. Change the X Offset to **4 pt,** the Y Offset to **4 pt** and the Blur to **2 pt**. Do not click OK.

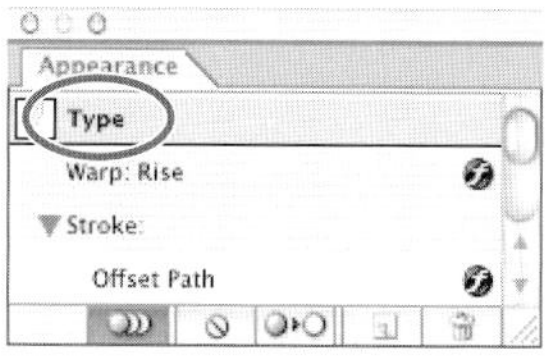

Select Text on the appearance palette.

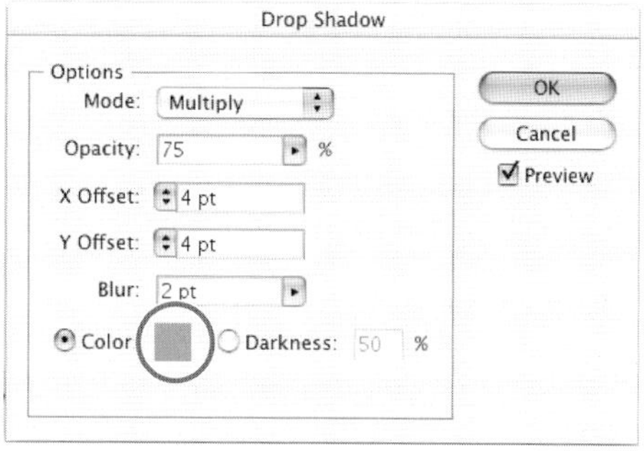

Change the Drop Shadow options, including the shadow color.

Result.

7 Click on the color square to the right of the Color radio button. Pick an orange color. (We picked C=10%, M=50%, Y=75%, B=0%.) Click OK.

8 Click OK to the Drop Shadow options window.

9 With the Selection tool, click off the artwork to deselect, or choose Select > Deselect.

10 File > Save. Leave the file open for the next lesson.

Using Brushes for decoration

In this next lesson you will create a decoration for the side panel using brushes. You'll select a brush from the many available brush libraries that come with Illustrator CS and are located in Window > Brush Libraries.

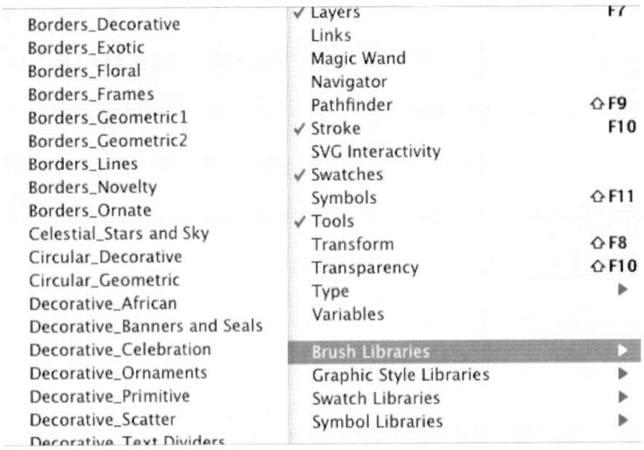

Illustrator CS comes loaded with lots of additional brush options.

1 First, you will create a path for the brush. If necessary use the Swatches in the toolbar to change the Stroke to Black and your Fill to None.

2 Choose the Pen tool (✒) and click on the left endpoint of the dashed guide under the artwork. Hold down the Shift key and click on the right endpoint.

3 Choose View > Guides > Clear Guides.

4 Choose Window > Brush Libraries > Circular_Decorative. This is a palette of brush art designed specifically for circular paths.

A separate palette opens with a choice of additional brushes.

5 Using the Selection tool (), select the path, scroll to locate the brush named Leaf.

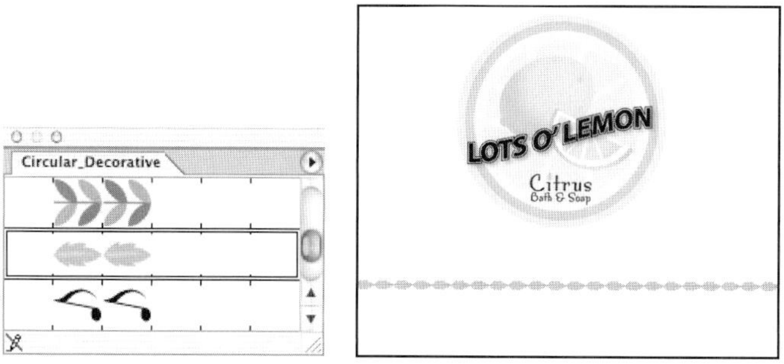

With the path selected, choose the Leaf brush.

The leaf is repeated the length of the path. Next, you will expand the leaf brush to change the Fill color from green to a yellow gradient.

6 Using the path still selected, choose Object > Expand Appearance. This converts the brush pattern into artwork that can be selected and edited. It is no longer linked to the Brushes palette.

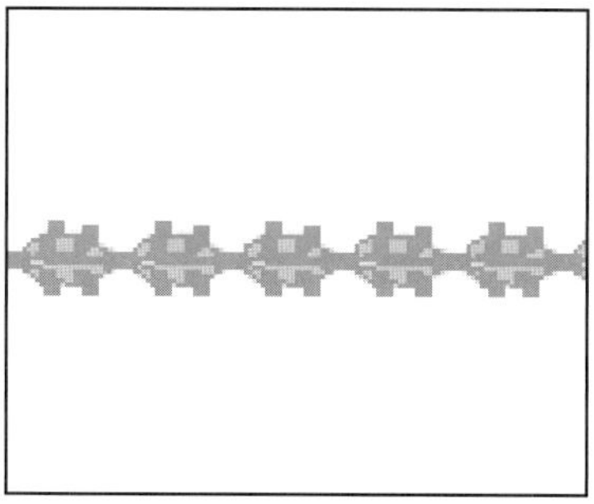

The Brush stroke expanded.

7 With the Selection tool, click off the artwork to deselect it.

8 Hold down on the Direct Selection tool to access the hidden Group Selection tool () and click on the green fill of any leaf. Choose Select > Same > Fill Color. All the green fills on the leaves are selected.

The Select Same feature is helpful when trying to find items of the same fill stroke or stroke weight.

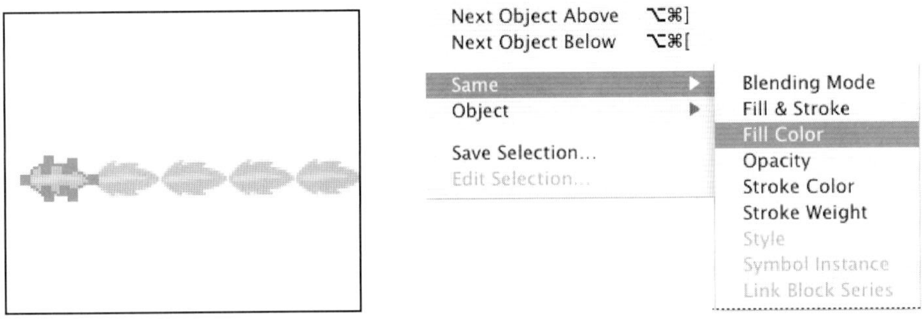

9 With the Fill swatch in the toolbar forward, choose Lemon gradient from the Swatches palette. All the green leaves are now filled with the Lemon gradient.

10 Choose Select > Deselect.

11 Using the Group Selection, tool click on the light green vein in one of the leaves.

12 Choose Select > Same > Same Fill Color.

13 Change the light green Fill to white.

Turning the artwork into symbols

You are finished with the artwork for the 3D shape. In order for these designs to be applied to the 3D shape, they must be turned into Symbols. The Symbols palette is used for a variety of things, from storing repeatedly used artwork, to creating a library of items that can be mapped 3D objects. Before Starting, make choose Window > Symbols if the Symbols palette is not visible.

1 Using the Selection tool (↖), click and drag a marquee surrounding all the yellow leaves.

2 Alt+click (Windows) or Option+click (Mac OS) on the New Symbol button in the lower right of the Symbols palette. Using the Alt/Option key in any palette will allow you to name the item as it is added to the palette.

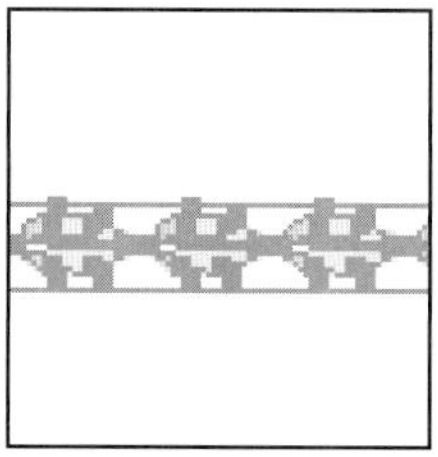

Select all the leaves.

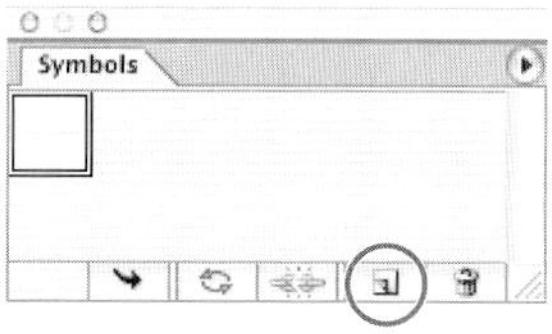

Alt/Option+Click on New Symbol button.

3 Name the Symbol **Leaves.**

4 With the leaves on the artboard still selected, choose Edit > Clear or press Delete.

5 Unlock Layer 1 by clicking on the padlock to the left of the layer name.

6 Choose Select > Select All, Control+A (Windows) or Command+A (Mac OS).

7 Alt+click (Windows) or Option+click (Mac OS) on the New Symbol button in the Symbols palette to add the label as a symbol. Name the symbol **Lemon.**

8 With everything still selected on the artboard, choose Edit > Clear or press the Delete key.

There should be nothing on your artboard at this time, and two symbols in the Symbols palette.

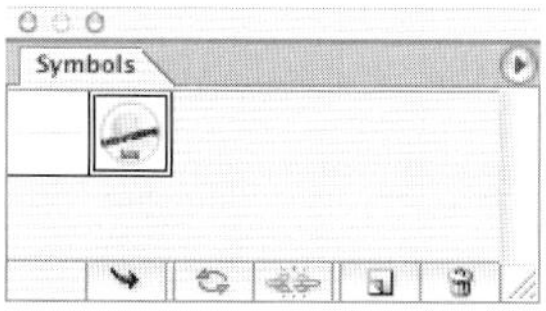

The artwork is now symbols.

9 File > Save.

Creating the 3D cylinder

In this part of the lesson, you'll use two-dimensional shapes as the foundation for creating three-dimensional objects. Using the 3D effect you can control the appearance of 3D objects with lighting, shading, rotation, and other properties.

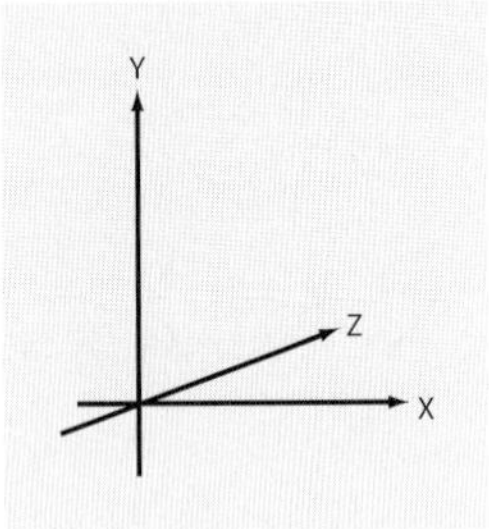

The 3D effect takes advantage of the x, y, z axes.

There are three ways to create a 3D object.

- Extrude and Bevel–Uses the Z axis to give a 2D object depth by extruding the object. For example, a circle becomes a cylinder.
- Revolve–Uses the Y axis to revolve an object around an axis. For example, an arc becomes a circle.
- Rotate–Uses the Z axis to rotate 2D artwork in 3D space and change the artwork's perspective.

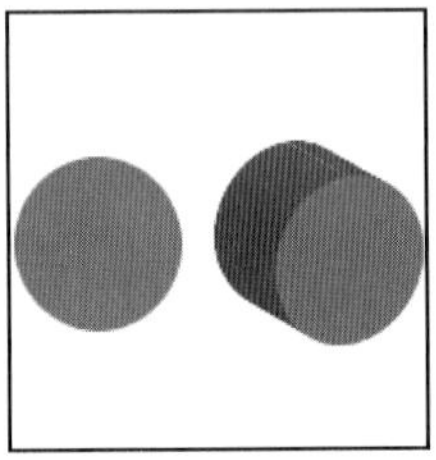

Extrude and Bevel.

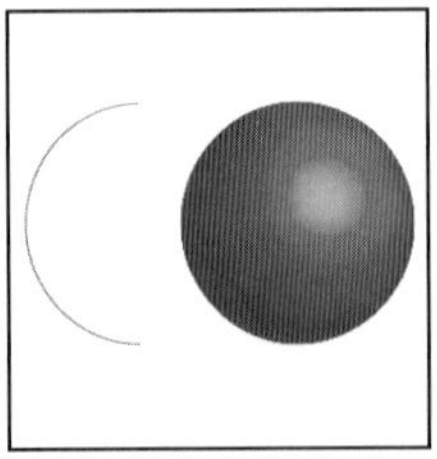

Revolve.

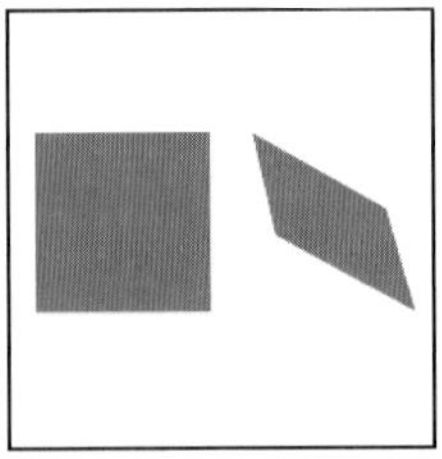

Rotate.

Using the 3D Extrude effect

In this next lesson you will create a can to hold the soap for which you have already created a label.

1 Choose the Ellipse tool (○) and click and release on the artboard. In the Ellipse options dialog box, type **285 pt** into the Width textbox and click on the word Height. The values are entered equally.

2 Fill the shape with the color Gray from the Swatches palette. Make sure that the Stroke is None.

3 Choose Effect > 3D > Extrude and Bevel, check the Preview checkbox. Click on the titlebar of the options window and drag it to a location that allows you to see your artwork.

The Extrude and Bevel effect has taken the two-dimensional circle and extruded it using the default settings. You will change several options including the depth and edges.

4 First, click on the position cube icon oo the left side of the dialog box. Experiment with rotating the object in space by clicking and dragging the cube. When you are finished experimenting, choose Off-Axis Bottom from the Position Pop-up menu.

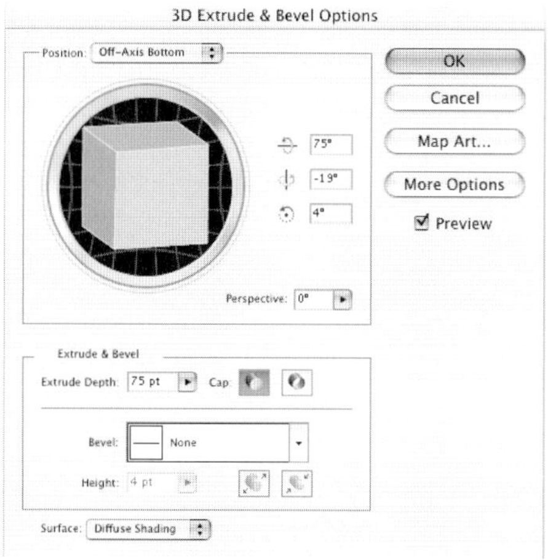

The Extrude and Bevel options.

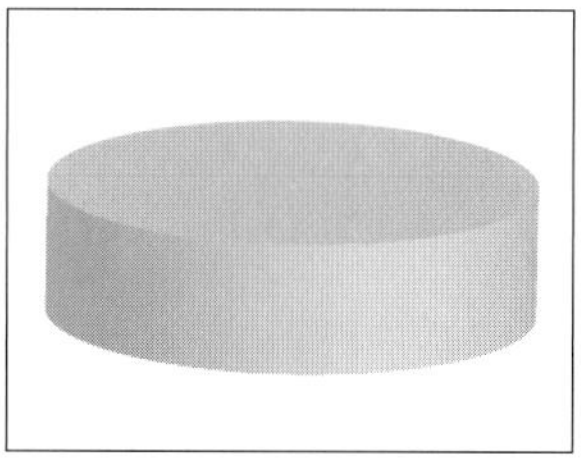

Result.

5 Make the cylinder taller by using the Extrude Depth slider or typing **75** into the Extrude Depth textbox. Check off and on the Preview checkbox to refresh the image.

Cap On or Cap Off?

In the Extrude and Bevel section of the 3D Options window (Extrude and Bevel and Revoive 3D effects) you have a choice to make your object appear solid or hollow.

- *Click the Revolve Cap On button to make the object appear solid.*
- *Click the Revolve Cap Off button to make the object appear hollow.*

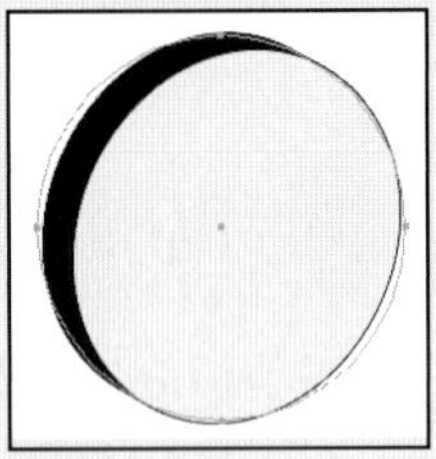

Cap On.

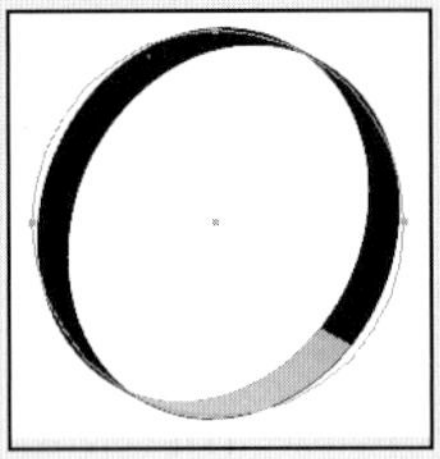

Cap Off.

6 Using the Bevel Pop-up box, experiment with the choice of different bevels to see different variations of edge effects you can easily create.

You can add beveling properties to carve away from or add to the object's surface.

- The Extent Out button adds the bevel to the object's shape.
- The Extent In button carves the bevel out of the object's original shape.

When you are finished experimenting return to None.

Note: *3D objects may display anti-aliasing artifacts on screen, but these artifacts disappear when the object is rasterized. Read more about rasterization in the flattening section of Lesson 10.*

For information about how to create your own bevels see Online Help.

8 Click OK.

9 File > Save. Leave the file open for the next lesson.

Applying the Symbol as mapped artwork

Take any 2D artwork stored as a Symbol in the Symbol's palette and apply it to selected surfaces on your 3D object.

Every 3D object is composed of several surfaces. For example, the shape that you just created has three external surfaces. It has a top, a bottom and a side surface that wraps around the shape. In this next lesson you will take the artwork that you created and map them to the cylinder.

1 Since you are editing the existing Extrude and Bevel effect, locate the Appearance palette, Go to Windows > Appearance if it is not visible, and double-click on 3D Extrude and Bevel. When the Extrude and Bevel options appear, drag the window to the side so that you can see your artwork as you make changes.

Note: *Any time that you apply an effect, double-click on the named effect in the Appearance palette to edit it.*

2 Press the Map Art button and check Preview.

When the Map Art window appears, notice the options to select a Symbol and a Surface. A window for positioning the mapped artwork appears below.

3 Click on the single arrow to navigate from one surface to another. Notice that as you rotate through the surfaces, a red highlight appears indicating what surface you have active in the preview window.

4 Choose 1 of 3. You see the top of the cylinder in the preview palette.

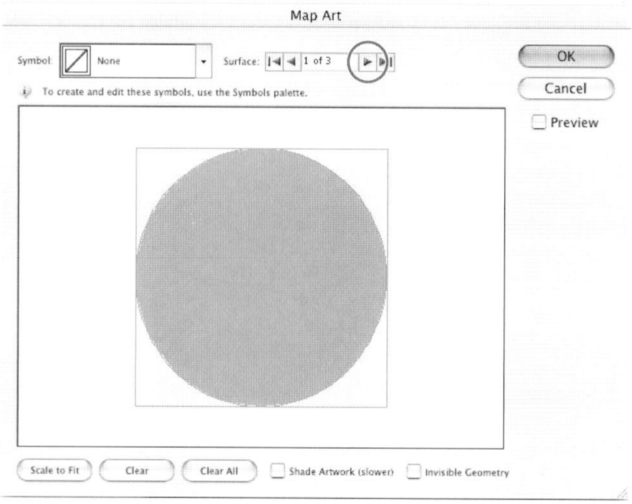

Click on the single arrow to navigate surfaces.

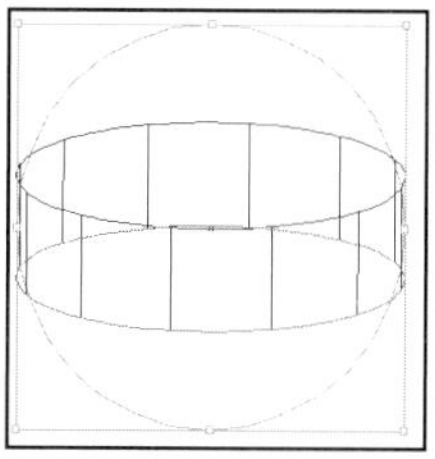

The highlighted Surface.

5 From the Symbol pop-up menu, choose the Symbol named Lemon.

The Lemon Symbol is placed in the preview palette.

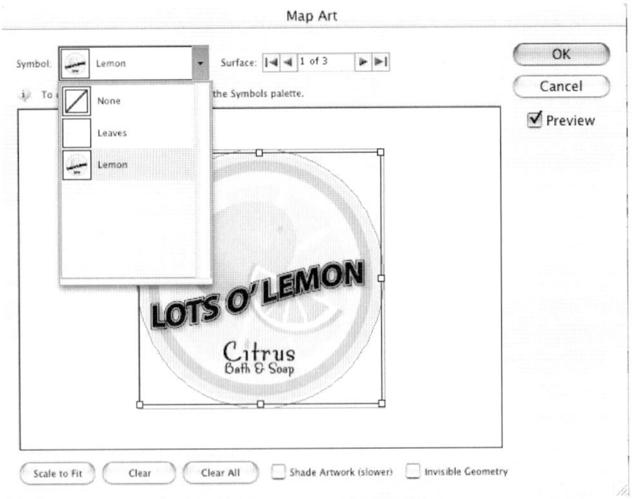

Select the Symbol.

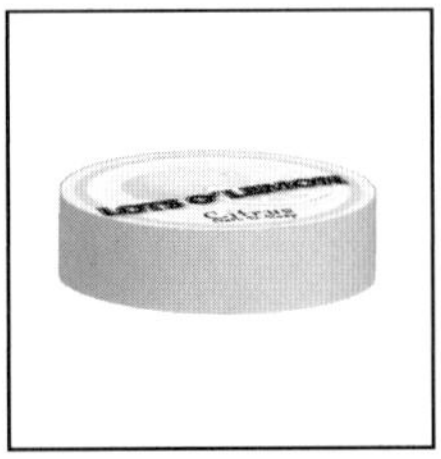

Result.

6 In Surface, click on the single arrow and choose 3 of 3.

7 Choose Leaves from the Symbol pop-up window.

8 Use the preview palette to position the Leaves. In this position, the light gray area is visible. If you like, check Shade Artwork to have the side and top art shaded.

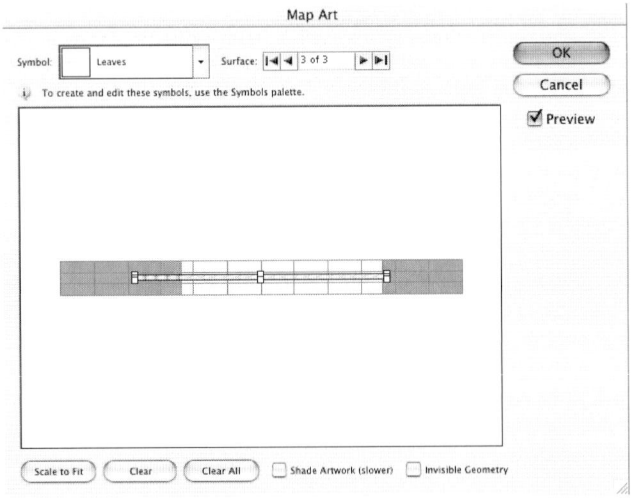

Position the leaves in the light gray area.

9 Click OK, and OK again.

10 File > Save.

Creating a revolved object

In this next lesson you will create the soap in the shape of a sphere. To begin with, create an arc that will be revolved to create the sphere.

1 Choose the Rectangle tool (▢) and click once on the artboard away from the artwork. When the Rectangle options dialog box appears, type **85 pt** for the Width and the **100 pt** for the Height. Click OK.

2 Press D to return the rectangle back to the default colors of black stroke and white fill.

3 Press Ctrl+5 (Windows) or Command+5 (Mac OS) or choose View > Guides > Make Guides, to turn the rectangle into a custom guide.

4 As a default, guides are locked. To verify that guides are locked, choose View > Guides if there is a check mark to the left of Lock Guides, they are locked. If there is no check mark, choose Lock Guides to lock them.

5 Using the Pen tool (✒) click on the lower right corner of the rectangle guide and drag to the left until the endpoint of the direction line reaches the lower left corner and release. This creates a directional line.

6 Click on the upper right corner and drag to the right until the endpoint of the directional line reaches the upper left corner and release. You have created an arc.

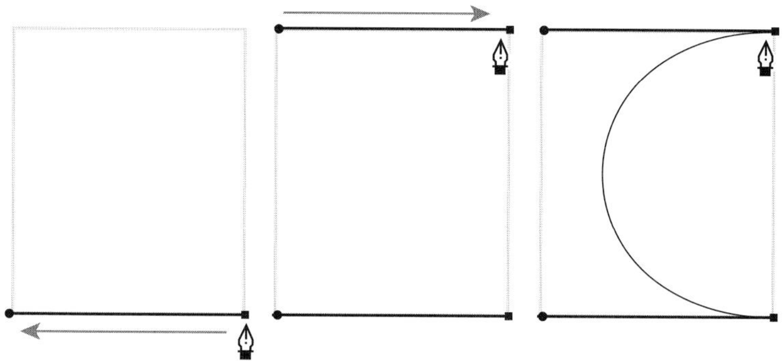

Click and drag to create a direction line. *The complete arc.*

7 Choose View > Guides > Clear Guides.

8 Use the Swatches at the bottom of the toolbar to change the Stroke to yellow and the Fill to None.

9 Choose Effect > 3D > Revolve. Click on Preview.

The Revolve option appears. The options appear similar to the Extrude options, but have quite a different effect.

10 Leave the position at the default position of Off-Axis Front.

11 Change the edge from Left Edge to Right Edge. Your arch revolves around the designated edge. The result varies dramatically depending upon the side that you choose. Leave it set to Right Edge. Click OK.

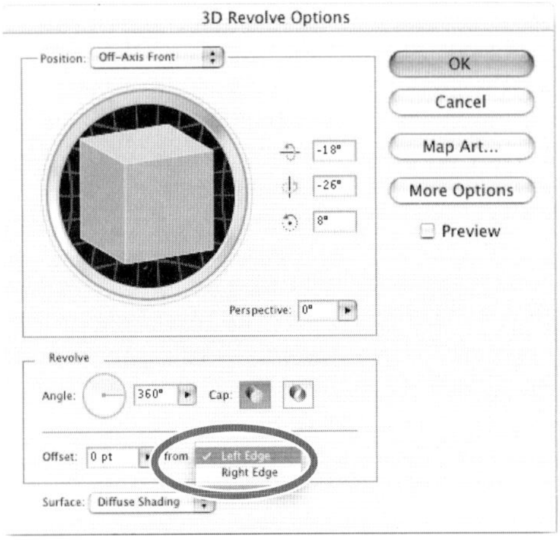

Choose which edge to revolve around.

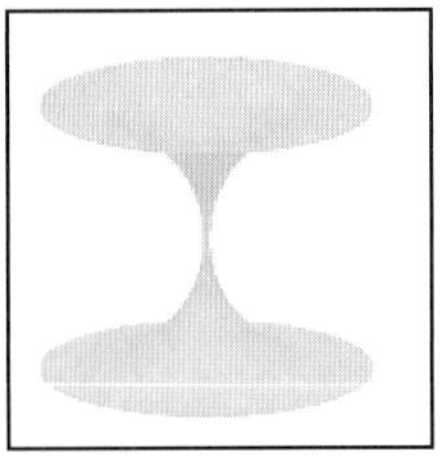

Revolve with Left Edge selected.

Revolve with Right Edge selected.

12 File > Save and keep the file open for the next lesson.

Changing the lighting

In this next lesson you will use additional options to change the strength and direction of the light source.

1 With the lemon soap shape still selected, double-click on 3D Revolve in the Appearance palette. If the Appearance palette is not visible, choose Window > Appearance.

2 Check on Preview and press More Options.

Using More Options gives you the opportunity to create custom lighting effects on your 3D object. You will use the preview window in the lower left to reposition the lighting and change the shade color.

3 From the Surface pop-up menu, choose Diffuse Shading.

4 In the preview window, click and drag the white square that represents the light source. This changes the direction of the lighting. For this exercise drag the light source at the top of the object.

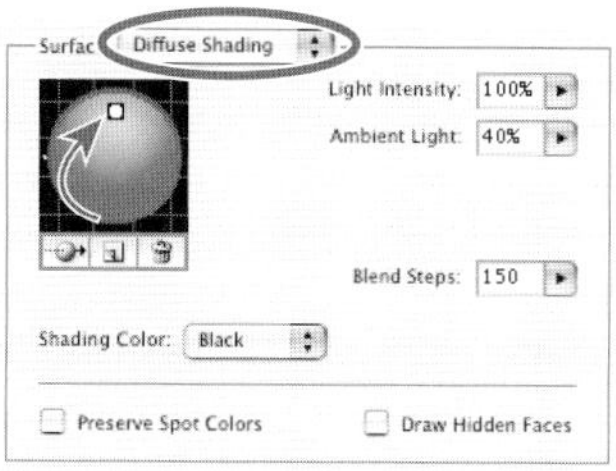

Move the light source by dragging it and change the Surface.

5 Click on the Shading Color Pop-up menu and select Custom. Click on the colored Red square to the right of Custom and use the Color Picker to select a green color, or enter values in the color textboxes to the right of the picker window. (We used C=90%, M=0%, Y=100%, B=0%.)

The yellow shape now has green shading applied to it.

6 Change the Ambient Light to **40%**.

Ambient light controls the brightness on the surface uniformly.

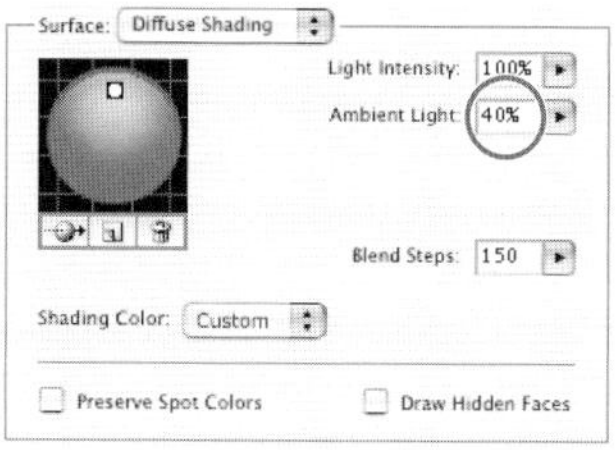

7 Position the soap closer to the soap tin.

8 File > Save.

Mapping a Photoshop image

You can map artwork from Illustrator, and also import artwork from other applications, such as Photoshop. In this next part of the lesson you will place a Photoshop texture into the document and apply it to the soap.

1 Choose File >Place and locate the image named Lemonskin.psd in the Lesson16 folder. Make sure that Link is unchecked. Files to be used as symbols must be embedded. Press Place.

2 With the Symbols palette visible, use the Selection tool to drag the image into the Symbols palette. Double-click on the new symbol in the Symbols palatte and name it **Texture**.

3 Delete the placed image.

4 Select the soap and double-click on 3D Revolve in the Appearance palette.

5 Click on Map Art and select Surface 1 of 2. Choose the Texture symbol from the Symbol pop-up menu.

6 Press Scale to Fit, and check Shade Art. Click OK.

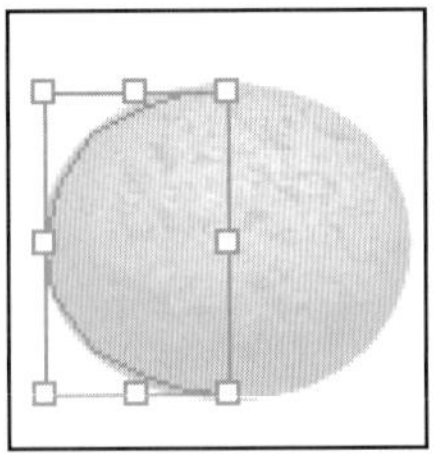

Map a Photoshop image.

The texture now wraps around the soap shape. Next you will clone the 3D objects to add more to the artboard.

7 Using the Selection tool, select the soap shape you just created. Hold down the Alt (Windows) or Option (Mac OS) key and drag the shape next to itself (left or right), releasing the mouse first. This clones the shape. Clone one more time to have a total of three spheres.

Use Alt/Option to clone the spheres.

Since 3D objects do not share lighting you will edit the existing Extrude and Bevel applied to the elipse you used to create the soap tin.

1 Using the Selection tool, click on the Lemon soap tin.

2 Double-click on 3D Extrude and Bevel to open the 3D options.

3 In the lighting preview pane, drag the light to the top of the shape. This makes the lighting more consistent with the soap shapes.

4 File > Save. Leave the file open for the next lesson.

What are Blend Steps?

In More Options is a textbox for Blend Steps. As a default this amount is low to process quickly and give optimum steps for on screen and web artwork. This low amount may cause banding (large shifts of value from one tone to the next) when printing. To learn more about techniques used to avoid banding in gradients, read "Calculating maximum blend length based on color change" in online Help.

Creating your own revolved artwork

This is when you have the opportunity to create your own 3D shape. In this next lesson you will create a path and adjust the offset to create a vase. An example of the path that we use is in the file named paths.ai the Lesson16 folder, but it can be much more worthwhile to apply your own path and see the interesting results you can achieve.

1 Choose View Show Rulers, or Ctrl+R (Windows) or Command+R (Mac OS).

2 Create a vertical guide by clicking on the vertical ruler and dragging it out to a blank area on your artboard.

3 Choose the Pen tool ( ) and create a vertical path with several curves, representing the curves that will be replicated in the 3D shape. If it is easier, use the Pencil tool ( ) to draw a path. The size of the path is not important at this time, it can be scaled later.

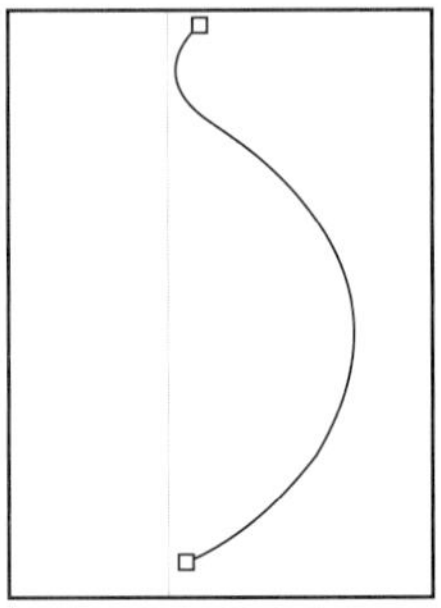

Create a path to revolve.

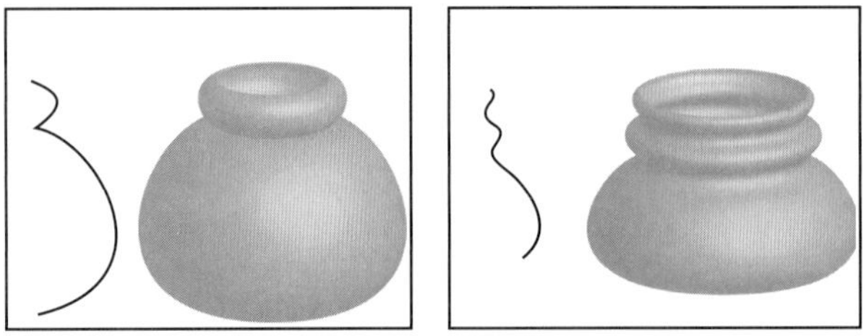

Example of curves and the resulting 3D shape.

4 Choose Effect > 3D > Revolve and click on Preview.

5 Depending upon the effect you want to achieve, you can change the axis from the Left Edge to the Right Edge.

6 To make the 3D object wider, choose an offset. The slider moves rather quickly, so type **50** into Offset textbox. If necessary, uncheck Preview and recheck preview to see the results.

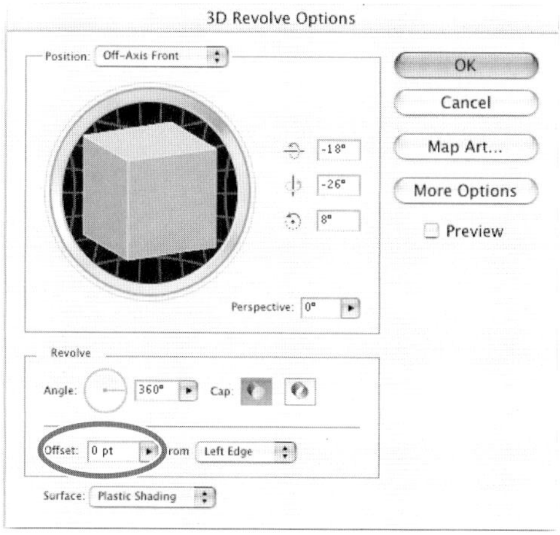

Offset at 0 pt.

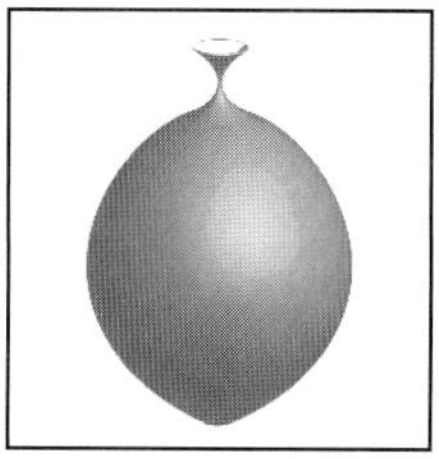

Result.

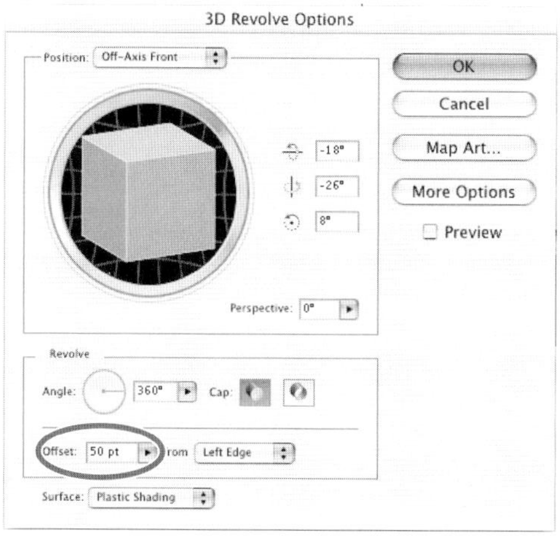

Offset at 50 pt.

Result.

If the lighting options are not visible, click on the More Options button to add an additional light source to the vase.

7 In the lighting preview window, click on the New button (▣) to add another light source. Position the lights so that one is on the lower left and the other is in the upper right of the preview object.

8 Change the Ambient Light to **25%**.

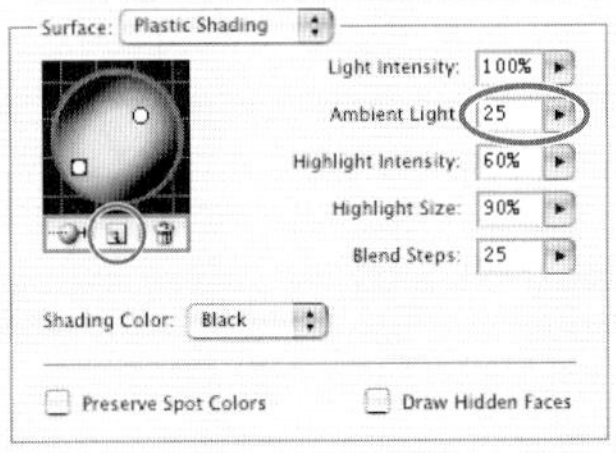

Click the new button to add additional light sources.

9 Click OK.

10 Using the Selection tool, move the vase in closer to the rest of the artwork and choose Object > Arrange > Send to back.

11 Use the Scale tool (![]) if you feel it is necessary to make your vase larger or smaller.

Move the Vase to the back.

12 File > Save. Leave this file open for the next lesson.

Using the 3D Rotate effect

Next you will create the placemat on which the objects are sitting. For this example you will create a rectangle, fill it with a pattern and use the Rotate effect to make it look as though it is lying down on a flat surface.

1 Create a rectangle that encompasses the entire artwork.

2 Making sure that the Fill swatch is forward in the toolbar, select the pattern Stripes from the Swatches palette.

3 Give the rectangle a stroke of None.

4 With the rectangle still selected choose Effect > 3D > Rotate and check Preview.

5 Using the text boxes enter **70%** for the rotation around the X axis. For the rotation around the Y axis specify **0%**. Specify **0%** for the rotation around the Z axis.

6 Enter **75%** for the amount of perspective. Click OK.

The rectangle now looks like a place mat sitting on a table. Notice how the pattern also has the perspective applied to it.

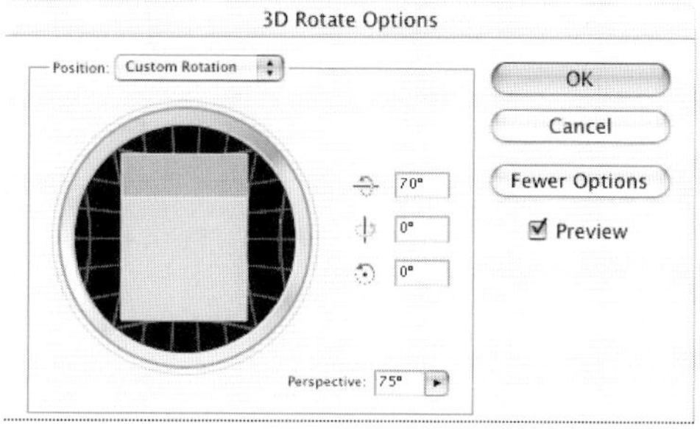

The Rotate Options window.

Result.

7 With the rectangle still selected, choose Object > Arrange > Send to Back. Using the Selection tool, position in place.

The completed illustration.

Once you have applied the 3D effect to an object it remains a live effect. In other words, you can change the scale of the object or change the color, and the 3D effect remains.

Note: *Do not rotate objects with the 3D effects applied to them, you will get unexpected results. To rotate a 3D object double-click on the Appearance palette 3D effect and rotate the item in space using the Position preview window.*

8 Once you have rearranged objects as you like, you have completed the lesson. File > Save, File > Close.

Exploring on your own

On your own, try to create an additional item for the artwork in this lesson. Choose File > Open and locate the file in the Lesson16 folder named L16strt2.ai.

1 Choose the Selection tool and then Select > Select All.

2 Drag the artwork into the Symbols palette.

3 Double-click on the Symbol in the Symbols palette and name it **Soap**.

4 With the artwork still selected, choose Edit > Clear, or press the Delete key.

5 Choose the Rectangle tool and click once on the artboard. Enter the values of **325 pt** for the width and **220 pt** for the height, click OK.

6 Choose Effect > 3D > Extrude and Bevel and experiment with different positions and settings.

7 Choose Map artwork and map the Symbol that you created (Soap) to the top of the box.

8 Click OK, and OK again when you are finished.

Take the illustration further by creating your own symbols and applying them to the other faces of the box.

Review questions

1 What are the three types of 3D effects that are available? Give a good example of why you would use each one.

2 How can you control lighting on a 3D object and does one 3D object's lighting affect other 3D objects.

3 What are the steps to mapping artwork to an object?

4 Once a 3D object is created, what is the best way to rotate it?

Review answers

1 Using the 3D effect, you can choose from Extrude and Bevel, Revolve and Rotate.

• Extrude and Bevel–Uses the Z axis to give a 2D object depth by extruding the object. For example, a circle becomes a cylinder.

• Revolve–Uses the Y axis to revolve an object around an axis. For example, an arc becomes a circle.

• Rotate–Uses the Z axis to rotate 2D artwork in 3D space and change the artwork's perspective.

2 By clicking the More Options button in the 3D options window, you can change the light, and the direction, as well as changing the shade color.
No, Options for one 3D object's lighting do not affect other 3D objects.

3 Map an artwork to an object by following these steps:

a Select the artwork and hold down the Alt/Option key and click on the New Symbol icon in the Symbols palette.

b Select the object that is to be 3D and choose Effects > 3D > Extrude and Bevel or Revolve.

c Click on Map Art.

d Select the surface using the arrows.

e From the Symbol pop-up menu, select the symbol.

f Click OK and OK again.

4 Once you have created a 3D object, it is best to double-click on the 3D effect in the Appearance palette and use the Position preview window to position it in space. Using the Rotate tool will lead to unexpected results.

Lesson 17

17 Printing Artwork and Producing Color Separations

The quality and color of your final printed output are determined by the process you follow to prepare an image for print. Whether you're printing a draft of your work on a desktop printer or outputting color separations to be printed on a commercial press, learning fundamental printing concepts helps ensure that your printed results meet your expectations.

In this lesson, you'll learn about the following:

- Different types of printing requirements and printing devices.
- Printing concepts and printing terminology.
- Basic color principles.
- How to separate your color artwork into its component colors for output to print.
- How to use spot colors for two-color printing.
- Special considerations when outputting to print.

Printing: An overview

When you print a document from a computer, data is sent from the document to the printing device, either to be printed on paper or to be converted to a positive or negative image on film. For black-and-white, grayscale, or low quantities of color artwork, many people use desktop printers. However, if you require large quantities of printed output, such as a brochure or magazine ad, you'll need to prepare your artwork for output on a commercial printing press. Printing on a commercial press is an art that requires time and experience to perfect. In addition to close communication with a printing professional, learning basic printing concepts and terminology will help you produce printed results that meet your expectations.

Note: *This lesson assumes that you have a desktop printer for use with the exercises. If you don't have a desktop printer available, read the sections and skip the step-by-step instructions.*

Different printing requirements require different printing processes. To determine your printing requirements, consider the following: What effect do you want the printed piece to have on your audience? Will your artwork be printed in black and white? Color? Does it require special paper? How many printed copies do you need? If you're printing in color, is precise color matching necessary, or will approximate color matching suffice?

Take a minute to consider several types of printing jobs:

- A black-and-white interoffice newsletter, requiring a low quantity of printed copies. For this type of printing job, you can generally use a 300-600 dpi (dots per inch) desktop laser printer to output the original, and then use a copy machine to reproduce the larger quantity.

• A business card using black and one other color. The term two-color printing typically refers to printing with black and one other color, although it may also refer to printing with two colors that are not black. Two-color printing is less expensive than four-color printing and lets you select exact color matches, called spot colors, which can be important for logos. For precise color matching, two-color printing is done on a printing press; if only an approximate color match is required, you might use a desktop color printer.

• A party invitation using two colors and tints of those colors. In addition to printing two solid colors, you can print tints of the colors to add depth to your printed artwork. Two-color printing is often done on colored paper that complements the ink colors and might be done on a desktop color printer or on a printing press, depending on the desired quantity and the degree of color matching required.

• A newspaper. Newspapers are typically printed on a printing press because they are time-sensitive publications printed in large quantities. In addition, newspapers are generally printed on large rolls of newsprint, which are then trimmed and folded to the correct size.

• A fashion magazine or catalog requiring accurate color reproduction. Four-color printing refers to mixing the four process ink colors (cyan, magenta, yellow, and black, or CMYK) for printed output. When accurate color reproduction is required, printing is done on a printing press using CMYK inks. CMYK inks can reproduce a good amount of the visible color spectrum, with the exception of neon or metallic colors. You'll learn more about color models in the next section.

About printing devices

Now that you've looked at several types of publications and different ways to reproduce them, you'll begin learning basic printing concepts and printing terminology.

Halftone screens

To reproduce any type of artwork, a printing device typically breaks down the artwork into a series of dots of various sizes called a halftone screen. Black dots are used to print black-and-white or grayscale artwork. For color artwork, a halftone screen is created for each ink color (cyan, magenta, yellow, and black); these then overlay one another at different angles to produce the full range of printed color. To see a good example of how individual halftone screens overlay each other at different angles on a printed page, look at a color comics page through a magnifying glass.

The size of the dots in a halftone screen determines how light or dark colors appear in print. The smaller the dot, the lighter the color appears; the larger the dot, the darker the color appears.

Enlarged detail showing dots in halftone screen.

Screen frequency

Screen frequency (also called line screen, screen ruling, or halftone frequency) refers to the number of rows or lines of dots used to render an image on film or paper. In addition, the rows of dots are broken down into individual squares, called halftone cells. Screen frequency is measured in lines per inch (lpi) and is a fixed value you can set for your printing device.

As a general rule, higher screen frequencies produce finer detail in printed output. This is because the higher the screen frequency, the smaller the halftone cells, and subsequently, the smaller the halftone dot in the cell.

However, a high screen frequency alone does not guarantee high-quality output. The screen frequency must be appropriate to the paper, the inks, and the printer or printing press used to output the artwork. Your printing professional will help you select the appropriate line screen value for your artwork and output device.

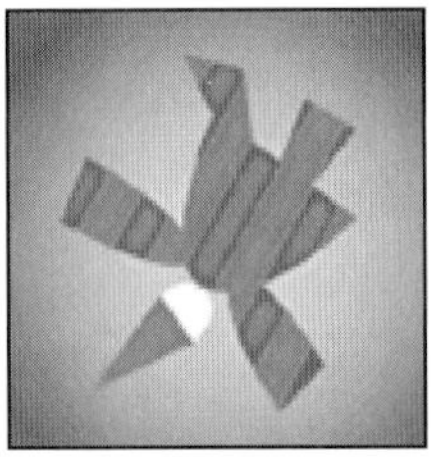

Low-screen ruling (65 lpi) is often used to print newsletters.

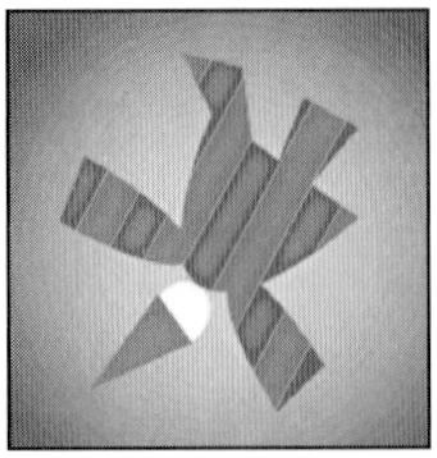

High-screen ruling (150–200 lpi) is used for high-quality books.

Output device resolution

The resolution of a printing device describes the number of dots the printing device has available to render, or create, a halftone dot. The higher the output device resolution, the higher the quality of the printed output. For example, the printed quality of an image output at 2400 dots per inch (dpi) is higher than the printed quality of an image output at 300 dpi. Adobe Illustrator is resolution-independent and will always print at the printing device's highest resolution capability.

The quality of printed output depends on the relationship between the resolution of the output device (dpi) and the screen frequency (lpi). As a general rule, high-resolution output devices use higher screen frequency values to produce the highest quality images. For example, an imagesetter with a resolution of 2400 dpi and a screen frequency of 177 lpi produces a higher quality image than a desktop printer with a resolution of 300 to 600 dpi and a screen frequency of 85 lpi.

About color

Color is produced by a computer monitor and printing device using two different color models (methods for displaying and measuring color). The human eye perceives color according to the wavelength of the light it receives. Light containing the full color spectrum is perceived as white; in the absence of light, the eye perceives black.

The gamut of a color model is the range of colors that can be displayed or printed. The largest color gamut is that viewed in nature; all other color gamuts produce a subset of nature's color gamut. The two most common color models are red, green, and blue (RGB), the method by which monitors display color; and cyan, magenta, yellow, and black (CMYK), the method by which images are printed using four process ink colors.

The RGB color model

A large percentage of the visible spectrum of color can be represented by mixing three basic components of colored light in various proportions. These components are known as the additive colors: red, green, and blue (RGB). The RGB color model is called the additive color model because various percentages of each colored light are added to create color. All monitors display color using the RGB color model.

The CMYK color model

If 100% of red, green, or blue is subtracted from white light, the resulting color is cyan, magenta, or yellow. For example, if an object absorbs (subtracts) 100% red light and reflects green and blue, cyan is the perceived color. Cyan, magenta, and yellow are called the subtractive primaries, and they form the basis for printed colors. In addition to cyan, magenta, and yellow, black ink is used to generate true black and to deepen the shadows in images. These four inks (CMYK) are often called process colors because they are the four standard inks used in the printing process.

For an illustration of RGB and CMYK color models, see figure 13-3 in the color section.

Spot colors

Whereas process colors are reproduced using cyan, magenta, yellow, and black inks, spot colors are premixed inks used in place of, or in addition to, CMYK colors. Spot colors can be selected from color-matching systems, such as the PANTONE® or TOYO™ color libraries. Many spot colors can be converted to their process color equivalents when printed; however, some spot colors, such as metallic or iridescent colors, require their own plate on press.

Use spot color in the following situations:

• To save money on one-color and two-color print jobs. (When your printing budget won't allow for four-color printing, you can still print relatively inexpensively using one or two colors.)

• To print logos or other graphic elements that require precise color matching. You want the printer in Boston to use the same color of red as the printer in New York.

• To print special inks, such as metallic, fluorescent, or pearlescent colors.

Getting started

Before you begin, you must restore the default preferences for Adobe Illustrator. Then you'll open the art file for this lesson.

1 To ensure that the tools and palettes function exactly as described in this lesson, delete or deactivate (by renaming) the Adobe Illustrator 11.0 preferences file. See "Restoring default preferences" on page 2.

2 Start Adobe Illustrator.

3 Choose File > Open, and open the L17strt1.ai file in the Lesson17 folder, located inside the Lessons folder within the AICIB folder on your hard drive.

For an illustration of the finished artwork in this lesson, see the color section.

4 Choose File > Save As, name the file **Circus.ai**, and select the Lesson17 folder. Leave the Format option set to Adobe Illustrator® Document, and click Save. In the Illustrator Options dialog box, leave at the defaults and click OK.

Color management

Although all color gamuts overlap, they don't match exactly, which is why some colors on your monitor can't be reproduced in print. The colors that can't be reproduced in print are called out-of-gamut colors because they are outside the spectrum of printable colors.

To compensate for these differences and to ensure the closest match between on-screen colors and printed colors, Adobe Illustrator includes a color management system (CMS) that lets you select profiles for your monitor and for the output device to which you'll print. Selecting a color profile controls the conversion of RGB values to CMYK values at print time. To select a color profile, you use the Color Settings command.

The point of color management is not to help you achieve better colors in print, but to help keep in check expectations as to how the artwork will print. Color management, essentially, makes your RGB monitor represent colors as they appear when printed in CMYK.

1 Choose Edit > Color Settings.

2 In the Color Settings dialog box, choose U.S. Prepress Defaults from the Settings menu.

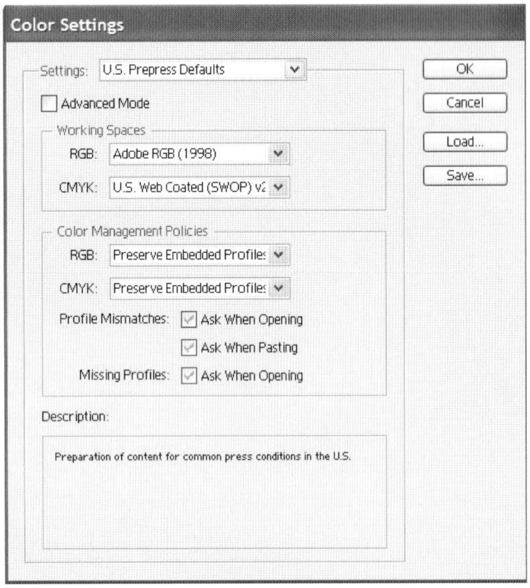

In this lesson, you'll use one of the predefined sets of color management settings provided in Adobe Illustrator. Each set has corresponding color profile and conversion options designed to preserve consistent color for a particular publishing workflow under typical conditions. For more information on color management settings, see "Using predefined color management settings" in online Help .

3 Leave the settings and options at their default values. Click OK.

Printing black-and-white proofs

As a general rule, you should print black-and-white proofs of all your documents at different stages of your work to check the layout and to verify the accuracy of text and graphics before preparing the document for final output.

Now you'll print a draft of the Circus.ai file.

1 In the Circus.ai file, notice the crop marks, the pairs of lines at each corner of the artwork. Crop marks define where the artwork is trimmed after it is printed. The crop marks indicate a bleed, the area of artwork that falls outside the crop marks, and which will be removed when the printed artwork is trimmed. The bleed is used to ensure that the artwork prints to the edge of the trimmed page. For more information on bleed, read "Specifying the bleed area" later in this lesson.

You can set crop marks where you want them directly in the artwork. See "Setting crop marks" in online Help.

2 If you're not connected to a black-and-white printer, go on to the next section.

3 Choose File > Print, leave all choices set at the defaults and click OK (Windows) or Print (Mac OS).

The circus logo is printed in black, white, and shades of gray. Next, you'll soft-proof the color on your monitor screen.

Soft-proofing colors

In a color-managed work flow, you can use the precision of color profiles to soft-proof your document directly on the monitor. Soft-proofing lets you preview on-screen how your document's colors will look when reproduced on a particular output device.

The reliability of soft-proofing completely depends, however, on the quality of your monitor, your monitor profile, and the ambient lighting conditions of your workstation area. In other words, if you are working in an inconsistent environment, with varying light throughout the day you might not get reliable results. For information on creating a monitor profile, see "Creating an ICC monitor profile" in online Help.

1 Choose View > Proof Setup > Custom. The profile is set to U.S. Web Coated (SWOP) v2. Leave it set to this profile and click OK.

The View > Proof Colors option is selected by default (indicated by a check mark) so that you can view the artwork as it will look when printed to the selected standard, U.S. Web Coated (SWOP) v2.

Next, you'll change the profile to see what the image will look like if printed on a different output device.

2 Choose View > Proof Setup > Custom.

3 Use the Profile menu to select Euroscale Uncoated v2, and click OK. Because the view is still set to Proof Colors, the image preview automatically shifts colors to display what it would look like were it printed according to the Euroscale Uncoated profile.

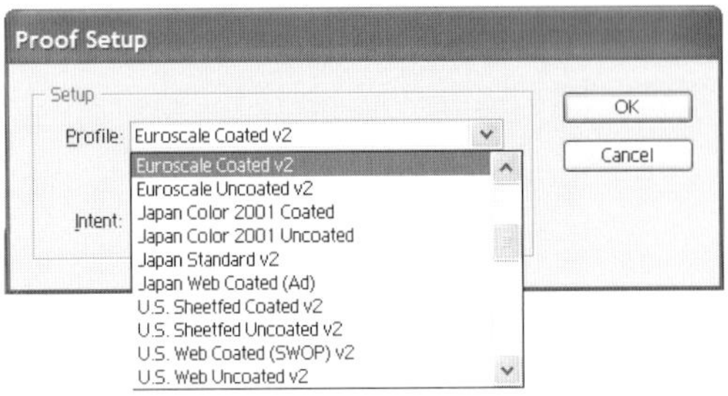

Use Proof Setup to change the color preview.

You'll now return the settings to the SWOP settings.

4 Choose View > Proof Setup > Custom. Set the profile to U.S. Web Coated (SWOP) v2 and click OK.

5 Choose View > Proof Colors to turn off the soft-proofing preview.

Next, you'll work with printing color artwork.

Using the Document Info command

Before you take your color artwork to a prepress professional or begin the process of creating color separations on your own, use the Document Info command to generate and save a list of information about all the elements of your artwork file. The Document Info command displays a palette of information on the objects, linked or placed files, colors, gradients, patterns, and fonts in your document.

If you're working with prepress professionals, be sure to provide them with the Document Info list before delivering your files; they can help you determine what you'll need to include with your artwork. For example, if your artwork uses a font that the prepress house does not have, you'll need to bring or supply a copy of the font with your artwork.

1 Choose Window > Document Info. The Document Info palette appears.

2 In the Document Info palette, select different subjects about the document from the palette menu in the upper right corner. The list box displays information about each subject you select.

3 If you have an object selected in the artwork, choose Selection Only from the Document Info palette menu to display information only on that selected object. A check mark indicates that the Selection Only option is turned on.

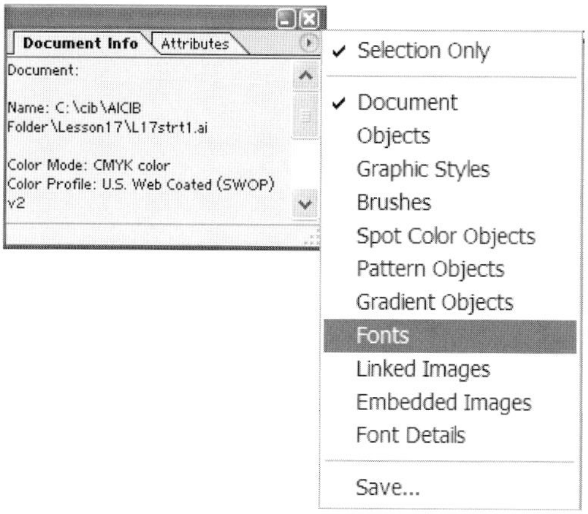

The Document Info palette.

You can also view or print the entire contents of the Document Info palette by saving it and then opening it in a text editor.

4 To save the Document Info text, choose Save from the palette menu, enter a name for the Document Info file, and click Save. You can open the file in any text editor to review and print the contents of the file.

5 When you have looked through the information on the file, you can leave the Document Info palette open on-screen or close it.

Creating color separations

To print color artwork on a printing press, you must first separate the composite art into its component colors: cyan, magenta, yellow, and black, and any spot colors, if applicable. The process of breaking composite artwork into its component colors is called color separation.

You set separation options in the Print dialog box. It's important to note that before setting separation options, you need to discuss the specific requirements of your print job with your printing professional. (You cannot separate to a non-PostScript® printer.)

For an illustration of color separations, see the color section.

1 Make sure that the Circus.ai artwork is still open.

2 Select the Selection tool (↖) in the toolbox. Then click various objects in the artwork to select them.

As you select different objects, notice that the Color palette reflects the current color's attributes. For example, if you click the flag atop the tent, a PANTONE color swatch appears in the Color palette; if you click the red or green stripe in the clown, the color is mixed using CMYK values.

Selecting a printer description file

The set-up for separations and other options are done in the Print dialog box.

Important: To be able to continue with this section, your computer must be connected to a PostScript printer. If you are connected to an ink-jet printer or not connected to a printer, the separation options will be dimmed in the Print dialog window.

1 Choose File > Print. The first pop-up window labeled Presets is left alone at this point. You will learn how to take your options and turn them into presets later in this lesson.

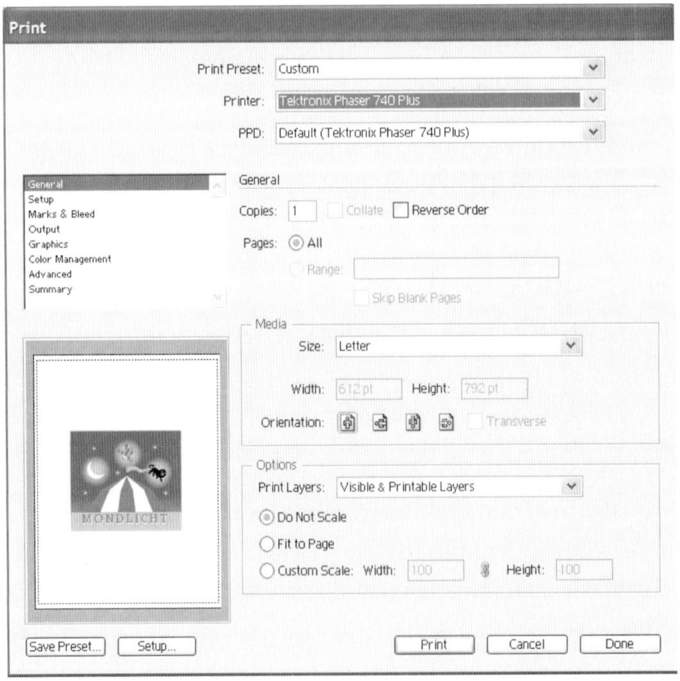

2 First off, make sure that you have a printer selected in the Printer pop-up box. If not select a Postscript printer at this point.

3 Select a PPD.

PostScript Printer Description (PPD) files contain information about the output device, including available page sizes, resolution, available line screen (frequency) values, and the angles of the halftone screens.

***Note:** A PostScript Printer Description file with limited selections has been placed in the Lesson17 folder for this exercise. When you install Adobe Illustrator, two PPDs are automatically installed in the Utilities folder within the Adobe Illustrator folder, and additional PPDs are provided on the Adobe Illustrator CD.*

4 In the PPD pop up window, choose Other.

5 Navigate to the General.ppd file, located in the Lesson17 folder, inside the Lessons folder within the AICIB folder on your hard drive. Click Open.

The Print dialog box is updated with general printer parameters, and a preview of your artwork is displayed on the lower left side of the dialog box. (The preview of your artwork depends on the page size selected in the Page Size menu. Each output device has a variety of page sizes available; select the desired page size from the Page Size menu in the Print dialog box.)

6 Choose US Letter for the paper size in the Media section.

7 Click on Marks and Bleeds in the options window on the left.

In this window you can choose which printer's marks are visible. Printer's marks help the printer align the color separations on the press and check the color and density of the inks being used.

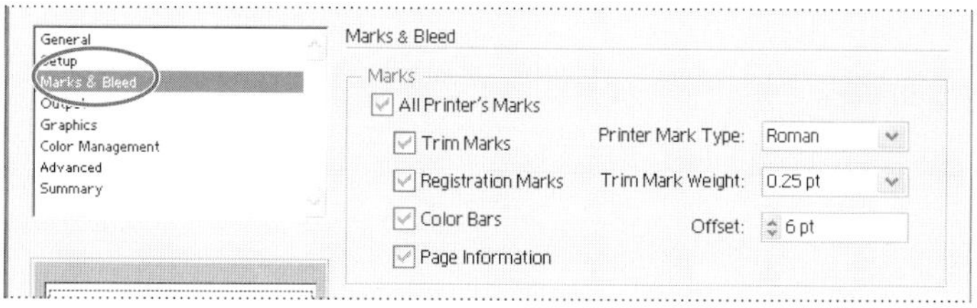

Add all printer's marks, or select just the ones that you want.

8 Click the checkbox to show all printer's marks.

The preview shows the crop and other marks in the preview.

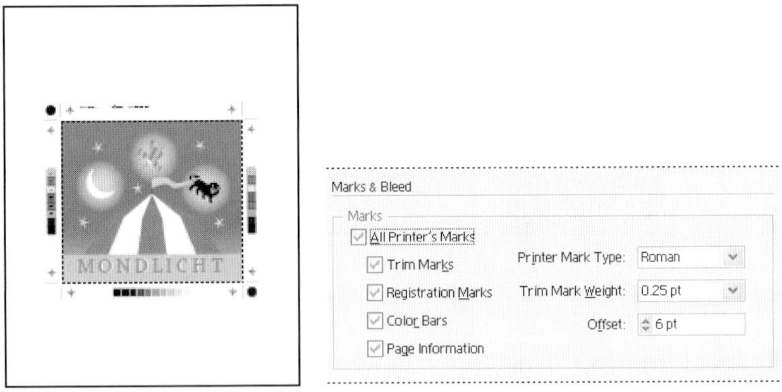

Select printer's marks.

A. *Registration mark.* **B.** *Page Information.*
C. *Crop mark.* **D.** *Color bar.*

Specifying the bleed area

Bleed is the amount of artwork that falls outside the printing bounding box, or outside the crop marks and trim marks. You can include bleed in your artwork as a margin of error—to ensure that the ink is still printed to the edge of the page after the page is trimmed or to ensure that an image can be stripped into a keyline in a document. Once you create the artwork that extends into the bleed, you can use Illustrator to specify the extent of the bleed.

Changing the bleed moves the crop marks farther from or closer to the image; however, the crop marks still define the same size printing bounding box.

Small bleed.

Large bleed.

1 Specify a bleed of **18 pt** by typing it in the Top bleed textbox. Click the Link icon to activate the bleed setting on all sides.

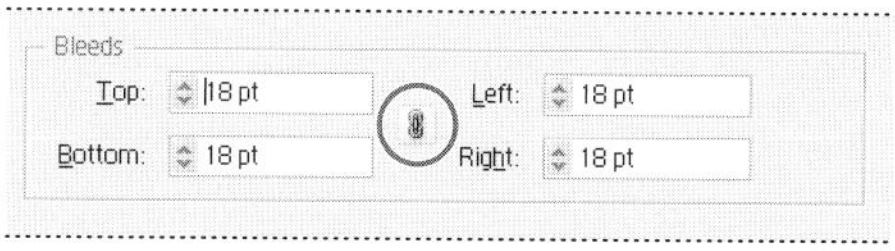

Add a bleed equal on all sides using the Link button.

This means that the artwork extends 18 points beyond the crop marks on your film. The maximum bleed you can set is 72 points; the minimum bleed is 0 points.

The size of the bleed you use depends on its purpose. A press bleed (that is, an image that bleeds off the edge of the printed sheet) should be at least 18 points. If the bleed is to ensure that an image fits a keyline, it needs to be no more than 2 or 3 points. Your print shop can advise you on the size of the bleed necessary for your particular job.

For more help, use online Help “Setting marks and bleed options”.

Separating colors

1 Click on Output in the Options window on the left side of the Print dialog window. Choose Separations (Host Based).

In the Mode pop-up box are three choices:

• Composite–This mode will leave the artwork as a one colored page for output, typical for your everyday printing to a color printer or a color copier.

• Separations (Host Based)–This is the typical separation mode that specifies the separation from computer which Illustrator is on.

• In-RIP Separations–At the output device's RIP (Raster Image Processor).

The circus artwork is composed of process colors and spot colors, which are displayed in the Document Ink Options window.

To the left of the process color names, a printer icon is displayed, indicating that a separation will be generated for each color. To the left of the spot color names, a spot color icon is displayed, indicating that the spot colors will be printed as separate colors.

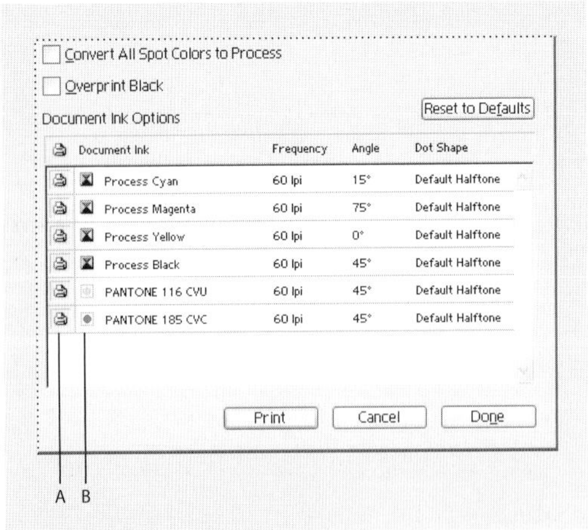

A. Indicates that the color will print.
B. Indicates a spot color.

If you were to print color separations at this point, all the colors, including the spot colors in the artwork, would be printed into 6 plates. Check the box to the left of Convert all Spot colors to Process and now the spot colors will be broken down into the CMYK builds.

Composite image.

Cyan separation.

Magenta separation.

Yellow separation.

Black separation.

2 Uncheck the Convert Spot Color To Process and the spot colors are no longer grayed out, and the process icon to the left returns to a spot icon, indicating that they are going to print.

As you learned earlier, you can print separations using process colors or spot colors, or you can use a combination of both. You'll convert only the first spot color (PANTONE 116) to a process color because a precise color match isn't necessary. The second spot color, PANTONE 185 CVC, will stay a spot color because a precise color match is desired.

3 To convert Pantone 116 to a process color, click the spot color icon to the left of its name in the list of colors.

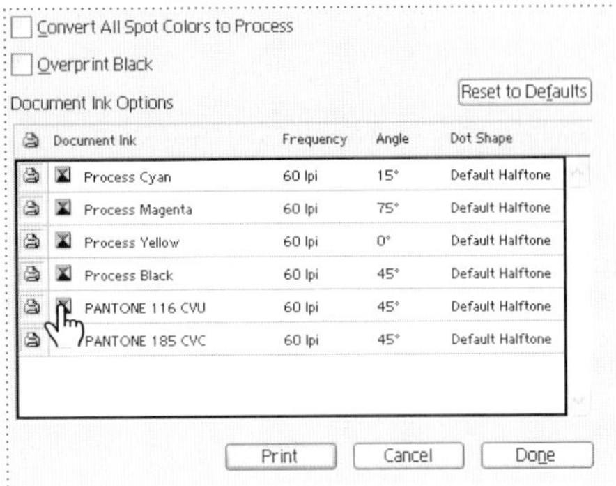

Click on the color swatch to the left of the color name to change it to process or spot.

If you were to print at this point, five separations would be generated: one each for the cyan, magenta, yellow, and black plates (including the spot color converted to a process color); and a single plate for the PANTONE 185 CVC spot color. (This job would require a more specialized press, capable of printing five colors, or the paper would have to be sent back through the press to print the fifth color.)

Composite image.

Cyan separation.

Magenta separation.

Yellow separation.

Black separation.

Spot separation.

Specifying the screen frequency

At the beginning of this lesson, you learned that the relationship between the output device resolution and the screen frequency determines the quality of the printed output. Depending on the output device you select, more than one screen frequency value may be available. Your printing professional will direct you to select the screen frequency appropriate to your artwork.

1 In the Printer Resolution pop-up dialog box, choose 60 lpi/300 dpi from the Halftone menu. The first value, 60, represents the screen frequency (lpi), and the second value, 300, represents the output device resolution (dpi).

Additional separation options, such as Emulsion Up/Down and Positive or Negative film, should be discussed with your printing professional, who can help you determine how these options should be set for your particular job.

For more information, see "Step 5: Set separation options" in online Help.

Printing separations

Before printing your separations to a high-resolution output device, it's a good idea to print a set of separations, called proofs, on your black-and-white desktop printer. You'll save time and money by making any needed corrections to your files after reviewing the black-and-white proofs.

2 Click on Save Preset button in the lower left of the Print dialog box to name and save this setting for future use. This customer always uses the same settings, so we will name it with their name "circus". In the future you can choose this Preset from the Preset pop-up window at the top.

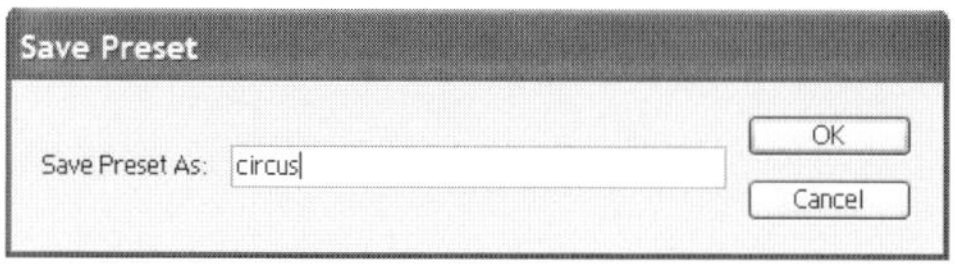

Save frequently used print settings as presets.

3 Choose Print and Click Print to print separations. Five pieces of paper should be printed–one each for cyan, magenta, yellow, and black, and one for the spot color.

Note: *Depending on your chosen printer, you may get a warning message that your PPD doesn't match the current printer. Click Continue to print the proofs.*

4 File > Save and close the Circus.ai file.

Working with two-color illustrations

As you learned earlier, two-color printing generally refers to black and one spot color, but may also refer to two spot colors. In addition to printing the two solid colors, you can print tints, or screens, of the colors. Two-color printing is much less expensive than four-color printing and lets you create a rich range of depth and color when used effectively.

Editing a spot color

In this section, you'll open a two-color version of the circus illustration containing black, a spot color, and tints of the spot color. Before you separate the illustration, you'll replace the current spot color with another from the PANTONE color library. Illustrator lets you make global adjustments to spot colors and tints of spot colors using a keyboard shortcut.

1 Choose File > Open, and open the L17strt2.ai file in the Lesson17 folder, located inside the Lessons folder within the AICIB folder on your hard drive.

Because you have set up Illustrator to work with a color management profile, you may be prompted each time you open a new file if you want to change how that file is color managed.

2 At the prompt, select Assign Current Working Space, and click OK.

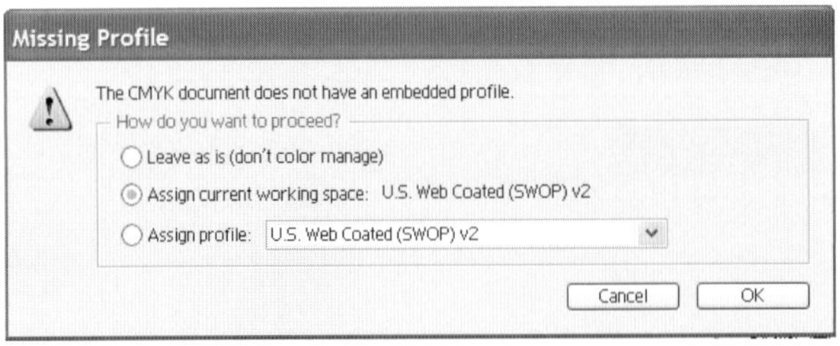

Since Color Management is turned on, you will be prompted with this window when opening files.

3 Choose File > Save As, name the file **Twocolor.ai**, and select the Lesson17 folder in the Save In menu. Leave the type of file format set to Adobe Illustrator® Document, and click Save. In the Illustrator Options dialog box, leave at the defaults and click OK.

4 Make sure that the Color palette and the Swatches palette are open and visible; if they aren't, use the Window menu to display them.

5 From the Color palette's menu (arrow in the upper right of the palette) choose to Show Options.

6 Using the Selection tool click any colored part of the circus tent. Notice the PANTONE 116 C swatch in the Color palette.

Next, you'll replace every instance of the spot color (including any tints of the color) with another spot color.

7 The Swatches palette, like most others, has three different views which you can use. In order to see the swatch color name and the swatch click on the palette menu in the upper right of the Swatch palette and choose List View. This provides you with information such as a visual of the swatch, its name and whether it is a process, RGB or spot color.

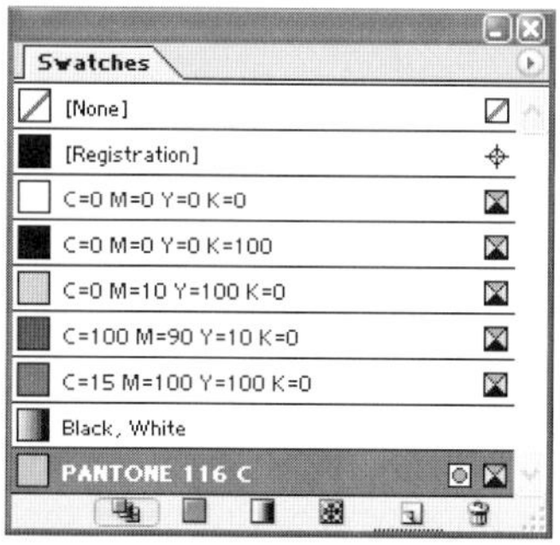

Change the Swatch palette to List View in order to read the swatch names.

8 Choose Select > Deselect or Ctrl+click(Windows) or Command+click (Mac OS) click away from the artwork to deselect it.

9 Choose Window > Swatch Libraries > PANTONE Solid Coated. The PANTONE swatch library appears. From the palette menu change this palette to be in list view.

You can choose new spot colors from the swatch library by typing the number of the color you want to use.

10 Click in the Find text box of the PANTONE Coated palette and type 193. PANTONE 193 C is selected in the palette, as indicated by the white outline around the swatch.

Next, you'll replace the current PANTONE color with the new PANTONE color.

11 Drag the title bar of the PANTONE Solid Coated swatch library closer to the Swatches palette.

12 If necessary, scroll down on the Swatches palette until Pantone 116 is visible, then hold down Alt (Windows) or Option (Mac OS), and drag the PANTONE 193 C swatch from the PANTONE Solid Coated swatch library onto the PANTONE 116 swatch in the Swatches palette.

As you Alt/Option-drag the swatch, the pointer changes to a crosshair.

The PANTONE 193 C replaces the PANTONE 116 C swatch in the Swatches palette, and the artwork is updated with the new PANTONE Solid color.

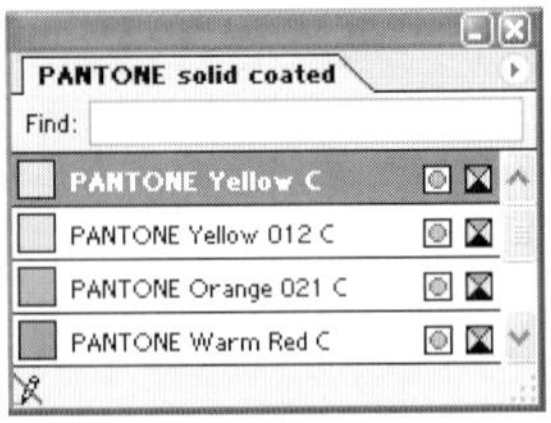

Open PANTONE Solid Coated swatch library.

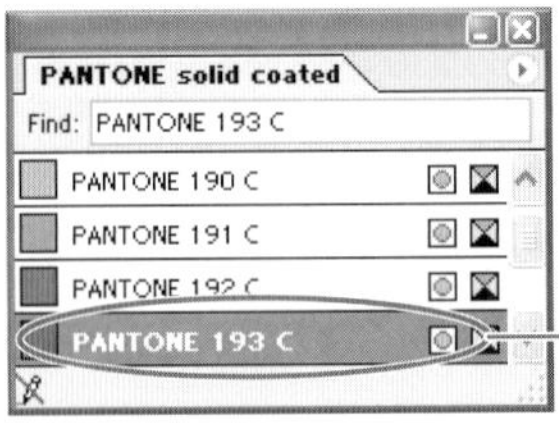

Select PANTONE 193 C swatch.

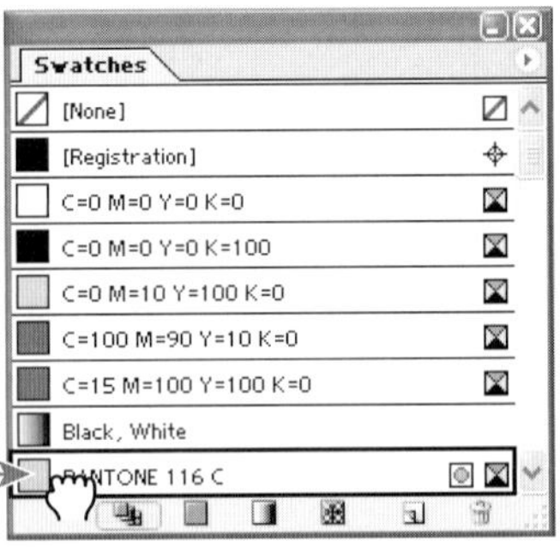

Alt/Option-drag onto swatch to replace in Swatches palette.

Notice that the updated red swatch still is named PANTONE 116 C. You need to rename the updated swatch to avoid confusion about the spot color when your artwork is printed by a commercial press.

13 In the Swatches palette, double-click the updated swatch (still named PANTONE 116 C), and rename the swatch to match its color, PANTONE 193 C. Click OK.

Separating spot colors

As you learned in "Separating colors" earlier in this lesson, you can convert spot colors to their process color equivalents, or you can output them to their own separation. When you're working with a two-color illustration, separating spot colors into their process color equivalents is less cost-effective than outputting the spot color to its own separation (converting to four CMYK plates versus one plate for each individual spot color). You'll deselect the Convert to Process option in the Separation Setup dialog box to output each spot color to its own separation.

Composite image.

Separation 1: Black.

Separation 2: Spot color.

1 Choose File > Print.

2 Click on Output in the Options window on the left.

3 Select Separations (Host-Based) for the Mode.

4 You may notice printer icons to the left of multiple colors. Since this is a two color job, make sure that you leave on only process black and PANTONE 193 C. Click on the printer icon of any unnecessary colors to turn off printing.

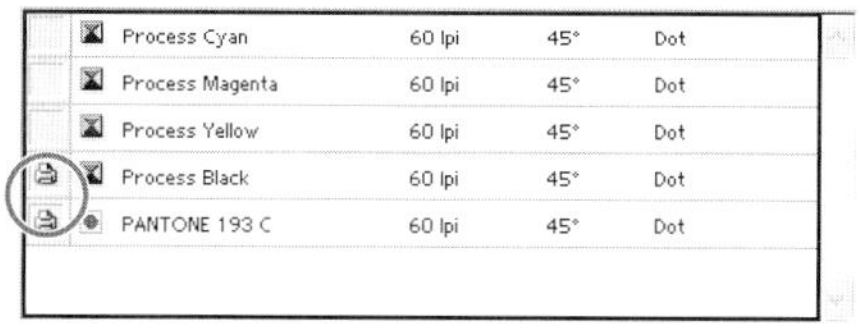

Process Cyan 60 lpi 45° Dot
Process Magenta 60 lpi 45° Dot
Process Yellow 60 lpi 45° Dot
Process Black 60 lpi 45° Dot
PANTONE 193 C 60 lpi 45° Dot

The printer icon indicates that the color will print.

5 Click Save Preset and name the Preset Circus 2-color to save these separation settings.

6 Click Done to save the settings, but do not print at this time.

7 Save and Close the Twocolor.ai file.

Creating a trap

Trapping is used to compensate for any gaps or color shifts that may occur between adjoining or overlapping objects when printing. These gaps or color shifts occur from misregistration, the result of the paper or the printing plates becoming misaligned during printing. Trapping is a technique developed by commercial print shops to slightly overprint the colors along common edges.

Gap created by misregistration.

Gap removed by trapping.

About traps

When overlapping painted objects share a common color, trapping may be unnecessary if the color that is common to both objects creates an automatic trap. For example, if two overlapping objects contain cyan as part of their CMYK values, any gap between them is covered by the cyan content of the object underneath.

Note: *When artwork contains common ink colors, overprinting does not occur on the shared plate—that is, the topmost overlapping printing ink appears opaque.*

There are two types of traps: a spread, in which a lighter object overlaps a darker background and seems to expand into the background; and a choke, in which a lighter background overlaps a darker object that falls within the background and seems to squeeze or reduce the object.

Spread: Object overlaps background.

Choke: Background overlaps object.

You can create both spreads and chokes in the Adobe Illustrator program.

It is generally best to scale your graphic to its final size before adding a trap. Once you create a trap for an object, the amount of trapping increases or decreases if you scale the object (unless you deselect the Scale line weight option in the Scale dialog box). For example, if you create a graphic that has a 0.5-point trap and scale it to five times its original size, the result is a 2.5-point trap for the enlarged graphic.

- From online Help.

Although trapping sounds simple enough, it requires a thorough knowledge of color and design and an eye for determining where trapping is necessary. You can create a trap in Adobe Illustrator using two methods: by applying the Trap filter or Trap effect, for simple artwork whose parts can be selected and trapped individually; and by setting a Stroke value for individual objects you want to trap. Like printing, creating a trap is an art that requires time and experience.

For more information on creating a trap, see "Step 3: Create a trap to compensate for misregistration on press" in online Help.

Now you'll practice creating a simple kind of trap called overprinting.

Overprinting objects

When preparing an image for color separation, you can define how you want overlapping objects of different colors to print. By default, the top object in the Illustrator artwork knocks out, or removes the color of, underlying artwork on the other separations and prints with the color of the top object only. Misregistration may occur when you knock out colors.

Composite image.

First plate.

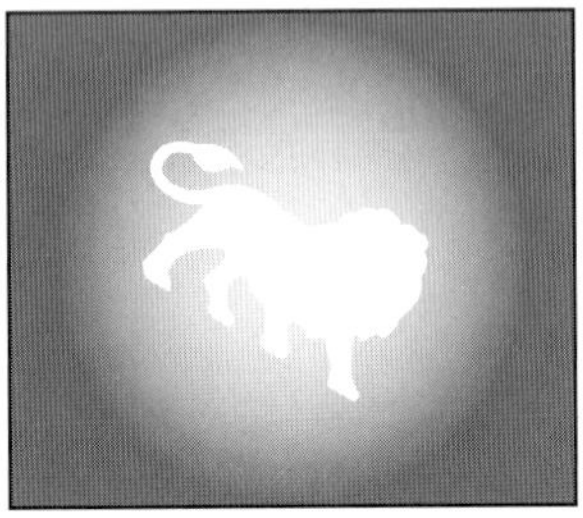

Second plate.

You can also specify objects to *overprint*, or print on top of, any of the artwork under them. Overprinting is the simplest method you can use to prevent misregistration (gaps between colors) on press. The overprinted color automatically traps into the background color.

Composite image.

First plate.

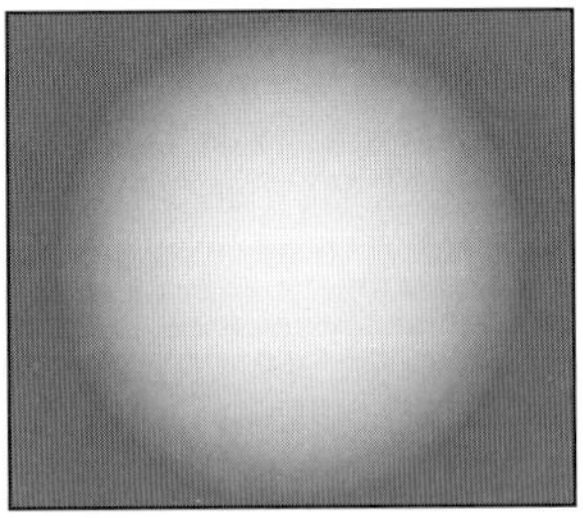

Second plate.

You'll select an object in the circus illustration and apply the overprint option. Then you will preview the overprint on-screen.

1 Choose File > Open. Locate and open the Circus.ai file, which you saved in the Lesson17 folder, inside the Lessons folder within the AICIB folder on your hard drive.

2 In the Missing Profile dialog box, select Assign Current Working Space: US Web Coated (SWOP) v2, and click OK.

The color version of the circus illustration appears.

3 Choose View > Zoom In to zoom in on the lion. You'll be able to see the overprint lines better if you magnify the view of the image. (We zoomed in to 400%.)

4 Select the Selection tool (↖) in the toolbox. Then click the lion to select it.

5 Click the Attributes tab to bring the palette to the front of its group. (If the Attributes palette isn't open, choose Window > Attributes.)

6 In the Attributes palette, select Overprint Fill.

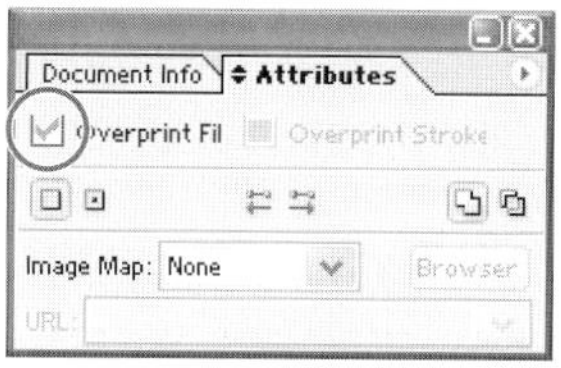

Now you'll see an approximation of how overprinting and blending will appear in the color-separated output.

7 Choose View > Overprint Preview to see the effect of the overprinted objects. The effect is subtle; look closely at the tip of the flag to see the overprinting.

If an object has a stroke, you can also select the Overprint Stroke option to make sure that the stroke overprints on the object below it as well. Next you'll add a stroke to an object to create a trap.

8 With the Selection tool (↖), select the yellow flag to the left of the lion.

9 Click the Color tab to bring the palette to the front.

10 In the Color palette, drag the yellow fill swatch onto the Stroke box to stroke the flag with the same color as its fill.

11 Click the Attributes tab to bring the palette to the front of its group. Select the Overprint Stroke option.

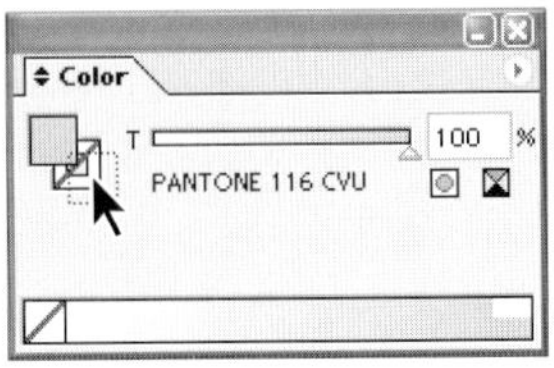

Drag the Fill swatch onto the Stroke box.

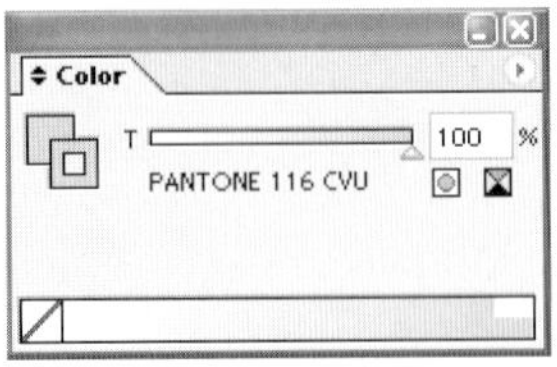

Result.

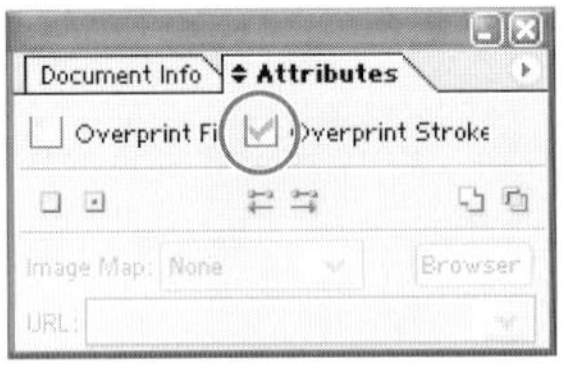

Select Overprint Stroke option.

Depending on what you have discussed with your printing professional, you may want to change the amount of trap specified. You'll try out changing the specified trap now.

12 Select the flag shape with the overprint stroke.

13 Click the Stroke tab to bring the palette to the front of its group. Increase the Stroke weight. In Overprint Preview to you can see the results.

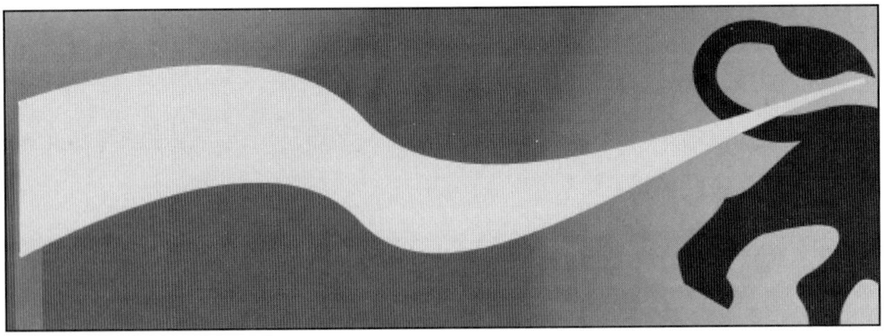
No Overprint preview.

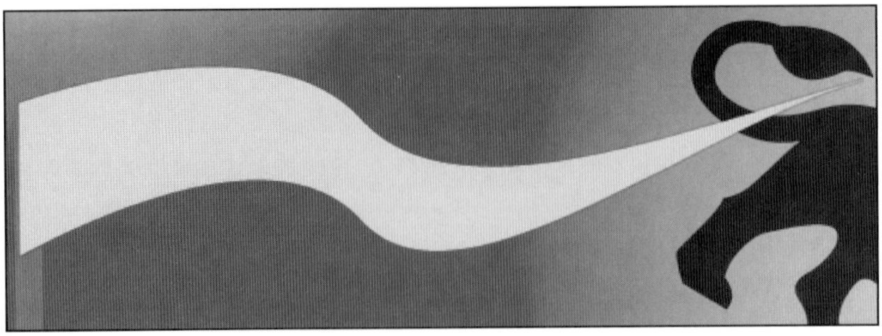
Overprint preview.

Strokes are centered over the object's path. This means that if an object is stroked with the same color as its fill, only half the stroke weight actually overprints. For example, if your printing professional wants a 0.5-point trap added to the yellow flag, you would use a 1-point stroke weight to achieve the trap. Half the stroke will appear inside the fill area and half will appear outside the fill area.

14 Choose File > Save. Choose File > Close to close the file.

You've finished the lesson. In an ordinary workflow situation, you would now be ready to send your artwork to a commercial press to be printed. Include proofs of color separation setups when you send your electronic file to a printer. Also tell your printer about any traps you created in the artwork. Keep in mind that you must remain in close communication with your printing professional for each print job. Each print job has unique requirements that you must consider before you begin the process of color separation.

Review questions

1 How do the RGB and CMYK color gamuts affect the relationship between on-screen colors and printed colors?

2 How can you create a closer match between your on-screen colors and printed colors?

3 What is the benefit of printing interim drafts of your artwork to a black-and-white desktop printer?

4 What does the term color separation mean?

5 What are two ways to output spot colors?

6 What are the advantages of one- or two-color printing?

7 What is trapping?

8 What is a simple method you can use to create trap?

Review answers

1 Each color model has a gamut of color that overlaps, but does not precisely match the others. Because monitors display color using the RGB color gamut and printed artwork uses the smaller CMYK color gamut, there may be times when a printed color cannot precisely match an on-screen color.

2 You can select one of Illustrator's built-in color management profiles to better simulate the relationship between on-screen colors and printed colors. You can choose View > Proof Setup and select an output device profile. Then choose View > Proof Colors to get an on-screen version of how the artwork will look when printed to the selected device.

3 It's a good idea to print black-and-white drafts of your artwork on a desktop printer to check the layout and the accuracy of text and graphics in your publication before incurring the expense of printing to a color printer or imagesetter (for separations).

4 Color separation refers to breaking down composite artwork into its component colors–for example, using the four process colors (cyan, magenta, yellow, and black) to reproduce a large portion of the visible color spectrum.

5 You can convert a spot color to its process color equivalents if a precise color match is not required, or you can output a spot color to its own separation.

6 One- or two-color printing is less expensive than four-color printing, and you can use spot colors for precise color matching.

7 Trapping is a technique developed by commercial print shops to slightly overprint the colors along common edges, and it is used to compensate for any gaps or color shifts that may occur between adjoining or overlapping objects when printed.

8 You can specify objects to overprint, or print on top of, any of the artwork under them. Overprinting is the simplest method you can use to create trap, which compensates for misregistration on press.

Lesson 18

18 Combining Illustrator Graphics and Photoshop Images

You can easily add an image created in an image-editing program to an Adobe Illustrator file. This is an effective method for seeing how a photograph looks incorporated with a line drawing or for trying out Illustrator special effects on bitmap images.

In this lesson, you'll learn how to do the following:

- Differentiate between vector and bitmap graphics.
- Place embedded Adobe Photoshop graphics in an Adobe Illustrator file.
- Create a clipping mask from compound paths.
- Make an opacity mask to display part of the image.
- Sample color in a placed image.
- Replace a placed image with another and update the document.
- Export a layered file to Adobe Photoshop and edit the type.

Combining artwork

You can combine Illustrator artwork with images from other graphics applications in a variety of ways for a wide range of creative results. Sharing artwork between applications lets you combine continuous-tone paintings and photographs with line art. Even though Illustrator lets you create certain types of raster images, Photoshop excels at many image-editing tasks; once done, the images can then be placed in Illustrator.

To illustrate how you can combine bitmap images with vector art and work between applications, this lesson steps you through the process of creating a composite image. In this lesson, you will add photographic images created in Adobe Photoshop to a postcard created in Adobe Illustrator. Then you'll adjust the color in the photo, mask the photo, and sample color from the photo to use in the Illustrator artwork. You'll update a placed image and then export your postcard to Photoshop to complete the type treatment.

Vector versus bitmap graphics

Adobe Illustrator creates vector graphics, also called draw graphics, which are made up of shapes based on mathematical expressions. These graphics consist of clear, smooth lines that retain their crispness when scaled. They are appropriate for illustrations, type, and graphics such as logos that may be scaled to different sizes.

Bitmap images, also called raster images, are based on a grid of pixels and are created by image-editing applications such as Adobe Photoshop. In working with bitmap images, you edit groups of pixels rather than objects or shapes. Because bitmap graphics can represent subtle gradations of shade and color, they are appropriate for continuous-tone images such as photographs or artwork created in painting programs. A disadvantage of bitmap graphics is that they lose definition and appear jagged when scaled up.

Logo drawn as vector art.

Logo rasterized as bitmap art.

In deciding whether to use Illustrator or a bitmap image program such as Photoshop for creating and combining graphics, consider both the elements of the image and how the image will be used. In general, use Illustrator if you need to create art or type with clean lines that will look good at any magnification. In most cases, you will also want to use Illustrator for laying out a design, because Illustrator offers more flexibility in working with type and with reselecting, moving, and altering images. You can create raster images in Illustrator but its pixel-editing tools are limited. Use Photoshop for images that need pixel-editing, color correcting, painting, and other special effects.

Getting started

Before you begin, you'll need to restore the default preferences for Adobe Illustrator. Then you'll open the finished art file for this lesson to see what you'll create.

1 To ensure that the tools and palettes function exactly as described in this lesson, delete or deactivate (by renaming) the Adobe Illustrator CS preferences file. See "Restoring default preferences" on page 2.

2 Start Adobe Illustrator.

3 Choose File > Open, and open the L18end.ai file in the Lesson18 folder, located inside the Lessons folder within the AICIB folder on your hard drive.

4 Choose View > Zoom Out to make the finished artwork smaller, adjust the window size, and leave it on-screen as you work. (Use the Hand tool ( ) to move the artwork where you want it in the window.) If you don't want to leave the image open, choose File > Close.

For an illustration of the finished artwork in this lesson, see the color section.

Now you'll open the start file to begin the lesson.

5 Choose File > Open, and open the L18strt.ai file.

The file has been prepared with three layers: the Text layer, and two additional layers, Layer 1 and Checkerboard, on which you'll place images. Checkerboard also contains objects that you'll make into a mask.

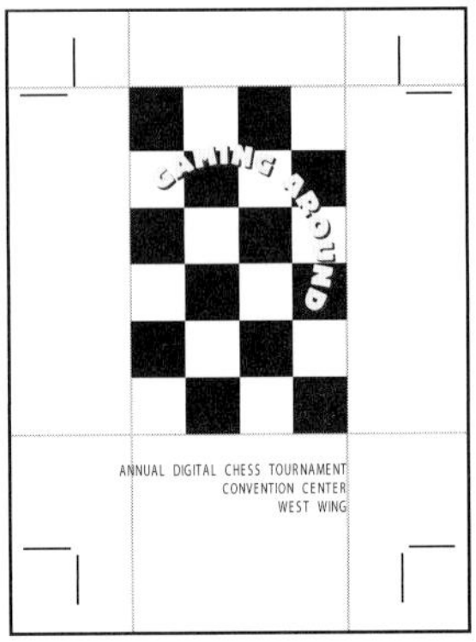

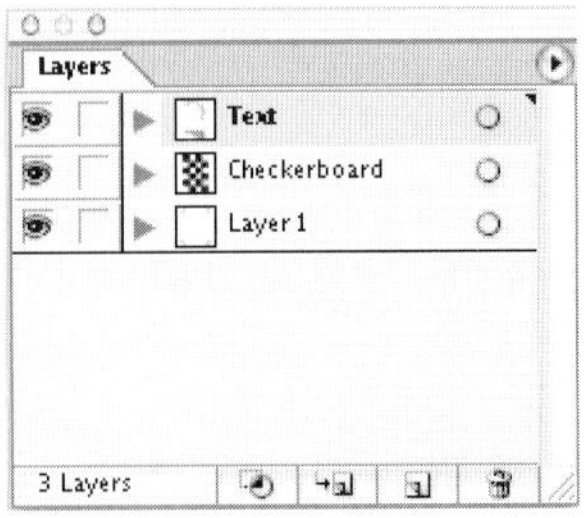

6 Choose File > Save As, name the file **Postcard.ai**, and select the Lesson18 folder. Leave the type of format set to Adobe Illustrator® Document, and click Save. In the Illustrator Options dialog box leave at the defaults and click OK.

Placing an Adobe Photoshop file

You'll begin by placing a Photoshop file in the Illustrator document as an embedded file. Placed files can be embedded or linked. Embedded files are added to the Illustrator file, and the Illustrator file size increases to reflect the addition of the placed file. Linked files remain separate, external files, with a link to the placed file in the Illustrator file. (The linked file must always accompany the Illustrator file, or the link will break and the placed file will not appear in the Illustrator artwork.)

1 Resize the Layers palette so you can see all the layers.

2 In the Layers palette, select the Checkerboard layer.

When you place an image, it is added to the selected layer. You'll use the Checkerboard layer for the placed image, because the layer includes artwork for a mask for the image that you'll create later in the lesson.

3 Choose File > Place.

4 Navigate to the Chess.psd file (in the Lesson18 folder inside the Lessons folder in the AICIB folder on your hard drive), and select it. Do not double-click the file or click Place yet.

5 If Link is checked, uncheck the Link option.

6 Click Place.

7 In the Photoshop Import dialog box, select the Convert Photoshop Layers to Objects option. Click OK.

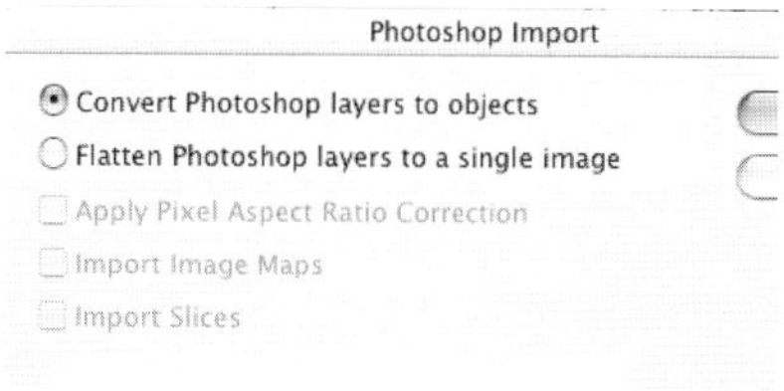

Rather than flatten the file, you want to convert the Photoshop layers to objects because the Chess.psd file contains two layers and one layer mask. You will use them later in the lesson.

Now you'll move the placed image, using the guides in the artwork to place the image precisely.

8 Choose the Selection tool (➤) in the toolbox. Drag the placed image at its edge (but don't grab a bounding box handle because that will resize the image), and drag the image onto the guides provided in the artwork. Release the mouse button when you have aligned the image with the guides.

You can use the arrow keys to nudge the selection into place.

The placed image covers up the squares in the Checkerboard layer. The placed image was added as a sublayer to the Checkerboard layer because it was selected when you chose the Place command.

9 Choose File > Save.

Now you will move the image below the squares and duplicate it.

Placing files

The Place command places files from other applications into Illustrator. Files can be embedded, or included in, the Illustrator file, or they can be linked to the Illustrator file. Linked files remain independent of the Illustrator file, resulting in a smaller Illustrator file. Depending on a preference you set for updating links, the linked image in the Illustrator file may change when the artwork in the linked file changes.

By default, the Link option is selected in the Place dialog box. If you deselect the Link option, the artwork is embedded in the Adobe Illustrator file, resulting in a larger Illustrator file. The Links palette lets you identify, select, monitor, and update objects in the Illustrator artwork that are linked to external files.

Placed bitmap images can be modified using transformation tools and image filters; placed vector artwork is converted to Illustrator paths (embedded images only).

If you place a Photoshop file and deselect the Link option, the Photoshop Import dialog box appears. For information on options in the Photoshop Import dialog box, see Opening Photoshop files in Illustrator in online Help.

Note: Do not place an EPS file containing mesh objects or transparency objects if it was created in an application other than Illustrator. Instead, open the EPS file, copy all objects and then paste in Illustrator.

— From online Help "Placing artwork".

Duplicating a placed image

You can duplicate placed images just as you do other objects in an Illustrator file. The copy of the image can then be modified independently of the original.

Now you'll reposition and duplicate the Chess.psd image in the Layers palette.

1 Click the Expand triangle (▶) to the left of the Checkerboard layer to expand it. Enlarge the Layers palette so that you can see all the contents of the Checkerboard layer.

2 Drag the Chess.psd layer down the list until it is at the bottom of the Checkerboard layer, and then release the mouse button when the indicator bar appears between the last <Path> layer and Layer 1.

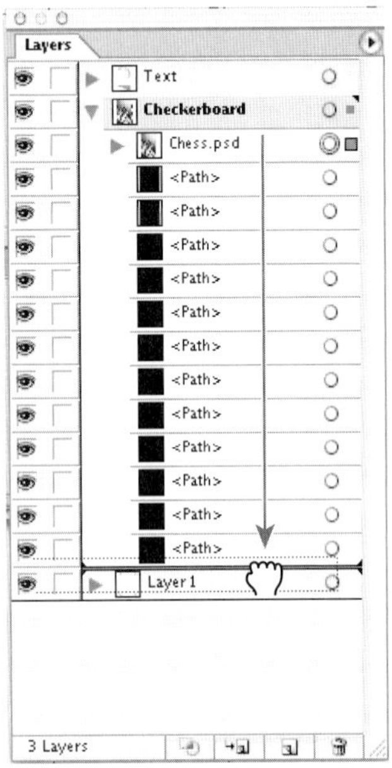

Indicator bar.

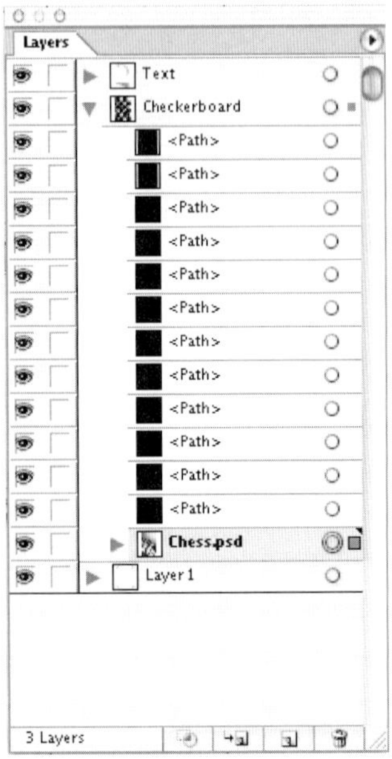

Chess.psd layer moved.

3 Click the triangle to the left of the Chess.psd layer to expand it. Notice that the Chess.psd layer has two sublayers, Masked King and Background. You will now duplicate the Background layer.

4 To duplicate the Background layer, click on the named layer and drag its thumbnail onto the New Layer button at the bottom of the Layers palette. Another layer called Background is created.

5 Double-click the lower Background layer and rename it Blue Chess.psd. Click OK. You will change the color of this image later in the lesson.

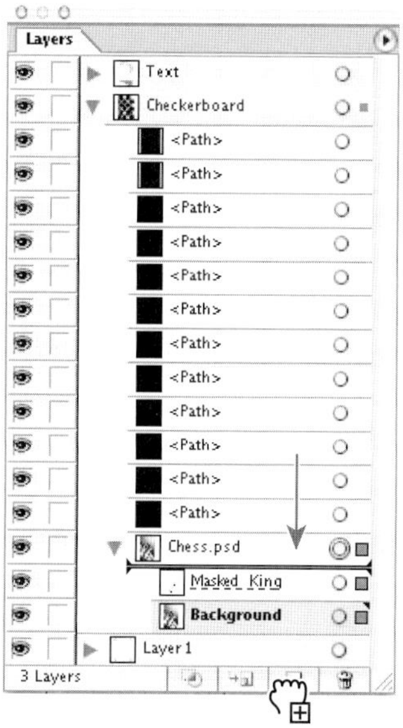

Duplicate Background layer.

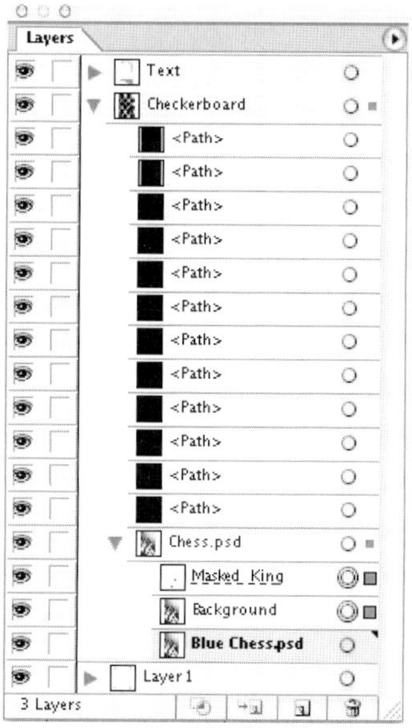

Rename layer.

6 Choose File > Save.

Adjusting color in a placed image

You can use filters to modify colors in placed images in a variety of ways. You can use filters to convert to a different color mode (such as RGB, CMYK, or grayscale) or to adjust individual color values. You can also use filters to saturate or desaturate (darken or lighten) colors, or invert colors (create a color negative).

For information on color modes and modifying colors with filters, see "About Color models and color modes" and "Applying filters and effects" in online Help.

In this section, you'll adjust colors in the Background layer. Later in the lesson, you'll apply a mask to this image and then adjust colors in the Blue Chess.psd layer so that the two layers appear in contrasting colors through the mask.

1 In the Layers palette, select the Background sublayer.

2 Click the eye icon to the far left of the Masked King layer to hide it.

When you hide a layer, all objects on that layer are deselected, hidden, and locked.

3 In the Layers palette, click the selection column to the far right of the Background layer to select its contents quickly.

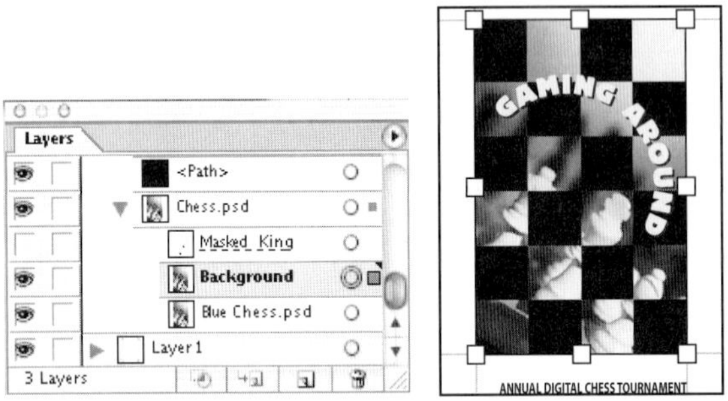

Masked King layer hidden and contents of Background layer selected.

4 Choose Filter > Colors > Adjust Colors.

5 In the Adjust Colors dialog box, select Preview so that you can see the color changes. Drag the sliders or enter values for the CMYK percentages to change the colors in the image. You can press Tab to move between the text boxes. (We used the following values to create an orange cast: C=–23, M=20, Y=74, and K=–52.)

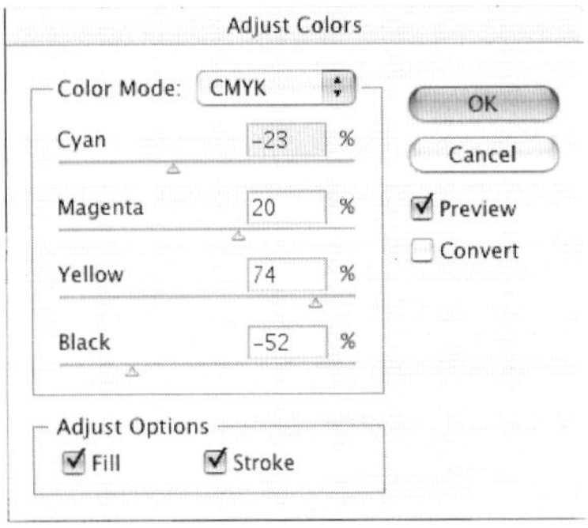

6 When you are satisfied with the color in the image, click OK.

7 Click outside the artwork to deselect the Background image, and then choose File > Save.

Besides using filters to adjust colors, you can also use filters to apply special effects to images, distort images, produce a hand-drawn appearance, and create other interesting effects. See "Changing the appearance of bitmap images with filters and effects" in Online Help .

Masking an image

Masks crop part of an image so that only a portion of the image appears through the shape of the mask. You can make a mask from a single path or a compound path. You can also import masks made in Photoshop files.

Creating compound path and opacity masks

In this section, you'll create a compound path from the checkerboard pattern on the Checkerboard layer and create an opacity mask from the compound path, so that the Background layer appears through the mask. Then you'll adjust the colors in Blue Chess.psd to contrast with the Background layer. You'll also use an opacity mask that was created in Photoshop and saved as a layer mask.

1 Select the Magic Wand tool ( ) in the toolbox.

2 Using the Magic Wand tool, click the upper left black square in the checkerboard pattern to select all the black squares. This action selects the checkerboard and deselects the background.

You can use the Magic Wand tool to select all objects in a document with the same or similar fill color, stroke weight, stroke color, opacity, or blending mode. See "Using the Magic Wand tool and palette" in online Help.

3 Choose Object > Compound Path > Make.

Notice how all the squares have been placed onto one layer, called <Compound Path>, in the Layers palette.

The Compound Path command creates a single compound object from two or more objects. Compound paths act as grouped objects. The Compound Path command lets you create complex objects more easily than if you used the drawing tools or the Pathfinder commands.

4 With the checkerboard still selected in the artwork, in the Layers palette Shift+click the selection column to the far right of the Background layer to select it and add it to the <Compound Path> selection. (The selection indicator (■) will appear and the Background layer will be added to the selection.)

Both the masking object and the object to be masked must be selected in order to create a mask.

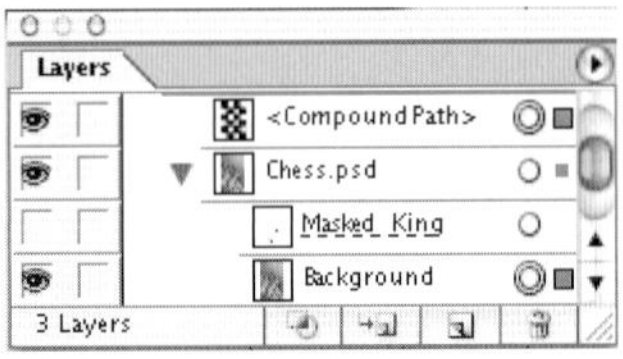

Background and <Compound Path> selected.

5 Click the Transparency palette tab to bring it to the front of its group. (If the Transparency palette isn't visible on-screen, choose Window > Transparency.)

6 From the Transparency palette menu, choose Show Options to expand the palette fully.

Now you'll mask the Background layer with an opacity mask that lets you use the change in luminosity in the overlying checkerboard to affect the background. Similar to a clipping mask, an opacity mask lets you make color and other fine adjustments that you can't make with a clipping mask.

7 From the Transparency palette menu, choose Make Opacity Mask. You will not see the effect until you select both the Clip and Invert Mask options.

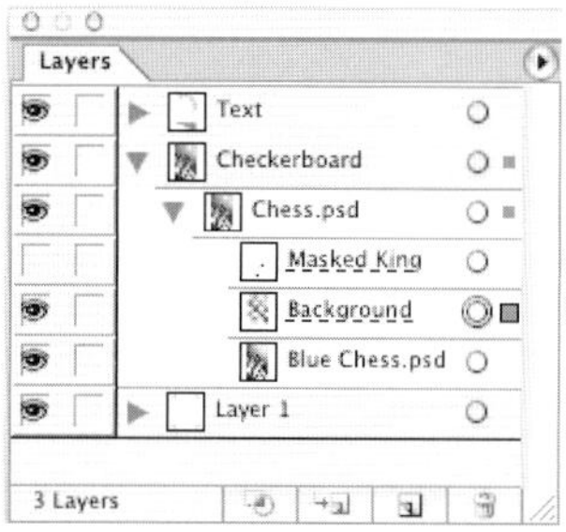

Dotted line indicates mask.

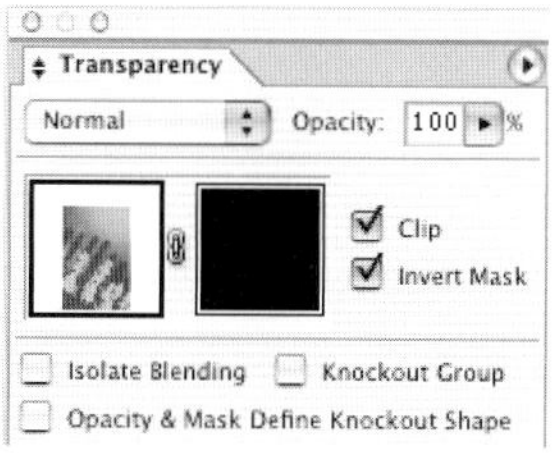

Preview includes opacity mask.

The checkerboard pattern is assigned a fill and stroke of None, and the Background layer is masked with the checkerboard pattern, as indicated by the dotted underline beneath the layer name. The Blue Chess.psd layer appears through the masked sections of the Background layer.

Now you'll apply the Adjust Colors filter to the Blue Chess.psd layer to create a stronger contrast between the two images.

8 In the Layers palette, click the selection indicator for the Blue Chess.psd layer to select only its contents.

9 Choose Filter > Colors > Adjust Colors.

The most recently used filter (in this case, Adjust Colors) appears at the top of the Filter menu, letting you easily reapply the filter. (Choosing Filter > Apply Adjust Colors would apply the filter with the same settings used on the Background layer.)

10 Click Preview to preview changes in the artwork.

11 Drag the sliders for the CMYK values to change the colors in the image. (We used the following values to create a blue cast: C=12, M=–10, Y=–74, and K=–31.) You can compare the color in Blue Chess.psd to that in the Background layer to choose a color that contrasts effectively.

12 When you are satisfied with the color, click OK. Using the Selection tool, click outside the artwork to deselect the Blue Chess.psd image.

13 Choose File > Save.

Editing an imported mask

You've made an opacity mask from artwork created in Illustrator. Now you'll use a mask that was created in Photoshop and imported when you placed the Chess.psd file. You'll experiment with changing the color of the image and then adjusting the transparency of the opacity mask to tone down the effect.

1 In the Layers palette, click the eye column to show the Masked King layer.

2 Click the selection indicator (■) for the Masked King layer to select its contents. (The dotted line under its layer name indicates that the Masked King layer has an opacity mask applied to it.)

3 Choose Filter > Colors > Adjust Colors.

4 In the Adjust Colors dialog box, click Preview to preview changes in the artwork. Drag the sliders for the CMYK values to change the colors in the image. (We used the following values to create a strong purple cast: C=60, M=60, Y=–46, and K=–60.) Click OK.

5 In the Transparency palette, change the opacity setting to **75%** for the Masked King layer.

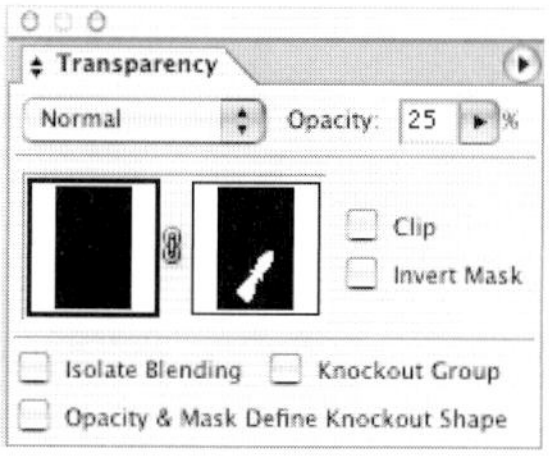

Mask opacity set to 75%

Result

For a dramatic effect you will now invert the opacity mask. This will subdue the Background and Blue Chess.psd layers and make the Masked King layer pop visually.

6 In the Transparency palette, select the Invert Mask option to reverse the effect of the opacity mask.

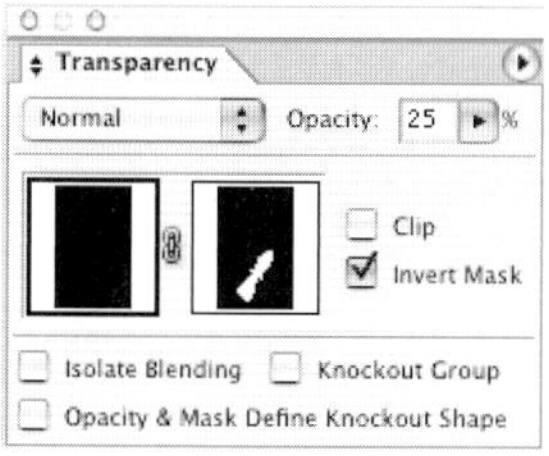

Mask inverted.

Result.

7 Click outside the artwork to deselect the Masked King layer.

8 Choose File > Save.

Sampling colors in placed images

You can sample, or copy, the colors in placed images, to apply the colors to other objects in the artwork. Sampling colors enables you to easily make colors consistent in a file combining Photoshop images and Illustrator artwork.

Copying attributes between objects

You can use the Eyedropper tool to copy colors from any object in an Illustrator file–from a paint swatch or from anywhere on the desktop, including from another application. You can then use the Paint Bucket tool to apply the current paint attributes to an object. Together these tools let you copy the paint attributes from anywhere on-screen to other objects.

By default, the Eyedropper and Paint Bucket tools affect all paint attributes of an object. You can use the tool's options dialog box to change the object's attributes. You can also use the Eyedropper tool and Paint Bucket tool to copy and paste type attributes.

— From online Help "Copying attributes between objects."

In this section, you'll use the Eyedropper tool to sample colors from the placed image, and apply the colors to selected type on the Text layer.

1 Use the Selection tool ( ) to click in the text at the bottom of the artwork to select the entire text block.

2 Select the Eyedropper tool ( ), and Shift+click in the image to sample a color to be applied to the selected text. (We chose a medium-purple color near the center of the image, between the king and queen chess pieces.)

The color you sample is applied to the selected text.

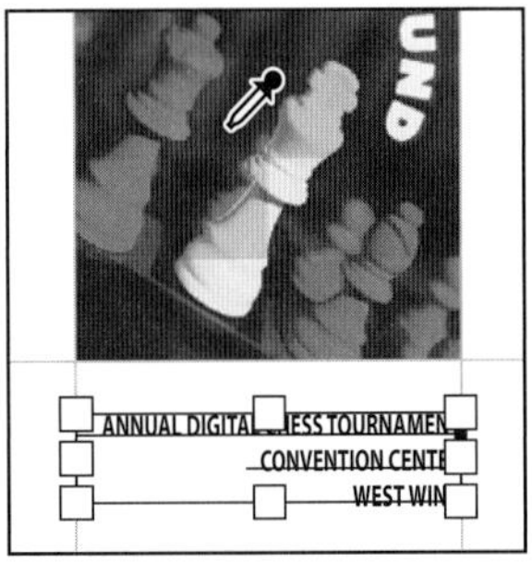

3 Choose File > Save.

Replacing a placed image

You can easily replace a placed image with another image to update a document. The replacement image is positioned exactly where the original image was, so you don't have to align the replacement image. (If you scaled the original images, you may have to resize the replacement image to match the original image.)

Now you'll replace the Blue Chess.psd image with the Chess2.psd image to create a new version of the postcard.

1 Choose File > Save As, name the file **Postcard2.ai**, and select the Lesson18 folder in the Save In menu. Leave the type of format set to Adobe Illustrator® Document, and click Save. In the Illustrator options dialog box, leave at the defaults and click OK.

2 Click the Links tab to bring the Links palette to the front of its group. (If the Links palette isn't visible on-screen, choose Window > Links.)

3 Click the last link in the Links palette to select it. (These links don't have names because we embedded them instead of linking them.)

4 Click the Relink button ( )at the bottom of the Links palette.

5 In the Place dialog box, navigate to the Chess2.psd image in the Lesson18 folder and select it. Make sure that the Link option is deselected. Click Place to replace the Blue Chess.psd image with the new one.

The replacement image appears in the Chess.psd layer with no color adjustments applied. When you replace an image, color adjustments you made to the original image are not applied to the replacement. However, masks applied to the original image are preserved. Any layer modes and transparency adjustments you've made to other layers also may affect the image's appearance.

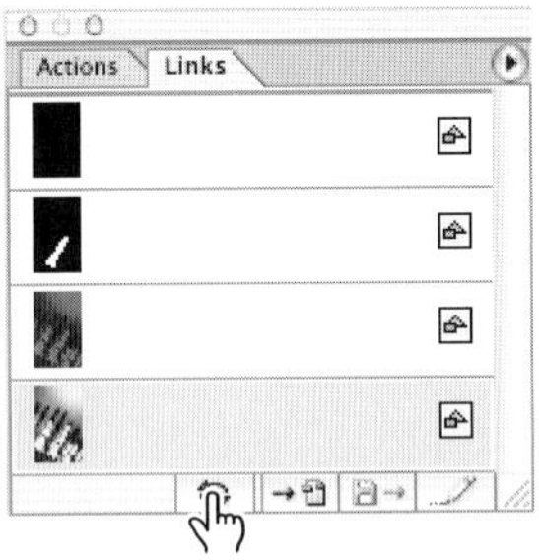

Select image in Links palette.

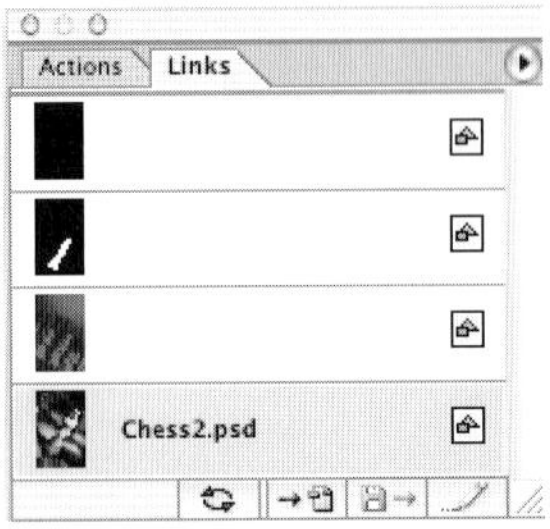

Click Replace Link button to replace with new image.

6 Choose File > Save.

You have completed the lesson. If you want to learn how to open and manipulate a layered Illustrator file in Photoshop, continue. If not, skip to "Exploring on your own".

Exporting a layered file to Photoshop

Not only can you open layered Photoshop files in Illustrator, but you can also save layered Illustrator files and then open them in Photoshop. Working with layered files between Illustrator and Photoshop is very helpful when creating and editing Web graphics. You can preserve the hierarchical relationship of the layers by selecting the Write Nested Layers option when saving your file. You can also open and edit type objects.

Now you'll adjust the Text layer and then you'll export the file, change its color mode and save it in layered Photoshop format so that you can edit it in Photoshop.

1 Click the Layers tab to bring the palette to the front of its group.

2 In the Layers palette, click the triangle (▶) to the left of the Text layer to expand its list.

3 Drag the Annual Digital Chess sublayer out of and above the Text layer. It is now its own layer instead of a sublayer nested in the Text layer.

To keep the Illustrator type layer editable when opened in Photoshop, the type layer must reside by itself on the topmost layer and not be nested inside another layer. Illustrator also cannot export area type, type on a path, or multicolored type to Photoshop as editable text.

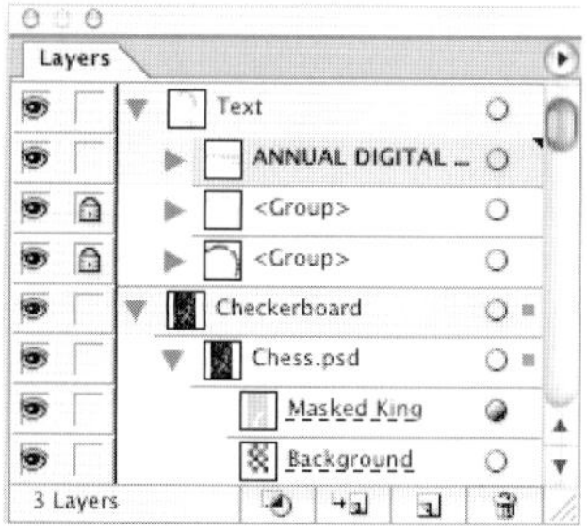

Select sublayer. Drag out of nested hierarchy to own layer.

4 Choose File > Export.

5 Navigate to the folder where you'll save the file, and name the file **Postcard2.psd.** Changing the file name preserves your original Illustrator file.

6 Choose Photoshop (PSD) from the Save as Type (Windows) or Format (Mac OS) pop-up menu, and click Save (Windows) or Export (Mac OS).

7 In the Photoshop Options dialog box, choose CMYK as the Color Model, select Screen (72 ppi) for Resolution, and check Write Layers. Leave Preserve Text Editability and Maximum Editability Checked. Check Anti-Alias. Click OK.

The Anti-alias option removes jagged edges in the artwork. The Write Layers option lets you export each Illustrator top-level layer as a separate Photoshop layer.

8 Start Adobe Photoshop.

9 Open the Postcard2.psd file that you exported in step 7.

10 If prompted to update text layers, click Update.

You'll edit the text you just exported to shorten it and increase its type size.

11 Select the Type tool in the toolbox.

12 Click the Type tool within the ANNUAL DIGITAL CHESS text, and choose Select > All to select all the text.

13 In the Options bar, click the Palettes button to display the Character palette. In the Character palette, edit the type by changing the point size to **24 pt** and the leading to **24 pt.**

14 In the Options bar, click the Flush Left button to move the text flush left.

15 Using the Type tool, select and delete the CONVENTION CENTER WEST WING text. (You may have to scroll to see the text.)

16 In the image, use the Selection tool to move the type so that its left edge aligns with the left edge of the image.

17 Choose File > Save. Choose File > Close to close the file.

You've completed the lesson on combining Illustrator graphics and Photoshop images, and learned how easy it is to work between the two applications.

Exploring on your own

Now that you know how to place and mask an image in an Illustrator file, you can place other images and apply a variety of modifications to the images. You can also create masks for images from objects you create in Illustrator. For more practice, try the following:

- Repeat the lesson using the Chess2.psd image in place of the Chess.psd image. In addition to adjusting color in the copies of the image, apply transformation effects, such as shearing or rotating, or filters or effects, such as one of the Artistic or Distort filters/effects, to create contrast between the two images in the checkerboard pattern.
- Use the basic shapes tools or the drawing tools to draw objects to create a compound path to use as a mask. Then place the Chess.psd image into the file with the compound path, and apply the compound path as a mask.
- Create large type and use the type as a mask to mask a placed object.

Review questions

1 Describe the difference between linking and embedding a placed file in Illustrator.

2 How do you create an opacity mask for a placed image?

3 What kinds of objects can be used as masks?

4 What color modifications can you apply to a selected object using filters?

5 Describe how to replace a placed image with another image in a document.

Review answers

1 A linked file is a separate, external file connected to the Illustrator file by an electronic link. A linked file does not add significantly to the size of the Illustrator file. The linked file must accompany the Illustrator file to preserve the link and ensure that the placed file appears in the Illustrator file. An embedded file is included in the Illustrator file. The Illustrator file size reflects the addition of the embedded file. Because the embedded file is part of the Illustrator file, no link can be broken. Both linked and embedded files can be updated using the Replace Link button in the Links palette.

2 You create an opacity mask by placing the object to be used as a mask on top of the object to be masked. Then you select the mask and the objects to be masked, and choose Make Opacity Mask from the Transparency palette menu.

3 A mask can be a simple or compound path. You can use type as a mask. You can import opacity masks with placed Photoshop files. You can also create layer clipping masks with any shape that is the topmost object of a group or layer.

4 You can use filters to change the color mode (RGB, CMYK, or Grayscale) or adjust individual colors in a selected object. You can also saturate or desaturate colors or invert colors in a selected object. You can apply color modifications to placed images, as well as to artwork created in Illustrator.

5 To replace a placed image, select the placed image in the Links palette. Then click the Replace Link button, and locate and select the image to be used as the replacement. Then click Place. The replacement image appears in the artwork in place of the original image.

Lesson 19

19 Creating a Web Publication

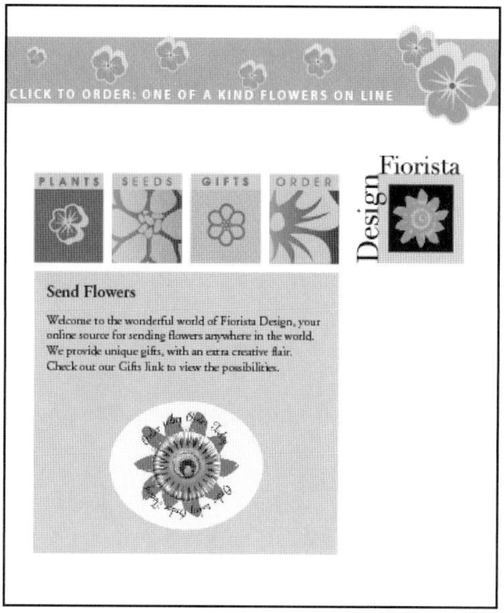

CLICK TO ORDER: ONE OF A KIND FLOWERS ON LINE
PLANTS
SEEDS
GIFTS
ORDER
Fiorista
Design
Send Flowers
Welcome to the wonderful world of Fiorista Design, your online source for sending flowers anywhere in the world. We provide unique gifts, with an extra creative flair. Check out our Gifts link to view the possibilities.

It's easy to design Web-ready, HTML pages in Illustrator that load quickly in browsers and maintain the artwork's integrity. Using slices, you can divide artwork and optimize it for size and quality in different Web file formats–including GIF or PNG-8 file format for flat-color art, JPEG or PNG-24 for continuous-tone photos and gradients, SWF for sound and animation, and HTML for text. You can animate slices, link them to URLs, or use them as HTML text.

In this lesson, you'll learn how to do the following:

• Determine which file format to use to publish different styles of artwork on the Web.

• Use Web-safe colors in your artwork.

• Link objects to URL addresses.

• Export different styles of artwork to GIF and JPEG formats.

• Create artwork for a simple animation and export it to the Macromedia® Flash™ (SWF) format.

• Export your Illustrator design as a completed HTML page with a folder of images ready to post to a Web site.

• Update artwork created in Adobe Illustrator and Adobe Photoshop, and then update your Web site with the edited image.

Important: During this lesson, you can preview the Web page, including links to URLs, on your local computer via your browser. However, you can only preview links to external URLs if your browser has a live connection to the Internet.

About Web format and compression options

Creating small graphic files is key to distributing images on the World Wide Web. With smaller files, Web servers can store and transmit images more efficiently, and viewers can download images more quickly. You decrease file size by saving your artwork in one of several compressed file formats like GIF, JPEG, or PNG.

Other formats used on the Web include SVG (Scalable Vector Graphics), Macromedia Flash (SWF), and HTML. SVG is an XML-based language for describing interactive, animated, two-dimensional graphics. The SVG format supports vector graphics (lines and curves), but it also supports text and raster images. Its feature set includes transformations, transparency, clipping paths, and filter effects. SVG files can easily be combined with HTML and JavaScript in Web pages.

For publishing vector artwork and sound in interactive Web sites and animations, the Macromedia Flash (SWF) file format works well with HTML and JavaScript.

The following table describes the file formats generally recommended for displaying specific types of artwork on the Web. Keep in mind, however, that the file format you choose for your artwork may also be determined by the quality and size of the image you want to place on the Web.

Slice format	Advantages and compression options
HTML	Ideal for plain HTML text.
GIF	Standard for logos and art with solid flat color. Choose dithering options, set transparency and interlacing.
JPEG	Standard format for photos and images with transparency and gradient color. Specify compression quality, whether the image loads progressively, and optimization controls.
PNG	Ideal for images when transparency is required. Specify whether to use PNG-8 or PNG-24 format, as well as other options including color reduction controls, dithering options, and more.
SVG	Ideal for vector-based graphics, especially when collaborating with developers. Choose whether fonts and images are embedded or linked as well as other compression options.
SWF	Ideal for vector-based graphics.

For more information on exporting images for the Web, see "Saving and Exporting Artwork" in online Help.

Image quality versus compression

There's always a trade-off between image quality and amount of compression: Higher quality images use less compression (and thus take longer to download) than lower quality images. The JPEG format uses a lossy compression method, in which data is discarded during compression. The JPEG compression method can degrade sharp detail in an image, such as type and line drawings. You specify the amount of compression to be applied by choosing a quality setting. A higher quality setting results in less data being discarded.

Note: *Data is discarded from a JPEG image each time you save the file. You should always save JPEG files from the original artwork, not from a previously saved JPEG file.*

The GIF format uses a lossless compression method, in which no data is discarded during compression. You can save a GIF file multiple times without discarding data. However, because GIF files are 8-bit color, optimizing an original 24-bit image (artwork created on a system displaying millions of colors) as an 8-bit GIF can degrade image quality.

The PNG-8 format is similar to the GIF format in that it is lossless and uses 8-bit color. It uses a more advanced compression scheme than GIF and depending on the image's color patterns, some PNG-8 files can be 10% to 30% smaller than GIF files. The disadvantage to using PNG-8, however, is that not all browsers support it. Thus, it may be advisable to avoid this format if your image needs to be accessible to the widest possible audience.

Using Web-safe colors to prevent dithering

Creating images in Web safe colors is becoming less of an issue as better equipment saturates the market. Creating in Web-safe colors should not be a concern if you are designing for an Intranet environment and know the company specifications for displays. But you should become educated as to what is involved with colors and the odd results that can occur if images are not saved with limitations in mind.

Most images viewed on the Web are created using 24-bit color displays, but some Web browsers are on computers using only 8-bit color displays, so that Web images often contain colors not available to those Web browsers. Computers use a technique called dithering to simulate colors not available in the color display system. Dithering adjusts adjacent pixels of different colors to give the appearance of a third color. (For example, a blue color and a yellow color may dither in a mosaic pattern to produce the poor illusion of a green color that does not appear in the color palette.)

Dithering can occur when you export artwork to GIF or PNG-8 formats if Illustrator attempts to simulate colors that appear in the original artwork but don't appear in the color palette you specify. It can also occur in GIF or JPEG images when a Web browser using an 8-bit color display attempts to simulate colors that are in the image but not in the browser's color palette. You can minimize dithering by shifting individual or groups of colors to their closest Web-palette equivalent. You can also control dithering done by Web browsers by painting your artwork with Web-safe colors from the Web palette. Web-safe colors can be displayed by any browser that uses an 8-bit or 24-bit color display.

For an example of dithering that occurs in a GIF image that has not been painted with Web-safe colors compared to a GIF image that has been painted with them, see the color section of this book.

Getting started

In this lesson, you'll create an HTML Web page along with a folder of images. You will optimize Web graphics by creating slices. The page will include links from several buttons to a URL, and a simple animation for a Web banner using symbols.

You'll start by previewing the completed Web page in your Web browser.

1 Launch your Web browser.

2 From the desktop, navigate to the Flwrhome.html file, located in the L19Web folder, inside the Lesson19 folder that is inside the Lessons folder within the AICIB folder on your hard drive. Drag and drop the Flwrhome.html into your browser. Notice the animation at the top, and the links in the navigation bar.

3 If you have a live Internet connection, click one of the navigation buttons to jump to its link.

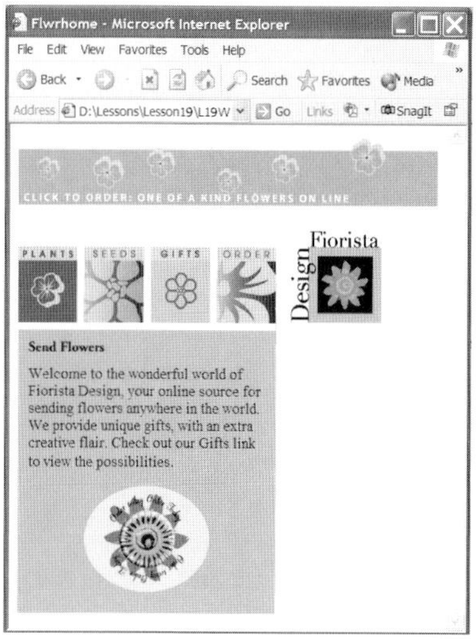

Flwrhome.html.

4 When you have finished exploring the page, close the browser window or exit the browser.

5 To ensure that the tools and palettes function exactly as described in this lesson, delete or deactivate (by renaming) the Adobe Illustrator CS preferences file. See “Restoring default preferences” on page 2.

6 Start Adobe Illustrator.

7 Choose File > Open, and open the L19comp.ai file in the L19Start folder, located in the Lesson19 folder that is inside the Lessons folder within the AICIB folder on your hard drive.

The artwork in this file is a design mock-up of a Web home page. The design for the completed page includes several styles of artwork, including flat-color, continuous-tone, and gradient-filled artwork.

CLICK TO ORDER: ONE OF A KIND FLOWERS ON LINE
Fiorista
Design
PLANTS
SEEDS
GIFTS
ORDER
Send Flowers
Welcome to the wonderful world of Fiorista Design, your online source for sending flowers anywhere in the world. We provide unique gifts, with an extra creative flair. Check out our Gifts link to view the possibilities.

L19comp.ai.

8 If the Layers palette isn’t visible on-screen, choose Window > Layers to display it.

9 Using the Selection tool (↖), click the various components in the artwork to examine them. Notice in the Layers palette which layers correspond to the styles of artwork in the design, as follows:

• Navigation bar–The four buttons incorporate two flat-color artwork and two gradient backgrounds. All four are made into buttons that link to a URL address.

• Sticker–This artwork includes a placed photograph, which is a continuous-tone bitmap image imported from Adobe Photoshop.

• Text–This layer is placeholder text for HTML text.

• Animation–created in Illustrator at the top of the page.

10 If you like, choose View > Zoom Out to make the design mock-up smaller, adjust the window size, and leave it on your screen as you work. (Use the Hand tool () to move the artwork where you want it in the window.) If you don't want to leave the artwork open, choose File > Close.

For an illustration of the finished artwork in this lesson, see the color section of this book.

Now you're ready to begin the Web page design.

Slicing artwork for Web pages

You'll create slices in the Web design to define its different Web elements. Slicing a design into small pieces lets you designate areas in an image as different file formats for different Web elements (such as GIF for a logo and JPEG for a gradient), to make the Web page load more quickly and to assign special behaviors, such as links to sections of a page.

When you save the artwork as a Web page, you can save each slice as an independent file with its own format, settings, and color palette. Using these slices, Illustrator creates an HTML table or cascading style sheet to contain and align the slices. (If you want, you can generate an HTML file that contains the sliced image along with the table of cascading style sheets.)

Creating slices from objects

You can create slices based on objects (or layers). Illustrator updates these slices automatically if you move or edit the selection, and uses these auto slices to create a valid HTML table if you save artwork as a Web page.

1 Choose File > Open, and open the L19strt1.ai file in the L19Start folder, located in the Lesson19 folder.

2 Choose File > Save As, rename the file **Flwrhome.ai**, and select the L19Start folder in the Save In menu. Leave the type of format set to Adobe Illustrator® Document, and click Save. In the Illustrator Native Options dialog box, leave at the defaults and click OK.

You'll start by slicing the buttons on the navigation bar.

3 In the Layers palette, Alt-click (Windows) or Option-click (Mac OS) the eye icon to the left of the Navigation Bar layer to hide all layers except the navigation bar. (Hiding the layers also locks them.) You won't use the hidden layers just yet.

The navigation bar contains two buttons with gradations and two buttons with flat color. You'll slice the buttons to optimize them individually with different format and compression settings.

4 Click the triangle next to the Navigation Bar layer to expand it. If necessary, resize the Layers palette to see all the layers.

5 Select the Selection tool (↖) in the toolbar. Then select the Gifts button in the artwork. Select the entire Gifts button layer by clicking the radio button (○) to the right of the named layer. Like the other buttons, the Gifts button elements have been grouped.

6 In the Layers palette, notice the blue square to the right of the layer, indicating that the sublayer is selected. You'll define your first slice based on this sublayer.

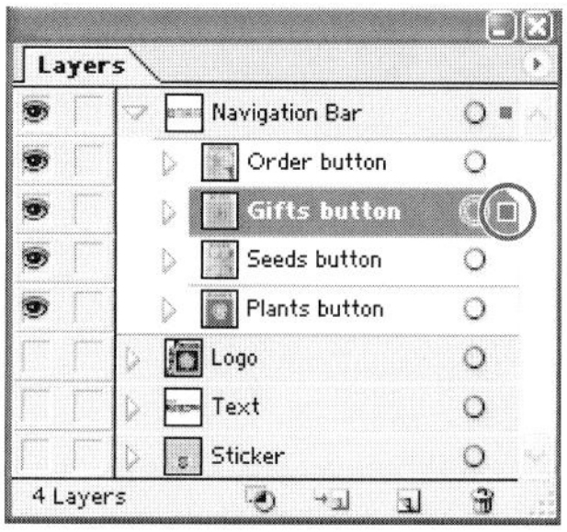

Selected sublayer.

7 Use the zoom shortcut, press Control+Spacebar (Windows) or Command+spacebar (Mac OS) and click once or twice on the selected Gift Button object on the artboard to zoom in to 150% on the artwork.

Now you'll create a slice that matches the boundary of one of the buttons in your artwork using the Make Slice command. This command defines the size of the slice according to a selection's rectangular bounding box.

8 Choose Object > Slice > Make. A series of numbered red outlines appear to indicate the position and order of the slices.

The Make Slice command creates auto slices for any areas of your artwork not already defined by slices.

9 Notice the semitransparent pink slices. These are subslices, also generated automatically by Illustrator, to indicate how overlapping slices will be divided.

Although subslices are numbered and display a slice symbol, you cannot select them separately from the underlying slice. Illustrator regenerates subslices every time you arrange the stacking order of slices.

10 Using the Selection tool (), move the Gift button to underneath the Plants button. Notice that the slices move with the object.

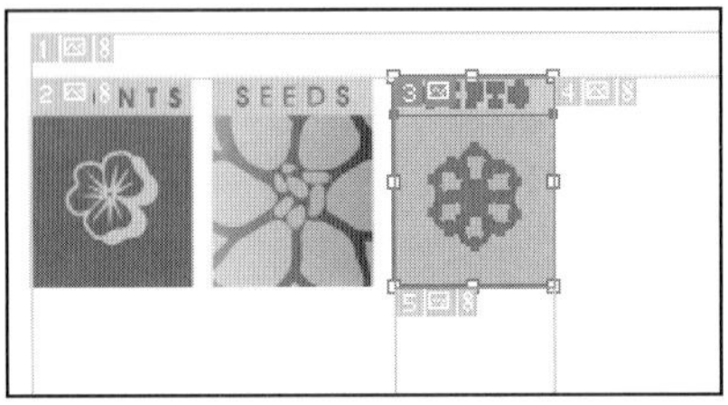

Sliced button.

Slice updated on moving object .

11 Return the slice to its original position by choosing Edit > Undo.

If you inadvertently create a slice from the wrong selection, you can delete the slices and start over. Simply choose Object > Slice > Delete All.

Creating slices from a selection

You can also define slices based on selections in the image, guides, or by using the Slice tool. Now you'll create slices using several other techniques to define the remaining buttons on the navigation bar.

1 In the Layers palette, click the triangle to the left of the Navigation Bar layer to collapse the sublayers. Then click the eye column to the left of the Sticker layer to make it visible.

2 Click the triangle next to the Sticker layer to expand it. Resize the Layers palette so that you can see the layer and its sublayers.

3 Choose View > Fit in Window to see the sticker clearly.

4 With the Selection tool, in the artwork, select the sticker. Its artwork, like the buttons, is grouped.

You can create slices from selections, guides, or objects–called custom slices. You can also define the slice dimensions separate from the underlying artwork.

5 Choose Object > Slice > Create from Selection.

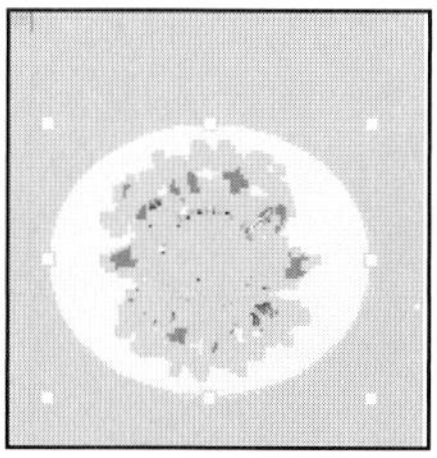

Select the Sticker.

Turn it into a slice.

Custom slices appear as items in the Layers palette, labeled as <Slice>. You can move, resize, and delete them in the same way as other vector objects. However, custom slices do not update automatically if you move them.

6 In the Layers palette, notice the sublayer <Slice>, the custom slice you just created.

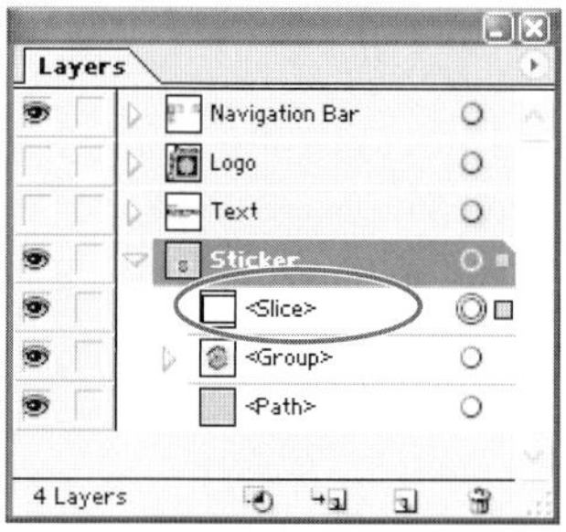

7 Select the remaining navigation buttons in turn, and repeat steps 4 and 5 to create a slice from the selection.

Now you'll try another way to create slices using the manual slicing tools—the Slice tool and Slice Select tool. Manual slices don't update automatically. But they let you dissect a single object into multiple slices or create slices that aren't tied to a specific object or group.

8 Position the pointer on the Slice tool ( ) in the toolbox. Drag to the right to select the small triangle to the right of the Slice tools, and then select the triangle to tear off the tools.

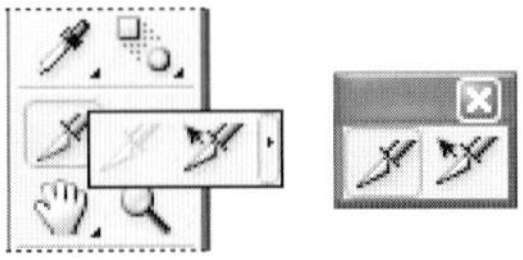

To separate a group of hidden tools from the toolbox, select the small triangle that appears at the right end of the group.

9 In the Layers palette, click the eye column to the left of the Logo layer to make it visible. Then select the Logo layer in the palette.

10 Using the Zoom tool ( ), zoom in to 150%.

11 Select the Slice tool in the tear-off slice tools. The Slice tool defines rectangular areas in your image as slices.

12 Position the pointer at the lower left corner of the logo artwork, below the Design text. Then drag diagonally up to draw a rectangle around the logo and its type, getting as close as possible to the shape to minimize the image size.

When you use the Slice tool, Illustrator creates auto slices for all the undefined areas surrounding the slice you drew. You can adjust a slice after you've drawn it.

13 Select the Slice Select tool ( ), and position it at the edge of the slice rectangle. The pointer changes to a double-headed arrow. Drag to adjust the size of the slice.

Note: *If you make a mistake, delete the slice by selecting the slice with the Slice Select tool and pressing Delete; then redraw the slice.*

Draw the slice with the Slice tool. *Drag with slice Select tool to adjust slice.* *Result.*

14 Choose Select > Deselect, and then choose File > Save.

Before you set optimization settings for these slices, you'll make sure that the colors are Web-safe.

Exporting flat-color artwork

Flat-color artwork with repetitive color and sharp detail, such as line art, logos, or illustrations with type, should be exported to GIF or PNG-8 format. Flat-color artwork appears best on the Web without any *dithering*–mixing colors to approximate those not present in the palette. To prevent computers from dithering colors, use Web-safe colors in your artwork, or if an exact match to the flat color is not necessary, turn off dithering when you export the file. This will be discussed later in this lesson.

In this part of the lesson, you'll prepare the artwork to be exported in the GIF format.

Painting with Web-safe colors

You'll start by painting the flat-color buttons in the navigation bar with Web-safe colors.

1 In the Layers palette, Alt/Option-click the Logo layer to turn on all layers. Turning on the layers also unlocks them.

You'll hide the slices so that they don't distract you.

2 Choose View > Hide Slices.

You'll select multiple objects and paint them with Web-safe colors.

3 Choose View > Zoom In to zoom in on the artwork to 200%.

4 Choose View > Pixel Preview to see the artwork as it will look in a Web browser. Notice that graphics that appeared smooth in the Preview view are now pixelated in the Pixel Preview. This is how your graphic will appear when it is placed in a Web page.

Preview.

Pixel preview.

You've been looking at a zoomed-in view of the graphic. Web browsers don't let you zoom in on graphics. You'll look at the graphic at actual size to see how the pixelization will appear.

5 Choose View > Actual Size to get a 100% view of the artwork.

You can continue to work in Pixel Preview for the rest of this lesson, or choose View > Pixel Preview to turn off the preview.

For more information, see "Working in Pixel Preview Mode" in online Help.

6 If necessary, scroll to the Plants button in the artwork.

7 Using the Direct Selection tool ( ), select the purple background of the Plants button.

8 Choose Select > Same > Fill Color to select all the objects in the artwork that are painted the same color as the selected object.

9 In the Color palette, choose the Web Safe RGB option from the palette menu in the upper right corner. (If the Color palette is not visible on-screen, choose Window > Color.)

Select purple background.

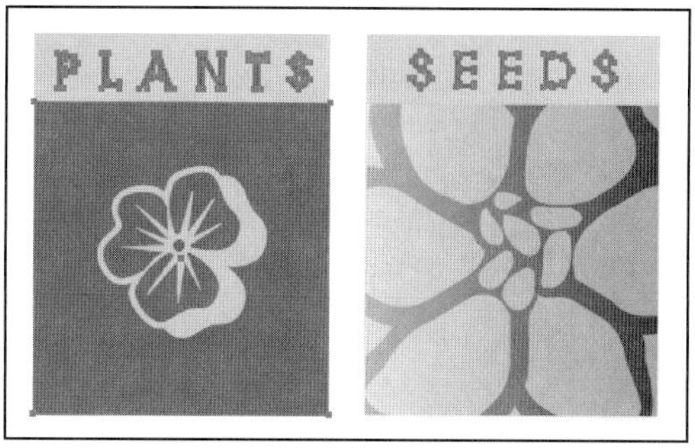

Auto-select objects with same fill color.

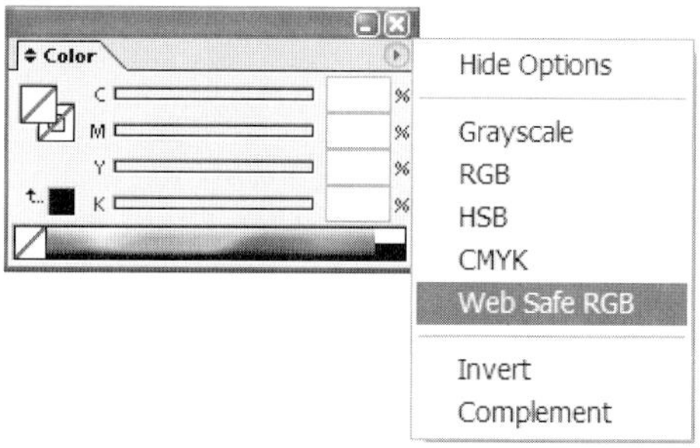

Change Color palette to Web Safe RGB.

The Web palette contains 216 RGB colors that are shared by both Windows and Mac OS platforms, so they can be viewed by anyone who has a system displaying at least 256 colors. If you have used a color that is not Web-safe, the Color palette displays a cube below the stroke and fill boxes in the Color palette and a small color swatch next to the cube containing the closest Web-safe color.

Now you'll select and correct the colors in the artwork that are not Web-safe.

10 In the Color palette, click Out of Web Color Warning button to change the fill color to the nearest Web-safe color.

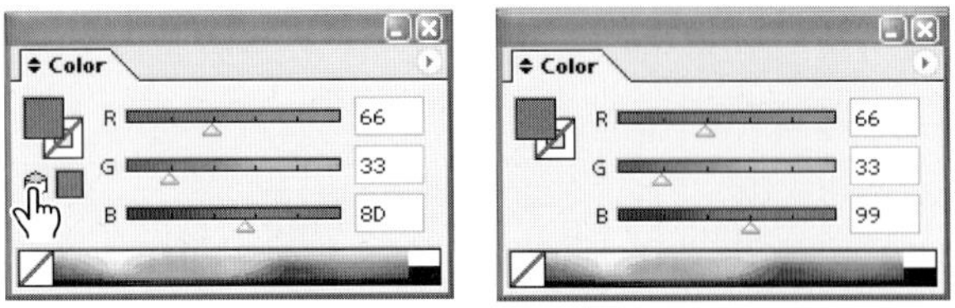

Click Out of Web Color Warning button to substitute nearest Web-safe color.

11 Press Ctrl+spacebar (Windows) or Command+spacebar (Mac OS) and click to zoom in on the Navigation buttons in the artwork.

12 Select the light blue rectangle behind the word Plants, and choose Select > Same > Fill Color to select all the objects with the same color.

13 In the Color palette, click the Out of Web Color Warning cube to change the fill color to the nearest Web-safe color.

The remaining objects in the artwork have already been painted with Web-safe colors.

14 Choose Select > Deselect. Then choose File > Save to save the changes to the artwork.

Creating slices for text and text formatting

Like flat-color artwork, type should be exported in the GIF or PNG-8 format. Now you'll create slices for text on the page.

1 Choose View > Show Slices to redisplay the slices.

2 In the Layers palette, click the selection column in the far right of the layer name to select the Text layer.

3 With the Selection tool (), click the paragraph of type to select it. This text is not outlined and is intended to be HTML text.

4 Choose Object > Slice > Make.

To create a slice with HTML Text content, you must select the text object and then use the Make Slice command. You cannot create HTML Text content using any other slicing method.

Next, you'll create a slice for the Send Flowers headline text. You'll create this slice as an image slice so that you can control its typeface in a browser.

5 With the Slice tool (), drag a rectangle around the text Send Flowers, being sure to include the yellow box behind the text. Start at the top left, and drag all the way to the edge of the yellow box. Do not drag on top of the slice you just made for the paragraph of text. If you drag slowly, the slice will snap to the top edge of the paragraph slice.

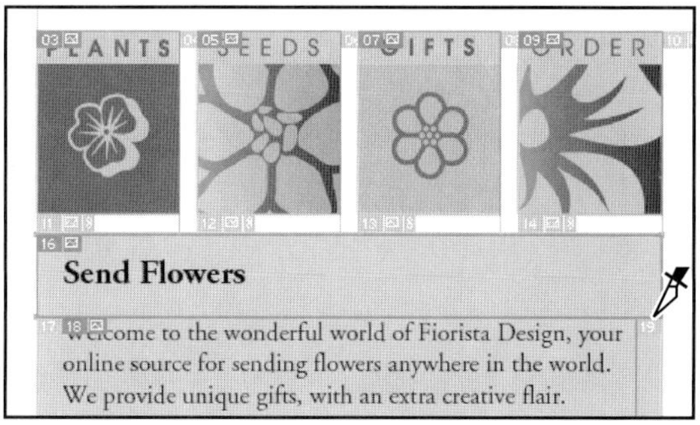
PLANTS
SEEDS
GIFTS
ORDER
Send Flowers
Welcome to the wonderful world of Fiorista Design, your online source for sending flowers anywhere in the world. We provide unique gifts, with an extra creative flair.
Selecting headline text.

Because you used the Slice tool to create the slice, by default it is an image slice and cannot be used for HTML text.

6 Choose File > Save to save the changes to the artwork.

Setting GIF export options

Now that you've created all the slices in your artwork to designate different Web elements, you're ready to optimize the artwork—that is, select export file settings that best trade off image quality, compression, and download speed.

1 Choose File > Save for Web.

The Save for Web dialog box displays all the slices of visible layers and lets you set optimization at the same time. Take a moment to familiarize yourself with this dialog box, using tool tips to identify the options. In Web production, you'll use this dialog box often.

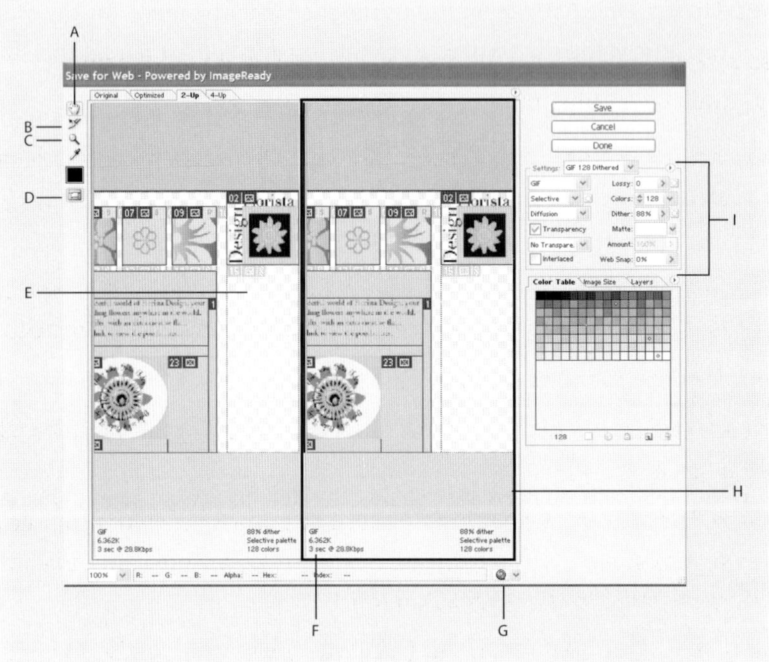

A. Hand tool. ***B.*** *Slice Select tool.* ***C.*** *Zoom tool.* ***D.*** *Toggle Slice Visibility.*
E. *Transparency checkerboard.* ***F.*** *File size/Download speed.* ***G.*** *Preview in Browser.*
H. *Selected view.* ***I.*** *Optimization settings.*

2 Click Done to close the Save for Web dialog box. We will come back to use this feature later in this lesson.

You'll start by optimizing the navigation bar.

3 In the Layers palette, Alt-click (Windows) or Option-click (Mac OS) the eye icon to the left of the Navigation Bar layer to hide all layers but that layer.

4 Choose File > Save for Web.

The View options in the Save for Web dialog box let you switch easily between optimized and original (non–optimized) versions of an image and view up to four versions of an optimized image simultaneously. The different views let you try out different settings before saving an optimized version.

5 Click the 2-Up tab.

Now you'll select two of the slices with flat color and select one of the preset optimizations available in Illustrator.

6 Make sure that the bottom (or right) preview (the Optimized view) is selected, as indicated by the black outline around the window. If it is not selected, simply click on the preview window.

7 In the Save for Web dialog box, select the Slice Select tool (). In the Optimized view, click the Plants button to select its slice. A selected slice is outlined in yellow.

8 In the Settings pop-up menu, choose GIF 128 Dithered.

9 Notice the file size in the bottom left corner of the window and the Color table in the bottom right corner.

10 Try GIF Web Palette from the Settings menu. The number of colors and file size decrease, but you have not lost any quality in this flat color button. You can compare the new setting on the bottom to the original on top.

11 Select the Toggle Slices Visibility button () to turn off the numbering of each slice, so that you can clearly see all the buttons.

12 Click the Toggle Slice Visibility button again to turn on the slicing.

13 In the bottom or right Optimized view, select the Gifts button. In the Settings pop-up menu, choose GIF Web Palette.

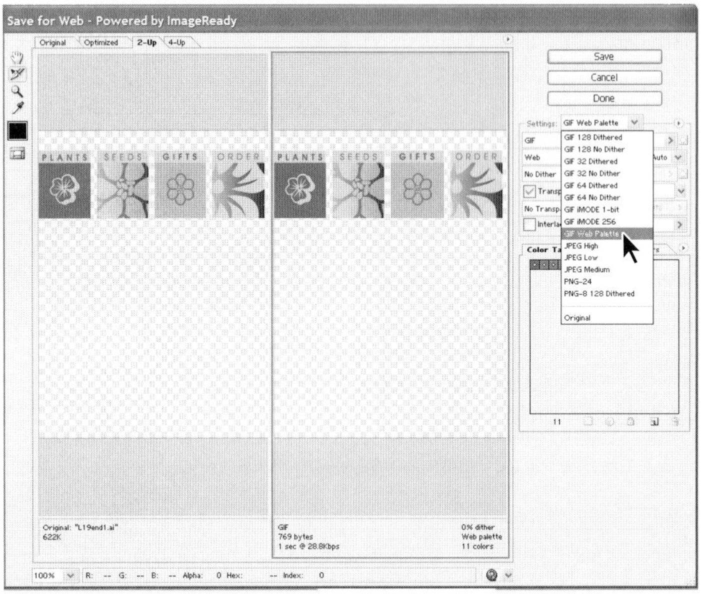

14 Click Done (not Save) to remember the current settings and close the dialog box. You won't save the settings until you've finished determining the settings for all the slices.

15 Choose File > Save to save the file.

You can also create your own custom settings. For more information on creating custom settings see "Applying Optimization Settings" in online Help.

More on Color Tables

GIF files are reduced in file size by reducing the number of colors. The lower the number of colors in the artwork, the smaller the file. Use the up and down arrow keys to the left of the colors textbox to reduce or increase colors one at a time.
If colors that are important to the artwork are eliminated, lock them so that they are the last to leave the palette.

***1.** Lock a color by clicking on an object containing that color in the artwork. It becomes a highlighted swatch in the Color Table.*

***2.** While the swatch is highlighted, click on the lock icon at the bottom of the color table.*

***3.** As colors are reduced using the Colors textbox or arrows, the locked color will be last to be dropped.*

***Note:** If you lock more colors than you have allowed in the colors palette, some will be dropped, but as you increase colors they will be the first to return.*

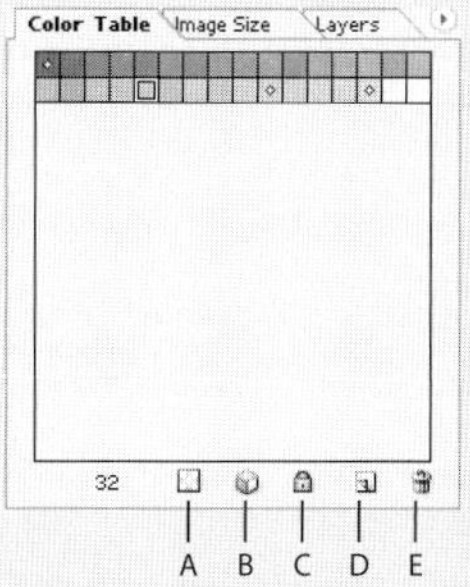

A. Map Selected Colors to Transparent.
B. Shifts/Unshifts colors to the Web Safe color palette.
C. Lock Color.
D. Adds Eyedropper color to palette.
E. Delete Color Swatch.

Do all colors need to be Web-safe?

Perhaps you are working on a company banner and when you shift to all web colors the colors are less than what you expected? In the Save for the Web dialog window you can selectively choose which colors should be web-safe, and which colors you want to look as accurate as possible in most browsers, and are not as concerned how they will appear in the few browsers that cannot accommodate the colors.

***1.** To selectively choose colors to be Web-safe, click on an object containing that color. The swatch becomes highlighted.*

***2.** Click on the cube icon at the bottom of the color palette. This button shifts or unshifts selected colors to the Web-safe palette.*

Exporting continuous-tone and gradient artwork

Next you'll optimize the logo and the sticker slices, and then optimize the remaining continuous-tone buttons in the JPEG and PNG-24 formats and compare these options.

To preserve the quality of continuous-tone and gradient-filled artwork, it's recommended that you use the JPEG image file format. Illustrator saves JPEG files using different compressions based on the specified image quality. The compression option you select determines how the color information in the artwork is preserved, which affects the size and quality of the image. It is important to keep in mind that JPEG doesn't support transparency.

Note: *Transparency makes it possible to place a nonrectangular graphic object against the background of a Web page. Background transparency, supported by GIF and PNG formats, preserves transparent pixels in the image, allowing the Web page background to show through in a browser.*

You can also export continuous-tone artwork to PNG-24 format—for example, to use background transparency or background matting with an image. However, not all browsers support the PNG-24 format. An image in the PNG-24 format usually is larger than in the JPEG format, because the PNG-24 format uses the same lossless compression method as the PNG-8 format, in which no data is discarded.

You'll start by selecting the logo and applying transparency.

1 In the Layers palette, Alt/Option-click the eye icon next to the Navigation Bar layer to display and unlock all layers.

2 Choose File > Save for Web.

3 In the Save for Web dialog box, select the Hand tool and scroll so that you can see the Logo slice in the upper right corner.

4 Select the Slice Select tool ( ), and then click the Logo slice in the Optimized view to select the slice.

5 Choose JPEG High from the Settings pop-up menu. Notice the white showing up in the open areas of the logo.

This color show-through–similar to color show-through in printing when colors aren't trapped–sometimes occurs when images are on top of a background.

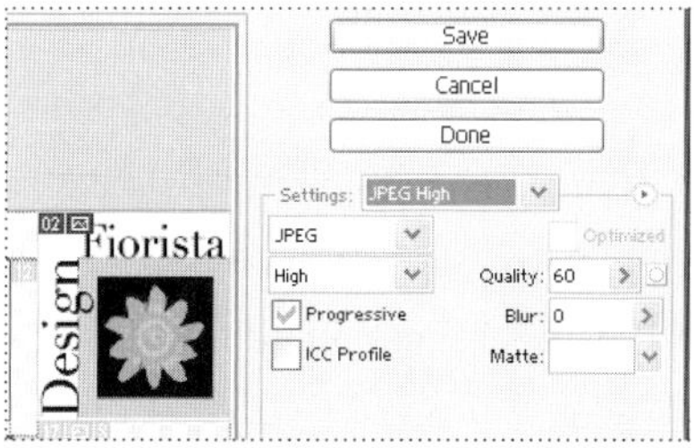

White in JPEG preview indicates color show-through.

The JPEG format maintains good quality in an image, but does not support transparency; if you choose the JPEG setting, the white background will show through in a browser.

If your image contains transparency and you do not know the Web page background color, or if the background will be a pattern, you should use a format that supports transparency (GIF, PNG-8, or PNG-24).

Now you'll try a file format that supports transparency, and see if it can also maintain the image quality.

6 In the Settings pop-up menu, choose GIF 128 Dithered. Notice the background display is now transparent, as indicated by the checkerboard, because the transparency option has been selected.

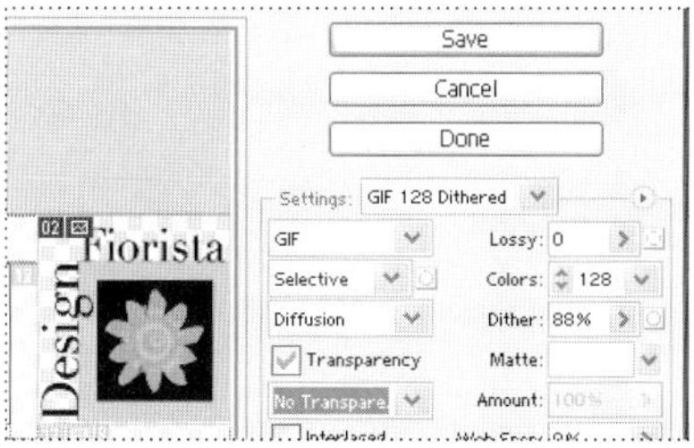

GIF 128 Dithered setting maintains transparency.

Next you'll optimize the sticker slice with the same setting.

7 Select the Zoom tool or Hand tool, and drag the sticker to bring it into view.

8 Using the Slice Select tool in the Optimized view, select the sticker slice. Choose GIF 128 Dithered from the Settings pop-up menu.

Now you'll compare the JPEG and PNG optimization settings.

9 Using the Zoom tool (🔍) and the Hand tool (✋) in the dialog box, zoom in to 200% on the Seed button preview in one of the frames and center the Seed button slice in the preview window.

Selecting or editing an object in one frame updates its preview in all frames.

You can also use the keyboard shortcuts to get the Hand and Zoom tools while in the Save for Web dialog box. Press the spacebar to get the Hand tool. Press Ctrl/Command+spacebar and click to zoom in on a preview. Press Alt+Ctrl+spacebar (Windows) or Option+Command+spacebar (Mac OS) and click to zoom out.

10 Click the 4-Up tab at the top of the Save for Web dialog box, so that you can preview four different settings. The original version appears in the upper left corner.

11 In the Save for Web dialog box, select the Slice Select tool, and then click the Seed button in the upper left of the dialog box to select the button. Make sure that a yellow outline appears around the Seed button, indicating it is selected.

First you'll compare JPEG settings.

12 Click the upper right version, and choose JPEG High from the Settings menu.

13 Click the lower right version, and choose JPEG Medium from the Settings menu.

14 Click the lower left version, and choose JPEG Low from the Settings menu.

15 Notice the difference in image quality between the four versions, particularly around the edges of the shapes where the colors blur.

16 Also note the file sizes of the different versions (approximately 2.752K for the JPEG High version, 1.61K for JPEG Medium, and 1.16K for JPEG Low).

The JPEG Low version will download more quickly than the JPEG High or Medium versions, but like the JPEG Medium version, is seriously compromised. Only the JPEG High version maintains the image quality.

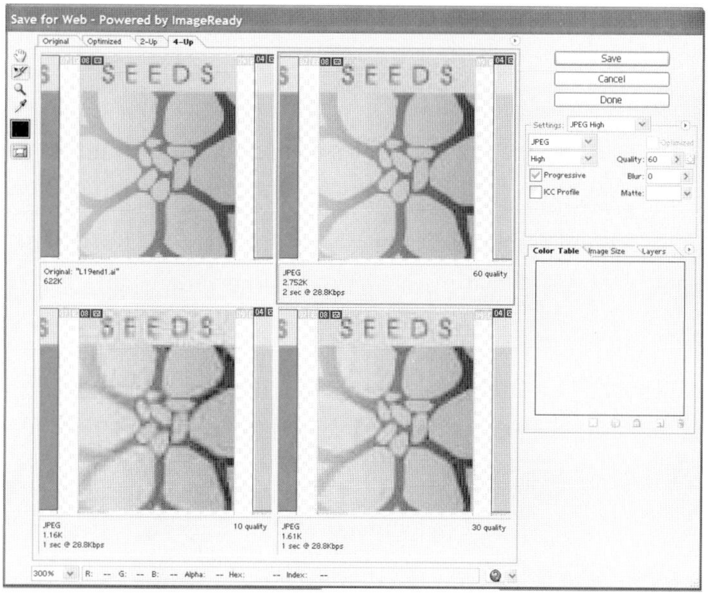

Now you'll compare the image quality and file size for the PNG-24 setting.

17 Click the lower left version if it is not already selected. Choose PNG-24 from the Settings pop-up menu.

Notice that the image quality of the PNG-24 version is very good, but the file size is now approximately 4.56K. Even though the image quality is slightly better than the JPEG High version, the increased file size will slow the Web site download time.

18 Choose JPEG High from the Settings pop-up menu.

You'll apply the same settings to the Order button.

19 Click the Optimized view tab. Double-click the Zoom tool to view the images at actual size.

20 In the dialog box, use the Slice Select tool to select the Order button.

21 Choose JPEG High from the Settings menu. Leave the Save for the Web window open.

You'll continue working in the Save for Web dialog box to set up links to URLs.

Linking slices to URLs

When designing Web pages, it's useful to attach links to objects that will load the specified Web page. You can link any object you create in Adobe Illustrator to a Uniform Resource Locator (URL) address, transforming the object into a button that links to an Internet Web site.

You can use either slices or image maps to link one or more areas of an image–called hotspots–to a URL. When a user clicks the hotspot in the resulting Web page, the Web browser loads the linked file. Slices with hotspots can link only to rectangular areas.

Image maps can link to polygonal or rectangular areas in your artwork. For more information on image maps, see "Creating image maps" in online Help.

1 Now you'll add URLs to the navigation bar slices.

Using the Slice Select tool ( ), double-click on the first button (Plants) to display the Slice Options dialog box. The Name text box lists the slice name, the default file name when you save the Web page.

You'll specify a URL to make the slice area a hotspot in the resulting Web page.

2 In the URL text box, type the URL for the destination of the link. You can enter a relative URL, a full URL (including http://), or choose a previously created URL from the pop-up menu. (We used http://www.adobe.com). Click OK to apply the changes.

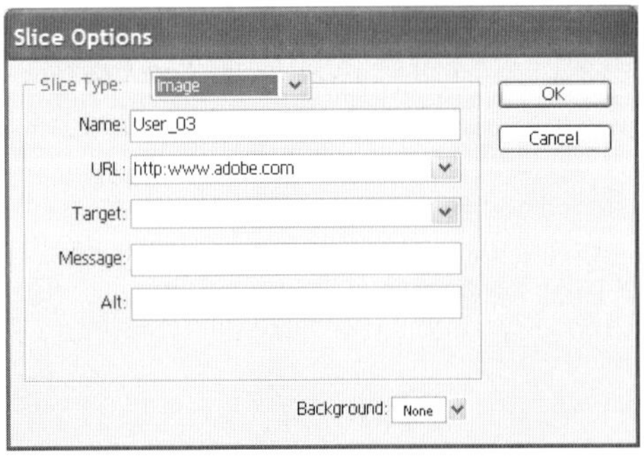

3 Select the remaining buttons (Seeds, Gifts, and Order) with the Slice Select tool and choose Object > Slice > Slice Options for them as well. Repeat step 2, typing in another URL to link the slice to a second destination URL. You can also select a URL from the URL pop-up menu. Click OK.

To clear the URLs shown in the pop-up menu, delete the Adobe Save For Web AI Prefs file located in Documents and Settings > User Name > Application Data > Adobe

> Save for the Web AI > 3.5 > Adobe Save For Web AI 3.5 Prefs (Windows) or Library > Preferences > Adobe > Save for the Web AI >Save for the Web Preferences (Mac OS).

After assigning the URLs to the buttons, you can test whether the URLs are valid.

4 If you have a live Internet connection, click the Preview in Browser button in the bottom right corner of the Save for Web dialog box. Valid URLs will jump to the address you entered in the URL text box.

Note: *Testing these URLs requires that you have a live Internet connection via your browser. If you don't have a live connection, testing the link will generate an error message. You can also enter a URL to your local computer in step 2 and test it locally.*

5 Close your browser window to quit the preview.

Now you'll have Illustrator remember the current settings in the Save for Web dialog box.

6 In the Save for Web dialog box, press Alt (Windows) or Option (Mac OS) and the Done button changes to Remember. Click Remember to remember the current settings and keep the dialog box open.

Setting HTML text options

Next you will replace the placeholder paragraph of text with HTML text.

Creating a slice as HTML text lets you capture text and basic formatting characteristics (such as the background color) of the text object in Illustrator. Text in HTML pages varies according to each browser setting. To control the exact typeface and size of a font you must convert text to an image.

1 In the Save for Web dialog box, click the Optimized tab if it is not already selected.

2 With the Slice Select tool, double-click the paragraph of text to display the Slice Options dialog box.

3 For Slice Type, choose HTML Text from the pop-up menu. The slice type and options determines how the content of the slice will look and function on the Web.

The text for HTML Text slices appears in the Slice Options dialog box, but you can't edit the content in the dialog box. To edit the text for HTML Text content slices, you must update the text in your artwork.

Note: *You can make HTML text editable in the Slice Options dialog box by changing the slice type to No Image. This breaks the link with the text object on the artboard.*

By default, the background color of the slice is none. You'll assign it a background color.

4 Using the Background pop-up menu at the bottom of the Slice Options dialog box, choose Other. The Color Picker appears.

5 In the Color Picker, select Only Web Colors. In the # text box, enter **FFCC00** for the background color. Click OK. Click OK again in the Slice Options dialog box.

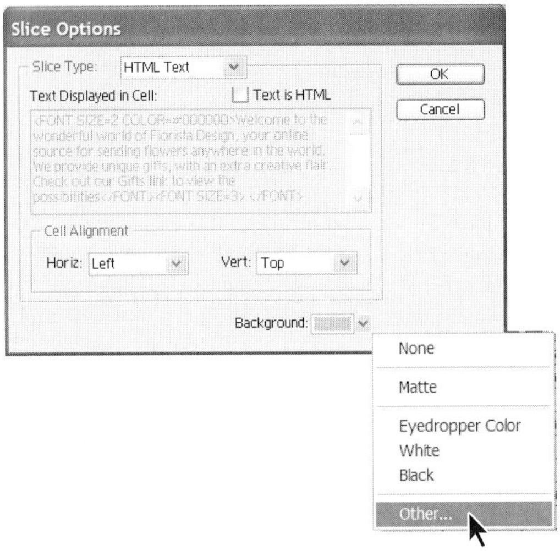

Selecting a background color.

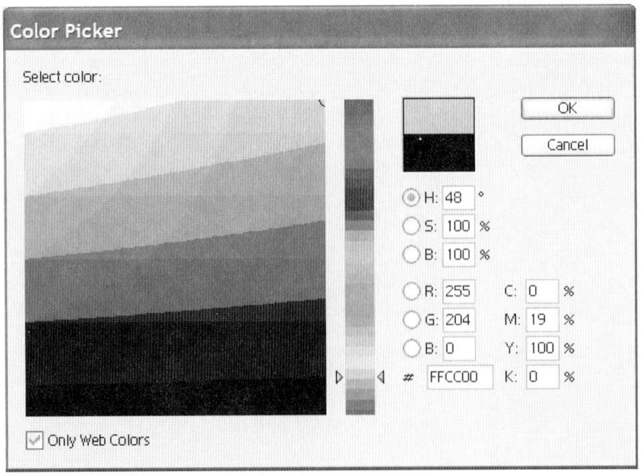

Selecting a Web color as the background color.

6 To view the HTML text, click the Preview in Browser button at the bottom of the Save for Web dialog box to launch your browser.

7 Look closely at the paragraph of text in the browser window. As HTML text, the font can change depending on the font preferences viewers have set for their browsers. (You can test how the font can change by changing the font preferences in your browser and seeing its effect on this text.)

8 Close your browser window to quit the preview.

Controlling the look of your type

You cannot control exactly how browsers display HTML text; you can only control the text size and weight, such as bold. The way to control the look of type–for example, if a design's look depends on using a specific typeface–is by setting a slice to be an image.

1 In the Save for Web dialog box, use the Slice Select tool and double-click the slice containing the words *Send Flowers* to display the Slice Options dialog box.

This slice includes both the text box and the background color that you selected when you created the slice, and is defined as an image. By default, slices are defined as images. When text is specified as an image slice, the text will be rasterized in the HTML page and the typeface will be maintained. However, you can't edit the headline text unless you return to Illustrator.

To see how text will appear in a browser when it's not specified as an image, you'll try another slice setting.

2 For Slice Type, choose No Image from the pop-up menu. In the Text Displayed in Cell text box, type the words **Send Flowers**. A No Image slice won't display text unless you enter it in the Text Displayed in Cell text box.

3 For Cell Alignment, select Horizontal Center and Vertical Middle. For Background, choose Other to display the Color Picker, change the background color to **FFCC00** in the # text box, and click OK. Click OK again in the Slice Options dialog box.

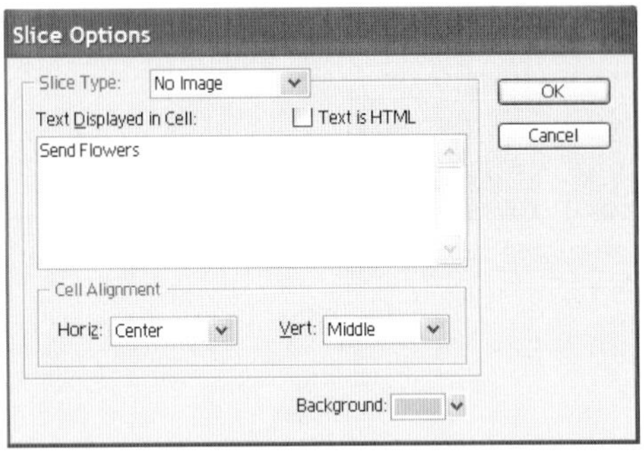

The No Image slice type lets you specify text or a solid color on the resulting Web page. You can't view No Image content in Illustrator; you must use a Web browser to preview it.

4 Click the Preview in Browser button at the bottom of the Save for Web dialog box to launch your browser. Notice that the headline type is now HTML text and follows the formats you set in the Slice Options dialog box.

5 Exit the browser.

Because it's important to control the typeface of this headline, you'll specify this slice as an image.

6 In the Save for Web dialog box, use the Slice Select tool to double-click the slice containing the words *Send Flowers* and display the Slice Options dialog box.

7 For Slice Type, choose Image from the pop-up menu. Click OK.

8 In the Settings pop-up menu, choose GIF 32 No Dither.

9 Click the Preview in Browser button at the bottom of the Save for Web dialog box to launch your browser. Notice that the type is exactly as you viewed it in Illustrator.

Headline as HTML Text loses formatting.

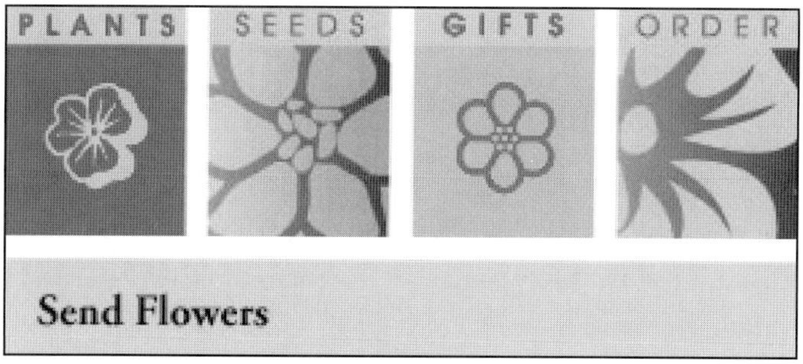

Headline as an image maintains typeface.

10 Exit the browser.

11 Alt/Option-click the Remember button to remember the current settings and keep the Save for Web dialog box open.

Saving your Web page as an HTML file with images

Once you've completed slicing your page for the Web, you are ready to save your page and create the HTML file with all your optimized images. The last artwork to optimize are the remaining auto slices that are filled with the yellow color.

1 In the Optimized view, use the Slice Select tool to double-click one of the long vertical yellow auto slices below the left edge of the heading *Send Flowers*. This action selects the slice and displays the Slice Options dialog box.

2 In the Slice Options dialog box, for slice type choose No Image, set the background color to yellow by choosing Other from the Background pop-up menu to display the

Color Picker. Select Only Web Colors, and then enter **FFCC00** in the # text box. Click OK to close the Color Picker; then click OK again.

3 Repeat steps 1 and 2 for the remaining yellow auto slices.

You've completed optimizing the file for the Web, and you're ready to save your settings.

4 In the Save for Web dialog box, click Save.

5 Click the New Folder button and navigate to your desktop. Select the Desktop and create a new folder on your desktop for the HTML file and images, and name it FlwrSite.

6 In the Save as type optimized dialog box, for Format choose HTML and Images to generate all files required to use your artwork as a Web page.

***Note:** If you want to fine-tune HTML settings, you can choose Other from the Settings pop-up menu.*

7 Click Save. Illustrator generates the HTML file and separate folder of image files within the folder you specified in step 5.

The HMTL file contains information that tells a Web browser what to display when it loads the page. It can contain pointers to images (in the form of GIF, PNG, and JPEG files), HTML text, linking information, and JavaScript code for creating rollover effects.

8 From the desktop, open the folder you just created, FlwrSite. Notice that the folder contains a folder of GIF and JPEG images, numbered according to the slices you created.

You now have the necessary elements to post your Web site to a server or hand it over to a developer for further enhancements.

9 Launch your browser. Then drag and drop the HTML file from the FlwrSite folder into your browser window to view the completed page. Close the browser window to quit the preview.

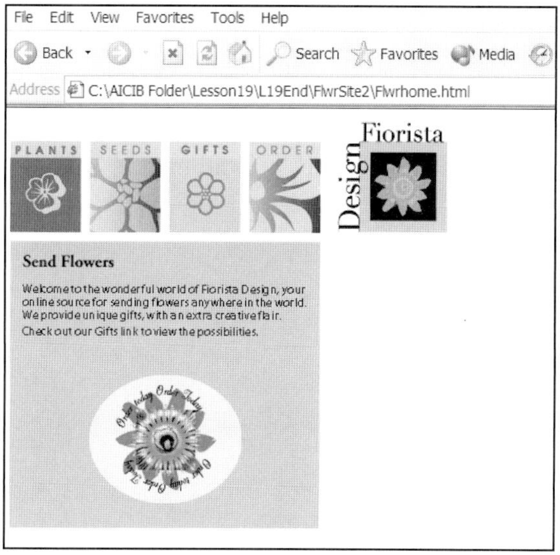
File Edit View Favorites Tools Help
Back
Search
Favorites
Media
Address C:\AICIB Folder\Lesson19\L19End\FlwrSite2\Flwrhome.html
Fiorista
Design
PLANTS
SEEDS
GIFTS
ORDER
Send Flowers
Welcome to the wonderful world of Fiorista Design, your online source for sending flowers anywhere in the world. We provide unique gifts, with an extra creative flair.
Check out our Gifts link to view the possibilities.

10 Return to Illustrator.

11 Choose File > Save to save the Flowerhome.ai file. Then choose File > Close.

Creating a Flash animation from symbols

To attract viewers to your site, you'll create a Web banner with an animated flower made up of symbols. You can also incorporate this artwork into your Web page.

Using symbols in your artwork minimizes file size. When you export a file containing symbols, the symbol is defined only once, resulting in smaller file sizes that are more Web-friendly.

1 Choose File > Open, and open the L19strt2.ai file in the L19Start folder, located in the Lesson19 folder.

The document contains a rectangular guide in the standard dimensions of a Web banner, 468 pixels by 60 pixels.

2 Choose File > Save As, name the file **Animate.ai**, and select the L19Start folder in the Save In menu. Leave the type of format set to Adobe Illustrator® Document, and click Save. Leave the Illustrator Options at the defaults and click OK.

You'll start by creating your artwork using symbol instances.

3 Click the Symbols tab to bring the Symbols palette to the front. (If the Symbols palette isn't open on-screen, choose Window > Symbol.)

You'll place a symbol instance in the artwork using the Symbols palette. You can also place multiple symbol instances as a set using the Symbol Sprayer tool.

4 In the Symbols palette, expand the palette to see all the symbols. Then select the Blue Flower symbol (the last symbol in the palette.)

5 Drag the symbol and place it inside the Web banner near the left edge. The symbol instance appears selected in the artwork with a bounding box around it, similar to grouped artwork.

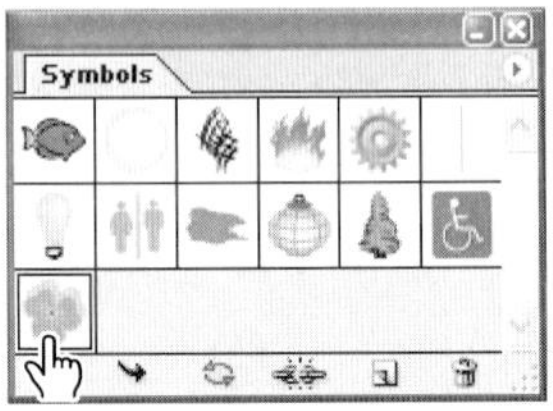

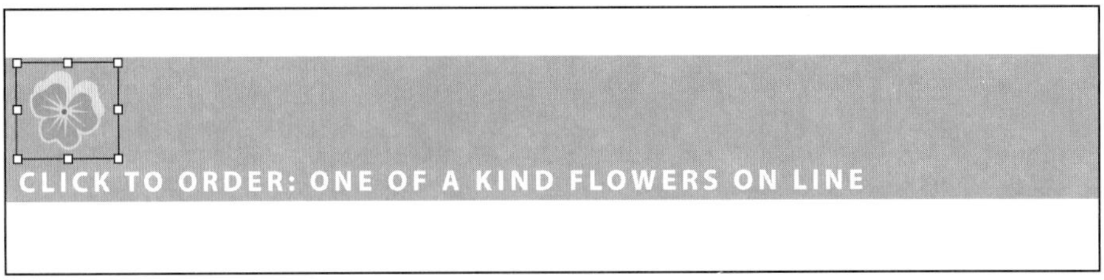

Placing Symbol instance in artwork.

Symbol instances placed using the Symbols palette are exact replicas of the original.

Now you will duplicate this symbol instance.

6 Using the Selection tool (), Alt-drag (Windows) or Option-drag (Mac OS) the symbol instance to the right of the first symbol. Do this several times (we used seven symbols) to fill in the banner with the flowers.

You'll change the size of some of the flowers. (We enlarged the symbols of the right end and reduced the symbols on the left).

7 Move the pointer over any corner of the selected symbol. The pointer changes to a double arrow. Hold down Shift as you drag to enlarge or decrease the symbol size.

8 Continue resizing the flowers until you're satisfied with the arrangement.

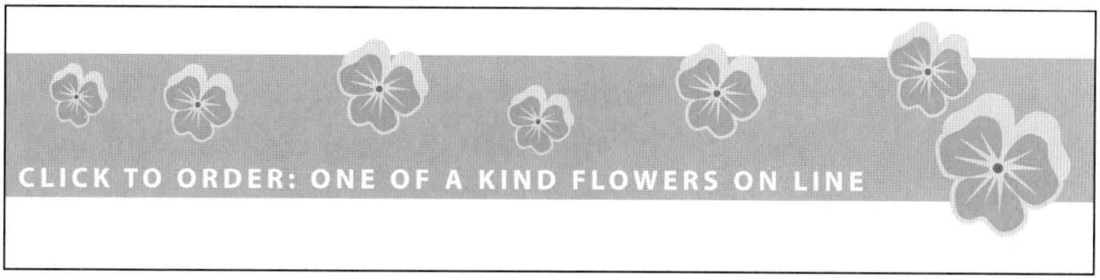

Symbol instances added to artwork and resized.

You're ready to set up the animation. To animate the artwork, you'll expand it so that each flower is placed on its own layer and becomes a separate frame in the animation.

9 In the Layers palette, click the triangle (▶) next to the Animation layer to display the symbol instances you created. (If the Layers palette isn't open, choose Window > Layers.)

To place the flowers, background, and text on separate layers and make each flower a different frame in an animation, you *release* the flowers to their own layers.

10 In the Layers palette, select the Animation layer.

11 In the Layers palette, choose Release to Layers (Build) from the palette menu. Each flower is now on its own layer, and all layers have been named and numbered.

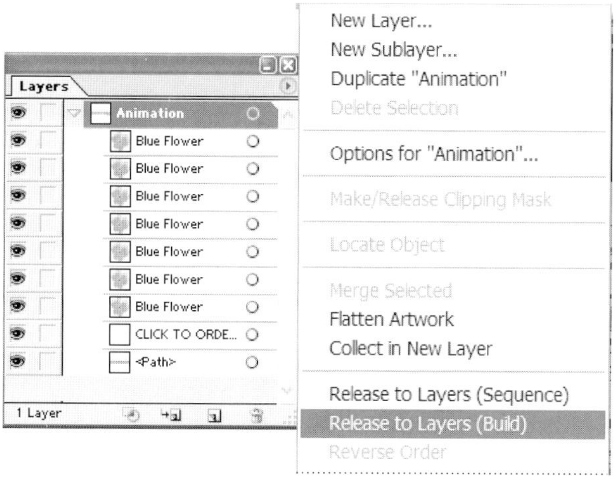

Releasing flowers to their own layer.

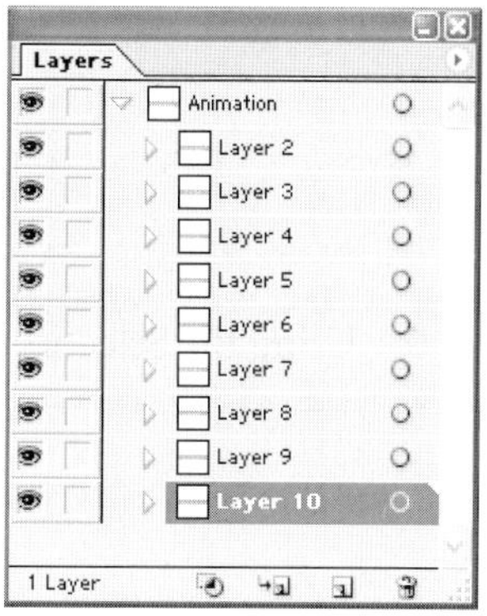

Result.

The Release to Layers command instantly distributes all the objects on one layer into separate, individual layers. You can use this feature to prepare files for Web animation applications that support layers, such as Macromedia Flash. For example, you can prepare different frames of an animation by first applying blend options to objects or by using the scatter brush to paint repeated copies of an object along a path. You can then release each object in the blend or scattered path to a separate layer and export the file as a Flash™ (SWF) file or to Adobe ImageReady™ CS to set up the animation.

Now you'll export the layered file to the SWF format. You can then open the animation in a browser and see the flowers dance across the page.

12 Choose File > Export. Choose Macromedia® Flash™(SWF) from the Save as Type (Windows) or Format (Mac OS) menu, name the file **Animate.swf**, and select the L19Start folder. Create a new folder inside the start folder titled **Banner**. Click Save (Windows) or Export (Mac OS).

Other formats that support symbols include SVG.

13 In the Macromedia Flash (SWF) Format Options dialog box, choose AI Layers to SWF Frames from the Export As menu. Adjust the Frame Rate and Resolution if desired (We used a frame rate of 6 fps (frames per second), selected Looping, and entered a resolution of 72 ppi.) Click OK.

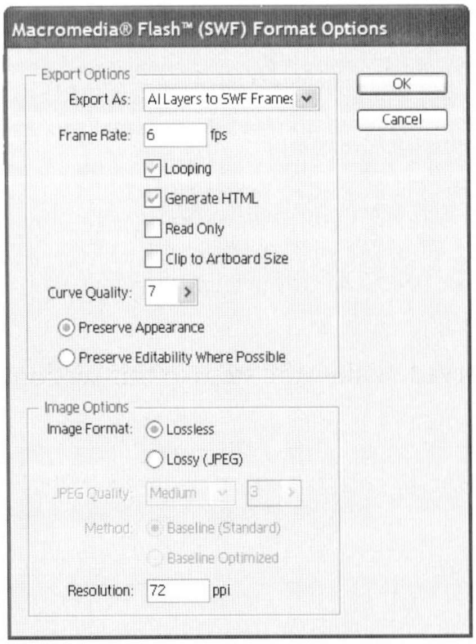

Illustrator creates two files, a SWF and an HTML file.

14 To view the Flash animation, open the Animate.html file in your browser window. Close the browser window to quit the preview.

Note: *Viewing the Flash animation requires the Shockwave plug-in. You can download the latest plug-in at http://www.macromedia.com/shockwave.*

15 Return to Illustrator.

16 Choose File > Save to save your work. Close your file.

You've completed the lesson in building a Web page. If you'd like more practice, you can continue fine-tuning your artwork using Adobe Photoshop, in the next section.

If you plan to convert several files to Web images or want to create animations from your artwork, consider Adobe ImageReady CS®, or Adobe GoLive® CS,–both programs for optimizing your graphics for the Web. For more information on these Adobe products and capabilities, visit the Adobe Web site at http://www.adobe.com.

Exploring on your own with Adobe Photoshop

Adobe applications are integrated so that you can go back and forth between them to fine-tune your artwork, depending on your design needs. Choose Adobe Illustrator for its tools for drawing and editing individual shapes, and for the full editing control it gives you over contours, scaling, and crisp, hard edges. When you want to blend photographic images and illustrative elements, choose Adobe Photoshop to let you integrate them visually by adjusting color, shading, transparency, and lighting.

Exporting an Illustrator image to Photoshop

Now you'll have a chance to work with Adobe Photoshop to alter the look of the sticker image at the bottom right of the flower Web page. This sticker was created in Adobe Illustrator and Adobe Photoshop. As you move a file between the two applications, layers, masks, and opacity settings are preserved. Follow the steps in this section to replicate the image for a Web page.

1 In Illustrator, choose File > Open, and open the L19strt3.ai file in the L19Start folder, located in the Lesson19 folder.

2 Choose Window > Layers to display the Layers palette.

3 Notice that the sticker flat-color artwork is separated into four separate layers—Type, Star, Flower, and Oval. All the objects in the artwork are painted with Web-safe colors.

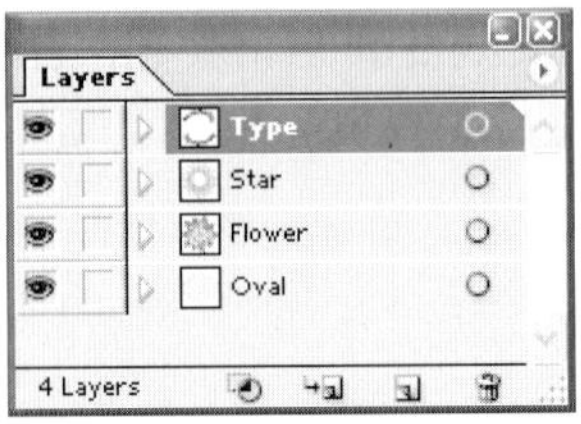

Now you'll export the artwork in the Photoshop format.

4 Choose File > Export. In the Export dialog box, choose Photoshop (PSD) from the Save as Type (Windows) or Format (Mac OS) menu, name the file **Sticker2.psd**, and select the L19Start folder inside the Lesson19 folder. Click Save (Windows) or Export (Mac OS).

5 In the Photoshop Options dialog box, choose RGB for Color Model and Screen (72 dpi) resolution. Check the Write Layers option and leave Anti-Alias selected, and click OK.

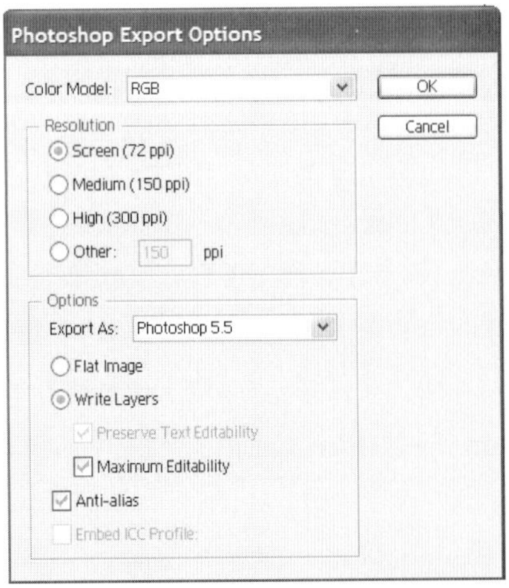

You'll switch to Photoshop, and then return to Illustrator to complete the lesson.

Adding a mask and applying effects in Photoshop

You'll work in Photoshop to create a mask for the sticker artwork and optimize it for the Web.

1 Start Adobe Photoshop.

2 In Photoshop, choose File > Open and open the file you just exported, Sticker2.psd, in the L19Start folder, located in the Lesson19 folder.

3 If the Layers palette isn't visible on-screen, choose Window > Show Layers. Notice how the layers in the artwork remain intact in the exported file.

4 Choose File > Open, and open the Flower.psd file in the L19Start folder, located in the Lesson19 folder. This file contains the bitmap image of a passion flower.

Note: *If the Missing Profile dialog box appears, click the Leave As Is (Don't Color Manage) option.*

5 Choose Select > All, and then choose Edit > Copy to copy the flower image to the Clipboard.

6 In the Sticker.psd file, choose Edit > Paste to paste the photo image into the sticker artwork. A new Layer 1 appears at the top of the Layers palette in the Sticker.psd file.

7 In the Layers palette, drag Layer 1 down between the Star and Flower layers.

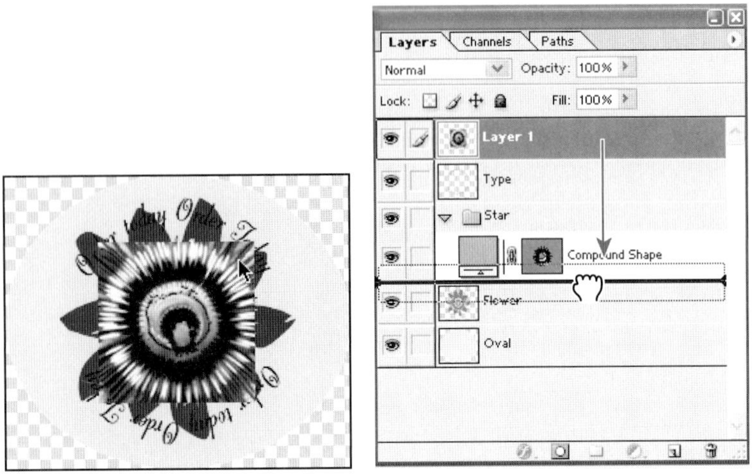

Paste flower into Sticker file.

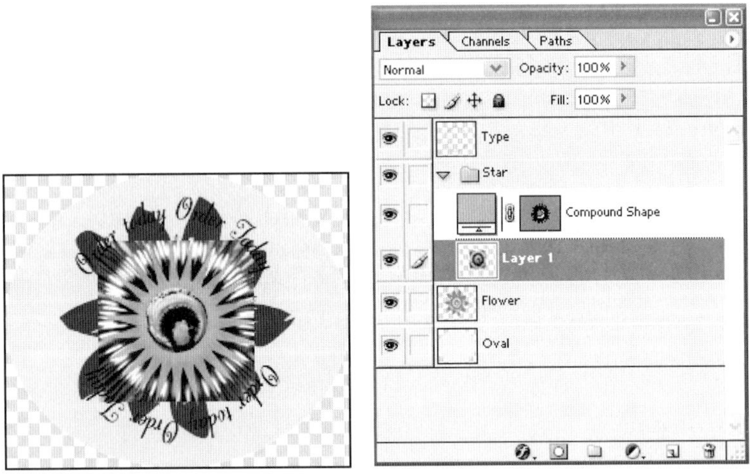

Move Layer 1 down between Star and Flower layers.

You'll mask the flower to replicate the artwork in the finished Web page.

8 Select the Elliptical Marquee tool (◌) under the Rectangular Marquee tool (⬚) in the toolbox.

9 Position the pointer in the center of the flower. Hold down Alt+Shift (Windows) or Option+Shift (Mac OS), and drag to draw a circle centered within the square photo.

10 Reposition the marquee within the square photo by positioning the pointer over the selection to change the cursor to a hollow pointer; then move the selection into place without moving pixels. Or press the arrow keys on the keyboard to nudge the selection into place.

11 With Layer 1 (the flower) active, choose Layer > Add Layer Mask > Reveal Selection. Now the image of the flower is masked within the circle.

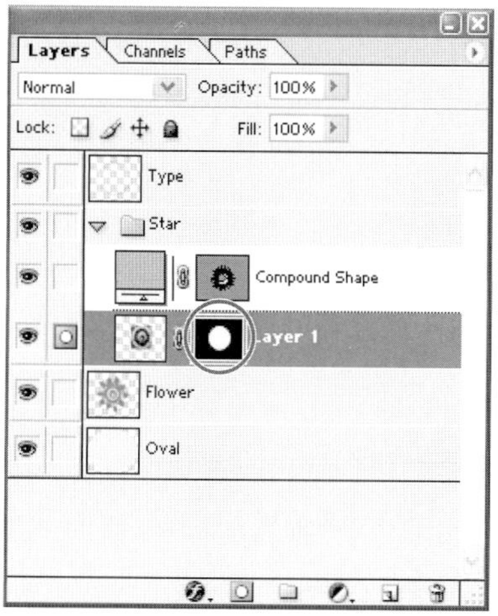

The layer mask.

Next you will adjust the color and simulated depth of the masked photograph.

12 In the Layers palette, select the layer thumbnail of the flower on Layer 1.

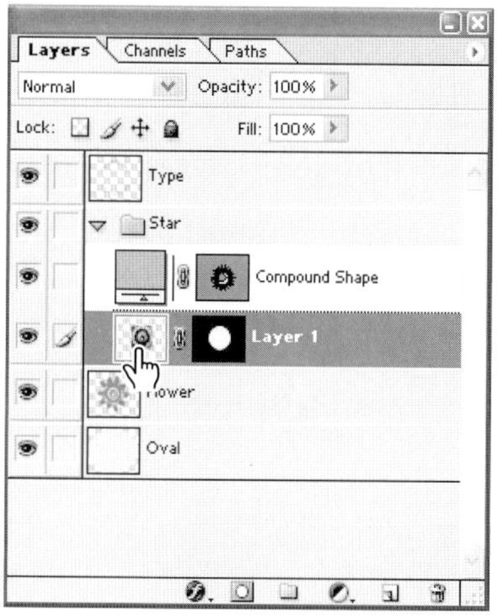

Selecting layer thumbnail of flower.

You'll adjust the color cast of the center of the flower, to complement the star points.

13 Choose Image > Adjust > Hue/Saturation. In the Hue/Saturation dialog box, select Colorize, and drag the sliders to adjust the Hue and the Saturation. (We selected a Hue of 124, and Saturation of 20, for a sea-green color.) Click OK.

Now you'll apply a live effect to give the flower a rounded embossed effect.

14 Choose Layer > Layer Style > Bevel and Emboss to apply a live filter to the image. In the Layer Style dialog box, change the Depth to **141%** and the Soften to **4 pixels**. Click OK.

15 Choose File > Save to save the Sticker2.psd file.

16 Quit Adobe Photoshop.

Optimizing a Photoshop file for the Web

You can optimize the sticker using the Save for Web dialog box in either Photoshop or Illustrator. The Save for Web feature has similar controls in both applications. In this case, you'll return to Illustrator to place the sticker artwork you just revised and then optimize the artwork.

1 Start Illustrator if it is not already running.

2 Choose File > Open, and open the file Flwrhome.ai in the L19Start folder, located in the Lesson19 folder.

3 If the Layers palette isn't visible on-screen, choose Window > Layers to display it.

4 Choose View > Show Slices to turn on the slices so that you can see their boundaries.

5 Select the Sticker layer. Click the triangle to the left of the Sticker layer to expand it.

6 To the right of the <Group> sublayer, click the target indicator (◎) to target only the sticker. You'll leave the slice and background sublayers intact.

7 Press Backspace or Delete to delete the sticker.

Next, you'll place the file you adjusted in Photoshop and scale the sticker so that it fits inside the existing slice.

8 Choose File > Place and locate the Sticker2.psd in the L19Start folder, located in the Lesson19 folder.

9 Using the Selection tool, align the bottom left corners of the slice and the sticker. Then Shift-drag the top right corner to scale the sticker to fit within the slice.

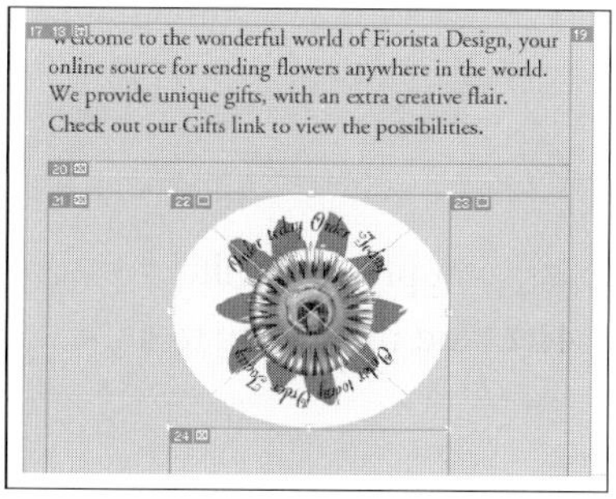
Welcome to the wonderful world of Fiorista Design, your online source for sending flowers anywhere in the world. We provide unique gifts, with an extra creative flair. Check out our Gifts link to view the possibilities.

Scaling the sticker to fit within the slice

Now you're ready to optimize the sticker image.

10 Choose File > Save for Web.

11 Using the Slice Select tool, select just the sticker slice. (A selected slice appears darker than other slices.)

12 Choose GIF 128 Dithered from the Settings pop-up menu. You can also try the GIF 64 Dithered and GIF 32 Dithered setting.

You'll create a new folder for the HTML file and its updated images.

13 In the Save for Web dialog box, click Save.

14 Click the New Folder button and navigate to your desktop. Create a new folder on your desktop for the HTML file and images, and name it FlwrSite2.

15 For type of format choose HTML and Images to generate all files required to use your artwork as a Web page. Click Save.

16 Quit Illustrator.

17 To view the edited Web page, drag and drop the FlwrSite.html file onto your browser window.

You can integrate your Web production process by working in both Illustrator and Photoshop to fine-tune your Web pages.

You can also open Photoshop files directly in Adobe GoLive CS. Slices, URLs, and other Web features in Photoshop files are accessible in GoLive for management and editing. Alternatively, you can open Photoshop files in GoLive as page templates. Page templates display as a shaded preview and provide a visual guide for building a Web page in GoLive.

Review questions

1 What determines the file format you should use when saving images for Web publication?

2 Name three styles of artwork that require different file formats for publication on the Web.

3 What is the benefit of selecting the Web palette when preparing images for publication on the World Wide Web?

4 What does the transparency option in a GIF file format do?

5 Does JPEG support transparency?

6 Describe how to select multiple objects and paint them with the same Web-safe colors.

7 Describe how to animate artwork for the Web.

8 Name some objects that lend themselves to animation.

Review answers

1 The style of artwork you're working with determines the file format you should use to save an image for publication on the Web. In addition, file size and image integrity may also affect which file format you use. In general, you should try to maintain the integrity of the image and keep the file size down.

2 Different styles of artwork include the following:

- Flat color (such as line art, logos, or illustrations with type).
- Full-color continuous-tone (such as bitmap images and photographs).
- Gradient-filled.
- Continuous-tone grayscale.
- Black and white.
- Animation.
- Artwork with URL links embedded in it.

3 Selecting the Web palette ensures that your images are displayed using the same color palette, regardless of the platform on which the image is displayed.

4 Transparency makes all the unpainted areas of the artwork transparent in a Web browser. You cannot select specific areas to be transparent; only the unpainted areas are defined as transparent.

5 The JPEG file format does not support transparency. When you save an image as a JPEG file, transparent pixels are filled with the Matte color specified in the Optimize palette.

6 Select an object and choose Edit > Select > Same Fill Color/Stroke Color/Paint Style to select the fill, stroke, or both, of all the objects in the artwork that are painted the same color. Then choose Web Safe RGB from the Color palette menu, and click a color to apply it to the selection. You can also click the Out of Web color warning cube in the Color palette to automatically switch to the nearest Web-safe color.

7 To animate artwork, you select the objects you want to animate and then expand them so that each object is placed on its own layer and becomes a separate frame in the animation. You can use the Release to Layers command to distribute all objects on one layer into separate, individual layers, for Web animation applications that support layers, such as Macromedia Flash (in the SWF format) or to Adobe Photoshop 6.0 to set up the animation.

8 To prepare different animation frames, you can begin by applying blend options to objects; by using the scatter brush to paint repeated copies of an object along a path; or by spraying symbols in your artwork.

Working with Version Cue

If you own Adobe® Creative Suite Standard or Premium, you can take advantage of Adobe Version Cue™, an integrated workflow feature designed to help you be more productive by saving you, and others you work with, valuable time.

With Version Cue, you can easily create, manage, and find different versions of your project files. If you collaborate with others, you and your team members can share project files in a multi-user environment that protects content from being accidentally overwritten.You can also maintain descriptive comments with each file version, search embedded file information to quickly locate files, and work with robust file-management features while working directly within each application.

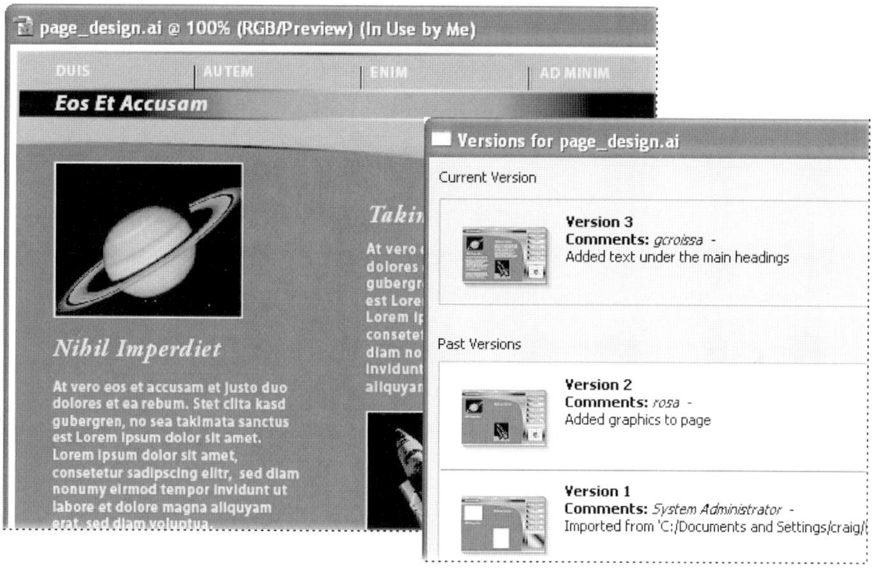

Note: *The Version Cue workspace is a feature of Adobe Creative Suite. If you purchased Adobe GoLive CS, Adobe Illustrator CS, Adobe InCopy CS, Adobe InDesign CS, or Adobe Photoshop CS separately, and don't own Adobe Creative Suite, you can use the Version Cue feature in your Adobe CS application only if an owner of Adobe Creative Suite gives you network access to their Version Cue workspace.*

Following are the steps you need to take before you begin working with Version Cue, and for how to use Version Cue.

1 Set up the Version Cue workspace.

You and others in your workgroup need access to a Version Cue workspace in order to work with the Version Cue feature. When you fully install Adobe Creative Suite, a Version Cue workspace automatically installs on your computer. Depending upon each project's needs, you may choose to work with other Version Cue workspaces located on your colleagues' computers or on a server.

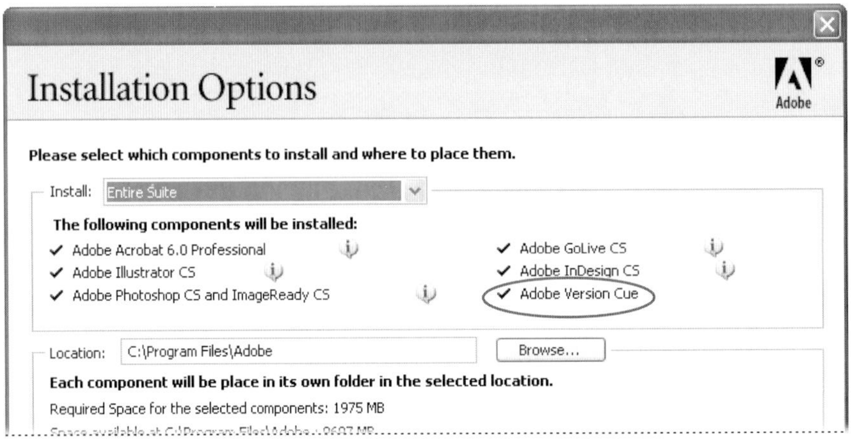

For projects and file versions that you don't need to share with others, or if you work on a laptop that isn't always connected to a network, it's easiest to use the Version Cue workspace located on your own computer. When you change your mind, Version Cue lets you immediately share any Version Cue project with other users. If you mostly intend to collaborate with others, make sure that a Version Cue workspace is located on a computer that everyone can access on a network and that the collaborative projects are kept in that workspace. For installation instructions, see "How To Install" on the Adobe Creative Suite CD.

2 Turn on the Version Cue workspace.

Before you can begin working with the Version Cue feature, you need to turn on the Version Cue workspace. Open the Adobe Version Cue preferences from Control Panel (Windows) or System Preferences (Mac OS) on the computer where the Version Cue workspace is located, and choose On from the Version Cue pop-up menu. To allow others to see and access the workspace over the network, choose This Workspace is Visible to Others from the Workspace Access menu, or, to keep it private, choose This Workspace is Private, and then click OK.

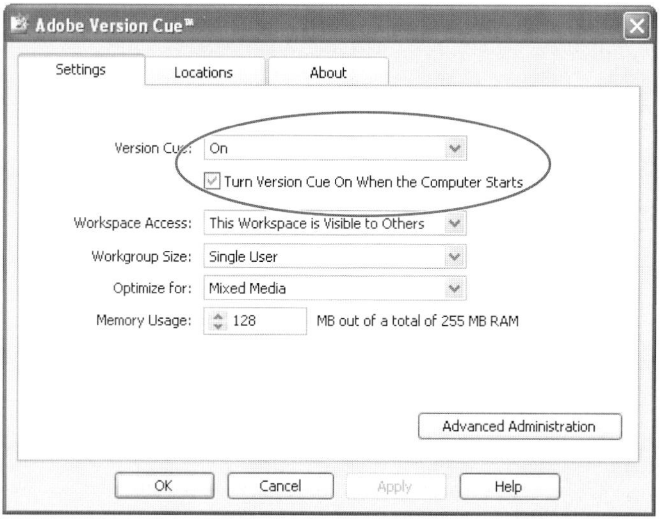

3 Enable the Version Cue preference in Adobe Illustrator CS.

In Illustrator CS, choose Edit > Preferences > File Handling & Clipboard (Windows) or Illustrator > Preferences > File Handling & Clipboard (Mac OS). Select Enable Version Cue, and click OK. To view the complete Version Cue documentation, click the Tell Me More button.

4 Create a Version Cue project for each set of related files.

Now you're ready to create a Version Cue project, which is used to organize related files. For example, to begin with, you can create a Version Cue project for files you want to keep private, and another project for those files you want to share with others. Choose File > Open and then click the Version Cue button; the Open dialog box then switches to display tabs, buttons, and menus for working with Version Cue projects. Double-click a Version Cue workspace to open it, and then choose New Project from the Project Tools menu. Enter a project name, information about the project (optional), and select Share This Project With Others if you want to give other users access to your project. Click OK.

5 Add files to the Version Cue project.

To add an existing file or new file to the Version Cue project, choose File > Save As. Then click the Version Cue button, open your Version Cue project and its Documents folder, enter comments for this version in the Version Comments text box, and click Save.

If you have several files to add to a Version Cue project, you can add the files to the project's Documents folder inside the My Documents/Version Cue (Windows) or Documents/Version Cue (Mac OS) folder on your computer . Then choose File > Open, click the Version Cue button, open your Version Cue project, and then choose Synchronize from the Tools menu.

6 Create file versions.

After you've saved a file to a Version Cue project, you can begin creating versions of the file and adding comments to it by choosing File > Save A Version.

File versioning with Version Cue ensures that no one overwrites the work of anyone else in a Version Cue project, but also prevents users from locking out others who need to work on the same file. You can use versioning to seamlessly retain multiple states of a single file as you work on it, in case you need to restore the file to a previous version. You can also use versioning to quickly compare file versions with team members or with a client before selecting a final version.

7 Review all versions of a file.

After you've created several versions of a file, you can choose File > Versions to view thumbnails of all versions of the file, alongside comments and dates for each, and then open, manage, or delete the versions.

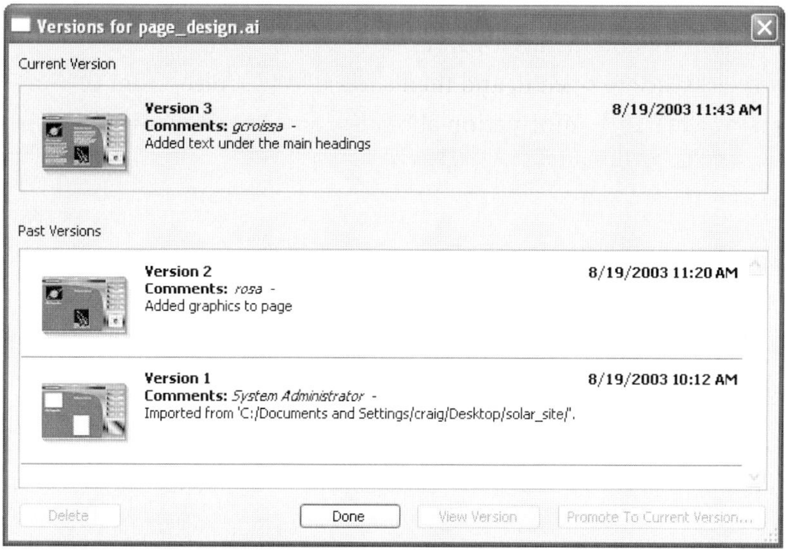

8 Collaborate on a Version Cue project.

When you want to work with other users on one of your Version Cue projects, you can instantly give them access to your Version Cue project. Choose File > Open, click the Version Cue button, and then open the Version Cue workspace that contains the Version Cue project you want to share. Select the project in the dialog box, and then choose Share Project from the Project Tools menu.

To access your Version Cue project, other computers need to be on the same subnetwork as the computer where the Version Cue workspace is installed. Computers outside the subnetwork can access the workspace by choosing Connect To from the Version Cue Tools menu and entering the Version Cue Client URL (IP address).

9 Locate files by searching embedded metadata.

Adobe Creative Suite lets users enter a wide variety of information in the File Info dialog box. This information gets embedded into a document as XMP metadata. For example, the metadata might contain a document's title, copyright, keywords, description, properties, author, and origin. Also, any comments you add to each file version are included in the file's metadata. With Version Cue you can quickly locate a file by searching the embedded metadata of all files in a Version Cue project, including Version Cue comments. You can also view a subset of metadata to quickly check the status of a file, its last comment, version date, and who is editing it.

Choose File > Open, click the Version Cue button, open the Version Cue workspace that contains the project you want to search, and then select the project. Select the Search tab and enter any text that may be embedded in the metadata of the file you want to locate or search by filename.

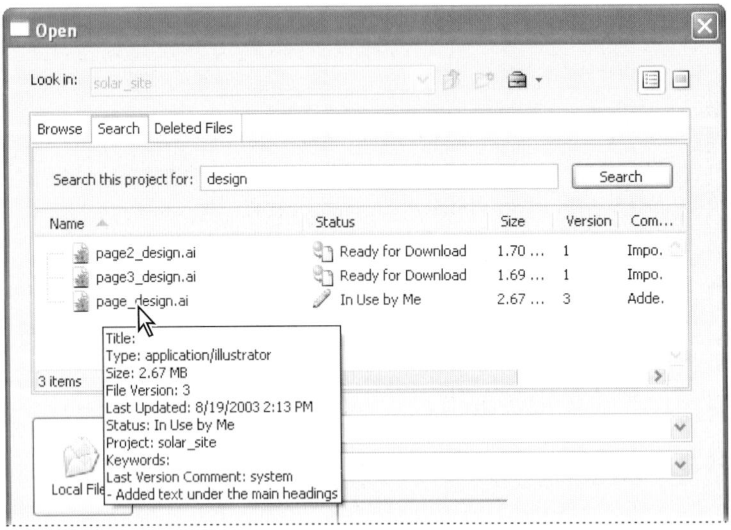

10 Perform advanced tasks with the Advanced Version Cue Workspace Administration utility.

You can choose to set up a simple collaboration where you share a Version Cue project with anyone using a Creative Suite application, or you can set up a more controlled environment in which users have to log in before accessing your project. Using the Version Cue Workgroup Administration utility, you can set up user IDs and define their project privileges, remove file locks, edit Version Cue Workspace preferences, and perform other project and workspace maintenance.

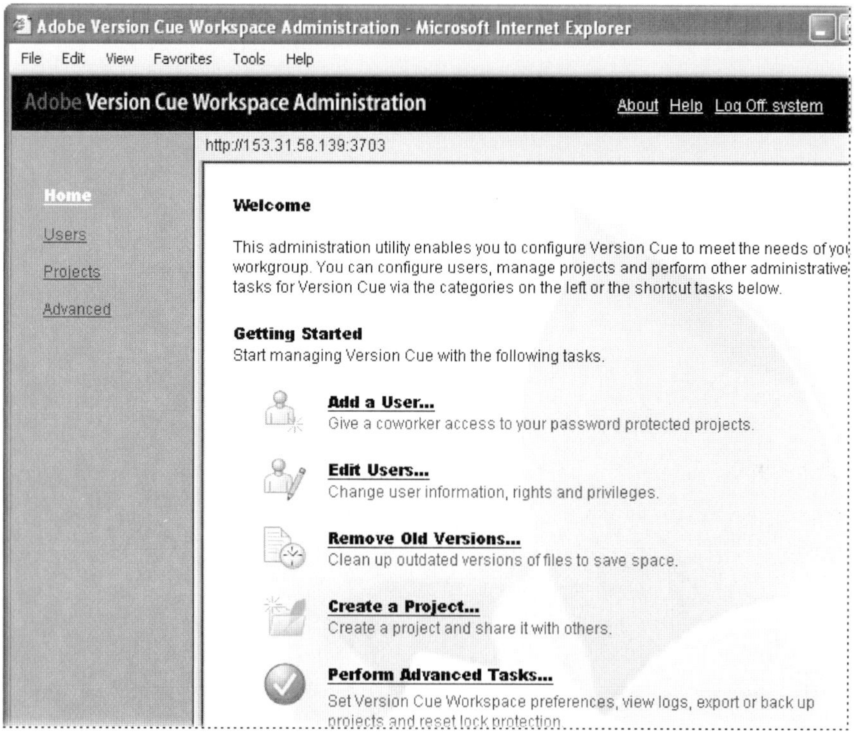

To display the Version Cue Workspace Administration utility log-in page, open the Adobe Version Cue preferences from the Control Panel (Windows) or System Preferences (Mac OS) on the computer where the Version Cue workspace is located, and click Advanced Administration.

Index

A

B

C

R

Production Notes

This Adobe Illustrator CS Classroom in a Book was created electronically using Adobe InDesign. Art was produced using Adobe InDesign, Adobe Illustrator, and Adobe Photoshop. The Myriad Pro and Minion Pro OpenType families of typefaces were used throughout this book.

References to company names in the lessons are for demonstration purposes only and are not intended to refer to any actual organization or person.

Images

Photographic images and illustrations are intended for use with the tutorials.

Clipart.com: Lesson 13 (ballplayer)

Passion flower: Lesson 19 (Kim Meuli Brown)

Typefaces used

Adobe Chaparral Pro, Adobe Garamond Pro, Myriad Pro are used throughout the lessons.

Team credits

The following individuals contributed to the development of new and updated lessons for this edition of the Adobe Illustrator Classroom in a Book:

Project coordinator, technical writer: Jennifer M. Smith

Production: AGI Training: Luis Mendes, Christopher G. Smith

Proofreading: Jay Donahue, Anne O'Shaughnessy

Technical Editors: AGI Training: Kelly Babik, Larry Happy, Greg Heald, Carl Leinbach and Cathy Auclair.

Adobe Certification

Adobe® Certified Expert

Adobe® Certified Training Provider

What is an ACE?

An Adobe Certified Expert (ACE) is an individual who has passed an Adobe Product Proficiency Exam for a specified Adobe software product. Adobe Certified Experts are eligible to promote themselves to clients or employers as highly skilled, expert level users of Adobe Software. ACE certification is a recognized standard for excellence in Adobe software knowledge.

ACE Benefits

• When you become an ACE, you enjoy these special benefits:

- Professional recognition
- An ACE program certificate
- Use of the Adobe Certified Expert program logo

What is an ACTP?

An Adobe Certified Training Provider (ACTP) is a Training professional or organization that has met the ACTP program requirements. Adobe promotes ACTPs to customers who need training on Adobe software.

ACTP Benefits

- Professional recognition
- An ACTP program certificate
- Use of the Adobe Certified Training Provider program logo
- Listing in the Partner Finder on Adobe.com
- Access to beta software releases when available
- Classroom in a Book in Adobe Acrobat PDF
- Marketing materials
- Co-marketing opportunities